The Gospels and Acts

THE GOSPELS AND ACTS
Fortress Commentary on the Bible Study Edition

Excerpted from the *Fortress Commentary on the Bible: The New Testament*
(Minneapolis: Fortress Press, 2014); Margaret Aymer, Cynthia Briggs Kittredge, David A. Sánchez, volume editors.

Fortress Press Publication Staff:
Neil Elliott and Scott Tunseth, Project Editors
Marissa Wold, Production Manager
Laurie Ingram, Cover Design.

Copyeditor: Jeffrey A. Reimer

Typesetter: PerfecType, Nashville, TN

Proofreader: David Cottingham and Linda Maloney

Library of Congress Cataloging-in-Publication data is available

ISBN: 978-1-5064-1589-5

eISBN: 978-1-5064-1590-1

The paper used in this publication meets the minimum requirements of American National Standard for Information Sciences—Permanence of Paper for Printed Library Materials, ANSI Z329, 48-1984. Manufactured in the U.S.A.

CONTENTS

PUBLISHER'S NOTE

About the Fortress Commentary on the Bible Study Editions

In 2014 Fortress Press released the two-volume *Fortress Commentary on the Bible*. See the Series Introduction (pp. 1–3) for a look inside the creation and design of the Old Testament/Apocrypha and New Testament volumes. While each comprehensive commentary volume can easily be used in classroom settings, we also recognized that dividing the larger commentaries into smaller volumes featuring key sections of Scripture may be especially helpful for use in corresponding biblical studies courses. To help facilitate such classroom use, we have broken the two-volume commentary into eight study editions.

Please note that in this study edition the page numbers match the page numbers of the larger Fortress Commentary on the Bible volume in which it first appeared. We have intentionally retained the same page numbering to facilitate use of the study editions and larger volumes side by side.

The Gospels and Acts was first published in Fortress Commentary on the Bible: The New Testament.

ABBREVIATIONS

General

AT	Alpha Text (of the Greek text of Esther)
BOI	Book of Isaiah
Chr	Chronicler
DH	Deuteronomistic History
DI	Deutero-Isaiah
Dtr	Deuteronomist
Gk.	Greek
H	Holiness Code
Heb.	Hebrew
JPS	Jewish Publication Society
LXX	The Septuagint
LXX B	Vaticanus Text of the Septuagint
MP	Mode of production
MT	Masoretic Text
NIV	New International Version
NRSV	New Revised Standard Version
OAN	Oracles against Nations (in Jeremiah)
P.	papyrus/papyri
P	Priestly source
PE	Pastoral Epistles
RSV	Revised Standard Version
TI	Trito-Isaiah

Books of the Bible (NT, OT, Apocrypha)

Old Testament/Hebrew Bible

Gen.	Genesis
Exod.	Exodus
Lev.	Leviticus
Num.	Numbers
Deut.	Deuteronomy

Josh.	Joshua
Judg.	Judges
Ruth	Ruth
1 Sam.	1 Samuel
2 Sam.	2 Samuel
1 Kgs.	1 Kings
2 Kgs.	2 Kings
1 Chron.	1 Chronicles
2 Chron.	2 Chronicles
Ezra	Ezra
Neh.	Nehemiah
Esther	Esther
Job	Job
Ps. (Pss.)	Psalms
Prov.	Proverbs
Eccles.	Ecclesiastes
Song.	Song of Songs
Isa.	Isaiah
Jer.	Jeremiah
Lam.	Lamentations
Ezek.	Ezekiel
Dan.	Daniel
Hosea	Hosea
Joel	Joel
Amos	Amos
Obad.	Obadiah
Jon.	Jonah
Mic.	Micah
Nah.	Nahum
Hab.	Habakkuk
Zeph.	Zephaniah
Hag.	Haggai
Zech.	Zechariah
Mal.	Malachi

Apocrypha

Tob.	Tobit
Jth.	Judith
Gk. Esther	Greek Additions to Esther
Sir.	Sirach (Ecclesiasticus)

Bar.	Baruch
Let. Jer.	Letter of Jeremiah
Add Dan.	Additions to Daniel
Pr. Azar.	Prayer of Azariah
Sg. Three.	Song of the Three Young Men (or Three Jews)
Sus.	Susanna
Bel	Bel and the Dragon
1 Macc.	1 Maccabees
2 Macc.	2 Maccabees
1 Esd.	1 Esdras
Pr. of Man.	Prayer of Manasseh
2 Esd.	2 Esdras
Wis.	Wisdom of Solomon
3 Macc.	3 Maccabees
4 Macc.	4 Maccabees

New Testament

Matt.	Matthew
Mark	Mark
Luke	Luke
John	John
Acts	Acts of the Apostles
Rom.	Romans
1 Cor.	1 Corinthians
2 Cor.	2 Corinthians
Gal.	Galatians
Eph.	Ephesians
Phil.	Philippians
Col.	Colossians
1 Thess.	1 Thessalonians
2 Thess.	2 Thessalonians
1 Tim.	1 Timothy
2 Tim.	2 Timothy
Titus	Titus
Philem.	Philemon
Heb.	Hebrews
James	James
1 Pet.	1 Peter
2 Pet.	2 Peter
1 John	1 John

2 John	2 John
3 John	3 John
Jude	Jude
Rev.	Revelation (Apocalypse)

Journals, Series, Reference Works

ABD	*Anchor Bible Dictionary*. Edited by David Noel Freedman. 6 vols. New York: Doubleday, 1992.
ACNT	Augsburg Commentaries on the New Testament
AJA	*American Journal of Archaeology*
AJT	*Asia Journal of Theology*
ANET	*Ancient Near Eastern Texts Relating to the Old Testament*. Edited by J. B. Pritchard. 3rd ed. Princeton: Princeton University Press, 1969.
ANF	*The Ante-Nicene Fathers*. Edited by Alexander Roberts and James Donaldson. 1885–1887. 10 vols. Repr., Peabody, MA: Hendrickson, 1994.
ANRW	*Aufstieg und Niedergang der römischen Welt: Geschichte und Kultur Roms im Spiegel der neueren Forschung*. Edited by Hildegard Temporini and Wolfgang Haase. Berlin: de Gruyter, 1972–.
ANTC	Abingdon New Testament Commentaries
AOAT	Alter Orient und Altes Testament
AbOTC	Abingdon Old Testament Commentary
AOTC	Apollos Old Testament Commentary
A(Y)B	Anchor (Yale) Bible
BA	*Biblical Archaeologist*
BAR	*Biblical Archaeology Review*
BDAG	Bauer, W., F. W. Danker, W. F. Arndt, and F. W. Gingrich. *Greek-English Lexicon of the New Testament and Other Early Christian Literature*. 3rd ed. Chicago: University of Chicago Press, 1999.
BEATAJ	Beiträge zur Erforschung des Alten Testaments und des Antiken Judentum
Bib	*Biblica*
BibInt	*Biblical Interpretation*
BJRL	*Bulletin of the John Rylands University Library of Manchester*
BJS	Brown Judaic Studies
BNTC	Black's New Testament Commentaries
BR	*Biblical Research*
BRev	*Bible Review*
BSac	*Bibliotheca sacra*
BTB	*Biblical Theology Bulletin*
BZAW	Beihefte zur Zeitschrift für die alttestamentliche Wissenschaft
CAT	Commentaire de l'Ancien Testament

CBC	Cambridge Bible Commentary
CBQMS	Catholic Biblical Quarterly Monograph Series
CC	Continental Commentaries
CH	*Church History*
CHJ	*Cambridge History of Judaism*. Edited by W. D. Davies and Louis Finkelstein. Cambridge: Cambridge University Press, 1984–.
ConBNT	Coniectanea biblica: New Testament Series
ConBOT	Coniectanea biblica: Old Testament Series
CS	Cistercian Studies
CTAED	*Canaanite Toponyms in Ancient Egyptian Documents*. S. Ahituv. Jerusalem: Magnes, 1984.
CTQ	*Concordia Theological Quarterly*
CurTM	*Currents in Theology and Mission*
ExpTim	*Expository Times*
ETL	*Ephemerides Theologicae Lovanienses*
ExAud	*Ex auditu*
FAT	Forschungen zum Alten Testament
FC	Fathers of the Church
FRLANT	Forschungen zur Religion und Literatur des Alten und Neuen Testaments
HAT	Handbuch zum Alten Testament
HBT	*Horizons in Biblical Theology*
HNTC	Harper's New Testament Commentaries
HR	*History of Religions*
HSM	Harvard Semitic Monographs
HTKAT	Herders Theologischer Kommentar zum Alten Testament
HTR	*Harvard Theological Review*
HTS	Harvard Theological Studies
HUCA	*Hebrew Union College Annual*
HUCM	Monographs of the Hebrew Union College
HUT	Hermeneutische Untersuchungen zur Theologie
IBC	Interpretation: A Bible Commentary for Teaching and Preaching
ICC	International Critical Commentary
Int	*Interpretation*
JAAR	*Journal of the American Academy of Religion*
JAOS	*Journal of the American Oriental Society*
JBL	*Journal of Biblical Literature*
JBQ	*Jewish Bible Quarterly*
JECS	*Journal of Early Christian Studies*
JJS	*Journal of Jewish Studies*
JNES	*Journal of Near Eastern Studies*

JNSL	*Journal of Northwest Semitic Languages*
JQR	*Jewish Quarterly Review*
JRS	*Journal of Roman Studies*
JSem	*Journal of Semitics*
JSJ	*Journal for the Study of Judaism in the Persian, Hellenistic, and Roman Periods*
JSNT	*Journal for the Study of the New Testament*
JSOT	*Journal for the Study of the Old Testament*
JSOTSup	Journal for the Study of the Old Testament Supplement Series
JSQ	*Jewish Studies Quarterly*
JSS	*Journal of Semitic Studies*
JTI	*Journal of Theological Interpretation*
JTS	*Journal of Theological Studies*
JTSA	*Journal of Theology for Southern Africa*
KTU	*Die keilalphabetischen Texte aus Ugarit*. Edited by M. Dietrich, O. Loretz, and J. Sanmartín. AOAT 24/1. Neukirchen-Vluyn: Neukirchener, 1976.
LCC	Loeb Classical Library
LEC	Library of Early Christianity
LHB/OTS	Library of the Hebrew Bible/Old Testament Studies
LW	*Luther's Works*. Edited by Jaroslav Pelikan and Helmut T. Lehmann. 55 vols. St. Louis: Concordia; Philadelphia: Fortress Press, 1958–1986.
NAC	New American Commentary
NCB	New Century Bible
NCBC	New Cambridge Bible Commentary
NedTT	*Nederlands theologisch tijdschrift*
Neot	*Neotestamentica*
NICNT	New International Commentary on the New Testament
NICOT	New International Commentary on the Old Testament
NIGTC	New International Greek Testament Commentary
NovT	*Novum Testamentum*
NPNF^1	*The Nicene and Post-Nicene Fathers*, Series 1. Edited by Philip Schaff. 14 vols. 1886–1889. Repr., Grand Rapids: Eerdmans, 1956.
NTL	New Testament Library
NTS	*New Testament Studies*
OBT	Overtures to Biblical Theology
OTE	*Old Testament Essays*
OTG	Old Testament Guides
OTL	Old Testament Library
OTM	Old Testament Message
PEQ	*Palestine Exploration Quarterly*
PG	Patrologia graeca [= Patrologiae cursus completus: Series graeca]. Edited by J.-P. Migne. 162 vols. Paris, 1857–1886.

PL	John Milton, *Paradise Lost*
PL	Patrologia latina [= Patrologiae cursus completus: Series latina]. Edited by J.-P. Migne. 217 vols. Paris, 1844–1864.
PRSt	*Perspectives in Religious Studies*
QR	*Quarterly Review*
RevExp	*Review and Expositor*
RevQ	*Revue de Qumran*
SBLABS	Society of Biblical Literature Archaeology and Biblical Studies
SBLAIL	Society of Biblical Literature Ancient Israel and Its Literature
SBLDS	Society of Biblical Literature Dissertation Series
SBLEJL	Society of Biblical Literature Early Judaism and Its Literature
SBLMS	Society of Biblical Literature Monograph Series
SBLRBS	Society of Biblical Literature Resources for Biblical Study
SBLSCS	Society of Biblical Literature Septuagint and Cognate Studies
SBLSP	*Society of Biblical Literature Seminar Papers*
SBLSymS	Society of Biblical Literature Symposium Series
SBLWAW	SBL Writings from the Ancient World
SemeiaSt	Semeia Studies
SJT	*Scottish Journal of Theology*
SNTSMS	Society for New Testament Studies Monograph Series
SO	Symbolae osloenses
SR	*Studies in Religion*
ST	*Studia Theologica*
StABH	Studies in American Biblical Hermeneutics
TD	*Theology Digest*
TAD	*Textbook of Aramaic Documents from Ancient Egypt.* Vol. 1: *Letters.* Bezalel Porten and Ada Yardeni. Winona Lake, IN: Eisenbrauns, 1986.
TDOT	*Theological Dictionary of the Old Testament.* 15 vols. Edited by G. Johannes Botterweck, Helmer Ringgren, and Heinz-Josef Fabry. Translated by David E. Green and Douglas W. Stott. Grand Rapids: Eerdmans, 1974–1995.
TJT	*Toronto Journal of Theology*
TNTC	Tyndale New Testament Commentaries
TOTC	Tyndale Old Testament Commentaries
TS	*Theological Studies*
TZ	*Theologische Zeitschrift*
VE	*Vox evangelica*
VT	*Vetus Testamentum*
VTSup	Supplements to Vetus Testamentum
WBC	Word Biblical Commentary
WSA	Works of St. Augustine: A Translation for the Twenty-First Century
WUANT	Wissenschaftliche Untersuchungen zum Alten und Neuen Testament

WUNT	Wissenschaftliche Untersuchungen zum Neuen Testament
WW	*Word and World*
ZAW	*Zeitschrift für die alttestamentliche Wissenschaft*
ZBK	Zürcher Bibelkommentare
ZNW	*Zeitschrift für die neutestamentliche Wissenschaft und die Kunde der älteren Kirche*

Ancient Authors and Texts

1 Clem.	*1 Clement*
2 Clem.	*2 Clement*
1 En.	*1 Enoch*
2 Bar.	*2 Baruch*
Abot R. Nat.	*Abot de Rabbi Nathan*
Ambrose	
Paen.	*De paenitentia*
Aristotle	
Ath. Pol.	*Athēnaīn politeia*
Nic. Eth.	*Nicomachean Ethics*
Pol.	*Politics*
Rhet.	*Rhetoric*
Augustine	
FC 79	*Tractates on the Gospel of John, 11–27.* Translated by John W. Rettig. Fathers of the Church 79. Washington, DC: Catholic University of America Press, 1988.
Tract. Ev. Jo.	*In Evangelium Johannis tractatus*
Bede, Venerable	
CS 117	*Commentary on the Acts of the Apostles.* Translated by Lawrence T. Martin. Cistercian Studies 117. Kalamazoo, MI: Cistercian Publications, 1989.
Barn.	*Barnabas*
CD	Cairo Genizah copy of the Damascus Document
Cicero	
De or.	*De oratore*
Tusc.	*Tusculanae disputationes*
Clement of Alexandria	
Paed.	*Paedogogus*
Strom.	*Stromata*
Cyril of Jerusalem	
Cat. Lect.	*Catechetical Lectures*
Dio Cassius	
Hist.	*Roman History*

Dio Chrysostom
- *Or.* — *Orations*

Diog. *Diognetus*

Dionysius of Halicarnassus
- *Thuc.* — *De Thucydide*

Epictetus
- *Diatr.* — *Diatribai (Dissertationes)*
- *Ench.* — *Enchiridion*

Epiphanius
- *Pan.* — *Panarion (Adversus Haereses)*

Eusebius of Caesarea
- *Hist. eccl.* — *Historia ecclesiastica*

Gos. Thom. — *Gospel of Thomas*

Herodotus
- *Hist.* — *Historiae*

Hermas, *Shepherd*
- *Mand.* — *Mandates*
- *Sim.* — *Similitudes*

Homer
- *Il.* — *Iliad*
- *Od.* — *Odyssey*

Ignatius of Antioch
- *Eph.* — *To the Ephesians*
- *Smyr.* — *To the Smyrnaeans*

Irenaeus
- *Adv. haer.* — *Adversus haereses*

Jerome
- *Vir. ill.* — *De viris illustribus*

John Chrysostom
- *Hom. 1 Cor.* — *Homiliae in epistulam i ad Corinthios*
- *Hom. Act.* — *Homiliae in Acta apostolorum*
- *Hom. Heb.* — *Homiliae in epistulam ad Hebraeos*

Josephus
- *Ant.* — *Jewish Antiquities*
- *Ag. Ap.* — *Against Apion*
- *J.W.* — *Jewish War*

Jub. — *Jubilees*

Justin Martyr
- *Dial.* — *Dialogue with Trypho*
- *1 Apol.* — *First Apology*

L.A.E.	*Life of Adam and Eve*
Liv. Pro.	*Lives of the Prophets*
Lucian	
Alex.	*Alexander (Pseudomantis)*
Phal.	*Phalaris*
Mart. Pol.	*Martyrdom of Polycarp*
Novatian	
Trin.	*De trinitate*
Origen	
C. Cels.	*Contra Celsum*
Comm. Jo.	*Commentarii in evangelium Joannis*
De princ.	*De principiis*
Hom. Exod.	*Homiliae in Exodum*
Hom. Jer.	*Homiliae in Jeremiam*
Hom. Josh.	*Homilies on Joshua*
Pausanias	
Descr.	*Description of Greece*
Philo	
Cher.	*De cherubim*
Decal.	*De decalogo*
Dreams	*On Dreams*
Embassy	*On the Embassy to Gaius (= Legat.)*
Fug.	*De fuga et inventione*
Leg.	*Legum allegoriae*
Legat.	*Legatio ad Gaium*
Migr.	*De migratione Abrahami*
Mos.	*De vita Mosis*
Opif.	*De opificio mundi*
Post.	*De posteritate Caini*
Prob.	*Quod omnis probus liber sit*
QE	*Quaestiones et solutiones in Exodum*
QG	*Quaestiones et solutiones in Genesin*
Spec. Laws	*On the Special Laws*
Plato	
Gorg.	*Gorgias*
Plutarch	
Mor.	*Moralia*
Mulier. virt.	*Mulierum virtutes*
Polycarp	
Phil.	*To the Philippians*

Ps.-Clem. Rec.	*Pseudo-Clementine Recognitions*
Pss. Sol.	*Psalms of Solomon*
Pseudo-Philo	
L.A.B.	*Liber antiquitatum biblicarum*
Seneca	
Ben.	*De beneficiis*
Strabo	
Geog.	*Geographica*
Tatian	
Ad gr.	*Oratio ad Graecos*
Tertullian	
Praescr.	*De praescriptione haereticorum*
Prax.	*Adversus Praxean*
Bapt.	*De baptismo*
De an.	*De anima*
Pud.	*De pudicitia*
Virg.	*De virginibus velandis*
Virgil	
Aen.	*Aeneid*
Xenophon	
Oec.	*Oeconomicus*

Mishnah, Talmud, Targum

b. B. Bat.	*Babylonian Talmudic tractate Baba Batra*
b. Ber.	*Babylonian Talmudic tractate Berakhot*
b Erub.	*Babylonian Talmudic tractate Erubim*
b. Ketub.	*Babylonian Talmudic tractate Ketubbot*
b. Mak.	*Babylonian Talmudic tractate Makkot*
b. Meg.	*Babylonian Talmudic tractate Megillah*
b. Ned.	*Babylonian Talmudic tractate Nedarim*
b. Naz.	*Babylonian Talmudic tractate Nazir*
b. Sanh.	*Babylonian Talmudic tractate Sanhedrin*
b. Shab.	*Babylonian Talmudic tractate Shabbat*
b. Sotah	*Babylonian Talmudic tractate Sotah*
b. Ta'an.	*Babylonian Talmudic tractate Ta'anit*
b. Yev.	*Babylonian Talmudic tractate Yevamot*
b. Yoma	*Babylonian Talmudic tractate Yoma*
Eccl. Rab.	*Ecclesiastes Rabbah*
Exod. Rab.	*Exodus Rabbah*
Gen. Rab.	*Genesis Rabbah*

Lam. Rab.	*Lamentations Rabbah*
Lev. R(ab).	*Leviticus Rabbah*
m. Abot	*Mishnah tractate Abot*
m. Bik.	*Mishnah tractate Bikkurim*
m. Demai	*Mishnah tractate Demai*
m. ʽEd.	*Mishnah tractate ʽEduyyot*
m. Git.	*Mishnah tractate Gittin*
m. Pesaḥ	*Mishnah tractate Pesaḥim*
m. Šeqal.	*Mishnah tractate Šeqalim (Shekalim)*
m. Shab.	*Mishnah tractate Shabbat*
m. Sotah	*Mishnah tractate Sotah*
m. Taʽan.	*Mishnah tractate Taʽanit*
m. Tamid	*Mishnah tractate Tamid*
m. Yad.	*Mishnah tractate Yadayim*
m. Yebam.	*Mishnah tractate Yebamot*
m. Yoma	*Mishnah tractate Yoma*
Num. Rab.	*Numbers Rabbah*
Pesiq. Rab.	*Pesiqta Rabbati*
Pesiq. Rab Kah.	*Pesiqta Rab Kahana*
S. ʽOlam Rab.	*Seder ʽOlam Rabbah*
Song Rab.	*Song of Songs Rabbah*
t. Hul.	*Tosefta tractate Hullin*
Tg. Onq.	*Targum Onqelos*
Tg. Jer.	*Targum Jeremiah*
y. Hag.	*Jerusalem Talmudic tractate Hagiga*
y. Pesaḥ	*Jerusalem Talmudic tractate Pesaḥim*
y. Sanh.	*Jerusalem Talmudic tractate Sanhedrin*

Dead Sea Scrolls

1QapGen	*Genesis apocryphon* (Excavated frags. from cave)
1QM	*War Scroll*
1QpHab	*Pesher Habakkuk*
1QS	*Rule of the Community*
1QSb	*Rule of the Blessings* (Appendix b to 1QS)
1Q21	*T. Levi*, aramaic
4Q184	Wiles of the Wicked Woman
4Q214	Levi^{d} ar (*olim* part of Levi^{b})
4Q214b	Levi^{f} ar (*olim* part of Levi^{b})
4Q226	psJub^{b} (4Q *pseudo-Jubilees*)
4Q274	Tohorot A

4Q277	Tohorot B[b] (*olim* B[c])
4Q525	*Beatitudes*
4QMMT	*Miqṣat Ma'aśê ha-Torah*
4QpNah/4Q169	4Q Pesher Nahum
4Q82	*The Greek Minor Prophets Scroll*

Old Testament Pseudepigrapha

1 En.	*1 Enoch*
2 En.	*2 Enoch*
Odes Sol.	*Odes of Solomon*
Syr. Men.	*Sentences of the Syriac Menander*
T. Levi	*Testament of Levi*
T. Mos.	*Testament of Moses*
T. Sim.	*Testament of Simeon*

INTRODUCTION

The *Fortress Commentary on the Bible*, presented in two volumes, seeks to invite study and conversation about an ancient text that is both complex and compelling. As biblical scholars, we wish students of the Bible to gain a respect for the antiquity and cultural remoteness of the biblical texts and to grapple for themselves with the variety of their possible meanings; to fathom a long history of interpretation in which the Bible has been wielded for causes both beneficial and harmful; and to develop their own skills and voices as responsible interpreters, aware of their own social locations in relationships of privilege and power. With this in mind, the *Fortress Commentary on the Bible* offers general readers an informed and accessible resource for understanding the biblical writings in their ancient contexts; for recognizing how the texts have come down to us through the mediation of different interpretive traditions; and for engaging current discussion of the Bible's sometimes perplexing, sometimes ambivalent, but always influential legacy in the contemporary world. The commentary is designed not only to inform but also to invite and empower readers as active interpreters of the Bible in their own right.

The editors and contributors to these volumes are scholars and teachers who are committed to helping students engage the Bible in the classroom. Many also work as leaders, both lay and ordained, in religious communities, and wish this commentary to prove useful for informing congregational life in clear, meaningful, and respectful ways. We also understand the work of biblical interpretation as a responsibility far wider than the bounds of any religious community. In this regard, we participate in many and diverse identities and social locations, yet we all are conscious of reading, studying, and hearing the Bible today as citizens of a complex and interconnected world. We recognize in the Bible one of the most important legacies of human culture; its historical and literary interpretation is of profound interest to religious and nonreligious people alike.

Often, the academic interpretation of the Bible has moved from close study of the remote ancient world to the rarefied controversy of scholarly debate, with only occasional attention to the ways biblical texts are actually heard and lived out in the world around us. The commentary seeks to provide students with diverse materials on the ways in which these texts have been interpreted through the course of history, as well as helping students understand the texts' relevance for today's globalized world. It recognizes the complexities that are involved with being an engaged reader of the Bible, providing a powerful tool for exploring the Bible's multilayered meanings in both their ancient and modern contexts. The commentary seeks to address contemporary issues that are raised by biblical passages. It aspires to be keenly aware of how the contemporary world and its issues and perspectives influence the interpretation of the Bible. Many of the most important insights of contemporary biblical scholarship not only have come from expertise in the world of antiquity but have also been forged in modern struggles for dignity, for equality, for sheer survival, and out of respect for those who have died without seeing justice done. Gaining familiarity with the original contexts in which the biblical writings were produced is essential, but not sufficient, for encouraging competent and discerning interpretation of the Bible's themes today.

Inside the Commentary

Both volumes of *The Fortress Commentary on the Bible* are organized in a similar way. In the beginning of each volume, **Topical Articles** set the stage on which interpretation takes place, naming the issues and concerns that have shaped historical and theological scholarship down to the present. Articles in the *Fortress Commentary on the Old Testament* attend, for example, to the issues that arise when two different religious communities claim the same body of writings as their Scripture, though interpreting those writings quite differently. Articles in the *Fortress Commentary on the New Testament* address the consequences of Christianity's historic claim to appropriate Jewish Scripture and to supplement it with a second collection of writings, the experience of rootlessness and diaspora, and the legacy of apocalypticism. Articles in both volumes reflect on the historical intertwining of Christianity with imperial and colonial power and with indexes of racial and socioeconomic privilege.

Section Introductions in the Old Testament volume provide background to the writings included in the Torah, Historical Writings, Wisdom, Prophetic Writings, and a general introduction to the Apocrypha. The New Testament volume includes articles introducing the Gospels, Acts, the letters associated with Paul, Hebrews, the General Epistles, and Revelation. These articles will address the literary and historical matters, as well as theological themes, that the books in these collections hold in common.

Commentary Entries present accessible and judicious discussion of each biblical book, beginning with an introduction to current thinking regarding the writing's original context and its significance in different reading communities down to the present day. A three-level commentary then follows for each sense division of the book. In some cases these follow the chapter divisions of a biblical book, but more often contributors have discerned other outlines, depending on matters of genre, movement, or argument.

The three levels of commentary are the most distinctive organizational feature of these volumes. The first level, "The Text in Its Ancient Context," addresses relevant lexical, exegetical, and literary aspects of the text, along with cultural and archaeological information that may provide additional insight into the historical context. This level of the commentary describes consensus views where these exist in current scholarship and introduces issues of debate clearly and fairly. Our intent here is to convey some sense of the historical and cultural distance between the text's original context and the contemporary reader.

The second level, "The Text in the Interpretive Tradition," discusses themes including Jewish and Christian tradition as well as other religious, literary, and artistic traditions where the biblical texts have attracted interest. This level is shaped by our conviction that we do not apprehend these texts immediately or innocently; rather, even the plain meaning we may regard as self-evident may have been shaped by centuries of appropriation and argument to which we are heirs.

The third level, "The Text in Contemporary Discussion," follows the history of interpretation into the present, drawing brief attention to a range of issues. Our aim here is not to deliver a single answer—"what the text means"—to the contemporary reader, but to highlight unique challenges and interpretive questions. We pay special attention to occasions of dissonance: aspects of the text or of its interpretation that have become questionable, injurious, or even intolerable to some readers today. Our goal is not to provoke a referendum on the value of the text but to stimulate reflection and discussion and, in this way, to empower the reader to reach his or her own judgments about the text.

The approach of this commentary articulates a particular understanding of the work of responsible biblical interpretation. We seek through this commentary to promote intelligent and mature engagement with the Bible, in religious communities and in academic classrooms alike, among pastors, theologians, and ethicists, but also and especially among nonspecialists. Our work together has given us a new appreciation for the vocation of the biblical scholar, as custodians of a treasure of accumulated wisdom from our predecessors; as stewards at a table to which an ever-expanding circle is invited; as neighbors and fellow citizens called to common cause, regardless of our different professions of faith. If the result of our work here is increased curiosity about the Bible, new questions about its import, and new occasions for mutual understanding among its readers, our work will be a success.

Fortress Commentary on the Old Testament

Gale A. Yee
Episcopal Divinity School

Hugh R. Page Jr.
University of Notre Dame

Matthew J. M. Coomber
St. Ambrose University

Fortress Commentary on the New Testament

Margaret Aymer
Interdenominational Theological Center

Cynthia Briggs Kittredge
Seminary of the Southwest

David A. Sánchez
Loyola Marymount University

Reading the Christian New Testament in the Contemporary World

Kwok Pui-lan

On Ascension Sunday in May 2012, the faculty and students of my school who were taking part in a travel seminar to China attended the worship service at the Shanghai Community Church. We arrived half an hour before the service began, and the church, which can accommodate about two thousand people, was already filled to capacity. Another two thousand people who could not get into the sanctuary watched the worship service on closed-circuit TV in other rooms in the church building. Through this experience and while visiting churches in other cities, we learned about and encountered the phenomenal growth of the Chinese churches in the past twenty-five years. The official statistics put the number of Chinese Christians at around 30 million, but unofficial figures range from 50 to 100 million, if those who belong to the unregistered house churches are counted. China is poised to become the country with the highest number of Christians, and China has already become the largest printer and user of the Bible in the world. In 2012, the Amity Printing Company in Nanjing celebrated the publishing of 100 million Bibles since its inception in 1987 (United Bible Societies 2012).

Besides China, sub-Saharan Africa has also experienced rapid church growth, especially among the African Independent Churches, Pentecostal churches, and Roman Catholic churches. By 2025, Africa will be the continent with the greatest number of Christians, at more than 670 million. At the turn of the twentieth century, 70 percent of the world's Christians were European. By 2000, that number had dropped to 28 percent (Flatow). The shift of Christian demographics to the South and the prospect of Christianity becoming a non-Western religion have attracted the attention of scholars and popular media (Sanneh 2003; Jenkins; Johnson and Ross). According to the *World Christian Encyclopedia*, almost two-thirds of the readers of the Bible are Christians from Africa, Asia, Latin America, and Oceania (around 1.178 billion) as compared to Europe and America (around 661 million) and Orthodox Eastern Europe (around 158 million) (Patte, xxi).

These changing Christian demographics have significant implications for reading the Bible as global citizens in the contemporary world. To promote global and intercultural understanding, we can no longer read the Bible in a narrow and parochial way, without being aware of how Christians in other parts of the world are reading it in diverse linguistic, cultural, and social contexts. In the past decade, biblical scholars have increasingly paid attention to global perspectives on the Bible to prepare Christians to live in our complex, pluralistic, and transnational world (Patte; Wicker, Miller, and Dube; Roncace and Weaver). For those of us living in the Global North, it is important to pay attention to liberative readings from the Global South and to the voices from the majority world. Today, the field of biblical studies has been enlivened and broadened by scholars from many social locations and culturally and religiously diverse contexts.

The New Testament in Global Perspectives

The New Testament touches on many themes highly relevant for our times, such as racial and ethnic relations, religious pluralism, social and political domination, gender oppression, and religious movements for resistance. The early followers of Jesus were Jews and gentiles living in the Hellenistic world under the rule of the Roman Empire. Christianity developed largely in urban cities in which men and women from different linguistic, cultural, and religious backgrounds interacted and commingled with one another (Theissen; Meeks). Christians in the early centuries lived among Jews and people devoted to emperor cults, Greek religion, and other indigenous traditions in the ancient Near East. Jesus and his disciples spoke Aramaic, the common language of Palestine. The New Testament was written in Koine Greek, the lingua franca of much of the Mediterranean region and the Middle East since the conquest of Alexander the Great. Living under the shadow of the Roman Empire, early Christians had to adapt to the cultures and social structures of empire, as well as resist the domination of imperial rule.

From its beginning in Palestine and the Mediterranean, Christianity spread to other parts of the Roman Empire and became the dominant religion during Constantine's time. Some of the notable early theologians hailed from northern Africa: Origen (c. 185–254) and Athanasius (c. 300–373) from Alexandria, Tertullian (160–225) from Carthage, and Augustine (354–431) of Hippo. While Christianity was persecuted in the Roman Empire prior to 313, it found its way to the regions east of the Tigris River possibly as early as the beginning of the second century. Following ancient trade routes, merchants and missionaries brought Christianity from the Mediterranean to the Persian Gulf and across central Asia all the way to China (Baum and Winkler, 8). In the early modern period, Christianity was brought to the Americas and other parts of the world, with the help of the political and military power of colonizing empires. Even though Christianity was a world religion, the study of church history in the past tended to focus on Europe and North America and to marginalize the histories in other parts of the world. Today, scholars of world Christianity have contested such Eurocentric biases. They have produced comprehensive accounts that restore the peoples of Africa, the Near East, and Asia to their rightful place in the rich and multilayered Christian tradition (Hastings; Irvin and Sunquist 2001; 2012; Sanneh 2007).

The translation of the Bible, especially the New Testament, into the native and vernacular languages of different peoples was and remains an important strategy of Christian missions. The United Bible Societies (2013) report that the complete Bible has been translated into at least 451 languages and the New Testament into some 1,185. The Bible is the most translated collection of texts in the world. There are now 2,370 languages in which at least one book of the Bible has been produced. Although this figure represents less than half of some 6,000 languages and dialects presently in use in the world, it includes the primary means of communication of well over 90 percent of the world's population.

Most Christians are more familiar with the New Testament than the Hebrew Bible. The New Testament is read and preached throughout the world in liturgical settings and worship services, taught in seminaries and church Sunday schools, studied in private devotions, and discussed in Bible study groups, women's fellowships, college campuses, and grassroots religious organizations and movements. Christians, Jews, Muslims, and atheists debate the meaning of Jesus and the gospel in books, mass media, and on the Internet. The life and the story of Jesus Christ have been depicted and interpreted in popular culture, such as films, songs, music videos, fiction, blogs, websites, photographs, paintings, sculpture, and other forms of art. The study of the New Testament is not limited to the study of the biblical text, but includes how the text is used in concrete contexts in Christian communities, popular media, and public spheres.

The Bible is taken to mean many things in our contemporary world. Christian communities regard the Bible as *Scripture*, and many Christians think that it has authority over their beliefs and moral behavior. In the academy, the Bible is treated more as a *historical document*, to be studied by rigorous historical criticism. Increasingly, the Bible is also seen as a *cultural product*, embedded in the sociocultural and ideological assumptions of its time. The meaning of the Bible is not fixed but is continually produced as readers interact with it in different contexts. The diverse understanding of what the Bible is often creates a clash of opinions. For example, Christians may think Lady Gaga's "Judas" video (2011) has gone too far in deviating from orthodox teaching. There is also a wide gap in the ways the Bible is read in the church and academy. The experts' reading may challenge the beliefs of those sitting in the pews.

In the field of biblical studies, Fernando F. Segovia (34–52) delineates three stages in the development of academic biblical criticism in the twentieth century. The historical-critical method has been the dominant mode of interpretation in academia since the middle of the nineteenth century. The meaning of the text is seen as residing *behind* the text—in the world that shaped the text, in the author's intention, or both. The second stage is literary criticism, which emerged in the middle of 1970s in dialogue with literary and psychoanalytic theory. The literary critics emphasize the meaning *in* the text and focus on genre, plot, structure, rhetoric, levels of narration, and characterization as depicted in the world of the text. The third stage is cultural studies or ideological criticism of the Bible, which developed also in the 1970s, when critics from the two-thirds world, feminist theologians, and racial and ethnic minority scholars in North America began to increase their numbers in the guild. They have increasingly paid attention to the flesh-and-blood readers *in front of* the text, who employ different methods, such as storytelling and reader-response criticism, in their interaction with the text to construct meaning in response to concerns arising from their communities.

The shift to the flesh-and-blood reader contests the assumption that there is a "universal" reader and an "objective" interpretation applicable to all times and places. The claim of an "objective" and "scientific" reading is based on a positivistic understanding of historiography, which presumes that historical facts can be objectively reconstructed, following established criteria in Western academia. But the historical-critical method is only one of the many methods and should not be taken as the "universal" norm for judging other methodologies. Its dominance is the result of the colonial legacy as well as the continued hegemony of Eurocentric knowledge and cultural production of our time. Nowadays, many methods are available, and biblical critics have increasingly used interdisciplinary approaches and a combination of theories and methods, such as postmodern theory, postcolonial theory, and queer studies, for interpretation (Crossley; Moore 2010).

What this means is the democratization of the study of the Bible, because no one group of people has a monopoly over the meaning of the Bible and no single method can exhaust its "truths." To understand the richness of the biblical tradition, we have to learn to listen to the voices of people from multiple locations and senses of belonging. Eleazar S. Fernandez (140) points out, "real flesh-and-blood readers assume a variety of positions—in relation to time, geography, geopolitics, diaspora location, social location, religion, ethnicity, gender, sexuality, and so on—in the power-knowledge nexus that inform their readings and cultural or religious discursive productions in the global market." Interpreting the Bible in global perspectives requires us to pay attention to the contextual character of reading and the relationships and tensions between the global and the local.

Reading the New Testament in Diverse Contexts

The shift from the author and the text to the reader means that we need to understand the ways the Bible functions in diverse sociolingusitic contexts (Blount 1995). Our critical task must go further than analyzing the text and the processes for production and interpretation, to include the cultural and social conditions that influence the history of reception. Let us go back to the examples of reading the Bible in the Chinese and African contexts. When Christianity arrived in China, the Chinese had a long hermeneutical tradition of interpreting Confucian, Buddhist, and Daoist texts. The missionaries and biblical translators had to borrow from indigenous religious ideas to translate biblical terminologies, such as God, heaven, and hell. The rapid social and political changes in modern China affected how the Bible is read by Christians living in a Communist society (Eber, Wan, and Walf). When the Bible was introduced to the African continent, it encountered a rich and complex language world of oral narratives, legends, proverbs, and folktales. The interpretation of oral texts is different from that of written ones. In some instances, the translation of the Bible into the vernacular languages has changed the oral cultures into written cultures, with both positive and negative effects on social development (Sanneh 1989). And if we examine the history of translation and reception of the English Bible, we will see how the processes have been affected by the rise of nationalism, colonial expansion, and the diverse forms of English used in the English-speaking world (Sugirtharajah 2002, 127–54).

Some Christians may feel uneasy about the fact that the Bible is read in so many different ways. For the fundamentalists who believe in biblical inerrancy and literal interpretation, multiple ways of reading undermine biblical authority. Even liberals might wonder if the diversity of readings will open the doors to relativism. But as James Barr has pointed out, the appeal to the Bible as authority for all doctrinal matters and the assumption that its meaning is fixed cannot be verified by the Bible itself. Both Jesus and Paul took the liberty to repudiate, criticize, and reinterpret parts of the Hebrew Bible (Barr, 12–19). Moreover, as Mary Ann Tolbert has noted, since the Reformation, when the doctrine of *sola scriptura* was brought to the forefront, the invocation of biblical authority by various ecclesiastical bodies has generally been negative and exclusive. "It has been used most often to *exclude* certain groups or people, to *pass judgment* on various disapproved activities, and to *justify* morally or historically debatable positions [such as slavery]" (1998, 142). The doctrinal appeal to biblical authority and the insistence on monocultural reading often mask power dynamics, which allow some groups of people to exercise control over others who have less power, including women, poor people, racial and ethnic minorities, and gay people and lesbians.

Multiple readings and plurality of meaning do not necessarily lead to relativism, but can foster deeper awareness of our own interpretive assumptions and broaden our horizons. In his introduction to the *Global Bible Commentary*, Daniel Patte (xxi–xxxii) offers some helpful suggestions. (1) We have to acknowledge the contextual character of our interpretation. There is no context-free reading, whether in the past or in the present. (2) We have to stop and listen to the voices of biblical readers who have long been silenced in each context. (3) We have to learn the reading strategies and critical tradition developed in other parts of the world, such as enculturation, liberation, and inter(con)textuality. Contextual readings do not mean anything goes or that interpreters may proceed without self-critique. (4) We have to respect other people's readings and assume responsibility for our own interpretation. (5) Other people's readings often lead us to see our blind spots, and invite us to notice aspects of the Bible we have overlooked. (6) We have to learn to read *with* others in community, rather than reading *for* or *to* them, assuming our reading is superior to others.

We can use the different readings of the story of the Syrophoenician woman (Matt. 15:21-28; Mark 7:24-30) to illustrate this point. Many Christians have been taught that the story is about Jesus' mission to the gentiles, because Jesus went to the border place of Tyre and Sidon and healed the gentile woman's daughter and praised her faith. Japanese biblical scholar Hisako Kinukawa (51–65), however, does not emphasize gentile mission but Jesus' crossing ethnic boundaries to accept others. She places the story in the cultic purity and ethnic exclusion of first-century Palestine and draws parallels to the discrimination of Koreans as minorities living in Japan. We shall see that the generalization of first-century culture may be problematic. Nevertheless, Kinukawa argues that the gentile woman changed Jesus' attitude from rejection to affirmation and created an opportunity for Jesus to cross the boundary. Jesus has set an example, she says, for Japanese people to challenge their assumptions of a homogeneous race, to overcome their prejudice toward ethnic minorities, and to respect other peoples' dignity and human rights.

On the African continent, Musa W. Dube, from Botswana, emphasizes the importance of *reading with* ordinary readers. She set out to find out how women in the African Independent Churches in Botswana read the Matthean version of the story (2000, 187–90). She found that some of the women emphasized that Jesus was testing the woman's faith. They said the meaning of the word "dog" should not be taken literally, as Jesus often spoke in parables. Several women did not read the story as if Jesus had insulted the woman by comparing the Canaanites as "dogs" to the Israelites as children. Instead, they saw the Canaanite woman as one of the children because of her faith, and the "dogs" referred to the demonic spirits. This must be understood in the context of the belief in spirits in the African religious worldview. The women interpreted the woman's answer to Jesus, that even the dogs eat the crumbs from the master's table (Matt. 15:27), to mean that no one is permanently and totally undeserving. The women believed that Jesus had come for all people, without regard for race and ethnicities.

These two examples show how social and cultural backgrounds affect the interpretation of the story and the lessons drawn for today. The majority of interpreters, whether scholars or ordinary readers, have focused on the interaction between Jesus and the woman. I would like to cite two other readings that bring to the forefront other details of the text that have been overlooked. Laura E. Donaldson reads the story from a postcolonial Native American perspective and places the "demon-possessed" daughter at the center of her critical analysis. In the text, the daughter does not speak, and her illness is considered taboo and stigmatizing. Donaldson challenges our complicity in such a reading and employs the insights of disabilities studies to demystify the construction of "able" and "disabled" persons. She then points out that the Canaanites were the indigenous people of the land, and the daughter might not be suffering from an illness pejoratively identified as "demon possession" by the Christian text. Instead, the daughter may be in an altered state of consciousness, which is a powerful form of knowing in many indigenous spiritual traditions. For Donaldson, the daughter may "signify a trace of the indigenous," who has the power to access other sites of knowledge (104–5).

While many commentators have noted the lowly position of dogs in ancient Mediterranean and Near East culture, Stephen D. Moore, who grew up in Ireland and teaches in the United States, looks at the Matthean story through the prism of human-animal relations. He contrasts the construction of the son of man with the dog-woman in Matthew. While the son of man is not an animal and asserts power, sovereignty, and self-control, following the elite Greco-Roman concept of masculinity, the dog-woman of Canaan embodies the categories of savages, women, and beasts. Jesus said that he was sent to the lost sheep of the house of Israel and it was not fair to take the children's food and throw it to the dogs. The problem of the dog-woman is that she is not a sheep woman. The image of Canaan as heathen, savage, and less than human justified the colonization of non-Christian people in Africa, the Americas, and other regions. Moore notes that the image of "heathens" in nineteenth- and twentieth-century biblical commentary conjured up the reality of "unsaved" dark-skinned people in need of Christ and in need of civilizing, and hence in need of colonizing (Moore 2013, 63). Moore's reading points out that mission to the gentiles may not be benign, and might mask colonial impulses.

These diverse interpretations of the Syrophoenician woman's story illustrate how reading with other people can radically expand our imagination. We can see how a certain part of the story is emphasized or reinterpreted by different readers to address particular concerns. Sensitivity to contextual and cross-cultural interpretation helps us to live in a pluralistic world in which people have different worldviews and assumptions. Through genuine dialogue and listening to others, we can enrich ourselves and work with others to create a better world.

Interpretation for Liberation

In the second half of the twentieth century, people's popular movements and protests led to the development of liberation theologies in various parts of the world. In Africa and Asia, anticolonial struggles resulted in political independence and people's demand for cultural autonomy. In Latin America, theologians and activists criticized the dependence theory of development, which continues to keep poor countries dependent on rich countries because of unequal global economic structures. Women from all over the globe, racial and ethnic minorities, and lesbian, gay, bisexual, and transgender people have also begun to articulate their theologies. People who are multiply oppressed began to read the Bible through the intersection of gender, race, class, sexuality, religion, and colonialism. I focus on liberative readings from the Global South here.

Following Vatican II (1962–1965), Latin American liberation theology began to develop in the 1960s and focused on social and economic oppression and the disparity between the rich and the poor. Using Marxist analysis as a critical tool, liberation theologians in Latin America argued that the poor are the subjects of history and that God has a preferential option for the poor. They insisted that theology is a reflection of social praxis, which seeks to change the oppressive situation that the majority of the people find themselves in. Juan Luis Segundo (9) developed a hermeneutical circle that consists of four steps: (1) our way of experiencing reality leads to ideological suspicion, (2) which we apply to the whole ideological superstructure, and especially theology, (3) being aware of how prevailing interpretation of the Bible does not take important data into account, resulting in (4) the development of a new hermeneutic.

Latin American theologians contested the formulation of traditional Christology and presented Christ as the liberator. The gospel of Jesus Christ is not about saving individual souls, without import for our concrete lives. In *A Theology of Liberation*, Gustavo Gutiérrez (102–5) argues that Christ is the liberator who opts for the poor. Jesus' death and resurrection liberates us from sin. Sin, however, is not private, but a social, historical fact. It is the absence of fellowship of love in relationship among persons and the breach of relationship with God. Christ offers us the gift of radical liberation and enables us to enter into communion with God and with others. Liberation, for Gutiérrez, has three levels: political liberation, liberation in the course of history, and liberation from sin and into communion with God.

Latin American women theologians have criticized their male colleagues' lack of attention to women's issues and *machismo* in Latin American culture. Elsa Tamez, from Mexico, is a leading scholar who has published extensively on reading the New Testament from a Latin American feminist perspective (2001; 2007). She has raised questions about Jesus' relation with women in the Gospels and the class difference between rich and poor women in the early Christian movement. The discussion of the Bible in the base Christian communities and women's groups helped spread the ideas of liberation theology among the populace. A collection of discussions of the gospel by Nicaraguan peasants who belonged to the Christian community of Solentiname was published as *The Gospel in Solentiname* (Cardenal). The peasants approached the Bible from their life situation of extreme poverty, and they connected with Jesus' revolutionary work in solidarity with the poor of his time. Some of the peasants also painted the scenes from the Gospels and identified biblical events with events leading to the 1979 Sandinista revolution (Scharper and Scharper). In response to the liberation movement, which had spread to the whole continent, the Vatican criticized liberation theology and replaced progressive bishops with conservative ones. But second-generation liberation theologians continue the work of their pioneers and expand the liberation theological project to include race, gender, sexuality, migration, and popular religions (Petrella).

Unlike in Latin America, where Christians are the majority of the population, Christians in many parts of Africa and Asia live among people of other faith traditions. Here, interpretation of the Bible follows two broad approaches. The liberation approach focuses on sociopolitical dimensions, such as the fight over poverty, dictatorship, apartheid, and other social injustice. The enculturation or the indigenization approach brings the Bible into dialogue with the African or Asian worldviews, popular religion, and cultural idiom. The two approaches are not mutually exclusive, and a holistic transformation of society must deal with changing the sociopolitical structures as well as the culture and mind-sets of people.

One of the key questions for those who read the Bible in religiously pluralistic contexts is how to honor others who have different religious identities and cultures. Some of the passages in the New Testament have been used to support an exclusive attitude toward other religions. For example, Jesus said that he is the way and no one comes to the Father except through him (John 14:6) and charged his followers with the Great Commission, to "make disciples of all nations" (Matt. 28:19). But as Wesley Ariarajah (1989) has said, the universality of Christ supports the spirit of openness, mutual understanding, and interfaith dialogue with others. In Acts 10:9-16, Peter is challenged in a vision to consider nothing unclean that God has made clean. He crosses the boundary that separates Jews and gentiles and meets with Cornelius, the Roman centurion, which leads to his conversion. When Paul speaks to the Athenians, he says that they are extremely religious, and he employs a religious language different from that when he speaks to the Jews (Acts 17:22-31). Ariarajah argues that openness to others and dialogue does not contradict Christian witness.

In their protests against political oppression and dictatorship, Asian Christians have reread the Bible to empower them to fight for human rights and dignity. *Minjung* theology arose in South Korea during the 1970s against the dictatorship of the Park Chung Hee government. The word *minjung* comes from two Chinese characters meaning the masses of people. New Testament scholar Ahn Byung Mu points out that in the Gospel of Mark, the *ochlos* ("crowd or multitude") follows Jesus from place to place, listens to his teachings, and witnesses his miracles. They form the background of Jesus' activities. They stand on Jesus' side, against the rulers of Jerusalem, who criticize and challenge Jesus (Mark 2:4-7; 3:2-22; 11:8; 11:27; 11:32). Jesus has "compassion for them, because they were like sheep without a shepherd" (6:34). Jesus proclaims to them "the kingdom of God has come near" (1:15). He identifies with the suffering *minjung* and offers them a new hope and new life. *Minjung* theology developed a political hermeneutics not for the elite but for the people, and spoke to the Korean reality at the time.

In India, the caste system has subjected the Dalits—the "untouchables"—to the lowest rank of society. Dalits are the oppressed and the broken. They are discriminated against in terms of education, occupation, social interaction, and social mobility. The prejudice against the Dalits is so deep-seated that they face a great deal of discrimination even in Indian churches. Dalit theology emerged because of the insensitivity of the Indian churches to the plight of the Dalits and to give voice to Dalits' struggle for justice. In constructing a Dalit Christology, Peniel Rajkumar (115–26) finds Jesus' healing stories particularly relevant to the Dalit situation. Jesus touches and heals the leper (Mark 1:40-45), and transcends the social norms regarding purity and pollution. Afterward, Jesus asks the man to show his body to the priest (Mark 1:44) to bear witness that he has been healed and to confront the ideological purity system that alienates him. Jesus is angry at the system that maintains ritual purity to alienate and classify people. In coming to ask for healing, the leper also shows his faith through his willingness to break the cultural norm of purity. Again, we will find that the generalization of Jewish culture and purity taboo may be open to criticism. Jesus' anger toward injustice and his partnership with the leper to create a new social reality would help Dalits in their present struggles. The emphasis of Jesus' crossing boundaries is a recurrent theme in other Dalit readings (Nelavala). Many of the Dalit women from poor rural and urban areas are illiterate and do not have access to the written text of the Bible. The use of methods such as storytelling and role-play has helped them gain insights into biblical stories (Melanchthon).

In Africa, biblical scholars have addressed poverty, apartheid, religious and ethnic strife, HIV and AIDS, and political oppression, all of which have wreaked havoc in the continent. During apartheid in South Africa, a black theology of liberation was developed to challenge the Western and white outlook of the Christian church and to galvanize people to fight against apartheid. Itumeleng J. Mosala developed a historical-materialist reading of the Bible based on black history and culture. Mosala and his colleagues from Africa have asserted that Latin American liberation hermeneutics has not taken seriously the history of the blacks and Indians. His reading of Luke 1 and 2 brings out the material condition of the text, focusing on the colonial occupation of Palestine by Rome and the imperial extraction from peasants and the poor. He then uses the history, culture, and struggle of black people as a hermeneutical tool to lay bare the ideological assumptions in Luke's Gospel, showing it to be speaking for the class interest of the rich and eclipsing the experiences of the poor. He charges that some of the black theologians have continued to use Western and white hermeneutics even as they oppose the white, dominant groups. What is necessary is a new hermeneutics based on a black working-class perspective, which raises new questions in the interpretative process and enables a mutual interrogation between the text and situation.

In order to develop this kind of hermeneutics, biblical scholars must be socially engaged and read the Bible from the underside. With whom one is reading the Bible becomes both an epistemological and an ethical question. Several African biblical scholars emphasize the need for socially engaged scholars to read the Bible with ordinary poor and marginalized "readers." Gerald O. West maintains that if liberation theology begins with the experience of the poor and the oppressed, then these persons must be invited and included in the dialogical process of doing theology and reading the Bible. He describes the process of contextual Bible study among the poor, the roles of engaged biblical scholars, and lessons gleaned from the process. In the contextual reading of Luke 4:16-22, for instance, the women living around Pietermaritzburg and Durban related the meaning of setting the prisoners free, healing of the blind, and the relief of debts to their society. They discussed what they could do following the insights from the story to organize their community and create social change.

The Circle of Concerned African Women Theologians, formed in 1989, has encouraged Christian women from the African continent to produce and publish biblical and contextual hermeneutics. Some of the contributions have been published in *Other Ways of Reading: African Women and the Bible* (Dube 2001). The authors discuss storytelling methods, reading with and from nonacademic readers, toward a postapartheid black feminist reading, and the divination method of interpretation. The volume demystifies the notion of biblical canon, showing how women of the African continent have read the Bible with the canon of various African oral cultures. Aspects of African cultures serve as theories for analyzing the Bible. The volume is also conversant with feminist readings from other parts of the world, and in particular with African American women's hermeneutical approaches.

The HIV and AIDS epidemic brings enormous loss of life and suffering in the African continent, and the virus has spread mostly among heterosexual people. There is an increasing concern that in the sub-Saharan region, HIV infects more women than men. Musa Dube has played a key role in helping the African churches and theological institutions in addressing HIV and AIDS issues. In *The HIV and AIDS Bible* (Dube 2008), she implores scholars to develop biblical scholarship that is prophetic and healing. She challenges patriarchy and gender justice, and urges the churches to move beyond their comfort zone to respond to people affected by the virus. The church is HIV positive, she claims. Reading with people living with AIDS allows her to see the potential of the Bible to liberate and heal. She brings new insights to reading the miracles and healing stories of Jesus, such as the healing of Jairus's daughter (Mark 5:21-45). Her reading breaks the stigma and silence around HIV and AIDS while calling for adequate and compassionate care, and placing the HIV and AIDS epidemic within the larger context of other social discrimination.

The biblical readings from the Global South contribute to a global scholarship that takes into account other religious texts and classics in what is called intercultural and cross-textual reading (Lee). It is also interpreted through the lens of oral texts and retold and performed through storytelling, role-play, and skits. The exploration of these methods decentralizes Eurocentric modes of thinking that have gripped biblical studies for so long. It allows us to see the Bible and the world with fresh perspectives and new insights.

Contemporary Approaches to the New Testament

Books that introduce the wide array of contemporary methods used to interpret the New Testament are readily available (Anderson and Moore; Crossley). I have selected a few approaches that have global significance, as scholars from both the Global North and the Global South have used them and commented on them to illustrate current discussions shaping biblical scholarship. We will look at feminist approaches, social scientific approaches, racial and ethnic minority approaches, and postcolonial approaches.

Feminist Approaches

The New Testament was written by authors who lived in a patriarchal world with androcentric values and mind-sets. For a long time, churches have used parts of the Bible to deny women's full participation and treat them as second-class citizens in church and society. For example, churches have denied women's ordination based on the argument that all of Jesus' disciples were male. People have also cited the household codes (Col. 3:18—4:1; Eph. 5:21—6:9; 1 Peter 2:18—3:7) to support wives' submission to their husbands. Paul's teaching that women should be silent in the church (1 Cor. 14:34-35) has often been used to deny women's religious leadership. It is little wonder that some Western feminists have concluded that the Bible is irredeemably sexist and have become post-Christian. But feminist interpreters around the globe have developed ingenious ways to read against the grain and to find the Bible's liberating potential.

Christian feminists in many parts of the world have focused on stories about women in the Gospels. They have shown that women followed Jesus, listened to his preaching, and were healed because of their faith. Even when the disciples deserted Jesus at the cross, women steadfastly showed their faith. Scholars have drawn from some of these Gospel stories of women to illuminate how the gospel may speak to women's liberation of our time (Kinukawa; Tamez 2001). Christian women have also reclaimed and retold these stories, imagining dialogues, and supplying different endings. For example, I have heard from Christian women that the ending of Mary and Martha's story (Luke 10:38-42) should not end in Jesus' praising Mary over Martha, but the sisters' inviting Jesus to help in the kitchen so that all could continue the dialogue.

Other scholars find that the focus on biblical women is rather limited, for it does not provide a comprehensive framework to interpret the whole New Testament and still gives primacy and authority to the biblical text. Elisabeth Schüssler Fiorenza's influential book *In Memory of Her* (1983) presents a feminist historical-reconstructionist model, which places women at the center of the reconstruction of the Jesus movement and early Christianity. She shows that women were apostles, prophets, missionaries, as well as founders of household churches. She suggests that the radical vision of Jesus' movement was the praxis of inclusive wholeness and "discipleship of equals" (105–59). But women's leadership was increasingly marginalized in the second century, as patriarchalization set in when the church became more institutionalized. Schüssler Fiorenza's feminist model of critical interpretation insists that women should have the authority to judge whether a particular text is liberating or oppressive in the context of its reception.

Another approach is to use historical data and social theories to investigate the social world of early Christianity and to present a feminist social history. These studies look at women's marriage, status in the family, work and occupation, slave women and widows, and women's resistance in the Roman Empire (Schottroff; Yamaguchi). The parable of the leaven, for instance, makes visible women's work and uses a woman baking bread to describe the kingdom of God (Matt. 13:33; Luke 13:20-21). These works examine the impact of Roman persecution on women, the exploitative economic system, and Jewish resistance movements to provide a wider context to read the New Testament. Influenced by liberation theology, Elsa Tamez (2007) employs class analysis to study the Pastoral Letters. She describes how the rich people had challenged the leadership of the elders and presbyters in the church to which 1 Timothy was addressed. The injunction that women should be silent and submissive (1 Tim. 2:11-12) targeted the rich women, who used their power and status to cause troubles in the church.

Feminist scholars have also used literary and rhetorical approaches. For example, Ingrid Rosa Kitzberger uses a literary approach to examine the women in the Gospel of John, paying attention to the characterization of the Samaritan woman, Mary Magdalene, Mary and Martha, and the mother of Jesus, the intention of the narrator, narrative devices and rhetorical strategies, and the sequential perception of the reader in the reading process. Her goal is to present a reading against the grain—a feminist hermeneutics that empowers women. Antoinette Clark Wire reconstructs a picture of the women prophets in the church of first-century Corinth by analyzing Paul's rhetoric in 1 Corinthians. She suggests that the Corinthian women prophets claim direct access to resurrected life in Christ through the Spirit. These women sometimes conflicted with Paul, but they were known for proclaiming God's thought in prophecy and responding for the people to God (11:5; 14:1-38). Others use rhetorical criticism not to reconstruct historical reality but to focus on the persuasive power of the text to motivate action and shape the values and ethos of the community. Schüssler Fiorenza (1992, 40–50) has suggested a rhetorical approach that unmasks the interlocking system of oppression because of racism, classism, sexism, and colonialism. She coins the term *kyriarchy* (from *kyrios*, the Greek word for "lord" or "master") to describe these multiple systems of domination and subordination, involving more than gender oppression. Her goal is to create an alternative rhetorical space that respects the equality and dignity of women and is defined by the logic of radical democracy. She uses the term *ekklēsia gynaikōn* or "wo/men church" to denote this political hermeneutical space. The Greek term *ekklēsia* means the democratic assembly, and "wo/men" signifies not the feminine gender (as ladies, wives, mothers, etc.) but full decision-making political subjects. She argues that "one can theorize *ekklēsia* of wo/men not only as a virtual utopian space but also as an already partially realized space of radical equality, as a site of feminist struggles to transform social and religious institutions and discourses" (2007, 73). Feminist biblical scholars have also begun to unpack the structures of masculinity in the ancient world and how they were embedded in the biblical text (Moore and Anderson).

Social-Scientific Approaches

As mentioned above, biblical interpreters have used social sciences to learn about the social and cultural world of New Testament texts. One of the early important figures is Gerd Theissen, who studied the sociology of early Palestinian Christianity by focusing on the three roles of the Jesus movement: the wandering charismatics, their supporters in local communities, and the bearers of revelation. The use of social scientific methods has broadened the scope and sources of the third quest or newest quest of the historical Jesus since the 1980s. Billed as interdisciplinary research, scholars claim to possess at their disposal the latest archaeological knowledge, sociological analysis, cultural anthropology, and other newest social-scientific tools. Scholars have employed theories from the study of millennial movements, Mary Douglas's theory of purity and pollution, and non-Western medicine, magic, and charismatic religion to scrutinize the Jesus movement (e.g., Gager; Crossan 1991; Borg).

Schüssler Fiorenza has criticized the social-scientific quest of Jesus. She notes that the emergence of this third quest coincided with conservative politics of the Reagan and Thatcher era and with growing right-wing fundamentalist movements. She chastises the restoration of historical positivism as corresponding to political conservatism and the proliferation of the historical Jesus books as feeding "into literalist fundamentalism by reasserting disinterested scientific positivism in order to shore up the scholarly authority and universal truth of their research portrayal of Jesus" (2000, 46). While these Jesus books are written for popular consumption with their authors featured in mass media, the works of feminist scholars are sidelined and dismissed as being too "political" and not "objective" enough.

From a South African perspective, Mosala asks whether the social-scientific approaches to the Bible are "one step forward, two steps back" (43). On the one hand, the social-scientific approaches are useful, he says, because they help us to see biblical texts as ideological products of social systems and power relations. Far too often, middle-class Christians have the tendency to psychologize or use an individualist lens while reading the Bible. On the other hand, the social-scientific approaches as practiced in the white, liberal, North American and European academy often reflect bourgeois interests. Many scholars, for example, have adapted interpretive sociology and structural-functionalist analysis to study the social world of the New Testament. The structural-functionalist approach looks at how social systems are related to one another so that society can function as a whole. Focusing more on integration, stability, and unity, it is less prone to analyze social confrontation and conflict. Using Theissen's study of Palestinian Christianity as an example, Mosala points out that Theissen fails to provide an adequate structural location of the Jesus movement in the political economy of the Roman Empire and does not deal with the real economic and political contradictions of the time (64–65). As such, Theissen's study will be of limited use for the black South Africans struggling against apartheid and other social oppression. Mosala challenges biblical scholars to be open about their own class interest and the limitations of their methods.

One of the important dimensions of social-scientific criticism is the introduction of models from social and cultural anthropology. In addition to the ancient Jewish, Hellenistic, and Roman cultures that biblical scholars have been studying, Bruce J. Malina, Jerome H. Neyrey, and others suggest a pan-Mediterranean culture, with values and ethos markedly different from those in North American culture. The pivotal characteristics of Mediterranean culture in the first century included honor and shame, patronage and clientele, dyadic personality, and rules of purity. They apply the study of Mediterranean culture to interpret the group development of the Jesus movement and Paul's Letters. Scholars have questioned whether it is appropriate to impose models of contemporary societies onto the ancient Mediterranean. They remain doubtful whether the pivotal values of honor and shame are so different from the values in North American and northern European cultures. James G. Crossley also notes that "the Mediterranean frequently blurs into the contemporary Arab world, an area of renewed interest in American and European politics and media in the past forty years" (27).

As a discipline, anthropology emerged during the colonial time and often served the interests of empire. The hypothesis of a distinct Mediterranean culture and personality as contrasted with those in Western society reinforces a binary construction of the colonizers and the colonized. Malina and others have imported twentieth-century anthropological studies to the study of first-century Galilean and Judean society, assuming that Mediterranean cultures had remained unchanged over the years. Furthermore, the honor and shame code is attributed to a strong division of sexual and gender roles in the region and to the anxiety of Mediterranean men over their manhood. Female scholars such as Marianne Sawicki have voiced concerns that the study of honor and shame has largely followed a masculinist script and that women's experiences are overlooked and different. She suggests that the honor-shame sensibility might simply be an ethnocentric projection of the Euro-American male researchers onto the people they are studying (77).

R. S. Sugirtharajah, from Sri Lanka, has criticized Orientalism in the work of biblical scholars who use social-scientific methods. In *Orientalism*, Edward W. Said questions the representation of the Middle East as inferior, exotic, and stagnant in Western scholarship. Sugirtharajah notes prevalent Orientalist tendencies and the recycling of Orientalist practices in biblical scholarship, especially in the study of the social and cultural world of Jesus. He surmises that designations such as "Israel," "Judah," "the Holy Land," "Mediterranean," "world of Jesus," and "cultural world of Jesus" are "ideologically charged rhetoric and markers of Eurocentric and Christian-centric conceptualizations of that part of the world" (2012, 103). New Testament scholars have reinscribed Orientalist messages by suggesting the idea of a static Orient, by generalizing and reducing complex Mediterranean cultures to a few essentials, by gender stereotyping, and by highlighting the contrast between the East and the West. Jesus is depicted as one who is secure in his culture and yet critical of it through redefining honor culture and rearranging Mediterranean values. Since the publication of Said's work, many disciplines have become cautious about Orientalist methods and tendencies. But such methods have resurfaced in biblical studies and books that display Orientalist biases. Sugirtharajah points out that some of them have even become best sellers in mainstream culture (102–18).

Racial and Ethnic Minority Approaches

Racial and ethnic minorities in the United States began to develop their hermeneutical approaches to the Bible during the struggles of the civil rights movement in the 1960s. The development of black theology, Hispanic/Latino theology, and Asian American theology in the United States could not be separated from the ferment and protest against imperialism and apartheid in the Global South. Tat-siong Benny Liew (2013) characterizes racial and ethnic minority readings of the New Testament as "border crossing"—transcending the border of theology and biblical studies and the border between biblical studies and other disciplines. He also succinctly delineates the different stages of the development of such readings. In the first stage, racial and ethnic minority theologians and biblical scholars interpreted the biblical message through their social realities and experiences. For example, James Cone's black theology (1969; 1973) relates the gospel of Jesus to black power and freedom and argues that Christ is black, because Christ identifies with the powerless in society. Mexican American theologian Virgilio Elizondo relates the story of the marginalized Galilean

Jesus who came from the borderland area of Galilee to the story of Hispanic/Latino people as a new *mestizo* people. Asian American Chan-Hie Kim sees parallels between the Cornelius story in Acts 10–11 and Asian immigrant experience because both Cornelius and Kim are outsiders. Other scholars began to find minority subjects in the Bible and presented positive images of them or more complex pictures, such as the Ethiopian eunuch in Acts 8:26-40 (C. J. Martin 1989), and discussed slavery in early Christianity and modern interpretations (Lewis; Martin 1991).

In the current, second stage, racial and ethnic minority scholars do not simply employ different methods of biblical criticism with a racial inflection; they are more thoroughly informed by scholarship in ethnic studies and cultural studies. Their interpretation of the New Testament no longer begins with the biblical texts but with their experience as racial and ethnic minorities living in the United States. Liew characterizes this shift of emphasis as the move from "reading Scripture reading race" to "reading race reading Scripture" (2013, 183). Instead of finding "race" in the biblical text, new frameworks and paradigms of engaging with the Bible are sought. This shift can clearly be seen in *African Americans and the Bible* (Wimbush), which considers the Bible in contemporary African American culture, including poetry, aesthetics of sacred space, gospel music and spirituals, rap music, folk oratory, and many other contexts. Liew's own volume *What Is Asian American Biblical Hermeneutics?* (2008) reads all the major genres of the New Testament with Asian American literature, ethnic studies, and current events. David A. Sánchez's study of Revelation includes significant resources from Latino/a studies and Chicana/o studies.

Another significant development in the second stage is the move beyond a unified and essentialized notion of race to an acknowledgment of internal diversity within each racial and ethnic minority group. African American women articulate the issues of womanist interpretation of the Bible, placing gender at the intersection of race, class, and other anthropological referents. Demetrius K. Williams examines the biblical foundation of understanding of gender in black churches, while Rachel Annette Saint Clair presents a womanist reading of Mark's Gospel. Within the Asian American community, heterogeneity can be seen not only in the addition of women's voices but also in readings by diverse ethnic groups, intergenerational interpretations, and readings by Asian American adoptees and queer people (Foskett and Kuan; Cheng). Likewise, the diversity of the Hispanic/Latino people has been highlighted, and notions of borderland and *mestizaje* differ among different ethnic groups. Manuel Villalobos has combined the insights from feminist and queer theories to read the Ethiopian eunuch in Acts to bring hope and affirmation to Latino queer bodies.

Moving into the third stage, racial and ethnic minority theologians and biblical scholars have begun collaboration across minority groups. The move from articulating minority experience vis-à-vis the white dominant culture to conversing with other racial and ethnic minorities signals a new awareness, which is much needed to prepare for 2040, when, if current trends continue, there will be no racial and ethnic majority in the United States. An important example of such endeavor is the volume *They Were All Together in One Place? Toward Minority Criticism*, coedited by African, Asian, and Hispanic Americans (Bailey, Liew, and Segovia). This collaboration shows a desire for mutual learning and communication across color lines. In the future, more attention needs to be paid both to engaging Native American readings and, given our transnational world, to linking minority criticism with readings in the Global South.

Postcolonial Approaches

Emerging in the late 1970s, postcolonial studies has had significant influence in the fields of the humanities and social sciences. The prefix *post-* does not simply signify the period after colonialism in a chronological sense, but also refers to reading and social practices that aim at contesting colonialism and lifting up the voices of the suppressed and formerly colonized. Postcolonial criticism has drawn from many disciplines and was introduced to biblical studies in the 1990s, particularly through the works and encouragement of R. S. Sugirtharajah (1998; 2002). Other scholars have included a postcolonial optic in the study of the New Testament; for example, Tat-siong Benny Liew (1999), Fernando F. Segovia, Musa W. Dube (2000), Laura D. Donaldson, Stephen D. Moore (2006), and me (2005).

During Jesus' time, Galilee was under Roman imperial occupation and ruled by Herod Antipas (4 BCE–39 CE), and the early Christian communities lived under the whims of empire. Postcolonial critics of the New Testament share common interests with those contributing to the emerging subfield of "empire studies," promoted enthusiastically by Richard A. Horsley (1997; 2002) and other scholars (e.g., Carter; Crossan 2007). This subfield consists of books and articles with the recurrent words *empire* or *imperial* in their titles and with the intention of using the theme of empire to reframe New Testament interpretation. While the authors of works in empire studies are interested in the ancient imperial contexts, and some have related their work to contemporary contexts, they may or may not use postcolonial studies to aid their research and few have shown particular interest in affixing the label "postcolonial" to their works (Moore 2006, 14–19).

Postcolonial critics emphasize that biblical texts are not innocent. Sugirtharajah, for instance, understands postcolonial criticism as "scrutinizing and exposing colonial domination and power as these are embodied in biblical texts and in interpretations, and as searching for alternative hermeneutics while thus overturning and dismantling colonial perspectives" (1998, 16). Postcolonial criticism shares similarities with liberation hermeneutics, but also diverges from it because postcolonial critics are more suspicious of the historical-critical method that many liberation critics use. Postcolonial critics see biblical texts as more complex and multilayered and do not construct rich/poor, colonizer/colonized, and oppressor/oppressed in binary and dichotomous ways, as some liberation theologians do. Liberation theologians from Latin America tend to be Christocentric, while postcolonial critics engage more fully with religious pluralism and popular religions (Sugirtharajah 2002, 103–23).

Applying postcolonial criticism to the Gospels, Sugirtharajah (2002, 86–91) finds that there is no mention of Jesus' explicit resistance against the colonial occupiers. Yet Jesus' critique of local profiteers who colluded with the Romans and some of his sayings about earthly rulers (Matt. 11:8; Luke 7:25; 13:32) suggest that his alternative vision was against those in power. Horsley (2002) takes a stronger stance that Jesus was against empire. He places the Jesus movement within the context of popular resistance movements in Judea and Galilee, and says that the anti-imperial nature of Jesus' movement can provide a basis for theological critique of the Roman Empire in the past and the American empire in the present. Postcolonial studies of Paul's letters have also appeared; for example, Joseph A. Marchal applies feminist and postcolonial theories to the study of Philippians. The 2011 volume *The Colonized Apostle: Paul through Postcolonial Eyes* (Stanley) is the most comprehensive study to date, discussing Pauline agency, Paul's supposed social conservatism, hybrid identity and ethnicity, gender and colonialism, and Paul's relation to struggles in South Korea and the Philippines, among other topics. Moore (2006) uses postcolonial theorist Homi Bhabha to read apocalypse in Mark and John and the book of Revelation and argues that these texts mimic to a certain extent Roman imperial ideology, even when resisting and eroding it. *A Postcolonial Commentary on the New Testament Writings* (Segovia and Sugirtharajah), published in 2007, showcases the diversity of approaches and is an invaluable resource for further studies.

Postcolonial feminist interpretation challenges white male and female metropolitan readings for ignoring the issues of colonialism and imperialism and shows how their readings might collude with empire (Dube 2000). As we have discussed, Dube has lifted up the readings of ordinary female readers in African Independent Churches. Other critical concerns of postcolonial feminist criticism include the investigation of how the deployment of gender and symbolization of women relate to class interests and colonial domination in the Bible and studying women in the contact zones and the borderlands, such as Rahab, Ruth, and the Syrophoenician woman (Kwok, 81–85).

The publication of *Postcolonial Perspectives in African Biblical Interpretations* (Dube, Mbuvi, and Mbuwayesango) in 2012 pushes the envelope of postcolonial criticism even further. It raises the possibilities of "unthinking Eurocentrism" in biblical studies and developing Afrocentric criticism. The volume discusses the politics of translation of the Bible, the Bible as read in and through African creative writings, the relation of the Bible and "the scramble of Africa," HIV and AIDS, and the roles of socially engaged biblical scholars. The volume offers much insight and food for thought for interpreters in other parts of the Global South as well as in metropolitan areas who want to decolonize their minds and their methods when approaching the Bible.

Contemporary Issues

In this final section, I would like to take up some contemporary issues to see how they have led to new readings of the New Testament from fresh angles. First, the Holocaust has prompted many scholars to be conscious of the long history of anti-Jewish and antisemitic biases in the history of biblical interpretation. Scholars have proposed new ways to interpret New Testament texts so that they will not be construed as anti-Jewish. Second, the vigorous debates on same-sex marriage in the United States and elsewhere require us to reexamine the teachings on marriage, family, and same-gender relationships in the New Testament. Third, the study of "Gnosticism" and other writings in early Christianity has made us keenly aware of the politics of inclusion and exclusion surrounding the New Testament canon. A group of scholars has produced a new version of the New Testament combining both traditional and newly discovered texts.

Anti-Judaism and Antisemitism

Anti-Jewish attitudes and prejudices have contributed to antisemitism and the tragic genocide in modern times of Jewish people in Europe. Jews have been blamed for killing Jesus. Jesus' accusations against the scribes and Pharisees as hypocrites and his polemical sayings about the Jews in

John's Gospel have been used to cast Jewish people as the other, who did not accept the good news of Jesus Christ. Jesus has been seen as the founder of a new religion, separate from his Jewish background. Paul's contrast of law and gospel has been taken as the foundational difference between the covenant of the old and the new. Christianity has often been hailed as a universal religion, accepting gentiles into its mix, while Judaism has been cast in a negative light as a religion belonging to a particular group. Many Christians continue to harbor a supersessionist viewpoint, believing that Christianity ultimately triumphs over Judaism.

Interpreters sensitive to the charges of anti-Judaism and antisemitism have presented alternative views and interpretations different from those often taught in Christian churches. New Testament scholars have emphasized Jesus' Jewishness and interpreted Jesus' movement as a movement *within* Judaism. For example, Géza Vermes regards Jesus as a Jewish Galilean charismatic, while E. P. Sanders sees Jesus as an eschatological prophet who believed that the promises to Israel would soon be fulfilled and restoration would be at hand. Jewish New Testament scholar Amy-Jill Levine (2011) calls Jesus "the misunderstood Jew," and her work helps Jews and Christians understand the Jewish context of the first century. In *The Jewish Gospels*, Daniel Boyarin, a professor of talmudic culture, argues that Jesus' teachings can be found in the long-standing Jewish tradition and the coming of the Messiah was imagined in many Jewish texts. Many also point out that Jesus' arguments with the Pharisees and Jewish leaders were not conflicts between Christian and Jews, but intra-Jewish arguments (Wills, 101–32).

Jewish scholars such as Judith Plaskow and Levine (2000) have cautioned against the blanket generalizations of Jewish culture as misogynist in order to construct Jesus as a feminist over against his cultural background. Sometimes, Christian feminists have used Jesus' critique of his culture to support their challenge of patriarchy in their own cultures. To heed these scholars' call, we must avoid generalization and not imagine "the Jews" as the same transhistorically and transculturally. Some of the characterizations of "purity" discussed earlier would seem to fall under this criticism. More attention must be paid to local practices, regional history, and religious views and political ideologies of different groups and factions in first-century Judaism. Levine also suggests reading in community so that we can be exposed to our biases and blind spots in our reading.

An exciting development is the publication of the volume *The Jewish Annotated New Testament* (Levine and Brettler) in 2011, a collaborative effort of an international team of fifty Jewish scholars, which presents Jewish history, beliefs, and practices for understanding the New Testament. The New Testament is interpreted within the context of the Hebrew Bible and rabbinic literature. Each book of the New Testament is annotated with references, and the volume includes thirty essays covering a wide range of topics, including the synagogue, the law, food and table fellowship, messianic movements, Jewish miracle workers, Jewish family life, divine beings, and afterlife and resurrection. It also addresses Jewish responses to the New Testament and contemporary Jewish-Christian relations. The book will facilitate Jewish-Christian dialogue because it helps Christians better understand the Jewish roots of the New Testament and offers Jews a way to understand the New Testament that does not proselytize Christianity or cast Judaism in a negative light.

It should be pointed out that there is a difference between antisemitism and the critique of the policies of the state of Israel and its unequal treatment of Palestinians. Some Jewish thinkers and leaders, such as Judith Butler and Rabbi Michael Lerner, have criticized political Zionism, the dispossession of land, and hard-line policies of the Israeli state. Palestinian liberation theologian Naim Stifan Ateek has challenged Christian Zionism, adherents of which believe that the Jews must return to the Holy Land as a prerequisite for the second coming of Christ. Ateek draws from the example of Jesus to discuss the relation between justice and peace, nonviolent resistance, and the peacekeeping imperatives of the church.

Same-Sex Marriage

Debates on same-sex marriage in United States, Europe, Latin America, and Asia saw both supporters and opponents citing the Bible to support their positions. In the United States, the influential conservative Christian leader James Dobson defends what he calls the biblical definition of marriage, and blames homosexuality and gay marriage for all kinds of social decline. A cursory search on the Internet can find numerous posts citing biblical passages to defend heterosexual marriage and label homosexual passions and acts as unnatural, shameful, and contrary to God's will. These posts usually cite the creation of Adam and Eve in Genesis and the views of Jesus and Paul on marriage and sexuality as support.

Many Christians believe that the modern nuclear family represents the Christian ideal, but the current focus on heterosexual nuclear family dates back only to the 1950s. Dale B. Martin argues that there are more sources in the New Testament to criticize the modern family than to support it. Jesus was not a family man, and the Gospels present Jesus as living in alternative communities that shared his vision of divinely constituted family. He refused to identify with his natural family, saying, "Whoever does the will of God is my brother and sister and mother" (Mark 3:35; cf. Matt. 12:50; Luke 8:21). Jesus forbade divorce, even though Mosaic law allowed it (Matt. 19:4-9; Mark 10:6-12). But Matthew follows this with the saying about those who have "made themselves eunuchs for the sake of the kingdom of heaven" (Matt. 19:12), which might imply that the avoidance of marriage and of procreation is preferable. Jesus also says in the Gospels that in the resurrection, marriage will be obsolete (Matt. 22:30; Mark 12:26).

Paul in 1 Corinthians 7 did not promote marriage or traditional family and preferred Christians to follow his example and remain single and celibate. He thought that marriage would become a distraction from the life of faith "in Christ." But he allowed marriage for those who were weak and could not control their passions, saying "it is better to marry than to be aflame with passion" (1 Cor. 7:9). In Paul's time, passion and sexual desires were associated with the body and had to be put under severe control. The letters to the Colossians and Ephesians contain the household codes, which propose the hierarchy and order of a patriarchal family. But these letters are generally considered deuteropauline and were written during the increasing patriarchal institutionalization of the church.

Opponents to same-sex marriage often cite Rom. 1:23-27 to support their claims that homosexual acts are unnatural. Scholars have offered different explanations of the context of this text to argue that it is not against homosexual relations as we have come to know them in the present day (Goss, 198–202). Some suggest that homosexual acts were considered part of unclean gentile culture and were condemned by Paul for that reason. Others claim that Paul was not speaking about adult homosexual relations but pederasty in the Greco-Roman world. Some even proffer that Paul might have in mind oral or anal sex as unnatural sexual intercourse, among opposite-sex partners as well. Bernadette J. Brooten comments that Paul's injunction against female homosexual relations was due to his understanding of gender roles. Paul did not want women to exchange their supposedly passive and subordinate desire for an active role (216). Feminist scholars have challenged the androcentric mind-set and patriarchal ideologies of Pauline and other New Testament writings.

The New Testament thus cannot be easily enlisted to support a reductionistic understanding of "Christian marriage" or "family values," as if these have not changed over time. While same-sex marriage has become a rallying cry for marriage equality and recognition of human rights, some lesbians and gay men have also expressed concerns that the legislation of marriage would give too much power to the state, which can legitimize one form of sexual relationship while excluding others. Dale B. Martin belongs to this latter group and encourages queer Christians to expand their imaginations to "allow scripture and tradition to inspire new visions of Christian community free from the constraints of the modern, heterosexual, nuclear family" (39). Tolbert (2006) adds that same-sex couples can find the ideals of friendship in the New Testament supportive of their relationship. In John, Jesus told the disciples that they were his friends and shared with them his deepest knowledge of God. The New Testament, Tolbert says, does not promote marriage, heterosexual or not, as the bedrock of Christian community, but rather values friendship; as Jesus says, "No one has greater love than this, to lay down one's life for one's friends" (John 15:13). Even though the notion of friendship in the ancient world might be quite different from ours, the shift from promoting marriage to friendship opens new horizons.

A "New" New Testament

In 1945, local peasants in Nag Hammadi in Egypt discovered papyrus codices in a clay sealed jar consisting of fifty-two gnostic writings that were previously unknown. Though the papyrus dated back to the fourth century, some of the texts in the manuscripts can be traced back to as early as the first or second century. The Nag Hammadi library contains texts such as the *Gospel of Thomas*, the *Gospel of Philip*, the *Gospel of Truth*, and writings attributed to Jesus' followers, such as the *Secret Book of James*, the *Apocalypse of Paul*, and the *Apocalypse of Peter* (Pagels). The discovery of these texts greatly expanded our knowledge of religious writings in the early centuries.

Just as Jewish scholars have challenged us to reexamine our assumptions about Christian origins and the Jewish roots of Christianity, the discovery and study of the Nag Hammadi library raised new issues about the conceptualization of the history of the early church. Before the discovery, all we knew about "Gnosticism" was that the orthodox heresiologists, especially Irenaeus and Tertullian, vilified it. Karen L. King (2003) argues that these polemicists had constructed the category "heresy" as part of their project of identity formation and to exclude Jews and pagans as outsiders. The Nag Hammadi writings show what scholars have called "Gnosticism" as highly pluralistic and the boundary between Christianity and "Gnosticism" as more permeable than previously assumed. Both the so-called orthodox and the heretical writings belonged to a common body of tradition and represented "distinct varieties of Christianity developed in different geographical areas, at a time when the boundaries of orthodox and heresy were not at all fixed" (152). Moreover, certain texts were excluded from the

New Testament canon because of ideological reasons, such as to marginalize women's authority and leadership. For example, the *Gospel of Mary*, which was excluded, depicts Mary Magdalene as having received special knowledge from Jesus and serving as a leader among the disciples after Jesus' resurrection. This portrait of Mary should be considered together with the depiction of her as one of Jesus' followers and a key witness to his resurrection in the New Testament (King 1998).

In addition to the Nag Hammadi library, other texts have been discovered in the nineteenth and twentieth centuries and scientifically verified to be almost as old as the manuscripts of the traditional New Testament. A group of scholars, pastors, and church leaders under the leadership of Hal Taussig have produced a New Testament for the twenty-first century that includes with the established canon a selection of some of the texts outside the canon and called it "a new New Testament." The newly added documents include ten books, two prayers, and the *Odes of Solomon*, which consists mostly of prayers. Now, within the same volume, we can read about Mary Magdalene in the traditional Gospels as well as in the *Gospel of Mary*. In contrast to the traditional book of Revelation, the *Secret Revelation of John* offers a different picture of how Christ rescues the world, not through apocalyptic battles, but by teaching about God's light and compassion. Taussig hopes that this new New Testament can offer readers a chance to form new opinions about the earliest traditions of Christianity and be inspired by the teachings, songs, prayers, letters, and meditations of Jesus' early followers (xviii–xix).

Conclusion

The New Testament has shaped human cultures for millennia and is read by Christians, people of other religious traditions, and secular people in different tongues, cultural backgrounds, social contexts, and life circumstances. As global citizens living in the twenty-first century, we have to remember how the gospel of Jesus Christ has been misused to oppress and construct the other, whether the other is Jewish people, women, racial and ethnic minorities, colonized people, or queer people, so that history will not be repeated. The availability of so many new resources and methods in New Testament studies and the addition of underrepresented voices from all over the world are cause for celebration. New Testament reading in the contemporary world has become more global, multicentered, and plurivocal, and contributes to interreligious understanding. The interpretation of the New Testament has also been brought to the public square, as people look for insights from the Bible to address problems of our day. I hope that those among the younger generation who profess that they are "spiritual but not religious" will also appreciate the wisdom in the New Testament, as one of the most fascinating and influential religious and spiritual literatures of humankind.

Works Cited

Ahn, Byung Mu. 1981. "Jesus and the Minjung in the Gospel of Mark." In *Minjung Theology: People as the Subjects of History*, edited by Kim Yong Bock, 136–52. Singapore: Commission of Theological Concerns, Christian Conference of Asia.

Anderson, Janice Capel, and Stephen D. Moore, eds. 2008. *Mark and Method: New Approaches in Biblical Studies*. 2nd ed. Minneapolis: Fortress Press.

Ariarajah, Wesley. 1989. *The Bible and People of Other Faiths*. Maryknoll, NY: Orbis.

Ateek, Naim Stefan. 1989. *Justice, and Only Justice: A Palestinian Theology of Liberation*. Maryknoll, NY: Orbis.

Bailey, Randall C., Tat-siong Benny Liew, and Fernando F. Segovia, eds. 2009. *They Were All Together in One Place? Toward Minority Biblical Criticism*. Atlanta: Society of Biblical Literature.

Barr, James. 1983. *Holy Scripture: Canon, Authority, Criticism*. Oxford: Clarendon.

Baum, Wilhelm, and Dietmar W. Winkler. 2003. *The Church of the East: A Concise History*. London: RoutledgeCurzon.

Blount, Brian K. 1995. *Cultural Interpretation: Reorienting New Testament Criticism*. Minneapolis: Fortress Press.

Borg, Marcus J. 1994. *Jesus in Contemporary Scholarship*. Valley Forge, PA: Trinity Press International.

Boyarin, Daniel. 2012. *The Jewish Gospels: The Story of the Jewish Christ*. New York: New Press.

Brooten, Bernadette J. 1996. *Love between Women: Early Christian Responses to Female Homoeroticism*. Chicago: University of Chicago Press.

Butler, Judith. 2012. *Parting Ways: Jewishness and the Critique of Zionism*. New York: Columbia University Press.

Cardenal, Ernesto. 1976–1982. *The Gospel in Solentiname*. Translated by Donald D. Walsh. 4 vols. Maryknoll, NY: Orbis.

Carter, Warren. 2001. *Matthew and Empire: Initial Explorations*. Harrisburg, PA: Trinity Press International.

Cheng, Patrick S. 2002. "Multiplicity and Judges 19: Constructing a Queer Asian Pacific American Biblical Hermeneutic." *Semeia* 90–91:119–33.

Cone, James H. 1969. *Black Theology and Black Power*. New York: Seabury.

———. 1975. *God of the Oppressed*. New York: Seabury.

Crossan, John Dominic. 1991. *The Historical Jesus: The Life of a Mediterranean Jewish Peasant*. San Francisco: HarperSanFrancisco.

———. 2007. *God and Empire: Jesus against Rome, Then and Now*. New York: HarperCollins.

Crossley, James G. 2010. *Reading the New Testament: Contemporary Approaches*. London: Routledge.

Dobson, James C. 2004. *Marriage under Fire: Why We Must Win This War*. Sisters, OR: Multnomah.

Donaldson, Laura E. 2006. "Gospel Hauntings: The Postcolonial Demons of New Testament Criticism." In *Postcolonial Biblical Criticism: Interdisciplinary Intersections*, edited by Fernando F. Segovia and Stephen D. Moore, 97–113. London: Continuum.

Dube, Musa W. 2000. *Postcolonial Feminist Interpretation of the Bible*. St. Louis: Chalice.

———, ed. 2001. *Other Ways of Reading: African Women and the Bible*. Atlanta: Society of Biblical Literature.

———. 2008. *The HIV and AIDS Bible: Selected Essays*. Scranton, PA: University of Scranton Press.

Dube, Musa, Andrew M. Mbuvi, and Dora R. Mbuwayesango, eds. 2012. *Postcolonial Perspectives in African Biblical Interpretations*. Atlanta: Society of Biblical Literature.

Eber, Irene, Sze-kar Wan, and Knut Walf, eds. 1999. *The Bible in Modern China*. Nettetal, Germany: Steyler.

Elizondo, Virgilio. 1983. *Galilean Journey: The Mexican-American Promise*. Maryknoll, NY: Orbis.

Fernandez, Eleazar S. 2013. "Multiple Locations-Belongings and Power Differentials: Lenses for Liberating Biblical Hermeneutic." In *Soundings in Cultural Criticism: Perspectives and Methods in Culture, Power, and Identity in the New Testament*, edited by Francisco Lozada Jr. and Greg Carey, 139–49. Minneapolis: Fortress Press.

Flatow, Sheryl. 2009. "Christianity on the Move." *Bostonia*. http://www.bu.edu/bostonia/fall09/christianity.

Foskett, Mary F., and Jeffrey Kah-Jin Kuan, eds. 2006. *Ways of Being, Ways of Reading: Asian American Biblical Interpretation*. St. Louis: Chalice.

Gager, John G. 1975. *Kingdom and Community: The Social World of Early Community*. Englewood Cliffs, NJ: Prentice-Hall.

Goss, Robert E. 2002. *Queering Christ: Beyond Jesus Acted Up*. Cleveland: Pilgrim.

Gutiérrez, Gustavo. 1988. *A Theology of Liberation: History, Politics, and Salvation*. Translated by Caridad Inda and John Eagleson. Rev. ed. Maryknoll, NY: Orbis.

Hastings, Adrian, ed. 1999. *A World History of Christianity*. Grand Rapids: Eerdmans.

Horsley, Richard A., ed. 1997. *Paul and Empire: Religion and Power in Roman Imperial Society*. Harrisburg, PA: Trinity Press International.

———. 2002. *Jesus and Empire: The Kingdom of God and the New World Disorder*. Minneapolis: Fortress Press.

Irvin, Dale T., and Scott W. Sunquist. 2001. *History of the World Christian Movement*. Vol. 1, *Earliest Christianity to 1453*. Maryknoll, NY: Orbis.

———. 2012. *History of the World Christian Movement*. Vol. 2, *Modern Christianity from 1454 to 1800*. Maryknoll, NY: Orbis.

Jenkins, Philip. 2007. *The Next Christendom: The Coming of Global Christianity*. Rev. ed. New York: Oxford University Press.

Johnson, Todd M., and Kenneth R. Ross. 2009. *Atlas of Global Christianity, 1910–2010*. Edinburgh: Edinburgh University Press.

Kim, Chan-Hie. 1995. "Reading the Cornelius Story from an Asian Immigrant Perspective." In *Reading from This Place*. Vol. 1, *Social Location and Biblical Interpretation in the United States*, edited by Fernando F. Segovia and Mary Ann Tolbert, 165–74. Minneapolis: Fortress Press.

Kinukawa, Hisako. 1994. *Women and Jesus in Mark: A Japanese Feminist Perspective*. Maryknoll, NY: Orbis.

King, Karen L. 1998. "Canonization and Marginalization: Mary of Magdala." In *Women's Sacred Scriptures*, edited by Kwok Pui-lan and Elisabeth Schüssler Fiorenza, 29–36. London: SCM.

———. 2003. *What Is Gnosticism?* Cambridge, MA: Harvard University Press.

Kitzberger, Ingrid Rosa. 1998. "How Can This Be? (John 3:9): A Feminist Theological Re-Reading of the Gospel of John." In *What Is John?* Vol. 2, *Literary and Social Readings of the Fourth Gospel*, edited by Fernando F. Segovia, 19–41. Atlanta: Society of Biblical Literature.

Kwok Pui-lan. 2005. *Postcolonial Imagination and Feminist Theology*. Louisville: Westminster John Knox.

Lady Gaga. 2011. "Judas." Posted on May 3. http://www.ladygaga.com/media/?meid=6765.

Lee, Archie C. C. 1998. "Cross-Textual Interpretation and Its Implications for Biblical Studies." In *Teaching the Bible: The Discourses and Politics of Biblical Pedagogy*, edited by Fernando F. Segovia and Mary Ann Tolbert, 247–54. Maryknoll, NY: Orbis.

Levine, Amy-Jill. 2000. "Lilies of the Field and Wandering Jews: Biblical Scholarship, Women's Roles, and Social Location." In *Transforming Encounters: Jesus and Women Re-viewed*, edited by Ingrid Rosa Kitzberger, 329–52. Leiden: Brill.

———. 2006. *The Misunderstood Jew: The Church and the Scandal of the Jewish Jesus*. San Francisco: HarperSanFrancisco.

Levine, Amy-Jill, and Marc Z. Brettler, eds. 2011. *The Jewish Annotated New Testament*. New York: Oxford University Press.

Lewis, Lloyd A. 1991. "An African American Appraisal of the Philemon-Paul-Onesimus Triangle." In *Stony the Road We Trod: African American Biblical Interpretation*, edited by Cain Hope Felder, 232–46. Minneapolis: Fortress Press.

Liew, Tat-siong Benny. 1999. *The Politics of Parousia: Reading Mark Inter(con)textually*. Leiden: Brill.

———. 2008. *What Is Asian American Biblical Hermeneutics?* Honolulu: University of Hawai'i Press.

———. 2013. "Colorful Readings: Racial/Ethnic Minority Readings of the New Testament in the United States." In *Soundings in Cultural Criticism: Perspectives and Methods in Culture, Power, and Identity in the New Testament*, edited by Francisco Lozado Jr. and Greg Carey, 177–89, Minneapolis: Fortress Press.

Malina, Bruce J. 1981. *The New Testament World: Insights from Cultural Anthropology*. Atlanta: John Knox Press.

Marchal, Joseph A. 2008. *The Politics of Heaven: Women, Gender, and Empire in the Study of Paul*. Minneapolis: Fortress Press.

Martin, Clarice J. 1989. "A Chamberlain's Journey and the Challenge of Interpretation for Liberation." *Semeia* 47:105–35.

———. 1991. "The *Haustafeln* (Household Codes) in African American Interpretation: 'Free Slaves' and 'Subordinate Women.'" In *Stony the Road We Trod: African American Biblical Interpretation*, edited by Cain Hope Felder, 206–31. Minneapolis: Fortress Press.

Martin, Dale B. 2006. "Familiar Idolatry and the Christian Case against Marriage." In *Authorizing Marriage? Canon, Tradition, and Critique in the Blessing of Same-sex Unions*, edited by Mark D. Jordan, 17–40. Princeton: Princeton University Press.

Meeks, Wayne A. 1983. *The First Urban Christians: The Social World of the Apostle Paul*. New Haven: Yale University Press.

Melanchthon, Monica Jyotsna. 2010. "Dalit Women and the Bible: Hermeneutical and Methodological Reflections." In *Hope Abundant: Third World and Indigenous Women's Theology*, edited by Kwok Pui-lan, 103–22, Maryknoll, NY: Orbis.

Moore, Stephen D. 2006. *Empire and Apocalypse: Postcolonialism and the New Testament*. Sheffield: Sheffield Phoenix Press.

———. 2010. *The Bible in Theory: Critical and Postcritical Essays*. Atlanta: Society of Biblical Literature.

———. 2013. "The Dog-Woman of Canaan and Other Animal Tales from the Gospel of Matthew." In *Soundings in Cultural Criticism: Perspectives and Methods in Culture, Power, and Identity in the New Testament*, edited by Francisco Lozada Jr. and Greg Carey, 57–71. Minneapolis: Fortress Press.

Moore, Stephen D., and Janice Capel Anderson, eds. 2003. *New Testament Masculinities*. Atlanta: Society of Biblical Literature.

Mosala, Itumeleng J. 1989. *Biblical Hermeneutics and Black Theology in South Africa*. Grand Rapids: Eerdmans.

Nelavala, Surekha. 2006. "Smart Syrophoenician Woman: A Dalit Feminist Reading of Mark 7:24-31." *ExpTim* 118, no. 2: 64–69.

Neyrey, Jerome H. 1990. *Paul, in Other Words: A Cultural Reading of His Letters*. Louisville: Westminster John Knox.

Pagels, Elaine. 1979. *The Gnostic Gospels*. New York: Random House.

Patte, Daniel. 2004. Introduction to *Global Bible Commentary*, edited by Daniel Patte, xxi–xxxii. Nashville: Abingdon.

Petrella, Ivan. 2005. *Latin American Liberation Theology: The Next Generation*. Maryknoll, NY: Orbis.

Plaskow, Judith. 1980. "Blaming the Jews for the Birth of Patriarchy." *Lilith* 7:11–12, 14–17.

Rajkumar, Peniel. 2010. *Dalit Theology and Dalit Liberation: Problems, Paradigms, and Possibilities*. Burlington, VT: Ashgate.

Roncace, Mark, and Joseph Weaver, eds. 2013. *Global Perspectives on the Bible*. Upper Saddle River, NJ: Pearson.

Said, Edward W. 1978. *Orientalism*. New York: Pantheon.

Saint Clair, Rachel Annette. 2008. *Call and Consequences: A Womanist Reading of Mark*. Minneapolis: Fortress Press.

Sánchez, David A. 2008. *From Patmos to the Barrio: Subverting Imperial Myths*. Minneapolis: Fortress Press.

Sanders, E. P. 1985. *Jesus and Judaism*. Philadelphia: Fortress Press.

Sanneh, Lamin O. 1989. *Translating the Message: The Missionary Impact on Culture*. Maryknoll, NY: Orbis.

———. 2003. *Whose Religion Is Christianity? The Gospel beyond the West*. Grand Rapids: Eerdmans.

———. 2007. *Disciples of All Nations: Pillars of World Christianity*. New York: Oxford University Press.

Sawicki, Marianne. 2000. *Crossing Galilee: Architectures of Contact in the Occupied Land of Jesus*. Harrisburg, PA: Trinity Press International.

Scharper, Philip, and Sally Scharper, eds. 1984. *Gospel in Art by the Peasants of Solentiname*. Maryknoll, NY: Orbis.

Schottroff, Luise. 1995. *Lydia's Impatient Sisters: A Feminist Social History of Early Christianity*. Translated by Barbara Rumscheidt and Martin Rumscheidt. Louisville: Westminster John Knox.

Schüssler Fiorenza, Elisabeth. 1983. *In Memory of Her: A Feminist Theological Reconstruction of Christian Origins*. New York: Crossroad.

———. 1992. *But She Said: Feminist Practices of Biblical Interpretation*. Boston: Beacon.

———. 2000. *Jesus and the Politics of Interpretation*. New York: Continuum.

———. 2002. "The Ethos of Biblical Interpretation: Biblical Studies in a Postmodern and Postcolonial Context." In *Theological Literacy for the Twenty-First Century*, edited by Rodney L. Petersen, 211–28. Grand Rapids: Eerdmans.

———. 2007. *The Power of the Word: Scripture and the Rhetoric of Empire*. Minneapolis: Fortress Press.

Segovia, Fernando F. 2000. *Decolonizing Biblical Studies: A View from the Margins*. Maryknoll, NY: Orbis.

Segovia, Fernando F., and R. S. Sugirtharajah, eds. 2007. *A Postcolonial Commentary on the New Testament Writings*, New York: T&T Clark.

Segundo, Juan Luis. 1976. *Liberation of Theology*. Translated by John Drury. Maryknoll, NY: Orbis.

Stanley, Christopher D., ed. 2011. *The Colonized Apostle: Paul through Postcolonial Eyes*. Minneapolis: Fortress Press.

Sugirtharajah, R. S. 1999. *Asian Biblical Hermeneutics and Postcolonial Criticism: Contesting the Interpretations*. Maryknoll, NY: Orbis.

———. 2002. *Postcolonial Criticism and Biblical Interpretation*. Oxford: Oxford University Press.

———. 2012. *Exploring Postcolonial Biblical Criticism: History, Method, Practice*. Malden, MA: Wiley-Blackwell.

———, ed. 1998. "Biblical Studies after the Empire: From a Colonial to a Postcolonial Mode of Interpretation." In *The Postcolonial Bible*, edited by R. S. Sugirtharajah. Sheffield: Sheffield Academic Press.

Tamez, Elsa. 2001. *Jesus and Courageous Women*. New York: Women's Division, General Board of Global Ministries, United Methodist Church.

———. 2007. *Struggles for Power in Early Christianity: A Study of the First Letter to Timothy*. Translated by Gloria Kinsler. Maryknoll, NY: Orbis.

Taussig, Hal, ed. 2013. *A New New Testament: A Bible for the Twenty-First Century Combining Traditional and Newly Discovered Texts*. Boston: Houghton Mifflin Harcourt.

Theissen, Gerd. 1978. *Sociology of Early Palestinian Christianity*. Translated by John Bowden. Philadelphia: Fortress Press.

Tolbert, Mary Ann. 1998. "Reading the Bible with Authority: Feminist Interrogation of the Canon." In *Escaping Eden: New Feminist Perspectives on the Bible*, edited by Harold C. Washington, Susan Lochrie Graham, and Pamela Thimmes, 141–62. Sheffield: Sheffield Academic Press.

———. 2006. "Marriage and Friendship in the Christian New Testament: Ancient Resources for Contemporary Same-Sex Unions." In *Authorizing Marriage? Canon, Tradition, and Critique in the Blessing of Same-Sex Unions*, edited by Mark D. Jordan, 41–51. Princeton: Princeton University Press.

United Bible Societies. 2012. "Celebrating 100 Millions Bibles printed in China!" November 12. http://www.unitedBiblesocieties.org/news/2902-celebrating-100-million-Bibles-printed-in-china.

———. 2013 "About UBS Translation Work." http://www.ubs-translations.org/about_us.

Vermes, Géza. 1973. *Jesus the Jew: A Historian's Reading of the Gospels*. London: Collins.

Villalobos, Manuel. 2011. "Bodies *Del Otro Lado* Finding Hope in the Borderland: Gloria Anzaldúa, the Ethiopian Eunuch of Acts 8:26–40, *y Yo*." In *Bible Trouble: Queer Reading at the Boundaries of Biblical Scholarship*, edited by Teresa Hornby and Ken Stone, 191–221. Atlanta: Society of Biblical Literature.

West, Gerald O. 1999. *The Academy of the Poor: Towards a Dialogical Reading of the Bible*. Sheffield: Sheffield Academic Press.

Wicker, Kathleen O'Brien, Althea Spencer Miller, and Musa W. Dube, eds. 2005. *Feminist New Testament Studies: Global and Future Perspectives*. New York: Palgrave Macmillan.

Williams, Demetrius K. 2004. *An End to This Strife: The Politics of Gender in the African American Churches*. Minneapolis: Fortress Press.

Wills, Lawrence M. 2008. *Not God's People: Insiders and Outsiders in the Biblical World*. Lanham, MD: Rowman & Littlefield.

Wimbush, Vincent L., ed. 2000. *African Americans and the Bible: Sacred Texts and Social Textures*. New York: Continuum.

Wire, Antoinette Clark. 1990. *The Corinthian Women Prophets: A Reconstruction through Paul's Rhetoric*. Minneapolis: Fortress Press.

Yamaguchi, Satoko. 2002. *Mary and Martha: Women in the World of Jesus*. Maryknoll, NY: Orbis.

Negotiating the Jewish Heritage of Early Christianity

Lawrence M. Wills

Any discussion of the dialogue between Jews and Christians in the twenty-first century must begin with some historical perspective as to what the traditional Christian view has been concerning the relations of Jews and followers of Jesus in the first century. In the first half of the twentieth century, for instance, the dominant Christian view was the following: on the one hand, there was one clear Judaism—viewed through the lens of Paul's critique of the law and represented by the Pharisees as depicted in Matthew—and on the other hand, one clear Christianity as a new entity that had separated from Judaism. If there was any disagreement among the first Christians, it was only that between the "correct" party—those who followed Paul—and the "incorrect" party—those who followed James in retaining Jewish law. How the divorce between Judaism and Christianity took place is treated in the book of Acts, which was taken as a historically accurate record of the intransigence of Jews in the face of Paul's preaching of the message of Christ. True, there were ambiguous passages throughout the Gospels, such as:

> When Jesus saw that he [the scribe] answered wisely, he said to him, "You are not far from the kingdom of God." (Mark 12:34)
>
> Jesus said to them, "The scribes and the Pharisees sit on Moses' seat; therefore, do whatever they teach you and follow it." (Matt. 23:2-3)

But these could be explained away by interpreting them in light of Paul's letters and Acts.

Over the last century, scholars have moved away from this simple view of the relation of ancient Judaism and early Christianity to a much more complex view, questioning almost every part of the description above. In the first half of the twentieth century, some Christian scholars argued that the variety of early Christian groups did not evolve out of one unified body of followers of Jesus, or even from the two divergent paths of "Paul Christians" and "James Christians." Rather, from the earliest period, there were already widely divergent practices and beliefs, without any clear sense of an agreed-on center. This challenge to a trunk-with-branches view of early Christian groups gave more weight to the "branches," groups formerly regarded as smaller, marginal, too Eastern, or heretical. Walter Bauer was a leading figure in this development; more recent scholars who exemplify this approach include James Robinson and Helmut Koester; Jack Sanders; and Stephen Wilson.

For instance, whereas it was traditionally assumed that the four Gospels were narrative depictions of a Jesus who taught essentially what Paul said in his letters using different language, now one had to take seriously the differences among the authors and audiences of these texts. The varied emphases that were found among the four Gospels, or between Paul's letters and Revelation, or between Acts and Jude, or between canonical texts and early Christian texts from outside the canon, came to be seen as reflective of widely divergent movements and eddies in this new religious movement. Scholars might retain the theological preferences of their own traditions, but in colleges and universities, and even in seminaries, the historical narrative no longer seemed like a tree with a clear trunk and branches, but followed the pattern of tubers and vines—widely propagating members with little clear order or lines of development.

In this process, Christian texts from outside the New Testament canon, even those that had been considered "heretical," came to be viewed as having an equal claim in the *historical* reconstruction of early Christianity, regardless of their theology. There was a larger and larger patchwork of groups, and a clear history of origins and development became ever more difficult to reconstruct. Very basic questions about the history of Judaism and Christianity were also introduced: Has the early Eastern history of Judaism and Christianity, all the way from Syria to India and later to China, been ignored as a result of the Western focus of much of the Christian church and of Judaism? To be sure, the Eastern church also included Paul in its canon, but was the relation between eastern Christians and Jews vastly different from that of their Western counterparts (Foltz)?

But another, parallel shift was also underway. In the last half of the twentieth century, scholars proposed a similar proliferation in the number of Jewish groups as well. Before about 1960, many scholars would have described Judaism in the first century as divided into three parties—Sadducees, Pharisees, and Essenes—based on a description of Judaism by the first-century Jewish historian Josephus (*J.W.* 2.117–66). But the discovery of the Dead Sea Scrolls, a new appreciation for the differences among the many Jewish texts of the period, and a growing realization that early rabbinic views were not authoritative for all Jews compelled scholars to recognize the wide variety of Jewish groups, beliefs, and practices (see Cohen 2006; J. J. Collins; Nickelsburg). The classic nineteenth-century history of the Judaism of this period by Emil Schürer (1886–1890) was enlarged in each of the many subsequent editions by the inclusion of more variety in terms of texts, theology, and practices.

Jewish scholars were also motivated by a desire to participate fully in the public discourse on the nature of religions. Judaism, they argued, should be studied in our colleges and universities as an important religious tradition alongside Christianity and other world religions. After World War II and the Shoah, or Holocaust—the genocide of six million Jews—there was an added motivation for both Jews and Christians: a more searching engagement about the origins of Jewish-Christian relations in the ancient world. If the historical assumptions behind a presumed Christian superiority could be challenged, then Christians, Jews, and others would have a chance of living in peace in the twentieth century and afterward without the corrosive effects of stereotypes derived from a misreading of ancient evidence.

Corresponding to the recognition of ancient variety was a new variety among the modern scholars who were studying it as well. During the twentieth century, there arose a full participation of Christian scholars in the study of Judaism and Jewish scholars in the study of Christianity—along with scholars from other religious backgrounds or with no religious affiliation at all. By the second half of the twentieth century, it came to be quite expected that New Testament scholars would know something about rabbinic literature and that Jewish historians of the Roman period would know something about the New Testament and early church. By the end of the twentieth century, there was not just one or two but a number of important studies on the New Testament by Jewish scholars and a number of important studies on rabbinic Judaism by Christians.

The situation at the end of the twentieth century, then, was drastically different from that at the beginning. Influenced by challenges in the social sciences, philosophy, and literary criticism, new issues came to be raised that only made the comparison more complicated, but in many cases, more interesting to modern audiences. Formerly, scholars compared Judaism and Christianity as two clearly defined bodies of people with separate identities, but increasingly many scholars realized that more elite voices within Judaism—for instance, the chief priests, Josephus, or Philo—were being unfairly compared to the less elite forms of Christianity—Mark or the sayings source of Matthew and Luke. The nonelite layers of the Christian movement seemed more revolutionary when compared with the aristocratic voices within Judaism, yet a comparison of Jewish prophetic movements (such as those reported in Josephus) to more elite Christian texts like Hebrews would look very different. Which is the "proper" comparison? Should popular movements among Christians be compared with popular movements among Jews, and more elite texts among Christians with elite Jewish authors, say, Hebrews with Philo? And further, would a female Christian who was the slave of a Christian master have had more in common with her master, or with a Jewish woman who was the slave of a Jewish master, or a female worshiper of Isis who was the slave of a master who worshiped Isis? The effects of geographical distance were also relevant, as both Jews and followers of Jesus were found in communities stretching well over a thousand miles, from Spain to the East, assimilating in each case to vastly different local customs. It was becoming increasingly difficult to define clearly separate bodies of "Jews" and "Christians."

The earlier consensus, then, might have compared the "three parties" of Judaism—Sadducees, Pharisees, and Essenes—and the "two parties" within Christianity—Pauline Christians and "Jewish Christians"—a comparison that could be depicted in this way:

Jewish groups: 1 1 1
Followers of Jesus: 1 1

But by the end of the twentieth century, in recognition of the great variety of subgroups, the comparison would appear more like this:

Jewish groups: 1 1 1 1 1 1 1 1 1 1 1 1 1 1
Followers of Jesus: 1 1 1 1 1 1 1 1 1 1 1

If many Jewish groups maintained strict observance of Torah, so did many followers of Jesus. If many followers of Jesus believed that the end of time was near, so did many Jewish groups. If many followers of Jesus believed that the community of believers was bathed in the holiness of God in a way that made the Jewish temple superfluous, so did some Jews. And finally: If the death of Jesus was the theological affirmation that supposedly separated Christians from Jews, what do we make of the fact that some followers of Jesus did not emphasize his death and some Jewish texts (for example, 4 Maccabees) did emphasize the death of Jewish heroes? Similarities and differences among the groups in *both* rows above introduced new challenges for comparing "Judaism" and "Christianity." The Gospel of Matthew, for instance, was clearly critical of Pharisees—*one* of the Jewish groups in the row above—but was it possible that Matthew was actually more similar to Pharisees than he was to Paul? The simple question of the relation of "Jews" and "Christians" could no longer be answered without pressing a more specific question: *Which* Jews? *Which* Christians?

Incorporating this new consensus concerning a variety of groups among Christians and among Jews, some scholars toward the end of the twentieth century began charting the history of the "partings of the ways" or the "divorce" between Judaism and Christianity (e.g., Dunn 1991; Townsend). A title that exemplified the new consensus of variety was James D. G. Dunn's *The Partings of the Ways* (1991), but challenges to the "new consensus" were, of course, inevitable. Dunn's title was countered by a collection of conference papers called *The Ways That Never Parted* (Becker and Reed; see also Boyarin). This volume asked: At what point were the followers of Jesus thoroughly parted from "Judaism" or "Israel"? True, differences among Jewish or Christian subgroups could be discerned, but could the line above of Christian subgroups really be clearly distinguished from the Jewish line? Thus it is somewhat ironic that, after a century of new studies emphasizing the distinctions among different Jewish groups and different Christian groups, some of the heirs of that consensus would amend it by deemphasizing the boundary line *between* Judaism and Christianity. As more and more subgroups were divided off, they began to fill out the *overall* circle of "Judaism and Christianity" approximately equally. It is even suggested that texts that seem at first to affirm a clear, separate identity are in some cases overstating the distinction, or even creating the illusion of separation, imposing distinctions that may barely exist, in order to instill a clearer sense of identity. (This may be true, for example, of Matthew.) As we learn from modern identity studies, the strongest assertions of difference, or the strongest assertions of a good "We" and an evil "Other," often appear between groups that are similar to each other, and almost indistinguishable by outsiders (Wills). Although this newest development appears at first to undo the previous consensus about variety and difference, it actually carries it forward by demonstrating that there is a wide, overlapping spectrum of beliefs and practices among Jews *and* followers of Jesus, and yet the differences that we perceive among groups and subgroups does not result in one clear line *between* Jews and followers of Jesus. Some Christian groups would admittedly be more clearly separated from Judaism—for example, the implied audience of the Letter to the Hebrews—but others would be more ambiguous in their separation than once thought. Again, it is as if the two lines of groups above should be merged into one indistinct set.

The Continuing Demand for Comparison, Despite the Complexity of the Data

While recognizing all of these challenging new questions, the effort to draw general conclusions about the relations of Jews and Christians continues, and is indeed necessary for a dialogue between Jews and Christians in the twenty-first century. The demands of modern Jews and Christians for dialogue have required some general observations about the first century in order to proceed. Some of the older conclusions still inform the present, more complex discussions among Jews, Christians, and others, and can be used as starting points.

Douglas R. A. Hare, for instance, divided the different assessments of Judaism found in the New Testament into three types. Some polemic in the Gospels is simply a critique of Jewish institutions by people who were, after all, also Jews. This he termed "prophetic anti-Judaism," the critique by a prophetic figure of his or her own institutions. (Even this use of the term *anti-Judaism* seems to separate the prophet from the people and imply that the prophet is *not* Jewish; it is tantamount to referring to Martin Luther King's "anti-Americanism." George Michael Smiga [12–13] tried to address this terminological problem.) According to Hare, Jesus himself would have fit in this category, and might be compared to figures such as Socrates, who, although he criticized his fellow Athenians, was not "un-Greek" or "anti-Greek." Nor did his students suggest that they must create a new entity in which to explore his philosophy (though Plato did eventually leave Athens to advise the king of Syracuse in a failed experiment to establish a "philosopher's state"). Other polemic in the New Testament, however, became progressively harsher, and pronounced a final condemnation on those Jews who did not accept Jesus as the Messiah. Hare termed this "Jewish-Christian anti-Judaism." Unlike the previous category, this type represents a division of groups within Judaism that is at the point of divorce, and the polemical language reflects the tension of being "mid-divorce" (Townsend). A third type is "gentilizing anti-Judaism," and is truly postdivorce: the critique of Judaism as a whole by gentile Christians (Wilson, 110–42, 258–84). Authors in this category are no longer realistically concerned with the conversion of Israel. It can be debated which texts of the New Testament or the early church would fall into these categories, but many scholars would consider the Gospel of Matthew as the first type, a prophetic critique of some (or even most) Jews from within Judaism; the Acts of the Apostles as a text of the second type, which condemns Jews for not accepting the message of Jesus as Messiah; and the Epistle to the Hebrews as an example of gentilizing anti-Judaism. But any of these might be and have been debated. Only if we could interrogate the authors could we be sure where they stood on key questions of the relations of the subgroups in a constantly differentiated Judaism.

In addition to historians and biblical scholars, theologians also entered into the dialogue and introduced terminology to define the various positions that Christians have taken in regard to their relation to Judaism. "Supersessionism" describes the traditional Christian view that in Jesus and Paul we find the belief that Judaism was superseded by God's new dispensation in Christ and the church. (Some New Testament scholars use the compound term rejection-replacement.) But even a doctrine of supersessionism can be more or less negative about the validity of the Jewish covenant. Does the old covenant have any continuing role in God's dispensation, or is it simply the precursor to Christianity (Novak; see also Soulen)? A so-called dual-covenant theology has arisen among liberal Christians, which is the notion that God's new dispensation in Christ did not cancel out the existing covenant with Jews. In this view, there are still two covenants operative, and thus there is no supersessionism, but rather a continuing coexistence of parallel covenants. Some passages from early Christian authors might be adduced in support of this position (see below concerning Paul).

Yet this overture only calls forth new questions. Even if Christians developed a benign view of the continuing validity of God's covenant with Jews, that does not begin to address the relations of Christians with religions other than Judaism. Jewish-Christian dialogue is an important beginning, but only a beginning, to dialogues with other faiths, and this should not be forgotten in discussions of the history of Jewish-Christian relations. Although it is understandable that Jewish leaders have often engaged in dialogue with Christian leaders in order to ameliorate the effects of antisemitism, for many Jews it would be unacceptable to achieve a recognition of God's continuing covenant with Jews if other religions still remained in a less favored status. In the twenty-first century, a broader notion of religious acceptance, beyond a "dual-covenant theology," has often arisen.

With these and similar analyses in mind, in the late twentieth century, scholars of the New Testament, including many Jewish scholars, proposed sweeping changes in regard to how the New Testament texts themselves evaluated Judaism. Vermes, Fredriksen, and Levine (17–52) returned to the Gospel accounts and Acts and argued that recoverable evidence about the historical Jesus depicts a teacher who may have *argued* about Jewish law—not surprising for a Jewish teacher—but who probably remained fairly observant to the end. A great deal of consensus has gathered around this view. If Jesus did reject certain aspects of Jewish law that were advocated by others, such as the Pharisees—again, not surprising for any non-Pharisaic Jew—he never made a blanket rejection of the markers of Judaism. Otherwise, why would Paul have been forced to argue so strongly with the disciples who actually knew Jesus (Galatians 1–2)? Some of Jesus' claims in the Gospels might actually constitute a *stricter* than usual observance of Jewish law, an "ultraorthodox" position! (These cases are sometimes ambiguous, and identifying something or someone as more or less orthodox is always a relative question—who defined the norm? Yet Jesus' rejection of divorce in Mark 10:2-12, or his constraints on accepted Jewish law in Matt. 5:17-48, could be considered a stricter "fence around the Torah" than that which became the norm in rabbinic literature. See also Vermes [80–81], and on the apparent exception in Mark 7:19, see below.)

It is likely that any observer in the year 30 CE would not have considered Jesus a "Reform" Jew (admittedly an anachronistic term), but more probably, a "strict" or "pious" Jew. As noted above, a compelling argument was also made that the Gospel of Matthew, although formerly viewed as "anti-Jewish" ("Scribes and Pharisees, hypocrites!" Matt. 23:13), was actually more anti-*Pharisaic* (Harrington, 1–3; Wills, 101–32). That is, Matthew does not perceive the movement of the followers of Jesus as opposing Judaism, but as opposing some within Judaism, especially Pharisees. To be sure, it is stated in Matthew that at the end, the gentiles will come in (28:19), but that is true of many Jewish texts as well. Matthew does not betray a "Pauline" critique of Jewish law and remains observant to the end.

Even if Jesus and the Gospel of Matthew assumed a continuing adherence to Jewish law, it has been assumed that Paul had irrevocably altered this situation by instituting a mission to gentiles without the law. But now this assumption as well has come in for a major reevaluation. The so-called new perspective on Paul has questioned the chasm that Christians have traditionally perceived between this apostle and the Judaism of his day (Dunn 1983). For the new-perspective scholars, Paul was more a missionary theologian than an abstract theologian or a psychologist of the human condition, and was rarely setting up an opposition between "Jews" and those in Christ. Rather than critiquing and rejecting Judaism as a form of legalism and "works righteousness" at odds with God's plan, almost all of Paul's apparent references to "Jews" are more likely referring to those *in the Jesus movement*, whether originally Jewish or gentile, who oppose his mission to gentiles without the law. This raises a challenging question: If gentiles had been allowed to enter freely into his churches without adhering to Jewish law, would Paul have voiced any reservations about the law for Jews at all?

The debate over the new perspective has been significant. The new perspective represents a direct challenge to strongly held tradition, and yet has achieved a large following. Still, conservative Protestant theologians have opposed it, and even those scholars who have self-identified as part of the new perspective can be divided into two groups, a moderate new perspective and a radical new perspective (Wills, 179–82). The distinction is based on how far they would push the questioning of the older consensus. The moderate new-perspective scholars hold that Paul was much less critical of Judaism than once thought. Says E. P. Sanders (552), whom we might consider a moderate new-perspective scholar: "In short, this is what Paul finds wrong in Judaism: it is not Christianity." That is, God (in Paul's view) is not "displeased" with Jews, Judaism, or Jewish law, but has simply, by the death of Christ, created a new door for all, both Jews and gentiles, to enter into the graces of God. The *discontinuity* between Judaism and Christianity is thus drastically reduced. This shift alone unsettled much Protestant tradition.

But the radical new-perspective scholars go further and argue a version of the dual-covenant theology mentioned above. For Paul, the death of Christ did indeed open a new door of access for gentiles that did not require Jewish law, but the old door for Jews remained open as well—without Christ and with the law still in effect! God was not closing one door to open a new one, but was opening an option for gentiles parallel to the one for Jews (Eisenbaum). Paul's letters are ultimately unclear on this question, but Eisenbaum's conclusions may be correct. However, as above with dual-covenant theology, the same demurral still applies: even if Paul envisioned a two-door access, for gentiles in Christ without the law and for Jews with the law only, he is quite explicit that gentile religion (apart from belief in Christ) is degraded and alienated from God (Rom. 1:2; Gal. 4:8; see

Wills, 179–82). There is no "newer perspective" on Paul that could soften his condemnation of the gentile religions, and in the twenty-first century this becomes a fundamental challenge for interfaith dialogue. (It would be speculative to try to imagine what Paul's views of Islam might have been, although the parallels to Paul's theology are significant. In Islam, Jesus is the Messiah of God, born of a virgin, who performed miracles, and the revelation in Islam came to a prophet who was also "last of all, as to one untimely born" [cf. 1 Cor. 15:8]. But even if, continuing this imaginative exercise on the analogy of the "two-covenant" understanding described above, we were to imagine Paul countenancing a third covenant, with Islam, what would we say of the status of other religions?)

Now, many passages in Paul, especially in Romans, would appear to fly in the face of the radical new-perspective scholars, but in each case an alternative interpretation is possible that would at least make this dual-covenant reading a plausible option. Consider the much-discussed case of Rom. 10:4: "For Christ is the end [*telos*] of the law so that there may be righteousness for everyone who believes." Like the English "end," *telos* can be translated as either "point of cessation" or "goal"; does Paul mean that Christ will bring the covenant of law to an end, or that Christ will constitute the goal of that law *for gentiles*? The interpretation of individual passages sometimes also comes down to whether Paul is speaking principally about Christ or God. For example, in Rom. 9:33, Paul quotes Isa. 8:14-15; 28:16.

> See, I am laying in Zion a stone that will make people stumble, a rock that will make them fall, and whoever believes in him will not be put to shame.

Is Paul referring here to Christ, as Christian tradition has generally held, or, like the Isaiah passages he quotes, to *God's* role in establishing Jerusalem? Note here that the Greek pronoun for "him" could equally be "*it*," that is, the stone (a masculine noun in Greek). Which is the center of Paul's vision, Christ or God? Is it necessary for Jews to have faith *in Christ*, or faith *in the promises of God for gentiles*? The radical new-perspective scholars point out that in Romans, Paul speaks of both.

Quite often, we see that the debate narrows to a microanalysis of individual verses. Indeed, interpretation can only proceed one passage at a time, and yet, if at each stop alternative understandings are possible, then the decision about the whole becomes more difficult to adjudicate. But for this, as for any important and difficult issue, the positions of scholars and of laypeople will likely not be based on "decoding" one or two passages, but rather on general dispositions to the texts. However, it is possible that the undisputed letters of Paul, really only about seventy-five pages in the English translations, simply do not unambiguously reveal Paul's view on this question. That in itself would still be news. If the supersessionist position were really so central to Paul's theology, should it not be easy to establish it in the letters without question? If the overall impression of ambiguity is sustained, does that not at least suggest that the assurance with which earlier interpreters spoke of Paul in supersessionist ways was unwarranted? If one sets aside the *later* Christian tradition on supersessionism, does the same view disappear in Paul's letters?

The issues found in the Gospel of John have also come under scrutiny. Unlike Matthew, which focuses its polemic stridently on the Pharisees, John equally insistently refers to opponents as "Jews"—*Ioudaioi* in Greek—which can also be translated "Judeans" (that is, those from Judea, where

Jerusalem was located). How does one explain the intense anti-Judaism of John, where it is stated that *Ioudaioi* are the "children of the devil" (8:44)? Was the audience of John an "introversionist sect," which turned the promise of salvation inward to a small group of followers who no longer identified with the *Ioudaioi*, meaning Jews who revered the temple authorities in Judea (Wills, 133–66; Reinhartz, 25; Kittredge, 49–63)? Or is the Galilean origin of the Gospel of John at play here, and should *Ioudaioi* be translated not as "Jews" but as "Judeans," those members of Israel who lived in Judea and exercised some control over the members of Israel (which may include Samaritans) who lived in Galilee and Samaria? Whatever sociological theory is asserted to explain the *Ioudaioi* in the Gospel of John, the text seems to express a polemical separation that is different from Matthew on one hand or Paul on the other. The distinction between good and bad people, or even good and evil people, is even stronger in John than in Paul or Matthew.

For twenty-first-century audiences, it is difficult to come to terms with the strong polemics voiced in our sacred texts. Should modern readers, both Christian and Jewish, simply conclude that the ancient writers of the now-sacred texts took group identity too far? Consider a passage from the Hebrew Bible and a passage from the New Testament.

> When the Lord your God brings you into the land that you are about to enter . . . and he clears away . . . the Hittites, the Girgashites, the Amorites, the Canaanites, the Perizzites, the Hivites, and the Jebusites, . . . then you must utterly destroy them. (Deut. 7:1-2)
>
> You [Jews] are from your father the devil, and you choose to do your father's desires. He was a murderer from the beginning and does not stand in the truth. . . . He is a liar and the father of lies. (John 8:44, referred to above)

One can imagine asking, "If you knew a Hittite well (or a Jew well), would you say that?" (On the ambiguity of these designations, see Wills, 21–51, 133–66.) But the many varieties of early followers of Jesus means that *different* lines were being drawn in the sand to differentiate groups, and while they defined the fissures between most Jews and followers of Jesus, they also defined serious breaches among different followers of Jesus. Would Paul, Matthew, or John have placed *each other* among the saved, or among the damned?

The Gospel of Mark as a Test Case

At the same time that bold new assessments were being raised in regard to the relations of Jews and followers of Jesus in Matthew, Paul, and John, there was relatively little rethinking of the situation in the Gospel of Mark, and this Gospel could become a test case for the *old* view. It has long been assumed that, *regardless of the original meaning of Paul's letters*, Mark understood Paul as Paul's followers did. The following assumptions seemed secure:

1. Mark was influenced by Paul and inherited a Pauline doctrine of faith.
2. Mark reflected a mission that was like Paul's; in Mark, Jesus moved into gentile territory to demonstrate an openness to gentile converts (Mark 7–9).

3. Mark must have been a gentile, because there are inaccuracies in regard to Jewish practice in the passion narratives and elsewhere, and Mark explains basic Jewish practices, often inaccurately (7:3-4).
4. Jesus is depicted as rejecting kosher laws across the board (7:19).

Now, however, these conclusions have also been challenged. First, it is not at all clear that Mark knew Paul's theology of faith *in contrast to law*. Faith was a constant element in the Hebrew Bible and also in the Jewish discourse of the period. The Hebrew word *'aman* ("to believe, have faith") and its related forms (in Aramaic as well) can be found behind the use of "amen" in liturgy and are related to the word truth (*'emet*, derived from *'aman*), and to the "faithful ones" (*ne'emanim*) among the Pharisees (*m. Demai* 4:6). In Neh. 9:38, the restored community in Jerusalem joins in a "faith covenant" (*'amanah*). The use of this root by Jews speaking Hebrew or Aramaic, and of the *pist-* root by those speaking Greek, only increases in the Hellenistic period. Thus, although the use of the language of "faith" and "believing" in Mark is pronounced, *it was also common in Judaism*, a fact that is almost totally ignored in assessments of Jewish-Christian relations in the first century. Further, the language of "faith" and "believing" in Mark is not explicitly contrasted with law as Paul would have it; it is used in the same way as other Jews were using it. (Parallels between Mark and Paul are often listed, but the Pauline passages are almost all found in Romans. Were Paul's words in this letter carefully chosen to respond to the *Jewish* discourse on faith in which that community would have been schooled?)

Second, although in Mark, Jesus does move into territories occupied by gentiles, these were also (with one exception, 7:1) part of the ancient borders of Israel. The Maccabees and their descendants had already conquered these lands in order to reestablish the boundaries of ancient Israel; so might we regard Jesus' itinerary in Mark as also reconstituting "Israel"? Jesus also heals gentiles, but so had the prophet Elisha (2 Kings 5); was the latter also "gentilizing" Israel? Third, Mark's Gospel does seem to include many *apparent* inaccuracies concerning Jewish practices, but these, too numerous to mention, are in some cases found in other Jewish texts or taken over in the "Jewish" Gospel Matthew, and other cases are much less clear than once thought (A. Y. Collins).

Last, we come to the argument that has often seemed conclusive: Mark's apparent cancellation of all kosher laws in Jesus' debate with the Pharisees and scribes at 7:1-23. The relevant verses are displayed here side by side with the equivalent section of Matthew. The parallel columns allow one to read Mark's words closely while at the same time noting the differences found in Matthew's treatment of this important issue. (Luke and John do not include this passage.)

Mark 7:1-23 (in part)	**Matthew 15:1-20** (in part)
1 When the Pharisees and some of the scribes who had come from Jerusalem	1 Then Pharisees and scribes came to Jesus from Jerusalem,
gathered around him, 2 they noticed that some of his disciples were eating with defiled hands, that is, without washing them.	
3 For the Pharisees, and all the Jews, do not eat unless they thoroughly wash their hands, thus observing the tradition of the elders;	
4 and they do not eat anything from the market unless they wash it; and there are also many other traditions that they observe, the washing of cups, pots, and bronze kettles.	
5 So the Pharisees and the scribes asked him, "Why do your disciples not live according to the tradition of the elders, but eat with defiled hands?"	and said, 2 "Why do your disciples break the tradition of the elders? For they do not wash their hands before they eat?"
[Several scriptural and legal arguments follow here.]	[Several scriptural and legal arguments follow here.]
14 He called the people to him again and said,	10 He called the people to him and said,
15 "There is nothing outside a person which by going in can defile, but the things which come out are what defile.	11 "It is not what goes into the mouth that defiles a person, but what comes out of the mouth, this defiles.
18 Do you not see that whatever goes into a person from outside cannot defile,	17 Do you not see that whatever goes into the mouth
19 since it enters not the heart, but the stomach,	enters the stomach,
and goes out into the sewer?"	and goes out into the sewer?
Thus he declared all foods clean [literally, "Thus he cleansed all foods"].	
20 And he said, "It is what comes out of a person that defiles.	18 But what comes out of the mouth proceeds from the heart, and this is what defiles.
21 For it is from within, from the human heart, that evil intentions come: fornication, theft, murder, 22 adultery, avarice, wickedness, deceit, licentiousness, envy, slander, pride, folly.	19 For out of the heart come evil intentions, murder, adultery, fornication, theft, false witness, slander.
23 All these evil things come from within, and they defile a person."	20 These are what defile a person, but to eat with unwashed hands does not defile."

Mark's words here are traditionally interpreted in a "Pauline" way, that is, that Jewish law now no longer applies among the followers of Jesus. However, challenges to that interpretation of this passage have also arisen. Jesus' debate with Pharisees about eating food with unwashed hands may not be a rejection of Jewish law but a debate *within* Judaism. Mark here may actually have Jesus endorse the majority Jewish position against the stricter Pharisees. Was the view Mark attributes to Jesus actually more typical of Jewish practice in the first century than the Pharisees'? One also notices that the run-on sentence in 7:3-4 may have resulted from the combination of a simple, and accurate, statement about Pharisees and additional comments about practices of "all the Jews" that were added later. (Note that these verses are not present in Matthew.) But Mark's explanation of Jewish customs may also not be as out of place in Jewish discourse as once thought (A. Y. Collins, 345; Regev 2000, 180–81, 188–89). To be sure, the passage indicates (if it was not inserted later in its entirety) that Mark is including gentiles in the audience of the Gospel, but it does not necessarily reveal a gentile *author*. Mark's reference to the practices of "all the Jews" certainly seems to distance himself from them, but we encounter here a hidden problem with English that affects interpretation. An English-speaking Jew might say, "All Jews do such-and-such," but not "All *the* Jews do such-and-such." The English definite article has the power in this construction to separate off the group in question and to distance the speaker from the group. In Greek, however, usage of the definite article is often quite different from English, and it is not clear that it would distance the speaker in this way. Did Mark mean, "All Jews wash their hands"—which could include Mark—or "All *the* Jews wash their hands"—which seems to distance the Markan Jesus from the Jews?

The last half of this passage has also been reassessed. The central statement—"There is nothing outside a person which by going in can defile, but the things which come out are what defile"—may not be a rejection of purity concerns, as long supposed, but simply an insistence that *moral* purity is as important, or even more important, than *ritual* purity. The prioritizing of moral motives over observance was well known in the Jewish background (Mic. 6:6-8, Hosea 6:6), but the insistence that Jewish observance remains in effect as well is also found in New Testament texts: "You Pharisees tithe mint and rue and herbs of all kinds, and neglect justice and the love of God. It is these you ought to have practiced, *without neglecting the others*" (Luke 11:42; Klawans, 147–48).

But Mark also broadens the discussion by the insertion of 7:19c, "thus he declared all foods clean" (*katharizōn panta ta brōmata*). This awkward and intrusive phrase, which does not appear in Matthew (the section as a whole, as noted, is lacking in Luke and John), may have been inserted later in the textual history of Mark (Booth, 49–50, 62–65), but even if these were Mark's own words, it is also possible that this clause has an entirely different meaning. The Greek literally says, "Jesus *cleansed* all foods," but translators, stumped by what that would mean, have chosen a paraphrasing translation that made perfect sense in the twentieth-century consensus: "Jesus declared all foods clean." This translation means that the "Pauline" Jesus was instituting a new policy canceling all kosher laws. However, in the ancient period, it was sometimes stated, in both Jewish and Christian texts, that at the end of time, for the special, saved community, there would be a *cleansing* of foods, vessels, or people. From Ezekiel (36:22-31) to Zechariah (14:16, 20-21) to *1 Enoch* (10:17—11:2) to Qumran (1QS 4:20-21), there are discussions of a shower of purity on the saved community, however that community is described (see also *Jub.* 1:17, 23; 4:26; 50:5; *Abot R. Nat. B* 42; *b. Erub.*

100b; Regev 2000; 2004). Indeed, with this notion in mind, one may look at other passages in Mark as well. Consider Jesus' healing of a leper, phrased in terms of "cleansing" (the *kathar* root in Greek).

> A leper came to him begging him, and kneeling he said to him, "If you choose, you can cleanse me [*katharisai*, cf. 7:19, discussed above]." Moved with pity, Jesus stretched out his hand and touched him, and said to him, "I do choose. Be cleansed [*katharisthēti*]!" Immediately the leprosy left him, and he was cleansed [*ekatharisthē*]. After sternly warning him he sent him away at once, saying to him, "See that you say nothing to anyone; but go, show yourself to the priest, and offer for your cleansing [*katharismos*] what Moses commanded, as a testimony to them." (Mark 1:40-44)

Although this passage is often understood, from the perspective of *later* Christianity, as the rejection of purity laws about leprosy, a close reading reveals that Jesus miraculously returns the leper to a state of being clean, but does nothing to alter the Jewish laws concerning purity. In fact, the man is instructed to go to the temple to make the offering that Moses commanded (Leviticus 14). The point is important. Technically, in Jewish law, a leper is not pure until after the temple offering is made, but the point of Mark's story is that purity is now made miraculously available as an eschatological event (see Regev 2000; 2004). In the similar but not identical case in the Hebrew Bible mentioned above (2 Kings 5), the prophet heals Naaman the Syrian from his leprosy. But just as it is not generally suggested in Jewish or Christian tradition that Elisha is opening Israel to gentiles, it is also not suggested that he is canceling Jewish purity laws concerning leprosy. And Mark is not the only Christian text to describe an end-time cleansing of the saints; in an otherwise puzzling passage, Paul finds a new cleansing in the community members themselves; note the juxtaposition of "cleansing" with holiness language (the *hag*- root in Greek):

> The unbelieving husband is made holy [*hēgiastai*] through his wife, and the unbelieving wife is made holy through her husband. Otherwise, your children would be unclean [*akatharta*], but as it is, they are holy [*hagia*]. (1 Cor. 7:14; see Johnson Hodge)

So just as the leper in Mark 1:40-45 is *cleansed*—purity rules are *not* abrogated—and in 1 Corinthians 7 an unbelieving spouse is made holy and the children cleansed, so in Mark 7 it is likely that in anticipation of an eschatological change, Jesus *cleanses* foods, as the Greek actually states. Thus, even if this verse was in Mark's original text, it may not have meant that Jewish kosher laws were being rejected, but that for this community, there is at the end of time a dispensation of purity that overwhelms impurity, and also defeats "impure spirits," Mark's more Jewish term for "demons." If, as Zech. 14:20 says, all vessels can be rendered pure at the end of time, and if, as 1 Corinthians 7 says, spouses can be rendered holy, why not lepers in the community, and foods? At the end of time, all heaven breaks loose, but only on the holy community, the *hagioi* ("saints"). There is a division of humanity for a simultaneous cleansing and judgment. The canceling of Jewish food laws, which is how Acts 10, for instance, has been traditionally interpreted, has been too hastily read back into Mark (see also Rom. 14:20).

This passage, then, which had been treated by scholars as a clear confirmation of the Pauline theology at the center of Mark, is much more ambiguous than was once supposed. Paul's letters were often used to justify a gentile mission and identity, but was Mark part of that development (as were Luke and Acts), or was it, like Matthew, part of that segment of the movement, perhaps the larger part, that had not abrogated Jewish law? What was once considered unlikely in regard to Mark now seems quite possible.

Conclusion

A common theme here is that Matthew, Paul, John, and Mark were likely much more rooted in Jewish tradition than Christians have generally assumed. The net effect of these newer investigations is to make discussions among Jews, Christians, and others much more unsettled, but also much richer. Much uncertainty has arisen about each old consensus, and this may seem daunting to contemporary audiences. But there is now a possibility of a wholly *new* dialogue, one that goes back to both the Jewish and Christian sources and asks again what the texts might have meant and what the relations were—both within each body and between the two bodies. The seeds of modern anti-Judaism and the Holocaust can still be seen in some of the ancient texts, but the varied relations also reveal the truth that the story is complex, and it includes many alternative visions of how religious subgroups could respond to each other. There is not just one blueprint for "the relations of Judaism and Christianity" in the first century.

Works Cited

Bauer, Walter. 1934. *Rechtgläubigkeit und Ketzerei im ältesten Christentum.* Tübingen: Mohr. Translated as *Orthodoxy and Heresy in Earliest Christianity.* Philadelphia: Fortress Press, 1979.

Becker, Adam H., and Annette Yoshiko Reed, eds. 2007. *The Ways That Never Parted: Jews and Christians in Late Antiquity and the Early Middle Ages.* Minneapolis: Fortress Press.

Booth, Roger P. 1986. *Jesus and the Laws of Purity: Tradition History and Legal History in Mark 7.* Sheffield: JSOT Press.

Boyarin, Daniel. 2004. *Border Lines: The Partition of Judaeo-Christianity.* Philadelphia: University of Pennsylvania Press.

Cohen, Shaye J. D. 2006. *From the Maccabees to the Mishnah.* 2nd ed. Louisville: Westminster John Knox.

Collins, Adela Yarbro. 2007. *Mark: A Commentary.* Hermeneia. Minneapolis: Fortress Press.

Collins, John J. 2000. *Between Athens and Jerusalem: Jewish Identity in the Hellenistic Diaspora.* 2nd ed. Grand Rapids: Eerdmans.

Dunn, James D. G. 1983. "The New Perspective on Paul." *BJRL* 65:95–122.

———. 1991. *The Partings of the Ways: Between Christianity and Judaism and Their Significance for the Character of Christianity.* London: SCM.

Eisenbaum, Pamela. 2009. *Paul Was Not a Christian: The Real Message of a Misunderstood Apostle.* New York: HarperOne.

Foltz, Richard. 2010. *Religions of the Silk Road: Premodern Patterns of Globalization.* 2nd ed. New York: Palgrave Macmillan.

Fredriksen, Paula. 1995. "Did Jesus Oppose Purity Laws?" *BR* 11:18–25, 42–48.

Hare, Douglas R. A. 1967. *The Theme of Jewish Persecution of Christians in the Gospel according to St. Matthew.* Cambridge: Cambridge University Press.

Harrington, Daniel J. 1991. *The Gospel of Matthew*. Sacra pagina. Collegeville, MN: Liturgical Press.

Johnson Hodge, Caroline. 2007. *If Sons, then Heirs: A Study of Kinship and Ethnicity in the Letters of Paul.* Oxford: Oxford University Press.

———. 2010. "Married to an Unbeliever: Households, Hierarchies, and Holiness in 1 Corinthians 7:12-16." *HTR* 103:1–25.

Kittredge, Cynthia Briggs. 2007. *Conversations with Scripture: The Gospel of John.* Harrisburg, PA: Morehouse.

Klawans, Jonathan. 2000. *Impurity and Sin in Ancient Judaism.* Oxford: Oxford University Press.

Levine, Amy-Jill. 2006. *The Misunderstood Jew: The Church and the Scandal of the Jewish Jesus.* San Francisco: HarperSanFrancisco.

Nickelsburg, George W. E. 2005. *Jewish Literature between the Bible and the Mishnah: A Historical and Literary Introduction.* 2nd ed. Minneapolis: Fortress Press.

Novak, David. 2004. "The Covenant in Rabbinic Thought." In *Two Faiths, One Covenant? Jewish and Christian Identity in the Presence of the Other*, edited by Eugene B. Korn, 65–80. Lanham, MD: Rowman & Littlefield.

Regev, Eyal. 2000. "Pure Individualism: The Idea of Non-Priestly Purity in Ancient Judaism." *JSJ* 31:176–202.

———. 2004. "Moral Impurity and the Temple in Early Christianity in Light of Ancient Greek Practice and Qumranic Ideology." *HTR* 97:377–402.

Reinhartz, Adele. 2001. *Befriending the Beloved Disciple: A Jewish Reading of the Gospel of John.* New York: Continuum.

Robinson, James M., and Helmut Koester. 1971. *Trajectories through Early Christianity.* Philadelphia: Fortress Press.

Sanders, E. P. 1977. *Paul and Palestinian Judaism: A Comparison of Patterns of Religion.* Philadelphia: Fortress Press.

Sanders, Jack T. 1993. *Schismatics, Sectarians, Dissidents, Deviants: The First One Hundred Years of Jewish-Christian Relations.* London: SCM.

Schürer, Emil. 1886–1890. *Geschichte des jüdischen Volkes im Zeitalter Jesu Christi.* 2 vols. Leipzig: Hinrichs.

Smiga, George Michael. 1992. *Pain and Polemic: Anti-Judaism in the Gospels.* Mahwah, NJ: Paulist.

Soulen, R. Kendall. 1996. *The God of Israel and Christian Theology.* Minneapolis: Fortress Press.

Townsend, John. 1979. "The Gospel of John and the Jews: The Story of a Religious Divorce." In *Antisemitism and the Foundations of Christianity*, edited by Alan T. Davies, 72–97. New York: Paulist.

Vermes, Géza. 1991. *Jesus the Jew: A Historian's Reading of the Gospels.* Philadelphia: Fortress Press.

Wills, Lawrence M. 2008. *Not God's People: Insiders and Outsiders in the Biblical World.* Lanham, MD: Rowman & Littlefield.

Wilson, Stephen G. 1995. *Related Strangers: Jews and Christians, 70–170 C.E.* Minneapolis: Fortress Press.

ROOTLESSNESS AND COMMUNITY IN CONTEXTS OF DIASPORA

Margaret Aymer

Rootlessness wanders through Christian imagination today as it has for thousands of years. Even today, hymns proclaiming "this world is not my home," and "I am a poor pilgrim of sorrow, I'm lost in this wide world alone," are sung by women and men whose families can trace their ancestry on any given land mass back multiple generations. Often, the Hebrew Scriptures are credited as the origin of themes of rootlessness, wandering, pilgrimage, and dispersion. However, the New Testament also contains themes of rootlessness and of the creation of community in times of diaspora.

Perhaps it takes an uprooted soul to notice these themes, this ongoing trope in the New Testament. Perhaps it takes the eyes of a woman between cultures, not fully American, and unquestionably not Caribbean—except when I unquestionably am—who emigrated as a child and has functioned as an interpreter of cultures for both my home and host cultures. Some Asian Americans call this the phenomenon of being "the 1.5 generation," the generation that stands between the deep memory of the first-generation immigrant who grew to adulthood in the country of origin and the deep acculturation of the second generation, born in the country of migration. As 1.5-generation people, we stand between homelands, always on a journey, negotiating when possible, turning away when endangered, forging a third way when necessary, and always being in the midst of creating and re-creating culture in ways that are at once rooted in the old, transplanted into a strange land, and bearing hybrid, sometimes nourishing fruit that may at times be unrecognizable as the result of transplantation.

I often read the New Testament with 1.5-generation eyes, eyes not only of an immigrant but also of an immigrant of color. And when I do, I notice that many of these New Testament texts bear marks of migration: evidence of negotiating one's way between home and host cultures, and of the work of forging culture and making meaning in the midst of displacement.

(Re)Considering the History and Rhetoric of New Testament Writings

To argue that the New Testament writings bear marks of migration is to make both a historical and a rhetorical argument. The historical argument is grounded in the accepted historical reconstruction of the creation of these writings by the majority of scholars. The rhetorical argument is grounded in the way in which the authors describe their displacement, their own rootlessness, and that of their community; and how they use that rhetoric to construct strategies of interaction with the wider world. Take, for example, the general consensus that Mark is the oldest canonical Gospel, written after the siege of Jerusalem (of which Mark 13 is understood as description after the fact rather than foretelling), and that it was not written in Judea or Galilee. Already that history suggests displacement, the Gospel narrative written in migration. This would not be the case if the story were an invention out of the imagination of "Mark" the Gospel writer. But if, as biblical scholars have claimed, "Mark" uses oral sources as well as written ones to construct a narrative that he believes to be factually true at least in part, then the ultimate origin of those oral sources would have had to be persons from Judea or Galilee whose bodies, or stories, had migrated to Mark's location. Thus we know with some certainty that at the very least, the stories are migratory.

Mark gives us more clues to suggest that the cultural home of his narrative is not his current audience. He includes and, of even more importance, he *translates* a number of Aramaic sayings of Jesus, among them *Talitha kum* (5:41), *Ephphatha* (7:34), and the cry from the cross, *Eloi, Eloi, lama sabachthani* (15:34). That there is Aramaic in Mark should come as no surprise. After all, Aramaic was one of the languages of Judea and the Galilee. The surprise is Mark's need to translate the Aramaic. This suggests, first, that either Mark or his oral source knows Aramaic, for the short passages are translated correctly. This makes Mark at least bilingual; the Gospel of Mark was composed in Greek. Second, it suggests that Mark is writing to an audience that is, at most, only partially literate in Aramaic.

All of these are traces, hints of the possible origins of the Gospel of Mark, which are, in reality, largely lost. However, these traces suggest a Gospel written in displacement and a writer bridging the distance between a story perhaps told in Aramaic and one written in Greek with Aramaic traces, translating the first generation to the second generation. If this is the case, Mark's Gospel not only tells the good news of Jesus Christ but also, like the older exilic writings of the Hebrew Scriptures, tells a story about a homeland and a home culture no longer accessible to a generation that may be in danger of forgetting. It is an immigrant's tale, a tale of which, if Mark 16:8 can be believed, Mark alone is the only faithful teller.

The other Gospels and the Acts of the Apostles might take issue with Mark's monopoly on faithful discipleship. As second- and third-generation readers (see Luke 1:1-2), they take the traditions of the migrants and rework them for their contemporaries, not unlike the transformation of English plum pudding into Caribbean Christmas cake or the twenty-first-century hip-hop recensions of Bob Marley's twentieth-century reggae hits. Some translation still needs to take place. Some original language still remains in place. And depending on the nature of the community, more of the home culture (Matthew) or more of the host culture (Luke) is emphasized. But the history remains the same: communities of persons outside of Judea and Galilee, and distant from the events of Jesus' life, inheriting a story told and retold in migration, a story possibly even recounted and written by migrants.

With the writings of Paul, one can demonstrate a case for their historical marks of migration much more simply. Paul is, after all, a wandering preacher writing to assemblies in cities and villages outside of his natal Tarsus. This alone is enough to make these writings migrant writings. But Paul, too, is engaging in translation: in this case, not translation from Aramaic to Greek, but the cultural work of translating a primarily Jerusalem-based, Jewish sect into an assembly that denies the distinctiveness between Jew and Greek, slave and free, perhaps even man and woman (Galatians 3). This is an assembly not just for gentiles, but even more powerfully for Diaspora Jews, those who for generations have lived away from but never completely separated from Jerusalem and Galilee. This group would have maintained some traditions and let others go, particularly others that would have made them peculiar or abhorrent to their majority-gentile neighbors. Indeed, by the time he writes to Philippi, Paul radically begins to imagine these assemblies not merely as bodies of believers gathered to pray but also as political entities in which those assembled had status, citizenship, and inheritance (Phil. 3:20). Paul's writing bears marks not only of his own migrant life but also of the diasporic migrant lives of his communities, and of a migrant imagination that forms new communities of migrants—persons living in one place with their citizenship in another.

Paul's interpreters, those who wrote the deuteropauline and Pastoral Epistles, are similarly involved in a work of translation: translation as cultural accommodation of the majority culture. Once Paul's apocalyptic insistence on the imminent return of Christ proves to be premature, these interpreters, perhaps a generation removed from Paul's migrant fervor, use their second-generation status to re-create a Christianity less dangerous to the empire in which it must survive.

Like Paul, John of Patmos seems to be a migrant, perhaps an involuntary migrant, if we take his self-description in Revelation 1:9 as evidence that he is in exile. His epistolary apocalypse then takes on the work of migrant writing, a writing both in migration (he is on Patmos) and to migrant communities. The letter does what John can no longer do, moving from place to place encouraging communities to hold fast and to remember that their final dwelling place is not the place where they currently abide and that their allegiances are not to the beasts of land and sea or to the dragon who gives them power. Rather, their allegiances are to the lion/slaughtered lamb on the throne and their true home is the new Jerusalem, which will come down from the new heaven on the new earth. They are thus to live as citizens of "an-other" place, as migrants in an evil world, waiting, like the souls under the altar, until all is accomplished and their nomadic God migrates to the new Jerusalem and pitches the divine tent among them (Rev. 21:3).

The writings attributed to John the Gospel writer and his community (the Gospel and the three pseudonymous epistles) betray a similar orientation to the world in which the community lives.

John 9, famously, has been held up by Raymond Brown and others as a narrative of the community's forced exile, its forced (e)migration from its community of origin (the synagogue/formative Judaisms) to an-other place, a location somehow outside of both "world" and "home" (John 1). Those who leave this other place are castigated in the first of the Johannine Epistles as antichrists. Within the Johannine community, forced migration on the basis of belief is virtuous; voluntary migration out of the community is satanic.

Migration as an underlying physical and/or rhetorical concern is thus evident in many of the New Testament writings. However, only two make it explicit: James and 1 Peter. James may well be a letter to, rather than by, migrant communities. Indeed, James's letter, addressed "to the twelve tribes in the Diaspora," strongly resembles other such Jerusalem-to-Diaspora missives sent by the Sanhedrin contemporary with this writing (Bauckham, 19–20). James's sermon-in-a-letter, or homiletic epistle, reminds those outside of the immediate influence of Jerusalem of the particular ethics expected of those who gather in synagogues (James 2), claim to follow the "royal law" (2:8), and consider themselves to be followers of the Lord Jesus Christ (2:1). Primarily, these communities should not resemble the stain of the world, but should be separate entities marked by an ethical concern for the workers, the widows and orphans, and the poor (1:27). However, they are not to consider their status permanent. They will continue in their involuntary migration only until the Parousia of the Lord (5:7). At that time, the injustices experienced in their exile will be adjudicated by the Lord of Sabaoth (5:4).

First Peter takes a similar tack. Writing specifically to those Diasporan exiles in Asia Minor, the advice of 1 Peter to these migrant communities is twofold. First, the author insists on the identity of these migrants as displaced royalty, exiled priests, and a people belonging to God (1 Peter 2). Their dispersal does not change their identity. Rather, it requires prudent interaction with the dominating culture of their exile until they can regain their inheritance as heirs to the kingdom of God. Second, the author requires that the migrant congregation act in ways that would be considered blameless during the time of their exile. For this author, this means that the community of faith must adopt even the norms of the kyriarchy of their community of exile. "Kyriarchy," a neologism coined by Elisabeth Schüssler Fiorenza, describes "the rule of the emperor, lord, slave master, husband, or the elite freeborn, propertied, educated gentleman to whom disenfranchised men and all wo/men were subordinated" (Schüssler Fiorenza, 9). Acceptance of such norms moved 1 Peter's Christian community away from less hierarchical structures such as those intimated by Galatians 3 and toward the more accommodationist stance of the second generation of the Pauline school. It was, among other things, a way for these migrants to "fit in." This kyriarchy-as-camouflage was, of course, counseled uncritically by a member of the literate class (or at least one who could pay for an amanuensis). Those who bore its burden most profoundly were the migrant community's least powerful members: women, children, and slaves.

Other New Testament writings give us far fewer clues about their migrant status. Yet even these reference comings, goings, and their impact on community identity. The pseudonymous letters of 2 Peter and Jude, for example, are unlikely to be of Galilean or Judean origin, although this is impossible to know. As such, they would also be migrant writings, strictly speaking. However, their discourse focuses less on the community's migrant nature and more on the danger of the immigration of other people—with other ideas about Christian identity—into their communities (2 Pet. 2:3; Jude 4). Even without a specific focus on the community's movement or clear evidence of displacement, these writings seek to create and strengthen communities that are outside the general population (e.g., not pagan, not Jewish, not licit), and there is still a sense of migration about them.

Hebrews, of course, stands as the New Testament enigma, giving its readers very few clues about authorship, dating, placement, or any other historical data. Yet even if one argues for Hebrews as an early Judean or Galilean document (as does DeSilva in this volume), there is still an overlay of migration in its rhetoric. For even if one depicts Hebrews as a letter/sermon written to, by, and in Judea or the Galilee, one cannot escape the trope of community-as-migrants and the rhetorical journey toward rest that wends its way through the homiletics of the unknown preacher. Hebrews too, although less explicit, bears the marks of migration.

Thus a phenomenon often overlooked marks at least a significant plurality of New Testament literature. The bulk of it, and perhaps all of it, could be categorized as migrant writing. As a result, although rootlessness is most frequently considered a concern of James and 1 Peter, and perhaps to a lesser extent of the rhetorics of Hebrews and Philippians, in truth, underlying all of the New Testament canon is a sense of rootlessness, of dispersion, and of the need to survive in a place that is not home, whether physically or culturally. The rest of this essay seeks to explore the implications of this underlying rootlessness, both in the New Testament writings and for those who appropriate these writings as Scriptures.

New Testament Writings as Diaspora Spaces

What difference might it make if the New Testament writings were considered to be migrant writings? Here, a brief consideration of theory about "diaspora spaces" might be helpful. Sociologist Avtar Brah proposes that diaspora space is that place

> where multiple subject positions are juxtaposed, contested, proclaimed or disavowed; where the permitted and the prohibited perpetually interrogate; and where the accepted and the transgressive imperceptibly mingle even while these syncretic forms may be disclaimed in the name of purity and tradition. [It is a space where] *tradition is itself continually invented even as it may be hailed as originating from the mists of time.* (Brah, 208, emphasis added)

This thick description reflects the struggle and promise of diaspora spaces, those spaces where migrants and host communities enter into the never-ending dance of self-definition. But what does it have to do with the New Testament? Simply this: If the New Testament writings are, indeed, migrant writings, these migrant rhetorics might be expected to create texts that are diaspora spaces, texts/spaces in which migrant writers and migrant communities struggle with the nature of faithfulness to their understanding of the new Christian movements while living in a majority-pagan world.

So, if the New Testament writings are migrant writings, one might expect to note the juxtaposition, contestation, proclamation, and/or disavowal of multiple subject positions (Brah, 208). Perhaps the quintessential example of such struggle is bound up in the person and history of Saul/Paul of Tarsus. He names himself a Jew, born of the tribe of Benjamin, circumcised and a Pharisee (Phil. 3:5). However, he is also named a citizen of the pagan, primarily Greek-speaking Roman Empire, and claims that status by birth rather than through financial or military transaction (Acts 22:25-28). He is Saul, named after the first king of Judea, but without fanfare becomes Paul as he begins his gentile evangelism, no doubt because his Hebrew name is transliterated *saulos* in Greek (Acts 13:9), and *saulos* is an adjective that describes "the *loose, wanton* gait of courtesans or Bacchantes" (Liddell and Scott, s.v. "*saulos*"). This is a person who claims to himself and to his entire community, Jew and Greek, the promises of the particularly Jewish Abrahamic covenant (Gal. 3:1-9). This same person claims to become "all things to all people" for the sake of his Christian evangelism (1 Cor. 9:22).

Of course, Paul is not alone in this place of juxtaposition, of negotiation between cultures. Other characters carry two names, two identities: consider Tabitha/Dorcas and John/Mark (Acts 9; 12). Neither is Paul alone is standing between cultures and negotiating different subject positions: consider Joanna, the wife of Chuza, Herod's steward, who stands between Roman client privilege in Herod's household and her support of Jesus—who would, no doubt, have been understood as a wandering Jewish prophet and social critic, and who was killed for sedition against the Roman Empire (Luke 8). However, not every New Testament figure makes the same choices that Paul makes when faced with this negotiation between cultures. The author of the Epistle of James, for instance, in his counsel to the "twelve tribes of the diaspora" (James 1:1), calls for withdrawal and self-preservation (1:27). Similarly, the seer on Patmos island, echoing the prophet's jeremiad, calls his people to "come out" of Babylon (Rev. 18:4, cf. Jer. 51:45). In a different response to the same question of positionality with respect to one's own culture and to "the world," John's Gospel suggests a third way, a way that is neither of the world nor of the home culture of the migrant outsiders. This way is signified by the Johannine phrase, "sons of God," and represents the formation of an-other position in society (John 1).

In addition to matters of the subject's positionality, New Testament writings also reveal the ongoing interrogation of permitted and prohibited, the mingling of accepted and transgressive, and ultimately the creation of syncretic forms that Brah describes as characteristics of diaspora space. Perhaps the most obvious New Testament example of the interrogation of the permitted and prohibited is the conflict regarding the inclusion of gentiles into the early churches without requiring of them the rite of circumcision. This early church-dividing conflict emerges in many of the undisputed Pauline writings, and differently in the Acts of the Apostles. Paul is usually the anticircumcision champion in his own writings; but the author of Luke-Acts makes Peter the standard-bearer after a theophany and an encounter with a gentile named Cornelius (Acts 10; 15). However, circumcision is not the only New Testament example of the interrogation and re-creation of traditions and forms. The "healing on the Sabbath" crisis seen in many of the Gospels is also part of this ongoing interrogation of what is and is not permitted to be done by faithful people during the Sabbath rest. Table fellowship is yet another example of the New Testament interrogation of permitted and prohibited: not merely who was admitted to the table (thus the Syrophoenician woman's protest in Mark 7) but even more the question of whether meat was to be served (1 Corinthians 8; Revelation 2). After all, meat was almost always sacrificed to the gods, whom Christians and Jews saw as idols. Should, then, Christians eat meat at their symposia, or was this a tacit acceptance of idolatry

(Taussig)? These discussions and debates about the interaction between the permitted and transgressive likely preceded the advent of Christianity among the Jewish migrants in Diaspora around the greater Mediterranean world. However, a new urgency in response to these questions would have been felt after the Roman destruction of the Jerusalem temple in 70 CE. After this destruction of the ritual and political center of Judaism, all claimants to the traditions of Abraham and Moses were in ongoing debates regarding what it might mean to be Jewish in a post-temple diasporic reality. This was not specific to the Gospel writers—or even to Christian writers. The rabbis, too, were beginning to argue about the nature of faithfulness after the fall of the temple.

Circumcision, Sabbath observance, and table fellowship were some of the more blatant ways in which this kind of cultural interrogation between permitted and transgressive took place. Other questions also arose, even if they were more subtly addressed. Should slavery persist in the Christian community, and how could one argue for slavery and yet argue that all have one master (see Col. 3:22-23)? What is the appropriate role of women, particularly of wives, in the early church and how might that intersect with the wider society's understanding of Christians (1 Cor. 7:12-13)? The answers are not straightforward. There are clear moves, particularly among the later Christian writings, to preserve kyriarchy, but the rationale for it is often a subtle rebuke of the dominating structures of the society, even if that rebuke does nothing to alleviate the distress of women, children, or slaves. In Colossians, for example, the command that slaves should obey their masters is followed by counsel to these slaves to perform their tasks "as for the Lord and not for your masters" and a promise that "the wrongdoer will be paid back for whatever wrong has been done" (3:23-25). When there is no rebuke, often there is a call for kyriarchal structuring of society as a mark of purity of the church, purity that makes the otherwise illicit church gathering unassailable by the pagan majority. Thus in 1 Timothy, slaves are told to obey their masters "so that the name of God and the teaching may not be blasphemed" (6:1).

Ultimately, as Brah posits, these ancient migrant writings represent the invention of a new tradition, a tradition we have come to call Christianity. For an example of this, one need look no further than to the name given to this ancient collection of writings: "New Testament." New Testament is an appropriation of the language of the Christian meal found in 1 Cor. 11:25 and Matt. 26:28. While most contemporary translations present this as a "new covenant," the Greek word *diathēkē* can be used either for "covenant" or "testament" (as in "last will and testament," see Galatians 3). So, "New Testament" also means "new covenant," and this in turn cannot be understood without reference to the "old covenant," as the early Christians would have understood it.

For many of these migrant groups, the "old" or Abrahamic covenant between God and God's people functioned not only as tradition but also as a fundamental identifier of the people (*ethnos*—the basis for the concept "ethnic group"). This identifier was traced primarily through the Abrahamic bloodline but could be extended to those who adhered to the identity markers of the covenant, among which were circumcision and the keeping of *kashrut*. So, when Paul and the Gospel writers, quoting the oral tradition that both trace to Jesus, speak of the table meal of the early church as a "new covenant" or "new testament," they are not only relating an important story in the birth of the church but also reinventing tradition, reinventing, not exorcising it. To speak of these stories and letters as a "new *diathēkē*" is both to invent a new way of being a covenant people in the world and to appropriate to the church—made increasingly of people from outside of the Abrahamic bloodline and covenant practices—the ancient *diathēkē* of the Abrahamic era.

Paul and the author of Luke-Acts do not explicitly value the new covenant as superior to the old covenant. However, for the writer to the Hebrews, the "new covenant" or "new testament" clearly supersedes the older. As the author of Hebrews argues, "if that first covenant had been faultless, there would have been no need to look for a second one" (Heb. 8:7). Yet even this assertion is premised on a reinterpretation of the received Scriptures of the people, the "Old Testament." The author to the Hebrews would probably not be claiming to invent tradition any more than would Paul or the author of Luke-Acts. Instead, he would assert that this new covenant is the real, heavenly variety—and thus ultimately more ancient than the human copy. And yet he, like Paul and Luke-Acts, is engaging in that diaspora-space activity of inventing, and claiming ancient provenance for, traditions (Brah).

All of this briefly suggests that, as a collection of primarily migrant writings, the writings of the New Testament can be shown to be diaspora space. The examples above are intended to be representative rather than exhaustive, and self-evident rather than nuanced. The struggle with subject positionality, juxtaposition of the permitted and transgressive, and (re)invention of tradition all appear in some of the most important theological discussions in the collection: discussions around identity, around who and what these Christians will be. However, to say that the New Testament writings constitute a kind of literary diaspora space is not to claim some uniformity of migrant reaction to their host cultures or their home culture. Rather, in the next section, four such possible migrant reactions will be explored, both for their presence or absence within the New Testament canon of writings and for their implications for the migrants who hold them.

New Testament Migrant Strategies

Just because one can argue that the New Testament writings constitute a kind of literary diaspora space, this does not mean that their migrant strategies for life as Christians in migration were identical. Psychologist John Berry's work proves helpful for unpacking these strategies. Berry outlines four migrants' strategies for interacting in their places of migration. He calls these four categories marginalization, separation, assimilation, and integration (Berry, 619).

Three of these strategies are readily observable in the New Testament writings. However, the strategy of assimilation is absent. Assimilation requires that migrants reject their home culture in favor of the host culture in which they find themselves. In twenty-first-century terms, this is the immigrant who intentionally loses her accent, forgets her native language, and claims only the nationality and culture of the nation in which she finds herself. Such assimilation does not exist in the New Testament canon; for, if it did, the writings would be pagan, extolling the virtues of the goddess Roma or the God Zeus/Jupiter. Indeed, an assimilationist of this time would have been found marching with the silversmiths of Ephesus crying out, "Great is Artemis of the Ephesians" (Acts 19:28).

In retaining their monotheistic theologies, both Jews and Christians set themselves apart from the majority-pagan polytheism of the ancient world in ways that were seen as misanthropic by their neighbors, regardless of how much else they mimicked the cultural norms of their host country. There seem to have been some Christians who did aspire to assimilate. To do so, they claimed a higher knowledge that allowed them to participate in pagan religiosity in all of its forms (including eating meat sacrificed to pagan gods) while at the same time claiming the faith of the early Christian church (see 1 Corinthians 7; Revelation 2). Such practices were condemned by those whose writings are preserved in the New Testament as misguided at best and satanic at worst. In fact, no New Testament writing counsels migrant assimilation; none offers a theology of assimilation. In the face of migration, each of the New Testament writings, regardless of how much they appear to mimic the greater society, preserves some separation from that society.

Liminal, or as Berry calls them, "marginalized" migrants take as their response to migration the rejection of both their home culture and their host culture. To determine that a migrant writing counsels such a stance for its audience, one must show *both* its rejection of the home culture, which in the case of early Christianity is Judaism and/or temple culture, *and* its rejection of the host culture in which it finds itself, which in many New Testament writings is simply called "the world." The Gospel according to John contains both of these kinds of counsel for its audience. Consider first this quotation:

> Then Jesus said to the Jews/Judeans who had believed in him, "If you continue in my word, you are truly my disciples; and you will know the truth, and the truth will make you free." They answered him, "We are descendants of Abraham and have never been slaves to anyone. . . .
>
> . . . Jesus said to them, "If you were Abraham's children, you would be doing what Abraham did, but now you are trying to kill me, a man who has told you the truth that I heard from God. This is not what Abraham did. You are indeed doing what your father does." They said to him, "We are not illegitimate children; we have one father, God himself." Jesus said to them, "If God were your Father, you would love me, for I came from God and now I am here. . . . You are from your father the devil, and you choose to do your father's desires." (John 8:31-33a, 39b-42b, 44a)

In this quotation, part of Jesus' longer diatribe against the "Jews" or the "Judeans," the author of John's Gospel, through Jesus, is disavowing any cultural consonance with those who would seem to be his own people, his home culture. There is no plea, here, that those who self-identify as Jews/Judeans are of the same family tree as the community to which John is writing. Raymond Brown posits that John's community has been forcibly removed from the synagogue worship out of which it sprang because of its assertion of the messianic nature of Jesus. This seems to suggest that the audience of John's Gospel has separated itself from its home culture.

However, in turning from its home culture, John's audience has not uncritically embraced its host culture. To the contrary. As part of the symposium dialogue in the fifteenth chapter, the Gospel of John records the following teaching of Jesus:

> If the world hates you, be aware that it hated me before it hated you. If you belonged to the world, the world would love you as its own. Because you do not belong to the world, but I have chosen you out of the world—therefore the world hates you. (John 15:18-19)

Here, John's Gospel is depicting Jesus, and through Jesus, his community, as rejected by its host culture, "the world."

In all fairness, a careful reader of John realizes this at the very outset of the Gospel. In the first chapter, John describes the incarnate Word (*logos*) and the community of those who accepted him this way:

> He [the Word/*logos*] was in the world, and the world came into being through him; yet the world did not know him. He came to what was his own, and his own people did not accept him. But to all who received him, who believed in his name, he gave power to become children of God, who were born, not of blood or of the will of the flesh or of the will of man, but of God. (John 1:10-13)

Perhaps no verse better illustrates John's liminality, the stance of a community leader—and thus of a community—rejected both by the world (host culture) and by his own people (home culture). The audience shaped by John's Gospel reflects such a liminality, neither being part of the world nor part of the home culture, a stance that requires the community of faith to strike out into unknown territory, creating an ostensibly brand-new culture apart from either of these cultural anchors.

The Gospel according to John is joined by the Johannine Epistles (1, 2, and 3 John) and possibly the Gospel according to Mark in this liminal stance. However, most New Testament writings do not use this migrant strategy to interact with their home and host cultures. The Epistle of James is illustrative of a more popular strategy: separation. Consider the following:

> Religion that is pure and undefiled before God, the Father, is this: to care for orphans and widows in their distress, and *to keep oneself unstained by the world.* (James 1:27, emphasis added)

and

> Those conflicts and disputes among you, where do they come from? Do they not come from your cravings that are at war within you? You want something and do not have it; so you commit murder. And you covet something and cannot obtain it; so you engage in disputes and conflicts. You do not have, because you do not ask. You ask and do not receive, because you ask wrongly, in order to spend what you get on your pleasures. [Adulterous women]! Do you not know that *friendship with the world is enmity with God*? Therefore whoever wishes to be a friend of the world becomes an enemy of God. (James 4:1-4, emphasis added)

Like the Gospel of John, the Epistle of James stands firm in its dismissal of the world. As in the Gospel of John, so here also the host culture is rejected. However, unlike John, James also says this:

> Do not speak evil against one another, brothers and sisters. Whoever speaks evil against another or judges another, speaks evil against the law and judges the law; but if you judge the law, you are not a doer of the law but a judge. (James 4:11)

Law, in this case, must be understood as Torah, the law of James's own people and community. James thus is not advocating a liminal migrant strategy. Instead, James is advocating a strategy of separation.

Luke Timothy Johnson has demonstrated that James is very possibly a letter written from the earliest Christians in Jerusalem, through the brother of Jesus, to the earliest diasporic communities of Jews/Judeans who have accepted Jesus as the Christ and son of God. From Jerusalem, James writes to migrant Christ-communities still worshiping in synagogues (James 2). He counsels the earliest believers to adopt a migrant strategy of separation: not to adopt gentile ways in their time of migration. Rather, they are to continue their adherence to the law, to be wary of accepting worldly ways, and to keep themselves unstained from the world.

The Epistle of James is not alone in this counsel. The Gospel of Matthew provides a similar strategy to its readers, almost until the Great Commission at the end; and even that commission is less about befriending the world and more about recruiting it to the "home culture" (Matthew 28). Likewise, the enigmatic book Hebrews, with its focus on Christian endurance, seems to counsel separation from the things of the world in favor of the "race that is set before us" (Hebrews 12). Jude, the often overlooked polemic toward the end of the canon, embraces this sort of strategy; and it is central to the theology of the Revelation to John with its admonition to "come out of" Babylon (Revelation 18). In each of these cases, the migrant strategy of separation calls the community of faith back to its roots and away from the world.

Liminality and separation define strategies in some of the more pivotal New Testament writings. However, the predominant migrant strategy within the literary diaspora space called the New Testament is accommodation. Consider, for example, these quotations from the writings of Paul of Tarsus:

> As many of you as were baptized into Christ have clothed yourselves with Christ. There is no longer Jew or Greek, there is no longer slave or free, there is no longer male and female; for all of you are one in Christ Jesus. And if you belong to Christ, then you are Abraham's offspring, heirs according to the promise. (Gal. 3:27-29)

and

> To the Jews I became as a Jew, in order to win Jews. To those under the law I became as one under the law (though I myself am not under the law) so that I might win those under the law. To those outside the law I became as one outside the law (though I am not free from God's law but am under Christ's law) so that I might win those outside the law. To the weak I became weak, so that I might win the weak. I have become all things to all people, that I might by all means save some. (1 Cor. 9:20-22)

These writings indicate a shift in strategy. Paul's overt inclusion of persons both from within and outside his own migrant culture, and his willingness to accommodate gentile inclusion in his ministry, suggests that he does not advocate a total avoidance of the gentile world. However, Paul simultaneously claims that his mixed community of Jews/Judeans and gentiles, a community comprising migrant Jesus-believers, somehow inherits the benefits reserved specifically for the Jews/Judeans: the covenant blessings of Abraham (Galatians 3). Paul thus not only invites "the world" in but also continues to embrace some of his home culture, a culture steeped in the Abrahamic covenant and the Mosaic law.

This Pauline migrant strategy I have termed accommodation, following sociologist Margaret Gibson, rather than using Berry's term *integration* (Berry, 618; Gibson, 20). According to Gibson, accommodation is marked by "the deliberate preservation of the homeland culture, albeit in an adapted form more suitable to life in the host country" (Gibson, 20–21). To argue that Paul is engaged in accommodation and not integration is to argue that he has deliberately preserved the Jewish narrative while adapting it so that faith communities may include gentiles. The result is an uneasy tension of a migrant strategy that both accepts and critiques home and host cultures. This uneasy tension is most clearly evident in Romans 12 and 13. In chapter 12, Paul famously counsels, "Do not be conformed to this world, but be transformed by the renewing of your minds, so that you may discern what is the will of God—what is good and acceptable and perfect" (Rom. 12:2). However, in Romans 13, this same Paul calls for a certain amount of conformity to the world *as a way to fully comply with the requirements of the Mosaic law.* Here, I quote Paul at length:

> Let every person be subject to the governing authorities; for there is no authority except from God, and those authorities that exist have been instituted by God. Therefore whoever resists authority resists what God has appointed, and those who resist will incur judgment. For rulers are not a terror to good conduct, but to bad. Do you wish to have no fear of the authority? Then do what is good, and you will receive its approval; for it is God's servant for your good. But if you do what is wrong, you should be afraid, for the authority does not bear the sword in vain! It is the servant of God to execute wrath on the wrongdoer. Therefore one must be subject, not only because of wrath but also because of conscience. For the same reason you also pay taxes, for the authorities are God's servants, busy with this very thing. Pay to all what is due them—taxes to whom taxes are due, revenue to whom revenue is due, respect to whom respect is due, honor to whom honor is due. Owe no one anything, except to love one another; for the one who loves another has fulfilled the law. The commandments, "You shall not commit adultery; You shall not murder; You shall not steal; You shall not covet"; and any other commandment, are summed up in this word, "Love your neighbor as yourself." Love does no wrong to a neighbor; therefore, love is the fulfilling of the law. (Rom. 13:1-10)

Despite the counsel in Rom. 12:1-2, one must read Romans 13 as advice to conform to the world—at least in part—even as you also attempt to conform to the law. Here Paul, deliberately holding to the law, counsels the Romans to adapt a form of his adherence better suited to accommodate the host culture in which they find themselves and the home culture to which they must cling.

Paul is not alone in his use of the migrant strategy of accommodation. Along with the thirteen writings written either by him or by imitators of him, this strategy is adopted by the writer of the Gospel of Luke and the Acts of the Apostles, and by the authors of the Petrine letters. This constitutes the majority of the New Testament writings, both by number of writings and by size of corpus.

These three migrant strategies—liminality, separation, and accommodation—reflect three competing New Testament canonical responses to the historical reality of migration and the literary trope of displacement encoded in this canon. It would be a mistake to read this description as though it were intended to denote some kind of progression from "unrealistic" to "realistic"; nor a decline from "purity" to "admixture." Liminality, separation, and accommodation are survival strategies in the face of displacement and dispersion adopted by these different migrant writings. Each adds to the Pentecost-like cacophony (Acts 2) of the diaspora space called the New Testament.

Migrant Writings as Twenty-First-Century Scriptures

Considering the extent to which New Testament writings may also be migrant writings is certainly of interest for the historical study of these texts, as well as for their academic and, perhaps, theological interpretation. But how might this information allow us better to understand the role of these writings in the twenty-first century? To respond, one must first consider the nature of Scriptures themselves: specifically, one must consider what makes certain cultural productions (writings, recitations, songs, etc.) into Scriptures.

Here, the work of Wilfred Cantwell Smith will be a helpful conversation partner. Smith's seminal work *What Is Scripture? A Comparative Analysis* traces the human activity of Scripture-making and Scripture-using across a variety of religious communities and traditions. He finds that

> scripture is a human activity. . . . The quality of being scripture is not an attribute of texts. It is a characteristic of the attitude of persons—groups of persons—to what outsiders perceive as texts. *It denotes a relation between a people and a text.* Yet that too is finally inadequate. . . . at issue is the relation between a people and the universe, in the light of their perception of a given text. (Smith, 18, emphasis added)

Smith's definition makes explicit that those who consider New Testament writings to be Holy Scripture are living in a particular relationship with these ancient texts. This relationship involves more than just a people and their Scripture. The relationship stretches "between a people and the universe, in light of their perception of a given text" (Smith, 18). To use another metaphor, for people of faith, their Scriptures function as a lens through which all things are considered. Scripture helps people of faith to clarify their proper relationships with one another, with the God of their understanding, and with the world.

For the New Testament, an added complication is that not every person of faith has considered every text as equally scriptural, or as scriptural at all. This conflict between what is and is not truly "Scripture" dates as far back as the early second century CE, when Marcion of Sinope rejected those Scriptures he considered "Jewish." Later Christians have had similar reactions to particular books. Reformers like John Calvin and Martin Luther had no love for the Revelation to John and the Epistle of James, respectively. As twentieth-century theologian Howard Thurman revealed, among African Americans descended from US chattel slavery, New Testament writings in favor of slavery were held in low esteem, and even "read out" of the Bible (Thurman, 30–31). In *Jesus and the Disinherited*, Thurman tells a story of his grandmother who would not let him read from the Pauline Epistles, with the exception, on occasion, of 1 Corinthians 13. Thurman recounts:

> What she told me I shall never forget. "During the days of slavery," she said, "the master's minister would occasionally hold services for the slaves. . . . Always the white minister used as his text something from Paul. At least three or four times a year, he used as a text: 'Slaves be obedient to them that are your masters as unto Christ.' Then he would go on to show how it was God's will that we were slaves, and how, if we were good and happy slaves, God would bless us. I promised my Maker that if I ever learned to read and if freedom came, I would not read that part of the Bible." (Thurman, 30–31)

Thurman's grandmother's quite candid assessment of the New Testament caused her to determine not to treat the proslavery writings of the New Testament as Scripture, even if she had to omit almost every word attributed to the apostle Paul. She refused, in so doing, to use the proslavery New Testament writings as Scripture—as lenses to help her negotiate her relationship to the universe.

Like Marcion, Luther, Calvin, and even Thurman's grandmother, Christian practitioners still very often select which among the New Testament writings they will treat as Scripture, although they may not do so consciously. More commonly, even among those who claim inerrant divine inspiration for all of the biblical writings, certain texts are seen as "favorites," or as "the heart of the gospel." As noted above, each of these writings is also a migrant writing. As a result, unsurprisingly, people of faith very often also end up incorporating into their scriptural lenses not only the theological concepts that the texts propose but also the migrant strategies toward home and host cultures embedded in them. Those for whom John's Gospel is paramount might find themselves valuing liminality as the ideal interaction with their world. Those who privilege the Revelation to John might find themselves valuing separation. Those who hold to Paul's letters might find themselves valuing accommodation. These migrant strategies become inseparable from scriptural lenses. As a result, Christians of the dominant culture of a particular country, whose families may not have experienced migration for many generations, may still interact with that culture as though they were migrants in a host culture because of their scriptural lenses.

Within twenty-first-century civic life, this adaptation of migrant strategies may take the form of groups that stay to themselves and are viewed with suspicion because they privilege a separate migrant strategy. In a society in which every detail of human life is readily accessibly through the Internet, the choice of such groups to distance themselves from society at large may be seen as inviting or, by contrast, quite suspicious. Alternatively, it may take the form of groups that vilify both Christian religion as it is typically practiced and the society at large, turning instead to an alternative way of being entirely. Certainly such practices might go unnoticed. On the other hand, when in positions of power, Christians adopting liminal migrant strategies might have profound impact on schools, political parties, and social policy—whether they are found on the left or right wing of the political spectrum. This may seem oxymoronic. However, the liminality in this case is not actual societal power. Rather, these persons adopt a liminal stance toward society because of the Scriptures through which they refract their world, and which counsel them regarding their appropriate interaction with the world.

However, perhaps the migrant strategy that has had the strongest historical stance and still continues to be heard from among Christian practitioners is that of accommodation. In the United States and the Western north, this is in part due to the outsize influence of the writings of Paul in the Protestant churches. It is this strategy that brings us the abolitionist and civil rights movements among African Americans and many other movements for social justice. It is also this strategy that brings us the proslavery movement within the church and the twenty-first-century church's willingness to accommodate unjust policies regarding poverty and human rights. In each of these opposing cases, Christian interaction with the world is governed not only by what the Scriptures say but also by the scriptural stance of holding on to tradition while finding a way to engage the "world," which may appear to be hostile. Thus an abolitionist holds on to one set of scriptural sayings and a slaveholder to another set; however, both take the Pauline tack that both holds to the tradition and engages the society. At stake is the argument over what aspects of the dominant culture shall be accommodated and what resisted. Faithful Christians have, over time, responded very differently to these questions.

Each of these strategies persists today, strengthened by the migrant strategies in these ancient writings that continue to be Scripture for twenty-first-century Christians. As students of these texts, paying attention to these strategies may help us to unpack some of the Christianity-related arguments in our civic commons. Pay attention, also, to the sense of rootlessness that undergirds some of the music and culture, particularly of the United States: the sense that "there's no place like home," but also that "we're not in Kansas anymore" that can emerge in the rhetoric even of people whose families have been resident since the days of European colonialism. For this is not simply a product of changing times; times have always changed. In a culture so steeped in these migrant writings, this literary diaspora space called the New Testament, surely some of that rootlessness, some of those uncritically employed migrant strategies can be traced back to these ancient writings, these migrant Scriptures of the Christian church.

Works Cited

Bauckham, Richard. 1999. *James.* New Testament Readings. New York: Routledge.

Berry, John W. 2001. "A Psychology of Immigration." *Journal of Social Issues* 57, no. 3:615–31.

Brah, Avtar. 1996. *Cartographies of Diaspora: Contesting Identities.* New York: Routledge.

Brown, Raymond. 1979. *The Community of the Beloved Disciple: The Lives, Loves, and Hates of an Individual Church in New Testament Times.* Mahwah, NJ: Paulist.

Gibson, Margaret A. 2001. "Immigrant Adaption and Patterns of Acculturation." *Human Development* 44:19–23.

Johnson, Luke Timothy. 2004. *Brother of Jesus, Friend of God: Studies in the Letter of James.* Grand Rapids: Eerdmans.

Schüssler Fiorenza, Elisabeth. 2009. "Introduction: Exploring the Intersection of Race, Gender, Status, and Ethnicity in Early Christian Studies." In *Prejudice and Christian Beginnings*, edited by Laura Nasrallah and Elisabeth Schüssler Fiorenza. Minneapolis: Fortress Press.

Smith, Wilfred Cantwell. 1993. *What Is Scripture? A Comparative Approach.* Minneapolis: Fortress Press.

Taussig, Hal. 2009. *In the Beginning Was the Meal: Social Experimentation and Early Christianity.* Minneapolis: Fortress Press.

Thurman, Howard. 1976. *Jesus and the Disinherited.* Boston: Beacon.

The Apocalyptic Legacy of Early Christianity

David A. Sánchez

a•poc•a•lyp•tic (adj): of, relating to, or involving terrible violence and destruction: of or relating to the end of the world

leg•a•cy (noun): something transmitted by or received from an ancestor or predecessor or from the past

(*Merriam-Webster Dictionary*, 2003)

Introduction: The Problem of a Suppressed Legacy

We twenty-first-century Christians find ourselves in a strange place in relationship to our apocalyptic biblical inheritance. In many of our churches, apocalyptic literature, especially the Revelation to John, is treated with benign neglect, yet its images continue to fascinate us, as witness the tremendous success of novels like the *Left Behind* series. This is especially true from my perspective as a Roman Catholic: the book of Revelation remains liturgically peripheral in my tradition (with the exception of December 12—the Feast of the Virgin of Guadalupe, when Revelation 12 is a focal reading—and, on occasion, during the Lenten season). Yet Roman Catholics, like most twenty-first-century Christians, remain remarkably vulnerable to conjuring apocalyptic scenarios, under the right circumstances.

Meanwhile, over the last several decades, a great deal of ink has been spilled by scholars attempting to specify matters like the genre, form, and content of those ancient texts that qualify as "apocalyptic" and thus have contributed to this legacy. As one might expect, the book of Revelation has been the most obvious focal point in those conversations. Indeed, according to the most learned biblical specialists, this is the *only* writing in the New Testament that meets the scholarly criteria regarding the form of the genre apocalypse. I, for one, am in total agreement with this assessment, but I remain unsatisfied with the emphases of the scholarly conversation because something tells me, deep in my soul, that there is more to our Christian apocalyptic legacy than is addressed by such formal considerations.

In this essay, I would like to suggest an alternative point of entry, other than the Revelation to John, for discussing our apocalyptic inheritance. I would like initially to consider the Synoptic Gospels, not, however, as we usually read them, conflated together, as if they are telling roughly the same story; that keeps us from seeing something important—that from the very beginning, Christians have struggled with the troubling legacy of a genuinely apocalyptic vision. The Gospel tradition has embedded within it, specifically within the Gospel of Mark, what functions as a genuinely apocalyptic text. By examining how Matthew and Luke altered that text, we see how early Christians negotiated the first apocalyptic legacy in their tradition by altering its eschatological moorings. More precisely, Matthew and Luke demonstrate how a Christian *apocalyptic* moment was turned into an ecclesiastical movement with the alteration to a less imminent expectation of the Parousia of Jesus Christ.

To start with, this less obvious biblical apocalyptic moment serves several purposes. (1) It prevents us from isolating the book of Revelation as if it were the only example of an apocalyptic worldview in the Christian canon, and from sequestering it in the category of prophetically anomalous literature, rendering it so much easier to ignore. (2) It demonstrates that Matthew and Luke believed they needed to domesticate the apocalyptic agenda of the Gospel of Mark in the wake of the delayed return of Jesus Christ. And (3) it challenges us to bring to consciousness, in a cultural-psychoanalytic sense, the way other scriptural sources, in addition to Revelation, are embedded in our psyches and contribute to our perduring fascination with apocalyptic solutions, prompting us to "act out" apocalyptically under the right circumstances.

Apocalypticism

At this point it is critical to be clear how I am employing the term *apocalyptic*, especially because much scholarly ink has been spilled on the contentious question of categorization. I rely on David Aune's summary in an illuminating 2005 article.

> "Apocalyptic eschatology" is the narrative theology, characteristic of apocalypses, centering in the belief that (1) the present world order, regarded as both evil and oppressive, is under temporary control of Satan and his human accomplices, and (2) that the present evil world order will shortly be destroyed by God and replaced by a new and perfect order corresponding to Eden before the fall. During the present evil age, the people of God are an oppressed minority who fervently expect God, or his specially chosen agent the Messiah, to rescue them. The transition between the old and the new ages will be introduced with a final series of battles fought by the people of God

> against the human allies of Satan. The outcome is never in question, however, for the enemies of God are predestined for defeat and destruction. (Aune, 236)

What I find most compelling in this definition—for the purposes of this essay and for my own personal relationship to apocalypticism—are the notions of cosmological dualism (with a war of heavenly proportions affecting, and afflicting, human actors), the introduction of the messianic agent (i.e., Jesus Christ), and the sense of temporal urgency. The present world order will be destroyed *soon*. It is this temporal consideration that I find most compelling when looking at an apocalyptic text like the Gospel of Mark—and at the Matthean and Lukan responses to Mark's acute temporality.

Excavating Mark as Another Example of Christian Apocalyptic

With this working definition of apocalypticism in mind, how does the Gospel of Mark function apocalyptically? Our first consideration is the moment in history when the Gospel of Mark was written. The majority of New Testament scholars date the Gospel between 66 and 70 CE, that is, squarely during the Jewish War with Rome, or shortly after the destruction of the Jerusalem temple. Thus Mark was written during a time of *real* political and cultural crisis (cf. Adela Yarbro Collins's language of *perceived* crisis; A. Y. Collins, 84–110) that may have indeed been an impetus for an apocalyptic response. Second, the Christology of the Gospel of Mark foregrounds the messiahship of Jesus. This is made explicit in the very first verse of the Gospel: "The beginning of the gospel of Jesus Christ" (i.e., Messiah). This christological emphasis is maintained throughout the Gospel (e.g., in the messianic secret motif: see the commentary on Mark). The relationship of a messianic figure to different apocalyptic scenarios is still under scholarly debate. I defer to Aune's assessment, noted above, which highlighted the expectation of God's oppressed people that an agent of God would act on their behalf at the critical and ultimate moment.

Other features of the Gospel of Mark that add to its apocalyptic tenor include its explicit cosmological dualism, as represented in the temptation of Jesus, after his baptism, by Satan (1:12-13) and the multiple exorcisms in the Gospel (e.g., 1:21-28; 5:1-20; 9:14-29). In comparison, the Gospel of John, arguably the least apocalyptic of the four canonical Gospels—has not one exorcism.

The Gospel of Mark also maintains a unique relationship to time. It is by far the most compressed of the four Gospels, narrating the ministry of Jesus from baptism to empty tomb. The Gospels of Matthew and Luke each begin with narratives of Jesus' birth, and end with accounts of his ascension into heaven. The Gospel of John goes even further, beginning "in the beginning" and ending with an ascension account. The Gospel of Mark employs the phrase "and immediately" some forty-one times in its narrative, twelve times in the first chapter alone. (The Greek phrase *kai euthys* occurs only nineteen times in the rest of the New Testament.) The phrase gives the reader/hearer the impression of a story moving very rapidly, and may remind the reader, ancient and modern alike, of the initial words uttered by Jesus in the Gospel: "The time is fulfilled, and the kingdom of God has come near" (1:15). Further, aspects of Mark's story reveal aspects of sectarian groups, as identified by modern theory: the requirement of severance of ties with one's biological family (e.g.,

1:16-20; 2:13-14; 10:28), the creation of a new eschatological family (3:31-35), and the mandatory renunciation of personal wealth for the benefit of the group (6:7-13; 10:17-27).

These observations crystallize the argument that Mark has apocalyptic features. This "excavation" goes beyond the usual characterization of Mark 13 as the "Little Apocalypse" to reveal that an apocalyptic character pervades the Gospel, and thus to foreground another apocalyptic moment in early Christian history; the Revelation to John does not stand in isolation. But consider next how both Matthew and Luke, unsatisfied with Mark's apocalyptic moorings some ten to fifteen years after the fact, chose to domesticate Mark when they incorporated his Gospel into their own. By means of this domestication, the legacy of Christian apocalypticism has been canonically offset, if not altogether suppressed, by the consequent conflated readings of the Gospel narratives.

Domesticating Mark: Matthew and Luke-Acts

I often imagine Matthew and Luke separately clinging to their manuscripts of Mark's Gospel and wondering just what on earth they were going to do with such an apocalyptically urgent Gospel. It is a humorous scene in my mind's eye, considering that apocalyptic movements have a short shelf life. How long can a preacher and/or teacher keep saying that deliverance is just around the corner? Thus I imagine Matthew and Luke questioning the validity of Mark's Gospel and how their Christian movements should proceed. In the wake of the delayed Parousia, with its delayed fulfillment of prophecy, do they quit the movement? Weren't the words of imminence placed on the very lips of Jesus himself (see esp. Mark 9:1; 13:30)? Perhaps they should bring about their own apocalypse, as subsequent Christian groups have done throughout the Christian era? Surely even slight provocation of Roman might accomplish that end. Or what if they took Mark's expected imminent Parousia and moved it into the distant future (by what scholars call "reserved eschatology")? If, as I contend here, this last was the option they chose, what were they to do with the rest of Mark, and even more acutely, what were they to do in the interim before the deferred Parousia?

These are fascinating questions that require some parsing. Note, first, that almost 90 percent of the Gospel of Mark is absorbed into Matthew's account. But how could one domesticate so apocalyptic a Gospel while absorbing so much of the original? Perhaps the best approach to this question is to assess how Matthew employed his sources. Arguably, the Gospel of Matthew can be reduced to three source-rich divisions. Chapters 1–2 are composed of material known as special M, biblical material unique to Matthew. This special source includes the (Matthean) birth narrative, the visitation of the magi, and the holy family's escape to Egypt in the wake of Herod's execution of Jewish male infants. This material accomplishes various purposes for Matthew, but most importantly for my point here, it expands the story of Jesus' life by almost three decades. Recall that the Gospel of Mark begins at Jesus' baptism, approximately one year before his death in his early thirties. Thus Matthew expands narrative time.

Matthew also proceeds in a much less rushed manner. The next section of the Gospel is made up primarily of materials gleaned from the sayings source Q. (See the essay on Jesus and the Gospels.) Embedded in this layer is a collection of words and teachings of Jesus apart from his deeds. In this material, we find the Sermon on the Mount, which takes up three chapters of Matthew's Gospel (chapters 5–7), and includes the Beatitudes and the Lord's Prayer. This saturation of Jesus' teachings in the middle of Matthew shifts the focus from Mark's apocalyptic Jesus to a more refined, rabbinic Jesus, one who certainly has much more time to teach and instruct his disciples on how to interact with the world in the interim before the Parousia.

We are finally introduced to the bulk of the Markan material as it is embedded in Matthew 12–28 (esp. after ch. 16). However, we have already been lulled into a more tranquil state of consciousness by the birth narrative and teaching discourse, so already the apocalyptic materials appear much more distant and future. The apocalyptic predictions imported from chapter 13 of the "Markan apocalypse" (Matthew 24) will come to pass (i.e., the destruction of the Jerusalem temple, wars and rumors of wars, persecution of the faithful, the desolating sacrilege, the appearance of false prophets, astronomical chaos, and the return of the son of man), but without the imminent tones of Mark's composition. This is also the case in the Lukan parallel to Mark 13 (Luke 21).

Even more brilliantly, Matthew incorporates ascension materials (28:16-20) to place Jesus back in heaven in the interim, thus overcoming what is, to Matthew, the more than slightly problematic lack of any indication where Jesus is during the interim according to the original ending of Mark (Mark 16:8, which, in my estimation, is a perfect ending for an *apocalyptic* Gospel). By conjoining it to the "Great Commission" in 28:18-20, Matthew has reframed Mark's apocalypticism into a template for a fledgling church movement that has much to accomplish before Christ's return. It is a brilliant piece of editorial work that simultaneously honors the primacy of Mark, by using so much of it as a source, *and* shifts Mark's emphasis from crisis and end-time speculation to an expanded story of the life of Jesus, with an emphasis on Jesus as aphoristic teacher and founder of a church. However, the point must not be overlooked that Matthew also felt the need for a complete eschatological overhaul of the Gospel of Mark, one that would privilege an emerging church. In my view, this was perhaps the most compelling reason for Matthew's privileged position in the New Testament canon. To place Mark at the beginning of the canon—noting its primacy among the Gospels—would have created an apocalyptic inclusio for the New Testament that would begin with Mark and end with the book of Revelation! The rhetorical brilliance of the canon as it now stands, however, is that the apocalypticism of the book of Revelation is now viewed as a futuristic culmination of the age of Matthew's developing and spreading church.

Luke, like his Synoptic cousin Matthew, had to make a tough decision regarding what to do with Mark's Gospel. I have always found it fascinating that both Luke and Matthew chose to retain and employ material from the Gospel of Mark. Surely, one avenue each author could have taken was to ignore the Gospel of Mark altogether and start from scratch. But neither did. Luke, as did Matthew, also employed special materials unique to his own Gospel, identified today as special L, and employed the 235 sayings of Jesus from Q. Unlike Matthew, however, the author of the Gospel of Luke used approximately one-half of the Gospel of Mark in the composition of his own Gospel (a large percentage even in relation to Matthew). Like Matthew, Luke also expanded the narrative time frame by introducing narratives of Jesus' birth and ascension. However, unlike any of his Gospel counterparts, Luke wrote a second contribution that would find its way into the New Testament canon, the Acts of the Apostles, which maps out the earliest years of the post-Easter church and the spread of the gospel from the Jewish world (foregrounding the apostleship of Peter) to the worldwide spread of the gospel to the gentiles (foregrounding the apostleship of Paul). In Lukan terms, this was the interim age of the Holy Spirit. The Parousia was delayed and Luke was prepared to encounter the delay, not as an unfulfilled prophecy, but as an opportunity to spread the gospel to the world. As in Matthew, the Gospel of Mark is relegated to the apocalyptic drama that would occur in the eschaton in the indeterminate future (again, reserved eschatology). Luke even hinted at an eschatology that we find most pronounced in the Gospel of John (that is, realized eschatology) when he hints at the benefits of the Parousia being accessible already, in the present, in Luke 17:20-21.

> Once Jesus was asked by the Pharisees when the kingdom of God was coming, and he answered, "The kingdom of God is not coming with things that can be observed; nor will they say, 'Look here it is!' or 'There it is!' For, in fact, the kingdom of God is among you."

It is evident from this brief analysis of both Matthew and Luke that both Gospel writers thought enough of the tradition of Mark to incorporate it into their literary productions while simultaneously toning down Mark's apocalyptic sensibilities to make it more palatable for Christians living in the 80s or later. Both spent much intellectual energy doing so. Matthew and Luke found themselves at least a decade removed from Mark's imminent apocalyptic prediction. The apocalyptic rhetoric had to shift because you cannot be an imminent apocalyptic preacher or sustain an apocalyptic community year after year after year.

Thus the Gospels present us with this curious combination of competing eschatologies. Because it has been a Christian interpretive practice to conflate our readings of the Gospels, emphasizing their presumed unity, the apocalypticism of Mark has been absorbed into the grander "gospel story." It is lost, or ignored, or projected into the undetermined future. The Markan legacy is a painful one, to be sure, because embedded within it is an unfulfilled prophecy of the imminent second coming of Christ, and so we can understand the energy that wants to avoid or defer it. But the presence of Mark among the Gospels means that even if we sequester the book of Revelation as some sort of apocalyptic anomaly, the intellectual fodder for subsequent apocalyptic movements and imaginings remains. Apocalypticism is embedded in our Gospel tradition itself, right in front of us, even if we choose not to acknowledge it. We may suppress it—and then act entirely surprised when apocalyptic inklings manifest themselves in us, like any other neurosis or psychosis would, given the right circumstances.

Expanding the Apocalyptic Landscape: The Pauline Tradition

Even the Pauline tradition—where scholars have long recognized the strength of apocalyptic influence on the apostle's thought—is not immune from a similar apocalyptic suppression. Paul's response to the church in Thessalonica regarding the fate of deceased Christians is illuminating:

> But we do not want you to be uninformed, brothers and sisters, about those who have died, so that you may not grieve as others do who have no hope. For since we believe that Jesus died and rose again, even so, through Jesus, God will bring with him those who have died. For this we declare to you by the word of the Lord, that we who are alive, who are left until the coming of the Lord, will

> by no means precede those who have died. For the Lord himself, with a cry of command, with the archangel's call and with the sound of God's trumpet, will descend from heaven, and the dead in Christ will rise first. Then we who are alive, who are left, will be caught up in the clouds together with them to meet the Lord in the air; and so we will be with the Lord forever. (1 Thess. 4:13-17)

Here, Paul speaks to the faithful in Thessalonica in no uncertain terms—imminent apocalyptic terms. Paul expects to be at the Parousia of Jesus Christ. And just as we saw in the Synoptic tradition, Paul faced a period of time (approximately five or six years, if we accept the dating of 1 Thessalonians c. 49 CE and Romans c. 55 CE) in which he personally was confronted with the delayed Parousia. Although Romans was written to a different congregation on a completely different set of issues, it is nevertheless surprising how completely lacking are apocalyptic tones in the letter. If we regard Pauline Christianity as an apocalyptic movement like other apocalyptic groups throughout history, we should expect apocalypticism to be the theological lens through which all things are assessed. How could it be otherwise? But then the absence of apocalyptic elements in Romans is altogether curious.

It appears, then, that any assessment of the apocalyptic legacy of early Christianity must begin with an expansion of the scriptural materials we delegate as apocalyptic. To continue to focus our consideration of apocalyptic material solely on the book of Revelation allows us to compartmentalize our assessment of early Christian apocalyptic wholly on the last book of the Christian canon. Thus any subsequent appropriation of apocalyptic worldviews by Christian groups is easily marginalized by placing the hermeneutic blame on simplistic and/or overly literal readings of the book of Revelation. The first step in recovery is acknowledgment: in this case, acknowledgment that our apocalyptic roots run much deeper than the book of Revelation. Therefore, the work of intellectually excavating texts such as the Gospel of Mark and Paul's First Letter to the Thessalonians is a positive first step in parsing how and why Christian apocalypticism has endured over two millennia. It is in our biblical DNA, present in the earliest letter from the apostle Paul and in the first Gospel ever written. And indeed, it is there, in all of its pure genre form, in the book of Revelation. It is more pervasive than we choose to admit, and scholarly discussions on matters of proper form have only distracted us from that fact. But Matthew, Luke, and Paul have left evidence not only of the prevalence of apocalyptic expectation but also of some measure of its unsustainability: that is, evidence that they tried to distance themselves from a perspective that had such a short shelf life. It appears that individuals and communities simply can't be perpetually apocalyptic. Nevertheless, our apocalyptic memories are short, and we Christians find ourselves bouncing to and fro, from postures of apocalyptic fervor to more tranquil, reserved eschatological expectation. It is a rhythmic dance that has played out over two Christian millennia.

The Book of Revelation and the Explicit Legacy of Christian Apocalypticism

Acknowledgment of the comprehensive influence of the book of Revelation on the Western Christian imagination goes unchallenged even with attempts by some denominations to altogether suppress it. It is, according to both form and content, the only true apocalypse in the New Testament (Collins 1979, 9; see the commentary on Revelation). Its rich imagery, full of beasts, martyrs, heavenly interlocutors, plagues, mysterious gematria, natural disasters, whores, and a great descending city is almost too much for the senses to comprehend, yet simultaneously hypersensual enough to draw even the casual reader into a hypnotic state of attention. It is like the car wreck on the highway that simultaneously repels and irresistibly attracts at least a momentary gaze as we cautiously pass by. It has been the source of Christian apocalyptic ambivalence and anxiety for the last two millennia. A summary of that interpretive history will bear out the alternating rhythm described above, in which our collective traditions have tried to come to terms with the last entry in the New Testament.

The apocalyptic legacy of the book of Revelation began early in the second century of the Common Era. According to Robert M. Royalty Jr. and Arthur W. Wainwright, proto-orthodox Christians like Justin Martyr (c. 100–165) and Irenaeus (c. 130–200) represented an interpretive position known as chiliasm (i.e., millenarian, from the Greek *chilia*, "thousand"). Chiliasm, which represented a literal interpretation of the book of Revelation, was theologically "mainstream" in the early second century. This position is best defined as the theological system that "believed literally in the thousand-year reign of the saints in Rev. 20:4 and the actual, physical new Jerusalem in Rev. 21–22" (Royalty, 285). Wainwright argues that "the chiliasts lived in an age of persecution. It was for such an age that they believed the Apocalypse was written. . . . During this period Chiliasm provided an antidote to the fear of persecution. When people are oppressed, they find consolation in dreams of a better life and focus their anger on the institutions and leaders that threaten them" (Wainwright, 22). Thus Wainwright makes the interpretive assumption that the Apocalypse functioned as a rhetorical call for endurance during times of persecution.

One of the first challenges to literal chiliastic readings of the book of Revelation came from Phrygia in Asia Minor. The "New Prophecy" (c. 150–175), or Montanism (as it was called by its opponents), was founded by Montanus, Prisca, and Maximilla. According to the New Prophecy, the new kingdom would be inaugurated by Christ—but in Pepuza, the geographical epicenter of the New Prophecy movement, and not Jerusalem. The New Prophecy thus challenged "normative" chiliastic expectations through a very selective literal approach to the text by its protagonists (including Tertullian, c. 160–220).

The chiliastic certainty of the of the mid-second century was also countered by emerging late second-century and early third-century allegorical interpretations of the book of Revelation forwarded by the likes of Dionysius, bishop of Alexandria (third century), Clement of Alexandria (c. 150–215), and Origen (c. 185–254). These allegorical readings came to full fruition under Augustine of Hippo (ca. 354–430), who himself was first a proponent of chiliasm until his "eschatological conversion" later in his career. Dionysius, Clement, and Origen began to challenge aspects of chiliasm, especially the literal interpretation of the new Jerusalem as a *physical* and earthly place where "the redeemed would eat, drink, marry, have children, and exercise dominion over other people" (Origen, *De princ.* 2.11.2–3). Thus the early challenges to the literal interpretations focused primarily on the location of the new Jerusalem (New Prophecy) and its physical nature, as depicted in Revelation 21–22. These challenges were just enough to begin to dislodge the mainstream chiliastic interpretations that nevertheless prevailed until the reign of Constantine, in the fourth century of the Common Era. That is a fascinatingly long tenure for literal apocalyptic musings. In some ways, the first three centuries of the Christian era mirror the apocalyptic tension that existed in the now emerging canon, representing both movements with apocalyptic sensibilities and those that countered them. Our ambivalence regarding apocalypticism and the variety of divergent interpretive possibilities were beginning to take shape in these earliest Christian centuries.

It could be argued, if one follows the logic of Wainwright, that the fourth century, with the shift in Rome's relationship to Christianity from one of indifference to persecution, then to tolerance and ultimately acceptance, also marked a shift in the Christian rhetorical posture toward apocalyptic literature in general, and the book of Revelation in particular. Violently imaginative and passive-aggressive fantasies of revenge of the Apocalypse were no longer necessary with Christianity's new and prominent relationship to the empire. This was especially the case after 381, when Emperor Theodosius endorsed orthodox Nicene Christianity over Christian Arianism and banned all pagan religious ritual. What was once peripheral was now central, and the Christian relationship to its apocalyptic legacy needed to be reevaluated. On this matter, Royalty notes, "after the Roman emperors moved from tolerance to acceptance and promotion of orthodox Christianity, millenarian views were even more strongly challenged. No imperial ruler, political or ecclesiastical, eagerly anticipated the destruction of the empire they now controlled" (Royalty, 286).

The influence of Augustine's allegorical reading of the Apocalypse was comprehensive and dominated orthodox circles from the fifth through thirteenth centuries of the Common Era. Perhaps the greatest challenge to traditional readings of the Apocalypse was Augustine's hesitance in speculating about the date of the end. Recall that Aune's working definition of apocalypse (see above) identified one of the key elements of literal apocalyptic readings as the expectation of the imminent end. This was not the case for Augustine, however, and in essence, by his very hesitation, he lowered the expectation of what is probably the most important aspect of apocalyptic eschatology: imminence. To challenge literal chiliastic views on the imminent apocalypse, derived from Revelation 20,

> Augustine offered two key interpretive points in the *City of God*, Book 20. First, the thousand year period is symbolic of "the whole duration of the world," the earthly fullness of time. Thus Augustine tried to put an end to speculations about dates and times for this millennium to start and end, a point for which he had plenty of biblical proof texts. Second, this symbolic millennium has already begun in the time of the church for that is what binds Satan until the final end. . . . And as for the final, *final* end, do not count the days, for the thousand year period is symbolic. (Royalty, 286–87)

Thus, with one powerful, stunning theological gesture, Augustine succeeded in shifting the emphasis from literal readings of the apocalypse to spiritual and nonmillennial readings that would last through the thirteenth century—until a Calabrian abbot named Joachim of Fiore (c. 1135–1202) would once again shift our relationship and understanding of the Apocalypse.

In contrast to Augustine's symbolic reading of the Apocalypse, Joachim of Fiore insisted on what he believed was a historical reading of the text. Joachim alleged that the persecution of Christians in his lifetime was evidence that the signs predicted in the book of Revelation were being realized.

Thus Joachim countered the allegorized reading promoted by Augustine by renewing a historicized reading of the Apocalypse similar to those first endorsed by Justin and Irenaeus. After his spiritual conversion and time spent in the Holy Land on pilgrimage, Joachim returned to Calabria and became a recluse, devoting his study and prayer time to deciphering the book of Revelation. Completely frustrated with his attempt to come to terms with the text, he reported that upon awakening one Easter morning, the meaning of the Apocalypse was revealed to him. Thus, unlike Augustine, Joachim is best understood—like John of Patmos—as an apocalyptic seer.

Joachim's primary contribution as a mystical seer was formulating a system (*concordia*) that divided human history into three historical epochs or states (*status* in Latin). The first *status* was the period from Adam to Jesus Christ, which Joachim called the period of God the Father, corresponding to the Hebrew Scriptures (and to the layperson's church). The *status* from Jesus Christ to 1260 was the period of God the Son and of the Christian Testament (corresponding to the papal church). This was the period in which Joachim himself lived. The third and final *status* began in 1260 and was the period of the Holy Spirit. This third epoch corresponded to the Friars' church. This age, according to Joachim, was the age of the new millennial kingdom:

> [The third epoch] was to be inaugurated by a new Adam or a new Christ who would be the founder of a new monastic order. The transition between the Papal Church of the second age and the Spiritual Church of the third age would be a time of great troubles during which the period of the Papal Church was to endure all the sufferings that corresponded to Christ's passion. The Papal Church would be resurrected as the Spiritual Church in which all men would live the contemplative life, practice apostolic poverty, and enjoy angelic natures. To this level Joachim's ideas were debased and popularized during the thirteenth century by a series of pseudo-Joachimite writings, which probably originated amongst the spiritual Franciscans themselves. St. Francis was identified with the messiah that Joachim prophesied. During the later Middle Ages Joachimism and the Apocalypse preserved their ideological union. (Phelan, 14)

Again, in contrast to Augustine's more domesticating and spiritual reading of the Apocalypse, Joachim revisited subversive interpretations of the text that were more at home in a historical interpretive framework. On this matter, Royalty notes, "Joachim reenergized historicized and potentially politically subversive readings of the Apocalypse, with one result being ideological challenges to ecclesiological and civil authorities in Europe within some monastic and mendicant religious communities" (Royalty, 289). And like the historicized readings of the first century, Joachim employed the powerful rhetoric of persecution. The echoes of his historicized reading reverberated most prominently from the thirteenth through the sixteenth centuries in Western Christendom and, in a few select traditions, are palpable even today (Sánchez).

The Protestant Reformation was also not immune from the perduring legacy of the Apocalypse to John. The onetime Roman Catholic German monk Martin Luther (1483–1546) also had an ambivalent relationship with the book of Revelation. In his early career, Luther remarked,

> I miss more than one thing in this book, and this makes me hold it to be neither apostolic nor prophetic . . . there is one sufficient reason for me not to think highly of it—Christ is neither taught nor known in it. (Luther 1960a, 399)

On a disenchanting trip to Rome, Luther felt betrayed by the "corruption" of the Catholic Church. This initiated an intense search of the Scriptures, which led him to conclude that salvation was a function of his own personal faith rather than derived from any corporate church entity—especially a church that he now found so dismaying. Luther set his own course with the posting of his Ninety-Five Theses in Wittenberg, Saxony, which ultimately led to his excommunication from the Roman Catholic Church.

One of the most significant appropriations of the book of Revelation among Protestant Reformers, including Luther, was the equating of the papacy with the beast(s) of the Apocalypse. Wainwright notes that Luther himself promoted "that . . . the papacy was the beast of the land [Rev. 13:11-18], [and] the empire was the beast of the sea [Rev. 13:1-10]. But the pope, he [i.e., Luther] argued, had control over the empire" (Wainwright, 61). Luther was not the first or the only critic of the papacy who employed negative apocalyptic accusations at Rome: "Some of the sharpest criticism came from Bohemia and England. In Bohemia John Milicz (d. 1374), Mathias of Janow (d. 1394), and John Hus (1369–1415) implied the pope was Antichrist" (Wainwright, 59).

Roman Catholicism in general and the papacy in particular came under a severe Protestant challenge. The need for a swift Catholic response was clear. In some circles, the Catholic response was simply to employ the same apocalyptic polemic against the Protestants. Catholic bishops like Bertold Pürstinger (1463–1543), bishop of Chiemsee (Germany), "explained that the locusts of the sixth trumpet vision [Rev. 9:13-19] were Lutherans. Serafino da Fermo described Luther as the star falling from heaven [Rev. 9:1] and the beast from the land [Rev. 13:11-18]" (Wainwright, 61).

Two other lines of interpretation employed by Catholics against Protestant antipapal interpretations were futurism, championed by the Spanish Jesuit Francisco Ribera (1537–1591), and preterism, developed most fully by the Portuguese Jesuit Luis de Alcazar (1554–1613). "Futurists contended that most of the prophecies in the Apocalypse were still unfulfilled, Preterists argued that most of them had been fulfilled already" (Wainwright, 63). Both methods of interpretation were effective. Futurism was attractive to Catholics, "because it dissociated the pope from Antichrist. It was cogent because it recognized the connection of the beast and the harlot of Rome, although it was a Rome of the future. Futurism challenged both the antipapal interpretation and the assumption that the Apocalypse provided a survey of church history" (Wainwright, 63). Preterism, by arguing that most of the prophecies of the Apocalypse had already been fulfilled, "was congenial to Catholics because it rejected the suggestion that the pope was Antichrist and it gave honor to the Roman Catholic Church" (Wainwright, 63).

One interesting offshoot of the Reformation era was the contemporary emergence of a group known as the Anabaptists. The name Anabaptist was not claimed by the group itself but rather came from other Christian groups opposed to their rejection of infant baptism (a common practice in Roman Catholic circles). The name is derived from the Greek *anabaptismos*, which is loosely translated as "being baptized (over) again." The Anabaptists were part of a movement classified today as the Radical Reformation, and it should be noted that both Protestant and Catholics persecuted Anabaptists. Beyond their baptismal practices, Anabaptists rejected organized religious hierarchies in favor of an idealized theocratic state. This ideology led to a faction of their membership occupying the German city of Münster, which they likened to the new Jerusalem (Revelation 21), to await the return of the heavenly Christ. Within the Anabaptist ranks, a Dutch national named Jan Bockelson declared himself the Messiah of the end times, and coins were minted that referenced the imminent apocalypse. The siege of Münster ended violently in 1535.

In the nineteenth century, three religious movements emerged that also took a historical interpretive approach to the Apocalypse. Those groups are the Church of Jesus Christ of Latter-Day Saints (Mormons) founded by Joseph Smith (c. 1830) shortly after the publication of the Book of Mormon; the Seventh-Day Adventists (Millerites), founded by William Miller (c. 1833); and the Jehovah's Witnesses, founded by Charles Russell (c. 1872). These three US-born movements are relevant for the current discussion because all three movements predicted an imminent apocalypse in their initial years, survived those unrealized predictions, and continue to remain with us today. Therefore, all three movements are interesting examples of how to negotiate an evolving apocalyptic expectation.

Latter-Day Saints (LDS) are an interesting example of a religious group that expanded on the Christian canon by including the Book of Mormon, *The Pearl of Great Price*, and the *Doctrine and Covenants* as church Scripture. LDS members also accept the prophecies of their church leadership as authoritative. (The head of the LDS Church at any given time in its history is recognized as prophet.) This combination of Scriptures and "[prophetic] pronouncement of their leaders has led them to expect both the rebuilding of Jerusalem in the old world and the erection of the New Jerusalem [Revelation 21] in North America. They look forward to the return of Christ to inaugurate his millennial reign over the earth" (Wainwright, 99). This bifurcated manner of dividing the old and new worlds is consistent with the LDS belief that Jesus Christ also visited the Americas shortly after his resurrection, in the first century CE.

Seventh-Day Adventists, like the earliest apocalyptic Christians, also had to deal with their own version of the delay of the Parousia. Their founder, William Miller, predicted that Christ would return in 1843. When his prophecy was not fulfilled, he changed the date to 1844, but that too was not realized. This unrealized prophecy was cause for the earliest Adventists to reconsider and reconfigure their intense apocalyptic hopes. What does an apocalyptic group do when their dated expectation is not realized? As noted above, these groups can abandon their expectations, they can initiate their own (violent) apocalypse (see below for modern examples of this option), or they can adjust the anticipated date—thereby adjusting their imminent expectation much as Matthew and Luke adjusted the Markan apocalyptic time frame. Such was the case with the Adventists; and the denomination still thrives today, some 170 years after the original apocalyptic prophecy. The rhetorical shift they made was to the notion that "another divine event, invisible to human eyes, had occurred in 1844. Christ, they said, had entered the heavenly sanctuary (Heb. 9:24-28)" (Wainwright, 99; cf. Froom, 889–99).

Note that the domesticating of apocalyptic imminence among Adventists did not sway the denomination away from their allegiance to the Apocalypse itself. Wainwright notes, "In arguing for the observance of Saturday as the holy day, they quoted the statement that those who did not keep God's commandments have the mark of the beast (Rev. 14:9-12). The Adventist John Nevis Andrews (1829–83) identified the beast from the land with the United States, whose two horns were civil and religious liberty. The beast from the sea and the whore of Babylon represented the papacy" (Wainwright, 99–100). Thus the continued Adventist appropriation of the Apocalypse shifted away from imminent temporal concerns toward an applied cosmological dualism, a trait common in most apocalyptic literature (as expressed, e.g., in the explicit distinction of insiders from outsiders, saved from unsaved, sinners from righteous).

At the forefront of Jehovah's Witness appropriations of the Apocalypse is their privileging of the 144,000 elect referenced in Revelation 7 and 14. Revelation 7:4-8 reads:

> Then I heard the number of those who were sealed: 144,000 from all the tribes of Israel.
>
> From the tribe of Judah, 12,000 were sealed,
> from the tribe of Reuben 12,000,
> from the tribe of Gad 12,000,
> from the tribe of Asher 12,000,
> from the tribe of Naphtali 12,000,
> from the tribe of Manasseh 12,000,
> from the tribe of Simeon 12,000,
> from the tribe of Levi, 12,000,
> from the tribe of Issachar 12,000,
> from the tribe of Zebulun 12,000,
> from the tribe of Joseph 12,000,
> from the tribe of Benjamin 12,000.

And Rev. 14:1 again refers to the 144,000: "Then I looked, and there before me was the Lamb, standing on Mount Zion, and with him 144,000 who had his name and his Father's name written on their foreheads." According to Jehovah's Witnesses, "the United Nations and the world's religious leaders will be on Satan's side in the Battle of Armageddon. Against them will be ranged the 144,000 and the other sheep, but Christ's heavenly army will actually win the victory, and the only survivors of the battle will be the Jehovah's Witnesses" (Wainwright, 100). This position is consistent with founder Charles Russell's original teaching that the 144,000 will constitute the foundation of God's people during the Christian millennium and will do battle with people marked with the mark of the beast (Wainwright, 100). Again, the acute dualism of this apocalyptic appropriation is evident in this end-time narrative. And like the Adventist Church, Jehovah's Witnesses have survived the crisis of unrealized apocalyptic prophecy.

> Mistaken prophecies have not daunted the Jehovah's Witnesses. Joseph Franklin Rutherford, who succeeded Russell as their leader, predicted that Abraham, Isaac, Jacob and other faithful Israelites would return to earth in 1925. More recent Witnesses have entertained the hope that the millennium might begin about 1975. In spite of the failure of these expectations, the organization continues to thrive. (Wainwright, 101)

The Apocalyptic Legacy Today

Looking back on this succinct review of how the apocalyptic legacy has endured over the Christian centuries, I, for one, am perplexed—yet not surprised—by the apocalyptically saturated culture in which we continue to live today. Over the last several decades, myriad films on the imminent end have been produced. Examples include *The Seventh Seal* (1958), *Fail Safe* (1964), *Planet of the Apes* (1968), *The Omega Man* (1971), *The Omen* (1976), *Apocalypse Now* (1979), *Pale Rider* (1985), *The Seventh Sign* (1988), the *Terminator* series (1984, 1991, 2003, 2009, and possibly a fifth episode in the series in 2015), *Independence Day* (1996), *The Matrix* series (1999, 2003, 2003), *Apocalypto* (2006), *Knowing* (2009), *The Road* (2009), *The Book of Eli* (2010), and *The Colony* (2013). At best, this is just a small representation of the hundreds of films produced in the recent past on an apocalyptic and catastrophic "end."

A great deal of apocalyptic music has also emerged over the same period: *The End*, by the Doors, 1967; *Burn*, by Deep Purple, 1974; *It's the End of the World as We Know It (And I Feel Fine)*, by R.E.M., 1987; *Idioteque*, by Radiohead, 2000; *When the Man Comes Around*, by Johnny Cash, 2002; and *Radioactive*, by Imagine Dragons, 2013.

From the literary world, one need look no further than Hal Lindsey and Carla C. Carlson's best-selling *The Late Great Planet Earth* (1970) and Tim LaHaye and Jerry B. Jenkins's sixteen books in the *Left Behind* series (1995–2007). Both pairs of authors were greatly influenced by another form of futurism known as dispensationalism, a term coined by British author John Nelson Darby (1800–1882) that "refers to the idea that all time can be divided into [seven] separate periods known as dispensations. The present dispensation spans the time between the first and second comings of Christ, and the next great dispensation will be the millennium" (Koester, 275). The reading and composition strategy of Lindsey and Carlson was to cut and paste a series of biblical passages to give the reader a comprehensive view of the end-time scenario. According to Craig Koester, "Hal Lindsey's *Late, Great Planet Earth* . . . linked the biblical text used in Darby's system [esp. Genesis 15; Daniel 9; 1 Thessalonians 4; 2 Thessalonians 2; 1 John 2; and the entirety of Revelation] to current newspaper headlines, giving readers the impression that scripture had predicted the dominant political trends of the Cold War. The *Left Behind* novels . . . present Darby's system through the medium of fiction" (Koester, 275).

Examples of Lindsey and Carlson's interpretation of current events as correlative of apocalyptic biblical scenarios include, but surely are not limited to examples like these:

> The seal visions . . . predict the outbreak of war in the Middle East. . . . They tell of economic distress, shortage of food, and the death of a quarter of the human race as a result of these disasters. . . . The sixth seal vision may describe the beginning of nuclear war, and the trumpet visions may foretell the disasters of that war. . . . The bowl visions describe the fearful punishment that will be inflicted on those who reject the Christian Gospel. (Wainwright, 84)

Unrealized scenarios, in Lindsey and Carlson's schema, are considered "still yet to come" rather than failed. Jack Van Impe, a popular apocalyptic and "historical" dispensationalist preacher on the Trinity Broadcasting Network, is another outstanding example of the ongoing hermeneutic tradition initiated by Darby and executed by Lindsey and Carlson. He too postpones unfulfilled prophetic expectations and continues to look to contemporary events as potential signs of imminent fulfillment.

The *Left Behind* series, as noted above, correlates apocalyptic biblical themes with fictional events (although the narrative can include real-world entities). For example, the first novel

> opens against a context of international food shortages, inflation (Rev. 6.5-6) and conflict (Rev. 6.4) in the Middle East. Amidst the upheaval, the rapture occurs. Children and Christian adults are taken up, but a few of those left behind appreciate what has occurred; most prefer the explanations offered by United Nations Secretary General Nicolae Carpathia, who promises a solution to the world's problems, heads a new ten-member (evoking the "ten crowns" of Rev. 13.2) Security Council, and brokers a peace deal for Israel. Carpathia is hailed as a great leader and replaces the United Nations with a totalitarian Global Community, as nations seeking peace and security willingly surrender their sovereignty. (Rev. 13; Wright, 2009, 81)

The popularity of the *Late Great Planet Earth* and the *Left Behind* series cannot be overstated. Combined sales of the books are well into the tens of millions. These books are, for many Christians, the primary source for their understanding of Christian apocalyptic. As Koester has noted, "The view of the future presented in [*Left Behind*] affirms that God is sovereign despite ominous world conditions. . . . The novels show that simple believers, who know the biblical script, are far better informed about global developments than the commentators on television" (Koester, 278). An appealing script for the apocalyptically inclined, indeed.

No survey of the apocalyptic legacy of Christian Scripture is complete without an acknowledgment of three of the most sensational and horrific demonstrations of that legacy in recent memory: Jonestown (1978), the Branch Davidians (1993), and Heaven's Gate (1997). As noted in the beginning of this essay, one generalized way to categorize the trajectories of apocalyptic groups is according to their responses when initial prophecies of an imminent event have been delayed. The group in question can disband; they can move the date of the end into the undefined future; or they can initiate a violent end within the parameters of their apocalyptic rhetoric. The three groups just named all chose the last option, under different circumstances. These three groups (and several others like them) pique our imaginations when we discuss modern apocalyptic groups. They represent the most extreme cases.

It may very well be that my own interest in apocalyptic groups began with the images I witnessed, as an eighteen-year-old, of the Jonestown debacle. The photos and film sent over the newswire were shocking: piles of bodies (many of whom were children) stacked up and grouped together in a jungle in Guyana, a dead US Congressman and reporters executed point blank lying on an airstrip, and syringes and vats of cyanide-laced, purple Kool Aid. Over 900 people died on a single day, March 18, 1978.

What we learned about the group and its leaders after the mass suicide was equally sensational. Pastor Jim Jones (1931–1978) had led his flock from its roots in Indianapolis, Indiana, to Redwood Valley, California, then to San Francisco, and ultimately to their final "utopian" location in Jonestown, Guyana. The group's migration to Jonestown began in 1977 and was executed in several stages: survey, development, occupation. Dominant in the group's rhetoric were themes of persecution, suffering, and potential martyrdom for the cause. The echoes of Christian apocalyptic are not difficult to discern in this rhetoric. Jones and his flock were committed to fighting what they perceived as "the injustices of a racist, classist, and capitalistic society" (Moore, 95). Jones believed that the group's new location in the jungles of Guyana would allow for the free exercise of their religion and the development of a socialist utopia.

The utopian beginnings of the relocated group were hounded by reports as early as 1972—the San Francisco years—"when a religion reporter for the *San Francisco Chronicle* wrote that a member wanting to leave the group had died under suspicious circumstances" (Moore, 97). Moore also reports that "the apostate group called the Concerned Relatives publicized an 'accusation of Human Rights Violations,' which detailed abuses that they believed were occurring in Jonestown" (Moore, 97). These accusations were the impetus for the visit of US Congressman Leo Ryan's visit to Jonestown in 1978. These accusations, combined with some current members desiring to leave Jonestown in conjunction with Jones's elevated paranoia (which may have included an increasing dependence on narcotics), fueled the volatile mix of the rhetoric of persecution and suffering and perceived external pressures. The pressure and paranoia became so acute that the infamous "white nights" (actual rehearsals of mass suicide) became more common in the latter stages of the group's existence. The actual performance was executed on the evening of March 18, 1978. In the words of the self-proclaimed messiah Jones, it was an act of "revolutionary suicide," an act no doubt influenced by apocalyptic ideation.

Fifteen years after the events of Jonestown, another apocalyptic group, the Branch Davidians, appeared on our apocalyptic landscape. The forensic analysis of the global press and the emerging World Wide Web allowed us our closest and most detailed look at an apocalyptic group and its violent end. Led by David Koresh (Vernon Howell, born 1959), another self-proclaimed messiah (Koresh is the Hebrew transliteration of Cyrus, a reference to the Persian king proclaimed messiah by the prophet Isaiah in Isa. 45:1), the Branch Davidians—an offshoot of the Seventh-Day Adventists Church—engaged in a lethal gun battle with US federal agents on April 19, 1993, in which their compound was destroyed by fire and seventy-six Davidians lost their lives. The source of the fire is still under debate: the two competing theories are that federal tear-gas canisters started the fire in the compound, or that members of the Davidians started the fire from within.

What is especially fascinating about this group was their explicit employment of the book of Revelation to map out their perceived apocalyptic destiny. Kenneth Newport argues, "The text [i.e., the book of Revelation] was at the very least an important factor . . . in the decision of the Branch Davidians to self-destruct (or 'act out their biblical destiny' as they would more probably have seen it)" (Newport, 213). He continues, "The community read the Book of Revelation (together with numerous other parts of the Bible, especially the Psalms) and what they read there, I suggest, together with the context in which they read it, led to the group's planned for and well executed apocalyptic self-destruction" (Newport, 213). Certainly texts like Rev. 10:7 were used by Koresh to depict himself as the seventh angel of the Apocalypse. The description of a lamblike beast in Rev. 13:11-18 was used to demonize the US government. Such passages were vital to group awareness. Thus, for the Branch Davidians, "the arrival of the ATF and then the FBI on the morning of 28 February, 1993, was highly significant and prophetically charged" (Newport, 219). For the Davidians (especially Koresh), as for Jonestown, all pressures from outside the group were biblically prophesied signs of the apocalyptic times. So when the *Waco Tribune-Herald* began publishing a critical exposé on Koresh, called "The Sinful Messiah," the day before the first day of the siege on the Davidian compound, all signs pointed to their impending end.

An interesting variation on the modern apocalyptic group coming to an abrupt end is Heaven's Gate. Founded in 1972 by Marshall Applewhite (1932–1997) and Bonnie Lu Nettles (1928–1985), the group chose to end their lives via ritualistic suicide by consuming a lethal combination of Phenobarbital (an anticonvulsant barbiturate) mixed with applesauce and chased with vodka. After law-enforcement authorities received an anonymous tip, thirty-nine bodies were discovered in a mansion in Rancho Santa Fe (an affluent suburb of San Diego), twenty-one women and eighteen men of various ages from twenty-six to seventy-two. The ritualistic suicides were performed over several days in 1997: fifteen on March 22, fifteen on March 23, seven on March 24, and the final two somewhere between March 24 and their eventual discovery on March 26.

The bodies (known as "vessels" by Heaven's Gate members) were all dressed in black shirts and trousers, black Nike sneakers, and a purple cloth covered their upper torsos. Each had an armband with the words "Heaven's Gate Away Team" embroidered on the band. The majority of the deceased had in their possession a five-dollar bill and three quarters.

The impetus for this ritualistic suicide is uniquely different from the rhetoric of persecution, suffering, and martyrdom commonplace in Jonestown and in Waco, Texas, among the Branch Davidians. Benjamin Zeller concludes that "while the movement surely experienced a sense of persecution and failure . . . these conditions are not in themselves sufficient to cause self-violence" (Zeller, 175). What motivated this group ritualistically to end their lives was their belief (according to their still-active website: heavensgate.com) that humanity needed to move beyond human existence to their rightful place at the "next level above human," the realm of God. For the members, the imminent timing of this transition was critical because it was their belief that the earth was soon to be "recycled."

It should be noted, however, that ritualistic suicide was not always a part of the group's theology. Rather, "for the first decade of the group's history it flatly rejected the very notion of suicide, arguing instead for the need to transition into the heavens while still embodied" (Zeller, 175). So what mechanism triggered the shift from embodied to disembodied transformation? The matter is still up for debate, but it should be noted that the death of cofounder Bonnie Lu Nettles of liver cancer in 1985 caused some cognitive dissonance among the membership. This period also marked the beginning of the group's devaluation of the body (from this point on, referred to as "vessels") that may have been a first step in their formulation of ritual suicide as spiritual release to the next level above human. This new understanding of the body, in combination with the belief that the earth was soon to be "recycled," played out when the comet Hale-Bopp manifested itself in the late-March skies of 1997. For Applewhite and the members of the Heaven's Gate group, this was *the sign.* A hypothesis was promoted by the group that located behind this comet was a spaceship that would gather the "elect" for the trip to the level above human. Although Zeller argued (as mentioned above) that the experienced sense of persecution and failure was not sufficient to explain the ritualistic violence that the group enacted, members were convinced in the days leading up to their end of "a massive government conspiracy to hide an extraterrestrial flying saucer trailing the comet" (Zeller, 177).

Epilogue

This essay began by questioning whether the book of Revelation was the sole source for the rich apocalyptic legacy in Western Christendom. It is, according to this essay, no doubt a tour de force in that history. Yet the history also reveals that Western Christians have had an ambivalent relationship with Revelation. The post-Augustinian shift from historical to spiritual readings is demonstrative of that point. That shift was, like Matthew and Luke's appropriation of Mark, a domestication of the apocalyptic tradition. And from roughly that point in history, Christians have both foregrounded and retreated from that position based on our interpretive agendas. The biblical tradition and the interpretive legacy have embedded within them *both* potentialities, for historicizing or for spiritualizing readings, and we are their inheritors.

With this inheritance comes great responsibility. History shows how easy it is for those enthusiastic for a final, definitive ending to risk actions that bring about lesser, still devastating ends. Today, however, more is at stake than the welfare of the members of an apocalyptic group. Apocalyptic scripts and a highly weaponized world make for a volatile mixture. As Catherine Wessinger observes, for example,

> In the 1980s Americans learned that President Reagan (Republican, served 1981–1989) had been influenced by [Hal] Lindsey's predictions about the roles of Israel and nuclear war in the final events. Throughout the Reagan administration Americans who did not believe in these apocalyptic prophecies contemplated the danger of having a Dispensationalist President as commander of the American nuclear arsenal. (Wessinger, 428; cf. Boyer, 140–43)

Apocalyptic scripts also make it much too easy to separate the world into sheep and goats, "axes of evil" and "elect nations"—perpetually seeking to identify antichrists for destruction. For example, George W. Bush's war on terror was often framed in the totalizing language of good versus evil. Again, Wessinger notes that the Bush administration's response to the attacks of 9/11 by Islamic jihadists was an act of "apocalyptic mirroring" (see Rosenfeld) in which "the radical dualism of the Bush administration matched that of jihadists, and Bush's apocalyptic war rhetoric mirrored that of bin Laden and colleagues" (Wessinger, 436). In a speech delivered on September 14, 2011, Bush declared that it was America's responsibility "to answer these attacks *and rid the world of evil*" (italics added; see Räisänen, 155). It should also be noted that the lyrics of hymns such as "Onward Christian Soldiers" and "The Battle Hymn of the Republic"—the musical selections for the Day of Prayer and Remembrance for the victims of 9/11 on September 14, 2001—reflect the anticipation of some fully to participate in the apocalypse on their time rather than God's. But all such appropriations are irrational and zealous impositions on the biblical texts—*all* of the texts we have identified as apocalyptic within the Christian canon (Jewett).

Perhaps it is our role as scholars, theologians, ministers, priests, and simply as rational human beings to remind those in our midst of the consequences of such human impositions on our sacred texts. The models of Jonestown, the Branch Davidians, and Heaven's Gate are just a few examples of the potential for disaster when we set the apocalyptic clock on our time. One could readily add other events and groups to an ever-expanding list (e.g., the Manson Family, Aum Shinrikyo, and the Solar Temple). Against the reflex to expedite the apocalyptic clock, we would do well to heed what the biblical texts actually have to say about the time frame of the end; for example, Jesus' words in Mark 13:32: "But about that day or hour no one knows, not even the angels in heaven, nor the Son, but only the Father." What is most tragic, however, is that our self-imposed acceleration of the apocalyptic clock has also accelerated the dangers of which the seer John issues an awesome warning against anyone who adds to his prophecy.

> I warn everyone who hears the words of the prophecy of this scroll: If anyone adds anything to them, God will add to that person the plagues described in this scroll. And if anyone takes words away from this scroll of prophecy, God will take away from that person any share in the tree of life and in the Holy City, which are described in this scroll. (Rev. 22:18-19)

The reflex to accelerate an apocalyptic schedule has actualized the calamities of which John warns. With or without explicit appeal to apocalyptic texts, the effort to determine the course of history through force has already begun to inflict plagues of biblical proportions on our world: the plague of war, the plague of famine, the plague of disease, the plague of a deteriorating ecosystem, and the plague of abject poverty are just a few prime examples. The time has come to stop and recognize the gravity, both explicit and implicit, of the scriptural inheritances that inform our apocalyptic legacy. Only then will we be able to begin to neutralize it.

Works Cited

Aune, David E. 2005. "Understanding Jewish and Christian Apocalyptic." *WW* 25, no. 3:233–45.

Boyer, Paul. 1992. *When Time Shall Be No More: Prophecy Belief in Modern American Culture*. Cambridge, MA: Harvard University Press.

Cameron, Averil, ed. 1989. *History as Text: The Writing of Ancient History*. Chapel Hill: University of North Carolina Press.

Chilton, Bruce. 2013. *Visions of the Apocalypse: Receptions of John's Revelation in Western Imagination*. Waco, TX: Baylor University Press.

Collins, Adela Yarbro. 1984. *Crisis and Catharsis: The Power of the Apocalypse*. Philadelphia: Westminster.

Collins, John J. 1979. "Introduction: Towards the Morphology of a Genre." *Semeia* 14:1–20.

———. 1984. *The Apocalyptic Imagination: An Introduction to Jewish Apocalyptic Literature*. New York: Crossroad.

Froom, LeRoy E. 2009. *The Prophetic Faith of Our Fathers*. Vol. 4. Hagerstown, MD: Review and Herald Publishing Association.

Hanson, Paul. 1979. *The Dawn of Apocalyptic: The Historical and Sociological Roots of Jewish Apocalyptic Eschatology*. Philadelphia: Fortress Press.

Jones, Ken Sundet. 2005. "The Apocalyptic Luther." *WW* 25, no. 3:233–45.

Koester, Craig R. 2005. "Revelation and the *Left Behind* Novels." *WW* 25, no. 3:274–82.

Kovacs, Judith L. 2005. "The Revelation to John: Lessons from the History of the Book's Reception." *WW* 25, no. 3:255–63.

Moore, Rebecca. 2011. "Narratives of Persecution, Suffering, and Martyrdom: Violence in Peoples Temple and Jonestown." In *Violence and New Religious Movements*, edited by J. R. Lewis, 95–111. Oxford: Oxford University Press.

Jewett, Robert. 1973. *The Captain America Complex: The Dilemma of Zealous Nationalism.* Philadelphia: Westminster.

Luther, Martin. 1960a. "Preface to the Revelation of John [I]." In *LW* 35.

———. 1960b. "Preface to the Revelation of John [II]." In *LW* 35.

Newport, Kenneth. 2009. "Be Thou Faithful Unto Death (cf. Rev. 2.10): The Book of Revelation, The Branch Davidians and Apocalyptic (Self-)Destruction." In *The Way the World Ends? The Apocalypse of John in Culture and Ideology*, edited by W. J. Lyons and Jorunn Økland, 211–26. Sheffield: Sheffield Phoenix.

Perkins, Judith. 1995. *The Suffering Self: Pain and Narrative Representation in the Early Christian Era.* London: Routledge.

Phelan, John Leddy. 1970. *The Millennial Kingdom of the Franciscans in the New World.* Berkeley: University of California Press.

Räisänen, Heikki. 2009. "Revelation, Violence, and War: Glimpses of a Dark Side." In *The Way the World Ends? The Apocalypse of John in Culture and Ideology*, edited by W. J. Lyons and Jorunn Økland, 211–26. Sheffield: Sheffield Phoenix.

Rosenfeld, Jean E. 2011. "Nativists Millennialism." In *The Oxford Handbook of Millennialism*, edited by Catherine Wessinger, 89–109. New York: Oxford University Press.

Royalty, Robert M., Jr. 2005. "The Dangers of the Apocalypse." *WW* 25, no. 3:283–93.

Sánchez, David A. 2008. *From Patmos to the Barrio: Subverting Imperial Myths.* Minneapolis: Fortress Press.

Wainwright, Arthur W. 1993. *Mysterious Apocalypse: Interpreting the Book of Revelation.* Nashville: Abingdon.

Wessinger, Catherine. 2014. "Apocalypse and Violence." In *The Oxford Handbook of Apocalyptic Literature*, edited by John J. Collins, 422–40. New York: Oxford University Press.

Wright, Melanie J. 2009. "Every Eye Shall See Him": Revelation and Film. In *The Way the World Ends? The Apocalypse of John in Culture and Ideology*, edited by W. J. Lyons and Jorunn Økland, 76–94. Sheffield: Sheffield Phoenix.

Wright, Stuart A. 2011. "Revisiting the Branch Davidian Mass Suicide Debate." In *Violence and New Religious Movements*, edited by J. R. Lewis, 113–31. Oxford: Oxford University Press.

Zeller, Benjamin E. 2011. "The Euphemization of Violence: The Case of Heaven's Gate." In *Violence and New Religious Movements*, edited by J. R. Lewis, 173–89. Oxford: Oxford University Press.

Jesus and the Christian Gospels

Raymond Pickett

Jesus in History and Interpretation

This is an essay about Jesus, about the significance of who he was and what he said and did. Any interpretation of Jesus' significance is based primarily on the narrative interpretations of his ministry, death, and resurrection in the four canonical Gospels in the New Testament. The operative word here is *interpretation*. The Gospels interpret the significance of Jesus' words and actions for his followers in order to shape the practices and beliefs of communities of faith, and hence they presume a faith commitment from the intended audiences. Although the Gospels recount select events in Jesus' life, they do not purport to be objective accounts of what happened. Therefore, reading them as straightforward historical reports of what Jesus did and said not only misconstrues the nature and purpose of the Gospels but also obscures the fact that history is itself always a matter of interpretation.

That there are four canonical Gospels and several Gospels that are not in the canon indicates that the memory and early traditions about Jesus were interpreted in various ways. A close comparison of the birth narratives in Matthew and Luke, the chronology of Jesus' ministry in the Gospels of Mark and John, or the resurrection narratives in all four canonical Gospels demonstrate how key events were interpreted differently. Not everything the Gospels depict Jesus saying and doing happened exactly as reported. Later in this essay, we will explore the character and purpose of the Gospels and various approaches to interpreting them in ancient and contemporary contexts. First, however, we investigate how these narrative interpretations of Jesus' significance have been used by modern scholars for historical reconstructions of the figure of Jesus based on critical analysis of the Gospels.

In 1906, Albert Schweitzer wrote a book that evaluated the works about the historical figure of Jesus that had been written in the previous two centuries. The English translation of the title of Schweitzer's book was *The Quest of the Historical Jesus.* The first quest began in the late eighteenth century, when a German scholar by the name of H. S. Reimarus, a philosopher who maintained that reason could arrive at knowledge of God and ethics from the study of nature, questioned the historicity of the Gospel accounts of Jesus' miracles. He was followed by David F. Strauss and others who sought to distinguish what they regarded as purely historical accounts of the life of Jesus from the faith perspective that originally shaped the Gospels. This first quest for the historical Jesus was influenced by Enlightenment-era rationality, which rejected certain aspects of the Gospel accounts of Jesus as problematic because they contradicted the laws of nature.

Schweitzer's review of this historical scholarship of Jesus demonstrated that the lives of Jesus produced during this era using historical-critical methods were themselves not objective, factual accounts. Rather, they reflected the interests and ideals of those who wrote them. In other words, the portraits of Jesus that emerged during the first quest betrayed the worldview and outlook of their authors. Just as the depictions of Jesus in the Gospels were conditioned by the cultural milieu in which they were written and by the faith convictions of their authors, so were the eighteenth- and nineteenth-century accounts of Jesus invariably shaped by the Zeitgeist of that historical period. Schweitzer's critique of historical Jesus research marks the close of what is often referred to as the first quest. However, Schweitzer's own contribution to the endeavor would have an enduring effect on historical Jesus studies. His interpretation of the Gospels in the context of early Judaism led him to conclude that Jesus was an apocalyptic figure who, along with his followers, expected the imminent arrival of God's kingdom. Unlike the liberal portraits of Jesus of the previous two centuries, which preserved his ethical message even as they stripped away the elements that were not consistent with a worldview that discarded the supernatural, Schweitzer's Jesus belonged more to the first-century world of apocalyptic Judaism and was therefore less familiar to Christians at the turn of the twentieth century. Schweitzer concluded that Jesus expected the imminent arrival of the kingdom of God. He wrote that Jesus "in the knowledge that he is the coming Son of Man lays hold of the wheel of the world to set it moving on that last revolution which is to bring all ordinary history to a close. It refuses to turn, and he throws himself upon it. Then it does turn; and crushes him" (Schweitzer, 369).

The first quest for the historical Jesus resulted in a number of important developments that significantly shaped subsequent study of Jesus and the Gospels. First, Mark came to be regarded as the earliest Gospel by scholars and hence was used as a primary historical source in historical Jesus scholarship. However, in 1901, Wilhelm Wrede's book *The Messianic Secret* contended that the secrecy motif was a literary device created by the author of Mark's Gospel to project the apostolic post-Easter faith in Jesus as Messiah back onto the Jesus of history. Although, according to Wrede, Jesus himself had actually made no claim to be messiah, Mark had incorporated this postresurrection belief into his narrative. Wrede's work highlighted the fact that the early Jesus traditions were creatively adapted to convey particular theological convictions. It also called attention to the literary quality of the Gospel, that is, the artistry of constructing such a narrative. These insights resulted in the development of new approaches to studying the Gospels. Redaction criticism, on the one hand, concentrated on how the Gospel writers used and edited source materials, and what this disclosed about the theological perspectives of the respective Gospels. The aim of form criticism, on the other hand, was to ascertain the earlier forms of the oral traditions used to craft the Gospel narratives. It asked questions about the function of the oral traditions in their original contexts and was interested in tracing the development of the Gospel tradition.

Another important consequence of the first quest for the historical Jesus was the distinction made between the "Jesus of history" and the "Christ of faith." One reaction to Schweitzer's historical reconstruction, which made Jesus as apocalyptic prophet less theologically relevant, was for others increasingly to emphasize the Christ of faith. Martin Kähler's book *The So-Called Historical Jesus and the Historical Biblical Christ*, published in German in 1892, claimed that the true Christ is a Christ of faith detached from the Jesus of history. However, the most important champion of this perspective, and one of the most famous New Testament scholars of the twentieth century, was Rudolf Bultmann. For Bultmann, Christianity begins with Easter, and so he downplayed the importance of the Jesus of history for theology. From Bultmann's perspective, it was God's action in the death and resurrection of Jesus that was decisive rather than what Jesus had said and done (Theissen and Merz, 6–7).

The "new quest for the historical Jesus," initiated by Bultmann's students, was interested in establishing a continuity between the Christ of faith and the historical Jesus that Kähler and Bultmann had so persuasively distinguished. In contrast to the first quest, which sought to strip away the theological elements of the traditions about Jesus used by the Gospels, the new quest was interested in supporting the connection between the Christ of faith and the historical Jesus (Theissen and Merz, 7). It was guided by the conviction that the Gospels presuppose the identity of the earthly Jesus and exalted Christ. Bultmann had made the case that presuppositions always influenced the interpretation of New Testament texts. This new quest was intentional in being guided by what they regarded as a foundational presupposition of the tradition, namely, the continuity between the earthly Jesus and the risen Christ. This more explicitly christological approach put history in the service of theology and resulted in representations of Jesus that were more Christian and therefore less Jewish.

In the early 1980s, a third quest for the historical Jesus, catalyzed by new approaches to the study of Judaism, used a variety of ancient Jewish sources. This produced a revitalized picture of early Judaism as much more diverse and nuanced than the caricature of the Pharisees in the Gospels that had been operative in much previous scholarship. Scholars such as E. P. Sanders, John Dominic Crossan, Géza Vermes, Marcus Borg, and many others in the last three decades have written books about the historical Jesus that depict him as thoroughly embedded and engaged in the Judaism of his day. One of the main insights that has emerged from this third quest is that Jesus was the leader of a renewal movement within Judaism (Sanders 1985). The debate has focused on the question of what kind of Jew Jesus was, and the relationship between his particular interpretation and embodiment of Jewish tradition to other forms and expressions of Judaism. This quest has been characterized by greater methodological variety and sophistication, including the use of social-science and anthropological models and, in many instances, greater awareness of the Roman Empire as an important part of the context to which Jesus was responding.

Inasmuch as there continues to be a proliferation of scholarly books on Jesus, we are still in the midst of this third quest. Although no consensus about the historical Jesus is forthcoming, a much more richly textured understanding of the Jewish and Greco-Roman contexts of Jesus and the Gospels has advanced the conversation. Nonetheless, what Schweitzer observed about earlier lives of Jesus reflecting the interests and biases of their authors is also true of more recent scholarship. Historical investigation is always guided to some extent by the presuppositions of those interpreting these texts and traditions. The Gospels are not objective historical accounts of what Jesus said and did. Jesus probably spoke Aramaic, lived in an oral culture, and never wrote anything himself. Remembrances of his teaching and activity were profoundly influenced by the belief that God had raised from the dead this Galilean Jew who had been crucified, and had made him both Lord and Christ. The task of reconstructing from the Gospels a purely historical account of Jesus, unencumbered by the perspectives and presuppositions of those who composed and preserved the traditions about him, seems unattainable. Nonetheless, there are important reasons not only for historians but also for those interested in the importance of Jesus for contemporary life to preserve the connection between the Christ of faith and what can be known about the significance of what Jesus said and did in his own historical context.

The Hermeneutical Circle

There are four canonical Gospels. Matthew, Mark, and Luke are referred to as the Synoptic Gospels because there is a literary relationship between them. The Gospel of John is different in many respects, and is typically not used in historical Jesus research. All four Gospels are a blend of faith and history. That is to say, followers of Jesus recounted the story of his ministry, death, and resurrection for the express purpose of fostering faithful disciples. In this essay, we want to use the methods of historical criticism to investigate how Jesus engaged his own cultural and religious context in a way that makes it possible to explore his significance for our world today. Although it is possible to take a strictly historical approach to an investigation of Jesus and the Gospels, our task calls for a strategy of interpretation that employs historical-critical methods but recognizes that any interpretation is shaped by the social location and cultural context of the interpreter. The hermeneutical circle provides a model, illustrated in figure 1, of what happens in the interpretive process.

To interpret the Gospels is to be drawn into the narrative *world of the text*. The world of the Gospels is a narrative world that has been constructed by the author using existing oral and written traditions to tell the story of Jesus. The *world behind the text* is the historical and cultural context in which the Gospels were originally written and heard as well as the cultural world of the historical Jesus. Although the cultural and religious norms of the world behind the text are reflected in the narrative world of the Gospels, the world of the text takes on a life of its own apart from its original historical context once it is disseminated to be read in other times and places.

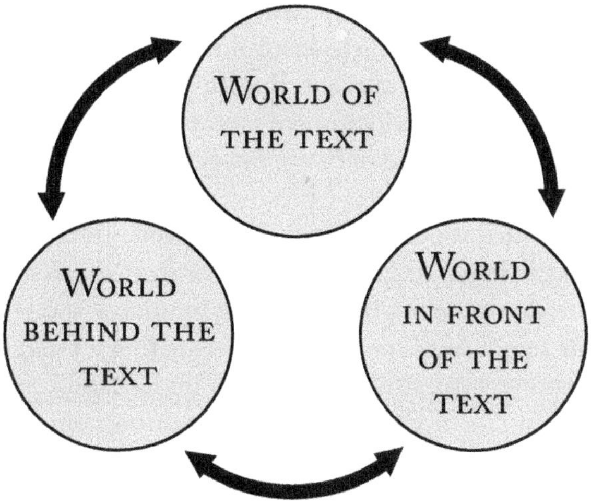

FIGURE 1. *The worlds behind, in front of, and in the text.*

The *world in front of the text* refers to subsequent interpretations of the text, which are always shaped by the social world of the interpreter. This includes the Gospels of Matthew and Luke, which reinterpret the Gospel of Mark in the light of their particular social situations, as well as contemporary interpretations of the Gospels that invariably construe the text through different cultural lenses. Every interpretation of the Gospel narratives about Jesus is influenced by a cultural context that is different from the ancient world in which it was produced and read. This is the reason that all reconstructions of the historical Jesus bear some resemblance to those who write them.

The arrows in the diagram illustrate the dynamic character of the interpretive process. The interpreter enters into the narrative world of the Gospels, but to some extent construes the story of Jesus in terms of the norms and conventions of his or her own social world. For example, modern American society values individual rights and tends to be guided by the ideal of the self-made person, who creates his or her own identity and determines his or her own fate. In the ancient world, however, a person's identity was defined by the group(s) to which he or she belonged and was thought to be vulnerable to numerous external forces, both terrestrial and celestial. So the predominant perception of Jesus as an itinerant charismatic leader held in scholarship on the historical Jesus today seems to reflect more modern ideas about the individual than the more communitarian ethos that was commonplace in antiquity.

The value of the hermeneutical circle is that keeping the worlds *of, in front of,* and *behind* the Gospels ever before the interpreter serves to promote awareness of the distinctive cultural values, conventions, and perspectives involved, and hence to magnify the difference between the world from which they come and the contemporary cultural contexts in which they are being interpreted.

Interpretations of Jesus and the Gospels that are interested primarily in their significance for life in today's world unwittingly collapse the distance of time and space between the worlds *in front of* and *behind* the text to make Jesus more relevant. But this is precisely how Jesus gets made over in our own image. The tools of historical criticism are used to travel the long, winding road from our world to the strange and wonderful world of first-century Judea, to better understand Jesus and the Gospels in their context.

It is, of course, impossible that we could somehow transcend the social milieu that formed us to fully fathom what it was like to live as a Galilean Jew under Roman rule in the decades leading up to the Jewish revolt. However, due diligence in attempting to understand Jesus in his context can also yield new insights into his significance for today. Just as visiting a foreign country casts one's own country in different light upon return, so efforts to better understand Jesus within the world that he inhabited can facilitate new angles of vision on our own cultural contexts and allow Jesus to speak to them in fresh and creative ways. The three worlds of the hermeneutical circle represent the three interacting contextual realities that are always in play in interpretation. In our attempts to grasp the significance of Jesus, we must navigate and negotiate the narrative or literary world of the text to ascertain the substance and force of what Jesus said and did in the world behind the text, and we are circumspect in this endeavor because we are mindful that our own social location colors what we see. Reflection on the significance of Jesus' words and actions for contemporary contexts should be predicated on our attempts to understand their force in their original historical and cultural context.

The Historical Figure of Jesus

The hermeneutical circle emphasizes the importance of context in interpreting the Gospel narratives about Jesus, and the primary task in this first portion of the essay is to place Jesus in his historical context. Any explanation of the significance of Jesus' teachings and actions should be based on an account of the circumstances and issues to which he was responding. However, before outlining the particulars of the historical and cultural framework for our sketch of Jesus, the content of and criteria for what should be regarded as historical need to be considered. This is a more challenging task than one might imagine because of the paucity of sources about Jesus outside the Gospels that can be used to verify the historicity of the tradition. The two basic aspects that need to be assessed historically are the sayings of Jesus and the actions of Jesus. Establishing the historical probability of what Jesus did is the less disputed of the two tasks, though it is complicated by how to interpret the healings, exorcisms, and other deeds of power attested by the Gospels.

In *The Historical Figure of Jesus*, E. P. Sanders offers a list of statements about Jesus that are almost beyond dispute and belong to the framework of Jesus' public career (Sanders 1993, 10–11).

- Jesus was born *c.* 4 BCE, near the time of the death of Herod the Great;
- he spent his childhood and early adult years in Nazareth, a Galilean village;
- he was baptized by John the Baptist;
- he called disciples;
- he taught in the towns, villages and countryside of Galilee (apparently not in the cities);

- he preached "the kingdom of God";
- about the year 30 he went to Jerusalem for Passover;
- he created a disturbance in the Temple area;
- he had a final meal with the disciples;
- he was arrested and interrogated by Jewish authorities, specifically the high priest;
- he was executed on the orders of the Roman prefect, Pontius Pilate.

Sanders adds another short list of what he regards as equally secure facts about the aftermath of Jesus' life:

- his disciples at first fled;
- they saw him (in what sense is not certain) after his death;
- as a consequence, they believed that he would return to found the kingdom;
- they formed a community to await his return and sought to win others to faith in him as God's Messiah.

With some qualifications, these lists serve as a foundation of most of the recent accounts of the historical Jesus. Jesus' birth is usually dated somewhere around 4 BCE. The birth narratives in the Gospels of Matthew and Luke are very different and are best seen as theological interpretations rather than historical accounts. The historical starting point for a reconstruction of Jesus' life and ministry is his baptism by John. The other historical bracket is his death by crucifixion. However, the Gospel traditions of both his baptism and death provide examples of historical traditions that have been expanded on. The Gospel accounts of the baptism highlight the superiority of Jesus to John and the voice from heaven, which announces that he is "Son of God." These, again, are theological appraisals that cannot be validated historically. The crucifixion, which is also on solid historical ground, is intertwined with chronicles of his trial which indicate that the Jewish authorities are ultimately responsible for his death. As Sanders suggests, it is likely that members of the priestly aristocracy were complicit in the trial and execution of Jesus, but from a historical perspective, Jesus was executed for sedition as an enemy of the Roman order. Historical information from other sources shows that Pilate summarily executed thousands of Jews and therefore was probably not as tentative in sending Jesus to his death as he is portrayed in the Gospels.

What the above comments demonstrate is that even the most basic historical information is interpreted in the Gospels in ways that reflect the circumstances and perspectives of faithful followers of Jesus. The four different accounts of the resurrection in the Gospels are further evidence of the interpretive process from the vantage point of such followers. All four Gospels narrate in different ways the common conviction that God raised Jesus from the dead, but that claim cannot be validated by historical investigation as such. What is clearly historical is the disciples' belief that they saw him after his death. So the resurrection faith of the first followers of Jesus is itself historical in some sense, but it is impossible to get behind the tradition to ascertain exactly what happened. What is historical is their conviction that the risen Jesus was alive and present to them and through them, and this conviction had an impact on the continued expansion and growth of the Jesus movement.

Probably the most challenging aspect of efforts to reconstruct the historical Jesus is deciding which words and deeds are authentic to Jesus. It is generally acknowledged among scholars that the Gospel of Mark was the first Gospel, and was written around 70 CE, shortly after the destruction of the Jerusalem temple. So there is approximately a forty-year period between the historical Jesus and the earliest narrative of his ministry, death, and resurrection. During that forty-year period, the memory of Jesus was first preserved and passed on in oral tradition and then written down in collections of Jesus' sayings, deeds of power, suffering and death, and resurrection before being crafted into a narrative of his ministry, death, and announcement of his resurrection by whomever wrote the Gospel of Mark. As the memory of what Jesus said and did passed through these various stages, it was transformed. The question is, How can what the historical Jesus said and did be ascertained from the narrative accounts in the Gospels, where the memory of him has been shaped by forty years and more of adapting the tradition to new contexts, and by the perspectives of the Gospel writers themselves?

Significant advances in the study of memory and orality in recent years have contributed to an understanding of the development of the tradition behind the Gospels. On the one hand, oral cultures tend to preserve traditions with more accuracy than literary cultures such as ours. On the other hand, memory is always selective and involves imagination. Since the Gospels and the traditions they used cannot be read uncritically as unvarnished historical records, scholars have developed criteria to determine what in the Gospels should be regarded as historical and what should be regarded as a creative reworking of the tradition. A brief consideration of a couple of these criteria illustrates the difficulty of getting behind the Gospels to establish a historical substratum of the Jesus tradition.

The *criterion of dissimilarity* was at first applied to posit that if a saying of Jesus could not be attributed to Judaism or to the early church's theological reflection on Jesus, then it was deemed to be something Jesus probably said. The problem with this approach is that it breaks off the lines of continuity with both Judaism and the earliest communities of his followers to put forward a minimal collection of genuine sayings of Jesus that depict him as unique. This approach reinforced a portrait of Jesus that is at the very least non-Jewish, and in some instances anti-Jewish. The *criterion of multiple attestation* maintains that if a saying of or tradition about Jesus is attested in multiple independent sources, it is likely authentic. Although this is a historically sound approach, there is still much debate about the relationship of the Gospels and their underlying sources. One of the main debates concerns the hypothetical document Q. Q is from the German word *Quelle*, for "source," and refers to the sayings of Jesus common to the Gospel of Matthew and the Gospel of Luke. Although Q is not an extant document, many scholars regard this hypothetical source as the earliest collection of Jesus' sayings from Galilee. Given the ongoing debate about the status of Q in scholarship, the material common to Matthew and Luke will be referred to as the *double tradition* in this essay.

Evaluation of what in the Gospel traditions goes back to the historical Jesus is a complex enterprise that requires a repertoire of tools and approaches. Although there have been gains from the application and refinement of these historical-critical methods to the study of the historical Jesus over time, they are typically focused on a particular aspect of the tradition. One of the most difficult challenges in these historical reconstructions of Jesus is that no single one of them can account for all the data in the tradition. Every interpreter of the Gospels, expert and nonexpert alike, brings to their reading of the text a working portrait of Jesus that privileges certain sayings or deeds and then interprets everything else in the Gospel tradition through that lens. In some instances, what one privileges in the tradition is the basis for bracketing something in the Gospel tradition as being less important or even inauthentic. Historical investigation is by its very nature circular inasmuch as it begins with a minimal amount of historical data and then builds a case informed by underlying assumptions that will inevitably have blind spots. The use of the various historical methods can contribute to this phenomenon because they tend to be used in ways that confirm one's preconceptions about Jesus. In other words, interpreters tend to find the Jesus they are looking for.

In view of this methodological impasse, I would propose that more emphasis should be placed on a holistic reading of the Gospel narratives of Jesus applying the *criterion of historical plausibility*. Theissen and Merz succinctly define the criterion of historical plausibility in this way: "Whatever helps to explain the influence of Jesus and at the same time can only have come into being in a Jewish context is historical in the sources" (116). The Gospels are realistic narratives that depict Jesus as a Judean, conversing and interacting mostly with other Judeans. Given the thicker and more richly textured view of first-century Judaism that has emerged in recent years, the primary task is to make sense of what the Gospels depict Jesus doing and saying *within his Jewish context*. This also pertains to the depiction of his contemporaries. For example, the portrait of the Pharisees in the Gospels is something of a caricature. It more likely betrays a conflict between them and the followers of Jesus after the destruction of the temple in 70 CE, which was then projected back onto the ministry of Jesus.

It is unlikely that there will ever be a definitive reconstruction of the historical Jesus that everyone will agree on. However, a critical reading of the Gospels, paired with a good working understanding of Judaism in its imperial context, provides the most promising path to a historically plausible interpretation of Jesus. Such an interpretation must account for the particularities of the Gospel tradition in relationship to a broader comprehension of what Jesus was trying to accomplish in Galilee and then Jerusalem. The attempt to construct a contextually credible account of Jesus' words and deeds will also benefit from the use of social-science models to examine the socioeconomic dynamics of Jesus' Galilean context. An important premise of this discussion of Jesus' significance is that he was addressing concrete circumstances in his own local context, and hence his message had practical significance for those who heard and followed him. The force of Jesus' teaching and ministry are more discernible when viewed against the backdrop of the local situation in Galilee, and so are those elements of the tradition that have been shaped by later theological reflection. From the standpoint of the hermeneutical circle, this requires greater awareness of and appreciation for the historical distance and cultural difference between Jesus' world behind the text and the interpreter's world in front of the text. Interpretations of Jesus' significance for contemporary contexts will be more socially relevant and less abstract when he is viewed as a Galilean Jew engaging local religious and social issues in Galilee.

The Jesus Movement in Galilee

This concise consideration of the historical Jesus will use the Gospel of Mark and the early-sayings source Q to present a historically plausible explanation of the significance of Jesus' words and actions in Galilee in the early 30s of the first century CE. The task of differentiating what the historical Jesus said and did from secondary interpretations of the tradition after the resurrection is complex. As has been noted, every reconstruction of the historical Jesus privileges certain aspects of the tradition that tend to reinforce one's preconceptions of Jesus. There are tensions in the Gospel tradition that cannot be resolved without positing that certain parts of it are the result of later theological reflection. Instead of beginning by outlining a method to distinguish what is authentic to Jesus from what is the product of later christological reflection, the priority here is to succinctly reconstruct the Galilean context as a framework for interpreting the earliest layer of the Jesus tradition. Context is the key to interpretation, and even a compact description of Jesus' Galilean environment elucidates the force of his words and deeds.

Jesus was born in the early years of the Roman Empire, which began when Augustus was declared emperor in 27 BCE. Herod the Great was the client king of the Roman Empire. Herod's allegiance to Rome was evident in his grand building projects, which included the rebuilding of the Jerusalem temple in Hellenistic-Roman style as well as temples dedicated to the divine Augustus. He also appointed high priests to replace the Hasmoneans, and together with other Herodians they formed a powerful aristocracy that collaborated with Rome. Herod's massive building program may have brought honor to him and his Roman patrons, but it was the cause of considerable economic distress for those living in Roman Palestine. It is not surprising that when Herod died in 4 BCE, there were rebellions in Galilee, Judea, and Perea that had to be suppressed. The Jewish historian Josephus relates the views of a delegation that went to Rome to complain about the repercussions of Herod's rule.

> He had indeed reduced the entire nation to helpless poverty after taking it over in as flourishing condition as few ever know. . . . In addition to the collecting of the tribute that was imposed on everyone each year, lavish contributions had to be made to him and his household and friends and those of his slaves who were sent out to collect the tribute because there was no immunity at all from outrage unless bribes were paid. (Josephus, *Ant.* 17.307–8)

The Roman Empire was an aristocratic empire. The example of Herod illustrates the dynamics in which the majority of resources are controlled by elite families who live off the labor of peasants. Roman Palestine was divided after Herod's death, and his son Antipas was given control of Galilee by Augustus. Herod Antipas was client king during Jesus' ministry, and the economic hardship that characterized his rule is reflected in the Gospels. The Jesus movement was a Galilean movement, and Galilee was an agrarian peasant society. Galileans were subjected to a triple tax system that consisted of a temple tax, a Roman tax, and a tax from the Herodian aristocratic administration that placed almost unbearable economic pressure on them. The political facet of this predicament was that this agrarian society was controlled by a ruling aristocracy, mostly from the neighboring cities of Sepphoris and Tiberias, who exploited local peasants through debt slavery. John's baptism of repentance and Jesus' message and enactment of the kingdom of God should be seen as responding to this social crisis in Galilee. Figure 2 is a graphic representation of an agrarian tributary society (from Lenski, 284; see Crossan 1991, 45–46).

The first task is to situate Jesus in his Galilean context in the 30s. All the Gospels agree that Jesus' ministry begins with his baptism by John in the Jordan River. John was an apocalyptic prophet announcing God's imminent judgment unless Israel repented. In the Gospel tradition, John's role is described as forerunner to Jesus. However, the Israelites who submitted to his baptism probably understood it as a reenactment of the exodus, as Crossan and Reed suggest, "taking penitents from the desert, through the Jordan, into the Promised Land, to possess it in holiness once again" (117–18). John's baptism, then, ritualized a hope for liberation from the political and economic oppression that characterized life in Galilee at this time. Jesus began his ministry under the auspices of John the Baptist, and whatever message and ministry he had was, initially at least, aligned with John's.

One of the main challenges in appreciating the significance of John and Jesus in their Galilean setting is the tendency to regard them simply as religious figures. However, in the ancient world,

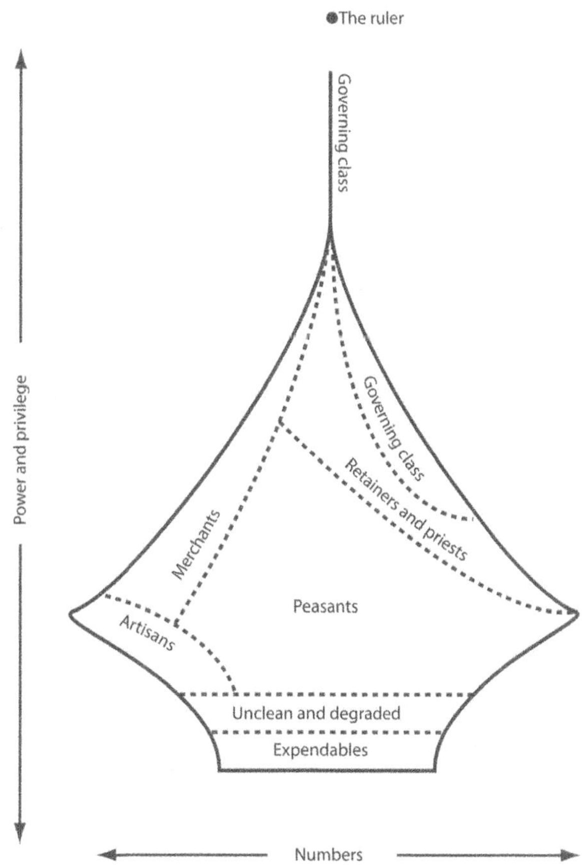

FIGURE 2. *Agrarian tributary society (after Lenski, 284).*

religion, politics, and economics were inextricably bound together. For Israelites, fidelity to God's covenant encompassed every dimension of life. The fact that Herod Antipas killed John indicates that he viewed John as a political threat. A passage from the Jewish historian Josephus elucidates both what John was doing and why Herod was concerned.

> For Herod had put him to death, though he was a good man and had exhorted the Jews to lead righteous lives, to practice justice towards their fellows and piety towards God, and so doing to join in baptism. When others too joined the crowds about him, because they were aroused to the highest degree by his sermons, Herod became alarmed. Eloquence that had so great an effect on mankind might lead to some form of sedition. (*Ant.* 18.117–18)

The Gospels report that Herod expressed the same concern about Jesus when he heard that Jesus had cast out demons and healed the sick.

> King Herod heard of it, for Jesus' name had become known. Some were saying, "John the baptizer has been raised from the dead; and for this reason these powers are at work in him." But others said, "It is Elijah." And others said, "It is a prophet, like one of the prophets of old." But when Herod heard of it, he said, "John, whom I beheaded, has been raised." (Mark 6:14-16)

Later when Jesus is in Jerusalem, Luke says that some Pharisees warned Jesus,

> "Get away from here, for Herod wants to kill you." He said to them, "Go and tell that fox for me, 'Listen, I am casting out demons and performing cures today and tomorrow, and on the third day I finish my work.'" (Luke 13:31-32)

The activity of John the Baptist and Jesus occurred in Galilee and surrounding villages, where taxation and subsistence agriculture served Herod Antipas's project of urbanization (Oakman). Richard Horsley has made the connection between the exploitation of the populace in these agrarian villages and the numerous incidents of resistance and rebellion that occurred around the time of Jesus. A related observation is that during Second Temple times most inhabitants of Galilee were descendants of the northern Israelite peasantry, and stood in the northern prophetic tradition calling for the revitalization of Israelite village communities and a return to covenantal principles as a means of redressing social, political, and economic injustices (Horsley 2003). Both John the Baptist and Jesus were shaped by this prophetic tradition and were committed to the renewal of village life in the face of these harsh circumstances. However, while Jesus was initially identified through baptism with John's more apocalyptic hope of God's coming in judgment to rectify matters, he is depicted throughout the Gospel tradition as having a different strategy of grappling with the distress and discontent that Galileans experienced.

Jesus and John the Baptist

In a passage common to Luke and Matthew, Jesus compares his reputation to that of John: "For John the Baptist has come eating no bread and drinking no wine, and you say, 'He has a demon'; the Son of Man has come eating and drinking, and you say, 'Look, a glutton and a drunkard, a friend of tax collectors and sinners!'" (Luke 7:33-34 // Matt. 11:18-19). Moreover, in this same passage, Jesus draws another sharp distinction between himself and John: "I tell you, among those born of women no one is greater than John; yet the least in the kingdom of God is greater than he" (Luke 7:28 // Matt. 11:11). Even as he affirms John's prophetic ministry, he signals that God is now present and active anew through him. The contrast between Jesus and John in this passage provides an important clue to understanding the distinctive character of Jesus' ministry, the focus of which was the kingdom of God. How do we account for Jesus' transition from participant in John the Baptist's ascetic movement, with its standard covenantal emphasis on repentance and cleansing from sins, to being stigmatized for keeping company with those in need of reform?

John's imprisonment and execution had a traumatic effect on Jesus, but another passage common to Luke and Matthew suggests that Jesus' views were developing in a different direction even before that. When John sends his disciples to ask Jesus, "Are you the one who is to come, or are we to wait for another?" Jesus replies:

> Go and tell John what you have seen and heard: the blind receive their sight, the lame walk, the lepers are cleansed, the deaf hear, the dead are raised, the poor have good news brought to them. And blessed is anyone who takes no offense at me. (Luke 7:22-23 // Matt. 11:4-6)

Paul Hollenbach proposes that this shift was caused by Jesus' experience of God's power being mediated through him to exorcise and heal, which he interpreted as the kingdom of God being present in some sense. The Gospels do consistently portray Jesus as having a distinct authority to enact the kingdom in word and deed that is markedly different from John's apocalyptic vision of awaiting God's approaching judgment.

As we attempt to situate Jesus in the Galilean context of his ministry, one question we must ask is: How did Jesus' message and embodiment of the kingdom of God deal with the hardship of that village populace? This is a difficult question for at least two reasons. First, as Bultmann famously said, already in the earliest strata of the tradition the proclaimer has become the proclaimed. That is to say, the kingdom of God is the primary focus of Jesus' activity, but in the Gospels, Jesus himself, his identity and significance, is the center of attention. The second complication follows from the first. Once Jesus' teaching about the kingdom of God became a set of beliefs about him, the metaphor of the kingdom of God became more abstract and spiritualized. A Galilean or Judean audience in the first century would have heard the phrase "kingdom of God" as a political metaphor and would have grasped the implicit contrast with the client kingdoms that were an extension of imperial rule, such as that of Herod Antipas. To examine Jesus' message and enactment of the kingdom of God in relation to the sociopolitical landscape of Galilee is to explore the politics of the kingdom, that is, how Jesus was organizing and mobilizing his followers to embody divine power in their local context.

Jesus and the Renewal of Local Community

In an article titled "Jesus and the Renewal of Local Community in Galilee," Jonathan Draper challenges the dominant scholarly perspective that Jesus was an itinerant charismatic leader and argues that more attention should be given to group formation in the Jesus movement as a response to the economic and social disintegration and threatened landlessness in Galilee. He contends that Jesus was attempting to "renew local community in villages and towns, to strengthen and renew family and community relations and reverse the downward spiral of violence" (40). Except for a few passages that describe specific instances in which disciples are sent out, the Jesus tradition presupposes the existence and support of settled local communities. Geographically, Jesus moves within a limited radius of a few villages until he goes to Jerusalem. Hence the emphasis on Jesus' itinerancy may be more a consequence of superimposing post-Enlightenment individualism on the Gospel tradition so that a focus on Jesus as a unique religious figure eclipses his "concrete program of action for social transformation" (Draper, 38).

A brief consideration of meals and some of Jesus' teachings as practical expressions of the kingdom of God will illustrate Jesus' strategy for the renewal of community life in Galilee. A place to start is the passage mentioned above that describes Jesus as "a friend of tax collectors and sinners." This phrase occurs with reference to Jesus in all three of the Synoptic Gospels, where it is leveled by scribes and Pharisees as a criticism of Jesus (Matt. 9:10; Mark 2:15; Luke 5:30; 7:34). This complaint about Jesus reflects his opponents' perception of him, and may come from an early stratum of the tradition rather than from Jesus himself. Nonetheless, the criticism preserves a reminiscence of Jesus as a social deviant that probably has some basis in history. In the world in front of the text, "sinner" has a moral connotation, but in the context of Judaism, a sinner is one who is not compliant with Torah. What sinners and tax collectors have in common is that while they represent opposite ends of the socioeconomic spectrum, both were dishonored and therefore socially marginalized. Douglas Oakman has made the interesting suggestion that the word for "sin" in Aramaic, which was the language Jesus spoke, was *hōvayin*, the word for "debtors." He points out that these debtors could have been farmers or fishers in heavy debt, women enslaved in prostitution, or members of trades endangered by taxes. According to Oakman, "In this understanding, Jesus dines with just these people in order to broker relief" (98).

Meals were an integral part of Jesus' enactment of the kingdom of God, and they play a prominent role in the Gospel tradition. In addition to their obvious material significance in satisfying the hunger of a preponderance of people who worked to eke out a subsistence living, they also had symbolic import on a number of levels. Crossan has interpreted the significance of Jesus' meals as a central aspect of what he calls a "brokerless kingdom" marked by "the just sharing of food as the material basis of life, of life that belongs to God" (Crossan, 1991, 341–44; 1994, 66–70). He sees this sharing of meals (commensality) as part of Jesus' program to restore, from the bottom up, a society fractured by urbanization and commercialization and, on a symbolic level, as a confrontation between the divine realm of God's kingdom and the temporal realm of Herod Antipas within the wider realm of the Roman Empire. The feeding stories in the so-called miracle tradition also operate at both material and symbolic levels. On the one hand, the appetites of five thousand and four thousand people respectively are satisfied by the multiplication of the loaves and fishes (Mark 6:30-44; 8:1-10). On the other hand, they also serve to declare God's abundant provision in the midst of ostensible scarcity.

Another important aspect of the kingdom of God signified by Jesus' meals is the manner in which social norms, boundaries, and social relations are reconfigured. According to Dennis Smith, there are four categories of meals in the Gospels: (1) meals with Pharisees, (2) miraculous feedings, (3) meals with "tax collectors and sinners," and (4) meals with disciples (D. E. Smith, 223). Smith maintains that only meals with "tax collectors and sinners" and with disciples offer a high degree of historical probability. "Sinner" and "tax collector" are both terms of slander that refer to two groups on the fringes of Jewish society, albeit at opposite ends economically. The scandal in Jesus' eating with them was his inclusion of two groups who were normally excluded by their social location. In eating with sinners and tax collectors, Jesus exemplified the kingdom of God as encompassing those on the margins of society.

Meals are a prominent theme in the Gospel of Luke, but what is striking about many of Luke's meal scenes is that they are depicted in the style of a Greco-Roman symposium, which provides the occasion for Jesus to teach (see Luke 7:36-50; 11:37-44; 14:1-24; 22:7-30). Formal meals in Greek or Roman settings were a microcosm of society, and meal etiquette served to reinforce the rigidly stratified Greco-Roman social order. In Luke's meal scenes, Jesus often challenges this hierarchical social ranking and teaches the "biblical" virtue of humility. For example, Jesus tells a parable that is only in Luke in which he gives this advice about the seating arrangement at a marriage feast.

> But when you are invited, go and sit down at the lowest place, so that when your host comes, he may say to you, "Friend, move up higher"; then you will be honored in the presence of all who sit at the table with you. For all who exalt themselves will be humbled, and those who humble themselves will be exalted. (Luke 14:10-11)

While the disregard for social honor and stratification evident in this passage is consistent with what is known about the historical Jesus, the challenge to social convention has been recontextualized for Luke's Greco-Roman audience. The historical Jesus' meals with "sinners and tax collectors" and Luke's meal scenes both subvert social convention and act out an inclusive vision of the kingdom of God. However, the original cultural context of Jesus' meals is Jewish, while Luke has set them in a Greco-Roman context, where they challenge conventions of status and honor.

The meal scenes in the Gospels illustrate just how difficult it is to separate history from tradition, to differentiate what Jesus said and did from their symbolic interpretations by his first followers. The prominence of meals in the Gospel tradition indicates that table fellowship was an important aspect of Jesus' ministry and that it had symbolic significance. However, what table fellowship with Jesus meant in the Jewish context of rural Galilee is somewhat different from the symbolic function of the meal tradition in the Gospels, which reflect a more Greco-Roman setting. In the agrarian context of Galilee under Antipas's rule, eating with sinners and tax collectors, and even the feeding stories, can be seen as dealing with the crisis of poverty and dispossession materially and socially through both a concrete and symbolic representation of the kingdom of God. Whatever meaning was originally ascribed to the meals Jesus had with Galileans, once they became a part of memory and tradition about him, their significance was largely symbolic. Jesus was eating with Galilean peasants who may not have kept all of Torah, or at least the traditions of the elders (Oral Torah), as the debate about his disciples' eating with defiled hands indicates (Mark 7:1-23). In the Gospel tradition, "sinners" and "tax collectors" become terms of slander used by Jesus' opponents, who accuse him of transgressing social and religious boundaries. The audiences of the Gospels were communities that included gentiles, who were de facto "sinners," and others who would not have been considered part of the covenant community. These communities were on the margins of Judaism and Greco-Roman society, so a key role of the meal tradition was to legitimate the inclusion of those on the fringe and to depict Jesus' inclusive vision of the kingdom of God as a reordering of social relationships.

Many if not most of the references to meals in the Gospels indicate a symbolic interpretation that connects them with communal meals shared by communities of Jesus' followers. The Lord's Supper tradition is the most obvious example (Mark 14:22-25 // Matt. 26:26-29 // Luke 22:15-20), but the feeding stories and other meal scenes also have eucharistic overtones. The "breaking of the bread" signifies the presence of the Lord at community meals, and this is also tied to an eschatological interpretation. Jesus expresses the eschatological significance of the last meal he eats with his disciples when he says: "Truly I tell you, I will never again drink of the fruit of the vine until that day when I drink it new in the kingdom of God" (Mark 14:25 // Matt. 26:29 // Luke 22:18). The meal anticipates a banquet at the end of time, which is described by Isaiah.

> On this mountain the Lord of hosts will make for all peoples
> a feast of rich food, a feast of well-aged wines,
> of rich food filled with marrow, of well-aged wines strained clear.
> And he will destroy on this mountain
> the shroud that is cast over all peoples,
> the sheet that is spread over all nations;
> he will swallow up death forever.
> Then the Lord God will wipe away the tears from all faces,
> and the disgrace of his people he will take away from all the earth,
> for the Lord has spoken. (25:6-8)

These images were associated with a future messianic banquet: victory over primordial enemies (e.g., death), eternal joyous celebration, abundance of food, the presence of the Messiah, and the pilgrimage of the nations (D. E. Smith, 169). All of these are important themes in the Gospels, but because the meal tradition is so entangled with communal meal practices that celebrate the presence of the risen Jesus and look forward to his return as Messiah, it is difficult to ascertain what exactly in these meal stories goes back to Jesus himself.

Jesus as Prophet

Jesus is depicted in the Gospel tradition as announcing the approach of God's future kingdom, which in some sense is experienced in the present through deeds of power such as exorcisms and healings, as well as gathering followers around particular covenantal practices. Although he is referred to as Son of God and Messiah in the Gospel narratives, these are honorific titles attributed to him by others that he does not explicitly use of himself. The designation that may best represent what Jesus was doing and saying in Galilee, and then in Jerusalem, is that of prophet. The Gospel of Mark indicates that Jesus regarded himself as a prophet. He tells those who took offense at him in his hometown synagogue at Nazareth, "Prophets are not without honor, except in their hometown, and among their own kin, and in their own house" (Mark 6:4). It is unlikely that the epithet "prophet" would have originated with the early church. A passage common to Luke and Matthew says that Jesus regarded John as a prophet, and so he was also linked to this role by virtue of his identification with him.

> When John's messengers had gone, Jesus began to speak to the crowds about John: "What did you go out into the wilderness to look at? A reed shaken by the wind? What then did you go out to see? Someone dressed in soft robes? Look, those who put on fine clothing and live in luxury are in royal palaces. What then did you go out to see? A prophet? Yes, I tell you, and more than a prophet." (Luke 7:24-26)

Jesus here associates John's prophetic activity with "wilderness," and contrasts it with powerful elites such as Antipas. A number of passages in the Gospels suggest that people surmise Jesus is a prophet: "But others said, 'It is Elijah.' And others said, 'It is a prophet, like one of the prophets of old'" (Mark 6:15).

There were different kinds of prophets in early Judaism, but Jesus and John the Baptist fit the profile of popular prophets who led movements of resistance and renewal, which were not uncommon in the first century (Horsley and Hanson). As William Herzog observes, this type of prophetic leader emerges because he or she embodies the values of the group they represent. As a peasant artisan in the village of Galilee, Jesus would have been steeped in the prophetic traditions of Israel (Herzog, 23). In contrast to the scribal subculture within Judaism, characterized by texts and interpretations, Jesus inhabited an oral cultural that related the foundational biblical stories and figures to their own local context. These popular messianic movements, as Horsley calls them, often began in the wilderness as reenactments of the foundational acts of God's deliverance in the exodus and the formation of the covenant community (Horsley 2012, 93). Moses was regarded as the prototypical prophetic leader (Deut. 18:15), and Elijah and Elisha were especially revered figures in the Galilean milieu of Jesus. They were prophets who responded to a crisis in the northern kingdom by challenging political authority. The prophetic renewal movement led by Elijah and "the children of the prophets" has left an indelible mark on the Gospel tradition and may even have provided inspiration for Jesus himself (Brodie).

It would be difficult to overstate the significance of the exodus as the defining event in Israel's history, especially in the popular imagination of Judeans who had lived under imperial rule since the Babylonian exile. John the Baptist's call to prepare the "way of the Lord" evokes Isaiah's theme of a new exodus signaling that God was acting anew through Jesus to effect the liberation of God's people (Mark 1:2-6 // Matt. 3:1-6 // Luke 3:1-7). While the new exodus is a scriptural motif used by the Gospel writers to characterize the movements initiated by John and Jesus respectively, it also symbolizes the phenomenon of power associated with the focus of Jesus' message and activity, namely the kingdom of God. The phrase "kingdom of God" is a political metaphor that has its roots in the biblical notion of God as king. However, it is also a spatial metaphor that highlights a tension between the principal conviction of Judaism, that God is the sovereign creator who rules the universe, and the reality of the Roman control of Palestine. Since Jesus was proclaiming God's reign in a Galilee that was under Roman rule, he was, in some sense, exemplifying an order or an experience of power different from and incompatible with the machinations of imperial power.

Given the anachronistic connotations of kingdom language in contemporary contexts, a constructive alternative translation that conveys the phenomenon expressed is "power." Oakman maintains that "when Jesus spoke of 'Kingdom of God,' his reference was to the presence and reality of the Power, the Power's ultimacy" (76). So, for example, when Jesus says to a group of Pharisees, "The kingdom of God is not coming with things that can be observed; nor will they say, 'Look, here it is!' or 'There it is!' For, in fact, the kingdom of God is among you" (Luke 17:20-21), he was speaking of the power "among you" or "in your midst." The language of power pervades the Jesus tradition and is used in a variety of ways. Jesus' healings are referred to as "deeds of power," and he is described as teaching with "authority." The Greek word translated "deeds of power," and erroneously in some translations as "miracle," is *dynamis* (e.g., Mark 5:20; 6:2, 5, 14; 9:1, 39; 12:24; 13:25-26; 14:62). The Greek term translated "authority" is *exousia* (e.g., Mark 1:22, 27; 2:10; 3:15). This is the same power that the Israelites identified with the one who delivered them from bondage in Egypt in the exodus (Horsley 2011, 45). It is also the power that formed the Israelites into a people, and the template for how that power was to operate among the people was set out in the Mosaic covenant. Principles of political-economic cooperation and justice distinguish it as a power shared in community (Horsley 2011, 43). Jesus uses the metaphor of "father" to speak of this power in personal terms as beneficent and merciful, as well as caring and providing for all creatures (see Luke 6:35-36; 11:2-4; 12:22-34).

The Gospel of Mark introduces the ministry of Jesus by announcing, "Now after John was arrested, Jesus came to Galilee, proclaiming the good news of God, and saying, 'The time is fulfilled, and the kingdom of God has come near; repent, and believe in the good news'" (Mark 1:14-15). Matthew and Luke follow Mark in making Jesus' assertion of the imminence of this "power" the central focus of the narrative by describing its effects. Although the plot of these narratives is a construction of the authors using a variety of traditions about Jesus, the major facets of what the Gospels describe Jesus doing and saying are historically consistent with the portrait of him as a popular prophet leading a local renewal movement that dealt with the severe social and economic conditions of Galilean life. "Kingdom of God" is a biblical catchphrase encompassing the various representations of power featured in the narratives.

If these portrayals of kingdom power in the Gospels are set within the exigent circumstances of Jesus' Galilean context, the shape of Jesus' prophetic program of renewal and the various responses to it become more intelligible as a historical phenomenon. Of primary importance are Jesus' efforts to gather the people of God. The gathering of the scattered people of God is a major theme in Israel's Scriptures, especially among the prophets (see Deut. 30:1-5; Isa. 11:12-13; 58:6). As Gerhard Lohfink observes, "gathering" Israel is often parallel to "liberating," "saving," "healing," and "redeeming" Israel (Lohfink, 60). The twelve disciples Jesus chooses represent the twelve tribes of Israel that were scattered; more importantly, it underscores the point that a primary purpose of the power is the formation of a community. In other words, "the reign of God must have a people" (Lohfink, 48). At the conclusion of an episode common to Luke and Matthew in which Jesus is accused of casting out a demon by Beelzebul, the prince of demons, he asserts: "Whoever is not with me is against me, and whoever does not gather with me scatters" (Luke 11:23). In a characteristically prophetic mode, he holds people accountable to the power operative through him to gather, restore, and heal.

The scene in which we find this saying, about participation in God's power at work in and among the people Jesus was gathering, is one of many exorcisms in the Gospel. Exorcisms can themselves be understood as episodes in a struggle for power. In commenting on the accusation in Luke 11:15 that Jesus "casts out demons by Beelzebul the prince of demons," Halvor Moxnes emphasizes that his response reveals assumptions about space and boundaries underlying the challenge: "Every kingdom divided against itself becomes a desert, and house falls on house. If Satan also is divided against himself, how will his kingdom stand?" (Luke 11:17-18). Moxnes sees the challenge that identified Jesus with Beelzebul as an attempt by opponents to put him outside the boundaries of "civilized" society, outside Israel. The household was the center of social and economic life, and it was at the intersections of household and kingdom that the people around Jesus lived their lives and experienced the power that "the strong man" (Luke 11:21-22) could use to exercise control (Moxnes, 338). Anthropological studies of exorcism in other societies suggest that there is a connection between spirit possession and forms of imperial domination, but such experiences of being occupied by an alien power were interpreted cosmologically rather than politically (Horsley 2011, 113–17). These exorcism stories allude to experiences of release from the effects of the oppressive and hegemonic powers that controlled people's lives as a consequence of Jesus imparting a restorative divine power.

Interpreting the exorcism and healing stories in the Gospels as a demonstration and experience of power that challenges existing structures of power not only demystifies the confrontation with cosmic forces but also sheds light on the conflict with the religious authorities. From a literary perspective, conflict drives the plot of the Gospel narratives just as it does any good story. Differentiating between conflict on the literary level of the narrative and in Jesus' Galilean context is complicated by the fact that the Gospels are written after the destruction of the Jerusalem temple. So the depiction of the conflict between scribes and Pharisees in the Gospels reflects post-70-CE disputes between Jesus' followers and Jewish leaders because the portrait of scribes and Pharisees is something of a caricature that does not completely fit with Jesus' Galilean context. However, if Jesus was mediating a power from outside the socioreligious system, then it follows that as its brokers, scribes and Pharisees would likely have regarded him as a disturbance and a threat.

In Mark's narrative, the conflict between Jesus' authority and scribal authority is introduced at the outset of his ministry where, in the context of teaching in a synagogue, he delivers a man with an unclean spirit (Mark 1:21-28). While it is the narrator who contrasts Jesus' authority to teach with that of the scribes, this passage points to the crux of the conflict between Jesus and the religious authorities both in Jesus' Galilean ministry and in the Gospels, namely the interpretation of Torah. First, it is important to note the setting of many of these conflicts is the local synagogue, which was a center for community life organized around the Torah. In a village context such as Galilee, scribes acted as administrators who related Torah to legal matters and the affairs of people's everyday lives. As prophetic leader of a renewal movement in Galilee, Jesus embodied the values of the people who followed him, and those values were rooted and grounded in Torah. Despite a long-standing view that Jesus transgressed or abrogated Torah, he is depicted in the earliest layers of the tradition as upholding the Decalogue in its entirety (Mark 12:28-31), espousing many of its individual demands (Mark 7:9-13, 21-23; 10:17-19), observing Levitical rule (Mark 1:44), confirming that the whole of Torah is binding (Luke 16:17), and refuting criticism that his behavior is lawless (Mark 2:23-28; 3:1-6; see Allison 2010, 165). What distinguished his interpretation of Torah from the more traditional interpretations of scribes and Pharisees was the conviction that God was speaking and acting through him. This prompted a prophetic approach to Torah that drew on its traditions of justice and judgment and was responsive to the socioeconomic stresses in Galilee.

The two nodal issues at the center of the dispute between Jesus and the scribes about how to interpret Torah were Sabbath observance and purity regulations. In Mark 2:23—3:6, there are two consecutive Sabbath controversy accounts. In the first, Pharisees complain that Jesus' disciples are violating Sabbath by plucking grain, and in the second, Jesus responds to those who are watching to see if he will heal on the Sabbath. Anticipating their criticism, he asks, "Is it lawful to do good or to do harm on the Sabbath, to save life or to kill?" (Mark 3:4). Both episodes have likely been embellished in the context of Mark's narrative, but even so they disclose the underlying issues in Jesus' historical context and a key interpretative principle for him. The matter in question in both incidents is the priority he gives to human distress—hunger and physical affliction, respectively. The purpose of Torah for Jesus was to support the health and well-being of human beings, and this is consistent with how Torah has been interpreted within historic Judaism. Similarly, in the conflict focused on Jewish purity regulations, he does not disregard purity so much as reinterpret it as a matter of interpersonal ethics rather than ritual practice (Mark 7:1-23).

Jesus' habit of fraternizing with "sinners and tax collectors" was also a matter of concern for those scribes and Pharisees who saw themselves as guarding the boundaries of the Mosaic covenant (Mark 2:15-17; Luke 5:30-32; 7:34, 39; 15:1, 7, 10; 18:13; 19:7). "Sinners" were by definition people who behaved contrary to the covenant, or, as Crossley remarks, to someone's definition of law and covenant (87). The most historically accurate aspect of the portrait of the Pharisees in the Gospels is their emphasis on purity or holiness. Some of the people who come to Jesus are depicted as being impure. While it is plausible that Jesus and his followers may have been somewhat lax in their observance of purity regulations, impurity was not regarded as a "sin" per se in early Judaism. Nonetheless, people who were ritually impure could be marginalized socially. The Gospel tradition does not elaborate on the specific reasons some around Jesus were deemed "sinners." Given that a majority of the people in Galilee would have lived around subsistence level, lack of time and resources may have impeded many from observing Torah according to the standards of local religious authorities. Those who were designated "sinners" give the impression of being on the margins of society for economic or social reasons, and Jesus was reintegrating them into the covenant community.

In contrast to the Pharisees, who stressed purity and boundaries, Jesus' teaching was more oriented to economic and social relations, and focused specifically on issues of poverty and debt. Followers were exhorted to give without expectation of return to everyone who begs (Luke 6:30-35). Several passages, including the prayer Jesus teaches his disciples, feature the problem of debt and emphasize the importance of release from indebtedness (Matt. 6:12 // Luke 11:4; Luke 7:41; 16:5, 7; Matt. 18:28, 30, 34). Jesus also instructs his followers regarding their relationship to possessions.

He urged them not to be anxious about material needs and to trust God's care for them. He enjoined them, "Sell your possessions, and give alms. Make purses for yourselves that do not wear out, an unfailing treasure in heaven, where no thief comes near and no moth destroys" (Luke 12:33; 14:33). Jesus also had a lot to say about the deleterious effects of wealth, and in several passages challenges the rich. In addition to aphoristic sayings such as "woe to you who are rich" (Luke 6:24) and "you cannot serve God and wealth" (Luke 16:13), the parables of the rich fool (Luke 12:13-21), the story of the rich man (Mark 10:17-22 // Matt. 19:16-22 // Luke 18:18-23), the parable of the great banquet (Luke 14:15-24), the parable of the dishonest steward (Luke 16:1-8), the parable of the rich man and Lazarus (Luke 16:19-31), the story of Zacchaeus (Luke 19:1-9), and the parable of the pounds (Luke 19:11-27) all challenge the prosperous in a manner that implies their fiscal habits were a cause of economic distress and oppression for others, and so he required them to repent and amend their ways.

Since Jesus lived in an oral culture, he did not regularly cite or refer to biblical texts, but his teaching is grounded in Israel's Scriptures. In the parable of the rich man and Lazarus, the rich man implores Abraham to warn his family so they can repent, but Abraham replies, "If they do not listen to Moses and the prophets, neither will they be convinced even if someone rises from the dead" (Luke 16:31). In a passage common to all three Synoptic Gospels, a scribe asks Jesus, "which commandment is the first of all?" Jesus answers by quoting Deut. 6:4-5 and Lev. 19:18.

> The first is, "Hear, O Israel: the Lord our God, the Lord is one; you shall love the Lord your God with all your heart, and with all your soul, and with all your mind, and with all your strength." The second is this, "You shall love your neighbor as yourself." There is no other commandment greater than these. (Mark 12:29-31)

This double command, as it is sometimes called, is the central precept in Jesus' interpretation and appropriation of Torah in the economically distressed milieu of Galilee. The parable of the good Samaritan in Luke 10:25-37 is an example of how Jesus illustrates the practical implications of these commandments in ways that promote inclusivity, beneficence, and accountability to others, especially those in need.

Jesus refers to the Torah and the prophets mostly in the context of debating with scribes and Pharisees. His disputes with them were predicated on some shared convictions, such as the authority of Torah and the importance of the Mosaic covenant. What differentiated Jesus from these other teachers and precipitated most of their disagreements, however, was his concern to connect the power of God's kingdom to the struggles of a peasant underclass who, for various reasons, found themselves on the periphery. Parables were his preferred medium for imparting the message of the kingdom. A parable is a short, narrative fiction that draws on the concrete particulars of nature and everyday life to subvert the status quo and reimagine the world (Scott 2001, 13–15). Jesus' parables employed poetic metaphors to engage hearers' imagination by painting a vivid a picture of kingdom power that was often set in contrast to grandiose images of power. A good example is the parable of the mustard seed.

> He [Jesus] also said, "With what can we compare the kingdom of God, or what parable will we use for it? It is like a mustard seed, which, when sown upon the ground, is the smallest of all the

> seeds on earth; yet when it is sown it grows up and becomes the greatest of all shrubs, and puts forth large branches, so that the birds of the air can make nests in its shade." (Mark 4:30-32 // Matt. 13:31-32 // Luke 13:18-19)

As the parable indicates, the mustard plant is more like a "shrub," which the ancient writer Pliny says, "grows entirely wild" and, once it has been sown, it "is scarcely possible to get the place free of it" (*Natural History* 29.54.170). This is a strange and provocative image for the kingdom of God, but Jesus was likely invoking a comparison with the mighty cedar of Lebanon, which was a common image for empire in Israel's Scriptures (see Ezek. 17:22-23; Dan. 4:10-12). The mustard shrub is a metaphor for an emergent phenomenon that was organic, recalcitrant, and disruptive. Moreover, it was the very antithesis of imperial power as control and order.

While it is not possible to comment on or categorize all of Jesus' parables, they are all part of a strategy to evoke the possibility of another reality, the world as it should be over against the world as it was. Some critique greed, patronage, preoccupation with status, and other Greco-Roman values (e.g., Luke 7:41-43; 12:16-20; 14:15-24; 16:19-31; 19:12-27), and others suggest countercultural dispositions and practices such as hospitality, generosity, mercy, forgiveness, vigilance, and so on (Matt. 18:10-14, 21-35; Mark 13:34-36; Luke 10:30-35; 15:11-32). All the parables, along with Jesus' other teachings, were inextricably tied to his effort to gather people into a cooperative form of life that would enable them to stand firm in the face of severe political and economic stress. The immanent power he mediated was the basis for a popular sovereignty, and as the movement organized around it galvanized and gained momentum, tensions with established authorities also intensified.

Journey to Jerusalem

The turning point in the Synoptic Gospel narratives and in the prophetic ministry of the historical Jesus was his journey to Jerusalem, where he caused a disturbance in the temple that eventually led to his trial and execution. Most scholars acknowledge the historicity of the temple incident and the subsequent trial and execution, but the interpretation of these incidents has been heavily shaped by later reflection on them from the perspective of Jesus' postresurrection appearances and in the light of the destruction of the Jerusalem temple in 70 CE. Therefore, the task is to distinguish a historically plausible account of what happened when Jesus went to Jerusalem from later interpretations of these events. This is a challenge because event and interpretation are inextricably woven together from very early in the history of the tradition. They key, however, is establishing the continuity of Jesus' prophetic ministry in Galilee with what he said and did in Jerusalem, and explaining the reaction of the authorities that resulted in his crucifixion. Then it will be possible to elucidate the development of the Gospel traditions about Jesus' passion and resurrection into their current canonical form.

From a historical point of view, Jesus went to Jerusalem as a prophet leading a renewal movement. In a passage from the tradition common to Luke and Matthew, Jesus laments over Jerusalem. The narrative context in which the saying occurs is different in the two Gospels. In Luke's version, some Pharisees warn Jesus that Herod wants to kill him.

> He said to them, "Go and tell that fox for me, 'Listen, I am casting out demons and performing cures today and tomorrow, and on the third day I finish my work. Yet today, tomorrow, and the next day I must be on my way, because it is impossible for a prophet to be killed outside of Jerusalem.' Jerusalem, Jerusalem, the city that kills the prophets and stones those who are sent to it! How often have I desired to gather your children together as a hen gathers her brood under her wings, and you were not willing!" (Luke 13:32-34)

This passage is significant both because it contains a saying of Jesus that links the portrayal of his prophetic ministry in Galilee with his presence in Jerusalem, and because it shows how the tradition has been appropriated in the narrative strategies of the Gospel writers. For the purpose of our historical reconstruction, it is noteworthy that Jesus depicts himself as a prophet who is attempting to gather the covenant community. In Luke's account, Jesus is still en route to Jerusalem, so this is not the proper setting for his lament. It is also questionable that Herod is seeking to kill Jesus before he even arrives. The point where history and interpretation converge in this passage is Jesus' reference to himself as a prophet, belonging to a long-standing tradition of Israelite prophets who confronted the authorities and suffered a similar fate in Jerusalem as well as outside Jerusalem. Joseph Fitzmyer observes that behind this statement lies a traditional belief about the fate of various prophetic figures in the city of Jerusalem. He suggests that the killing of the prophet Uriah in Jerusalem by King Jehoiakim might be envisaged (Jer. 26:20-23), or the attempt on Jeremiah's life in Jerusalem (Jer. 38:4-6). However, there are many other examples of prophets who meet a similar fate (Fitzmyer, 1032).

In Mark's Gospel, Jesus enters Jerusalem as he approaches the city from the Mount of Olives. Although this event, like many of the incidents in the passion narratives, is recollected as a performance of Israel's Scriptures, especially the prophets and psalms, Mark's account preserves the historical kernel of a symbolic action typical of prophets. The crowd construes his arrival as the coming kingdom of David and shouts,

> Hosanna!
> Blessed is the one who comes in the name of the Lord!
> Blessed is the coming kingdom of our ancestor David!
> Hosanna in the highest heaven! (Mark 11:9-10)

However, in this passage as well as the story of blind Bartimaeus (Mark 10:46-52), the view of Jesus as Davidic Messiah is rejected. Rather, Jesus' action in Mark and in its original historical context is best understood as a parody of royal processions common in antiquity. In contrast to political or military rulers who entered a conquered city in a war chariot or on a ceremonial steed, the symbols of violent power, Jesus entered on a donkey (Crossan and Reed, 220). The fact that this satirical public action was performed during Passover, when Israel celebrated liberation from its oppressors, made it even more provocative, and in itself could have been enough to result in crucifixion (Crossan and Reed, 220).

Upon his arrival in Jerusalem, this symbolic act was followed by another disruptive action in the temple itself. According to Mark, Jesus "entered the temple and began to drive out those who were selling and those who were buying in the temple" (Mark 11:15). In the Synoptic Gospels, this is the incident that leads to Jesus' arrest, trial, and execution. Although Jesus' action in the temple is recognized by most scholars as having some basis in history, the significance of this event is a matter of some debate. The episode is often referred to as the "cleansing of the temple," but that is a misnomer because it does not accurately indicate the focus of Jesus' critique. Jesus is portrayed here as teaching, and the words he uses to convey the reason for his indignation are from Isa. 56:7 and Jer. 7:11: "Is it not written, 'My house shall be called a house of prayer for all the nations'? But you have made it a den of robbers" (Mark 11:17). Although it is improbable that Jesus quoted Scripture verbatim on this occasion, the Jeremiah text in particular associates Jesus' outburst with Jeremiah's temple sermon and is used to interpret the underlying issue in a manner consistent with the focal point of his prophetic praxis in Galilee, namely economic hardship.

The verse from Jeremiah is taken from the prophet's oracle against the temple and its priests. Jeremiah indicts them for presuming that sacrificial worship in the temple could be the basis of the covenantal relationship with God without upholding its standards of justice and moral obligations to the most vulnerable.

> For in the day that I brought your ancestors out of the land of Egypt, I did not speak to them or command them concerning burnt offerings and sacrifices. But this command I gave them, "Obey my voice, and I will be your God, and you shall be my people; and walk only in the way that I command you, so that it may be well with you." (Jer. 7:22-23)

As in Jeremiah, in condemning the temple Jesus was denouncing a priestly aristocracy who presided over it by accusing them of acting like "thieves" who have turned the temple into a "den" where they hide out. Their administration of the temple system disclosed their own elite interests at the expense of the people. As Herzog puts it, the wealth of the temple, which was also a treasury, was an inevitable corollary of the poverty of the peasantry (167). The temple extracted tribute from people through the temple tax, tithes, and sacrifices. It was an economic institution with the priestly aristocracy bearing responsibility for collecting tribute to Rome, so in opposing the ruling class of Jerusalem Jesus was by implication opposing Roman rule (Horsley 2012, 144).

The Gospel of Mark, followed by Luke, suggests that Jesus' prophetic action in the temple was the cause of his subsequent arrest and execution. Within the narrative, after Jesus expresses his dissatisfaction with the temple using the words of Isa. 56:7 and Jer. 7:11, the narrator observes: "And when the chief priests and the scribes heard it, they kept looking for a way to kill him; for they were afraid of him, because the whole crowd was spellbound by his teaching" (Mark 11:18; Luke 19:47). While this is the narrator's interpretive perspective, it is also the most plausible historical explanation. Not only did Jesus' pronouncement against the temple challenge the authority of the priestly aristocracy, but it also roused the multitude of pilgrims in Jerusalem for Passover. In Luke, the narrator's report of the chief priests' and the crowd's response to Pilate's acclamation of Jesus' innocence echoes a similar sentiment: "He stirs up the people by teaching throughout all Judea, from Galilee where he began even to this place" (Luke 23:5). Therefore, even though passages are constructions of the Gospel writers, they underline the fact that Jesus was leading a movement that may have gained momentum in Jerusalem as the Jewish people were celebrating liberation from slavery in Egypt. If so, then Roman authorities would likely have regarded his behavior as seditious and therefore as deserving of execution.

The Gospel accounts of the arrest and trial of Jesus, and of the role of the different Jewish groups in these events, are at variance with one another. This indicates that details of what happened to Jesus in Jerusalem are highly interpreted and cannot be taken at face value historically. The traditions about Jesus' trial and crucifixion have been comprehended through the lens of Israel's Scriptures and shaped both by the experiences of his followers and the destruction of the temple in 70 CE. The development of the passion narratives in the Gospels will be discussed in the next section. What can be established beyond reasonable doubt is that Jesus was arrested and taken before Pilate, the Roman prefect of Judea, who authorized his crucifixion. Temple authorities may have played a role in handing him over, but the trial before the Sanhedrin is historically questionable. There is no historical precedent for such a trial, and the high priest's question, "Are you the Messiah, the Son of the Blessed One?" (Mark 14:61), reflects later christological reflection and debate. Moreover, the charge of blasphemy brought against Jesus by the high priest was not an offense punishable by death (Mark 14:64).

One aspect of the trial before the Jerusalem council that may be historically accurate is the false accusation that Jesus said he would destroy the temple (Mark 14:58). Jesus is also reported to have spoken against the temple earlier in the long discourse set on the Mount of Olives, in Mark 13. He tells his disciples who marvel at the grandeur of the temple, "Do you see these great buildings? Not one stone will be left here upon another; all will be thrown down" (Mark 13:2). Jesus then goes on to predict the tribulation that will occur before the son of man returns. Mark 13 is a dense and complicated passage that has been heavily redacted by Matthew and Luke (Matt. 24:1-44; Luke 21:5-38), and it is difficult to disentangle what might be authentic in these sayings of Jesus from material that was retrojected into the story after the destruction of the temple and in anticipation of Jesus' return. There are, however, two elements in the passage that are important to our historical reconstruction and can serve as points of transition to a discussion of the development of the Gospel tradition. On the Temple Mount, Jesus tells his disciples that "not one stone will be left here upon another; all will be thrown down" (Mark 13:1). Although Jesus does not say that he would destroy it, when he is taken before the chief priests and the council some falsely testify that they heard him say, "I will destroy this temple that is made with hands, and in three days I will build another, not made with hands" (Mark 14:57-58). Jesus' prediction that the temple would be destroyed may have been ascribed to him after the fact. However, given that the ruling class of Judea presided over a long-standing situation of economic distress that eventually resulted in the Jewish wars and the destruction of Jerusalem, it is conceivable that a prophet like Jesus could have foreseen the eventual downfall of the city (Goodman).

Jesus' prophetic warning about the impending destruction of the temple in Mark 13 is associated in this section with his sayings about the return of the son of man. This raises what is probably the most disputed aspect of historical Jesus studies, the eschatological or apocalyptic dimension of Jesus' proclamation and enactment of the kingdom of God. There are essentially two basic views. One view regards Jesus as more of a sage or teacher who propounded a subversive practical wisdom, and attributes the eschatological material to a later layer of the tradition that has its origins in the early church. On this view, what Jesus says about judgment, tribulation, and the imminence of God's kingdom is best explained as the result of Jesus' earliest followers interpreting his memory and tradition in the light of the resurrection, which was itself viewed as an apocalyptic event. This perspective is shaped more by social analysis of the Gospel tradition, which understands Jesus' sayings to be responding to the concrete realities of the local Galilean milieu, and therefore regards sayings more oriented to the future as inauthentic.

Concentrating on the Galilean context tends to highlight the social and pragmatic force of Jesus' words and deeds, but this perspective also tends to downplay Judaism as the framework of his teaching and activity. On the other hand, those who emphasize the apocalyptic or eschatological aspects of the Jesus tradition tend to regard Jesus primarily as a religious figure and make sense of his sayings and activity in relation to other voices and groups in Judaism. Both perspectives have merit and use different approaches to call attention to important but divergent facets of the Jesus tradition that should be held together, even if there is an ostensible tension. As noted in the outset of this essay, the distinction between social, religious, political, and economic dimensions of life is anachronistic and artificial when projected onto the Jesus tradition, because they were correlative facets of Jewish life. The portrait of Jesus as leading a renewal movement in Galilee needs to be combined with the view that regards him as an eschatological prophet within Judaism. As Dale Allison (1998, 100) points out, if Jesus did prophesy the temple's demise and replacement, then he was operating within the framework of restoration eschatology.

The role of prophet in Judaism encompasses the message and praxis of Jesus' Galilean ministry as well as his prophetic pronouncements and actions in Jerusalem. It is impossible to do justice to the complexity of the issues surrounding the debate about whether Jesus had an apocalyptic outlook, but much of what has been construed as apocalyptic in the tradition can also be explained as part of Israel's prophetic tradition. The term "apocalyptic" comes from the Greek word *apokalypsis*, which means "revelation"; and "eschatology" comes from the Greek word *eschatos*, which means "last" or "coming at the end or after all others." Both words denote an orientation to the future. Crossan represents the common understanding of "apocalyptic eschatology" when he says that it refers to "the darkening scenario of the end of the world" with an expectation of divine intervention (1991, 238). Along with a majority of scholars, he sees John the Baptist as a harbinger of an imminent apocalyptic intervention by God, who will enact eschatological judgment on those who don't repent. Those who downplay the eschatological aspects of Jesus' message want to dissociate Jesus from John's apocalypticism. But as Horsley contends (2012, 18), the message that on "the day of the Lord" God would come in judgment to either deliver or punish was typical of the prophets.

Both John and Jesus were prophets who called people to repent as part of a summons to covenant renewal, and this involved holding people accountable, especially those in power, through pronouncements of judgment. Themes of reversal, final judgment, resurrection of the dead, restoration of Israel, and the great tribulation are stock prophetic themes that run throughout the sayings of Jesus (e.g., Mark 10:31; Luke 14:11; 17:33). A good example of a saying that includes themes of tribulation, covenant, eschatological banquet, judgment, and the restoration of Israel is a passage in Luke.

> You are those who have stood by me in my trials; and I confer on you, just as my Father has conferred on me, a kingdom, so that you may eat and drink at my table in my kingdom, and you will sit on thrones judging the twelve tribes of Israel. (Luke 22:28-30; see Matt. 19:28)

The Greek verb translated as "conferred" means "to make a covenant with." Jesus speaks as an eschatological prophet mostly in the context of Jerusalem, where he must face his own imminent end, but this was consonant with his prophetic activity in Galilee. As Allison suggests (1998, 110), eschatology is, among other things, an expression of dissatisfaction with the present. Jesus went to Jerusalem as prophet, addressing issues of poverty and exploitation in Galilee, and there his focus shifted from a strategy of renewal in the present to future judgment. What is not a part of his prophetic warnings, however, was an emphasis on the end of the world. This is a misunderstanding of the message of Jesus and of Jewish apocalyptic.

Mark 13 is sometimes referred to as the "little apocalypse" because it is regarded as the most explicitly apocalyptic passage in the Gospels, with parallels in Matthew and Luke. Jesus speaks to his disciples about tribulations that include wars, earthquakes, famines, trials, betrayal, and false prophets and messiahs, and then exhorts them to stay vigilant. Since many of the particulars in this passage could allude to the Jewish wars that began in 66 CE, ascertaining which parts of the discourse can be traced back to Jesus is difficult. Although many interpreters read the passage with an accent on the end-time scenario, Jesus emphasizes that "the end is not yet. . . . This is but the beginning of the birth pangs" (Mark 13:7-8). After he warns his disciples of these impending disasters, he then assures them that after the ordeal "they will see 'the Son of Man coming in clouds' with great power and glory. Then he will send out the angels, and gather his elect from the four winds, from the ends of the earth to the ends of heaven" (Mark 13:26-27). These words in quotation marks are from Dan. 7:13. Daniel is an apocalyptic book in the sense that it contains "revelation." That revelation assured Jewish people during the reign of Antiochus Epiphanes that "one like a son of man" would mediate divine sovereignty by judging the empires of the world and gathering the elect. However, Daniel 7 is not about a judgment that signals the end of the world, but rather, as Horsley puts it, a judgment that "leads to the renewal of the world as the place where the restored people can finally live in justice" (2012, 49).

The Synoptic Gospels tell the story of Jesus in two parts. In the first part, Jesus is a popular prophet leading a renewal movement in the exploited environs of Galilee, and in the second part, he goes as a prophet to the capital city of Jerusalem to confront those in charge of the temple. Jesus' engagement with the authorities in Jerusalem continued to be on behalf of the Jewish populace. By invoking the apocalyptic vision of Daniel 7, he reiterated and reinforced the connection between the reign of God and the people of God that characterized his Galilean ministry. In that vision, a heavenly court is assembled to judge all the world empires, especially the beasts. The symbols of lion, bear, leopard, beast, and finally "son of man" represent successive societies. Lohfink's comments about the political force of this vision are worth quoting at length.

> The fifth society is, of course, very carefully dissociated from those that precede it. It is no longer brutal, no longer bestial but finally a human society. Therefore it is symbolized not by beasts but by a human being. . . . The fifth society does not arise out of the sea of chaos but comes from

> heaven. It comes "with the clouds of heaven" (Dan 7:13). Thus the new, eschatological society comes from above. It cannot be made by human beings. It is God's gift to the world. It is the end of violent rule. (43)

Along with a number of scholars, Lohfink understands "son of man" as a symbol for the ultimate and final royal rule of God, but at the same time a figure for the true Israel or eschatological Israel that serves God alone. Jewish and Roman authorities recognized that Jesus' pronouncements against and demonstration in the temple were, like his proclamation of God's kingdom, patently political. The Gospel accounts of the trial(s) that led to his execution may vary, but what is beyond dispute is that the historical reason for the Roman prefect Pilate sentencing him to death by crucifixion was the charge of sedition.

Crucifixion was a form of execution reserved primarily for slaves and criminals; it was meant to make an example of those who would dare to subvert the imperial order, the *Pax Romana*. This is precisely what was indicated by the inscription on the cross, "The King of the Jews" (Mark 15:26). Although obviously intended to mock Jesus as falsely claiming to be ruler of the Jewish people even while they lived under Roman rule, it nonetheless betrayed Pilate's grasp of the seditious potential of Jesus and the community forming around him. The portrayal of Pilate as a principled official, reluctant to allow the crucifixion but ultimately succumbing to the pressure of the crowd, is in tension with what is known about him from other sources. Philo and Josephus, ancient Jewish writers from the first century, describe incidents that took place during Pilate's tenure that caused near insurrections among the Jews because of his insensitivity to Jewish customs. Philo describes him as "a man of a very inflexible disposition, and very merciless as well as very obstinate" (Philo, *Embassy* 38.299–305). He was removed from office two to three years after the death of Jesus, accused of murdering innocent Samaritans (Josephus, *Ant.* 18.4.1–2). Despite the fact that Pilate authorized Jesus' execution, all of the Gospels shift responsibility for the death of Jesus to the Jewish authorities and, to some extent, the Jewish crowd assembled at his trial. Therefore, it is with the stark and bleak reality of the crucifixion ordered by Pilate that this historical account of Jesus comes to a close and we begin to focus on the interpretive process.

Throughout this account of Jesus in his historical context, it has been evident that the details of events are so tightly interwoven with their interpretation that it is difficult to disentangle them. The most effective approach to ascertaining the historical contours of Jesus' public ministry is setting out a plausible account of the Synoptic Gospels' narrative of Jesus in the cultural-historical milieu of Galilee and Jerusalem. The next step is to show how the memory of what Jesus said and did was preserved and shaped by the first followers of Jesus. After the death of Jesus, his followers continued the movement he initiated and developed the tradition into what became the four literary productions known as the Gospels.

Followers of Jesus and the Development of the Gospel Tradition

The memory of what Jesus said and did, of his trial, and of his crucifixion was preserved by his followers. Also inscribed into each of the four canonical Gospels is the conviction that God raised him from the dead. The Gospel accounts of Jesus' postmortem appearances to his disciples were not included in the discussion of the historical Jesus because resurrection intimates an experience of transcendence that cannot be verified by historical method. What can be explored historically are the effects that belief had on his followers, and on the formation of the Gospels. In the Gospel of Mark, the risen Jesus does not appear to his disciples. Rather, a young man tells the women who go to the tomb, "He has been raised; he is not here. Look, there is the place they laid him. But go, tell his disciples and Peter that he is going ahead of you to Galilee; there you will see him, just as he told you" (Mark 16:6-7). The Gospels of Matthew, Luke, and John all have different appearance stories, which betokens not only multiple encounters with the risen Jesus but also that the narration of the event is itself an interpretation of its significance (see Matt. 28:1-20; Luke 24:1-53; John 20:1-29; 21:1-23). The earliest reference to the resurrection of Jesus is the tradition Paul cites in 1 Corinthians, which says that the risen Jesus "appeared to Cephas, then to the twelve. Then he appeared to more than five hundred brothers and sisters at one time, most of whom are still alive, though some have died" (1 Cor. 15:5-6). Paul goes on to mention Jesus' appearance to James and to himself, and then asserts that in raising him from the dead God had inaugurated the general resurrection of the dead (1 Cor. 15:12-13).

An important element of the resurrection accounts in all four Gospels that is absent from Paul's discussion is the empty tomb tradition. The empty tomb tradition belongs to the earliest conceptualization of Jesus' resurrection. In all four Gospels, it features women who go to the tomb where Jesus was buried to anoint his body, only to discover that it is not there. The initial message from the young man in the tomb in Mark's account, who become angels in Matthew and Luke, is that Jesus is not here because he has been raised. The interpretation of the empty tomb is not self-evident, and indeed raises the question of how an ancient audience would have understood this tradition. Daniel Smith contends that a first-century person (Jewish or Greek) would have interpreted an inexplicably disappearing body or an unaccountably empty tomb as evidence, not of "resurrection," but of "assumption" (D. A. Smith, 4). He notes this is an idea found in almost every ancient culture that, in certain special cases, God or some divine being or beings could take a person immediately and bodily into the divine realm. The significance ancient audiences would have inferred from the empty tomb tradition in the Gospels is that God had vindicated Jesus. In other words, since Jesus was executed as an enemy of the Roman order for sedition, the view that he had been raised from the dead was regarded as a divine response that validated his prophetic message and activity.

The various accounts of Jesus' postmortem appearances have a different function from the empty tomb tradition in the Gospel narratives. The phrase "he appeared" in 1 Corinthians 15 likely denotes a visionary experience of the risen Jesus, but in the Gospels, Jesus' appearances to his disciples are depicted as more than an apparition or a resuscitation. In Matthew, Luke, and John, the risen Jesus walks and talks, and in Luke and John, he even eats with his disciples, thus providing narrative accounts of what in Paul's discussion of resurrection he describes as a "spiritual body": "It is sown a physical body, it is raised a spiritual body. If there is a physical body, there is also a spiritual body" (1 Cor. 15:44). One concern addressed by the appearance stories, especially in Luke and John, may have been the belief, which came to be known as docetism, that Jesus only seemed to be human, and that his physical body was a phantasm. The primary purpose of the appearance stories in all the

Gospels, however, was to show Jesus commissioning his disciples to carry on with his mission. Those who had seen the risen Jesus could claim distinctive authority for leadership in the movement. In the shorter ending of Mark's Gospel, which does not include an appearance account, the young man instructs the women to "go, tell his disciples and Peter that he is going ahead of you to Galilee; there you will see him, just as he told you" (Mark 16:7). Galilee here is not just a geographical location but also symbolic of any place where the ministry of Jesus was continued by his followers. Therefore, within the narrative strategy of the Gospels, appearances of the risen Jesus serve to validate his message and mission vis-à-vis the imperial system that executed him and to inspire his followers to continue the movement he initiated in Galilee.

The empty tomb and the appearance traditions first circulated orally among Jesus' followers. They were related and handed down in the context of instruction or proclamation. These traditions were shaped by the conviction that Jesus was risen from the dead, and then woven together with other traditions about Jesus to form the narrative accounts that are the canonical Gospels. The memory of Jesus was, from the very beginning, shaped by followers who reflected on the significance of his message and actions for their own lives in diverse contexts. The earliest traditions about him were transformed as they were appropriated by communities of his followers throughout the Roman Empire. Form usually follows function, and this is no less true of the Jesus tradition, as followers made use of them to define their identity and develop practices of communal patterns of life.

Jesus was crucified sometime around 30 CE, and there is general agreement that Mark was written shortly after the destruction of the temple in Jerusalem in 70 CE. In this forty-year period between the time of Jesus and the time of the Gospels, stories and sayings circulated as oral tradition in what was an oral culture. In contrast to Western societies predominated by written media, the fundamental dynamic of communication in the ancient world was between speaker and hearer. The literacy rate was low, somewhere between 5 percent and 10 percent, and most written texts were scripts to be performed in public. Performative storytelling was the ordinary medium of literary production in the Greco-Roman world. As Michael White puts it, written texts served as scripts *of* and *for* oral presentations (White, 92). Stories about and sayings of Jesus that were disseminated in an oral culture were not static or fixed in the same way written texts are. Oral tradition is conservative in seeking to preserve authentic memories, but it is also malleable in that it changes with each new performance. As the Jesus tradition was transmitted in new contexts, it reflected the interests, values, and ideals of the community in which it was performed (White, 101–3). In this respect, the constructed memories of oral tradition do not simply relate the facts of what happened. They are also scripts for communal practice and belief.

During the forty or so years between Jesus and the Gospel of Mark, the memory of Jesus circulated orally. However, Mark and the other Gospels used sources, some of which were written down. There were likely collections of stories about Jesus' deeds of power, aphoristic sayings and parables, accounts of his suffering, death, and resurrection, and eventually nativity stories. As noted earlier in this essay, the sayings of Jesus common to Matthew and Luke are regarded by many scholars as an example of such a sayings collection, and are together referred to as Q. The sayings are not identical in the two Gospels because they were edited by the Gospel writers, but the sayings in Luke are generally regarded as closer to the original than Matthew (Robinson, Kloppenborg, and Hoffmann).

Q contains some of the most memorable sayings of Jesus and is important because it is purported to be an example of an early source for the Gospels; the best guess for its date would be somewhere between 50 and 70 CE. But because there is no manuscript evidence for Q or any references to it in any ancient Christian texts, this dating is at best a working theory that has been questioned by a growing number of scholars (e.g., Goodacre).

What is interesting about scholarship on the Q sayings source is that it provides a window, albeit one based on conjecture, onto the period of oral tradition between Jesus and the Gospels. While there are no extant copies of Q, the *Gospel of Thomas* is an analogous example of a collection of Jesus' sayings that has no narrative structure. The *Gospel of Thomas* is one of the most famous of the cache of texts found in 1945 in the Egyptian town of Nag Hammadi. It is an extant sayings collection that contains 114 logia, or sayings, of Jesus. Half of the sayings have parallels in the Gospels, and half were formerly unknown. So whether there was an actual Q document or not, the *Gospel of Thomas* is an example of a collection of Jesus sayings that makes no allusion to the passion or resurrection. This would suggest that the individuals and communities for whom this document was of value probably tried to live in accordance with these particular sayings of Jesus. Similarly, scholars who work on Q maintain that it describes a particular way of life of Jewish disciples of Jesus, who regarded themselves as itinerant prophets, moving from town to town and announcing, "The kingdom of God has come close to you." Many of the sayings in Q also imply that these followers of Jesus called for repentance and experienced persecution.

There are a number of observations to be made from this brief treatment of collections of sayings during the period between Jesus and the Gospels before we turn to discuss the canonical Gospels. Although there is no evidence for the existence of the Q sayings source as a document, it is probable that this collection, or ones like it, existed as oral tradition. In other words, whether there is a Q source or not, the *Gospel of Thomas* confirms that collections of Jesus' sayings did circulate and were a source for the narratives of Jesus constructed by the Gospel writers. Perhaps even more significant for understanding the development of these Jesus traditions into the Gospels is how the tradition was simultaneously preserved and modified as Jesus' followers sought to embody his teachings. For some communities in the Jesus movement, the sayings functioned as practical wisdom to live by. Not only was the Jesus tradition being performed for followers, followers were themselves performing the tradition with their lives. The Jesus movement was, in its first decades, a messianic movement within Judaism that, if Paul's letters are any indication, included an increasing number of gentiles so that by the end of the first century they were a majority. Jews and gentiles alike were drawn into the movement by the communal pattern of life, predicated on Jesus' teaching and prophetic praxis and on the conviction that, though he had been executed for sedition, God had raised him from the dead and hence had inaugurated the new age.

The Genre and Relationships of the Gospels

As works of ancient literature, the canonical Gospels do not fit neatly into any particular genre. Some have stressed their Jewish character, especially their continuity with the narrative traditions and themes of Israel's Scriptures, while others look for analogies in Greco-Roman literature.

Although the oral qualities of the Gospels have been underlined so far, when the story of Jesus was committed to writing in the second half of the first century CE, the authors made use of literary forms available in the culture. Before the Gospel of Mark, the memory of Jesus was preserved and recounted orally in story and ritual. The Gospel of Mark is the first known attempt to render into a cohesive narrative the oral legacy of Jesus. In this respect, the Gospel of Mark signals an important transition in which a more fluid oral tradition was transformed into a more fixed literary tradition that became the standard and primary source for subsequent narrative interpretations of Jesus. Since the Gospels emerged from a Jewish messianic movement, Israel's Scriptures provided a lens for interpreting the Jesus tradition, and also served as a literary template. At the same time, to communicate the message of and about Jesus to a growing number of followers and would-be followers, it was essential to find some common cultural ground. So there are points of connection with both Jewish and Greco-Roman literary forms.

As Richard Burridge has argued, there are similarities between the Gospels and Greco-Roman biographies (Burridge, 185-211). The structure of the Gospels is broadly biographical, tracing Jesus' public ministry in chronological sequence. However, the disproportionate amount of narrative space devoted to the last week of Jesus' life distinguishes it from the typical Greco-Roman biography. Some elements from the ancient biography genre, such as anecdotes and sayings of particular teachers, known as *chreiai*, bear some resemblance to Justin Martyr's description of the Gospels as "the memoirs of the apostles," but, as Loveday Alexander points out, "the precise literary form adopted by Mark's performance of the Jesus story is hard to match in the Greek biographical tradition" (Alexander, 27). She suggests that the Gospel narratives have more in common with the folktale, which blends some characteristics from biographical tradition with oral traditional literature. The folktale is more a mode of composition and performance than a genre. Like folktales, the Gospels are focused to a remarkable degree on the action of the hero (Alexander, 18). This is especially true of the Gospel of Mark. Alexander cautions against drawing too firm a distinction between action and teaching in the Gospels because many of the action episodes are didactic. Nonetheless, the narratives as a whole give prominence to Jesus' public activity, and this is different from Hellenistic biographies of the philosopher or poet whose life exemplified virtues to be emulated. The Gospels provide virtually no information about Jesus' private existence nor insight into his interior life. A counterpart to the Greco-Roman biography in Jewish literature is the "biography of the prophets," which was concerned with office and function. Helmut Koester has suggested that the Gospel of Mark in particular follows the framework of the "biography of the prophets" because the primary concern in the story of Jesus' suffering and death is the legitimation of his office (Koester, 27–28).

A strong case can be made for the literature of the Hebrew Bible having the greatest influence on the literary form of the Gospels. Much of the narrative of the Hebrew Bible is composed of biographical "story cycles" that feature the exploits and achievements of key protagonists such as Abraham, Moses, or Elijah (Alexander, 27). The paradigmatic significance of the Moses and Elijah traditions in the depiction of Jesus as a prophet has already been discussed, but another critical aspect of the Hebrew Bible narratives is that the tales of these heroic figures were, in Alexander's words, "subordinated to the overall narrative style and goals of a purposeful religious, ethical, and national work" (Alexander, 27). Like the biblical narratives on which they are patterned, the Gospels tell the story of Jesus as a continuation of the story of Israel after the destruction of the Jerusalem temple. They are organized around key themes from the Hebrew Bible such as covenant, kingdom, exodus, prophecy, Suffering Servant, Messiah, Son of God, son of man, and so on, which were pressed into service to cast Jesus as the divinely appointed leader of the covenant community

Among the various reasons the Gospels were written, the destruction of the temple in 70 CE was a watershed event that profoundly influenced the composition of all four canonical Gospels. There is general agreement that the Gospel of Mark was written shortly after Jerusalem was conquered. The rebellion against Rome that began with the wars that broke out in 66 CE culminated with the burning of the temple in Jerusalem. There is general agreement that the Gospel of Mark was written around this time, either just before or after 70 CE, the date that marks the end of Second Temple Judaism. For more than five hundred years, the temple stood not only as the main religious institution of Judaism but also the axis around which its view of reality revolved. Jews regarded it as the *axis mundi*, the center of the cosmos, and believed that when the temple liturgy was performed properly it perpetuated a symmetry between heaven and earth. So the end of the temple not only raised theological questions about faithfulness, both God's and the covenant people's, but also ignited a debate about the future of Israel.

Mark's story of Jesus engaged this debate by presenting Jesus as the leader of the covenant people and therefore as the key to Israel's future after the destruction of the temple. At the beginning of the narrative, at his baptism by John in the Jordan, Jesus is described as being anointed by the Spirit and hearing a divine voice from heaven that declared, "You are my Son, the Beloved; with you I am well pleased" (Mark 1:11). These words are a conflation of Ps. 2:7 and Isa. 42:1. Psalm 2 is an enthronement psalm acclaiming the newly anointed king as God's son. So before Jesus even began his renewal movement in Galilee and the surrounding villages, hearers are informed that he has already been designated as the one through whom God will lead the people. (The "son of God" title ascribed to Jesus defines his role as God's representative who mediates divine power and sovereignty; it should not be confused with later creedal formulations in which language of Jesus as "Son" is interpreted to mean that he has a divine nature.) Mark's story operates on two levels. On one hand, historical sources are used to recount Jesus' activity in Galilee and Jerusalem. But the story is told from a post-70-CE perspective, after Jesus, having been executed by that same imperial power that destroyed the temple, is believed to have been vindicated and appointed by God to lead Israel and the nations in the "way of the Lord" (Mark 1:3). The phrase "way of the Lord" comes from Isaiah and is an allusion to the hope and promise of a new exodus. But in Mark, the "way," as in, Jesus and the disciples were "on the way," is also a metaphor for the pattern of life taught and modeled by Jesus (e.g., Mark 4:4, 15; 8:27; 9:33; 10:32).

The word that is translated "Christ" (*christos*) simply means "anointed one." It has the connotation of "messiah," and occurs in the opening line of Mark with the other term for political leader of Israel, "The beginning of the good news of Jesus *Christ*, the *Son of God*" (Mark 1:1). The use of the designation "Christ" or "messiah" is contested in Mark because it was typically associated with a national model of leadership. The turning point in Mark's narrative is when Jesus begins his journey to the capital city of Jerusalem. At Caesarea Philippi, he redefines the role of messiah for his followers by associating it with his impending suffering and death. Three times in Mark 8–10, Jesus explains that it is necessary for the "son of humanity," his preferred self-designation, to be delivered to the authorities and condemned, only to rise after three days (Mark 8:31-33; 9:30-32; 10:32-34). However, the main thrust of these predictions of his passion and resurrection is to teach his disciples that his path of rejection, suffering, death, and resurrection is the new paradigm of faithfulness for the covenant community in a post-70 imperial world.

Jerusalem is the setting for Mark 11–16, and the predominance of the temple theme in this section takes on new significance in light of the audience's knowledge that the temple has recently been destroyed. Jesus criticizes the temple establishment and forecasts the ruin of a temple that for the audience no longer exists. After Jesus is arrested, he is taken before the chief priests and the council who, according to the narrator, bear false witness against him, saying, "We heard him say, 'I will destroy this temple that is made with hands, and in three days I will build another, not made with hands'" (Mark 14:58). Although the testimony is false in the sense that within the narrative Jesus never said that he would destroy the Jerusalem temple and replace it with a temple "not made with hands," the audience understands that this new temple that will replace the one that has been destroyed is the covenant community. It seems likely that the word "temple" here echoes Paul's metaphor of the "body of Christ," which could also be translated "body of the Messiah." The inscription on the cross that sarcastically acclaims Jesus as "the king of the Jews" also has ironic force because, for the audience, Jesus has been divinely appointed to lead the lead the people of God into a new future and way of life at variance with the imperial power and social order. Finally, as Jesus breathes his last, "the curtain of the temple was torn in two, from top to bottom," and a centurion exclaims, "Truly this man was God's Son!" (Mark 15:38-39). Having a Roman centurion, someone implicated in Jesus' execution, acknowledge that Jesus is God's anointed leader portends that gentiles will also be included in the movement as it spreads throughout the empire.

Matthew and Luke as Interpreters of Mark

In the transition from oral tradition to written narratives about Jesus, the Gospel of Mark established the basic plot of the story followed by Mathew and Luke. Together, these three Gospels are referred to as the Synoptic Gospels. The term *synoptic* comes from two Greek words, *syn* ("with") and *optikos* ("seeing"), and denotes the literary relationship between them. There is an ongoing debate about whether the Gospel of John also used Mark as a source or is an independent Gospel tradition. All four Gospels were likely written in last third of the first century, though some scholars would date Luke and John early in the second century. The earliest traditions about the four canonical Gospels stem from the second century and are reflected in the titles prefaced to the Gospels. Matthew and John were attributed to apostles, and Mark and Luke were attributed to companions of the apostles. However, the names of the apostles were attached to the Gospel manuscripts much later. The oldest witness is Bishop Papias of Hierapolis, who is quoted by Eusebius (*Hist. eccl.* 3.39.3–4). Papias's writings are dated between 100 and 150 CE. Helmut Koester makes three important observations about the Papias tradition. First, Papias does not use the term "Gospel," but says that Matthew composed "the sayings." Second, in their written form, these traditions about Jesus do not carry any greater authority for Papias than what was transmitted orally: in other words, these texts are not regarded as Scripture. Third, Papias shows that these written documents came with the names of apostolic authors, or of men who had followed the apostles, which guaranteed the trustworthiness first of the oral tradition and then of the written documents (Koester, 33).

A close reading of the Synoptic Gospels side by side in a Gospel parallel shows that while they have a great deal in common, there are also a number of inconsistencies and contradictions in details. The birth narratives of Matthew and Luke, for example, are completely different, as are the resurrection narratives. The tendency throughout church history was to harmonize the differences, which had the consequence of minimizing the distinctiveness of each Gospel. In the second century, an early Christian apologist by the name of Tatian combined the four Gospels into a single narrative called the *Diatesseron.* But as scholars began to compare the four Gospels and study them critically, it became evident that the authors were not eyewitnesses. New theories about the interrelationship of the Gospels emerged.

In the eighteenth century, scholars realized that the parallels in the Gospels are so similar in wording that one of the three Synoptic Gospels must have been the basis for the others. Since Luke states in the preface to his Gospel that he made use of other narrative accounts (Luke 1:1-4), this Gospel must have been dependent on either Matthew or Mark. From the time of Augustine in the fourth century, the canonical order of the Gospels was regarded as the order of dependence, so Matthew was thought to have been written first. According to Papias, the Greek version of Matthew was a translation of an earlier Hebrew edition. So, for centuries, the common view was that Mark abbreviated Matthew. Toward the end of the eighteenth century, however, J. J. Griesbach proposed a theory, based on the early view that Matthew was the first Gospel, which claimed that Mark used both Matthew and Luke for his abbreviated version. The main problem with the Griesbach hypothesis is that it is difficult to account for why Mark would omit material in the double tradition common to Matthew and Luke. Therefore, the theory that is most widely accepted by scholars is the two-source theory, which posits that Matthew and Luke depended on Mark and wrote independently of each other. The other main source used by both Matthew and Luke was Q. The distinctive material in Matthew and Luke is designated "M" and "L" respectively. Although the theory posits four sources, it is called the two-source theory because Matthew and Luke both use Mark and Q as primary sources. The two-source theory is illustrated in figure 3.

There is no one solution that solves all the difficulties, but since 80 percent of Mark is reproduced in Matthew and 65 percent in Luke, Markan priority is seldom questioned. The existence of Q, however, continues to be debated, with the majority of scholars who question the existence of Q maintaining that Luke used both Mark and Matthew.

One of the main benefits of the study of the relationships among the Gospels is that it led to a deeper appreciation for the distinctive narrative vision of each Gospel. Although the study of the use of sources in the Gospels involves a certain amount of conjecture, it has also put more emphasis on how the evangelists redacted and shaped the Jesus tradition to address particular contextual and theological issues. In using Mark as a source, Matthew and Luke can be read as the first interpreters of Mark, or better, as performances of Mark. A close analysis of how Matthew and Luke modify Mark's narrative provides some insight into their respective narrative strategies. This, along with an examination of the material unique to Matthew and Luke and the distinct themes and uses of

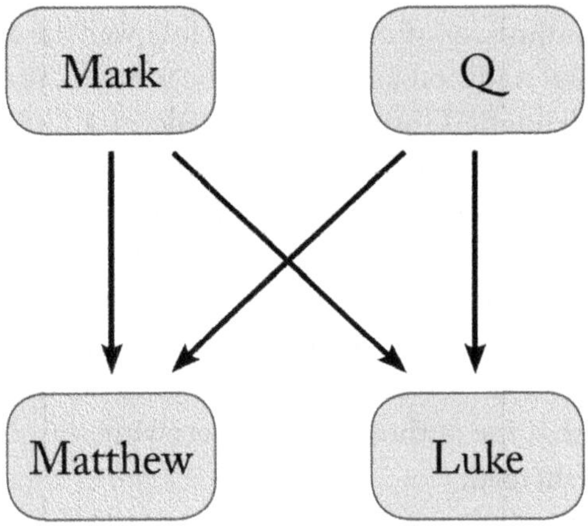

FIGURE 3. *The Two-Source Hypothesis*

Israel's Scriptures, suggests how Matthew and Luke adapted Mark's story of Jesus to shape the convictions and practices of audiences negotiating particular concerns and circumstances. While there is no external information outside the Gospels themselves that would make it possible to situate them geographically, the overarching perspective and key emphases of each Gospel can be inferred from the narrative itself.

Matthew and Luke both follow the basic framework of Mark's Gospel, and both also add infancy narratives to set the stage and introduce the story. Since it is only possible to touch on the broad contours of their narratives in this essay, the main point to be inferred from the divergent accounts of Jesus' birth, including irreconcilable genealogies, is that in different ways they are at the outset connecting their respective stories of Jesus to the history of Israel. Matthew establishes that Joseph belongs to the house of David so as to depict Jesus as the Davidic Messiah. Throughout the Gospel, Matthew makes a point to show that Jesus' ministry, death, and resurrection were a fulfillment of Israel's Scriptures. Luke's genealogy goes back to Adam to underline the universal scope of Jesus' mission. The main themes of Luke's Gospel are set out in the canticles of Mary (Luke 1:46-56) and Simeon (Luke 2:25-35), and the prophecy of Zechariah (Luke 1:67-80). The focus in all three passages is on the redemption of Israel, in particular the restoration of Israel that includes the nations. This central theme of the restoration of Israel is woven throughout the narrative and expressly highlighted in the final scene as two disciples, walking on the road to Emmaus with the risen Jesus whom they do not yet recognize, say, "we had hoped he was the one to redeem Israel" (Luke 24:21). This theme is then carried over into Acts, the only sequel to a Gospel in which the mission of Jesus is continued by his followers.

In each Gospel, there are key passages vital for understanding the narrative as a whole, and that also provide a window on the communal context of the Gospel. Matthew's Gospel is organized around five major discourses that include the Sermon on the Mount (Matthew 5–7), the discourse on mission (Matthew 10), parables of the kingdom (Matthew 13), discourse on community life (Matthew 18), and an eschatological discourse (Matthew 24–25). The Sermon on the Mount contains material that is also in Luke, but Matthew's Jesus is portrayed as the authoritative interpreter of Torah who teaches and models a righteousness characterized by "meekness" (Matt. 5:5; 11:29; 21:5) and "mercy" (Matt. 5:7; 9:13; 12:7; 23:23). Since Jesus tells his followers, "Do not think that I have come to abolish the law or the prophets; I have come not to abolish but to fulfill. . . . For I tell you, unless your righteousness exceeds that of the scribes and Pharisees, you will never enter the kingdom of heaven" (Matt. 5:17, 20), a number of scholars have inferred that the setting for this Gospel was a Torah-observant community of Jesus' followers that was involved in a dispute with scribes and Pharisees (who are likely represented by the religious authorities in Matthew's context). The vitriolic diatribe against scribes and Pharisees in Matthew 23 acknowledges their authority but criticizes them because they "do not practice what they teach" (Matt. 23:3). Matthew's story of Jesus can be read as a narrative portrayal of a righteousness, a central theme in Torah, that can be practiced by all. Hence the final authoritative command of the risen Jesus to "Go therefore and make disciples of all nations . . . *teaching* them to obey everything that I have commanded you" (see Matt. 28:19-20).

Luke's story of Jesus tells of God fulfilling promises of salvation for Israel and the nations. Only Luke's account of John the Baptist includes the phrase from Isaiah 40, "and all flesh shall see the salvation of God" (Luke 3:6). This vision of salvation is given more specific definition in Jesus' programmatic first speech at his hometown synagogue in Nazareth, where he reads from the Isaiah scroll.

> The Spirit of the Lord is upon me,
> because he has anointed me
> to bring good news to the poor [Isa. 61:1].
> He has sent me to proclaim release to the captives
> and recovery of sight to the blind,
> to let the oppressed go free [Isa. 58:6],
> to proclaim the year of the Lord's favor. (Luke 4:18-19)

This passage signals to the audience that Jesus' ministry will engage various forms of oppression and injustice. There is more material on economic relations in Luke than any other Gospel, so issues of poverty and marginalization were specific contextual issues facing the author (e.g., Luke 6:20-21, 27-36; 12:13-21, 32-34; 14:15-33; 16:1-13, 19-31). The hope of salvation in Luke is defined as deliverance from social ills, and so Jesus is cast in the role of prophet on the model of Elijah, who was engaged in renewing society. However, the offer of salvation requires a human response of "repentance" that entails participation in Jesus' mission. Luke's story of Jesus offers an alternative vision of life and practice. This vision promises God's deliverance from the dehumanizing effects of imperial society for the covenant community that hears Jesus' words and does them (see Luke 6:46-49).

The Gospel of John

The Gospel of John has not been discussed because its narrative about Jesus is different from and probably independent of the Synoptic tradition. At least we can say it radically departs from it. The literary relationship among Matthew, Mark, and Luke indicates that they share a similar form, structure, and content. All three Synoptic Gospels, on the one hand, use many of the same sources and traditions to tell the story of Jesus. Their authors edited the material in ways that reflected the concerns and interests native to the communities and contexts in which they were writing, but Matthew and Luke are essentially following and adapting Mark's story of Jesus. The Gospel of John, on the other hand, is so different from the Synoptic Gospels that we must begin with what is distinctive so that John's story of Jesus can be interpreted on its own terms.

On a basic level, the chronology and geography of the Gospel of John are at variance with the Synoptic Gospels. In the Synoptic Gospels, the temple incident is the turning point in the plot of the story inasmuch as it leads to his trial before the Sanhedrin and, ultimately, to his death. In the Gospel of John, the incident in the temple occurs at the beginning of the Gospel, in chapter 2. Jesus moves back and forth between Galilee and Jerusalem throughout the Gospel. John and the Synoptic Gospels are obviously referring to the same incident, even though they place it at different points in the chronology. They also interpret its significance in different ways. In the Synoptic Gospels, Jesus' prophetic challenge to the temple administration belongs to a longer section that deals with temple themes and sees his trial and execution as the direct consequence of what he said and did in the temple. In John, the plot to kill Jesus is hatched after Jesus raises Lazarus from the dead (John 11:45-53), something that does not happen in the Synoptics.

Among some of the other important differences between John and the Synoptic Gospels is the fact that in John, Jesus' ministry spans three years, while in the Synoptic chronology it lasts only a year. There are no exorcisms or parables in John. There are fewer healings and other deeds of power in John, and those that are narrated are called "signs." In the Synoptic Gospels, the exorcisms, healings, and other deeds of power are evidence of the presence of the "kingdom of God." But the "kingdom of God" is not the focus of the Gospel of John. Rather, the "signs" serve to reveal the true identity of the one who performs them. Perhaps the most striking difference between John and the Synoptic Gospels is the manner in which Jesus speaks. Instead of short, pithy sayings, or parables, Jesus speaks in long, extended discourses. The metaphors and symbols of John are also different from those in the Synoptic Gospels. Jesus' metaphorical way of speaking is self-referential and does not point to the "kingdom of God," the root symbol of the Synoptic tradition. This is because John depicts Jesus preeminently as the "Revealer." He comes from God and he reveals God. Even the healings are occasions for long monologues in which Jesus "reveals" the deeper significance of his identity and the nature of his work.

The Gospel of John begins with a hymn that succinctly tells the story of Jesus in poetic form. John's prologue sets out many of the main themes and the essential plot of the Gospel. At the outset, the hymn evokes the creation and introduces the "Word" as the central character who "was in the beginning with God. All things came into being through him, and without him not one thing came into being" (John 1:2-3). In Stoic philosophy, *logos*, translated "Word" here, referred to the cosmic reason holding the universe together. The counterpart to this idea in Judaism was the important concept of Wisdom as a preexistent divine being. This personification of Wisdom found in Proverbs 8 and other Jewish literature is probably the frame of reference for this poetic description of the descent of the Word into the world. Wisdom was perceived to be a female figure, present with God at creation, who comes to dwell on earth. In Jewish tradition, she is identified with Torah, but in John, Jesus is the expression of this divine Wisdom.

In the Gospel of John, Jesus is the incarnation of this preexistent divine Wisdom. He came to "take up residence" in the cosmos in order to lead people to life (John 1:14). But as the prologue and the Gospel both attest, this story takes a tragic turn when those who inhabit the cosmos reject this particular embodiment of the divine presence. Another feature that makes this Gospel so different from the Synoptic Gospels is that it is plotted along a vertical axis, whereas the Synoptics are plotted along a more historical, horizontal axis. John's Jesus is the "man from heaven" who "tabernacles" among the people of God, only to return to the Father. Although the Synoptic Gospels affirm the divine presence and power in and through Jesus, they do not go so far as to suggest that he was with God from the beginning. John tells the story of Jesus as a cosmic tale, while in the Synoptic Gospels the story unfolds on the horizontal plane of history (see figure 4).

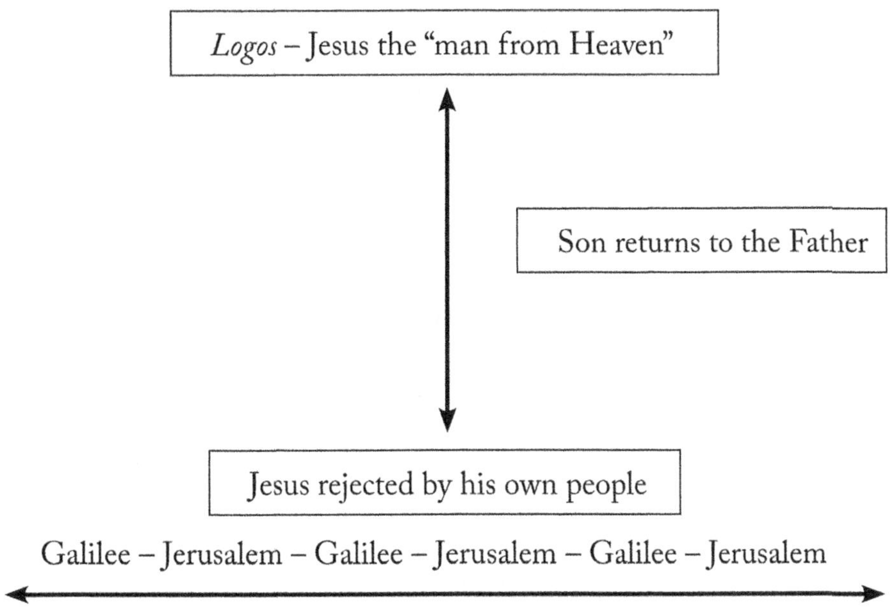

FIGURE 4. *Vertical and horizontal axes of the Johannine narrative.*

So while the Johannine Jesus moves back and forth between Galilee to Jerusalem and interacts with various characters, the main narrative arc is from heaven to earth and then back again. What Jesus says and does, the conflicts he is embroiled in, and even his death and resurrection are presented from the point of view of the cosmological tale set out in the opening hymn. John essentially replaces the Synoptic Gospels' proclamation of the kingdom of God with a present experience of "life" that is "eternal" (see John 3:15-16; 4;14, 36; 5:24, 39; 6:27, 40, 47, 54, 68; 10:28; 12:25, 50; 17:2). The phrase "eternal life" (*zōē aiōnion*) in John virtually replaces the proclamation of the kingdom and denotes a quality of life peculiar to the new age that is experienced in the present.

The clearest window onto the world behind the text of this Gospel is the skillfully narrated healing of the man born blind in John 9. This healing story operates on at least two levels, in the sense that the story of the blind man who receives his sight also discloses something about the story of the Johannine community. After Jesus heals the blind man, he is brought before the Pharisees to be interrogated. Since the Jewish authorities do not believe the man had been blind, they call the man's parents to explain how he now sees. They reply:

> "We know that this is our son, and that he was born blind; but we do not know how it is that now he sees, nor do we know who opened his eyes. Ask him; he is of age. He will speak for himself." His parents said this because they were afraid of the Jews; for the Judeans had already agreed that anyone who confessed Jesus to be the Messiah would be put out of the synagogue. (John 9:20-22)

There are other references in the Gospel to being put out of the synagogue (12:42; 16:2). We should, however, be careful about taking such statements at face value as indicating believers were actually expelled from the synagogue. This Gospel was written fifteen to twenty-five years after the destruction of the Jerusalem temple, during a time when Jewish leaders were shoring up boundaries as they attempted to redefine what it meant to be Jewish in a world without a temple. As a result, there developed some kind of strife between the Johannine community and the local Jewish community. The language of enmity against "the Jews" in this Gospel was born of intense emotional pain and social bereavement due to strained relationships with and perhaps separation from their Jewish compatriots. The Gospel itself suggests that the main issue may have been the community's claims regarding Jesus' unique relationship to God. There was a perception among Jewish rabbis early in the second century that Christians believed that there were "two powers in heaven." This was thought to compromise the foundational monotheistic confession in Judaism that there is one God. There are passages in John that suggest this may have been a point of contention between the Johannine community and the synagogue.

Concluding Summary

This essay about Jesus has shown that, from the beginning of his ministry in first-century Galilee, people have interpreted the significance of what he said and did in various ways. The four canonical Gospels are the primary sources for understanding who Jesus was, but they are not straightforward historical accounts. Rather, they are narrative interpretations that relate Jesus' message and mission to new historical circumstances for followers. The Enlightenment gave rise to historical criticism and attempts to get behind the text of the Gospels to distinguish the Jesus of history from the faith perspectives of his followers. However, as Schweitzer saw at the turn of the twentieth century, interpretations of the Jesus tradition always reflect the social location of the person who is doing the interpreting. History and interpretation are so intertwined in the Gospels that there continues to be a robust conversation and a diversity of views about the historical reliability of the Gospels and how they are used to construct a portrait of the historical Jesus.

This essay has suggested that a thick and nuanced description of the sociohistorical context of Galilee and Jerusalem in the 30s of the Common Era is needed to provide a framework for deciphering the significance of what Jesus said and did in his own context, and for understanding how the Gospel writers adapted the traditions about Jesus to their contexts after the destruction of Jerusalem in 70 CE. The canonical Gospels represent four similar yet different narrative performances of the story of Jesus. Each has its own rhetorical strategy, designed to shape the identity and practices of a particular community, or perhaps multiple communities. In his Galilean context, Jesus was leading a renewal movement that addressed issues of economic and political oppression, and social and religious marginalization. He went to the capital city of Jerusalem as a prophet to challenge the priestly aristocracy that collaborated with Rome, and was executed as an enemy of the imperial order. The four Gospels all attest that his followers experienced him as alive after the crucifixion and commissioned them to continue the movement, which then spread throughout the Roman Empire. The Gospels were all shaped by the conviction that God had raised Jesus from the dead and inaugurated a new messianic age. Each Gospel narrates what Jesus said and did, and the events of his life, as the basis for a distinctive vision of an inclusive and communal pattern of life that was countercultural and had the power to transform the lives of individuals and the world in which they lived.

Works Cited

Alexander, Loveday. 2006. "What Is a Gospel?" In *The Cambridge Companion to the Gospels*, edited by Stephen Barton, 13–33. New York: Cambridge University Press.

Allison, Dale C. 1998. *Jesus of Nazareth: Millenarian Prophet*. Minneapolis: Fortress Press.

———. 2010. *Constructing Jesus: Memory, Imagination, and History*. Grand Rapids: Baker Academic.

Barton, Stephen C., ed. 2006. *The Cambridge Companion to the Gospels*. New York: Cambridge University Press.

Borg, Marcus J. 1994. *Jesus in Contemporary Scholarship*. Valley Forge, PA: Trinity Press International.

———. 1998. *Conflict, Holiness, and Politics in the Teachings of Jesus*. Harrisburg, PA: Trinity Press International.

———. 2008. *Jesus: Uncovering the Life, Teachings, and Relevance of a Religious Revolutionary*. San Francisco: HarperOne.

Brodie, Thomas L. 2000. *The Crucial Bridge: The Elijah-Elisha Narrative as an Interpretive Synthesis of Genesis-Kings and a Literary Model for the Gospels*. Collegeville, MN: Liturgical Press.

Burridge, Richard. 2004. *What Are the Gospels?: A Comparison with Graeco-Roman Biography*. Grand Rapids: Eerdmans.

Crossan, John Dominic. 1991. *The Historical Jesus: The Life of a Mediterranean Jewish Peasant*. San Francisco: Harper.

———. 1994. *Jesus: a Revolutionary Biography*. New York: HarperCollins.

Crossan, John Dominic, and Jonathan L Reed. 2001. *Excavating Jesus: Beneath the Stones, Behind the Texts*. San Francisco: HarperSanFrancisco.

Crossley, James G. 2006. *Why Christianity Happened: A Sociohistorical Account of Christian Origins (26–50 CE)*. Louisville: Westminster John Knox.

Draper, Jonathan. 1994. "Jesus and the Renewal of Local Community in Galilee." *Journal of Theology for Southern Africa* 87:29–42.

Fitzmyer, Joseph A. 1985. *The Gospel According to Luke X–XXIV*. Garden City, NY: Doubleday.

Goodacre, Mark S. 2002. *The Case Against Q: Studies in Markan Priority and the Synoptic Problem*. Harrisburg, PA: Trinity Press International.

Goodman, Martin. 1987. *The Ruling Class of Judaea: The Origins of the Jewish Revolt against Rome, A.D. 66–70*. New York: Cambridge University Press.

Herzog, William R. 2005. *Prophet and Teacher: An Introduction to the Historical Jesus*. Louisville: Westminster John Knox.

Hollenbach, Paul. 1982. "The Conversion of Jesus: From Jesus the Baptizer to Jesus the Healer." In *ANRW* 2.25.1:196–219.

Horsley, Richard A. 2003. *Jesus and Empire: The Kingdom of God and the New World Disorder*. Minneapolis: Fortress Press.

———. 2011. *Jesus and the Powers: Conflict, Covenant, and the Hope of the Poor*. Minneapolis: Fortress Press.

———. 2012. *The Prophet Jesus and the Renewal of Israel: Moving beyond a Diversionary Debate*. Grand Rapids: Eerdmans.

Horsley, Richard A., and John S. Hanson. 1999. *Bandits, Prophets, and Messiahs: Popular Movements in the Time of Jesus*. Harrisburg, PA: Trinity Press International.

Koester, Helmut. 1990. *Ancient Christian Gospels: Their History and Development*. London: SCM; Philadelphia: Trinity Press International.

Lenski, Gerhard. 1966. *Power and Privilege: A Theory of Social Stratification*. Chapel Hill: University of North Carolina Press.

Lohfink, Gerhard. 2012. *Jesus of Nazareth: What He Wanted, Who He Was*. Collegeville, MN: Liturgical Press.

Moxnes, Halvor. 2010. "Ethnography and Historical Imagination in Reading Jesus as an Exorcist." *Neot* 44, no. 2:327–41.

Oakman, Douglas E. 2012. *The Political Aims of Jesus*. Minneapolis: Fortress Press.

Robinson, James McConkey, Paul Hoffmann, and John S. Kloppenborg. 2009. *The Sayings Gospel Q in Greek and English*. Minneapolis: Fortress Press.

Sanders, E. P. 1985. *Jesus and Judaism*. Philadelphia: Fortress Press.

———. 1996. *The Historical Figure of Jesus*. New York: Penguin.

Schaberg, Jane. 2002. *The Resurrection of Mary Magdalene: Legends, Apocrypha, and the Christian Testament*. New York: Continuum.

Schweitzer, Albert. 1910. *The Quest of the Historical Jesus*. London: Black.

Scott, Bernard Brandon. 1989. *Hear Then the Parable: A Commentary on the Parables of Jesus*. Minneapolis: Fortress Press.

———. 2001. *Re-imagine the World: An Introduction to the Parables of Jesus*. Santa Rosa, CA: Polebridge.

Smith, Daniel Alan. 2010. *Revisiting the Empty Tomb: The Early History of Easter*. Minneapolis: Fortress Press.

Smith, Dennis Edwin. 2003. *From Symposium to Eucharist: The Banquet in the Early Christian World*. Minneapolis: Fortress Press.

Theissen, Gerd, and Annette Merz. 1998. *The Historical Jesus: A Comprehensive Guide*. Minneapolis: Fortress Press.

Vermes, Géza. 1981. *Jesus the Jew: A Historian's Reading of the Gospels*. Philadelphia: Fortress Press.

———. 1993. *The Religion of Jesus the Jew*. Minneapolis: Fortress Press, 1993.

White, L. Michael. 2010. *Scripting Jesus: The Gospel Authors as Storytellers and Their Images of Jesus*. San Francisco: HarperOne.

Wrede, William. 1971. *The Messianic Secret*. Trans. J. C. G. Greig. London: James Clarke.

MATTHEW

Warren Carter

Introduction

Matthew's story of Jesus unfolds in six sections. The opening section introduces Jesus (1:1—4:16). He is located in the story of Israel (1:1-17); conceived and commissioned by God to manifest God's saving presence (1:18-25); threatened by Herod, recognized by the magi and a star, protected by Joseph (ch. 2); witnessed to by John the Baptist (3:1-12); sanctioned by God in baptism (3:13-17); tested by the devil (4:1-11); and interpreted by the Scriptures (4:12-16). Then in the second section, Jesus carries out his commission to manifest God's saving presence (4:17—11:1) by announcing God's reign or empire (4:17); calling disciples (4:18-22); teaching (chs. 5–7, 10); and performing actions such as healings and exorcisms (chs. 8–9).

The third section highlights diverse responses to Jesus and his activity of recognition and rejection (11:2—16:20). In the fourth section (16:21—20:34), Jesus announces a further dimension to his commission. The ruling alliance of Jerusalem elite and the Roman governor Pilate will crucify him. In his teaching (ch. 18) and while journeying from Galilee (chs. 19–20), he elaborates the implications of his death for his disciples' "way of the cross." The fifth section narrates his increasing conflict with the ruling powers in Jerusalem, his curses and judgment on their imperially allied world, and his crucifixion as rebel king and death (chs. 21–27). The final section reveals that Roman power does not have the last word as God raises Jesus (ch. 28).

This story of Jesus' birth, activity, teaching, death by crucifixion, and resurrection exhibits standard features of the genre of ancient biography. We do not know its author. Though the Gospel twice mentions a disciple named Matthew (9:9; 10:3), he is probably not the author. This disciple plays a minor role in the Gospel. And the name "Matthew" is not linked with the Gospel until late in the second century, some one hundred or so years later.

The Gospel's references to Rome's destruction of Jerusalem in 70 CE (see below) and its apparent citing by writings from Syrian Jesus-followers early in the second century (e.g., *Didache*, letters of Ignatius) establish a window of c. 80–c. 100 CE for its composition. The Gospel, then, is not an eyewitness account or day-by-day record of Jesus' ministry. It shapes its sources—Mark's Gospel and a collection of Jesus' sayings called Q—to address its audience's circumstances in the 80s or 90s CE. It was written perhaps in Galilee or in Syria, notably the city of Antioch. The prominence of Peter, the surprising reference to Syria in 4:24, and its early citing by writings from Syria suggest the latter.

Narrative Pastoral Theology at Work

Why tell this story of Jesus? The devastating assertion of Roman power in destroying Jerusalem and its temple in 70 CE, events that concluded the 66–70 war of revolt, had momentous consequences for emerging Judaisms. The Gospel's telling of the story of Jesus, one crucified by Rome as a rebel king, functions to interpret these events, to secure the distinct and differentiated identity of the community of Jesus-followers, to discredit other groups, and to envision practices and a societal vision that constitute a way ahead. The Gospel is thus a work of narrative pastoral theology, addressing its audience's particular circumstances.

These circumstances comprised conflict, competition, pressure, and vulnerability. Syria had significant involvement in the 66–70 war. In 67, the Roman general and later emperor Vespasian marshaled there three or four legions of troops (more than 20,000 troops in a city of perhaps 150,000). Syrian grain was levied to support Titus's troops in the subsequent siege of Jerusalem. The practice of *angaria* requisitioned transport, labor, lodging, and supplies from local people (see Matt. 5:41; 27:32). As Roman presence and pressure increased, conflicts among Jews in Antioch erupted. A highly acculturated member of the Jewish elite by the name of Antiochus accused other Jews of plotting to burn Antioch. Antiochus banned identity-defining practices (Sabbath observance) and required sacrifices to city and/or imperial gods. Some complied, some refused, some were martyred, and some gentiles violently attacked Jews (Josephus, *J.W.* 7.47–53).

After the war, the victorious Roman general and future emperor Titus paraded Jewish captives and booty through Antioch. Some Antiochenes urged him, unsuccessfully, to expel Jews from the city. The emperor Vespasian levied a tax on Jews as a subjugated people, diverting the tax formerly paid to the Jerusalem temple to maintain and rebuild the temple of Jupiter Capitolinus in Rome. This move added insult to injury. Jupiter was the sponsoring deity whose blessing had ensured Roman victory over Judea, its God, and temple.

Jerusalem's devastation made an example out of Jewish people. It reminded the rest of the empire that Roman power was not to be challenged. It also raised significant theological issues and questions about the identity, way of life, and future of Jewish communities in the empire. What was God doing? Had God withdrawn God's presence and blessing? Was the event punishment? If so, was there forgiveness? How should they live so as to prevent such a terrible thing happening again?

And this military-political event posed special challenges for Jesus-followers. They followed one who had been executed on a cross. Rome used crucifixion, a cruel form of the death penalty, to punish runaway slaves, bandits who attacked elite personnel and their property, and insurrectionists against Roman rule. Jesus' death by crucifixion placed him in such company. The alliance comprising the Roman governor Pilate, the face of Roman power in Judea, and the Jerusalem leaders with whom Pilate shared power, had viewed Jesus as a threat for attacking the temple that was the basis for their power, for proclaiming an alternative empire, and for being understood as a king not sanctioned by Rome.

In telling the story of Jesus, Matthew's Gospel interprets and addresses this post-70 situation. How did followers of one crucified by Rome negotiate a world defined by a fresh assertion of Roman power?

One consequence of the 70-CE defeat of Jerusalem was added pressure on and suspicion of the significant Jewish population of Antioch. The reality that when a ruling power exerts downward pressure on a subordinated group, horizontal verbal, structural, and physical violence frequently breaks out among group members is well attested. This phenomenon is evident in Antioch, as noted above, and in Matthew's Gospel. The Gospel exhibits considerable verbal hostility toward and conflict with leaders, at least, of the synagogue or synagogues of which these Jesus-followers were members.

The Gospel explains the destruction of Jerusalem and its temple as punishment on the rulers of Galilee and Judea for rejecting Jesus (22:1-10). Jesus declares the temple leadership (allied with Rome) to be "robbers" or "brigands." Their rule attacks and harms the people's well-being (21:12-13; quoting Jer. 7:11). Through several parables (21:33—22:10; esp. 21:41; 22:7), Matthew interprets Jerusalem's fall to the Romans in 70 CE as God's judging the leaders for rejecting Jesus (21:45-46).

This explanation presents Rome as chosen by God to be agents of this punishment. But following a well-established Hebrew Bible pattern, the Gospel also presents Rome as under God's judgment. Chapter 24 offers the fantasy of Jesus' return to establish God's empire or reign in full, destroying Rome's empire (24:27-31). Rome and other nations will be condemned for not caring for the broken and powerless (25:31-46). The sinful structures of power that benefit elites at the expense of the rest created unjust and harmful circumstances.

Worse, the Gospel presents this Roman-ruled, sinful world as being in the devil's hands. In tempting Jesus, the devil asserts control over all the empires of the world, of which Rome is the leading empire. The devil offers Jesus these empires if he will bow down to the devil (4:8-9). Jesus' exorcisms of demons, the devil's agents, show his victory over the devil's control (8:28-34).

Moreover, the Gospel declares that this judgment on the Jerusalem leaders and Rome is not the end. It presents Jesus as God's anointed agent (Christ/Messiah, 1:1; Son, 3:17). He represents and reveals God's saving presence (1:21-23) and will for the way ahead. Jesus challenges the ruling powers with a different societal vision. He announces and enacts God's empire or kingdom (4:17). He calls disciples to form a new community (4:18-22) and teaches them (chs. 5–7). Many sick people occupy the world of the Gospel (4:23; 9:35) because Rome's imperial structures ensure that the ruling elite have plenty to eat while most struggle for daily sustenance. In such a context, diseases of deprivation and contagion are rife. Jesus' healings, exorcisms, and feedings (see 14:13-21; 15:32-39) enact and anticipate the physical wholeness and abundant fertility that the prophets picture when God's reign/empire is established in full (Isa. 26:6-10; 35:1-7).

Jesus forgives sin (9:1-8; 26:26-29). He also declares that he represents God's presence wherever his followers gather (18:20) and engage in mission (28:18-20). In five teaching blocks, Jesus reveals God's will and purposes, shaping the identity and way of life of his followers (chs. 5–7; 10; 13; 18; 24–25). Jesus' teaching announces the surprising situations in which God's blessing is encountered—among the poor (most of the population!) whose poverty corrodes their being or spirit (5:3), and in deeds of mercy (5:7; 9:13; 12:7; 18:21-35). Mercy is demonstrated in actions that relieve harsh socioeconomic conditions (25:31-46). Quoting from Deut. 6:5 and Lev. 19:18, Jesus declares that the double command to love God and neighbor is central to God's will (22:34-40).

Through this presentation of Jesus' actions and teaching, Matthew's Gospel reassures people after Rome's destruction of Jerusalem and the temple in 70 CE that God has not abandoned them or withdrawn God's presence, forgiveness, and blessing. God's agent, Jesus, provides a future. God has commissioned him to reveal God's purposes in his actions and teaching, shaping their identity and way of life.

How, then, are followers of Jesus, crucified by Rome, to live in this imperial world? Despite opposition (5:10-12), they are to understand that the empire's power is not ultimate. It could not keep Jesus dead. God raised him from the dead (ch. 28), and he will return to establish God's reign (chs. 24–25). Disciples are not to "resist violently" but are to negotiate Rome's power in active, nonviolent ways (5:39-42). They pay taxes while recognizing that the earth belongs to God, not to Rome (17:24-27; 22:15-22). They pray for God's will and rule to be established (6:9-13). They reject hierarchical structures of power (20:20-28). They care for and support one another with practical mercy, love, and forgiveness (5:42; 6:9-13; 18:1-35; 22:34-40; 25:34-36). The Gospel thus shapes the identity and way of living of Jesus-followers in a world often not structured according to God's purposes of abundant life for all people.

Enemies and Verbal Violence

The Gospel's presentation indicates, though, that other members of the synagogue do not accept Jesus' credentials, explanations, and teaching. Considerable tension exists between Jesus-followers and the rest of the synagogue communities. Though Jesus is active in synagogues (4:23; 9:35), he often finds opposition. The Gospel's verbally violent rhetoric associates synagogues with conflict and rejection (12:9-14; 13:54-58). Jesus describes them as full of hypocrites (6:2, 5) and violent toward his followers (10:17-18, as are rulers). Throughout, Jesus is in conflict with leaders such as scribes, Pharisees, and chief priests who, along with the Roman governor Pilate, crucify him (9:2-8; 12:1-14; 16:1-12; 26:3-5, 57-68). They clash over how to interpret the Scriptures and practice God's will in Sabbath observance (12:1-14), elder care (15:1-9), divorce (19:3-12), and paying taxes (22:15-22). They think he is a blasphemer (9:3), the devil's agent (9:34; 12:24), lacking authority for his actions and teaching (21:23-27). In turn, he declares them disqualified from God's purposes (15:6-9), warns against their teaching (15:13-14), and in the terrible chapter 23 curses them as hypocrites who neglect justice, mercy, and faithfulness (23:23).

At the heart of this conflict is the issue of Jesus' identity. Those who oppose him in synagogues do not recognize him as God's agent commissioned to manifest God's will, presence, forgiveness, reign/empire, and purposes. In the difficult situation of post-70 Antioch, perhaps various synagogue leaders and members thought that a group committed to one who had been crucified was likely to attract unwelcome hostile attention. Perhaps they considered the Gospel's analysis of Roman power as diabolical and dangerous. Perhaps they found its certainty about Jesus' return to end the Roman world similarly provocative. Perhaps they found it incredible that a crucified one could manifest God's saving presence and reign/empire. Perhaps they found the eschatological declaration that God had raised him untenable, because clearly the world continued unchanged, with, in fact, Roman power strengthened.

The Gospel, then, tells the story of Jesus so as to address the circumstances of its own time. This situation is marked in part by struggles among synagogue members to make sense of the events of 70 CE and to discern a faithful way ahead. The Gospel sees Jesus as the key figure in offering a way ahead; others in the synagogue do not. The Gospel inscribes this bitter conflict in its story of Jesus.

A word of warning, though, is necessary. This Gospel presents this conflict between Jesus, synagogues, and Jewish leaders in harsh terms. Jesus makes nasty statements that are problematic for contemporary readers (e.g., ch. 23). The history of reading this Gospel over the last two millennia shows that its language has readily been a source of hostile anti-Jewish thought, rhetoric, and actions among Christians. The Gospel provides no warrant for such responses by contemporary readers. Its hostile rhetoric emerges from particular circumstances that no longer apply. And the Gospel holds out a different and greater vision of love for neighbors that accompanies love for God (22:37-40).

In the following commentary, I elaborate this reading and engage the Gospel's contemporary address. In the bibliographies, I regularly cite two quite different commentaries from among many fine Matthean commentaries. One is my own, *Matthew and the Margins*, which elaborates this interpretation of Matthew. The other is the magnificent commentary by Ulrich Luz, from which I have drawn much material in the sections on the interpretive tradition. I wish to acknowledge my debt to this fine work.

Part 1: God Commissions Jesus (Matthew 1:1—4:16)

The first chapters of Matthew make clear that Jesus has been commissioned by God. A new section of the narrative is marked by the statement in 4:17 that "from that time Jesus began to preach . . ."

Matthew 1:1-17: A Genealogy

The Text in Its Ancient Context

While repeating a formula "*a* was the father of *b*" some thirty-nine times may not strike modern sensibilities as a gripping beginning, first-century readers found this opening genealogy to be of great significance. Genealogies linked the present with the past. They named prestigious ancestors, creating identity through an ancestral line to which some belonged and some did not. Jesus and his followers are set in a line that originates with the eminent figures of David and Abraham.

This genealogy, though, is not primarily about biology. The artificial patterning of 3 × 14 generations, the lack of match between the number of generations and the likely time spans, the false link between Salmon and Rahab (1:5), and missing generations (1:8, 11) indicate a different focus.

Matthew narrates a distinctive version of the biblical story in which the purposes of God are worked out through the ages and generations, and especially through Jesus. Jesus' significance is defined by divine purposes and not, for example, by cultural markers such as elevated social status, noble birth, wealth, and power. The selected biblical traditions provide a theological framework for the rest of the Gospel, where everything and everyone are evaluated in relation to God's workings (Carter 2000, 53–66; Waetjen).

This theological focus is polemical in the context of Matthew's audience. Jewish traditions included various tellings of the biblical story. Matthew's account chooses to highlight the key role of Jesus. Further, in the context of the Roman Empire, Rome's self-presentation in coins, public festivals, buildings, and literature written by elite authors emphasized Rome as chosen by the gods. Jupiter had chosen Rome to manifest the gods' will and blessing throughout the earth. The genealogy's concern with God's purposes contests those claims and offers an alternative. God's purposes are displayed through Israel and Jesus, not Rome.

The genealogy establishes that God intends life for all people, not only the empire's privileged elite. The opening verse ("the book of the origin") evokes God's life-giving act of creation (Genesis 1). Abraham recalls God's declaration of blessing through him for all the nations of the earth (Gen. 12:1-3), a promise elaborated in terms of fertility, food, health, and safety in the covenant blessings of Deuteronomy 28–29. Linking Jesus to David recalls the kingly tradition that was to represent God's reign, justice, and protection for the vulnerable (Psalm 72). The genealogy also uses a common technique in the ancient world involving numbers to emphasize David's importance. The number fourteen, which structures the three sets of fourteen generations, underlines David's importance (1:17). The numerical value of the consonants in David's name in Hebrew adds up to fourteen.

The genealogy demonstrates that God's purposes are wide and inclusive, embracing gentiles (Ur, Babylon) and Jews (Israel, Judah), men and women (five in 1:3, 5-6, 16), the celebrated (Abraham, David) and the nobodies that even the tradition has forgotten (1:3b-4, 13-15), the powerful (kings) and those on the cultural margins (the women). Nor is God bound by human structures such as imperial power (Babylon), patriarchy (the women), or primogeniture (Isaac not Ishmael; Jacob not Esau). God is not confined by human boxes.

The Text in the Interpretive Tradition

At least two issues have dominated interpretive discussions. Interpreters have long noticed that Matthew's genealogy differs significantly from that of Luke 3:23-38. Tertullian explained the difference by claiming that Matthew offers Mary's genealogy while Luke provides Joseph's. Others have tried to distinguish between a "natural" genealogy and a "legal" genealogy, though which Gospel offers which continued to be debated. Both approaches are unsatisfactory because they do not recognize the theological and narrative functions of the genealogy.

As christological debates and formulations unfolded through the second to fifth centuries, interpreters read the genealogy as underscoring the humanity of Jesus. It showed the birth of the human Jesus. John Chrysostom saw the marvel of the incarnation in observing the skeletons that rattled in

Jesus' closet. These rattling ancestors included sinful characters such as the women, Judah who had sex with an apparent prostitute (his daughter-in-law Tamar), and the adulterer David.

The Text in Contemporary Discussion

The genealogy is often regarded as irrelevant for contemporary congregations and is not often utilized in preaching. Yet it contains important perspectives both for the Gospel narrative as a whole and as a subsection of the Gospel.

For example, every name evokes a story of encounter with God and a role in the divine scheme. What emerges from these individual stories is a mosaic attesting that God's work embraces all people through diverse circumstances: faithfulness or sinfulness (many of the kings in 1:6b-11 were unfaithful to the vision of kingship in Psalm 72) or gender (male and female) or ethnicity (Jew and gentile) or imperial power (Babylon cannot thwart God's faithfulness, 1:11-12) or even anonymity when some of the characters, especially in verses 12-15, are unknown. Human sinfulness and assertions of imperial power are caught up in, but cannot derail, God's faithful efforts to be with God's people and enact God's will. Preaching and informed Bible study can explore these numerous stories.

The presence of the women, unusual but not unique in ancient genealogies, provides another point of connection. They also underline God's inclusive and unconventional ways of working. The naming of Tamar (1:3; cf. Genesis 38), Rahab (1:5; cf. Joshua 2), Ruth (1:5; cf. Ruth), the wife of Uriah (Bathsheba, 1:6; 2 Samuel 11–12), and Mary (1:16) disrupt the pervasive and patriarchal "*a* was the father of *b*" pattern. Why are they included? Numerous suggestions have included their gentile origins or connections, and unconventional sexual roles (Tamar, seducer; also Ruth; Rahab, prostitute; Bathsheba, adulterer; Mary, pregnant virgin) that bypass and even threaten conventional patriarchal structures. They occupy socially marginal and often culturally powerless locations in which they exercise initiative and participate in God's plans. They often exhibit faithfulness lacking from their attendant males (Levine 1998, 340–41).

Matthew 1:18—2:23: Jesus' Conception, Commission, and Vulnerability

The Text in Its Ancient Context

Framed by the theological context of the genealogy, the Gospel story commences with the conception, commissioning, and endangerment of Jesus as God's agent (Carter 2000, 66–89).

First, Jesus is conceived at God's initiative. Twice Mary's pregnancy is attributed to the Spirit (1:18, 20), and twice she is said to be pregnant before having sex with Joseph (1:18, 25). Stories of miraculous conceptions involving divine power circulated about great conquering military men and rulers such as Alexander "the Great" and the emperor Augustus. Jesus is placed among heroes, though for very different reasons (Horsley).

Second, God commissions Jesus as the agent of God's purposes. Named "Jesus," he is to save from sin (1:21) and, as Emmanuel, to manifest God's presence (1:23). As God's chosen agent ("son," 2:15), Jesus joins and exceeds other agents such as Moses (5:21-22), David (22:42-43), Solomon

(12:42), as well as chosen places such as the temple (12:6). He also contests Roman claims to be the designated agent of divine purposes, will, and blessings among humans (Carter 2001, 57–107).

Third, the Scriptures interpret Jesus. Five times (1:22-23; 2:5-6, 15, 17-18, 23), the narrator stops the action to underscore God's shaping of events by quoting the Hebrew Bible. Four of these instances involve prophets: Isaiah (1:22-23), Micah (2:5-6), Hosea (2:15), Jeremiah (2:18). The fifth is attributed to the collective entity of "the prophets," with no one particular source able to be identified (2:23). The citations do not mean that prophets predicted events in Jesus' life or his messianic identity centuries ago. None of these texts mentions a messiah. Rather, the prophets addressed a word from the Lord to circumstances in their own time. Matthew, reading with "Jesus-glasses," sees God doing similar things in Jesus' life and uses Hebrew Scriptures to interpret his significance.

Fourth, Jesus is opposed by King Herod. Herod ruled Judea as Rome's client king and agent of Rome's interests. Introducing both Herod (2:1) and Jesus (2:2) as kings sets up the conflict. Herod uses various methods typical of an imperial tyrant to eliminate Jesus as a threat to his and Roman interests. He gains information from his allies, the Jerusalem leaders (the chief priests and scribes; 2:3-6). He tries to turn the magi into spies (2:7-8). He tells lies, claiming that he wants to pay homage to Jesus (2:8). He tries to kill Jesus (2:13), creating misery in killing all the male babies two years and under in the vicinity of Bethlehem (2:16-18). His attempts are thwarted by divine intervention through an angel and dreams (2:13). He dies, an event the narrative attests three times by way of emphasizing God's protection of Jesus and God's purposes being worked out through him (2:15, 19, 20). The threat of imperial power to Jesus continues with Herod's son Archelaus (2:22).

Fifth, the magi and a star witness to Jesus. The gentile magi "from the East" are astrologers, interpreting events in relation to the stars. Stars were commonly associated with important events or the births of important figures such as emperors (Augustus, Nero). Magi often had some marginal and destabilizing role as political advisors. They come to pay homage to Jesus, thereby threatening Herod (2:2-3). They bring gifts for Jesus (2:11), which in Matthew's narrative recalls Hebrew Bible traditions of gentile homage in Jerusalem (Isaiah 60; Ps. 72:10-11). Their witness emphasizes Jesus' significance for gentiles and Jews.

And sixth, Jesus is protected from Herod by the righteous Joseph (1:19). In chapter 2, Joseph's righteousness comprises his receptivity in dreams to the angel's leading and his instant obedience (2:13-15, 19-21, 22). The narrative underscores his obedience by narrating his actions with wording almost identical to the angel's instructions.

The Text in the Interpretive Tradition

This section has a rich interpretive history (Luz 2007, 89–131). The passage itself engages in reinterpretation of biblical texts, reading them in a new context in relation to Jesus. It also employs numerous echoes of the Moses story—killing male children, conflict with rulers, divine protection, Egypt—thereby linking Moses and Jesus.

In the church's history, Matthew's reading of Hebrew Bible texts in relation to Jesus has often provoked anti-Jewish attitudes in Christian readers. These citations have often been misread in mechanistic, predictive terms with prophets "obviously" referring to Jesus. Accordingly, when Jewish readers of the Hebrew Bible texts did not see references to Jesus, condemnations from Christians have been harsh. Martin Luther, for instance, fumes about "obstinate damned Jews" who did not see Isa. 7:14 (addressing an eighth-century-BCE crisis with Assyria) as a reference to Jesus. As with many readers, Luther fails to see Matt. 1:22 and all Matthew's citations of the Hebrew Bible as distinctively Christian readings.

Mary's conception has been much debated. The Roman Catholic tradition has defended her perpetual virginity, while Protestant interpreters have noted Matt. 13:55's references to Jesus' brothers and sisters. Other interpreters have read this verse in terms of Joseph's children from another marriage (Epiphanius), or cousins (Jerome).

Since the Enlightenment, Mary's virgin birth has been both strongly defended by those who understand God to intervene in human history to accomplish anything and dismissed as improbable by rationalists and those committed to cause-and-effect historical inquiry. The latter can, nevertheless, find meaning in the narrative in terms of God's gracious initiative of the events of Jesus' life.

The magi have spawned extensive traditions (Powell, 131–84). They have been turned into kings, numbered (three? twelve?), named (in the sixth century), celebrated in festivals (thirteen days after Jesus' birth: Augustine), and paid homage in a Middle Ages cult of relics and devotion that was opposed by the Reformers. Their gifts have been interpreted christologically (gold for kingship, frankincense for high priesthood or divinity, myrrh for humanness or death) or as denoting discipleship qualities (variously, prayer, faith, good works, reason, mercy, etc.).

The Text in Contemporary Discussion

Often read around the Christmas season, this rich text counters popular sentimentality and materialism with a profound theological claim ("God is with us"), a christological revelation of Jesus as agent of God's saving presence, examples of faithful discipleship (Joseph, the magi), and a warning that empires always strike back, resisting to death divine efforts for a transformed world (Herod).

Matthew 3:1—4:16: Witnessed to by John and the Scriptures, Tempted by the Devil

The Text in Its Ancient Context

Chapters 1–2 have introduced Jesus and his mission as agent of God's saving presence (1:21-23). He is initiated and commissioned by God, interpreted by (as he interprets) the Scriptures, opposed by Herod, ignored by the Jerusalem leaders, attested to by a star and the gentile magi, and protected by Joseph. This section continues to prepare for his public ministry (Carter 2000, 90–116).

In 3:1-12, John the Baptizer appears, a popular prophet, like others in the first-century Judean context (Taylor). His mission is to purify people in preparation for God's coming reign and the agent of that reign. Isaiah 40:3, originally a reference echoing the exodus to describe God's saving the Babylonian exiles, is reinterpreted to sanction John's work. Perceiving life in Rome's empire to be inconsonant with God's empire/kingdom, John demands repentance (3:2), expressed, at least initially, in the cleansing sign-action of baptism (3:6).

His ministry, oriented to God's empire, is opposed by Pharisees and Sadducees. The phrase "coming for baptism" is much more adequately translated "coming against baptism." The exchange is ugly, with John's harsh rebuke and threat of divine judgment (3:7-10). These groups, with the chief priests and scribes (2:4), constitute the religious-societal leaders who, as allies and retainers of Rome, embody a societal vision and practices that Jesus contests throughout. Their presence may reflect post-70-CE debates over societal practices such as observance of the Sabbath, food purity, and interactions with gentiles. The scene ends with John witnessing to Jesus as the dispenser of the Spirit and eschatological judge (Murphy). The Gospel emphasizes the latter role, with Jesus as the agent of God's judgment of a world ruled by Rome, which is allied with the Jerusalem leaders (e.g., 25:31-46).

In 3:13-17, Jesus appears as an adult. His baptism by John is presented as a revelatory occasion with the "heavens opened" (compare Ezek. 1:1-2), the Spirit descending on him, and God speaking (which happens again in 17:5). God endorses Jesus as God's agent or beloved Son, empowered and sanctioned to carry out the mission of manifesting God's saving presence (1:21-23). For first-century readers, the language of "son" employs Hebrew Bible language denoting God's people (Hos. 11:1) and kings (Ps. 2:7) as representatives or agents of God's will. It does not yet bear the high christological meanings that will develop in subsequent centuries.

As God's agent/son, Jesus demonstrates loyalty to God by resisting the devil (4:1-11). Numerous Jewish traditions attest the devil as tempter. The central issue concerns whether Jesus will remain faithful to his identity as God's son/agent (3:17; 4:3, 6), or whether he will be directed by the devil. Even when the temptation has a noble end—turning stones into bread—the issue remains one of authorization. The third temptation positions the devil as the power in control of Rome's empire. Though not the Gospel's only statement about the empire, it is nevertheless an important perspective for Jesus-followers who live in the Roman Empire. While the empire claims to be chosen by the gods (as Jupiter) to manifest their blessings and worldwide rule, this temptation scene "reveals" that the actual power "behind the throne" is the devil. Jesus-followers are cautioned to be careful in ascribing absolute power to the empire.

Witnessed to by John, sanctioned by God, tempted by the devil, Jesus is now interpreted and legitimated by the Scriptures (4:12-16). Prompted by John's arrest (unelaborated until 14:1-12), Jesus withdraws to Galilee and Capernaum in Zebulon and Naphtali. These regions, bearing the names of two Israelite tribes, were land allocations in the promised land (Josh. 19:10-16, 32-39). Jesus thus withdraws to territory that the tradition attests God had given and over which God should have sovereignty. Now Galilee is "of the Gentiles" (4:15). The genitive case indicates possession and suggests translations such as "Galilee under the Gentiles" or "Galilee possessed by the Gentiles." The gentiles are Rome, whose world is described as "darkness" and "death." The citation from Isa. 9:1-2 referred, in the eighth century, to Assyrian domination. Matthew reads it in relation to Roman control and deliverance ("light") in Jesus, the eschatological judge.

The Text in the Interpretive Tradition

Two of the scenes, Jesus' baptism and his temptation, have presented interpreters with significant challenges (Luz 2007, 133–60). Mark's Gospel narrates Jesus' baptism as a revelatory event without explanation or rationale. Matthew's addition of the dispute between John and Jesus over who should baptize whom (3:14-15) reflects concern or embarrassment among Jesus' followers over Jesus' submission to John, and the implication of Jesus' need for forgiveness. Matthew's solution is to present the event as enacting the divine will and saving action ("fulfill all righteousness"). Subsequent interpreters found the scene difficult for high Christologies, rejecting notions that Jesus the eternal Son was adopted as God's Son at baptism or that the fully incarnated eternal Logos was somehow devoid of the Spirit until baptism. Others, like Calvin, saw the scene witnessing to the triune God with Father, Son, and Spirit acting in concert, with the revelation of Jesus' Sonship not for his benefit but as a public witness. The problem of course is that Matthew presents the revelation of the Spirit's presence as something Jesus alone sees (3:16) even while recasting the heavenly voice. Mark's private word to Jesus ("You are my Son, the Beloved," Mark 1:11) becomes in Matthew a public announcement ("this is my Son, the Beloved").

Interpreters have, predictably, connected the scene with the ecclesial practice of baptism. Ignatius saw Jesus purifying water. Augustine celebrated the connection of water and word. In Eastern traditions, epiphany became the occasion for baptisms. Interestingly, the New Testament writers do not make the argument that believers should imitate Jesus in being baptized. Some have seen this absence as indicating, using the criterion of dissimilarity, the historicity of Jesus' baptism. (The criterion of dissimilarity has been used by scholars questing for the historical Jesus; it states in its classic form that if an action or saying is dissimilar to Jewish culture and to early church practice or teaching, the saying or action probably derives from Jesus.)

The Text in Contemporary Discussion

The scenes in this section can be difficult for contemporary readers looking for ready guidance for daily living. John the Baptist can seem to us to be something of a caricature: weird and remote, involving anger issues, bad wardrobe, and an obsession with judgment. Clearly Matthew's presentation takes him very seriously. The temptation scene with the devil is also difficult for some readers, many of whom have not found quoting Bible verses to be an effective strategy for countering temptations.

A more useful reading strategy might be found in understanding the scene's roles in the unfolding narrative of the Gospel. Each scene underscores aspects of Jesus' mission and identity in preparation for his public ministry, which begins in 4:17.

Part 2: Jesus' Public Ministry Begins (Matthew 4:17—11:1)

A new section begins with the transitional statement that "from that time, Jesus began to preach . . ." (4:17). In this section Jesus commences his public ministry (Carter 2000, 119-27).

Matthew 4:17—5:48: God's Empire Displayed in Jesus' Actions and Teaching

The Text in Its Ancient Context

Jesus declares that "the kingdom/empire of the heavens has come near" (4:17, author's translation; cf. 3:2). The term "kingdom/empire" is also used to denote Rome's rule. Jewish traditions used the image of rule to celebrate God delivering God's people (Psalms 47; 72). Here it expresses Jesus' commission to manifest God's saving presence (1:21-23). This reign originates in God's domain, heaven (cf. 6:10); the verb "come near" tensively holds together nearness and arrival.

The following two scenes illustrate the disruptive and restorative impact of God's rule/empire. In 4:18-22, it overturns the lives of four fishermen embedded in the empire's socioeconomic structures of a fishing economy, providing new allegiance, mission, and community (Hanson and Oakman, 106–10). Then Jesus heals numerous sick people (4:23-25). The sick embody the damage of imperial structures, especially elite control on food supply whereby the powerful few ate well while many struggled for regular adequate nutrition, resulting in diseases of deficiency and contagion. God's reign, manifested in Jesus' healings, restores wholeness and anticipates the physical wholeness of the eschaton.

Having enacted God's grace in calling disciples, Jesus instructs them (5:1-2) in the Sermon on the Mount (chs. 5–7; Betz; Patte). The sermon's placement after their call is decisive for its interpretation as an identity-forming, practice-shaping discourse. God's empire (5:3, 10, 19-20; 6:10, 33; 7:21) provides the central image of this first of five major teaching blocks (chs. 5–7; 10; 13; 18; 24–25). Its setting on an unidentified mountain evokes God's giving of the Decalogue to Moses on Mt. Sinai. Other traditions anticipated the establishment of God's reign over all nations at Mt. Zion (Isa. 2:3).

The sermon opens with nine beatitudes or blessings (5:3-12). Beatitudes were common in Greco-Roman writings and in Jewish wisdom and apocalyptic texts. They are not concerned with individual feelings and emotions. The inaccurate translation "Happy are" makes these declarations into the "Be-Happy attitudes." Rather, they announce God's favor on certain situations and actions (see Ps. 1:1-2), both present and future, when God reverses and transforms current injustice (Hanson). They reassure people experiencing distress that God's favor is with them.

They also function to exhort human actions consistent with God's favor. They thereby identify actions characteristic of the community of disciples. These situations (being poor) and practices (being merciful) are commonly not those valued by the Roman elite. Hence a countercultural quality to the community of disciples contests and challenges the status quo.

The first four beatitudes (5:3-6), shaped by Isa. 61:1-3, name situations of oppression and distress in which God's just and transforming favor is already manifested in Jesus' ministry, in anticipation of the future transformation in the eschatological completion of God's purposes. Specifically, these four beatitudes identify God's transformation of the destructive sociopolitical, economic, and religious consequences of Roman rule. The "poor in spirit" are not to be spiritualized. They are the literal poor whose material poverty has crushed their very being (e.g., 4:23-25). They mourn their desperate circumstances. The meek are not what contemporary culture would consider "wimps," but are, in Jesus' citation of Ps. 37:11, 22, 29, the powerless poor who trust God to deliver them from "the wicked" (elite control) by inheriting the basic resource of land. They hunger for justice, transformed societal structures, and access to life-giving resources. They will not be disappointed at the completion of God's purposes.

The second group of five beatitudes (5:7-12) moves from God's reversal of these circumstances to human actions that enact God's purposes. Acts of mercy, integrity of action and worship (evoking

Ps. 24:4), peacemaking and nonviolent dissent from Roman rule, and enduring the backlash result in divine approval and participation in God's good reign (line two of each beatitude).

Two further images of discipleship follow, in 5:13-16. Salt flavors, purifies, transforms. Light, used in 4:15-16 to describe Jesus' manifesting God's saving presence and reign, now describes the continuing lifestyle and mission of the community of disciples.

Six further examples of the actions of "exceeding justice/righteousness" that God's empire shapes follow in 5:17-48. Verses 17-20 indicate that these examples are consistent with and do not abolish "the law and the prophets." Accordingly, the six scenes in 5:21-48 are not antitheses, where Jesus quotes from the biblical tradition and then abolishes it. Rather, he quotes the passage and interprets it. He instructs disciples to be a reconciled community (5:21-26), to curb male lust and power concerning adultery and divorce in a patriarchal society (5:27-32), to speak trustworthy words (5:33-37), to employ active, nonviolent resistance to evil (5:38-42; Wink), and to love neighbors and enemies (5:43-48).

The Text in the Interpretive Tradition

Debates about the sermon's meaning have been extensive (Luz 2007, 161–294). Does it offer an impossible ideal, thereby provoking repentance? Is it an interim demand until the kingdom comes in full? Or does it shape discipleship, as Anabaptist traditions, for example, have argued? Particular scenes have caused much controversy especially in relation to other parts of the Gospel. For example, how does the prohibition of divorce cohere with the mercy of new relationships (5:7; 9:13; 12:7)? How does the scathing attack on Jewish leaders in chapter 23 display love for enemies?

The Text in Contemporary Discussion

This rich sequence challenges contemporary readers to careful reading, informed reflection, and communal action. If the sermon is practicable, how are contemporary Jesus-followers to live the practices shaped by the identity of being salt and light, of the Beatitudes, or of the examples in 5:21-48? For example, the renouncing of violence in 5:38-42 and urging of love for enemies in 5:43-48 offer the church a practice that is out-of-step with the aggressive assertion of personal will and military power typical of our world. To embody this teaching requires both a firm witness to this alternative, nonviolent practice matched by pragmatic efforts for justice that remove occasions for violence.

Matthew 6:1—7:29: Jesus Continues Teaching on the Mountain

The Text in Its Ancient Context

The sermon continues in these two rich chapters (Carter 2000, 158–95; 2007, 8–35). The first section (6:1-18) assumes three conventional Jewish acts of "justice" (misleadingly translated in verse 1 as "piety").

Verse 1 establishes the basic principle. Disciples live for God's approval, not public approval. First-century values of honor and shame required public displays of beneficence by wealthy elite members (funding food distributions, buildings, festivals). These "honorable" actions enhanced power and societal status. Disciples do not imitate this value system.

The first act of justice concerns almsgiving or acts of mercy (the root meaning of the Greek word; 6:2-4; cf. 5:7). Almsgiving was a normal part of Jewish faithfulness (Prov. 25:21-22). The negative example of blowing a trumpet is a caricature (6:2). The polemical tone may suggest strained relationships with synagogues. The "how-to-do-it" of 6:3-4 presents acts of mercy as normative and uncalculated in enacting God's redistributive justice through providing resources for all.

The second act of justice concerns prayer (6:5-15). Matthew 6:5-6 contrasts prayer with the false practice of public performance; 6:7-15 contrasts prayer with a false theology comprising unknowing, uncaring, and vain gods, manipulated by repetition and verbosity. Many gentiles would rightly protest this polemical caricature. Disciples, by contrast, engage God as a knowing and caring Father (6:8; Sheffield) and align themselves with God's purposes for the world.

The Lord's Prayer sets out these purposes (6:9-13). The first petition, hallowing or sanctifying God's name, concerns God's saving will (Lev. 22:31-32; Ezek. 36:22-38). The parallel petition, "Your kingdom/empire come," similarly asks God to accomplish God's life-giving and just reign in Rome's world. Jesus enacts this mission (4:17), as do disciples (10:7-8). This is the doing of God's will, which shapes "earth" in accord with God's domain, heaven (6:10).

The fourth petition requests God's provision of food that is "necessary for existence" (the difficult word translated "daily"). God's forgiveness requires forgiveness of others (6:12, 14-15). The "testing" petition of 6:13 concerns perhaps general temptation, or deliverance from eschatological woes, or God's overcoming of all evil in transforming the world.

The third act of justice concerns fasting (6:16-18). How is divine, not societal, approval gained through fasting? Isaiah 58 emphasizes that fasting participates in the struggle against societal injustice by doing God's will.

The second major section (6:19-34) concerns justice and materialism. Previously, the destructive impact of Rome's empire has been evident on the poor, who are deprived of access to adequate resources (5:3-6). And disciples have been instructed to do economic justice in the three acts of 6:1-18. Now they are warned against pursuit of and distraction by material things (6:19-21), exhorted to focus on God's empire (6:22-23), alerted to the incompatibility of serving God and wealth (6:24), and urged to rely on God's provision of daily necessities (6:25-34).

The third section highlights three characteristics of discipleship. Disciples are to embody compassionate correction, not condemnation (7:1-6), persistent prayer (7:7-11), and indiscriminate love for all as the key interpretation of the biblical tradition (7:12). This "golden rule" exists in both positive and negative forms in various ancient cultures.

The fourth section (7:13-27) contextualizes discipleship in God's future. This eschatological goal provides incentive (reward/inclusion, not punishment/exclusion) and perspective on the present. So 7:13-14 adapts the common "two ways" metaphor (Deut. 30:15-20) to underscore the countercultural way of discipleship. Verses 15-23 warn against false prophets, urge attention to their lifestyle, and provide assurance of their final condemnation. And verses 24-27 contrast two responses to (doing/not doing) and two eschatological consequences (of vindication/condemnation) Jesus' teaching. Verses 28-29 note the crowds' positive responses (cf. 5:1-2) and contrast Jesus' teaching with that of the scribes.

The Text in the Interpretive Tradition

The interpretive traditions concerning this material are extensive (Luz 2007, 295–397). The Lord's Prayer has been used in personal piety (the *Didache* instructs its use three times a day), communal worship, and teaching, both as a summary of doctrine in catechesis and for ethical instruction. Interpretive questions have explored whether the prayer is answered by God's actions alone, or through the actions of disciples, or a partnership of both. Is the prayer answered in the present or in the eschatological future, when God's purposes are finally established?

The passage on trusting God to provide (6:19-34) has posed substantial difficulties. Many in the Matthean world knew degrees of poverty, and hence God's lack of provision, a situation repeated throughout history. The passage has seemed simplistic and naive. Others have found it to exhort laziness, at odds with the apostolic command to work (2 Thess. 3:8-12). Yet others, some hermits, have interpreted it literally—giving away possessions, not working, and not providing for the future. Some have spiritualized it to say that God meets spiritual needs. Others have interpreted it to permit possessions, but focus on their use in almsgiving. Others have read it as forbidding worry about earthly matters but legitimating concern over heavenly matters. Verse 34 has been central for some in pointing to a way of life focused on God's kingdom/empire, a way that is an alternative to seeking security in things, careers, and cultural conformity.

The Text in Contemporary Discussion

Contemporary interpreters interact with this text in a number of productive and often difficult ways. Attention to economic justice, for example, is pressing in a global village where many lack adequate resources. For rich Christians, the petition for daily bread (6:11), for example, recognizes this lack because of human greed, misuse of power, and unjust access to and distribution of resources. The petition, then, counters greed and incessant questing for "more stuff." It requires appropriate actions of redistribution and disinvestment. Along similar lines, we can note the use of debt forgiveness as a strategy of international justice.

Some have experienced "dis-ease" with the eschatological judgment of 7:13-27. Matthew regularly ends teaching blocks with eschatological threats and rewards. For some, this "bullying" tactic imitates the strategy of the empire and stands at odds with the Gospel vision of God's indiscriminate love (5:45).

Matthew 8:1—9:38: God's Empire Displayed in Jesus' Actions

The Text in Its Ancient Context

After three chapters of teaching, chapters 8–9 present Jesus' actions (Carter 2000, 196–231). Miracles dominate with six healings—leprosy (8:1-4), paralysis (2×; 8:5-13; 9:2-8), fever (8:14-15), hemorrhage (9:20-22), blindness (9:27-31)—two exorcisms (8:28-34; 9:32-34), a rescue-epiphany (8:23-27), and a raising from the dead (9:18-26). Two summary passages (8:16; 9:35-36) indicate widespread preaching, healing, and exorcism (Wainwright). There are also dialogue scenes about discipleship—faith (8:9-12), the cost of following (8:18-22), calling (9:9), eating with the marginalized (9:10-13), and not fasting (9:14-17). A well-established tradition of itinerant teachers and miracle workers exists from the ancient world (Meier, 509–1038).

Five perspectives on Jesus' actions emerge.

1. His actions express God's empire (8:11-12; 9:35). They enact his commission to manifest God's saving presence (1:21-23), elaborating the initial presentation of the impact of God's reign in 4:17-25 (proclamation, calling disciples, healing, exorcism). The Scripture citation of 8:17 confirms he does the divine will.

2. Three statements declare Jesus' purposes and motivation. In 9:13, citing Hos. 6:6, his actions perform mercy. In 9:16-17, his actions mean interactions between the old and the new. In 9:36, he enacts compassion for harassed and afflicted people.

3. These displays of the transforming power and wholeness that God's empire effects interfere with and repair Rome's world. A centurion cannot heal his servant (8:5-13). And the demon-possessed empire, depicted by demons named after the central unit of the Roman army, the "Legion," faces inevitable destruction: the boar was the mascot of the tenth Fretensis legion, which played a key role in Jerusalem's defeat in 70 CE (8:28-34). The destruction of the demon-controlled pigs in the sea depicts God's sovereignty and portends Rome's eventual destruction.

4. Elites oppose Jesus. Town leaders ask him to leave (8:34). Scribes (retainers) deny that his ministry enacts God's authority (9:3). Pharisees question his association with "tax collectors and sinners" (9:11) and declare he is the devil's agent, not God's (9:34). Jesus echoes the indictment of Israel's leaders in Ezekiel 34 for failing to provide for the poor and weak. He laments that the Rome-allied Jerusalem leaders oppress, rather than provide for, the people (9:36).

5. By contrast, the marginalized and broken receive Jesus' ministry positively in being healed and exorcized.

Miracle stories dominate the chapter. The prevalence of the sick and demon-possessed is not surprising, given a context of disease-promoting social conditions such as urban and rural squalor, poor water supply, limited medical knowledge, poor nutrition, diseases of deficiency and contagion, overwork, and tough daily living conditions. The miracle scenes often follow a predictable fourfold form. An introduction assembles participants (Jesus, crowd, distressed person) and narrates a respectful request for Jesus' help. Verbal exchanges often elaborate the distress or involve conflict. The miracle takes place, involving touch or word, distance, and a report or demonstration. The scene's conclusion can involve wonder, dismissal, an alternative explanation, secrecy, or spreading the news.

Miracle stories function to demonstrate God's power in a Roman world in which inhabitants experienced the powers of numerous gods and goddesses. They also manifest compassion in a context in which many understood ailments to result from sin, the devil and demons, angry gods, and hostile people. God's empire rules over all forces in compassionate and transformative ways. The emphasis on somatic wholeness anticipates the final transformation effected by God's reign (11:2-6). In the meantime, healings and exorcisms enact the blessing of God's empire on the poor (5:3), transforming destructive economic circumstances (no work, poverty), social isolation, political oppression, and religious marginalization.

The Text in the Interpretive Tradition

Interpretive questions have commonly centered on the nature of miracles (Luz 2001, 1–65). While some readers have readily accepted the stories as accurate accounts of actual events, numerous others have not done so. The latter have adopted various interpretive strategies. Rationalists have looked for natural explanations of events. Others have declared all life to be miraculous, but failed to account for the distinctiveness of miracles. A dominant line has spiritualized the scenes, overlooking the physical or social in favor of spiritual lessons. So Augustine saw in 8:1-5 a man freed from "spiritual leprosy" or the mortal sin of not observing the Sermon on the Mount. The centurion of 8:5-13 exhibits true humility and faith (Chrysostom). For Luther and other Protestant Reformers, the physical healing of the paralyzed man (9:2-8) recedes before the word of forgiving grace understood in antithesis to legalism and works. The raising of the dead daughter (9:18-26) anticipates Jesus' resurrection. On the basis of Romans 11:25-32, she and the hemorrhaging woman have represented the inclusion of both gentiles and Jews in salvation history.

A similar symbolizing strategy has been used for the storm scene in 8:23-27 (Bornkamm). Since Tertullian, this story has been read as depicting the church tossed about by various crises but assured of Jesus' protective presence. Another line of interpretation comprises an individualistic reading with the boat as the human heart that Jesus enters.

The Text in Contemporary Discussion

Miracle stories remain contentious in contemporary faith communities. Those who read them literally and/or claim contemporary miracles face the challenge of explaining their relative dearth in contemporary society. Hospitals remain full, and most dead people remain so. Those who reject the narrated events and experiences as actual events, but nevertheless find "spiritual" significance in the scenes, face the challenge of explaining why God's healing or liberative action might be experienced spiritually but not materially or somatically. In a faith tradition that affirms the importance of the material and somatic from the perspectives of both creation and incarnation, this ready dismissal of the somatic requires examination.

The emerging discipline of disability studies seeks, among other things, to honor the suffering and physical challenges of people, past and present, whom the Gospel often presents as "photo ops" for the larger christological and theological agenda. This approach, along with imperial-critical studies that locate the Gospel's numerous sick and demon-possessed in a context of imperial power, at least moves attention to responses of compassion and justice (9:13). Jesus' description of his imperial world as "harassed and helpless" by illegitimate leaders and structures (9:36) points similarly toward transformative actions.

Matthew 10:1—11:1: Mission Work for Disciples

The Text in Its Ancient Context

Jesus has manifested his God-given commission to disclose God's saving presence in calling and teaching disciples (chs. 5–7) and in various, especially miraculous, actions (chs. 8–9). In chapter

10, the mission discourse, Jesus elaborates for disciples their call to mission from 4:19 ("fish for people") and 5:13-16 (salt, light). The ancient world knew numerous individuals and nations who were on missions. Israel was to be God's light to the nations (Isa. 49:6). Zeus sends itinerant Cynic teachers (Epictetus, *Diatr.* 3.22.19–26). The poet Virgil presents Jupiter giving "empire without end" to Rome to be "lords of the world" (*Aen.* 1.254–82) and to "crown peace with justice, to spare the vanquished, and to crush the proud" (*Aen.* 6.851–53).

The disciples' mission continues Jesus' manifestation of God's empire (Carter 2000, 232–46). So in 10:1-4, Jesus calls a community of twelve "apostles" (the only use of "apostle" in Matthew). Peter is named first. Jesus commissions them to continue his mission of repairing imperial damage through proclamation, exorcism, and healing (10:1, 7-8). The community is apostolic in being "sent out" in mission (10:2).

The second section (10:5-15) identifies four aspects of their mission. Its arena is, at this point, Israel (10:5b-6). Its task is to continue Jesus' mission, proclaiming God's life-giving empire, and performing the transformative, miraculous actions Jesus performs in chapters 8–9 (10:7-8a). Their material support is minimal. They give without payment or profit, traveling inconspicuously, being vulnerable and sustained by recipients (10:8b-10). And the impact of the disciples' mission is both positive and negative (10:11-15).

The third section (10:16-23) underscores the challenge of God's empire to the vested interests of the powerful and of households (10:17-22). Suffering and persecution are inevitable consequences. Mission means danger. The image of sheep among wolves (10:16) picks up Jesus' "sheep" description of 9:36, which evoked Ezek. 34:5, 10, where the people are food for "wild beasts," consumed by their rapacious leaders (Matt. 10:17-18). Faithful endurance, sustained by "the Spirit of your Father," is required (10:20-22) until the son of man returns (10:23).

The fourth section identifies the courage, impact, and reward of faithful mission (10:24-42). As Jesus was resisted, so are disciples (10:24-31). But disciples can "fear not" (10:26, 28, 31) because God rules the future (10:28, 32) and the present (10:29-31). The mission's exclusive loyalty to Jesus disrupts households (10:34-39). Yet some will be receptive and vindicated in the judgment (10:40-42).

This mission discourse underscores key features of the community of disciples. As a mission community commanded by Jesus, it imitates and continues his mission. Disciples do so in poverty, single-mindedness, itinerancy, vulnerability, and interdependence. They engage society, neither fleeing from it nor accepting imperial society as normative. Mission comprises transformative practices of proclamation, healing, and exorcisms. It is not a sporadic or optional activity but is central to the community's identity and practice. It requires courage, hope, and conviction about its life-and-death importance in the face of resistance and persecution. The existence of persecution highlights its contestive and conflictual nature.

The Text in the Interpretive Tradition

This chapter has provoked numerous debates as interpreters have read it in circumstances that differ greatly from its original context concerning itinerant preachers (Luz 2001, 66–128).

In the Reformation and Counter-Reformation, for example, Catholics understood the placement of Peter first in the list of apostles (10:2) as an indication of his superior qualities or merits, and thus found support for the primacy of the papacy. Protestant interpreters have maintained the view (drawing on Chrysostom, from the fourth century) that the placement reflects only Peter's call as the first disciple (4:18-22) and says nothing about his merits or authority.

The restriction of the mission to Israel (10:5-6) stands in contradiction to the Gospel's final command to "Go therefore and make disciples of all nations" (28:19). Some have explained the difference by arguing that 10:5-6 originated from the historical Jesus (pre-Easter) while 28:19 originated from an early believing community some time after Jesus' resurrection (a post-Easter community). Others have seen a reflection of a struggle in the Matthean community between Jewish members favoring mission to Israel, and a growing gentile presence supporting gentile mission. The inclusion of both statements reconciles and endorses both missions. Others have seen the verses reflecting not a community struggle but a succession in the narrative. That is, there is a narrative movement from an initial mission to Israel, in chapter 10, that is subsequently expanded, after the resurrection in chapter 28, into the wider world.

The very difficult instruction in 10:9-10 concerning mission, marked by poverty and defenselessness and unencumbered by money, bag, spare tunic, sandals, or staff has received various interpretations. Some have obeyed it literally. According to one source, St. Francis of Assisi is said to have thrown away his shoes after reading these verses. There is also a long tradition that avoids a literal reading and diminishes the severity of the demands by using the verses in polemic against opponents, especially against their (presumed) pride and greed. The verses also appear in debates over whether clergy should be paid, and if so, how much. Luther supported some modest payment; Calvin disagreed.

The chapter underscores frequent rejection of the mission, hostility to it, and division of households over it. How are disciples to respond? Clearly they are to endure (10:22), even embracing martyrdom (10:28). But how are they to treat hostile and hurtful responders? How are the actions of social (10:14) and eschatological (10:32) reprisals consistent with the demand of love for enemies (5:44)?

The Text in Contemporary Discussion

The assertion of the church's identity and practice as a mission community challenges all images and practices of contemporary mainline and emerging churches (Luz 1994, 39–55). At least since the Reformation, the marks of the one, holy, apostolic, and catholic church have comprised word (preaching) and sacrament (baptism, Eucharist). But here the marks of the church comprise mission, powerlessness, vulnerability, poverty, suffering. For Matthew, the church is about actions consistent with the mission and qualities of Jesus. The chapter points churches in this direction. In societies where creature comforts, wealth, security, power, and status are so important, this chapter offers the massive challenge for churches to be always moving obediently to embrace active, countercultural mission for others.

Part 3: Responses to Jesus' Ministry (Matthew 11:2—16:20)

Chapter 11 begins the Gospel's third section (11:2—16:20), which narrates a growing division of responses to Jesus' ministry (11:1; Carter 2000, 249–79). The section is bookended with two scenes that pose the question of Jesus' identity (11:3; 16:13). Increasing opposition emerges from scribes and Pharisees (12:2, 14, 24, 38). Along with the issue of Jesus' identity is that of his societal vision and claim to reveal God's will. The section has been understood to reflect a post-70 context of conflict between Jesus-followers and other synagogue members.

Matthew 11:2—12:50: Discerning and Responding to Jesus' Mission and Identity

The Text in Its Ancient Context

The opening scene provides both the central question and the means of answering it (11:2-6). Jesus responds to John's disciples by summarizing his activity from chapters 8–9 and evoking visions from Isaiah of a society shaped by God's life-giving reign/empire (Isa. 26:19; 29:18-19; 35:5-6; 42:7; 61:1). Jesus favors the marginalized, repairs elite-inflicted damage, and creates new social participation. Those who perceive his identity and activity as manifesting God's saving presence and empire are blessed (11:6).

In 11:7-15, Jesus asks the crowds six rapid-fire questions about John. The point is that understanding John's mission (3:1-12) prepares one, through repentance and understanding, to receive Jesus. Negative responses, however, dominate, with John misunderstood as demonic (11:18) and Jesus rejected as not God's faithful or wise son (11:19; Deutsch). Jesus curses the unrepentant Galilean towns of Chorazin and Bethsaida, which cannot see the significance of Jesus' actions (11:20-24).

Yet some receive his revelation. Verses 25-27 affirm his identity and role as revealer of God based in intimate relationship of Father and Son. They also affirm, despite 11:20-24, that the "infants" or lowly, the weary and burdened, accept his yoke (God's reign rather than Rome's) and find "rest" (11:28-30; Carter 2001, 108–29). By contrast, the subsequent narrative shows the "wise and intelligent" (powerful leaders and elite) not receiving him.

Chapter 12 opens with rejection. Two scenes concern whether procuring food and healing are acceptable Sabbath practices. Pharisees, retainers in the imperial system with a societal vision extending temple practice to everyday life, protest. The issue is not whether one party observes Sabbath or not, but *how* Sabbath is honored—by mercy (12:7) and doing good (12:12), or by rest, as God did? Anticipating Jesus' passion, they plan to kill him (12:14).

More responses concerning the authority and origin of Jesus' ministry follow. Matthew now applies Isa. 42:1-4, a text originally declaring Israel as God's servant and light to the nations in the midst of the Babylonian Empire, to Jesus' activity in Rome's empire (12:15-21). An exorcism/healing produces three verdicts: from the crowds (Son of David, 12:23), the Pharisees (the devil, 12:24), and Jesus (12:25-37). Scribes and Pharisees demand a sign despite Jesus' previous actions

(12:38-42). Jesus identifies these leaders as an "evil generation." The chapter ends with Jesus identifying true followers, or "family," as those who do God's will, which he reveals.

The Text in the Interpretive Tradition

Among the interpretive challenges of these chapters (Luz 2001, 129–227), one has concerned the "violence" statement in 11:12. Challenges in translating this verse have produced different meanings. One understanding is that the kingdom is aggressively (violently) breaking in and people readily seize it. Another reading sees violence inflicted on the kingdom as people aggressively embrace its proclamation. A variation of this reading sees gentile believers stealing the kingdom from Israel. Both readings, though, are unsatisfactory, because the verb and noun denoting violence and the violent usually have negative associations.

Another reading sees the kingdom suffering because violent people like Zealots blasphemously co-opt it and force God's hand. This reading, though, ignores the saying's context in chapter 11. A more convincing, fourth reading understands the language and the context to refer to opponents of John, Jesus, and disciples as agents of the kingdom (3:2; 4:17; 10:7-8). Opponents include synagogues, governors, kings (Herod), leaders, and households (10:17-18, 21, 34-36; 12:14).

Matthew 11:27 featured in the fourth-century Arian christological controversy. Arians understood the claim that God had "handed over" all things to the Son to indicate a time when "all things" had not been delivered to him, thereby denying the eternal divinity of the Son. The orthodox either dismissed the reading, thereby preserving a trinitarian understanding, or with Athanasius, saw the handing over as the moment when the eternal Logos became incarnate in the human Christ. Others, notably nineteenth-century Protestant exegetes, abandoned any trinitarian framework to focus on the historical Jesus' special insight into or consciousness of God's plan of salvation.

In 12:32, Jesus declares speaking against the Holy Spirit unforgivable. Interpreters have suggested three explanations for what this speaking consists of. Some see it as denying the divinity of Christ. Others see it as sins committed by Christians despite good knowledge of God's will. And others, such as Augustine, understand it as resisting the unity of church, an especially useful interpretation for denouncing heretics.

The Text in Contemporary Discussion

A concern with unforgivable sin remains ongoing among some people. Concern over whether one has committed the unforgivable sin usually indicates one has not. In Matthew's context, its primary sense seems to involve a sustained refusal to see the Spirit at work in Jesus in manifesting God's saving presence and empire (3:16-17).

While conflict between Jesus and the leaders increases in the narrative, Christian readers must be careful not to perpetuate anti-Jewish sentiments and practices in interpretations. Jesus' association of the resisting leaders with demons in 12:43-45 is one such instance. Related to this matter is the understanding that all leaders in the Gospel (Pharisees, priests) are not accurately identified as "religious" leaders akin to contemporary clergy. Rather, they are societal leaders. Their conflicts with Jesus do not involve merely "religious" questions but matters of societal visions and practices.

The Sabbath controversies raise questions about Sunday observance among contemporary believers. In an age of shopping, sports, entertainment, family events, and seven-days-a-week work, in what sense is the day "honored"?

Matthew 13:1-58: Explaining Different Responses to Jesus

The Text in Its Ancient Context

Chapter 13 comprises seven parables as Jesus addresses alternatively disciples and crowds (Carter 2001, 280–300). Parables were a familiar form in the Hebrew Bible (2 Sam. 12:1-4: the ewe lamb; Ezek. 17:2-21), rabbinic literature, and collections such as Aesop's fables. The word *parable* literally means to "throw something alongside," indicating a comparison in which one thing—God's empire—is compared to the situation of the subsequent, short narrative.

The parables in chapter 13 interpret the division increasingly evident in responses to Jesus in chapters 11–12. While some people discern Jesus' identity as the agent of God's saving presence and empire, others—especially powerful leaders—do not. The parables explain why this division occurs. The lack of receptivity derives not from failure on God's part but from human sinfulness and the devil's activity. The parables also affirm the Gospel audience's welcoming response and further illumine God's empire.

The opening section features the parable of the seed and soils and an allegorical explanation (13:1-23). The sower is compared to Jesus proclaiming God's empire (the seed). Three-quarters of the seed falls on unproductive ground and produces nothing because of the evil one (13:19), opposition (13:21), and the "cares of the world and the lure of wealth" (13:22). These three factors explain in part the dominant negative response to Jesus' ministry. Only a quarter of the seed finds receptive people (13:23).

The second section (13:24-43) comprises three parables. The parable of the weeds and wheat, interpreted allegorically in 13:36-43, depicts God's empire coexisting in Jesus' ministry with evil/the devil (and the devil's agents). Disruptive weeds, sown by the devil, grow together until the final harvest/divine victory.

The parable offers another reason that some/many do not respond positively. They fail to recognize a "now but not yet" dynamic. God's empire is present in part but not yet fully.

The mustard seed (13:31-32) offers a further explanation, namely, the strange and mysterious nature of the reign's present manifestation. The mustard seed denotes invisibility (is anything happening under the ground?), contrast (small seed, big shrub), continuity or inevitability (the seed becomes a shrub), and growth (it takes time). These features describe the present state yet also the future goal of God's work, explaining why some/many fail to see it, but assuring disciples of God's work.

A third parable repeats these factors (13:33). God's reign, like yeast or leaven, works over time, in a hidden manner, yet its transforming work continues inexorably.

A further section (13:44-50) presents three final parables. In the parable of hidden treasure, the focus moves from a contrast of small beginnings and cosmic completion to a person's encounter with the empire. Searching, joy, setting aside all else, commitment, and disruption of priorities mark the encounter, and confirm its great value. The pearl offers a similar experience. The repetition underscores the point (13:45-46). The parable of the fishnet rehearses emphases from the weeds and the wheat. Evil coexists with God's empire, as do negative and positive responses until the final division and God's triumph (13:47-48).

The chapter ends with a rejection scene (13:54-58). People in Jesus' hometown wonder about his teachings, actions, and origin, but cannot recognize God's commission. The scene enacts the rejection that the parables explain.

The Text in the Interpretive Tradition

One theme that emerges in the diverse and multivalent interpretations of the parables concerns how God works in the church and world (Luz 2001, 228–304). Some interpreters of the sower/seed/soil parable, for example, emphasized the quality of the soil in exhorting lives receptive to the gospel. Others, such as Luther in the Reformation, emphasized the truth of the word sown by preachers even when it does not produce fruit, thereby encouraging disheartened preachers. Some interpretations of the mustard seed equated God's kingdom with the church in its growth to dominance, while others understood the seed as Christ or the preached word at work in an individual.

Interpreters of the wheat and weeds parable have variously understood the field or arena of God's activity to comprise an individual, the church, and the world (cf. 13:38). The weeds have been understood as specific heresy existing alongside the pure doctrine of the church, or the presence of evil coexisting with the gospel, or the presence of sinners within the church. What is to be done about them, and what is the role of church discipline? Chrysostom offers that heretics should be expelled but not killed. Others saw the parable justifying religious wars against enemies (Aquinas). Others saw it justifying patience in recognizing God's role in judgment. Others saw the parable urging a restrained and realistic use of church discipline, and recognizing the futility of expecting a perfect church. People should be wheat and produce good fruit in faithful living.

The Text in Contemporary Discussion

Current questions of what, how, and where we understand God to be active in the church and in the world are live ones. Some pieties understand God to be active in arranging all sorts of personal matters and circumstances on a daily basis. When things do not work out well, it is not a matter of divine inactivity but an opportunity to trust and learn whatever God is teaching the individual. The larger world is largely not in view.

Other pieties take a more global perspective and understand themselves to be active partners with God's life-giving and just work in the world. The challenge here often comes with the recognition that, despite much effort, injustice and human needs seem to continue unabated. This situation raises questions about both the power and the will of God. Is God uncaring and/or powerless in the face of vast human need? Why does God's reign not seem more evident? Matthew's chapter offers a range of perspectives on God's current activity, simultaneously recognizing human resistance or indifference, God's persistent and faithful activity in the midst of the world, and the certainty of God's eschatological completion.

Matthew 14:1-36: God's Empire at Work

The Text in Its Ancient Context

The emphasis on discerning Jesus' identity and God-given mission to manifest God's saving presence and reign (1:21-23; 4:17) continues in the four scenes of chapter 14 (Carter 2000, 301–13). First, God's empire arouses opposition from Rome's client ruler Herod, who was tetrarch of Galilee until 39 CE (14:1-12). Then Jesus attests the fertility and abundance of God's reign in a feeding (14:13-21). He demonstrates his identity as God's agent in walking on water (14:22-33). He exhibits the healing, restorative work of God's empire in more healings (14:34-36). That is, the divisive effect of his ministry continues. The powerful Herod rejects God's work, the crowds benefit from feeding and healing, and the disciples receive the disclosure of Jesus' identity as God's agent or son (14:33).

The Herod scene elaborates the brief references in 4:12 and 11:2 to John's arrest and imprisonment. John is arrested and executed because of his prophetic criticism of Herod's liaison with Herodias, wife of Herod's brother Philip. Given the close allying of John and Jesus in relation to God's empire (3:2; 4:17), Herod's action against John is consonant with the negative or hostile responses to God's work that are depicted in the divisions in the parables of chapter 13 (between weeds and wheat; different kinds of fish), and in the rejection of Jesus in his home town at the end of chapter 13 (13:54-58).

It is also consonant with the Gospel depiction of kings and rulers as opposing God's work—the disobedient kings of 1:6-11, Herod (ch. 2), Archelaus (2:22), persecuting governors and kings (10:18), the great men of the gentiles (20:25-26), and Pilate and his Jerusalem allies (27:11-26). The powerful elite protect their interests and societal structures against God's empire and its agents. They do so characteristically with violence, as Herod (2:16) and his sons Archelaus (2:22) and Herod Antipas (14:1-12) demonstrate. By contrast, the martyred John remains faithful (10:28).

After the extravagant and violent, elite birthday feast with its grotesque image of John's head on a platter, the next scene presents Jesus compassionately enacting God's will to feed hungry people (Isa. 58:6-7). The act echoes Moses and the exodus wilderness feeding. It also addresses the social reality that a significant proportion of the population struggled for adequate nutrition. And it anticipates the final establishment of God's reign, marked by fertility and abundant food for all (Isa. 25:6-10; Matt. 8:11; 22:1-10).

With the disciples in a boat (14:22), Jesus performs more Godlike actions. He again calms stormy seas (Exod. 14–15; Ps. 69:1-3, 30-36; cf. Matt. 8:23-27) and walks on water (Job 9:8; Ps. 77:16-20). These acts demonstrate God's control over the waters (Gen. 1:6-10) and contest an imperial tradition in which emperors claim sovereignty over land and sea. They also demonstrate God's concern for disciples battered by the storm. Peter imitates Jesus walking on the water, exhibiting both faith and unbelief, and evoking Psalm 69, a psalm of deliverance. The scene ends with the storm calmed and the disciples' confession, for the first time in the Gospel, of Jesus' identity as God's agent (14:33).

The chapter closes with another summary scene of Jesus' healings (14:34-36).

The Text in the Interpretive Tradition

The scene of Herod's execution of John has drawn attention in various ways (Luz 2001, 305–24). Numerous artists have depicted John's head on the platter. Ironically, it is Herodias's daughter (unnamed in Matthew's version) who has often received attention. Some writers, including Chrysostom and Ambrose, were drawn to yet appalled by her dancing. They dwell on her voluptuous and seductive movement but are equally sure that her dancing is sinful and/or provokes sin. A nineteenth-century tradition gives the daughter a makeover, freeing her from ecclesial condemnation in (re-)presenting her with positive sensuality, in love with John, and appalled at his execution (Oscar Wilde; Richard Strauss). Both images are, of course, fantasies created by men that focus on sexuality, while ignoring other dimensions such as the scene's murderous assertion of imperial power.

Interpretations of the feeding story have often found ways to avoid taking seriously the literal feeding of people. Some interpreters, highlighting echoes of Moses and the wilderness journeys, read it in supersessionist terms of salvation history. The five loaves represent the five books of the Torah, and the twelve baskets represent the apostles. Jesus transforms the tradition into life-giving spiritual food. Another line of interpretation, including a number of current interpreters, reads it as a eucharistic scene, noticing the similarities between the distribution of 14:18-19 and the Last Supper scene of 26:26-27. Yet another approach has extended both lines in an ecclesiological interpretation that sees the disciples as priests or pastors in mediating Christ's benefits and the Eucharist to the laity. Such readings ignore the feeding of people's bodies.

The Text in Contemporary Discussion

What does contemporary discipleship look like? This chapter offers various vignettes of discipleship shaped by God's reign. John, for example, loses his head for courageously speaking truth to power. He remains faithful to his word in the face of life-and-death opposition. His speech in the midst of evil embodies dynamics depicted in the parables of chapter 13. And his disciples display their own courage and loyalty, honoring him in burial. Jesus' disciples serve food to the people. Peter emerges from the group of disciples with an initiative that imitates Jesus in walking on the water. In responding to Jesus' command (14:28-29), he courageously and obediently trusts Jesus' word to forsake the safety of the boat and undertake a task that seems impossible. Having started well, however, his faith gives way to fear and doubt, and Peter the rock sinks like a stone. He knows enough, though, to cry out in the words of a psalm of deliverance and experiences rescue through Jesus. In turn, his experience and the calming of the storm provide the occasion for a revelation of Jesus' identity and the disciples' confession. What contemporary situations and experiences do such vignettes address, and how do they shape authentic discipleship?

Matthew 15:1—16:20: Jesus' Authority as God's Agent

The Text in Its Ancient Context

Disclosure, conflict, and confession continue (Carter 2000, 314–37). Jesus reveals his authority and identity as God's agent (15:1-20; 16:13-20). He dispenses God's wholeness and abundance to a Canaanite woman's daughter, in healings, and in another feeding (15:21-39). He conflicts with scribes, Pharisees, and Sadducees from Jerusalem (15:1; 16:1-12). Peter confesses Jesus' identity (16:13-20).

Jesus' opponents constitute an alliance of groups with some status, political power, and wealth. Sadducees, absent since 3:7, and scribes, legal agents and interpreters of traditions, have not recognized Jesus' identity (2:4; 12:38). The Pharisees participate in the ruling group centered on the Jerusalem temple and allied with chief priests and Rome's governor (15:1). They have some political power and a religious-societal vision involving table companions (9:11), Sabbath observance (12:1-14), hand-washing (15:2), and support for the temple (15:3-7). They think Jesus is an agent of the devil (9:34; 12:24) and want to kill him (12:14).

Jesus reciprocates the antagonism. He disparages their traditions as "human precepts" contrary to "the commandment" and "word of God" (15:3, 6, 9). He rebukes them for teaching that gifts to God (priests and temple) void parental support (15:5). He declares them to be leaders not sanctioned by God (15:13), blind and unreliable guides (15:14). He accuses them of majoring on minor matters (hand-washing) while ignoring disruptive societal practices (murder, theft, slander; 15:19).

In 16:1-12, things deteriorate when the Pharisees and Sadducees ask Jesus again for a sign (cf. 12:38-42). Their repeated demand shows an unwillingness to listen and learn. Verse 1 presents this request negatively, as a "test." The temptation scene uses the same verb when the devil tempts or tests Jesus (4:1, 3). They thus behave as the devil, tempting Jesus to address their demands rather than maintain his allegiance to God. Jesus rebukes them for failing to discern God's saving presence and empire in his activity. Jesus calls them evil (16:4), the same term he uses for the devil (6:13). They, like Rome (4:8), are agents of the devil.

Jesus follows up this nasty polemic by warning the disciples against the Pharisees' and Sadducees' teaching (16:5-12). Given their position as political-societal leaders, this warning embraces more than limited religious questions. Jesus warns against the societal structures and practices that they uphold.

Between these conflict scenes, Jesus blesses the crowds with further healings (15:29-31) and a feeding (15:32-39). He displays God's care for physical well-being, repairing damage inflicted by imperial structures through inadequate availability of land and food, and diseases of deprivation and contagion. Two confessional scenes—the Canaanite woman who successfully seeks mercy from Jesus for her demon-possessed daughter (15:21-28; Ringe 1985; Levine 2001) and Peter's confession of Jesus as "Messiah, the Son of the Living God" (16:16; cf. 14:33)—counterbalance the conflicts. The section 11:2—16:20 has depicted growing division in response to Jesus' activity.

The Text in the Interpretive Tradition

Perhaps there is no more significant a passage for the disunity of the worldwide church than 16:13-20 (Luz 2001, 325–77). Peter confesses Jesus' messianic identity. Jesus blesses him, announces this answer to be divinely revealed, declares that "on this rock I will build my church," and assigns to him "the keys of the kingdom of heaven" (16:16-19). The interpretive issues, discussion, and tradition are immense; space permits only a brief naming.

One question concerns whether, in confessing Jesus' identity (16:16), Peter functions as a representative or ideal spokesperson for all disciples (appealing to the previous confession of 14:33), or has a unique and preeminent role (appealing to 4:18; 10:2; and 16:18).

Another concerns the meaning of "on this rock" in verse 18. Does it refer to Christ himself or to Peter? Augustine argued for Christ, appealing to 1 Cor. 3:11 and 10:4, among other passages. If it refers to Peter, in what role? One view emphasizes Peter as representative of all believers, particularly in confessing Jesus' identity. This line was favored initially by Origen and Tertullian, and was developed by Reformers like Zwingli and Melanchthon in arguing against the papacy. Another option focused on Peter the model bishop and head of the church succeeded by bishops of Rome. This option had clearly emerged by the mid-third century in relation to the bishop of Rome; in the fifth century, it was developed by Leo the Great in arguing that Peter is present in the bishops of Rome as his successors.

A third issue concerns the identity of the "keys" in verse 19. Does this refer to the authority of the pope and the church (for example, forgiveness from sins and the sacrament of penance) or, as in Protestant interpretation, to preaching and communal confession that reflects Peter's confession?

These centuries-old interpretive debates, of course, continue to influence contemporary ecclesial traditions and practices.

The Text in Contemporary Discussion

In this rich section is the story of the Canaanite woman who successfully overcomes Jesus' initial indifference and procures healing for her demon-possessed daughter and commendation for her faith. Troubling, though, is both the disciples' (15:23) and Jesus' reluctance to assist a non-Israelite woman (15:24), despite substantial traditions about God's blessing for all people (e.g., Abraham, Gen. 12:1-3). Worse, Jesus dismisses her in a demeaning and sexist fashion by calling her a dog (15:26). As one contemporary commentator has observed, Jesus is caught with his compassion down. Yet despite this treatment, the woman refuses to be humiliated, perseveres, and outwits Jesus in verbal sparring as she turns his metaphor back on him. She affirms Israel's temporal priority in God's purposes along with their universal and inclusive reach (15:27). This "teachable moment" for Jesus results in healing and commendation for this gentile woman's daughter.

The text has proved disturbing for readers who impose on it later christological formulations of Jesus' divinity. Some deny any poor treatment of the woman or that Jesus has anything to learn. Other readers recognize a difficult yet intriguing text, which displays courageous faith and, eventually, inclusive divine mercy.

Part 4: Jesus Will Be Crucified and Raised (Matthew 16:21—20:34)

The Gospel's fourth major section begins in 16:21 (Carter 2000, 341–60). God has commissioned Jesus to manifest God's saving presence and reign (1:1—4:16). Jesus enacts that commission in his words and actions (4:17—11:1). Responses of division and conflict follow (11:2—16:20). Now, the narrative establishes that Jesus' commission involves his death by Jerusalem's ruling elite and his resurrection by God (16:21—20:34).

Matthew 16:21—17:24: The Way of the Cross for Jesus and Disciples

The Text in Its Ancient Context

Jesus' announcement of his imminent suffering in 16:21 provides a plot summary for the rest of the Gospel. His confrontation with the alliance of power in Jerusalem is the inevitable consequence of challenging the status quo with an alternative vision and practices. Yet his opponents do not have the final word or ultimate power. God will raise him from the dead. The understanding of resurrection as God's vindication of those who suffer faithfully, even to death, emerged in the second century BCE under the tyranny of Antiochus Epiphanes (Dan. 12:1-3; 1 Macc. 1–2; 2 Maccabees 7).

Jesus' death has implications for disciples. Peter, the hero of the previous scene, rejects Jesus' teaching; Jesus allies him with the devil against God (16:22-23). Jesus also declares that disciples walk the way of the cross, thereby specifying how he will die (16:24). Crucifixion was a shameful form of execution reserved for those who challenged the imperial status quo. Jesus calls his followers to discipleship of this same style and consequence, continuing his mission until his return (16:27-28).

The transfiguration scene confirms Jesus' instruction in two ways (17:1-8). First, Jesus appears in glory, foreshadowing his resurrection and return (cf. 17:2 and 13:43). Second, God speaks, repeating the intimate blessing from Jesus' baptism (3:17), but adding a key clause, "listen to him" (17:5). With this imperative, God confirms Jesus' disclosure of his forthcoming death, resurrection, and return, and his teaching about discipleship as the way of the cross.

Jesus performs his final exorcism (17:14-20) after the disciples' faith fails in the face of Satan's reign. They are unable to manifest God's liberating and merciful empire, despite Jesus' commission to them (10:8). Jesus again predicts death and resurrection in Jerusalem (17:22-23). The repetition underscores its importance.

The chapter ends with an enigmatic scene about taxes (Carter 2001, 130–44). In the Gospel's post-70-CE context, the scene instructs Matthew's audience to pay an imperial tax (17:24-27). After Rome's destruction of Jerusalem, the emperor Vespasian imposed a humiliating and punitive tax on Jews as a defeated people. Vespasian co-opted the temple tax and used it to rebuild and maintain the temple of Jupiter Capitolinus in Rome, the sponsoring deity of Rome's victory in 70 CE. The scene instructs disciples to pay the tax, though with an understanding that—for disciples in the know—it subverts Roman claims of sovereignty and asserts God's sovereignty. Jesus' instruction in verse 27, about catching the fish and finding in its mouth the tax coin, evokes and counters imperial claims that Rome's sovereignty subdued even wild animals and fish. Jesus' instruction reasserts God's sovereignty over God's creation, represented by the fish (8:23-27; 14:13-21; 15:32-39). God supplies the tax. It is paid to Rome. For disciples in the know, it testifies subversively to God's sovereignty.

The Text in the Interpretive Tradition

Jesus' statement in 16:28 promises his return before some of his generation die (Luz 2001, 378–420). Various interpretations have arisen to account for its nonfulfillment. The *Gospel of Thomas* (log.

1) individualizes and spiritualizes the saying by claiming that those who understand Jesus' words do not die. An extensive tradition found its fulfillment in the transfiguration scene that immediately follows with the "some" comprising Peter, James, and John. Among the Reformers, it was common to interpret the resurrection as attesting Jesus "coming in his kingdom" (Luther, Calvin, Bucer). For nineteenth-century interpreters, one way of avoiding the problem of Jesus' reliability was to declare that it was not an authentic saying of Jesus.

Not surprisingly, many interpreters understood the transfiguration story as a revelation of, and therefore a confirmation of, the church's subsequent elevated christological teaching regarding Jesus' divine being. Another tradition, though, has seen it as a scene in which believers participate. In believers, too, the glory of God's reign is present, and in Jesus' experience is prefigured the eschatological experience of transformation.

The Text in Contemporary Discussion

This passage contains provocative and disparate material about discipleship. The call to self-denial in 16:24 has often been understood to negate the world and personal, somatic existence that God created and declared to be good. As recently as 15:29-39, Jesus has demonstrated in his healings and feeding God's commitment to physical, created, somatic well-being and flourishing. Yet as Bonhoeffer rightly observes, following Jesus requires a way of life out of step with dominant cultural values. To "take up the cross" (16:24) is to commit to a way of life that does not conform to, but challenges, self-serving societal and personal practices and structures. Hence Jesus does not remain transfigured but comes down the mountain (17:9-13) and repeats his declaration about going to Jerusalem to be killed (17:22-23).

Yet such a life is not monolithic in cultural opposition. The chapter recognizes the humanness of disciples (17:19-20). It also includes the scene about paying taxes. Disciples are to pay taxes that signify submission to Roman rule, yet the story reframes them so that payment simultaneously signifies covert dissent. Taxes for contemporary disciples do not necessarily represent submission to ruling power, but they do provide funding for governmental programs that followers of Jesus might decide are contrary to Jesus' teaching. The military provides a center of concern, causing some contemporary followers to withhold or redirect a percentage of taxes as a sign that simultaneously expresses cooperation and dissent.

The juxtaposition of such material indicates the complexities and challenges of discipleship, and the need for communities of discourse to discern together appropriate and intentional practices of faithfulness.

Matthew 18:1-35: A Community of Sustaining Relationships and Practices

The Text in Its Ancient Context

Jesus has declared that the way of discipleship is the way of the cross (16:24). The image immediately locates disciples committed to God's empire/reign in the difficult societal place of both being at cross-purposes with Roman power, while also simultaneously accommodating its demands (17:24-27). How, then, to live?

Chapter 18 constitutes the Gospel's fourth block of teaching material (see chs. 5–7, 10, 13; Carter 2000, 361–75). Known as the community discourse, it establishes that the difficult and ambiguous way of the cross is communal. This life is constituted as, and sustained by, a network of practices and interdependent relationships. These practices emerge in Jesus' teaching throughout the chapter.

The first section names humbleness as basic practice among disciples (18:1-5). Empires and "greatness" form a natural pair. Alexander "the Great" and Rome's Pompey "the Great" personified greatness in terms of power (through military subjugation), privileged birth, wealth, office, and status. Jesus rejects such a definition, replacing it with the humbleness of the child (18:4). If we define "child" in terms of our contemporary values—children are pure and innocent—we miss the point. In the ancient world, children were understood to be insignificant nobodies, vulnerable, powerless, and defenseless. By some estimates half died by age ten. They lacked status and resources and were often regarded as unpredictable, even threatening. Matthew 2, particularly verses 13-18, shows children vulnerable in a dangerous political world. They are further depicted as sick (8:6; 9:2), hungry (14:21), demon-possessed (15:22; 17:18), and dead (9:18). The community of disciples knows vulnerability and powerlessness, but also mutual support and protection.

Moreover, disciples do not cause one another to stumble nor despise one another (18:6-9, 10-14; Loader, 20–36). Aware of God's protection through guardian angels, they are vigilant in communal interactions that reflect God's valuing of and vigilance for each one. God, like a shepherd, lovingly searches for any that "go astray" (18:10-14).

Such interactions do not mean, though, that disciples always agree with one another. Verses 15-20 recognize the reality that among human beings, especially among a hard-pressed community, conflict and offense are inevitable (Duling). Typical of numerous groups in the ancient world, the verses set out a general process of communal accountability involving reproof and restoration. The one who is wronged initiates the process with the offender (18:15), perhaps involving witnesses (18:16) and the church (18:17). To be treated as "a Gentile and a tax collector" is not to be shunned but to be the object of restorative efforts that are ratified by God (18:18-20). Verses 21-22 confirm the limitless commitment to reconciliation and forgiveness.

The emphasis on the practice of forgiveness continues with the parable of the unforgiving servant (18:23-35). The point is straightforward in establishing forgiveness as a communal norm—God's forgiveness requires disciples to forgive one another. But the parable sits uneasily here. Verses 21-22 exhort forgiveness, but the parable depicts its opposite with two examples of not forgiving! The king takes back the forgiveness he initially offered (18:27, 32-34), and the forgiven slave refuses to forgive another slave (18:28-30). The parable warns that not forgiving means the loss of God's forgiveness (cf. 6:14-15).

The discourse exhorts a network of community relationships and practices among disciples marked by humble receptivity to the other, mutual support and active respect, accountability, relentless commitment to reconciliation, and repeated forgiveness. Such a communal life sustains and embodies vulnerable discipleship on the way of the cross.

The Text in the Interpretive Tradition

This chapter as a whole has not often played a significant role in discussions about "marks" of the church (Luz 2001, 421–83). The commonly accepted marks of the church—whether "one, holy, catholic, and apostolic," or preaching and sacraments—do not, in and of themselves, highlight the relationships, practices, and structures evident in this chapter.

Yet while the chapter's relative lack of influence as a whole is evident, significant interpretive discussions about many of its subsections exist. Its most striking image concerns the repeated instructions to cut off the hand, foot, or eye if they cause one to stumble (18:8-9). Some have placed the saying in a tradition of ancient medical practice whereby people sacrificed a body part to ensure their own survival. Others note a link to torture and martyrdom traditions (cf. 2 Maccabees 7). Some, reading the passage in relation to Mark 9:43-48 and in the context of Matt. 18:1-5, have seen a warning to protect (literal) children from pederastic activity. Others have seen a more generalized, metaphorical reference that graphically exhorts self-protection against sinful behavior, whether one's own or of others such as evil friends. Another line of interpretation has seen the body imaging, as it commonly did in ancient thinking, an ecclesial or social context (akin to 1 Corinthians 12–14). On this reading, the "cutting off" refers to expelling offending members. There are, though, difficulties with this last reading. Matthew does not use the "body" image for the church, and verses 15-20 and 21-35 exhort reconciliation.

The Text in Contemporary Discussion

This chapter's insistence on the central place of "church as community" in following Jesus challenges some contemporary understandings of discipleship. Some frame discipleship in terms of individual salvation and emphasize "my personal walk with the Lord" to such an extent that, in actuality, there is no place for or accountability to any community. While such individual understandings protect against manipulative communal practices, they have no room for the sort of humility, accountability, and interdependence envisioned in Matthew 18.

The chapter's vision also challenges ecclesial understandings that see the "true" church constituted by particular rituals, or structures of ministry, order and authority, or doctrinal tests, or positions on social issues. That is not to say these things do not matter; each aspect is important for ecclesial life. But in Matthew's vision, they do not matter as much as relational community that sustains and embodies disciples on the way of the cross. The chapter urges followers to nurture such communities.

Matthew 19–20: Alternative Households Shaped by God's Empire

The Text in Its Ancient Context

Jesus has declared twice that he must walk the way of the cross (16:21; 17:22-23). In 19:1, he and his disciples leave Galilee for Jerusalem, where the ruling elite will execute him. Chapters 19–20 narrate the journey as he continues to instruct disciples about the way of the cross (Carter 2000, 376–410; Loader , 80–81, 102–20, 127–35).

The content of his instruction concerns household matters: marriage and divorce (19:3-12), children (19:13-15), wealth (19:16-30), a parable about a wealthy householder and day laborers (20:1-16), and being slaves (20:17-28), concluding with a healing story (20:29-34). Why this cluster of material on households?

Various philosophical traditions (Aristotelian, Stoic, neo-Pythagorean) as well as Hellenistic Judaism (first-century writers Philo and Josephus) understood the household as the basic unit of a city or empire. They envisioned ideal households as a microcosm of imperial society. Households were, then, to be patriarchal and androcentric, reflecting and constituting elite imperial society in privileging male "power over." The husband/father/master was to "rule over" wife/children/slaves. He provided the household's economic well-being and represented it in society.

Given this link between households and empires, Jesus' manifestation of "the empire of the heavens" predictably includes instruction on households. The Gospel imitates this cultural pattern, just as it continues to privilege male power in recognizing twelve special male disciples (among other disciple figures, including women). Yet simultaneously, it also contests this dynamic to some extent. The first scene, on divorce and remarriage, while maintaining a male perspective, limits male power in divorce (advocated by Pharisees "for any reason," 19:3) with a vision of "one flesh" reciprocity and mutuality (19:6) and by specifying only one situation of "unchastity" (Allison).

In 19:13-15, instead of maintaining the dismissal and insignificance of "little children" (practiced by disciples, 19:13), Jesus affirms their central place in God's empire (19:15). He identifies all disciples as children ("such as these," 19:14-15). He envisions the community of disciples as comprising only children (brothers and sisters, 12:46-50) and without "power-over" parental figures (18:1-5; 23:9). In 19:16-30, he endorses not the pursuit of wealth but its disinvestment. He instructs the rich man to divest himself of his household wealth and redistribute it to the poor (19:21). The poor, not the elite wealthy, have a special place in God's empire (19:24; cf. 5:3) in anticipation of the abundance of God's new age for all people (19:27-30).

A parable about a wealthy householder and day laborers exemplifies God's empire. It in part treats all people equally (20:12), reversing hierarchy. In 20:17-28, Jesus repeats his explanation about going to Jerusalem and co-opts the exploitative and humiliating image of being a slave to present himself acting for the benefit of others (20:28). His actions contrast those of his disciples and the "great men of the Gentiles" who seek power and "lord it over" others. Disciples are to imitate Jesus and seek each other's good (20:20-27).

The section ends with a display of transforming mercy in response to two determined (faith-full) blind men (20:29-34). The same mercy can empower disciples in unlearning cultural values and structures as they live into societally contestive household structures.

The Text in the Interpretive Tradition

Catholic and Protestant traditions have interpreted the teaching on divorce in 19:9 quite differently (Luz 2001, 484–551). Catholic interpretation has generally read the verse as forbidding divorce and remarriage (complementing 5:32), though recognizing that partners live apart. Protestant interpretation has increasingly come to accept divorce and remarriage without restrictions and increasingly without stigma, although some more conservative expressions are not supportive. The interpretive difficulties multiply. What does "unchastity" mean—adultery, or incestuous marriages as defined by Leviticus 18? Does it modify divorce alone or remarriage also?

The verse assumes a very different world of arranged marriages, younger participants, much shorter life spans, and patriarchal cultural assumptions that only women commit adultery and that men divorce. Contemporary expectations of loving, fulfilling, chosen relationships are not in view. Yet the Gospel values love in urging love for God and neighbor (22:37-39). It also knows the importance of mercy (9:13; 12:7), which surely means, among many things, not only empowering and transforming broken situations (forgiveness), but also the possibility of fresh starts that do not trap people in loveless relationships but sets them free for new life. The verse (19:9) does not seem to be informed by this rich Gospel thread of love and mercy, thereby creating an opportunity for interpreters to put verse and context into conversation.

The saying about eunuchs in 19:10-12 has been read, in the context of 19:3-9, as referring to divorced men who cannot remarry and produce children because of restrictions in verse 9 on remarriage. It has also been read in relation to subsequent ascetic practices of voluntary celibacy, and particularly priestly celibacy as a way of life shaped by God's reign.

The Text in Contemporary Discussion

The passage raises numerous issues: male power, gender roles, household and societal structures, and discipleship and cultural practices.

Two further brief comments can be made. The "ransom" saying (20:28) has informed a personal piety concerning Jesus' self-giving death "for me." A reading that points to a much broader societal scope for God's work is possible. The verse's language is plural ("for many"), and "ransom" language often evokes God redeeming or liberating people from imperial powers (Egyptian, Exod. 6:6; Deut. 7:8; Babylonian, Isa. 43:1). Jesus' death and resurrection expose the limits of Roman power and demonstrate God's life-giving work for the world.

Second, the Gospel's concern with wealth and the poor continues in 19:21. This instruction has been read literally, whereby the wealthy should give all their wealth away. The definition of "wealthy" is complex and contested. Interpretation has also moderated the demand to giving, not everything, but something to the poor (almsgiving) and has focused on attitudes to wealth. Clement of Alexandria argued that the threat is not possessions themselves, but emotional attachments to wealth, so the rich who are not attached to wealth can be saved. What do rich, comfortable Christians in a poor global village do with this verse?

Part 5: Jesus in Jerusalem: Conflict and Death (Matthew 21–27)

The Gospel's fifth section (chs. 21–27) centers on Jerusalem and Jesus' fatal conflict with the temple-based rulers allied with the Roman governor Pilate (Carter 2000, 413–31). What Jesus predicted three times now takes place (16:21; 17:22-23; 20:17-19).

Matthew 21: Conflict in Jerusalem

The Text in Its Ancient Context

The entry scene is full of irony, imitating celebratory imperial entry processions yet with an "antitriumphal" parody (21:1-11). It borrows features of entry processions that celebrated conquering generals or the arrival of governors and emperors in a city representing imperial grandeur and "power over" subjugated peoples: procession, crowds, hymns, temple worship. Yet it creates street theater to critique imperial practice and mind-set. Entry processions defined greatness in terms of military violence, defeat of enemies, power, plunder, and public gratitude. Jesus, though, rides not a war horse but a donkey, a poor person's working animal, yet also one that evokes the scene in Zech. 9:9 of God's eschatological king, establishing God's reign triumphantly over all enemies in Jerusalem on the Mount of Olives (Zechariah 14; Matt. 21:1, 4-5). Continuing ironically to mimic imperial ways even while reinscribing them, verse 9 reinforces this emphasis by quoting a Passover processional psalm celebrating God's victory over the nations (Ps. 118:10-18).

Jesus does not attack empty temple ritual or the futility of Jewish efforts to encounter God. Rather the scene focuses on the temple's economic practices, which Jesus deems exploitative, turning a place of prayer into a "den for robbers" (21:13; Hanson and Oakman, 99–159). He cites Isa. 56:7 and Jer. 7:11, which condemn injustice and envision just communities. The scribes and priests are angered by his action, healing (21:14), and appreciation from children (21:15-16). A cursed and withered fig tree symbolizes God's judgment on the temple (21:18-20; Jer. 8:12-13), the first of several explanations for Rome's destruction of it in 70 CE. Jesus envisions a different community marked by prayer and faithfulness (21:21-22).

The offended "chief priests and elders" initiate open conflict as they check Jesus' credentials (21:23-27). The conflict is between Jesus and the leaders, not between Jesus and Israel. He prevails in verbal sparring through posing the question of the origin and the legitimacy of John's baptism. To evaluate John is to evaluate Jesus (11:7-19). The chief priests and elders do not recognize either as commissioned by God.

Jesus counterattacks these societal leaders with three parables (the third comprising 22:1-14). Jesus introduces and ends the first parable, concerning two sons, with a question that requires their response (21:28, 31). They correctly identify the one who does his father's will. In so doing, they endorse an important emphasis in Jesus' teaching on obeying God's will (7:24-27; 12:46-50). They condemn themselves, though, as people who do not welcome God's agents—unlike the prostitutes and tax collectors (21:31-32).

The second parable—that of tenants who do not pay rent from a vineyard—interprets Jerusalem's fall to the Romans in 70 CE as punishment on the leaders' violent unfaithfulness in crucifying Jesus (21:33-43). The landowner planting a vineyard evokes the picture of God choosing Israel (Isa. 5:1-7). But the tenants refuse to pay the rent—the good and just works of obedient living—killing slaves (prophets) and the landowner's son (Jesus). The temple leaders correctly identify the tenants' eviction and replacement, thereby announcing their own penalty at the hands of the angry landowner (21:35-41). The vineyard (Israel) is not destroyed, but God replaces the leaders as tenants.

On realizing their condemnation by Jesus, "the chief priests and Pharisees" want to arrest Jesus (21:45-46).

The Text in the Interpretive Tradition

Across the church's history, interpretation of the chapter has emphasized God's rejection, not of the Jerusalem leaders as in the reading offered above, but the rejection of Israel as a whole from God's story of salvation (Luz 2005, 1–44). Regularly the chapter's scenes have been allegorized to underscore the passing of God's favor from Israel to the church. Even the entry-to-Jerusalem scene was so read. Justin and Origen interpreted the mother donkey as the sin-bound, law-yoked synagogue and the colt as gentiles who leave Jericho (the world) to enter the church (Mount of Olives) and the heavenly Jerusalem. The cloaks on the road are church dogma. In a twist uncommon in the Christian tradition, a few understood the mother donkey (Israel) to follow the colt; she too will enter the heavenly Jerusalem, though after the gentiles. Other interpretations, especially dramatic liturgical reenactments, emphasized Christ as the victorious king, anticipating the Easter victory over sin and death.

The cursed fruitless fig tree was similarly understood, from the second century on, as condemned Israel (not the temple as proposed above). Jesus' hunger depicted his unsatisfied yearning for faith in Israel. Likewise, the parable of the two sons was read, since Origen, as one of salvation history. The second son, who says "yes" but does not go, represents disobedient Jews or Israel (not only leaders), while the son who obeys represents gentiles. The parable of the vineyard was likewise interpreted as a story of Israel's rejection. Some, however, like Calvin, rejected such allegorization and read it as a warning to the church to produce fruit.

The Text in Contemporary Discussion

Such interpretations of Christian Scriptures constitute a long, shameful, and tragic tradition of anti-Jewish attitude and practices among Christian groups that should not be forgotten, but should never be replicated. Such readings pose an ongoing challenge to Gospel readers. Has God forever abandoned Israel, revoking covenant with God's people? Has God withdrawn love and grace once and for all? It is both tragic, given the history of interpretation, and hopeful, for a different future, to recognize that these supersessionist or replacement readings are not inevitable or necessary. They can be interrupted. One option is to read against the grain. Another option is to formulate readings such as in the first section above that endorse not a general repudiation of Israel and breaking of covenant but a specific targeting of an institution (temple) and group (leaders).

This solution, though, remains imperfect because of a further issue, namely the notion of judgment that pervades the Gospel (7:24-27; 10:40-42; 13:47-50; 18:21-35; 25:31-46). God the householder acts like an imperial tyrant in destroying the leaders and their temple. The Gospel enacts the imperial practice of requiring acceptance of God's empire or else punishment follows for those who reject and defy. While verses like 5:45 depict God's mercy and goodness extending to all people, the Gospel is not convinced that God's mercy draws everyone into loving relationship with God. Hence judgment plays a significant role. Disturbingly, in this regard, the Gospel constructs God as acting like an emperor.

Matthew 22: Conflict over Jesus' Authority

The Text in Its Ancient Context

The conflict between Jesus and the Jerusalem-based socioreligious leaders continues from chapter 21 (Carter 2000, 432–48).

The chapter's opening scene comprises the third of three parables Jesus tells against the "chief priests and Pharisees" (not all Israel). After the second parable, they want to arrest him, yet he continues the attack (21:45; 22:1). This parable, concerning rejected invitations to the wedding banquet of the king's son, rehearses the leaders' rejection of Jesus as God's agent and their judgment, enacted in Jerusalem's destruction in 70 CE. Banquets and eating often signal participation in God's purposes, including their full establishment (Prov. 9:1-2; Isa. 25:6-10; Matt. 8:11-12). The reference in verse 7 to the burning city is a particularly Matthean feature, missing from the Q version of Luke 14:21, interrupting the sequence between verses 5 and 8, and creating an improbable scenario of a banquet among the smoldering ashes of the burned city. Josephus records Jerusalem's burning in 70 CE (*J.W.* 6.249–408), and the city's fall was widely interpreted as divine punishment enacted by Rome. The reasons for the punishment differed (*2 Bar.* 1:1-5; *4 Ezra* 3:24-26); Matthew's is explicitly christological: the rejection of the Son. Verses 11-14 extend the reach of the judgment. Guests at the banquet who, once admitted, do not behave in a manner appropriate to that identity (they are not appropriately attired) are also excluded.

Verse 15 narrates the response of Pharisees. They now attempt to trap Jesus. Allied with Herodians, presumably supporters of the Herodian dynasty and Rome, they ask Jesus about tax payment to the emperor. The question is astute. Tax payment expressed submission to Roman rule over God's people and land. Refusal was serious dissent. Coins bore forbidden images of emperors. Most accommodated; a few openly resisted. Jesus dissembles, first not having the tax coin, then with a naive, perhaps mocking question, then with a riddle (21:21). What is the relationship of the two clauses? Does Jesus endorse paying the tax as part of the things of God, or, in privileging the second cause, as a strategy for removing the blasphemous and idolatrous coin from the land, or, reading the "and" in an adversative sense, does he disqualify payment because the land and people belong to God, not to the impostor Rome? It is indeed an amazing answer (22:22).

The conflict scene involves another power group, the Sadducees, and resurrection. Resurrection is not just a religious matter. The notion arose during the second century BCE in the context of the Seleucid tyrant Antiochus Epiphanes' martyrdoms of faithful followers of God's law (1 Maccabees 1-2; 2 Maccabees 7). Resurrection denoted God's faithful justice even through and beyond death. The Sadducees parody resurrection with a ridiculous scenario that utilizes the patriarchal structure of levirate marriage that was concerned to continue a dead man's name (Deut. 25:5-10). Jesus bests them rhetorically, declaring their errors both in their general rejection of resurrection and in their particular construction (22:29-34).

Further conflict follows with the Pharisees (22:34, 41), first in ranking the commandments, then concerning his identity as Messiah. The question about the greatest commandment *could* be a fair one. Various summaries of the tradition prioritize its requirements (Isa. 56:1; Mic. 6:8). But the verb "test" (22:35) recalls previous confrontational scenes (16:1; 19:3) and the devil's testing (4:1, 3).

Jesus' prioritizing of love for God and neighbor draws from the heart of the tradition, envisioning societal interaction at odds with an imperial, hierarchical social structure that favored a few. Unable to answer his question about Ps. 110:1, the Pharisees join the Sadducees in being silenced (22:34). Question time ends (22:46).

The Text in the Interpretive Tradition

The wedding-feast parable has most commonly, and troublingly, been read as another allegory of salvation history (Luz 2005, 45–91). On this reading, Jewish rejection of Jesus (refused invitations) means Israel's rejection by God from the covenant and from their status as God's chosen. Gentiles replace them (22:9-10) in a full wedding hall (22:10b), where there is no room any more for Israel.

While many interpreters have readily found judgment on Israel in 22:1-10, they have been less happy about finding it extended to the wedding guests in the added scene of 22:11-14. The debates are long-standing. Origen engaged the question of this display of God's rejecting anger. Luther called it a "terrible Gospel." The referent for the requisite "wedding robe" has been debated. Initially, the dominant reading identified it with good works, particularly works of love (Augustine). Others, though, saw it as baptism or Christ put on in baptism (Aquinas), or the Holy Spirit. The Reformers (Zwingli, Luther, Calvin) saw it as active faith expressed in works of love. This church-centered reading of 22:11-14 regards Israel's rejection (supposedly presented in 22:1-10) as providing a warning to the church.

The Text in Contemporary Discussion

The tax-payment scene continues to raise the question of the relation of Jesus-followers to political and civic authority. A long tradition in both Catholic and Protestant traditions reads this scene through a division of responsibilities between the church (spiritual matters, rites and piety, word and Spirit) and civic authorities (civic and political order). However, such a division separates civic and political order from divine accountability as well as from the voices and input of Christian citizens who are rendered quietistic and automatically compliant by such a dualistic schema (contrary to Acts 5:29). For many Jesus-followers, such forced nonparticipation in the processes of government is unacceptable.

The double-love commandment, drawing from Deut. 6:5 and Lev. 19:18, continues to be central for contemporary Christian practice. Always the question of how we love God has to be addressed. This question includes issues of worship, emotion, mind, mystical communion, and obedience. Yet however we answer the question, it cannot be separated from love for neighbor and for oneself.

Matthew 23: Jesus Attacks the Scribes and Pharisees

The Text in Its Ancient Context

Though none of the Jerusalem leadership "dared to ask him any more questions" (22:46), Jesus is not finished attacking them. In the notorious chapter 23, he curses them with seven woes, while differentiating the practices of the community of disciples (Carter 2000, 449–65).

Three factors indicate that Jesus directs his attack not to all Israel but against its Jerusalem-based, Rome-allied leaders. First, the chapter continues conflict with Israel's leaders evident since

Jesus entered Jerusalem in chapter 21. He has tangled with "chief priests and scribes" (21:15), "chief priests and elders" (21:23), "the chief priests and Pharisees" (21:45), "Pharisees and Herodians" (22:15-16), Pharisees (22:34, 41), and Sadducees (22:23). This sequence parades Israel's leaders in accord with Jesus' passion predictions (16:21; 20:18-19).

Second, this animosity is usually understood to reflect post-70 conflicts with leaders in a synagogue to which Matthew's Jesus-followers belong. Chapter 23 details their unfaithfulness, and distinguishes Matthew's supporters from them. It does not claim God's rejection of all Israel.

Third, the chapter employs common polemical language to identify these leaders as opponents. Just as modern political rhetoric conventionally paints opponents and their policies as too expensive, too late, and too little, ancient polemic had a standard lexicon. It was common to attack enemy groups as snakes, blind persons, hypocrites, sexual and socioeconomic offenders, deceivers, and murderers. We are not reading objective discourse about "all Jews," but polemic against specific enemies.

The opening eight verses present the leaders as hypocrites. The image denotes actors who play a part, who represent someone they are not. Here the leaders lack integrity in the disparity between their living and their teaching. They also love and benefit from their position as retainers in hierarchical, imperial society. Verses 9-12 contrast different social interactions among disciples.

The first two woes against "the scribes and Pharisees" appear in 23:13-15. Woes, especially in prophetic traditions, conventionally announce divine judgment (Isa. 3:9-11). Jesus declares divine judgment on them as hypocrites who hinder access to God's purposes. The third and fourth woes (23:16-24) condemn them as blind for majoring on minor matters and neglecting important societal and covenantal practices, namely the "weightier matters of the law: justice and mercy and faith(fullness)." The fifth and sixth condemn disparities between actions and motivation, especially their greed and self-indulgence, hypocrisy, and lawlessness (23:25-28). The final woe (23:29-36) places them in a long line of leaders who have violently rejected the prophets to preserve the status quo. The woes target their societal leadership concerned with their own position and benefit and not with representing God's justice among the people.

The chapter ends with a lament over Jerusalem, the leaders' city. Again the leaders are in view (not all Israel), with the repeated emphasis on their violent rejection of prophets and of God's agents who manifest God's maternal care and guidance. Verse 38 again interprets the fall of Jerusalem and its temple in 70 CE by Rome as divine punishment. Verse 39, though, offers some relief from the insistent judgment in citing Ps. 118:26 to anticipate Israel's final salvation.

The Text in the Interpretive Tradition

Early second-century interpretation extended the polemic in chapter 23 against Jewish leaders to target *all* Jews as "hypocrites" in practices of prayer and fasting (Luz 2005, 92–177). This extension enabled Christian interpreters to distinguish Jewish practice from Christian practice (*Didache* 8). But once the separation of gentile Christ-believers and Jews was more widely established, chapter 23 generally (and surprisingly) seems to play little explicit part in expressing hostility toward Jews, though its continued negative influence should not be underestimated. Instead, readings became more ecclesially centered in attacking vices and exhorting virtuous behavior. The chapter is, then, understood textually to rebuke Jews but functionally to teach and warn Christians. Polemical readings continue but are directed against ecclesial opponents or against inappropriate Christian behavior. Scribes and Pharisees, for example, are understood to represent not Judaism but stingy and greedy actions (23:23, 25). Jerome called Christians who seek public applause "scribes and Pharisees" (23:5). In terms of polemic, Dante called Pope Boniface VIII a Pharisee, and Luther labeled Catholic opponents Pharisees. More generally among the Reformers, Pharisees came to represent those who trust in works and are hypocrites. In our time, the *Shorter Oxford English Dictionary* includes "self-righteous" and "hypocritical" in its entry on "Pharisees."

The Text in Contemporary Discussion

The presence of the woes of chapter 23 in a canonical Gospel is most troubling (Saldarini). Whatever the interpretive tradition, the chapter has exercised continuing negative influence on Christian anti-Jewish attitudes and practices. Attempts to read the tradition against the grain, in terms of warnings for Christians, have some merit, but they cannot be the only way forward. This dreadful past cannot be glossed over, set aside, and forgotten; repentance is required. Such Christian readings assume in their very language attacks on Jewish practices, and they maintain the hostility by presenting Jews as types of deficient Christian piety.

Moreover, the presence of such language in this Gospel poses the very difficult question of its relationship to the command in 5:44 to love one's enemies. Chapter 23 is as far from 5:44 as the east is from the west. No definition of love stretches to include condemning one's opponents to God's judgment. Yet 23:39 should not be completely forgotten. As much as it offers some hope—the punishment of the leaders' city is not a final dismissal—it compounds the contradictions. What is the relationship between the divine condemnation of the woes and this glimmer of hope?

In a different direction, 23:8-12 continues the vision of the church in chapters 18–20 as an alternative society marked by egalitarian structures (no teacher, no father) and contrary to hierarchical imperial society. In the history of interpretation, its import has been mollified by emphases on humility and against pride in defending ecclesial hierarchy and power. Matthew's vision for different social interactions is more radical, its continued challenge underscored by the theological and christological affirmations of 23:9-10.

Matthew 24–25: Jesus Announces the Final and Full Establishment of God's Empire

The Text in Its Ancient Context

Chapters 24–25 continue the conflict and condemnation of Jesus' final days in Jerusalem (Carter 2000, 466–97). The two chapters form the eschatological discourse, the Gospel's fifth major teaching section. Jesus addresses "signs of his coming/return and of the end of the age" (24:3)—his intervention to end Rome's empire and its Jerusalem allies, and fully establish God's reign/empire.

The chapter opens with another reference to the temple's destruction by the Romans in 70 CE. The discourse is located on the Mount of Olives and evokes Zechariah 14, which presents the Mount as the place where God enters the city, overcomes Israel's enemies, and establishes God's reign. The disciples ask about Jesus' "coming" or "arrival" (24:3; Gk. *parousia*), a term that refers to the arrival of generals or emperors parodied in 21:1-11. Now, though, there is no parody as his powerful and triumphant coming outmuscles the empire. The time until his coming, however, is difficult, marked by false agents misrepresenting God (24:4-5), wars (24:6-7a), natural disasters (24:7b-8), persecution, betrayal and faithfulness (24:9-13), mission (24:14), violation of the temple (24:15), flight and false alarms (24:16-26). The son of man's coming, however, will be unmistakable. He overcomes Roman power (represented in 24:28 by eagles, not vultures) and cosmic deities, before gathering God's people (24:27-31; Carter 2003a).

Exhortation takes over, as Jesus underscores the importance of recognizing the signs of his imminent coming with a lesson from the leafy fig tree (24:32-35). Subsequently, several passages warn that while his return is imminent, its timing is unknown and disciples must be ready (24:36-44). Three parables make the same point with slight variations. The first employs the imperial institution of slavery without any questions, and adds a picture of frightful punitive violence (24:45-51). A second parable uses a wedding scenario to show the joy of Jesus' return and the necessity of being ready (25:1-13). The third employs the common imperial scenario of the wealthy absentee landowner who entrusts his estate's management to his slaves (25:14-30). Returning, he holds them accountable for the talents entrusted to them. The faithful slaves are joyfully rewarded (25:21, 23); the unfaithful slave is punished (25:30).

The final scene portrays the judgment of the nations to take place at Jesus' return (25:31-46). Jesus appears as son of man and king in representing God's rule over the nations (25:34). The key interpretive question concerns the criterion for vindication (25:34-40) and condemnation (25:41-46). The participants themselves do not know (25:37-39, 44). One reading sees the nations judged on the basis of how they have treated those in need. Another reading sees the nations judged on the basis of their response to Christian proclamation of the good news. This latter view highlights the mission of 24:14 to all the nations (gathered in 25:31), and understands positive response to "the least of these" (25:40, 45) as referring not to the needy but specifically to receiving disciples and their Gospel message (so 10:40).

The Text in the Interpretive Tradition

Chapter 24 has been read along various, but at times overlapping, lines (Luz 2005, 178–296). One approach, beginning with the *Didache*, and present from Irenaeus through the Reformers, has read it as an eschatological text culminating in Jesus' parousia. Verses 3-26 are understood as depicting the final collapse, with references often focusing on the personification of evil in an antichrist (imported from 1 John 2:18 and not specifically mentioned anywhere in Matthew). The antichrist is identified variously with the "false prophets" (24:11), the "desolating sacrilege" (24:15), and the "false" Messiahs (24:5, 23-24). A second approach, beginning with Chrysostom, has read the chapter historically, not in relation to the end of the age but in relation to the Roman destruction of Jerusalem in 70 CE. This approach understands the "desolating sacrilege" as something done by a Roman to profane the temple, such as introducing an image of the emperor or a legionary standard into the temple. The historical approach handles much of verses 4-31 but struggles with the question of verse 3b and with verses 27-31. To solve these problems, a mixed interpretation emerged with Augustine that notes concerns with both the fall of Jerusalem and the end of the age and tries to read the chapter as moving between these two events. Another line emerging from this approach found connections with contemporary ecclesial and world situations. (Spener, for instance, identified the "desolating sacrifice" with the papacy.) This approach was often combined with a sense that the end was near in the time of the interpreter (true of both Luther and contemporary TV preachers).

The Text in Contemporary Discussion

These two chapters pose numerous questions for contemporary readers. Perhaps the most basic question concerns how we engage eschatological thinking, both the notion of divine intervention to affect the end of history with the establishment of God's purposes, and its bleak, hopeless perspective on the present. Two thousand years later and counting, the imminent expectation of 24:34 has not materialized. Some parts of the contemporary church live in such thinking; other parts find no resonance with it at all. A related issue is the language in which this divine intervention is described. Throughout, the eschatological discourse borrows imperial language (*parousia*), structures (slavery, absentee landowners), and strategies (punishing violence) to depict divine actions. The ways of Caesar are attributed to God without hesitation. There is no questioning of the violent assertion of cosmic power in 24:27-31 in the defeat of Roman military power (24:28). There is neither critique of slavery in 24:45-51 nor restraint in depicting the horrendous violence of hacking a slave to pieces in 24:51. Violent punishment continues in 25:31-46. How does this strand of violent judgment interact with the depictions of universal divine favor in 5:45 and the elevation of mercy (9:13; 12:7)? And what are we to make of the presentation of judgment by works and the privileging of the poor in the assertion of God's kingly power in 25:31-46?

Matthew 26–27: Jesus Is Crucified

The Text in Its Ancient Context

After two chapters of eschatological discourse (chs. 24–25), the path to the cross via conflict with the Roman governor and the Jerusalem elite resumes from chapters 21–23. The transition from chapters 25 to 26 is stunning. The king who judges the nations is now judged by their rulers even while he exposes the vicious and self-serving ways of the imperial world.

These two long chapters move quickly with short and interwoven scenes, changing characters, and varied settings (Carter 2000, 498–540). The turning point comes in 26:47-56 as Judas betrays Jesus in Gethsemane, Jesus is arrested, and the disciples flee. From 26:57 to 27:26, Jesus is condemned first by the high priestly leadership and then by governor Pilate (Carter 2003b). Matthew 27:27-66 narrates his crucifixion as "king of Israel" (27:37, 42)—a treasonous claim in Roman rule—death (27:50), and burial in a guarded tomb.

The early Christian movement had to account for Jesus' death by crucifixion and for its own loyalty to one who had been crucified. Doing so clearly posed an enormous challenge. These chapters, as do other New Testament writings, devote considerable effort to offering explanations of that significance both for divine plans and for the life of discipleship. The challenge originates with the act of crucifixion itself.

In the Roman system, the punishment fit the social status of the convicted. Crucifixion, the "most pitiable of deaths" (Josephus, *J.W.* 7.202–3), was reserved for lower-ranked, more marginal, and provincial folks like violent criminals, unruly slaves, and rebellious provincials or foreigners who claimed kingship not sanctioned by Rome and attacked the personnel and property of elites. Crucifixions were carried out publicly along well-traveled roads so as to intimidate as many as possible.

Jesus' death by crucifixion puts him—and his followers—in such company. So, in 27:38-44, two rebels (bandits or brigands) are crucified with Jesus for rebellion against Roman order. Matthew's chapters take up the questions: What was God doing? What is the significance of this event? How does it shape discipleship? The two chapters can be read as a catalog of interpretations of his crucifixion, viewed through the perspective of resurrection. Among Matthew's affirmations are the following:

- Jesus' crucifixion is the inevitable consequence of a prophetic challenge to the imperial powers that be (26:1-5). The empire always strikes back. This is the way of the cross.
- An unnamed woman—a model disciple—recognizes that Jesus dies not in defeat but willingly (26:36-46), in God's service (26:6-13) and will (26:56). This service includes the establishment of a covenant for release from sins in anticipation of the full establishment of God's life-giving will (26:17-30). Jesus' death exposes the sinful nature of the imperial world.
- Jesus' death results from the betrayal by one disciple, Judas (26:14-16, 47-56; 27:3-10), and his abandonment by Peter (26:31-35, 69-75) and all the male disciples (26:56). By contrast, it is witnessed by courageous women followers (27:55-56).
- Jesus' death results from the concerted and effective effort of the alliance of Jerusalem and Roman imperial power to kill a challenger to the imperial status quo. This alliance involves the high priest Caiaphas (26:57-68), the Roman governor Pilate (27:1-2, 11-26), Roman soldiers (27:27-31, 54, 62-66), and the chief priests, scribes, and elders (27:41-43).

The Text in the Interpretive Tradition

The interpretive tradition concerning Jesus' passion is rich and diverse, expressed through art, drama, music, and theological reflection (Luz 2005, 297–589, with images). One history identifies four broad approaches across the last two millennia. Initial interpretations, viewing crucifixion and resurrection as one connected event, emphasized not its suffering but its triumph (indicated in the eschatological anticipations of resurrection in 27:51-53). A second emphasis emerged in seeing the cross as an act of love (cf. Rom. 5:8). A third emphasis, especially in medieval exegesis, emphasized the suffering of the cross in which believers emotionally share and suffer through various contemplative practices, including self-flagellation, so as to learn love, pity, and thankfulness, and live a world-denying life. Protestant Reformation piety commonly associated with Luther, Calvin, and Melanchthon emphasized the benefits—both judgment and grace—of Jesus' death as *pro me* ("for me") or *pro nobis* ("for us"), encountered through preaching and sacraments, and responded to with faith.

Contemporary strands of interpretation have continued emphases from the past such as ransom theories (Anselm: Jesus' death satisfies God's honor and justice and buys release from sin and the devil), God's wooing love that draws humans into divine relationship (Abelard), *Christus victor* formulations of triumph over sin, and the *pro nobis* benefits of Jesus' sacrificial death. Other contemporary approaches, such as feminist and liberation work, have reacted strongly against sacrificial emphases, regarding "God giving God's son to die" as more akin to child abuse and as encouraging submission to abusive power and suffering. Instead, in focusing on life-giving and liberating dimensions, they have, for example, emphasized Jesus as one who suffers with us and strengthens all who are poor and oppressed. A similar approach has countered spiritualizations of the cross by seeking to restore it to its Roman imperial context. On this approach, the cross exposes human (imperial, systemic) evil, violence, and scapegoating (Girard) in the resistance to Jesus' alternative societal vision and practices.

The Text in Contemporary Discussion

Creative reflection on the significance of Jesus' death continues, though often ecclesial communities seem wary of this diversity and favor traditional, especially sacrificial, interpretations without exploring the diversity in the New Testament writings and the tradition across the ages.

These two chapters are full of characters that provide numerous points of entry into discipleship as the way of the cross. These characters include the anointing woman (26:6-13), the betrayer Judas, the overconfident but fragile Peter, the disciples who sleep through the Gethsemane prayer meeting, Caiaphas, who represents Jewish identity and allies with Roman power, Pilate, not spineless but concerned to maintain Roman rule and score a victory over his begging provincial allies (27:22-23), Simon of Cyrene, who is compelled to carry the cross (27:32), and the faithful and brave women at the tomb (27:55-56).

Part 6: God Thwarts Imperial Power and Raises Jesus (Matthew 28)

On normal expectations, the Gospel story should end with Jesus' death and the ruling elites' victory. Chapter 28, though, boldly declares God's miraculous intervention, which creates a different future with the raising of Jesus (Carter 2000, 541–54). The worst that imperial power can do is thwarted and reversed.

Matthew 28: Jesus' Resurrection and the Commissioning of Disciples

The Text in Its Ancient Context

Verses 1-10 emphasize this divine intervention. The raising of Jesus is assumed and declared, not described, thereby augmenting its mystery. The narrative focuses on the two women who come to "see" the tomb. Unlike Mark 16, they do not bring spices to anoint a dead body. That omission and the significant verb "see," with which Matthew frequently denotes understanding (Matt. 9:2) and insight into Jesus' mission (13:13-17), suggest they expect resurrection.

The descent from heaven of "an angel of the Lord," the earthquake, and the angel's divine-like appearance and reassuring words "do not be afraid" underscore God's presence and intervention.

God's action renders the empire's military agents powerless, "like dead men," in this place of new life (28:3-5a). The angelic proclamation underscores both divine intervention with its passive, "he has been raised" (28:5-8), and the need to reveal this activity. The notion of resurrection emerged in contexts of imperial tyranny to affirm God's triumph over death caused by imperial tyrants, and to provide assurance of participation in God's eschatological purposes (Dan. 12:1-3; 2 Maccabees 7). With joy and fear, the women obey the instruction to proclaim this message to the disciples in Galilee, an instruction renewed in their worshipful, fearful encounter with the risen Jesus (28:8-11; Cotter).

While the chapter's first section interprets the empty tomb in terms of God's life-giving intervention, its second scene presents the ruling powers' perspective (28:11-15). The now-revived soldiers, representing the power of the alliance of Pilate and the Jerusalem leaders (27:62-66), report "everything that had happened." The chief priests, assuming the governor's support, bribe the soldiers to declare an alternative story: the disciples have stolen the body. Regrettably, the scene presents those who do not believe or accept the angel's story as corrupt, deceiving, greedy—and not very smart.

In this conflictual context, the all-powerful Jesus commissions the disciples (28:16-20). The obedient disciples worship and doubt Jesus on a mountain, echoing Mts. Sinai and Zion. Jesus' massive assertion that God has given him "all authority in heaven and earth" declares a share in God's reign over all creation (contrast 4:8). The assertion both contests yet imitates Roman imperial claims to rule land, sea, and people. Jesus commissions the disciples to worldwide mission, making disciples, baptizing, and teaching Jesus' instruction (evoking the teaching of chs. 5–7, 10, 13, 18, 24–25; Carter 2004). Again the commission contests yet imitates imperial practice. Rome paraded its Jupiter-given mission to be "lords of the world" and to "crown peace with justice, to spare the vanquished, and to crush the proud" (Virgil, *Aen.* 1.254–82; 6.851–53).

The scene closes with Jesus' promise to be present with the small community of disciples as they undertake this mission in the resistant world of 28:11-15 (28:20). The Gospel ends by repeating its opening claim, that Jesus' presence manifests God's saving presence and reign/empire throughout the world (1:21-23; 4:17).

The Text in the Interpretive Tradition

The four Gospels present significantly different resurrection accounts comprising different characters, events, appearances, and settings (Luz 2005, 590–636). Early interpreters regularly combined these different versions to reconstruct a narrative sequence of "what actually happened." With the Enlightenment emerged new understandings of historical inquiry that dismissed miracles, gave prominence to rationality, and emphasized cause-and-effect explanations and the importance of analogous situations. This approach has meant for much—but not all—contemporary interpretation a shift in focus from the narratives as providing a historical account to their significance or meaning.

Interpreters have found meaning variously in allegorizing the accounts, with a primary focus on hearing the word that the stories narrated. The Reformers urged attention to the "for us" quality of the narratives, particularly focusing attention on the women. Calvin, for example, interprets the women in terms of 1 Cor. 1:27 and God's choice of those who are regarded as weak and foolish. Others have highlighted the emotional, rather than cognitive, components of joy and fear, worship and doubt in Matt. 28:8, 17, as alternative but appropriate, meaning-making responses.

The Text in Contemporary Discussion

Evangelism is a significant issue for contemporary congregations, both its strong advocates and those troubled by the practice. The history of interpretation shows that 28:19-20, a central text for contemporary debates, gained that central place as recently as the late eighteenth century. Early interpretation and the Reformers interpreted the verses as referring only to the disciples' mission. Catholic practice centered on territorial expansion such as the Spanish and Portuguese missions in the Americas and Asia. It was among Anabaptist and Protestant pietists that a missional interpretation developed. The English Baptist William Carey argued in 1792 for 28:19-20 as a central missional text, commanding worldwide mission to convert non-Christian individuals to Christianity. Such understandings have informed both Protestant and Catholic evangelistic missions.

Others, however, have become increasingly uncomfortable with assertions of ecclesial power and the association of the church with the damage done by colonial powers on local ways of life. Interfaith dialogue has also questioned evangelistic practices as triumphalistic and disrespectful of diverse traditions. Does 28:19-20 authorize such practices, or does its location at the end of the Gospel point to an interpretation in relation to the Gospel's previous teaching, such as Jesus' emphasis on the praxis of love for God and neighbor as demonstrated in "good works" more than words (5:16; 22:37-39)?

The Gospel's final promise raises questions as to how the continuing presence of the risen Jesus is experienced. Interpreters have suggested the Spirit, otherwise not prominent in the Gospel, the Eucharist, and the proclaimed word. Perhaps also this presence is experienced in worship and joy in the midst of fear and doubt.

Works Cited

Allison, Dale. 1993. "Divorce, Celibacy, and Joseph (Matthew 1:18-25 and 19:1-12)." *JSNT* 49:1–10.

Betz, Hans Dieter. 1995. *The Sermon on the Mount.* Minneapolis: Fortress Press.

Bornkamm, Günther. 1963. "The Stilling of the Storm." In *Tradition and Interpretation in Matthew*, by Günther Bornkamm, Gerhard Barth, and Heinz Held, 52–57. London: SCM.

Carter, Warren. 2000. *Matthew and the Margins: A Sociopolitical and Religious Reading.* Maryknoll, NY: Orbis.

———. 2001. *Matthew and Empire: Initial Explorations.* Harrisburg, PA: Trinity Press International.

———. 2003a. "Are There Imperial Texts in the Class? Intertextual Eagles and Matthean Eschatology as 'Lights Out' Time for Imperial Rome (Matt 24:27-31)." *JBL* 122:467–87.

———. 2003b. *Pontius Pilate: Portraits of a Roman Governor.* Collegeville, MN: Liturgical Press.

———. 2004. "Matthew and the Gentiles: Individual Conversion and/or Systemic Transformation?" *JSNT* 26:259–82.

———. 2007. "Power and Identities" and "Embodying God's Empire in Communal Practices." In *Preaching on the Sermon on the Mount: The World That It Imagines*, edited by David Fleer and Dave Bland, 8–21 and 22–35. St. Louis: Chalice.

Cotter, Wendy. 2001. "Greco-Roman Apotheosis Traditions and the Resurrection Appearances in Matthew." In *The Gospel of Matthew in Current Study*, edited by David Aune, 127–53. Grand Rapids: Eerdmans.

Deutsch, Celia. 2001. "Jesus as Wisdom: A Feminist Reading of Matthew's Wisdom Christology." In *A Feminist Companion to Matthew*, edited by Amy-Jill Levine with Marianne Blickenstaff, 88–113. Sheffield: Sheffield Academic Press.

Duling, Dennis. 2012. "'Egalitarian' Ideology, Leadership, and Factional Conflict within the Matthean Group," "The Matthean Brotherhood and Marginal Scribal Leadership," and "Matthew 18:15-17: Conflict, Confrontation and Conflict Resolution in a 'Fictive' Kin Association." In *A Marginal Scribe: Studies in Matthew in a Social-Scientific Perspective*, 145–78, 179–211, and 212–44. Eugene, OR: Cascade.

Hanson, K. C. 1994. "How Honorable! How Shameful! A Cultural Analysis of Matthew's Makarisms and Reproaches." *Semeia* 68:81–111.

Hanson, K. C., and Douglas Oakman. 1998. *Palestine in the Time of Jesus: Social Structures and Social Conflicts.* Minneapolis: Fortress Press.

Horsley, Richard. 1989. *The Liberation of Christmas: The Infancy Narratives in Social Context.* New York: Crossroad.

Levine, Amy-Jill. 1998. "Matthew." In *Women's Bible Commentary: Expanded Edition*, edited by Carol A. Newsom and Sharon H. Ringe, 339–49. Louisville: Westminster John Knox.

———. 2001. "Discharging Responsibility: Matthean Jesus, Biblical Law, and Hemorrhaging Woman." In *A Feminist Companion to Matthew*, edited by Amy-Jill Levine with Marianne Blickenstaff, 70–87. Sheffield: Sheffield Academic Press.

Loader, William. 2005. *Sexuality and the Jesus Tradition.* Grand Rapids: Eerdmans.

Luz, Ulrich. 1994. *Matthew in History: Interpretation, Influence, and Effects.* Minneapolis; Fortress Press.

———. 2001. *Matthew 1–7.* Trans. James E. Crouch. Hermeneia. Minneapolis: Fortress Press.

———. 2005. *Matthew 8–20.* Trans. James E. Crouch. Hermeneia. Minneapolis: Fortress Press.

———. 2007. *Matthew 21–28.* Trans. James E. Crouch. Hermeneia. Minneapolis: Fortress Press.

Meier, John P. 1994. *A Marginal Jew: Rethinking the Historical Jesus.* Vol. 2, *Mentor, Message, and Miracles.* New York: Doubleday.

Moss, Candida R., and Jeremy Schipper, eds. 2011. *Disability Studies and Biblical Literature.* New York: Palgrave Macmillan.

Murphy, Catherine. 2003. *John the Baptist: Prophet of Purity for a New Age.* Collegeville, MN: Liturgical Press.

Patte, Daniel. 1999. *The Challenge of the Sermon on the Mount: A Critical Study of the Sermon on the Mount as Scripture.* Harrisburg, PA: Trinity Press International.

Powell, Mark Allan. 2001. *Chasing the Eastern Star: Adventures in Biblical Reader-Response Criticism.* Louisville: Westminster John Knox.

Ringe, Sharon. 1985. "A Gentile Woman's Story." In *Feminist Interpretation of the Bible*, edited by Letty Russell, 65–72. Philadelphia: Westminster.

Saldarini, Anthony. 2001. "Reading Matthew without Anti-Semitism." In *The Gospel of Matthew in Current Study*, edited by David Aune, 166–84. Grand Rapids: Eerdmans.

Sheffield, Julian. 2001. "The Father in the Gospel of Matthew." In *A Feminist Companion to Matthew*, edited by Amy-Jill Levine with Marianne Blickenstaff, 52–69. Sheffield: Sheffield Academic Press.

Taylor, Joan. 1997. *The Immerser: John the Baptist within Second Temple Judaism.* Grand Rapids: Eerdmans.

Waetjen, H. 1975. "The Genealogy as the Key to the Gospel of Matthew." *JBL* 95:205–30.

Wainwright, Elaine. 2001. "The Matthean Jesus and the Healing of Women." In *The Gospel of Matthew in Current Study*, edited by David Aune, 74–95. Grand Rapids: Eerdmans.

Wink, Walter. 1992. "Beyond Just War and Pacifism: Jesus' Nonviolent Way." *RevExp* 89:171–214.

MARK

Raquel S. Lettsome

Introduction

No one knows exactly who wrote the Gospel of Mark. The ancient church historian Eusebius wrote that Bishop Papias of Asia Minor attributed the Gospel to John Mark (Acts 12:12; Col. 4:10), who was a follower and interpreter of Peter (*Hist. eccl.* 3.39). This would suggest that it was not a first-hand account of Jesus' ministry. The general consensus is that Mark, whoever he may be, wrote the Gospel somewhere in the Roman Empire between 66 and 70 CE. The precise dating of the Gospel hinges on the interpretation of the events prophesied by Jesus in Mark 13. For some scholars, the similarity between Jesus' prediction that there will be left of the temple "no stone upon a stone" and Josephus's narrative of the temple being razed in 70 suggests that Mark should be dated after the fall of the temple (Marcus; Pesch; Theissen). I find this a compelling argument (St. Clair). Therefore, the context of Mark's Gospel is the Jewish War: It is one of several Jewish and Christian responses to the fall of the temple.

The setting first posited for Mark's Gospel was Rome. This is where John Mark was believed to have written it, according to Papias. But the Gospel's use of Latin involves only a few military terms like "legion" (5:9) and "centurion" (15:39); there are no Latin words that reflect the social, domestic, or religious areas of Roman life (Kelber, 129). Based on this evidence, it is more probable that Mark wrote somewhere in the Roman Empire other than in Rome itself. Scholars have since identified Galilee and southern Syria as possible locales, suggestions that would also disqualify John Mark as the author. The viability of each of these locations primarily depends on how well they account for certain characteristics of Mark's Gospel: geographical discrepancies (his knowledge of the Galilean locales is lacking beyond their names, and his topology is often inaccurate: 1977); the use of a number of Hebrew (7:11; 11:9) and Aramaic words in transliteration (5:41; 7:34; 14:36; 15:22, 34), most of them translated into Greek, suggesting that Mark's community included Jews and gentiles in close association (Waetjen, 14); the explanation of Jewish traditions (e.g., 7:3-4) to at least some readers unfamiliar with them; the author's and presumed audience's familiarity with Jewish Scriptures, which are cited on twelve occasions, without further explanation (1:2-3; 4:12; 7:6-7; 10:6-8, 19; 11:17; 12:10-11, 36; 13:24-26; 14:27, 62; 15:34); and the representation of Jesus' ministry to gentiles, suggesting the presence of some gentiles, at least, in the audience. Both Rome and southern Syria had large gentile populations with a significant number of Jewish inhabitants, but given the limited use of Latinisms mentioned above, southern Syria seems more probable. Moreover, the Gospel's setting seems to be more rural than urban. All of Jesus' parables use agrarian imagery, and the majority of Jesus' ministry occurs in the villages, towns, farms, and countryside (1:38; 6:56; 8:27; 11:1, 2, 11, 12; 14:3).

Until the 1800s, Mark's Gospel was neglected, for the most part, by both church tradition and scholarship because it was not a firsthand account and because it was dated after Matthew (Catholic scholars) or after both Matthew and Luke (Protestant scholars). Nevertheless, it boasts some unique literary features. The author highlights key points and narrative themes by "sandwiching" one story in the middle of another, arranging episodes into concentric patterns, using two similar stories to begin and end a large section of the Gospel (Rhoads, Dewey, and Michie 1999). Mark's style is terse and literal. This led Augustine to conclude that Mark was an abbreviated version of Matthew. It was not until 1838 that Mark's priority was established (by C. J. Wilkes and C. H. Weisse). Mark's Gospel then gained popularity because its simplistic style suggested historical accuracy, until form critics argued that the Gospel was not historically accurate but reflected the beliefs of early Christian communities. They examined the literary units to reveal the *Sitz im Leben* of the various forms in the Gospel. Next, the redaction critics focused on the author's arrangement of the tradition, thereby uncovering the author's theological approach to it.

Interest in the Gospel shifted from the historical to the literary. Mark was then primarily viewed as narrative, understood as a "communication event between a writer and an audience" (Juel, 13). The narrative approach to the Gospel drew attention to the contemporary audience or reader and how they engaged the text. This brought to the fore theological concerns that are of importance to people in local churches, rather than only literary and historical issues (Placher, ix–xi). Contemporary Mark scholarship examines the traditional themes of discipleship, Christology, and kingdom of God in the text. However, these are now reexamined through different cultural and theological lenses to expose the liberative strains of Mark's Gospel.

Mark 1:1-13: The Beginning of the Good News

The Text in Its Ancient Context

According to Mark, his story is "good news" (*euangelion*). Although his tidings of "good news" announce a beginning, they do not stand as an isolated experience. Rather, he connects his story to the story of Israel. Moreover, the content of his story will not focus on a single event but on a singular person: Jesus, whom he labels as both "Christ" and "Son of God." For those in his audience who are familiar with the Hebrew Scriptures, the title Christ brings to fore communal memories of exile and foreign rule under Babylon and subsequent deliverance under Cyrus. According to Isa.

44:28, Cyrus was God's anointed (*christos*), and his release of the captives was seen by Isaiah as a result of God's intervention. By employing the designation "Christ," Mark identifies Jesus as the anointed of God who will be used for a divine purpose. In the context of first-century Palestine languishing under foreign (Roman) rule, it would be hard to walk away from these opening lines without having expectations of deliverance raised. Mark compounds this further by his use of "Son of God." Jesus is more than God's anointed; he is in fact God's Son. Textual experts disagree about whether this title in Mark 1:1 is part of Mark's original text or a later inclusion. The title is missing from a few important manuscripts (e.g., Sinaiticus) and present in others (e.g., Vaticanus). However, the presence of the title in important manuscripts like Vaticanus, along with Mark's penchant for identifying Jesus as God's Son throughout the Gospel (1:11; 3:11; 5:7; 9:7; 12:6; 13:32; 14:61; 15:39), suggests that its inclusion here is the work of an omniscient narrator clearly stating his point of view from the start.

Against the backdrop of Old Testament prophecy, Mark sets the stage for the events that follow. Although he opens with a quote that he ascribes to Isaiah (1:2), the first portion of the quotation ("I am sending a messenger ahead of you") is better attributed to Exod. 23:20 and Mal. 3:1. Exodus 23:20 evokes images of wilderness wanderings in which God sends forth a messenger (*angelos*) to keep watch over the Israelites as they sojourn to the promised land. Malachi 3:1 describes the sending of the messenger prior to the coming of the Day of the Lord. The second portion of the quotation, found in Isa. 40:3 (Mark 1:3), announces the coming of the Lord but without the tones of impending judgment found in Malachi. Instead of condemnation, the prophet heralds the end of the exile and Babylonian captivity.

By detailing both John's proclamation and performance against the landscape of Old Testament prophecy, Mark conveys a sense of hope and expectancy to his original readers. As an introduction to his work, this citation of the prophets implicitly offers the theme of judgment as a means of understanding the destruction of the Jerusalem temple by the Romans and unites it here with a theme of comfort. Just as John preaches and baptizes in preparation of the Lord's arrival (1:3, 7-8), so Mark sets the narrative stage for Jesus' appearance.

The narrative lens then turns to Jesus, who has come to the Jordan to be baptized by John. Mark has already introduced him as "Christ" and, depending on how one interprets the textual evidence for Mark 1:1, also "Son of God," perhaps to counter any negative preconceived notions that his audience may have about the next bit of information that he shares. Jesus is from Nazareth of Galilee, a small village off the main roads that is about seventy miles from Jerusalem. Jesus' hometown has no geographic, religious, or political importance of its own. However, about four miles northwest lies the city of Sepphoris. Not only was Sepphoris highly influenced by Rome, but it also greatly angered the rest of Galilee when it refused to rebel against Rome in 66 CE. Had not Mark given the titles in the first verse, his audience's initial perception of Jesus might be as a "nobody from nowhere," or worse, a Roman sympathizer. The titles "Christ" and "Son of God" help to persuade his readers that it is his personage rather than his address that is significant.

Mark tells us nothing of Jesus prior to this moment. It seems that his baptism is the beginning of his story and nothing before matters. The heavens, the barrier separating the human and divine realms, are torn. The Greek verb, *schizein*, suggests that the tear is irreparable. There will be no mending of this breach: God is now accessible to human beings and human beings are accessible to God (Juel, 34–35). Through this divide comes the Spirit in the form of a dove, perhaps intimating the birth of a new creation (Gen. 1:2; 8:8). Mark notes that the dove descends "into" (*eis*) him—not "upon" (*epi*) him (Matt. 3:16; Luke 3:22). Jesus is indwelled by the Spirit. Finally, a voice speaks from heaven affirming that he is God's Son, who is both "pleasing" and "well loved."

No sooner does the Spirit descend into Jesus than it "drives" him into the wilderness. Jesus is cast out from human company, much like the demons he will cast out in his ministry. Both his location and length of stay are important to note. They allude to the children of Israel's sojourn in the wilderness for forty years. Jesus is also in a place of testing, suggesting that his departure from this place will be the fulfillment of another divine promise. However, it will not be without opposition. Otherworldly lines of demarcation are being drawn: Satan tests him and angels minister to him, leaving his audience to wonder how this will play out in the human realm.

The Text in the Interpretive Tradition

Questions about Jesus' (divine and/or human) nature have caused Mark's account of Jesus' baptism to be ignored and/or conflated with Matthew's version. Until the late eighteenth century, Matthew was believed to be the first written Gospel. According to Augustine, Mark was Matthew's abbreviator. Therefore, Matthew's Gospel, which included an infancy narrative and an explanation of why Jesus was being baptized (Matt. 3:14), was preferred. Once Markan priority was established, it became clear that the early church had been uncomfortable with Mark's presentation and preferred Matthew, often called the "church's Gospel," because it corrected Mark's lack of episodes such as the infancy narrative, which depicts the miraculous nature of Jesus' birth, and the lack of explanation for Jesus' receiving John's "baptism of repentance," which implicitly called into question early Christian belief in Jesus' sinlessness.

Rather than focus on what this passage says about Jesus' (divine or human) nature, contemporary scholars explore the connection between Jesus' baptism and his ministry. His baptism is understood as Jesus' surrender to God's will, his divine commissioning by God, his rejection of the dominant culture, and/or his identification with sinners. Questions of divine origin hinge more on whether "Son of God" (1:1) was originally included in Mark's manuscript than on an examination of Mark's baptism account alone.

The Text in Contemporary Discussion

If we are to follow the trajectory of contemporary scholars and focus on Jesus' ministry, baptism becomes intimately connected to discipleship. We can no longer stop with the question of who Jesus is but must ask, how can others follow him? Matthew, Mark, and Luke record John's proclaiming a "baptism of repentance." It may be helpful for readers of Mark's Gospel to think about repentance as changing one's heart or mind and then read the Gospel with this question in mind: How does Mark's story of Jesus get us to change our minds about the world around us and our participation in it?

Mark 1:14-39: An Invitation to Follow

The Text in Its Ancient Context

Unlike John, who ministered in the southern region of Judea near the urban center of Jerusalem, Jesus' ministry begins in the northern region of Galilee. Galilee was known for its farming and fishing, both industries sustained through the labor of a predominantly peasant population. It was a largely rural area surrounded by foreign nations whose inhabitants would later be strongly resistant to the Romans during the war (66–70 CE). They reaped none of the benefits Rome bestowed on the Jewish political and religious elites in the south. Instead, their labor fueled an economy that kept them at the lowest economic and social strata of ancient Palestinian society. It is here that Jesus proclaims the impending arrival of God's kingdom.

The first thing Mark shows his community is that the kingdom has both social and economic implications. As Jesus "pass[es] along" the Sea of Galilee, he calls four fishermen to follow him: Simon, Andrew, James, and John (vv. 16-20). Each of them responds without hesitation. They leave behind all ties to their current livelihood, which will affect them economically and affect their relationships with their families. James and John work with their father, Zebedee. We will soon see that Simon is married; he has a mother-in-law (v. 30). If we are to begin to understand the appeal of Jesus' invitation, we must first refrain from equating the modern industry of fishing and our understanding of entrepreneurship with the profession in its ancient Palestinian form. According to K. C. Hanson, the fishing industry was highly regulated and governed by political and kinship ties. The profits routinely made their way to the coffers of the urban elites, leaving many fishermen indebted to brokers for leases and money needed to run their businesses. Fisherman often formed cooperatives to survive. If they did not have enough people in the cooperative, they hired laborers, as Zebedee did (Hanson, 104). In effect, the four men forsake the highly regulated vocation that is controlled by the Jewish elites and accept Jesus' invitation to follow and fish for people.

Next, Mark demonstrates that the kingdom of God is manifest in both Jesus' word and deed (vv. 21-18). When Jesus enters the synagogue and begins to teach, he astonishes the audience with the level of authority he possesses. In the midst of his teaching, a man with an unclean spirit interrupts him and identifies him as the "Holy One of God." The presence of the man is not surprising: the world was believed to be inhabited by spirits, which were mainly malevolent in nature. Both Judaism and the pagan religions of the Greco-Roman world saw the need for people to be freed from the power of unclean spirits/demons. In Judaism, the presence of unclean spirits symbolized the struggle between God and the forces of evil (Mann). Therefore it is ironic that the people who are supposed to be on the side of God, namely, the religious leaders and members of the congregation, are not the first characters in Mark's narrative to recognize who Jesus really is. Instead, it is the unclean spirit who knows what the people of God do not. Jesus responds by silencing and exorcizing the demon with a verbal command, thereby confirming the audience's original assessment of his authoritative teaching. His is a "performative utterance" (Tolbert). Jesus speaks and things happen; demons obey.

Finally, kingdom life involves service. Jesus and his four followers return to Simon's house, where they find Simon's mother-in-law sick with a fever. Jesus takes her by the hand and heals her of the fever. In return, she begins to serve them. She is the second character in Mark's story to serve (*diakonein*) Jesus; the first are the angels in the wilderness (1:13). These acts of service foreshadow Jesus' teaching and example of discipleship as servanthood (10:43, 45).

The Text in the Interpretive Tradition

As early as the Middle Ages, the church interpreted the kingdom (*basileia*) of God as a sphere of influence (reign of God) rather than a spatial reality (physical kingdom). However, they equated God's reign with ecclesial rule (Mann). In the mid-1800s, Albrecht Ritschl awakened scholarly interest in this theological concept. He argued that the kingdom of God was the sociopolitical transformation of this world and that it would result in the overthrow of oppression. His work laid the foundation for the social gospel movement, which peaked in the early 1900s. However, Ritschl's work lacked the apocalyptic edge that other scholars believed was present in the Gospel's articulation of the kingdom of God. Scholars such as Johannes Weiss, Albert Schweitzer, and Rudolf Bultmann maintained the apocalyptic notion of time that is divided into two eras: the now and the not yet. For these scholars, the kingdom is a future reality that is beyond human control. C. H. Dodd rejected this otherworldly, future orientation and advocated a realized eschatology. For him, the kingdom of God was already present whenever and wherever God's rule was established.

In the mid-1900s, the next wave of scholarship sought to mediate between the apocalyptic and realized eschatological thrusts of kingdom language. They attempted to bridge the academic chasm between the now and the not-yet, on the one hand, and the kingdom as beyond human control and the participatory nature of the kingdom, on the other (Blount). In addition, scholars moved away from a "pan-Synoptic" approach to the kingdom, in which they studied the kingdom-of-God concept across the Gospels. Instead, they began to explore how individual Gospels presented the kingdom of God (France). Liberation theologians who have equated the kingdom with sociopolitical acts of liberation have taken the symbol full circle, bringing scholarship back to the groundbreaking work of Ritschl as well as to its critiques (Blount).

The Text in Contemporary Discussion

During the last few years, the emerging church movement, which has been defined as "a growing, loosely-connected movement of primarily young pastors who are glad to see the end of modernity and are seeking to function as missionaries who bring the gospel of Jesus Christ to emerging and postmodern cultures" (Driscoll 2006, 22), has shown renewed interest in the kingdom of God. They claim that the kingdom of God is, or at least can be, here and now: "Our [principal] desire is to see God's kingdom come on earth as it is in heaven. We believe this happens when God's people are renewed around God's mission of love and justice in the world" (Maddock and Maddock, 80). This mission of love and justice in the world includes addressing ecological, moral, economic, and social ills. The focus is, therefore, communal, as relationships are of primary importance. However, it is not only human relationships that matter but also humanity's relationship with all of creation.

The communal emphasis of the emerging church movement is similar to that of liberation theologians, who see the redistribution of wealth and a sociopolitical reordering of society that brings in those who have been relegated to the margins as part of the kingdom of God agenda. However, liberation theologians believe that the presence of evil is so pervasive that the kingdom agenda as they understand it cannot be brought about completely by human initiative. It will require divine intervention for its fulfillment, including judgment on those people and systems that oppose God's work. For the emerging church movement, the future is bright. Heaven will eventually come to earth as the kingdom of God is manifested through good works.

As we read Mark's presentation of Jesus' proclamation of the kingdom and Jesus' ministry, how are we to articulate its meaning in a postmodern setting? However we define it, we must be mindful that our definitions have implications for both mission and eschatology.

Mark 1:40—3:6: Following beyond the Boundaries

The Text in Its Ancient Context

Jesus' ministry in Galilee continues to grow. However, it brings to him not only the crowds but also the criticism of the scribes and Pharisees. Mark's presentation of Jesus' ministry and the response of the religious leadership in Galilee show a fundamental difference between the two. By narrating a series of boundary-crossing ministry acts in a concentric pattern, Mark highlights for his audience both the growing tensions between Jesus and the religious leaders in Galilee and the reasons for Jesus' popularity among people in the region.

The first episode in this section (1:40-45) reveals that Jesus' fame has now reached the lowest social strata—the outcasts. A leper approaches Jesus. Despite the hopelessness of his situation, he does not question Jesus' ability to cleanse him. The only barrier the leper perceives to his deliverance is Jesus' willingness to cross the boundaries of ritual purity in order to engage and aid him. Jesus is willing and sends the cleansed man to the priests, commanding that he offer what Moses commanded in the law (Lev. 14:1-7). The leper does not do as Jesus commands, however, but instead tells what Jesus has done for him. Jesus' fame increases to the point that he cannot go into the town but must remain in the country.

As Jesus' popularity grows, so does his conflict with the religious leaders in Galilee. In the remainder of this section of his Gospel (2:1—3:6), Mark shows this by setting up these stories in a series of concentric circles (Rhoads, Dewey, and Michie, 52). He frames this section with two healing stories (2:1-12 and 3:1-6) placed at the beginning and end of this section. The first pericope details the healing of a paralytic. Jesus heals the man so that the scribes who accuse him of blasphemy will know "that the Son of Man has authority on earth to forgive sins" (2:10). In the last, he heals a man with a withered hand. It appears to be a setup since "they watched to see whether he would cure him on the sabbath, so that they might accuse him" (3:2). In both passages, Jesus' power, his "ability to exercise control over the behavior of others" (Pilch, 139), is unquestionable. He has the power to affect the functioning of both men's bodies. The real issue is Jesus' authority, whether he has the "socially recognized and approved ability to control the behavior of others" (Malina, 11). The scribes in 2:1-12 and the Pharisees and Herodians in 3:1-6 do not believe Jesus has the authority to forgive sin or transgress Sabbath law just because he has the power to heal. They do not share the same willingness demonstrated by Jesus when he healed the leper: a willingness to use both power and authority to help those in need. Therefore, Mark shows his audience that if things are left up to the current religious leadership, nothing will change for the vast majority of people.

The second and fourth episodes deal with eating regulations (2:13-17 and 2:23-28). In the second episode, Jesus calls a tax collector by the name of Levi to follow him. Later that evening, he is eating with Levi and many tax collectors and sinners are eating with them. Although the tax collectors represent an economically stable cadre of individuals, they were considered social outcasts and the greatest sinners. They were exploiters of the common people; they raised funds that supported the oppressive regimes of Herod and Rome. Moreover, they increased their salaries by extorting from the people additional money in excess of the tax rate. At first glance, Mark's audience might get the impression that Jesus' table fellowship with tax collectors and sinners implies his approval of them. However, Mark makes it clear to his readers, just as Jesus makes it clear to the scribes that question him, that Jesus is calling sinners because they are the ones in need of assistance. His ministry is directed to those outside the pale of Jewish law, and he goes where they are in order to get them.

The fourth pericope also has to do with eating. In this story, Jesus is criticized for allowing his disciples to eat plucked grain on the Sabbath. Plucking the grain is work and therefore puts them in violation of Sabbath law. Jesus responds to this criticism by reminding his detractors of what David did while fleeing from Saul (1 Sam. 21:1-6). Although there are differences between David's story and the episode at hand (Donahue and Harrington, 111), the reference to David serves to parallel Jesus and David. The implicit argument was a common Jewish technique in which one argues from "light to heavy" (*qal we chomer*). The logic is that if David could claim special authority, then how much more so could Jesus, a point Marks makes explicit in 12:35-37. This special authority extends to his interpretation of what is proper to do on the Sabbath (2:28). He reminds them that the Sabbath was created to serve humans, not the other way around, a notion not foreign to Judaism (Hooker, 104; Juel, 54). This interpretation represents Jesus' basic view of the law—it is to help people, not hurt them.

In the middle of this section is the third episode (2:18-22), which illumines the surrounding stories. In response to questions raised about his disciples' lack of fasting, Jesus compares himself to a bridegroom. A wedding is a time of celebration, not of fasting. In the same manner, his disciples do not fast while he is with them. There will be time to fast when he is no longer there. Right now, a new thing is transpiring. It is symbolized by the images of wine, wineskins, and cloth, highlighting the two very different applications of the faith of Mark's day. The new wine and the new cloth of Jesus cannot fit within the current tradition. If the old does not change, it will cause the two to tear apart. By using the word *schisma* ("tear"), Mark calls his audience's attention back to Jesus' baptism, in which he uses the verbal form of *schisma* to describe the irreparable tearing of the heavens. Mark suggests that just as God ripped through the heavens to destroy the boundary between the Creator and creation, so God will rip through the current religious practices and traditions to destroy the social and economic systems that separate God's people from their God.

This tearing away emphasizes both the severity of the growing conflict between Jesus and the religious leaders and the intensity of the religious leaders' commitment to the prevailing social structure. With each successive story, more people are involved in the conflict. It starts with the scribes, who functioned as low-level officials and religious leaders invested with the authority to interpret Scripture. The Pharisees, who represented perhaps the most influential leadership group among the common people, show up next. It ends with the Pharisees and Herodians, most likely the courtiers of Herod, joining forces to kill Jesus (3:6). Moreover, as Jesus' opponents increase, so has the level of animosity against him. It begins with the scribes questioning in their hearts (2:6) and ends with a conspiracy to assassinate Jesus (3:6). Jesus' response to his challengers also intensifies. He begins by merely responding to their questions and ends with outright anger (5:5), showing that his commitment to change the status quo is just as profound as the religious leaders' opposition.

The Text in the Interpretive Tradition

"Son of man" (*ho huios tou anthrōpou*), first mentioned in Mark 2:10, is the Greek translation of the Aramaic phrase *bar nasha*. The earliest commentators saw the son of man as a reference to the humanity of Jesus as it related to his earthly parentage. In the writings of Tertullian and Ignatius, both qualified "son of man" with the phrase "according to the flesh" to highlight Jesus' humanity and juxtaposed it to "Son of God," which highlighted his divinity. The early church fathers followed the Jewish understanding of the Hebrew form (*ben 'adam*), which refers to humanity in general. Within its Jewish context, "son of man" was believed to highlight the weakness and frailty of humanity. This is where the early church fathers' understanding of son of man differed from the Jewish understanding. For them, Jesus' divinity could in no way be compromised by human weakness.

The understanding of "son of man" as an affirmation of and emphasis on Jesus' humanity continued through the 1600s. However, new theories emerged after the Protestant Reformation. The two most predominant were from scholars who asserted that son of man was a messianic title based on Dan. 7:13 and those that argued that it was simply a self-reference. The understanding of "son of man" as a messianic title gained ground during the 1700s and 1800s. Yet the stress on Jesus' humanity remained. "Son of man" referred to a very human Messiah.

By the mid-1800s, this changed when an Ethiopic manuscript of *1 Enoch* was discovered that mentioned a preexistent heavenly son of man. For nearly a century, scholars asserted that Jesus' use of the phrase was based on this figure (France). During this same time period, scholars posited various theories: namely, that Jesus identified himself with the son of man that he expected to arrive during his lifetime (Joachim Jeremias); that the son of man was an allusion to and Jesus' acceptance of his role as an obedient servant (Morna Hooker); that the phrase was a creation of the early church; and that "son of man" was an idiom meaning "I," and therefore a nontitular self-reference (Géza Vermes). Scholarship remains divided on the theological interpretation of this phrase and whether it should be understood as a title or a simple self-designation. The lack of scholarly consensus has caused son of man studies to be described as "a prime illustration of the limits of New Testament scholarship" (Burkett, 5).

The Text in Contemporary Discussion

Scholars identify three types of son of man sayings in the Synoptic Gospels. They refer to (1) Jesus' earthly ministry, (2) his suffering, or (3) his future glory. The initial two son of man sayings in Mark's Gospel (2:10, 28) are located within the controversy cycles and refer to Jesus' earthly ministry. At the heart of the conflict are the boundary-breaking actions of Jesus that upset the social structure of his day. Interestingly enough, twenty-first-century American life reflects this aspect of Mark's world, a world in which 1 to 2 percent of the population controlled the vast majority of resources, leaving the rest barely able to survive (Saldarini, 40–41). We also live in a time and place in which scriptural interpretation and theological perspectives are used to support public policies and practices that deny people equal access under the law and basic forms of societal maintenance. Although we do not use the language of "unclean" to exclude people, we hear the labels "lazy," "deviant," and "dangerous" used to suggest that certain people are undeserving and unworthy of medical care, decent food and housing, equal rights under the law, or quality education because they are morally unfit or unqualified to reap societal benefits. Therefore, the ministry of the son of man in the controversy cycles poses questions to us: Who benefits from our interpretations of Scripture and practices of the faith? Who is excluded?

Mark 3:7-35: Following in Ministry: Expansion and Opposition

The Text in Its Ancient Context

Just as Mark recounted the upsurge of Jesus' fame due to the testimony of the leper (1:45), followed by the rise of opposition (2:1—3:6), so the pattern now continues. The crowds from Galilee are joined by those from Judea, Jerusalem, Idumea, beyond the Jordan (Perea), and the area of Tyre and Sidon. Although mentioned cursorily, the expansion of Jesus' following by people in these locales is significant in that it foreshadows the continued antagonism toward Jesus.

Initially of note is the fact that Mark mentions Judea and Jerusalem separately. At this time, the area that had long ago been the kingdoms of Israel and Judah comprised three regions: Judea, Samaria, and Galilee. Jerusalem was located in the region of Judea. However, Mark highlights the fact that people came not only from the smaller Judean towns and villages but also from the urban religious and political center of Jerusalem, the residence and spiritual base of the upper echelon of the Jewish religious leaders. It was also the political domain of the Roman procurator Pontius Pilate and the Roman client king Herod Antipas.

The inclusion of Idumea and Perea ("beyond the Jordan") as key places from which the multitudes have come gives further reason for the Herodians' animosity (3:6). The Herodians were most likely servants, courtiers, and/or officials of Herod. As supporters of Herod's rule, the Herodians would have found Jesus' preaching of a coming kingdom and (if known) his connection to the Davidic royal line to be a threat to their political interests (Meier, 744). At this point in the narrative, Jesus' ministry has been exclusively within the region of Galilee. Both Galilee and Perea were the original provinces given to Herod Antipas by Rome upon the death of his father, Herod the Great. Moreover, Idumea is the ancestral home of the Herodian dynasty.

Joining the people from Galilee, Judea, Jerusalem, Idumea, and Perea are the crowds that come from the area around Tyre and Sidon. Jesus' ministry has now attracted gentiles from two of the leading Phoenician maritime merchant provinces of Rome. Their inclusion suggests that at some point, Jesus will also find himself in conflict with Rome.

The crowd has now swelled to "crushing" proportions. Despite the potentially deadly repercussions, Jesus does not scale back ministry but expands it. He calls twelve people to "be with him" and participate in ministry by preaching his kingdom message and having the authority to exorcize unclean spirits (3:14-15). Again, opposition will follow expansion. One of the twelve whom Jesus has chosen, Judas Iscariot, will betray him (3:19).

The pattern continues into the final portion of this section. Again, Mark notes the size of the crowd (3:20). What follows is a Markan inclusio—one story "sandwiched" between the beginning and end of another story—that highlights the opposition. The first conflict comes from an unexpected place, Jesus' own family. They believe that he is no longer in his right mind and are on their way to get him. Mark then turns the narrative lens to the "scribes from Jerusalem" who accuse Jesus of demon possession. They attribute his power to Beelzebul, the prince of demons. The story shifts back to Jesus' being told that his family is looking for him. Jesus redefines his family as those who "do the will of God" (3:35), which is precisely how Mark has depicted Jesus' ministry. Howard Clark Kee argues that this new eschatological family is a break from the actual family unit that allows followers of Jesus to form a new kinship group. It represents Markan "eschatological existence," which "involves the acceptance of present opportunities and obligations in view of the age to come" (Kee, 109).

The opposition to Jesus has arisen from every possible vantage point. He is confronted by his family and will soon face betrayal from one of his handpicked apostles. The spread of his fame and the increasing number of people drawn to him potentially threaten to exacerbate the tensions between him, the religious leaders in Jerusalem, and the supporters of Herod. Eventually, Jesus' ministry will catch the attention of Rome.

The Text in the Interpretive Tradition

One of the initial concerns for Roman Catholic interpreters of Mark 3:31-35 was reconciling the presence of Jesus' siblings (also mentioned in 6:3) and the perpetual virginity of Mary. Bede states emphatically, "the brothers of the Lord must not be thought to be the sons of the ever-virgin Mary." Jerome in his treatise *Against Helvidius* argues that Jesus' brothers were actually his cousins. Another argument for the perpetual virginity of Mary asserts that the siblings of Jesus were the children of Joseph from a previous marriage. However, the majority of scholars from the patristic period to the present focus on the formation of Jesus' new family.

John Chrysostom and John Calvin believed Jesus' actions demonstrated the primacy of spiritual relations over fleshly ones. Pseudo-Jerome held that these spiritual relations were not limited by gender. The inclusion of "sisters" in Jesus' new family (Mark 3:35) causes him to conclude: "He [Jesus] discerns us not by sex but by our deeds." Donald Juel avoids spiritualizing Jesus' words. Instead, he points out the controversial nature of denying the most basic social institution of the time, the family, and forging a new one (Juel, 65). Ched Myers articulates the eschatological role of Jesus' new family: it will socialize people into the kingdom just as the natural family socializes individuals into society (Myers, 168).

The Text in Contemporary Discussion

The phrase "family values" hit the national political scene in 1976, when the Republican Party decried the "erosion of family structures and family values." At the 1992 Republican National Convention, Pat Robertson and Dan Quayle claimed that "family values" were what the Republican Party stood for. Since then, the GOP has been criticized for its narrow definition of "family," often specified as a mother, a father, and their child/ren, when only 20 percent of US households fit this particular model. The phrase "family values" often works as code to refer to policies opposing reproductive and homosexual rights. But as historian Lawrence Stone observed while delivering the Tanner Lectures on Human Values at Harvard University, family values actually include several wider areas of social life: how children are socialized to fit into definitions of societal and individual roles, and a range of values concerning work, the accumulation of goods, sexual behavior, religion, and race (Stone, 70). In practice, any political party's policies will affect people's lives in all these areas.

In Mark 3:31-35, Jesus redefines his family. How might Mark's story of Jesus shape our behavior and affect our attitudes in terms of "family values," that is, our attitudes toward and behaviors concerning the areas just named?

Mark 4:1-34: Parables of the Kingdom

The Text in Its Ancient Context

Chapter 4 opens with the first discourse found in Mark. It contains three parables that use the common images of Galilean agrarian life: seeds and sowers. Jesus uses the parables to explain the kingdom he proclaims. The parables also serve to explain the rejection of Jesus and his kingdom message to Mark's readers.

The first parable describes a sower whose seed falls on four types of soil: a path, thorny ground, rocky ground, and good ground. The sower initially appears to be carelessly scattering seed. He has not identified a particular plot or portion of land to sow; nor is he careful about seed placement. Consequently, the majority of the parable is dedicated to describing the consequences: the seed does not grow from bad soil. However, the good soil produces an unimaginable harvest of thirty, sixty, and a hundredfold. These numbers vastly exceeded the 10 percent increase that a farmer would have considered a "bumper crop." Yet, no explanation is given about why the good soil produces such an unheard-of harvest. The assumption of the parable is that the seed is inherently good and only needs the right or good soil to produce copiously.

Producing a harvest at the level Jesus describes would have been a life-changing event for the masses that listened to him. Those gathered were more than likely dispossessed landowners or day laborers whose lack of employment and/or land enabled them to wander the countryside following Jesus (St. Clair, 105). They were ensnared by debt for their entire lives. The burden of Roman taxes, Jerusalem tithes, and the money required to seed the land and take care of a family left many people living at a subsistence level. The result is that those who had land often lost it because of debt. Those living on the land as tenant farmers could never earn enough to buy the land they worked. However, a harvest of thirty, sixty, or a hundredfold meant not only the difference between life and death but also freedom from a debt system that kept them in financial slavery (Myers, 177).

Although Jesus admonishes the crowd to listen, not everyone understands what he is saying. When the crowds have dispersed, those "around him" ask him to explain the parable. Before giving the explanation, he tells them that what they are in receipt of is the "mystery of the kingdom of God" (v. 11). Something is about to be revealed to them that will remain in parables to those "outside." This mystery is a dividing line that demarcates outsiders and insiders.

Mark's Jesus stresses the insider-outsider distinction by quoting Isa. 6:9-10. Whether the lack of understanding and subsequent repentance is the product of Jesus' intention or the consequence of one's failure to hear and accept Jesus' words depends on one's interpretation of *hina* in the Isa. 6:9-10 quotation as either an expression of purpose ("so that") or of result ("in order that"). Although C. S. Mann argues that determinism is a characteristic of apocalyptic and that an interpretation of purpose would not be surprising to Mark's audience, the subsequent parable in this chapter suggests a reading that implies *consequence*. Mark asserts that the meaning of Jesus' parable is "to be disclosed" and "come to light" (4:22). In addition, Mark will show the repeated misunderstanding of the Twelve, who are recipients of the parable's explanation. Originally cast as insiders, their misunderstanding suggests a refusal on their part to heed what they have been taught. Thus the line Mark draws is traversable. Insiders could be "anyone" who has "ears to hear" and listen (v. 9). These receive the mystery of the kingdom that Jesus is giving to them. However, a refusal to hear and listen can relegate one to the outside.

What follows is an explanation of the parable that is critical for understanding all of the parables in Mark (v. 13). It begins simply: "The sower sows the word" (v. 14). The primary sower in Mark's Gospel is Jesus, whose ministry began with proclaiming the good news of God. His sowing, too, seems wasteful. The vast majority of those who gather around him when he is giving the word are poor, diseased, demon-possessed, or considered sinners. They lack economic means and social acceptance and cannot attain the standards of ritual purity. Although their lack relegates them to the margins of their current society, it will not hinder their participation or production in the kingdom of God. According to the parable, Satan, persecution or trouble, and wealth or worldly desires cause spiritual barrenness. But if people will hear, accept, and act on the word, then they, too, can be fruitful (v. 20).

In short, the kingdom is not what people would expect. It is hidden (vv. 22) like a seed on the earth that is not readily seen but takes time to grow and make its presence known (vv. 26-29). It starts small and looks insignificant but becomes great (vv. 30-32). One could easily dismiss the kingdom and its messenger. For this reason, Jesus admonishes those around him (and Mark, by extension, is telling his readers) to "listen" (v. 22) and "pay attention" (v. 23), lest they too become the bad soil that rejects the seed of this sower.

The Text in the Interpretive Tradition

The earliest interpretations of Jesus' parables were allegorical in nature. The early church read parables as stories that used earthly symbols to communicate heavenly truths. Pseudo-Jerome wrote that Jesus spoke in parables so that "those who could not take in heavenly things, might conceive what they heard by an earthly similitude." The first major departure from an allegoristic approach was by Adolf Jülicher in 1888. He argued that Jesus would not have used coded language; therefore, the allegorical interpretations of the parables were the creation of the Gospel writers. Interestingly enough, the patristic and medieval interpreters had no problem with the coded language of the parables. Although they believed the ability to see or understand was a result of God's grace, the lack of understanding was attributed to human unwillingness (Pseudo-Chrysostom), specifically people "mak[ing] themselves not to see" (Theophylact).

Scholars who followed in the wake of Jülicher, like Joachim Jeremias, believed that by studying the parables one could reconstruct the situation in which they developed and uncover the original sayings of Jesus. The next shift occurred when the focus of study moved from the world behind the text to the narrative world of the text. Contemporary scholars now look at the literary context of the parables to ascertain their meaning and seek to be mindful of the insider-outsider dynamic of the text by acknowledging both the comfort and the discomfort created by the text.

The Text in Contemporary Discussion

Parables are tricky. One the one hand, they use familiar imagery to communicate a message. This lends an air of accessibility; it makes one feel like the parables can be easily understood. Yet this is not the case for those around Jesus in Mark's Gospel. He must explain the parables, and then only does so in private, thereby erecting a wall between those on the inside, who understand, and those on the outside, who do not. Coded language separates, and the inevitability of its separating function is often uncomfortable. The first major interpretive shift in the study of parables occurred precisely because of a scholar's discomfort with Jesus' use of coded language. Yet some people are comfortable with coded language. They see the boundaries that the code erects as necessary for survival and communication. The apocalyptic language of Daniel and Revelation and the use of spirituals by African Americans are two examples.

Mark 4:35—6:6: Ministry and Rejection

The Text in Its Ancient Context

Writing shortly after the fall of the Jerusalem temple, Mark responds to the religious crisis by encouraging his readers to follow Jesus. In this section, Mark makes it clear to the Jews and gentiles that constitute his audience that following Jesus will require the inclusion of the gentiles as well as Jews like the woman with the hemorrhage, who have found themselves marginalized by Jewish law.

After a day of public and private instruction on the kingdom of God, Jesus decides to take his disciples to the "other side" of the lake (4:35). Before they reach gentile soil, however, a storm arises that threatens to keep them from reaching their destination. It also causes the disciples to fear for their lives (4:38). Within the narrative context, the storm could be symbolic of the Jewish attitudes that oppose the inclusion of the gentiles. Since Jesus is able to subdue nature in the same way he has been able to subdue demons, the disciples do not perish as they follow Jesus' command to cross over. Mark, therefore, shows his readers that this ministerial direction is by divine proclamation and under divine protection.

According to Mark, Jesus and his disciples disembark in the land of the Gerasenes (5:1). Although the name of this region differs from that given in Matthew (Gadarenes, 8:28) and its location is unknown, it is a gentile territory near the Decapolis, a group of ten Greek city-states southeast of the Sea of Galilee. This area represents the height of uncleanness for Jews. The first person Jesus and the disciples encounter is a man possessed by so many demons that they refer to themselves as "Legion" (5:9). He lives among the tombs, a place inhabited by the dead (5:3). There is a "great herd" of pigs nearby (5:11).

It seems that Jesus has entered the "strong man's house" (3:27) by invading enemy territory both spiritually and politically. "Legion" is the name of a Roman military unit composed of about six thousand soldiers. During this time, the soldiers stationed in Palestine displayed a wild boar as their symbol. Although the demons possess the man, their control of him is secondary to their desire to remain within that particular geographical locale. After begging Jesus not to send them out of the region (*chora*, 5:10), they beg him to send them into the swine (5:12). By exorcizing the demons, Jesus has "plundered [the strong man's] property" (3:27). He is strong enough to subdue the demoniac (5:4) because he is the stronger one whom John foretold (1:7). Mark shows his readers that this foray into gentile territory does not result in the demise of Jesus or his disciples. Neither does it contaminate them. On the contrary, it results in the drowning of the demon-possessed pigs in the sea, like Pharaoh's army in Exodus, and produces another disciple who follows Jesus in his preaching ministry (5:20).

Next, Jesus and his disciples return to Jewish soil. Mark now links the stories of Jairus's daughter and the woman with the issue of blood. Both are referred to as "daughter" (5:23, 34), a familial designation that suggests they are part of the Jewish community. Given that the number twelve, the number of Israel's tribes, is used with reference to both women, perhaps Mark intends these two females to symbolize Israel.

This passage begins with Jairus's begging Jesus to heal his daughter. If the two women are meant to represent Judaism in some way, then Jairus's daughter might represent Jews whose lives are properly circumscribed by the law. The little girl is the legitimate offspring of her father (5:23). He speaks on her behalf and solicits the aid she needs. Moreover, he is a leader of a synagogue. He and his family would have been fully included in the community. Furthermore, her age suggests that she is still virginal. Her presence within the home suggests that she is ritually clean. However, none of this prevents her from being sick to the point of death and needing Jesus to heal her.

Before the girl is healed, Jesus is stopped by the touch of a woman who has suffered from hemorrhages for twelve years. She may represent those who have been marginalized by the law. Her condition renders her status as perpetually ritually unclean (Leviticus 15), and she has found no one to help her. Like the little girl, she is sick. She has gone to physicians, but the physicians have not made her better. She too needs Jesus in order to be healed. However, her healing will restore more than her health. It will restore her place within the community. She will no longer be excluded by virtue of her disease.

Critical to each story is Jesus. If these women are meant to represent classes of people, Mark may be showing that Jesus' ministry is needed not only for the gentiles to be delivered (5:1-20) but also for Israel to be healed. By placing the little girl's healing last, perhaps Mark suggests that Israel will not be healed until not only the gentiles but also the Jews who have been marginalized by the law are included. Like the father who was told to "only believe" (5:36) and the woman whose "faith made [her] well" (5:34), Israel must heed Jesus' kingdom message and believe the good news.

Unfortunately, the prospect of this occurring does not look good. Earlier, the gentiles begged Jesus to leave their neighborhood (5:17). Now, although a crowd is pressing in on Jesus, only one person has enough faith to get Jesus' attention (5:30-31). Rather than celebrate the fact that the little girl is not dead, the mourners laugh at Jesus (5:40). Even the people from Jesus' hometown are offended (*skandalizein*) by him (6:3). Their unbelief amazes Jesus (6:6). Yet the only scandalous thing Mark has shown Jesus do is minister to those who have been left out.

The Text in the Interpretive Tradition

This section contains four of the most extraordinary miracles in the Gospel. During the late nineteenth and early twentieth centuries, scholars from the history of religions school began to explore the Hellenistic origins of Christianity. In 1935, Ludwig Bieler published a two-volume work, *Theios Anēr*, which cataloged the characteristics of the Greek "divine man" (*theios anēr*) and listed examples of the divine man in ancient literature including the Bible. One of the characteristics of the divine man was the performance of miracles. Based on the similarities discovered between Hellenistic figures and Jesus, a *theios anēr* or god-man Christology arose. Redaction critics who accepted the existence of a *theios anēr* Christology argued that Mark was written as either a modification of it (Keck) or an outright rejection of it (Weeden). Other scholars, such as Barry Blackburn, deny a *theios anēr* Christology in Mark and argue that the miracle stories are derived from a Jewish rather than a Hellenistic context. Narrative critics, on the other hand, were not concerned about the miracle stories' connection to a cultural milieu. Instead, they looked at how these stories moved Mark's plot forward and attended to the expansion of Jesus' ministry and mission.

The Text in Contemporary Discussion

On January 20, 2009, Barack Hussein Obama was inaugurated as the forty-fourth president of the United States of America. He was the first African American to hold this nation's highest political office. This led many to conclude that the United States was now a "post-racial" society. Somehow President Obama's election was believed to be the death knell of racism, race-based discrimination, and prejudice. It proved that America was whole, or at the very least no longer divided by race. Yet Sunday mornings remain the most segregated time of the American day, and church pews remain one of the most segregated places.

At the time of President Obama's election, approximately 5 percent of US churches were racially integrated or had 20 percent or more of their members represent a different racial/ethnic background from the majority group. Half of these congregations were trending toward a single ethnic identity, which was a reflection of the basic preference among all racial groups: homogeneity. In order for a congregation to be truly multicultural, no single racial identity can dominate its religious life or practice. This means that more than the face of the congregation must change. The congregation must be prepared for changes in things like leadership, worship practices, mission projects, and financial priorities.

As we reflect on this passage in Mark, it is important for us to consider honestly who the gentiles would be to us—whose racial/ethnic background is not only different from our own but also what separates us from each other. Who would be the outcasts—the people who share a similar racial/ethnic background but whose social, cultural, and/or economic status separates us from them? What storms could potentially arise if we were to "cross over to the other side"? Would our declining and dying congregations be resurrected if we, too, included the modern-day equivalent to Mark's "outsider" (gentile) and "outcast"? What would national policies like immigration, health-care reform, and welfare reform look like?

Mark 6:7-29: Ministry and Murder

The Text in Its Ancient Context

Whereas the parable of the sower in chapter 4 focuses on the condition of the soil (4:3-8), this section reveals the possible consequences of sowing the word. The theme began with the sending out of the Twelve whom Jesus called to be with him, proclaim the message, and have authority over unclean spirits (3:14-15). This is the same ministry work that Mark records Jesus doing and that the disciples now perform (6:12-13). Jesus gives them specific instructions on how to govern themselves and what to bring with them. It is clear that Jesus expects the people to welcome the itinerant ministers because he tells them to take nothing with them except a staff (6:8). The *Didache* also shares this expectation of hospitality (*Did.* 11.1–12). However, Jesus is aware that not everyone will receive the Twelve. In this instance, they are to shake the dust from their feet (6:11), thereby disassociating themselves from the bad soil that does not listen and accept the word.

The ministry of the Twelve is apparently successful. People begin to speculate that John the Baptist or Elijah has been raised from the dead (6:14-15). The ministry work of the disciples, work that clearly mirrors the ministry of Jesus, is now connected to John the Baptist. Prior to this point, Mark has told the reader that John was arrested (1:14). Now the reader finds out that John has been beheaded by Herod (6:16) and his death was orchestrated by Herodias (6:19-24). Like Jezebel, who sought to kill Elijah for condemning the worship of her gods and killing her prophets (1 Kings 19:1-2), Herodias wanted John executed for speaking against her marriage to Herod (6:18-19).

At this point in the narrative, one sower is dead, and sowing the word lies at the root of his death. Members of Mark's community, who already know of Jesus' death, would also know that John will not be the only casualty in Mark's story. Jesus will die, and Mark is laying the foundation to connect his death to John's. In Mark's narrative, both men are "handed over" or "betrayed" (*paradothēnai*, 1:14; 3:19; 14:41). The means of death (beheading and crucifixion) are the most shameful ways of executing a person during this time. Mark shows their words to be the precipitating factor in their deaths (6:18; 14:62). The people's assertion that John has been raised from the dead (6:14) prepares Mark's audience for Jesus' prediction of his own resurrection (8:31; 9:31; 10:34).

Upon the disciples' return, Jesus decides that they should get away from the crowds and rest (6:31). However, they cannot escape the multitudes. The people flock to where they are. The scene is reminiscent of Israel in the wilderness, whose hunger is satisfied by manna, bread from heaven. In this instance, Jesus looks up to heaven, blesses and breaks five loaves, divides two fish, and gives them to his disciples to distribute (6:41). At least five thousand people are fed (6:44). Once again, Jesus and his disciples are aligned in ministry. Yet Mark will show that they still do not grasp the significance of who Jesus is, and therefore cannot possibly understand the consequences of following in a ministry like his.

The Text in the Interpretive Tradition

In 1901, Wilhelm Wrede published his groundbreaking work, *Das Messiasgeheimnis in den Evangelien*. He is credited with being "the first to appreciate the theological nature of the synoptics" (Dunn, 92). His basic thesis was that Jesus' silencing of demons, healed persons, Peter after his confession at Caesarea Philippi, and the disciples after the transfiguration as well as the private instruction, parabolic teachings, and continued misunderstanding of the disciples (like the misunderstanding about the loaves in 6:52 noted above) are all a part of the "messianic secret." The messianic secret was Mark's attempt to resolve the tension between the early church's claim that Jesus is the Messiah and Jesus' not claiming this role for himself in the Gospel. Wrede believed that the messianic secret was not historical in origin, but rather a theological motif created by and imposed on the Gospel by Mark.

James Blevins traces three waves of reactions during the first seventy years after the release of Wrede's monograph. The first decade was characterized by a widespread rejection of his theory. The few who accepted it did so in modified form. For example, Albert Schweitzer accepted Wrede's theory but did not attribute the secrecy theme to Mark. Modifications of the theory continued into the next wave of reactions. During the second and third decades, scholars tried to connect the motif to the historical Jesus. Form critics who accepted Wrede's argument noted that certain elements included in the secrecy motif, like the silencing of demons, was not the work of Mark, but preredaction material. During the years just before and after World War II (fourth and fifth decades), a primary issue was whether the secrecy motif originated with Jesus, and was therefore historical in nature, or with Mark, thereby making the Gospel a wholly theological construction.

This interplay between history and theology also emerges in this section, when Mark lays the death of John the Baptist at the feet of Herodias (Mark 6:19, 24; cf. Matt. 14:8). Mark portrays Herod as easily manipulated and an unwilling partner in Herodias's deadly scheme. However, Josephus attributes John's death to Herod's fear of John's popularity (*Ant.* 18.116–19), not Herodias's "grudge against him" (6:19). According to Bede, it is not Herod's fear but Herodias's fear of Herod repenting of his marriage to her that is the impetus for her murderous designs. Theophylact also implied Herodias's culpability by claiming that lust is what prompted Herod to comply with his wife's wishes. Despite Josephus's assertion and the Herodian rulers' hunger for political power, both biblical scholarship and popular culture have left Herodias's diabolical role in John's death unquestioned.

In medieval Europe, Herodias was said to fly through the night once a year and was purported to be the leader of a cult of witches. During the nineteenth century, Flaubert and Massanet both wrote stories in which Herodias bore all the features of a stereotypical femme fatale. Contemporary Mark scholars pay little attention to the historical Herodias. Their focus tends to be more theological as they note the similarities between John's and Jesus' death, the analogous roles Herod and Pilate played in their respective deaths, and the parallels between John, Herod, and Herodias and Elijah, Ahab, and Jezebel.

The Text in Contemporary Discussion

Although much of Wrede's thesis has been dismissed or modified by subsequent scholars, any discussion of Mark's Gospel must take it into consideration. C. S. Mann correctly asserts, "The 'secrecy' motif is too strongly entrenched in the narrative to be dismissed lightly" (Mann, 216). However, it is almost universally agreed that Wrede's "messianic secrecy" is too limiting a category to house such "disparate phenomena" (Donahue and Harrington, 28) that have a "variety of motives" at work (Dunn, 98). Since the World War II years, scholarship remains divided on whether the secrecy motif finds its genesis in Jesus or Mark. On one end of the debate are those who locate the motif's origin with Jesus, who was afraid that revealing himself would incite a military revolt. On the other end are those who say it is a creation of Mark, who seeks thereby to explain why Jesus does not claim to be the Messiah in his Gospel. At the heart of the issue is whether the origin of Mark's Gospel is historical or theological.

Meanwhile, the work of feminists, which has drawn scholarly attention to the negative portrayal of Herodias, struggles with the historical and theological interplay in Scripture. They admonish readers of the biblical text to beware when reading stories about women because historically these have been "stories by men about women" (Schüssler Fiorenza, 50). They reveal the patriarchal language in the text in which Herodias is referred to as a possession belonging to Herod's brother (6:18). They call attention to the contradiction between Herodias's alleged power in having John killed and her absence from Herod's birthday celebration, which suggests she was not important enough to attend. They examine the roles of women within the sociocultural world that shaped the Gospels. This allows them to show how women have been misrepresented, overlooked, or even vilified.

Narrative readings allow scholars to hold the story world of Mark together with its theological import while examining the historical background of the text. Narrative critics see Mark as an author with an important story to tell. In the case of Herodias, narrative critics look at how a woman has been characterized: What does the author show and tell us about her? Does she espouse or reject the evaluative point of view (the belief system or moral disposition) of the narrator? What are her character traits? If the portrayal in Mark's Gospel is negative, it is also important to ask if her role is consistent with Mark's characterization of other women his Gospel, or does he present a variety of female characters? While her story as presented by Mark may not be historically accurate, it can help the reader understand Mark's story better.

Mark 7:1-23: Ministry and Tradition

The Text in Its Ancient Context

Jesus' popularity among the masses has gotten the attention of the religious leaders in Jerusalem (7:1). Previously, the scribes who had come from Jerusalem accused Jesus of being possessed by Beelzebul (3:22). Now the Pharisees join the scribes. The point of contention is the "tradition of the elders," the oral law that was eventually written in the Mishnah, as it relates to hand washing. The scribes and Pharisees notice that Jesus' disciples do not wash their hands before eating, and question why (7:2, 5). At the root of their concern is more than hand washing; it is the practice of their faith.

Whereas Mark's response to post-temple Judaism is to encourage following Jesus, the Pharisees' response was to bring holiness into everyday life. In their opinion, Jews could uphold God's requirement for holiness (Lev. 11:44, 45; 19:2) by ordering life in such a way that all they did and touched was sanctified. This required avoiding anything that defiled a person. To disregard the practices that helped to cleanse daily life was to dismantle the faith and disregard the oral tradition. This dismantling was, in their eyes, as destructive to Judaism as was the destruction of the temple. For the Pharisee, on the one hand, the Torah as interpreted by the oral tradition mediated the relationship between God and God's people. Mark, on the other hand, sees Jesus fulfilling that role (Juel, 106–7).

According to Mark, Jesus asserts that "human tradition" and the commands of God are at variance with one another (7:8-9). At the heart of Jesus' concern is the inclusion of those heretofore excluded from the practice of the faith. When Mark writes that "all the Jews" do not eat with unwashed hands (7:3), he is using "Jews" to refer to those who adhered to the teachings of Pharisaic Judaism because he has not shown this to be the practice of the Jewish followers of Jesus. It would have been virtually impossible for the five thousand men fed in the wilderness to have washed their hands before eating (6:44). Neither does he record any hand washing before the meal at Levi's house (2:15). Moreover, it is doubtful that many of the people who came to Jesus would have been concerned with, or had the means of maintaining vigilant hand-washing practices, since these persons were predominantly indigent, ill, or demon-possessed. Consequently, Mark's use of "all of the Jews" is inaccurate. However, saying "all the Jews" allows him to separate the practices of his community not only from Pharisaic Judaism but also Judaism in general. Therefore, Jesus' refusal to uphold the tradition of hand washing is no longer a difference of opinion with those from a particular branch of Judaism but represents a rift with Judaism itself. It also allows gentiles and Jews who do not or cannot keep the traditions of the elders to follow Jesus.

Jesus begins his critique of the tradition by quoting Isa. 29:13. He uses the words of the prophet to argue against the practices of the Pharisees. In short, they are hypocritical (7:6). Their tradition actually militates against true worship of God (7:7). Consequently, the Jews in Mark's community need not feel obligated to follow the Pharisees or feel excluded by them. Moreover, the gentiles in Mark's community can reach the same conclusion, as it is clear that Mark is writing to them also. He explains what "defiled hands" mean (7:2), expounds on the "tradition of elders" (7:3-4), and translates the Aramaic word *korban* (7:11).

Jesus pushes his kingdom agenda further by using this opportunity to explain what truly defiles a person. Mark refers to Jesus' teaching here as a "parable" (7:17). As with the telling of the parables in chapter 4, Jesus commands those around him to "listen" (7:14). Moreover, he explains the meaning of the parable to his disciples in private. These similarities intimate that Jesus is telling his listeners something about the kingdom of God.

Specifically, Jesus teaches that an understanding of defilement in terms of the kingdom of God is not about what goes in but what goes out (7:15, 20). There is a difference between the stomach and the heart (7:19). What comes out of the heart corrupts. What goes in the stomach does not have the power to defile, leaving Mark to conclude that Jesus has "declared all foods clean" (7:19). How one eats (whether the hands are washed or unwashed) and what one eats (whether the food is deemed clean or unclean according to dietary laws) no longer has the power to deny persons a relationship with God or prevent participation among the people of God.

The Text in the Interpretive Tradition

Readings of this passage have primarily focused on the dispute between Jesus and the Pharisees over the validity of oral law. Many commentators equated "oral law" with "man-made" law because they were unaware that the Pharisees believed in a dual Torah, written and oral, that was revealed to Moses on Sinai (Donahue and Harrington, 228). However, interpretations became more nuanced as scholars began to examine the Jewish context of Jesus' ministry and no longer to view first-century Judaism in monolithic terms. Instead, scholars began to see the varied strands of Judaism and how they responded to the fall of the Jerusalem temple. Consequently, descriptions of Pharisaic Judaism went beyond labels of "religious legalism." Attention to the sociocultural context of Mark's Gospel filled out the flat characters that Mark presented. It also prompted contemporary scholars to view this passage as breaking the barriers that would have prevented gentile participation in the early church. This passage clarified for Mark's community its stand on issues that would have distinguished it from Pharisaic Judaism.

The Text in Contemporary Discussion

In almost every religious tradition, there is a belief that certain things or people have the power to defile individuals or the community. There are usually two basic approaches to dealing with the pollutant: washing machine or garbage disposal. At the heart of the washing-machine approach is the conviction that the power to cleanse is greater than the power to contaminate. Therefore, the polluted thing or person can be cleaned up and restored to inclusion. When one opts for the garbage-disposal approach, there is a belief that the power to contaminate is greater than the power to cleanse. Consequently, the pollutant must be removed before it corrupts another individual or community. One's approach depends on the particular contaminant being addressed, and both approaches can be utilized within the same religious tradition. For example, unwashed hands, certain foods, and table fellowship with the wrong people were just a few of the contaminants that first-century Pharisees believed made a person unclean. Hands could be purified by washing (the washing-machine approach) and certain foods and people could be avoided (the garbage-disposal approach).

What are the pollutants that we fear in our contemporary practice of the faith? Which ones do we believe have a power to contaminate that is greater than the power to cleanse (requiring us to use a garbage-disposal approach)? Over what pollutants is the power to cleanse greater than the pollutants' power to defile (so we may use the washing-machine approach)? According to Mark, Jesus redefines what defiles a person and thereby pronounces all food clean (7:19). By so doing, he eradicates the need to employ either the washing-machine or the garbage-disposal models because there no longer exists any need for cleansing. Do we need to amend our understanding of what defiles and therefore our approach to some things and/or some people?

Mark 7:24—8:26: Receptivity and Misunderstanding

The Text in Its Ancient Context

Jesus again journeys into gentile territory. This trip reveals the receptivity of the gentiles to Jesus' ministry and proves that there is room for them to be included. Mark, then, uses the receptivity of the gentiles to highlight the growing lack of perceptivity of the Jews whom Jesus encounters throughout this section.

Jesus' first stop is in the region of Tyre. There, he meets a Syrophoenician woman who begs him to cast a demon out of her daughter (7:26). Initially, Jesus seems disinclined to help her. He dismisses her by insisting that "the children" (Israel) are to be fed (*chortasthēnai*) first (7:27). To do otherwise is tantamount to giving their food to dogs (7:28). Although Jesus calls her a dog (7:27), the woman is not dissuaded. She insists that even the dogs get crumbs (7:28). Jesus validates her statement by casting the demon out of her daughter (7:29-30). However, the veracity of her statement has farther-reaching implications than the fulfillment of an individual request.

By recounting the feeding of the five thousand in a manner that alluded to Israel's experience of manna in the wilderness, Mark had shown that "the children" have already eaten to the point of satisfaction (6:42). There he used the same verb that occurs in 7:27 (*chortasthēnai*) to convey that the desert meal filled them. He also noted that the disciples collected twelve baskets of leftovers, symbolically suggesting a basket from each of the twelve tribes of Israel. Indeed, there are crumbs from the children's table, and now Jesus meets a woman so hungry for his help that she is willing to receive these scraps. Mark further emphasizes the gentile woman's hunger for Jesus' ministry by placing her story immediately after Jesus' confrontation with the scribes and Pharisees. While the Pharisees and scribes were concerned with the purity of one's hands and one's food, the gentile woman is willing to eat off the floor to get what she needs from Jesus. By linking her story to the feeding of the five thousand and positioning it immediately after Jesus' argument with the scribes and Pharisees, Mark argues that the inclusion of gentiles will neither prevent nor lessen what God has for the Jews.

Upon leaving Tyre, Jesus travels to the region of the Decapolis. Mark identifies this place as the locale of the former demoniac's preaching ministry. It is here that he proclaimed what Jesus had done for him (5:20). Earlier, the people of this region begged Jesus to leave (5:17). Now they beg Jesus to heal a deaf and mute man (7:32). Jesus heals the man "in private, away from the crowd"

(7:33) and forbids the people from telling it. Yet they proclaim it "zealously" (7:36), thereby joining the former demoniac in his preaching ministry by again proclaiming what Jesus has done.

The two preceding events occur at the initiative of gentiles. They seek out Jesus and request his aid. The feeding of the four thousand, which is the last act Mark records as occurring on gentile soil, happens at Jesus' initiative. Like the feeding of the five thousand on Jewish soil, the motivation behind this miracle is Jesus' compassion. However, Jesus had compassion for the Israelites because they lacked leaders (6:34). Here, Mark emphasizes the receptivity of the gentiles to Jesus' ministry by noting that the crowd has been with Jesus for three days (8:2). As a result, they are hungry. However, their physical hunger is the direct result of their hunger for Jesus, a hunger that causes them to remain with him for three days without food. Therefore, Jesus responds.

Using seven loaves and a few small fish, he feeds the four thousand gathered around him. Jesus has now used a total of twelve loaves to feed both Jews and gentiles. The number twelve may allude to the twelve tribes of Israel. If this is the case, then Mark is letting his community know that what has been given to Israel is more than enough to satisfy both groups. The supply is so great that neither group can exhaust it. Like the Jews who were fed in the wilderness, the gentiles are filled (*chortasthēnai*) and there are still leftovers (8:8).

After the feeding of the four thousand, Jesus immediately returns to Jewish territory. Here he is met with skepticism and misunderstanding. His first encounter is with Pharisees who demand a "sign from heaven" (8:11). Jesus refuses to oblige them (8:12). However, Mark has answered their question for the reader, with the details he has included in his Gospel. He has recounted the heavens opening (1:10), a voice from heaven at Jesus' baptism (1:11), Jesus looking to heaven as he blessed the five loaves he used to feed five thousand people (6:41), and Jesus looking up to heaven before healing the deaf mute (7:34). Although Mark never mentions the presence of the Pharisees at the aforementioned events, his narrative flow makes the Pharisees appear obtuse to the reader. Because Mark's audience has been given all these "signs from heaven," they are left to assume that the Pharisees should understand rather than argue.

Misunderstanding is not a quality reserved for Jesus' enemies alone. There is much his disciples do not get. Mark shows their lack of understanding in the next episode. Jesus warns them about the "yeast of the Pharisees" and the "yeast of Herod" (8:15). They do not grasp the symbolic use of yeast as a corrupting agent (Donahue and Harrington, 252). Instead, they think Jesus is talking about their lack of physical bread. Even if they could not appreciate the full intent of Jesus' warning, the fact that they think Jesus is troubled by a lack of bread after feeding at least nine thousand people with only twelve loaves shows their imperceptivity.

This section closes with Jesus' healing a blind man. What is unique about this account is that Jesus must lay his hands on the man twice to fully restore his sight (8:23, 25). Given Jesus' command of nature, authority over demons, ability to multiply fish and loaves, and healing virtue that is so strong that touching his garments restores people to full health, the need to touch the blind man twice does not suggest a diminishment of Jesus' power. Instead, it points to the persistent imperceptivity of the disciples. They are blind like this man. They do not get it on the first encounter. They see a little, but they do not yet grasp the whole thing.

The Text in the Interpretive Tradition

Some of the earliest commentators on the story of the Syrophoenician woman (7:24-30) focus on the woman as model of faithful persistence. Bede describes her reply to Jesus' initial refusal of her request as both "humble and faithful." He asserts that these are the qualities that garnered her request. Calvin observes, "she adhered firmly to . . . [her] sentiment of faith" despite the fact that Jesus "[makes] trial of her faith" (Calvin 1845, 2:266-68). Although he describes her actions as "presumptuous," most early commentators downplay her transgression of social boundaries by finding qualities such as humility and service in her behavior. Pseudo-Chrysostom goes so far as to say her reverence was demonstrated by placing herself at the level of a dog. Feminist and womanist scholars broke from this tradition by highlighting her disregard of social convention and applauding her bold behavior. They point to her "sass" (womanists) and her wit (feminists), rather than traditional female virtues of passivity and submission, as the reason she got what she needed from Jesus.

The Text in Contemporary Discussion

Scholars have attempted to soften the impact of Jesus' calling the Syrophoenician woman a "dog," by (1) drawing attention to more positive gentile understandings of "dog" as a house pet (!); (2) pointing out that Jesus actually referred to her and her child as "little dogs" (*kynaria*), which is less offensive than "dog" (*kyōn*); or (3) arguing that Jesus' words represented prevailing Jewish opinion about gentiles, rather than his own perception of the woman, in order to counter opposition to gentile inclusion. The fact remains, however, that this ethnic slur is found on the lips of Jesus.

Now consider how common it has become in some parts of popular culture today to refer to women in general, and African American women in particular, as "bitches" (female dogs). The lyrics of many hip-hop songs equate "bitch" with "woman." Reducing women to the level of animals allows men outright to exploit them or treat them as pets (Collins). Moreover, women are also referred to as "hoes" (whores), thereby relegating them to the status of sex objects, or as "chickenheads," persons of intellectual inferiority. Social theorists and feminist scholars acknowledge that while it is easy to point out the vulgar references to women in hip-hop and especially its subgenre gangsta rap, these are merely the blatant expression of a wider societal misogyny.

The attempts by Mark scholars to neutralize the "dog" language in the text is akin to the efforts of some women and that of some African Americans to defuse the racist and misogynistic import of the *b* and the *n* word. As people argue both sides of the issue, the question remains: Are there words that are so negative that it is impossible to redeem their meaning or their use? If so, what do we do with a text like Mark 7:24-30?

Mark 8:27—10:52: Following on the Way

The Text in Its Ancient Context

Jesus' lessons on discipleship and the misunderstanding of his disciples typify this section. Although Jesus' lessons have the disciples as their narrative audience, Mark shows that anyone can follow Jesus

(Malbon 1986). Like Jesus' original disciples, however, many will misunderstand. Therefore, Mark employs Jesus' passion prediction and lessons to prepare a would-be disciple for both the call and consequences of discipleship (St. Clair 2008).

Discipleship is not for the fainthearted; no one finds it easy (Malbon 1983, 29). Defined primarily in terms of servanthood, discipleship runs counter to a social structure that advances persons with access to wealth, power, authority, and even purity to the highest levels of the social order. Those without access to this social currency remained at the lowest levels. Thus the way of Jesus reverses the honor-shame codes that structure the cultural world in which Mark's audience lives (St. Clair, 109–64).

Mark first attends to Jesus' identity. Peter declares Jesus to be the "Messiah" (*christos*, 8:27), and for the first time within the narrative, someone uses the same title as that found in the opening line of the Gospel (1:1). Jesus' response confirms the veracity of Peter's answer. He orders Peter and the disciples to keep silent for the same reason he forbade the demons to speak: they knew him (1:25, 34; 3:11).

On the heels of Peter's confession, Jesus foretells his suffering, death, and resurrection (8:31). Although Peter has correctly identified Jesus as the Christ, he does not fully grasp the consequences of Jesus' messianic ministry. He therefore attempts to silence Jesus by rebuking (*epitimān*, 8:32) him as Jesus has rebuked the demons. Rather than silencing Jesus, Peter's actions precipitate Jesus' first lesson on discipleship. Jesus teaches that following him will necessitate two things that run counter to the cultural values of ancient Mediterranean society. First, a would-be disciple must deny himself or herself (8:34). For Mark's original audience, self-denial meant leaving behind one's primary group affiliation (usually the family or kinship group) and solely identifying with Jesus and his gospel. The would-be disciple would need to do "the will of God" so that Jesus and his followers become his or her "brother and sister and mother" (3:35). She or he would then seek approval from Jesus rather than their original group or society at large (St. Clair, 135–36). Second, she or he must "take up the cross" (8:34). The cross represented the most painful and humiliating death that Rome could exact on its subjects. Therefore, Jesus' disciples needed to be able to face pain and shame as a result of following Jesus. In short, a follower of Jesus needed to be prepared to die (St. Clair, 138).

Six days later, Jesus takes Peter, James, and John up a high mountain, where he is transfigured in the presence of Moses and Elijah. Their presence with Jesus suggests that the law (Moses) and the prophets (Elijah) reach their fullest expression in Jesus. Their disappearance, leaving Jesus standing alone, suggests that Jesus has the final authoritative word. Once again, Peter misunderstands. Whether he proposes the booths to prolong the mountaintop experience (Donahue and Harrington, 270) or he believes this event signals the time Zechariah foretold (14:12-21) in which the survivors of the war against Jerusalem would celebrate the Feast of Booths (Juel, 128), he knows he stands at a critical moment. However, the correct response is neither speaking nor building: he needs to listen.

Peter, however, is not the only one struggling to follow Jesus. The remaining nine disciples have also been having difficulty. They have been unable to cast a spirit out of a little boy (9:17). Before rebuking the spirit, Jesus criticizes those around him, including his disciples, for their lack of faith. Faithlessness both characterizes their generation (9:19) and reveals the disciples' lack of identification with Jesus and his words. They are more like the people around them than they are like Jesus.

Jesus must start from the beginning. He foretells his suffering and death for the second time (9:31). Rather than ask Jesus for clarification, the disciples argue about who is the greatest (9:34). Jesus' teaching again reverses the honor-shame codes: status comes through service (9:35). The one willing to humble oneself to the level of the least is the greatest. Jesus illustrates this point by taking a child, the person with the least social status, in his arms (9:36). If one can welcome such a person of low estate in Jesus' name, it will be like welcoming Jesus (9:32). Mark then highlights Jesus' lesson by presenting four episodes that deal with the treatment of the least.

The first episode concerns an exorcist who casts out demons using Jesus' name but does not follow Jesus like the disciples (9:38). For this reason, the disciples try to stop him. Jesus forbids them to stop him and warns them about putting a "stumbling block before one of these little ones" (9:42). "Little ones" are the followers of Jesus who are called to be the servant(s) of all (9:35). Though society may view them as small in social stature and having little power, the "little ones" are great in the kingdom. The sin of hindering their discipleship is so egregious that it is better to cut off the offending body parts rather than risk hellfire (9:43-47).

Jesus' description of the "little ones" as those who believe in him suggests that the exorcist is a disciple. The exorcist believes in Jesus enough to use his name successfully. Unlike the disciples, who could not exorcize the demon in the little boy, this exorcist has been able to cast out unclean spirits (9:38). Rather than hinder kingdom work by trying to erect boundaries that exclude, Jesus admonishes his followers to be at peace with one another (9:50).

The next episode addresses another low-status group in Mark's social world: women. When the Pharisees come to test Jesus, their question references the law, which only allows men the right to divorce (10:2-12). This practice leaves women vulnerable because they are financially and socially dependent on their husbands. Jesus declares that Moses allowed divorce because of their hard hearts. Quoting Gen. 1:27 and 2:24, he argues that divorce was not the original plan but a concession made due to their inability to live up to the original intent of Scripture. Jesus' words show that the Pharisees are not in line with teachings of Moses. When Jesus explains divorce to his disciples, he puts men and women on equal footing. His teaching gives both genders the same right to divorce as well as the same culpability should the divorced person remarry (9:10-12). Thus Mark continues to demonstrate the same concern for women he has shown with the positive portrayals of Peter's mother-in-law (1:31), the woman with the hemorrhage (5:25-34), and the Syrophoenician woman (7:26-30), as well as the intentional inclusion of "sister[s]" as part of Jesus' redefined family (3:35).

The narrative moves from the treatment of women to that of children. Jesus reiterates the principle of his last discipleship lesson. Greatness in the kingdom of God will not be the result of wealth, power, or ritual purity. On the contrary, the kingdom belongs to the least (10:14). This is precisely why one must become the least and servant of all to enter it (10:15). Jesus blesses the children (10:16), thereby sealing his reversal of the honor-shame codes. The ones who are blessed are the ones society has relegated to the lowest social level.

The last episode deals with wealth. The underlying issue is the treatment of another group considered least in Mark's social world, the poor. When a rich man approaches Jesus wanting to know how to gain eternal life (10:17), Jesus tells him to sell all he has, give the money to the poor, and then follow him (10:21). His command to give the money from the sold possessions is an attempt to restore to the poor what was unfairly taken from them. These instructions seek to remediate economic practices that consign the majority of the people to poverty. Discipleship that forbids the oppression of the poor protects these who are also among the least. Jesus' teaching about wealth runs counter to the prevailing notions of wealth in Mark's day. Wealth gave people access. Yet Jesus claims it is a hindrance to those who desire to enter the kingdom of God (10:23). Even for those who have little to no wealth, Jesus' declaration is so shocking that the disciples question the possibility of anyone being saved (10:26).

Despite Jesus' teaching on wealth and a third passion prediction, James and John still clamor for status by asking for positions of honor (10:37). Jesus presents his final discipleship lesson and again emphasizes the need to be a servant (10:43). He concludes by pointing out how he has modeled the behavior he is teaching them. He has not come to be served. Instead, he gives his life in service as he ministers to the least. He will give his life in death because the opposition to this ministry will be fatal. However, his service will ransom "many" (10:45), thereby releasing them from the "strong man's" clutches.

Mark finishes this section with the healing of blind Bartimaeus (10:46-52). He is the first person to call Jesus the "Son of David" (10:47-48) and thus to convey the political implications of Jesus' journey to Jerusalem. According to the Hebrew Scriptures, God promised the throne of Israel to David and his descendants forever (2 Sam. 7:16). It was therefore expected that the Messiah would be a descendant (son) of David (Isa. 11:1; Jer. 23:5-6). As son of David, Jesus is a threat to both Roman and Jewish leadership. The blind man sees the very thing that Jesus has foretold in his passion predictions.

The Text in the Interpretive Tradition

Jesus' passion predictions introduce a new theme into the Gospel: suffering. Since discipleship characterizes this portion of the Gospel, the relationship between suffering and discipleship is worth exploring. Historically, Mark scholars have understood suffering to be a condition or requirement of discipleship. Many interpret *dei* (8:31) as divine necessity. In other words, God sent Jesus to suffer. Others use this section of the Gospel as their interpretive key. They highlight themes of suffering and servanthood, and suffering and death. They claim that the key to understanding Jesus is in relation to his suffering and therefore describe him as a suffering Messiah. Others posit a scriptural necessity for suffering, by interpreting Mark 9:12 and 10:45 as allusions to Psalm 118 and Isaiah 53 respectively. Most recently, Mark scholars have argued for *dei* to be interpreted in terms of inevitability. They cite the opposition to Jesus' ministry in the narrative as the reason for his death. For these scholars, suffering is not a condition but a consequence of discipleship (St. Clair).

The Text in Contemporary Discussion

The relationship between suffering and discipleship is especially important for people who have endured personal or communal suffering. Womanist scholars have found it helpful to distinguish between suffering, on one hand, that arises from oppressive systems and circumstances and results in a static condition that will not change until its sources are confronted, and pain, on the other hand, that is a result of challenging the causes of one's oppression and therefore has the possibility of being eliminated. Jesus' passion is then understood in terms of pain. To follow him is not a call to perpetual suffering for the sake of suffering. To follow him is to accept pain as a consequence of discipleship that requires one to participate in boundary-breaking ministry like his (St. Clair, 145).

The work of womanist scholars causes exegetes (1) to be mindful, when interpreting passages about self-denial, of people who have been denied access to basic necessities, and (2) to be aware, when interpreting passages about taking up the cross, of people who have and are functioning as surrogates (persons who take the place of another by performing the roles and responsibilities of said person). How one interprets these passages may justify, prolong, or even sacralize the suffering and oppression that Jesus in Mark's Gospel seeks to eradicate.

Mark 11:1—12:44: Following to Jerusalem

The Text in Its Ancient Context

Jesus now arrives at Jerusalem, the center of Jewish religious power (11:1). His entry into the city is replete with messianic overtones. Jesus rides into Jerusalem on a colt. The scene depicts the fulfillment of Zech. 9:9. People spread their cloaks for Jesus to tread on like officers did when Jehu was anointed King (2 Kings 9:13). Hosanna, "save, please," conveys the people's desire for deliverance. It is clear from their shouts that they view Jesus' entry into the city as heralding the reinstitution of the Davidic monarchy (10:10). Like Bartimaeus, they recognize Jesus as the promised son of David. They quote Ps. 118:26 as they cry out, "Blessed is the one who comes in the name of Lord!" Yet the second portion of that verse, "we bless you from the house of the Lord," will not be realized. The ministry that has the crowds following him and his entry into the city amid cries of messianic expectation makes Jesus a threat to both Jewish and Roman leaders.

Mark adds new groups to those he has already shown to be arrayed against Jesus. The chief priests and the elders, whose rejection Jesus foretold in 8:31, confront him in the temple (11:27). The Sadducees join the chief priests, elders, scribes, Pharisees, and Herodians as interrogators of Jesus (12:18). The common link among them all is their support of and participation in the temple system, a system Jesus finds corrupt.

The temple is not functioning as intended. Therefore, one of Jesus' first undertakings is symbolically to cleanse the temple. He uses the language of the prophets to describe what has happened to the temple. Instead of being a "house of prayer for all nations" (Isa. 56:7), it has become "a den of robbers" (Jer. 7:11). In Mark, Jesus specifically uses the Greek word for "bandits" (*lēstai*). He equates temple practices with those of first-century highway robbers who plunder people by force. He also depicts Jesus as the stronger one who enters the strong man's house (3:27). And he uses the language of exorcism (*ekballein*) to describe the driving out of the buyers and sellers (11:15).

Additionally, Mark shows the temple system to be representative of a tree that does not produce fruit. He does this by "sandwiching" the temple cleansing (11:15-19) between the story of the cursed fig tree (11:12-14, 20-25). The temple is like the fig tree. It was the crowning achievement of Herod's building projects, but it only has the appearance of fruitfulness, like the fig tree in leaf suggests. On closer inspection, however, there is nothing to it. The fig tree imagery alludes to Old Testament Scriptures that compare Israel to barren fig trees (Jer. 13:13; Hosea 9:10; Mic. 7:1). Jesus' cursing of the fig tree, therefore, intimates the destruction of the temple.

The corrupt temple system and its impending demise is the result of corrupt leadership. In the parable of the vineyard (12:1-12), Jesus implicitly compares the scribes, chief priests, and elders to the evil tenants who kill the vineyard owner's beloved son (12:7-8). He warns people about the scribes' pride (12:38-9), unscrupulous financial practices that result in the "devouring" of widow's property (12:40), and hypocrisy (12:40). It is important to note that Mark uses the scribes to connect Jesus' enemies. He lists the scribes with the chief priests and elders (8:31; 11:27; 14:43, 53; 15:1) and with the Pharisees (7:1), whom Mark pairs with the Herodians (3:6; 12:13). Therefore, Jesus' condemnation of the scribes can be applied to all of the Jewish leaders whose opposition has increased in numbers and in intensity as the scribes and chief priests also look for a way to kill Jesus (11:18).

The Text in the Interpretive Tradition

Couched between Jesus' scathing condemnation of the scribes and his foretelling of the temple's destruction is the story of the widow's offering. Leo the Great, Gregory the Great, and John Chrysostom lifted her as an example of faith and generosity. Based on his interpretation of this story, Calvin concluded that one who "offers to God the little that he has, is more worthy of esteem than that of him who offers a hundred times more out of his abundance" (Calvin, 3:113). From their earliest readings until the present time, scholars have commended the widow whose actions Jesus is believed to have extolled. Most recently, however, scholars have interpreted this story as an indictment of the temple system that victimizes the poor and vulnerable.

The Text in Contemporary Discussion

In 2012, the *Chronicle of Philanthropy* reported their findings on giving patterns in the United States by state, city, and zip code. What they found was that people in higher-income brackets gave less to charitable causes than people with less income. Persons earning between $50,000 and 75,000 per year gave 7.6 percent of their income to charity. People earning more than $200,000 per year, and living in areas where at least 40 percent of their neighbors shared their economic status, gave only 2.8 percent to charity. The divide between income and generosity encourages us to take another look at the widow's offering in Mark's Gospel.

Much of contemporary discussion around this text no longer offers a commendation for the widow's gift but rather a condemnation of the systems of oppression, both religious and political, that persuade those with less to give out of their lack and the rich to keep what they have. They note the juxtaposition of Jesus' condemnation of the scribes as those who "devour widows' houses" (12:40) and the story of the widow's offering. The widow is now seen as a victim of predatory practices rather than a woman whose faith in God results in generosity. Her once positive portrayal is threatened as she becomes a passive character who is duped into supporting something that Jesus condemns and predicts will be destroyed.

As we interpret and apply this passage to our current context, it is important to tease out the strands of condemnation and commendation. How we understand the relationship between the woman and the temple influences how we use this passage to either encourage or discourage relationship between giver and the faith community to which they give.

Mark 13:1-37: Following to the End

The Text in Its Ancient Context

Chapter 13 contains the largest block of teaching found in Mark's Gospel. Commentators have referred to this chapter as the prophetic discourse, believing it to foretell the future; the eschatological discourse, because it speaks of "the end"; the Olivet Discourse, because Mount Olives is the setting for the passage (Brooks, 204); and the "Little Apocalypse," because it reveals the future and discloses the heavenly realm. The description of this chapter as the Little Apocalypse, however, is often debated because certain apocalyptic features such as visions, resurrection, and final judgment are missing. Neither is there a juxtaposition between heaven and earth, the present age and the age to come, or those inside and outside of the church that characterize Christian apocalyptic writings (Edwards, 384). In addition, there is no heavenly intermediary revealing the future events.

Although Mark 13 is different from most examples of apocalyptic literature, there are enough features to categorize it as such. Since apocalyptic literature is a form of sociopolitical resistance by people who have little chance of achieving the political, economic, or military overthrow of their oppressors, Mark, written in the context of the Jewish War, reflects the exact setting out of which apocalyptic literature develops. Moreover, the description of wars, conflicts among nations and kingdoms, famines, and earthquakes are common Christian and Jewish apocalyptic features. Mark specifies that Jesus teaches from the Mount of Olives, the eschatological location of YHWH's final deliverance of Israel from her enemies (Zech. 14:4). Mark 13:19 parallels Dan. 12:1, which is an undisputed apocalyptic portion of the book. Both Mark and Daniel foretell suffering using the same Greek word, *thlipsis*, and record the magnitude of the suffering in similar fashion. Daniel states that it is "such as never occurred since the nations existed"; Mark says it is "such as has not been from the beginning of the creation."

Because apocalyptic literature arises from situations of oppression and/or persecution, its writers often promote both patient endurance and hope. In a manner of speaking, apocalyptic literature is "good news," not in the sense of a literary genre but in terms of the message it proclaims. There is confidence in the fact that although things look bleak now, God is in control and will be victorious. Therefore, Jesus encourages the disciples to "endure" (13:13) and "keep awake" (13:35, 37). The events Jesus foretells in verses 5-23 are described as "birth pangs" (13:8). Read in this context, Mark communicates to his readers that while their situation will get worse before it gets better, their suffering is connected to a greater purpose (Juel, 176). It is not the end; their salvation is (13:13). Mark thus inspires a present hope in his readers as he communicates Jesus' revelation of future events.

It is important to note that some apocalyptic literature "describes the course of history as well as a climactic cosmic transformation" (Donahue and Harrington, 378). In other words, one of the functions of apocalyptic literature is to explain the current circumstances of its readers in light of God's unfolding plan. As expectations for liberation erupted into social protests such as banditry and messianic movements (Horsley 1984, 482), messianic expectations raised eschatological hope, since the Messiah was expected to arrive before "the end." Therefore, Mark needed to address these first-century Palestinian expectations while protecting his community (13:5-6, 21-22). The warnings against false prophets and messianic pretenders found on Jesus' lips frame the discourse so that Mark's readers will not be led astray (13:6, 22).

According to Mark, Jesus foretells the destruction of the temple (13:2) as well as the persecution of his followers (13:9, 11-12). These prophecies prepare Mark's readers for their current state of affairs. First, they are reassured that the temple was not intended to be the center of the community's faith. Mark presses this point by reminding them (through words he attributes to Jesus) that those in Judea are supposed to flee when the temple's destruction, signaled by the "desolating sacrilege," is about to take place (13:14). In Dan. 9:27, the "desolating sacrilege" referred to the pagan altar set up in the temple by Antiochus Epiphanes. Mark uses the phrase to refer to another desecration of the sacred space. By using the masculine form of the Greek participle for "stand" (*estēkota*) rather than the neuter, Mark informs his readers that the "desolating sacrilege" is not an "it" but a "he." There are three main proposals for identifying this person: (1) Caligula, who ordered the erection of a statue of himself in the temple in 40 CE (Josephus, *Ant.* 18.261), (2) the rebel Eleazar, who used the inner temple as his headquarters from the winter of 67–68 CE until 70 CE, and (3) Titus, who entered the temple in 70 CE as it was being destroyed. Since the "desolating sacrilege" is a sign to flee Judea, Caligula would be too early and Titus would be too late, which leaves Eleazar as the best option (Marcus). The attention Mark pays to the "course of history," namely, the temple's destruction and the desolating sacrilege, provides clues for dating his Gospel as well.

By recounting Jesus' prophecy about the persecution of his followers, Mark parallels his community's suffering with that of Jesus. Like Jesus, they will be "handed over to councils" (15:1), beaten (14:65), brought to trial (14:55-64) and before governors (15:1-15), and betrayed by their own families (14:43-45). Given Jesus' redefinition of family (3:35), the betrayal by family members may not come from one's biological kin but those who are part of the community of disciples.

After twenty-three verses that focus on the "course of history," Jesus' discourse gives way to "cosmic transformation." In the background of Jesus' teaching is the disciples' question of when "these things" will take place (13:4). The contextual referent for "these things" is the destruction of the temple. However, as Jesus answers their question, he speaks of "the end" twice (13:7,13) and concludes with the appearance of the son of man and the gathering of the elect (13:24-27). The son of man's appearance in Mark 13:26 mirrors that of the apocalyptic son of man who also comes in the clouds in Dan. 7:13.

Although his style is not typical of apocalyptic literature, Mark does juxtapose heaven and earth in his own way. The destruction of the temple signals transformation on an earthly scale, but the appearance of the son of man does so on a celestial scale. Famines, earthquakes, and wars are signs on earth that will eventually give way to the heavenly signs of a darkened sun, a lightless moon, falling stars, and shaken heavenly powers. Thus salvation takes on a spiritual, eschatological dimension as those who "endure to the end will be saved" (13:13).

Ultimately, the disciples' question is never answered. Jesus informs them that he does not know when "that day or hour" (13:32) will come. Instead, he tells them how to interpret the events so that they know when he is "near, at the very gate" (13:29). However, Jesus does tell them that it will not happen before the good news is preached to all nations (13:10). This statement extends the timetable of Jesus' return for Mark's readers. It reminds them that the end is imminent but not yet. Therefore, he tells them what to do: "Watch" (13:5, 9, 23, 33, *blepete*).

"Watch" characterizes Mark's ethical stance (Donahue and Harrington, 378). The inclusion of this ethical/exhortation component makes this chapter practical and immediately applicable. It also caused James A. Brooks to conclude that Mark 13 "combines two literary forms, apocalyptic and testamental" (Brooks, 204). This fusion enables Mark to achieve his purpose for this chapter: keep eschatological hope alive while balancing it with vigilance (Donahue and Harrington, 378). His message to his readers is clear: This is not the end. It is only birth pangs, and they are just as unpredictable as labor. So, keep awake!

The Text in the Interpretive Tradition

In Mark 13:32, Jesus states that he does not know the day or hour of the son of man's return. This statement resulted in three words, "nor the Son," becoming a point of interpretive contention since its earliest readings. For interpreters such as Arius, this verse posed no problems. Instead, they saw it as scriptural affirmation of their theological position that subordinated both the Son and the Holy Spirit to the Father. Using Mark 13:32 (and its parallel Matt. 24:36), they rejected the equal divinity of Jesus with the Father. However, the majority of interpretations of this verse have been fueled by the same discomfort as described by John Calvin: "But since it is manifest that the same kind of ignorance is ascribed to Christ as is ascribed *to the angels*, we must endeavor to find some other meaning which is more suitable" (Calvin, 1845, 3:37).

The quest for a "more suitable" meaning began with Matthew's Gospel. Although the most reliable manuscripts of Matthew's parallel text (Matt. 24:36) include "nor the Son," several omit the phrase due to the doctrinal problems it raised (Harrington, 342). Athanasius, who defended the doctrine of the Trinity against the Arian heresy of subordinationism, affirmed the divinity of Jesus by arguing that Jesus was "speaking according to his humanity" in this verse. Chrysostom, Gregory of Nazianzus, Martin Luther, and John Wesley also espoused this interpretation of Mark 13:32. Ambrose seems to have had the Matthew text with the omission of "nor the Son" since he accused the Arians of inserting the phrase into Mark's text because the other Gospels did not include it.

For Augustine, the issue was not from which nature Jesus' words derived, but an exercise of choice. Jesus chose not to disclose what he knew because "he had not been sent by the Father with this commission, so long as he lived among mortals." Theophylact concurred, reasoning that this concealment was "better for us; for if, now that we know not the end, we are careless, what should we do if we knew it?" Hilary of Poitiers argued that Jesus' apparent lack of knowledge was not a reflection of his ignorance, but that it "must be connected with the hiding of the treasures of wisdom, which are in Him." Contemporary options for those who take Mark literally follow one of the three interpretive trajectories: subordinationism, in which Jesus (and by implication the Holy

Spirit) are ignorant of the Father's timetable; "official ignorance," in which Jesus purposely conceals the day and hour; or what might be called the "nonuse" approach, in which Jesus does not use the omniscience of his divine nature but rather speaks from a human point of view (Carl).

The Text in Contemporary Discussion

The material in the first twenty-three verses of Mark 13 can be linked easily to events shortly before or after the fall of the Jerusalem temple. However, verses 24-27 foretell the coming of the son of man, an event that has not yet occurred. On one end of a spectrum today are readers who have interpreted Mark 13 in its ancient setting and concluded that Jesus expected the fulfillment of verses 24-27 in his lifetime, but died a failure (Schweitzer). On the other end are premillennialists, who read Rev. 20:1-6 literally and believe that Jesus will physically return to rapture the righteous prior to the tribulation and that he will subsequently inaugurate a thousand-year reign. They see the signs of Jesus' coming in contemporary events.

During the twentieth century, the possibility of nuclear destruction, the reality of ecological collapse, the creation of the state of Israel along with the Six Day and Yom Kippur Wars, and the perceived threats to US exceptionalism fueled premillennial expectations of Jesus' return. Despite the statement in 13:32 that the timing of the son of man's return remains a mystery, some readers still attempt to correlate current events with those listed in Mark 13 so as to describe contemporary timetables that will lead up to Jesus' appearing. Examples in popular culture include *The Late, Great Planet Earth* (Lindsey 1970) and, more recently, the *Left Behind* series (LaHaye and Jenkins 1995–2007).

The underlying premise of such interpretations is the expectation that apocalyptic passages like Mark 13 accurately and precisely predict the future. Should supposedly predicted events not take place as expected, then the passage might become a failed apocalyptic text or proof that Jesus was wrong (Schweitzer). Yet, premillennialists like Tim LaHaye and Hal Lindsey can avoid Schweitzer's conclusion if the events that signal "the end" are seen as still forthcoming. If Jesus does not return as expected, then calendars can be readjusted. This way, the *interpretation of the text*, rather than the text itself, fails. The "prophet," rather than Jesus, is wrong. However, this attempt fails to preserve the integrity of the text. Instead, it risks undermining the text's integrity by using current events to predict the "end," when the historical context of Mark's Gospel points to the events surrounding the Jewish War.

Mark 14:1—15:47: The Cost of Following

The Text in Its Ancient Context

Mark gives great attention to Jesus' passion. He lays the foundation for his passion narrative with three passion predictions and then devotes one third of his Gospel to detailing Jesus' final days. He takes great pains to highlight what contemporary readers might identify as the sociopolitical reasons behind Jesus' death. Although Jesus is executed by Rome as a criminal, his death does not represent a failure on his part. Rather, Mark shows that there has been a failure of justice, a failure of discipleship, and a failure of sight on the part of Roman and Jewish leadership.

Mark tells the story of Jesus' death against the backdrop of the Passover. The day before the feast, the day of preparation, the chief priests and scribes are preparing to arrest Jesus (14:1). A woman enters the room where Jesus is sharing a meal with Simon the leper and anoints him (14:3). Amid criticisms for wasting the money on the perfume and accusations of neglecting the poor, Jesus defends her actions. Jesus states that the deed was done "for me" (14:6). Just as the disciples' lack of fasting while the "bridegroom" is present (2:18-20) showed an understanding of the significance of Jesus' presence among them, so this woman's kindness highlights the same (Myers, 359). Moreover, acts of kindness can be shown to the poor at any time, but he will not always be with them (14:7). His statement is neither a consignment of people to perpetual poverty nor an encouragement to neglect the poor. Jesus does not set up an "either/or" dynamic. Personal acts of kindness are no substitute for public care of the poor or vice versa, and "one should not be harassed for doing either" (Tolbert, 271). By performing a "good service," this nameless, speechless woman fits the predominant image of women in Mark's Gospel as those who serve and provide for Jesus (1:31; 15:41). Her prophetic act helps to move the reader into Mark's passion narrative. She is not anointing Jesus as king but is preparing his body "beforehand for its burial" (14:8). Jesus will not be given a crown, but a cross.

The Last Supper (14:17-25); Jesus' betrayal (14:41-45), arrest (14:46-49), and trial before the Sanhedrin (14:53-65); his prayer in Gethsemane (14:32-40); the desertion of his disciples (14:50-52); and Peter's denial (14:66-72) all occur on the day of Passover. The Passover is not simply a remembrance of divine intervention, but of divine intervention with sociopolitical implications. It is a Jewish feast that commemorates Israel's liberation from Egyptian slavery or the freeing of God's people from an oppressive government. Just as the Passover celebrates the ransoming of Israel from Egypt (Exod. 6:6, *lytroō*), so Mark presents Jesus' life and death as part of a ransoming work (10:45, *lytron*). This time, the oppressive regime is Rome.

During the Passover meal, Jesus reinterprets the bread and wine in light of his impending death. The bread is his body, which will soon be broken (14:22). The wine is the "blood of the covenant" (14:24). The "blood of the covenant" has two possible references to the exodus story. First, it may refer to the blood that Israelites painted on their doorposts to protect their firstborn from the death angel (Exod. 12:7). According to Exod. 4:22, Israel is God's firstborn. Therefore, Jesus intimates that the deliverance and protection of Israel is tied to his spilled blood. The second reference to the "blood of the covenant" is the blood sprinkled on the Israelites at Sinai to establish their relationship as the people of God and confirm their covenant with God (24:1-8). Jesus' spilled blood verifies that God's commitment to Israel is still in effect. However, Mark shows that what God is doing through the death of Jesus will not be for Israel alone. Instead, he once again pushes for gentile inclusion.

Israel's deliverance from Egyptian slavery was necessary for God to fulfill God's promise of land and progeny to Abraham (Gen. 15:5-7). According to Gen. 17:5, Abraham would not be the ancestor of the Israelites alone, but of "many [*pollōn*] nations" (Gen. 17:5). Mark links the language of the "many" (*polloi*) to Jesus. Jesus will give his life as a ransom for "many" (10:45, *polloi*). His blood is described as being "poured out for many" (14:24, *polloi*).

It is important to note that the Passover language in Mark is not expiatory; it points instead to the sociopolitical dimensions of Jesus' death (Blount). Mark simply states that Jesus' body is broken. Unlike Luke, he does not add "for you" (Luke 22:19). Moreover, the breaking and blessing of the bread alludes to the feeding stories in which Jews (6:33-44) and gentiles (8:1-9) are filled. In addition, the "blood of the covenant" is not specified as being for the "forgiveness of sins" (as in Matt. 26:28). Jesus forgave sin prior to his death (Mark 2:5).

At the heart of the animosity toward Jesus on the part of scribes, Pharisees, and other authorities in Jerusalem are the sociopolitical implications of his ministry. Jesus is a threat to the temple system and their control of the people, both of which ingratiate them to Rome. When Jesus is arrested, the only accusation Mark records is someone claiming that Jesus said, "I will destroy this temple that is made with hands, and in three days I will build another, not made with hands" (14:58). When Jesus drove the animal sellers and money-changers out of the temple, it resulted in the chief priests and scribes looking for a way to kill him (11:18). Jesus has predicted the temple's destruction (13:1-2). Later, when he dies, Mark will report that the temple curtain is torn (*eschisthē*) in two (15:38) like the heavens were ripped asunder (*schizomenous*) during Jesus' baptism (1:10). Because the tearing of the temple curtain occurs during the darkness that covers the land at noonday (15:33), it is probably best read as an omen of God's judgment against the temple. However, Mark's use of *schizein* at both Jesus' baptism and death suggests that the latter event, like the former, grants access to God, rather than the temple system. Moreover, the tearing (*schizein*) of the curtain suggests that the breach between the old way represented by the temple and the new way represented by Jesus is as irreparable as the tear (*schizma*) created from sewing together new and old cloth (2:21).

Such bold political counteractions require authority. At Jesus' trial before the Sanhedrin, the high priest's question is therefore one about identity. He asks if Jesus is "the Messiah [*christos*], the Son of the Blessed One?" (14:61). The high priest's question mimics what Mark has already told his readers is Jesus' true identity. According to Mark, Jesus is the Messiah (*christos*, a political designation), and the Son of God (a theological designation, 1:1). Jesus affirms both by responding with an answer that has political and theological undertones. He begins with "I am" (*egō eimi*), which is a play on the divine name (Exod. 3:14) revealed to Moses during his divine commission to free Israel from Egyptian bondage. Next, Jesus declares that those questioning him will see him "seated at the right hand of the Power" (14:62). For Jesus' interrogators, his position next to God may be seen as a threat to the sovereignty and/or the oneness of God. In either case, they view him as "infringing on God's prerogatives" (Juel, 208–9). Consequently, they charge him with blasphemy, which is punishable by death. Yet they take Jesus to the Roman procurator, Pilate (15:1), where the accusation against Jesus becomes purely political, not theological. In an effort to present Jesus' offense as a crime punishable by Rome, blasphemy disappears from everyone's vocabulary. Instead, the charge is treason: his alleged claim to be a king. Three times Pilate refers to him as "king of the Jews" (15:2, 9, 12). The crowds as well as "the whole cohort" mock him as such (15:16-20). The sign placed over his cross reads the same (15:26). Even the chief priests and scribes refer to him using two political titles: "king of Israel," a variant of "king of the Jews," and "Messiah" (15:32).

Mark further highlights the sociopolitical nature of Jesus' death through his use of bandit (*lēstēs*) language. In first-century Palestine, bandits were typically highway robbers or guerrilla warriors who opposed Rome and Judean collaborators with Rome. They were viewed by Rome and Roman sympathizers as seditious and traitors (Horsley 1985). When taken into custody, Jesus likens his arrest to that of a bandit (14:48). Mark tells us that he was crucified between two bandits (15:27). Moreover, Mark juxtaposes Jesus and Barabbas. Jesus is arrested as if he were the rebel; Barabbas has been arrested for actually participating in an insurrection. There is no historical evidence that attests to the existence of Barabbas or the Passover custom that allows the crowd to choose which man goes free. Jesus and Barabbas may be Mark's way of representing two sociopolitical responses to Roman oppression. Jesus represents those in favor of nonviolent opposition. Barabbas, whom Myers says is described by Mark as a Sicarii operative, is the choice of those who advocate outright rebellion to Rome (Myers, 380). Meanwhile, Jewish leaders who have made the temple a den of bandits (11:17) are behind Jesus' arrest.

In the end, Jesus is crucified. He suffers a horrifically painful and humiliating death reserved for crimes against the state, high treason, and as punishment for slaves, prisoners of war, rebels, robbers, freedmen, and *peregrini*, that is, free persons without Roman citizenship (Hengel). Mark shows Jesus' death to be a failure of justice. The Sanhedrin does not follow jurisprudence found in the Torah (or, later, the Mishnah), nor does Pilate free him when he believes Jesus to be innocent (Juel). Jesus' death highlights the failure of his followers, who cannot stay awake and pray with him in Gethsemane (14:37); who betray him (14:10, 43), desert him (14:50), deny him (14:66-72), turn against him (15:14), and follow only from a great distance (15:40-41). Mark uses verbal irony to reveal the failure of sight on the part of Jewish and Roman leadership. They repeatedly identify him correctly as "King of the Jews," but fail to recognize who he really is.

However, none of these failures come as a surprise to Jesus, nor should they surprise Mark's readers. Jesus has predicted it all, and so it has come to pass. Yet one things remains to be accomplished: a resurrection!

The Text in the Interpretive Tradition

Readings of Mark's passion narrative have often been influenced by the ransom and the substitutionary/penal-substitutionary theories of atonement. Scholars who argue for a theory of atonement in Mark's Gospel point to 10:45 and 14:24 as justification for their position. In addition, some read Mark's passion narrative against the backdrop of Isaiah 53 and contend that Mark presents Jesus as Isaiah's Suffering Servant. Jesus then becomes one who suffers vicariously for humanity as payment for our sin. Once one assumes an atonement theory is at play, one interprets other portions of the Gospel in light of the theory rather than the narrative context. For example, Morna Hooker interprets Jesus' "cry of dereliction" (15:34) as his experiencing "what Paul elsewhere describes as 'becoming a curse' (Gal. 3:13) or 'being made sin' (2 Cor. 5:21)" (Hooker, 375).

In the last thirty years, however, scholars have argued against the presence of any atonement theories in Mark. Instead, they opt to make meaning of Jesus' death on the basis of evidence within the text rather than by imposing theological constructs formulated outside it (Myers; Tolbert; Blount).

Therefore, Mark 15:34 can be explained within the context of the narrative using the historical reality of the crucifixion as its backdrop. The cry of dereliction becomes "Jesus' final emotional and psychological torment, in addition to his physical suffering" (Powery, 150). By quoting Psalm 22:1 and alluding to Psalm 22 throughout the passion narrative, Mark holds in tension the horrific conditions of Jesus' death and the hope for his vindication as a righteous sufferer.

The Text in Contemporary Discussion

The shift to a narrative reading of Mark as described above also enables us to recognize Christian anti-Judaism in Mark's Gospel. Mark portrays the Jewish leadership (3:6; 11:18; 14:1; 15:11) and the crowds (14:43; 15:8-14) as the instigators of Jesus' death, causing some to conclude that Mark's Gospel is inherently antisemitic. William A. Johnson argues that "every kind of Jew" is presented negatively in the Gospel, which he describes as a "carefully devised theological attack on the Jews" (Johnson, 183). He concurs with S. G. F. Brandon that Mark's reader "is led to see Jesus as both rejected by, and in turn rejecting his fellow-Jews" (Brandon, 274). Fortunately, this shift to narrative readings has also sensitized scholars to the potential antisemitic implications of their analyses. Therefore, attention is given to certain aspects of the Gospel in an effort to prevent readers from forming antisemitic attitudes based on Mark's story.

Contemporary scholars note that Mark's Gospel reflects the historical tensions between Jews who followed Jesus and Jews who did not in Mark's day (Hooker, 24). Initially, the dispute between Jews and Jewish Christians was an internal dispute among *Jews* about accepting Jesus as the Messiah. Thus Mark writes about a time when followers of Jesus will be "beaten in synagogues" (13:9).

In addition, scholars highlight Jesus' Jewish background. Indeed, Jesus was a Jew whose ministry was directed to the Jewish people. His use of Scripture and adherence to the law (1:44; 3:4; 10:19; 12:29-31) demonstrate his fidelity to Judaism. The main contention with his opponents over Mosaic tradition was whether he or they were more faithful in interpretation and application (Hooker, 24–25).

Narrative readings of Mark's Gospel are also careful to point out the divergence between historical data and Mark's story. Historically, Jesus' death cannot be attributed to the Jewish leaders as Mark portrays. Scholars appeal to extrabiblical literature to see if the image of the easily manipulated Pilate in Mark's Gospel matches what other writers say about him. It seems highly unlikely that Pilate would have left the decision to execute Jesus to the crowd, especially since there is no extrabiblical evidence of any custom to release a prisoner of the crowd's choosing (15:8). Legally, Pilate would have had to sentence Jesus to death, and the means of Jesus' death—crucifixion—was a Roman practice, not a Jewish one.

Contra Johnson, Mark does not present all of the Jews in a negative light. Mark's Gospel distinguishes itself with a very positive portrayal of women, the majority of which are Jewish, who serve as examples of discipleship (Dewey; Malbon 1983; Miller; Kinukawa; Mitchell). Jairus, a synagogue leader, had enough faith to have his petition granted (5:36) and be allowed to remain in the room after Jesus put everyone out (5:40). Although Jesus' disciples betray, deny, and desert him, he still commands them to meet him in Galilee after the resurrection (16:7).

Mark 16:1-8: Will You Follow?

The Text in Its Ancient Context

Despite the variety of endings given to Mark, the evidence suggests that the version of Mark's Gospel available to his original readers ended with 16:8 (see below). Chapter 16 begins with three women journeying to Jesus' tomb at first light (16:1-2). Mary Magdalene heads the list of women. Mark tells us that she provided for Jesus' ministry and witnessed his crucifixion (15:40), followed to see where he was buried (15:47), and came to anoint his body (16:1). Absent is any reference to her deliverance from seven demons (Luke 8:2) or any information that would suggest she was the harlot that the later interpretive and especially artistic tradition claimed. There is some inconsistency around the identity of "Mary, the mother of James." It is not certain whether she is also "Mary, mother of James and Joses" (15:40), "Mary, mother of Joses" (15:47), or even Mary, Jesus' mother, who is mentioned with Jesus' brothers, also named James and Joses (6:3). Salome only appears here and in 15:40, among those who provided for Jesus' ministry and were present at the crucifixion. These women anticipate providing for Jesus one last time. They come to anoint his body, apparently oblivious to the fact that he was "anointed beforehand for [his] burial" in Bethany (14:3-9). Yet, even the narration of Jesus' predicting his own death and resurrection three times (8:31; 9:31; 10:33-34), the first being declared "quite openly" (8:32), had not caused them to expect a resurrection, only a dead body.

The timing of the women's visit is also inconsistent. "Early morning" would have been between three and six in the morning. Nevertheless, Mark adds that they came after sunrise, perhaps wishing to assure his readers that the women were able to see clearly what follows. As they journey to the tomb, they worry about the stone at its entrance (16:3). The stone, however, is an afterthought, as they do all the preparations for the anointing and depart for the tomb, thinking about the stone only as they arrive. This afterthought, Hooker asserts, is probably an attempt to emphasize the fact that the tomb was indeed sealed (Hooker, 384) and to confirm that the absence of Jesus' body is due to a resurrection, not a theft.

When the women arrive at the tomb, the stone has already been rolled away (16:4). However, there is no resurrection appearance, only a young man with a message. Mark describes him as a "young man dressed in a white robe" (16:5). Some interpreters identify the young man as an angel, citing his white robe; the similarity between the women's alarm at seeing the young man and the fear that often accompanies angelic appearances (Gen. 21:17; Matt. 28:5; Luke 1:13, 30; 2:10); Luke's (24:4) and Josephus's (*Ant.* 5.277) use of the word "man" (*anēr*) to describe angelic appearances; and the fact that the young man knows about the postresurrection meeting in Galilee (14:28)—information R. T. France argues no human being apart from the disciples would have known (France, 676). Others, however, link the young man in the tomb to the young man in the garden who lost his garment during Jesus' arrest.

The Greek words used for "young man" (*neaniskos*) and "dressed" (*peribeblēmenos*) occur only here (16:5) and in 14:51-52. Mark connected Jesus with the young man in the garden, writing that the latter "followed" (*synēkolouthe*) Jesus. (Throughout the Gospel, Mark uses "follow" [*akolouthein*] to signify discipleship: 1:17, 20; 2:14, 15; 3:7; 5:24, 37; 6:1; 8:34; 10:21, 28, 32, 52; 11:9; 14:54; 15:41. By adding the preposition *syn* to the word, Mark suggests a close relationship between the young man and Jesus.) Both are dressed in linen fabric, the young man wearing a linen cloth (*sindon*) when Jesus is arrested (14:51) and Jesus wrapped in a linen cloth (*sindon)* before Joseph places him in the tomb (15:46). Mark also links Jesus with the young man in the tomb, recording that both appear in white garments: Jesus in "dazzling white" at the transfiguration (9:3) and the young man in the tomb (16:5).

Finally, Mark specifies the location of the young man in the tomb as being "seated on the right" (16:5). Individuals positioned on the right side figure prominently in Mark's Gospel: James and John request to sit at the right and left of Jesus (10:40); the Messiah's place is at the right hand of the Lord according to Ps. 110:1 quoted in Mark 12:36; and Jesus prophesies the coming of the son of man "seated at the right hand of the Power" (14:62). Myers defines the right side as denoting "true power of solidarity" (Myers, 397). Although there is no scholarly consensus on the identity of either young man (in the garden or at the tomb), the connections Mark makes between them and Jesus suggest that the young man was someone close enough to Jesus to have insider information and familiar enough to Mark's community to need no explanation.

The young man tells the women that "Jesus of Nazareth" has been raised (16:5-6). He does not employ a christological title, but rather situates Jesus historically as a real man from a real place. The women are commanded to carry the news to Jesus' disciples "and Peter" (16:7). It is most likely that the young man mentions Peter by name because Peter needs special encouragement (Juel, 232). As one who denied being a disciple by denying Jesus (Hooker, 385), he is specifically welcomed back here into the community of followers.

Unlike the people in the Gospel who are commanded to be quiet but tell what Jesus has done anyway (1:44; 7:36), the women who are commanded to speak here remain quiet. Mark highlights this with a double negative construction in Greek: "they said nothing to no one" (16:8). Instead, the women flee like the disciples (14:50-52). Narratively, there is a failure of discipleship for all who have followed Jesus. Yet the fact that Mark's community has access to his Gospel proves that someone said something. The message was indeed proclaimed.

Neither the absence of a resurrection appearance nor the fear and silence of the women nullifies Mark's description of his work as "good news." Emerson Powery states that for Mark, "hope is not defined by a resurrection or a physical appearance *but* by an empty tomb and a promised re-gathering" (Powery, 152). Herein lies the good news: not only is the tomb empty, but Jesus also has gone ahead of them to Galilee, "just as he said" (14:28; 16:7). There is no need to doubt Jesus' words, as Mark has taken great pains to prove his trustworthiness. His instructions concerning his entry into Jerusalem (11:2-6), the preparation for the Passover meal (14:16), and the events surrounding the passion have all come to pass (Juel, 233). Moreover, Mark has kept his word. He promised to tell "the beginning of the good news of Jesus Christ." Whether by accident or intent, this is exactly what he has done.

The Text in the Interpretive Tradition

Interpretations of Mark's last chapter must contend with a problem unique to his Gospel. The Gospel has four endings: 16:8, the longer ending (vv. 9-20), a shorter ending, and the longer and shorter endings combined. The most reliable codices, Sinaiticus and Vaticanus, end with 16:8. Both Clement of Alexandria and Origen knew only of this ending. However, Eusebius and Jerome report that they are aware of the longer ending, but the longer ending is not found in the majority of Greek manuscripts. Both Irenaeus, who quotes 16:19, and Tatian, who includes the longer ending in his *Diatessaron*, do so without any acknowledgment of its being a later addition. By the second century, either the longer and/or shorter endings were added and were copied onto the majority of manuscripts.

In 1546, the Council of Trent canonized the old Latin Vulgate edition, which included Mark's longer ending. The Protestants also accepted the longer ending by including it in the King James Version. Modern scholarship reverted to the ending at 16:8 after Adolf von Harnack contended, in 1893, that Mark's original ending was lost. The textual evidence above as well as the stylistic, syntactical, vocabulary, and theological differences between the material prior to and after 16:8 have been the basis for contemporary arguments in favor of an ending at 16:8.

Whereas some of the earliest readers of the Gospel felt it necessary to create an ending for Mark's Gospel that is more consistent with the endings of Matthew, Luke, and John, contemporary readers may find the ending at 16:8 to be theologically consistent with the preceding narrative. Unlike von Harnack, they may consider that Mark intentionally ended his Gospel at 16:8. Donald Juel argues that the ending at 16:8 leaves the reader without any reason to trust human response: one "can only trust that God will one day finish the story, as God has promised" (Juel, 235). Others may see the abruptness of 16:8, with its unusual grammatical structure, to be an invitation by the author for readers to finish his story of discipleship for themselves. Early readers did something similar, codifying their supplemental endings by including them in ancient manuscripts. Contemporary readers will have to decide how they will complete "the beginning of the good news of Jesus Christ, the Son of God" (1:1).

The Text in Contemporary Discussion

Traditional African American preaching lends homiletical support to Mark's Gospel being good news despite the ending at 16:8. In *Celebration and Experience in Preaching*, Henry Mitchell argued that celebration, which has been defined as "the joyful and ecstatic reinforcement of the truth already taught and delivered in the main body of the sermon" (Thomas, 85), is a distinctive of African American preaching (Mitchell 1990). In the overwhelming majority of African American sermons, the moment of celebration centers on the resurrection of Jesus. However, the celebration often begins, like Mark's passion narrative, with a detailed account of the crucifixion. Classic African American preaching often punctuates the story with rhetorical questions like "He died, didn't he die?" and describe how Jesus was "hung high and stretched wide" until "the earth reeled and rocked like a drunken man, and the sun refused to shine." At this point, worshipers are often already standing on their feet, clapping their hands, shouting the preacher on, or engaged in some other form of congregational celebration in response to the Word. This celebration is not a reflection of masochistic or death-glorifying tendencies but a manifestation of the congregant's confidence in the end of the story.

Like Mark's community, the worshipers are not physical witnesses to Jesus' resurrection. However, the proclamation of it is enough to elicit praise because the one who foretold it and the witness of other believers are enough. There is every reason to expect death to give way to life, even in the midst of the darkest circumstances. So, before the preacher can say "early Sunday morning," the celebration has begun. It is not based on what people did but on what God did. They believe God raised Jesus from the dead, even if they have not yet seen the risen Lord. They do not need to end the story. Instead, they can be a part of it, by following the resurrected one.

Works Cited

Blevins, James L. 1974. "Seventy-Two Years of the Messianic Secret: A Review Article." *Perspectives in Religious Studies* 1, no. 2:192–200.

Blount, Brian K. 1998. *Go Preach! Mark's Kingdom Message and the Black Church Today.* Maryknoll, NY: Orbis.

Brandon, S. G. F. 1967. *Jesus and the Zealots.* New York: Oxford University Press.

Brooks, James A. 1991. *Mark.* The New American Commentary 23. Nashville: Broadman & Holman.

Burkett, Delbert. 1999. *The Son of Man Debate: A History and Evaluation.* New York: Cambridge University Press.

Calvin, John. 1845. *Commentary on a Harmony of the Evangelists Matthew, Mark, and Luke* (Vols. 2 and 3). Trans. the Rev. William Pringle. Edinburgh: The Calvin Translation Society.

Carl, Harold F. 2001. "Only the Father Knows: Historical and Evangelical Responses to Jesus' Eschatological Ignorance in Mark 13:32." *Journal of Biblical Studies* 1, no. 3. http://www.mountainretreatorg.net/articles/only_the_father_knows.shtml.

Collins, Adela Yarbro. 1992. *The Beginning of the Gospel: Probings of Mark in Context.* Minneapolis: Fortress Press.

Dewey, Joanna. 2006. "Women in the Gospel of Mark." *WW* 26, no. 1:22–29.

Donahue, John R., and Daniel J. Harrington. 2002. *The Gospel of Mark.* Sacra Pagina 2. Collegeville, MN: Liturgical Press.

Driscoll, Mark. 2006. *Confessions of a Reformission Rev.: Hard Lessons from an Emerging Missional Church.* Grand Rapids: Zondervan.

Dunn, James D. G. 1970. "The Messianic Secret in Mark." *TynBul* 21:92–117.

Edwards, James R. 2002. *The Gospel according to Mark.* Pillar New Testament Commentary. Grand Rapids: Eerdmans.

France, R. T. 2003. *Divine Government: God's Kingship in the Gospel of Mark.* Vancouver, BC: Regent College Publishing.

Haber, Susan. 2003. "A Woman's Touch: Feminist Encounters with the Hemorrhaging Woman in Mark 5:24-34." *JSNT* 26 no. 2:171–92.

Hanson, K. C. 1997. "The Galilean Fishing Economy and the Jesus Tradition." *BTB* 27:99–111.

Harrington, Daniel J. 1991. *The Gospel of Matthew.* Sacra Pagina. Collegeville, MN: Liturgical Press.

Hengel, Martin. 1977. *Crucifixion.* Minneapolis: Fortress Press.

Hooker, Morna D. 1999. *The Gospel according to St. Mark.* Peabody, MA: Hendrickson.

Horsley, Richard A. 1984. "Popular Messianic Movements around the Time of Jesus." *CBQ* 46:471–95.

———. 1985. *Bandits, Prophets, and Messiahs: Popular Movements at the Time of Jesus.* Harrisburg, PA: Trinity Press International.

Johnson, William A. 1989. "'The Jews' in Saint Mark's Gospel." *Religion and Intellectual Life* 6, nos. 3–4:182–92.

Juel, Donald H. 1990. *Mark.* Augsburg Commentary. Minneapolis: Fortress Press.

Keck, Leander E. 1965. "Mark 3:7-12 and Mark's Christology." *Journal of Biblical Literature* 84, no. 4: 341-48.

Kee, Howard Clark. 1977. *Community of the New Age: Studies in the Gospel of Mark.* Philadelphia: Westminster, 1977.

Kelber, Werner H. 1974. *The Kingdom in Mark: A New Place and Time.* Philadelphia: Fortress Press.

Kinukawa, Hisako. 1994. *Women and Jesus in Mark: A Japanese Feminist Perspective.* Maryknoll, NY: Orbis.

LaHaye, Tim F., and Jerry B. Jenkins. 1995–2003. *Left Behind Series.* Carol Stream, IL: Tyndale House Publishers.

Lindsey, Hal, and Carole C. Carson. 1970. *The Late Great Planet Earth.* Grand Rapids: Zondervan.

Maddock, Sherry, and Geoff Maddock. 2007. "An Ever-Renewed Adventure of Faith." In *An Emergent Manifesto of Hope*, edited by Doug Pagitt and Tony Jones, 79–88. Grand Rapids: Baker Books.

Malbon, Elizabeth Struthers. 1986. "Disciples/Crowd/Whoever." *NovT* 28:104–30.

———. 1983. "Fallible Followers: Women and Men in the Gospel of Mark." *Semeia* 28:29–48.

Malina, Bruce J. 1993. "Authoritarianism." In *Biblical Social Values and Their Meaning: A Handbook*, edited by John J. Pilch and Bruce Malina. 11-17. Peabody, MA: Hendrickson.

Mann, C. S. 1986. *Mark: A New Translation with Introduction and Commentary.* AB 27. New York: Doubleday.

Marcus, Joel. 1992. "The Jewish War and the *Sitz Im Leben* of Mark." *JBL* 111:441–62.

McLaren, Brian. 2004. *A Generous Orthodoxy.* Cajon, CA: Youth Specialties Books.

Meier, John P. 2000. "The Historical Jesus and the Historical Herodians." *JBL* 119:740–46.

Miller, Susan. 2004. *Women in Mark's Gospel.* New York: T&T Clark.

Mitchell, Henry H. 1990. *Celebration and Experience in Preaching.* Nashville: Abingdon.

Mitchell, Joan L. 2001. *Beyond Fear and Silence: A Feminist-Literary Approach to the Gospel of Mark.* New York: Continuum.

Myers, Ched. 1988. *Binding the Strong Man: A Political Reading of Mark's Story of Jesus.* Maryknoll, NY: Orbis.

Pesch, Rudolf. 1976–80. *Das Markusevangelium*, 2 vols. HTKNT. Freiburg: Herder.

Pilch, John J. 1993. "Power." In *Biblical Social Values and Their Meaning: A Handbook*, edited by John J. Pilch and Bruce Malina. 139-42. Peabody: Hendrickson.

Placher, William C. 2010. *Mark.* Belief: A Theological Commentary on the Bible. Louisville: Westminster John Knox.

Powery, Emerson B. 2007. "Mark." In *True to Our Native Land: An African American New Testament Commentary*, edited by Brian K. Blount, 121–57. Minneapolis: Fortress Press.

Rhoads, David, Joanna Dewey, and Donald Michie. 2012. *Mark as Story: An Introduction to the Narrative of a Gospel.* 3rd ed. Minneapolis: Fortress Press.

Saldarini, Anthony J. 1998. *Pharisees, Scribes, and Sadducees in Palestinian Society.* Grand Rapids: Eerdmans.

Schüssler Fiorenza, Elisabeth. 1992. *But She Said: Feminist Practices of Biblical Interpretation.* Boston: Beacon.

Schweitzer, Albert. 2001. *The Quest for the Historical Jesus: The First Complete Edition.* Trans. and ed. John Bowden. Minneapolis: Fortress Press.

Stone, Lawrence. 1994. "Family Values in a Historical Perspective." Tanner Lectures on Human Values, Harvard University, November 16 and 17.

St. Clair, Raquel A. 2008. *Call and Consequences: A Womanist Reading of Mark.* Minneapolis: Fortress Press.

Theissen, Gerd. 1991. *The Gospels in Context: Social and Political History in the Synoptic Tradition*. Translator Linda M. Maloney. Minneapolis: Fortress Press.

Thomas, Frank A. 1997. *They Like to Never Quit Praisin' God: The Role of Celebration in Preaching*. Cleveland: United Church Press.

Tolbert, Mary Ann. 1989. *Sowing the Gospel: Mark's World in Literary Perspective*. Minneapolis: Fortress Press.

Waetjen, Herman C. 1989. *A Reordering of Power: A Socio-Political Reading of Mark's Gospel*. Minneapolis: Fortress Press.

Weisse, Christian Hermann (1838). *Die evangelische Geschichte kritisch und philosophisch bearbeitet*. Leipzig: Breitkopf und Härtel.

Wilke, Christian Gottlob. 1838. *Der Urevangelist oder exegetisch kritische Untersuchung über das Verwandtschaftsverhältniß der drei ersten Evangelien*. Dresden und Leipzig, G. Fleischer.

Weeden, Theodore. 1971. *Traditions in Conflict*. Philadelphia: Fortress Press.

LUKE

Robert L. Brawley

Introduction

Luke's Gospel is embedded in Israel's story of God's relationship with humanity and the world. Though it was canonized sometime after its writing, it extends Israel's scriptural tradition. Special emphasis falls on covenants. Abrahamic promises in particular are synthesized with other covenants in Israel's traditions. Luke is composed from individual episodes that are here arranged in three primary sections: the setting and preparation for Jesus' ministry (1:5—4:13); proclamation and extension of God's commonwealth (4:14—21:28); passion and resurrection (23:1—24:53).

Luke is also embedded in Israel's relationships with surrounding cultures. It participates in Hellenism not only in its language but also in its literary conventions. The Roman Empire especially bleeds through every page (Carter 2006). Luke's audience seldom experienced the empire's upper stratum directly. Rather they confronted systems that flowed down through client kings, governors, and local elite collaborators, including a high-priestly hierarchy, magistrates, and tax collectors. These systems sustained a world divided between unpropertied and propertied populations, those who subsisted from their own labor (90 percent) and those who lived from the labors of others (10 percent) (De Ste. Croix).

Luke's Jesus proclaims God's commonwealth as an alternative to these imperial systems. Anything new in God's commonwealth is also in continuity with Israel's covenant community. Continuity comes with critiques aimed at abuses in imperial systems, but the critiques also aim at renewing Israel's heritage. Luke anticipates extending God's commonwealth to the nations, but this too is grounded in God's promises to bless all the nations of the earth.

An early third-century manuscript, P^{75}, contains most of the Third Gospel, but its first lines, presumably including the title, are missing. Nevertheless, the ending attributes the writing to "Luke." A coworker of Paul bears this name in Philem. 24. But there are two problems with identifying the author. Though early, P^{75} already represents development from an original writing, indicated by variants of the title in other manuscripts but also by the standardization of Gospel titles in P^{75}. Original writings like the separate Gospels were unlikely to have used the same titular formula. The earliest attribution is at the stage of standardizing the Gospels. Second, the name Luke was common, and it is impossible to determine if the name on the manuscript refers to the same person as Philem. 24. Consequently, we know virtually nothing about the author.

Attempts to locate the place of writing or the destination produce only speculations. Again, we know virtually nothing about the place of writing or destination. When apparent historical allusions and time to allow for the use of sources are considered, a date in the last decades of the first century CE is likely.

A strong consensus takes Acts to be a sequel to Luke. Therefore, at times one volume elucidates the other. Furthermore, just as Luke presumes Israel's prior story, it also presumes a sequel, even beyond Acts.

Luke 1:1-2 acknowledges the use of "many" sources. Close agreement with passages in Mark and Matthew have led to widely accepted hypotheses that Luke used Mark and Q. A minority of scholars rejects the hypothetical source Q without denying the use of sources (e.g., Goulder). This has led to highlighting differences between sources and Luke's use of them in order to discover particular emphases. Here, scholars have encountered difficulties. Literary relationships among the Gospels are too complicated for hypotheses as simple as the use of Mark and Q, indeed too complicated to allow any solution (Sanders and Davies, 97–111). If "many" in 1:1 is literal, other sources may have been oral. Further, when authors use sources, emphases cannot be deduced from differences any more than from duplication. Therefore, reading Luke as a coherent document is a highly valued approach for interpretation today. Interpreters approach reading with constructs of authors and contexts in their minds, but images of authors and contexts ultimately develop from reading.

Note: in the following I translate *Ioudaioi* as "Jewish people." Most of the time in Luke, "Jewish people" are not to be confused either with institutional Judaism or the entire populace. All translations are mine unless otherwise noted.

Luke 1:1-4: Prologue: What and How

The Text in Its Ancient Context

Ancient parallels demonstrate that the prologue (1:1-4) follows literary conventions. It orients audiences to the literature they will hear, which the author calls a "narrative." With only hints of the contents as "things that happened," emphasis falls on methods and purposes. The author's involvement is analytical, communal, and dependent on antecedents. The things that happened "among us" (communal), already appeared in "many" other narratives that comprise chains of traditions. If "many" is literal, previous narratives included oral traditions. The purpose, addressed to Theophilus with a noble title, *kratiste,* is to ensure order and increase certainty for people who already have received instruction.

The Text in the Interpretive Tradition

Almost universally, interpreters assume Mark and another written source that Luke shares with Matthew (Q) among antecedent narratives. Whether "the things that have happened" includes events in Acts is debated. If so (this is quite likely), Acts 1:1-2 provides a secondary prologue. Parallels with Josephus and other Hellenistic authors imply that the author is writing history, but only as modified by previous sources and Israel's Scriptures (Alexander).

The Text in Contemporary Discussion

Traditions that Luke was a physician who accompanied Paul persist. The only reference the author makes to himself is a masculine participle ("having investigated"). Assuming that the author is Paul's companion, therefore, is beyond evidence in the text.

Some interpreters claim that if the genre is history, this enhances Luke's "authority." Readers encounter a narrative, and the prologue notwithstanding, the narrative itself unfolds the kind of literature that audiences perceive. Can authority be determined by the prologue, or does it rest in the power of persuasion in the reading itself?

Luke 1:5—4:13: Setting and Preparation for Jesus' Ministry

Luke 1:5—3:20: Divine Promises, Infancy Narratives, Global and Local Settings

The Text in Its Ancient Context

Immediately after the prologue, Luke establishes a setting before Herod's death (4 BCE). But more than establish chronology, the narrator starts with a local personal story that is set in global systems of social order, religion, and politics. Zechariah and Elizabeth belong to a priestly order of low status that contrasts with high-priestly elites. Piety makes them exemplary, but in an ethos where children manifest God's blessings, childlessness blemishes them. Sterility *before* menopause and *advanced age* are characteristic of biblical stories of extraordinary births. Their privacy cannot escape the foreground of imperial systems (see also 2:1-2; 3:1-2). Systems involving an imperial client king (1:5) and high-priestly collaborators (implied by Zechariah's status under a priestly hierarchy, 1:5, 8) affect their lives.

The setting jumps inside the Jerusalem sanctuary (1:8). Outside, a multitude prays; inside, incense goes up like prayers. Gabriel has to do with both. Inside, he promises God's remedy for the couple's childlessness. For the outside, his promise is for Israel. Zechariah's question "how will I know" encompasses *both* sides, and his inability to speak until the child's birth is a sign that validates God's promises for Israel as well as for him and Elizabeth.

Dramatically the narrative becomes gendered. It shifts from masculine characters to women. Elizabeth celebrates her pregnancy as God's inversion of disgrace, and the term of her pregnancy links her to Mary in Galilee. Gabriel speaks to Mary, and aside from overarching imperial systems, her impending marriage is the context. Promises to her are also both private and communal—a child for her; restoration of David's commonwealth for Israel. In keeping with 2 Samuel 7, the restoration is everlasting—with a twist. In 2 Samuel, David's "seed" is a collective noun for David's dynasty. Gabriel makes it literally singular. Gabriel promises *Jesus'* everlasting enthronement (1:32-33).

Like Zechariah, Mary asks "how" (1:34). Gabriel's response makes her conception a matter of divine initiative and correlates it with Elizabeth's pregnancy by means of an astounding claim: "Any prediction [thing] will not be impossible with God" (1:37). Mary avows remarkable consonance with Gabriel's announcement: "[I am] the Lord's servant; may it be with me according to your prediction" (1:38).

When Mary journeys to Elizabeth, they join forces. In contrast to mute Zechariah, women deliver the first speeches of consequence. By concealing herself, Elizabeth occupies the social margin but transforms it into creative space by playing a prophet's role. She blesses Mary and Mary's child, and affirms her own place in God's eyes in something greater than themselves.

Mary adds the antiphonal voice of another prophet from the margins. She identifies with the low social class and affirms God's power to bless. This takes the shape of God's "class conversion." Against powerful thrones (implicating imperial systems), God manifests mercy to generations of those who have inadequate access to the earth's resources. Her references to Abrahamic promises also supplement Gabriel's allusions to David's commonwealth (1:46-55).

Then a male prophesies creatively from the margins (the Judean backcountry, 1:68-79). Zechariah reiterates Gabriel's allusions to Davidic promises, synthesizes them with Abrahamic promises, and views God's fidelity to the promises as liberation from oppression. John and Jesus are ways God keeps ancient promises. When Zechariah calls this "forgiveness of sins," he means corporate consequences beyond individual transgressions: in context, complicity in Israel's subjugation. John's role as preparing the way of the Lord, recalling prophecies of Israel's restoration from captivity, likewise embraces liberation from oppression.

Luke 2:1 fills in the foreground of imperial systems. Emperor Augustus and Governor Quirinius in Syria complement the picture of King Herod and an implicit priestly hierarchy in chapter 1. Another imperial agent in Bethlehem, an unmentioned local clerk, awaits Joseph's enrollment. Geographical horizons reflect the interplay between local and global—Herod's Judea (1:5), all the world (2:1) (Wolter, 121). Distinctions in political status between Judea and Galilee also affect the setting, as does the village atmosphere reflected in a manger and shepherds. Augustus's might, contrasted with peasants caught homeless at childbirth, is full of pathos. Irony snags imperial powers, who force a journey that matches divine purposes for Jesus to be born in David's city. Like Mary, shepherds measure low culturally and are unanticipated recipients of the message that a Savior-Messiah is born to *them*. The inauspicious becomes auspicious, and out of character for their marginal status, shepherds become witnesses to others.

Joseph and Mary comply with cultic expectations of circumcision and purification. Offering two turtledoves underlines their peasant status (Lev. 12:8). But the inauspicious is also confirmed in the temple by sagacity, commitment, and hope. This also is gendered. First, venerable Simeon anticipates peace through God's restoration of Israel. He labels Jesus a light of revelation for the nations and for the glory of Israel, but also predicts the falling and rising of many in Israel (Luke 2:34). This reiterates Mary's prophecy about the downfall of the powerful and exaltation of the lowly (1:52) and anticipates conflict between elites and the oppressed. Second, venerable Anna witnesses to God's promises to deliver Jerusalem from oppression.

Most interpreters present 3:1-20 as a new literary unit. A reference to Tiberius's fifteenth year (c. 29 CE) lures many commentators to focus on chronology. But 3:1-2 elaborates and extends the local and global political and economic setting of chapters 1–2 and depicts how Jewish people experienced imperial systems from the emperor to local collaborators. Furthermore, like Elizabeth, Mary, Zechariah, Simeon, and Anna, the Baptizer plays a prophet's role within this imperial setting. His baptism for forgiveness has implications for individuals (3:10-14) but is also tied to Isaiah's message of national restoration (Isa. 40:3; Luke 3:3-6). Individual behavior has communal consequences for Israel in imperial contexts in both Isaiah and Luke. When John deals with instances of behavior in 3:14, they have to do with covenant values of equitable access to resources, economics, and the power of the strong over the weak. By contrast, 3:18-20 portrays another imperial client ruler, Herod Antipas, suppressing covenant values by imprisoning John.

Abraham, who figures in Mary's and Zechariah's prophecies, reappears in John's. First, he challenges Abrahamic descent unless it bears fruit in covenant ethics (3:8). Simultaneously, he espouses God's ability to raise up children of Abraham. Most interpreters take the metaphor of raising up children from stones as devaluing Abrahamic descent. But does it not also, like 1:37, affirm God's power (see 19:40)? In Luke, does God (metaphorically) raise up children of Abraham from stones?

The Text in the Interpretive Tradition

Most interpreters underplay the context of imperial systems and social struggles among the elite and the oppressed and focus instead on chronology (1:5; 2:1; 3:1-2). From the beginning of the second Christian millennium, Elizabeth's prophecy concerning Mary and her child became a liturgical prayer, with emphasis on Mary's roles as the mother of the Lord and mediatrix. This reduced the complementarity of the prophecies of Elizabeth, Mary, and Zechariah. The virginal conception also dominated interpretation and eclipsed scriptural traditions of divine initiative in birth wonders; indeed, it overshadowed parallels between Elizabeth's conception and Mary's, and diverted emphasis from God's initiative to Mary's character.

Moreover, emphasis on John as a forerunner and Jesus as Savior tended to write off antecedents in Israel's history and neglected continuity with Israel in portrayals of John and Jesus in the traditions of Elijah, David, and Abraham.

The Text in Contemporary Discussion

Debates persist over the virginal conception. The narrative lacks specificity about how conception occurred. When Gabriel predicts that Mary will bear a son, her engagement implies conception in her impending marriage (see Fitzmyer 1973, 566–67). However, Mary presumes not her marriage but her virginal condition (Brown 1979, 298–309). In addition, some deduce that Luke conceals Mary's pregnancy outside marriage. This too can be intensely theological if one assumes pregnancy due to rape or abuse. This intensifies God's inversion of shame among the marginalized (Schaberg). Either option underscores God's initiative in the births of Jesus and John. Such divine initiative, however, remains mysterious. Karl Barth once remarked that the virginal conception is "inconceivable."

Luke's use of sources leads interpreters to emphasize individual episodes, but increasingly, narrative continuity is also accented. Speeches of Gabriel, Elizabeth, Mary, and Zechariah fit together in one story. The context of imperial systems is also overarching.

Mid-twentieth-century interpretations made a sharp break between Jesus' proclamation of God's commonwealth and Israel's heritage (Conzelmann), sharpened even into "anti-Judaism" (J. Sanders). This will come under consideration again, but continuity with God's promises to Israel is undeniable.

Similarly, some interpreters judge Luke deficient in neglecting significant roles for women (Reid). Elizabeth and Mary are prominent exceptions. Interpreters often read the silence imposed on Zechariah as punishment for failing to believe Gabriel and contrast this with Mary's assertion of conformity to divine purposes. Actually, both ask "how?" Further, when it is clear that Gabriel's promises are for Israel as well as for Zechariah and Elizabeth, rather than punishing Zechariah, Gabriel declares that the inability to speak is a sign that confirms predictions both to him *and* to Israel.

How does the serene and contemplative Mary as the servant of the Lord (1:38) in popular piety and art fit her role as a prophet in 1:46-55? As with servants of the Lord in Israel's traditions such as Moses and the prophets, in her role as God's servant she also confronts oppressive powers and correlates God's mercy and promises to the plight of poverty, hunger, and oppressive powers. Today the Virgin of Guadalupe has been used as just such a prophet among the disadvantaged in Mexico, especially among indigenous populations. An image of her accompanied César Chávez and the striking United Farm Workers in the 1960s, and some feminists have adopted her as an advocate of liberation.

Luke 3:21—4:13: Unfolding Jesus' Identity and Endowment with the Spirit

The Text in Its Ancient Context

Jesus' baptism unfolds his identity. A heavenly voice declares: "You are my beloved son" (3:22, reiterating 1:32), and he is endowed with the Spirit.

More than monotonous lists, genealogies establish relationships and continuity. Jesus is related to Israelites in whom God was at work: Zerubbabel in Israel's restoration after exile (Ezra 3:2, 8); David in God's promises of rulers on Israel's throne (2 Sam. 7:13; Luke 1:32-33); Abraham, Isaac, Jacob, and Adam—continuity with stories of both Israel and humanity.

The devil (4:1-13) advances Jesus' identity by questioning, "If you are God's son" (4:3, 9). The devil proposes that Jesus dramatize sonship, but Jesus' first words as an adult demonstrate what he is not—he is not what the devil proposes. Forty days in the desert echo Israel's wilderness wandering. Further, allusions to Scripture evoke their larger contexts. Turning stones into bread recalls wilderness feedings of Israel, personified as God's Son. Will God likewise feed Jesus, God's Son? For Jesus, "one does not live by bread alone" (Deut. 8:3) means that Israel's *hunger* rather than the *feeding* taught them to live under God's care. The devil's promise to give Jesus the world's kingdoms for worshiping him (violating monotheism) is a deceitful shortcut to David's throne (Luke 1:32).

Jumping from the temple is a challenge to trust the words of Scripture: "God will keep you" (Ps. 91:11-12). Citing Deut. 6:16, Jesus asserts that testing whether God is "among us or not" is a failure of trust (Brawley 1995, 15–26).

The Text in the Interpretive Tradition

Some interpreters argue that by reporting Jesus' baptism after John's imprisonment, Luke conceals that Jesus was baptized by John (Conzelmann, 21). This is excessive. In Luke 3, Jesus' baptism stands in continuity with John's baptism of the crowds (3:7). He is baptized along with them (3:21). Many take the devil's claim to exercise power over all kingdoms to mean that Luke thinks all governments are demonic. But the deceptive devil is unreliable! In keeping with Gabriel's interpretation that *Jesus* is David's seed (singular, 1:32-33), the genealogy avoids David's descendants who ruled, and links Jesus more directly to David (2 Sam. 7:8-16) (Wolter, 175).

The Text in Contemporary Discussion

Jesus' genealogy is masculine, but the hint about Joseph's paternity ("as was supposed," 3:23) may be the only reference outside the birth narratives to the virginal conception or alternatively, to a problem pregnancy (rape, abuse) (Schaberg). Descent from Adam gives Jesus a role in God's relationship with all humanity. Jesus and the devil challenge each other by interpreting Scripture. When used deceptively, Scripture is false (Brawley 1995, 20–26).

Luke 4:14—21:38: Proclamation and Extension of God's Commonwealth

Luke 4:14-41: Hopes and Manifestations of Jesus' Mission

The Text in Its Ancient Context

Interpreters often call Jesus' proclamation in Nazareth his inaugural sermon, but the preceding summary (4:14-15) shows that it is an instance of his ministry already underway. The incident has four foci. Jesus reads Isaiah, announces a word-event that occurs when the congregants hear the reading, implicates himself in this word-event, and provokes a response.

Luke's audience would hardly have understood God's sending Jesus as one anointed with the Spirit in terms of a developed Christology. With thematic emphasis on the Spirit (annunciation, baptism, temptation), they would have heard that where God's Spirit is, God's favor is manifest, like the Jubilee Year (Green 1997, 212–13). The poor who receive good news are the bottom 90 percent, dominated by elites in a two-tiered system. Their social status is that of Rome's vanquished victims. Concretely, debts are annulled, debtors are released from prison, blindness is overcome, brokenness is mended. Jesus assumes the power of God's Spirit in his ministry. This is what God's commonwealth is (4:43).

Blindness plays on Jesus' hearers who fix their *eyes* on him (Green 1997, 211). They see Isaiah's gracious words (originally spoken also in an imperial context), but reject Jesus as sent by God (see "sent" in 4:18, 43). Luke gives no motivation for the people of Nazareth to reject Jesus. However, rejection verifies the proverb demonstrated by Elijah and Elisha: "No prophet is accepted in his own countryside." Their rejection confirms Jesus' prophetic mandate (Brawley 1987, 6–27). Conversely, Jesus' ministry in Capernaum manifests the favor God's Spirit generates (4:31-41).

The Text in the Interpretive Tradition

Since the development of Chalcedonian Christology, Jesus' claim to be anointed has directed attention to his messianic identity, often associated with doctrines of human and divine natures. Emphasis is on his God-sent ministry rather than his ontological essence. Possibly Luke intends only a prophetic anointing (Fitzmyer 1981, 1:529–30). But "anointed" in Acts 4:27 (citing Psalm 2) speaks against restriction to a prophetic anointing.

The Text in Contemporary Discussion

It is significant that Jesus' ministry has a major focus on release from prison. In Luke's world, prisons were primarily short-term facilities. Debtors, however, were subject to long-term incarceration ("until you have paid the very last penny" [Luke 12:59]). Today "restorative justice" places emphasis on building relationships between victims and offenders and offers the latter opportunities to make restoration—obviously impossible if offenders are incarcerated.

Recent discussion tends toward Jesus' anticipation of his ministry in terms of poverty and exploitation in addition to personal or figurative meanings (Wolter, 192–93). Many interpreters take the Nazarenes' rejection of Jesus as anticipating Jewish rejection of Jesus, even revealing Luke's anti-Judaism in favor of gentiles (J. Sanders). This ignores Jesus' prior successful ministry in Galilean synagogues, his subsequent ministry and acceptance in Capernaum, and his programmatic statement of his *sending* to the *synagogues* of Judea (4:14-15, 31-41, 42-44) (Brawley 1987, 7–11). In Luke, particular Israelites respond positively and negatively to Jesus and his followers. A corporate rejection by Jewish people distorts the data. Given the setting in imperial systems, the citation from Isaiah, and Jesus' claims of fulfillment, the Nazareth incident initiates the realization of the covenant promises claimed by Mary in 1:50-55.

Luke 4:42—5:11: Initial Extensions of Jesus' Mission

The Text in Its Ancient Context

Luke 4:44 summarizes Jesus' proclamation in synagogues. Then 5:1-11 shifts the setting precipitously to public space, where his auditors are a crowd closely identified with the 90 percent of the subdominant population—earlier called "the poor." Merely the appearance of crowds is a sign of differentiation from reigning imperial systems (Scott, 63). Again, Jesus' proclamation is summarized and gives way to a brief narrative about recruiting coworkers. Following Jesus' suggestion, Simon and his partners net an abundant catch of fish. Sequence alone leads hearers to presume causation by Jesus and to be astonished, like Simon and his companions. Simon then recognizes a manifestation of the numinous that threatens him, a "sinner." Thematically, this has to do with manifesting

God's Spirit in God's commonwealth, a manifestation that dramatizes what God's commonwealth is. Jesus makes it analogous to collaborating in mission—catching people. They leave all and follow.

The Text in the Interpretive Tradition

The catch of fish is often called a nature "miracle." Beyond prescience, little is extraordinary. Abundant catches are remarkable but natural, and Jesus makes this one a parable of mission. Developments of church hierarchy have appealed to Simon's priority and apostolic office. Here, however, there is no "calling" or "sending." The fishermen follow on their own initiative.

The Text in Contemporary Discussion

This incident culminates in a dramatic change. "Leaving everything" entails striking changes personally (e.g., Peter), economically (the fish are not marketed), socially (relationships are fundamentally altered), and decisively (commitment to mission to the poor/crowds) (4:18; 5:1). These disciples have a special status in Luke and are hardly models for every reader, but the call for change, commitment, and ministry are unavoidable.

Luke 5:12—6:11: Faith and Restorations in Contexts of Oppression

The Text in Its Ancient Context

Luke 5:12—6:11 presents concrete cases of good news to the poor (4:18) in other Judean cities (4:43). Three incidents focus on Jesus (5:12-14; 5:17-26; 6:6-11), three on his followers (5:29-32; 5:33-39; 6:1-4).

The healing of a leper is a remarkable deed of compassion pared to essentials (5:12-14). Luke's hearers understand the sparse description of leprosy as a skin disorder (not Hansen's disease) that required heartrending exclusion from normal society (Lev. 13:46; Josephus *Ant.* 3.264: "as good as dead" [author's trans.]). Prostration and supplication reflect the gravity of the ailment. Purification is primary; healing, the means to it. The leper links restoration with Jesus' desire: "If you *want to* . . . you can make me clean" (5:12 Phillips). Exceeding mere healing, Jesus proclaims good news: "Certainly I want to." Touching affirms his desire. Thus an instance of God's Spirit that blesses occurs. Luke's hearers cannot understand Jesus' charge not to tell to mean suppressing the deed, since the story itself makes it known. Rather, procedures in the law, rather than rumors, confirm the man's restoration to his community.

The second episode is closely related because it is stimulated by the cleansing of the leper (5:15). The priest's confirmation of the purification should have served as a witness to some Pharisees and teachers of law who show up in 5:17-26. Whereas the leper's purification is a bare-bones account, complex narrative tensions surface in the healing of a paralytic. The paralytic and the men who bring him beat the competition for space by a dramatic act of breaking through barriers to gain access to Jesus. They are virtually pallbearers who let the paralytic down through the roof. When the narrator says that Jesus *saw* their faith(fulness) (5:20), faith(fulness) is not confessed, but dramatized. (Confession does not thereby become irrelevant; see on 12:8-9 below.) Faith(fulness) looks like this. Jesus' reaction to their faith(fulness) is a non sequitur—an assurance of pardon that perhaps reflects beliefs that sin produces maladies. Some scribes and Pharisees create a narrative need by questioning: Who can forgive sins but God alone? Luke's audience understands that Jesus assures *God's* forgiveness (divine passive, 5:20) on the basis of action that overcomes obstacles to life. But Jesus provokes theological considerations by arrogating power (5:24) to grant assurance of pardon on earth (on the basis of the dramatic act) and offers healing as evidence that forgiveness is not in word only but in deed as well. Luke's audience hears Jesus refer to himself as "son of man" for the first time and understands that he claims a special commission from God. When the paralytic arises and carries his bed, he and *everyone*, including scribes and Pharisees, glorify God and acknowledge this as a "sign" with a double meaning—a sign of the power of the Spirit in God's commonwealth, and of Jesus' power to assure God's forgiveness.

Two additional episodes also produce conflict and prepare for what follows—for Jesus' proclamation of God's commonwealth, recruiting followers, and developing themes of mission (5:27-32; 5:33-39). Like the catch of fish (5:4-11), calling Levi is a recruitment story. The first person Jesus "calls" is not Simon, but this tax collector. Like Simon and his partners, he leaves all and *follows*. This does not merely provide a setting for the subsequent conflict over table fellowship. Rather, Levi's banquet is an instance of *following*. For Levi, following Jesus means including in God's commonwealth people who are of questionable repute, like himself, because they participate in systems of economic abuse (see 3:13) and/or transgress social norms. Thus the banquet is an act of following that becomes a conflict story. Pointedly, not the narrator, but critics label the guests "sinners" and question Jesus' inclusive table fellowship. Jesus defends his relationships by a parabolic image associating his "companionship" ("eating bread together") with healing those who are not in good health. Astute hearers of Luke would recognize thematic development on Jesus' mission to proclaim God's commonwealth not only to those who are economically poor but also to people like lepers whose social status is problematic. Jesus then expresses his mission thematically: to call sinners to repentance. This explanation also proclaims God's commonwealth to his critics.

Anonymous interlocutors then question the failure of Jesus' followers to practice special prayer while fasting ("praying and fasting" go together as one act, 5:33-39). The first time Jesus' followers are called "disciples" in Luke is on the lips of interlocutors who compare them with disciples of John and the Pharisees. Thereafter, the name sticks. Jesus responds with two figurations. His answer in the second person plural places his interlocutors at a wedding feast where fasting is absurd; under different conditions, fasting is appropriate (see 22:18). Garments and wineskins old and new depict *preservation* and *innovation* simultaneously.

The fifth incident (6:1-5) is a controversy story. A small amount of harvesting and eating grain on Sabbath raises protests against the behavior of Jesus' disciples. "Some" Pharisees object that harvesting on Sabbath is unlawful. Jesus tacitly affirms their premise, but also makes it contextually dependent by appealing to David's precedent, in which need supersedes regulations. Luke's audience would find Jesus' reference to the "son of man" (6:5) ambiguous. Do needs of *any* human supersede restrictions? Or do Jesus' prerogatives outshine David's?

The sixth episode (6:6-11) is another conflict story that clarifies this question somewhat by refocusing on Jesus. Luke 6:6 makes this incident an instance of Jesus' mission in other synagogues of

Judea (4:44). But his prior activity also invites a test. His examiners are some scribes and Pharisees with ulterior motives to find fault. The only question on the examination is: Will Jesus heal on Sabbath? Jesus' response first restates Sabbath law positively: instead of prohibiting what is unlawful, he proposes that doing good is lawful. *His* only "work" is words: "Stretch out your hand" (6:10). When the man does, Jesus' critics discuss: What are we going to do with Jesus? This question deliberates possibilities, which makes the translation of *anoia* as "fury" (NRSV) unlikely. Rather they lack "understanding" (6:11).

The Text in the Interpretive Tradition

The cleansing of a leper, the raising of a paralytic, and the restoration of a withered hand are all healing stories, but controversy over forgiveness and Sabbath behavior in the last two also mix with conflict stories about table fellowship and harvesting grain on the Sabbath. Conventionally, the healings are called "miracles." But antiquity does not distinguish between "natural" and "supernatural," as common definitions of miracle imply. The term in 5:26 means "something remarkable." Tradition understands the leper's cleansing as an act of Jesus' authoritative will. But the leper's supplication and Jesus' response are at the level of desire: "If you want to" (5:12-13). When conflict arises with scribes and Pharisees, almost all interpreters presume that Jesus' critics are unyielding. But 5:26 includes them among "all" who glorify God and acknowledge a remarkable deed. The other conflict stories end with Jesus' explanations of his and his followers' behavior. The restoration of a man's hand, however, ends with his critics' reaction: What are we going to do with Jesus? English translations of 6:11 that make his critics "furious" are simply inadequate. Rather, they "misunderstand." This is one among other cases where the interpretive tradition has set Jesus in opposition to his interlocutors in a way that is unjustified.

Interpretations of garments and wineskins have overwhelmingly emphasized innovation to the point of incompatibility between old and new. Both cases depend indispensably on *preservation* of the old. Indeed, the image of the wineskins ends with the value of old wine (5:39) (Green 1997, 250; against Wolter, 232–33).

The Text in Contemporary Discussion

Studies of Jesus' remarkable deeds have highlighted features that are prominent in Luke. Virtually all involve descriptions of oppressive restrictions, which either Jesus or persons in need violate in order to produce transformation (Theissen, 134–37; Wire, 109–10). In the healing of the paralytic, sin (not merely personal but also corporate and systemic), the pardon of which Jesus assures, plays a role in oppression. Demonic possession may be psychosocial expressions of domination and protests against social oppression (Theissen, 255–56). Some interpreters portray Jewish society generally as oppressive, against which Jesus produces a new order.

Two features resist such negative portrayals of Israelite communities. One is the larger context of oppressive imperial systems. Although some Jewish people collaborated problematically in these systems, such imperial systems do not represent Israelite covenant communities in general. Second, there is no supplanting of Israelite covenant communities here. Invariably, the transformations reintegrate people into Israelite communities. Violations of barriers are clear in the leper's healing, where

Jesus' touch violates a social quarantine in order to reintegrate the man into his community. Similarly, the healing of the paralytic violates controlled channels of access to divine power. This produces conflict, but the story ends in reintegrating the paralytic and Jesus' critics into common affirmations of God. Controversies over the practices of Jesus' followers highlight behavior appropriate to contexts, and continuity with the old balances innovation. Conflict over Jesus' table fellowship and questions about fasting receive Jesus' explanations of his and his followers' behavior. If Luke finds these responses persuasive for his hearers, should contemporary interpreters not also suppose that some of Jesus' critics were also persuaded? With post-Holocaust sensitivities, it is important to note that only "some" Pharisees scrutinize Jesus and his followers (see 6:2). Interpreters should refrain from taking them as characteristic of all Pharisees. Luke's Gospel is a narrative of persuasion (see 1:4). But unloading on Jesus' interlocutors as irreparable antagonists forestalls possibilities for either the antagonists or readers who are, like them, to be persuaded. Early Jewish tradition, a bit later than Luke, reflects a similar controversy resulting in a ruling that allows crushing small quantities of straw with the hands on Sabbath, without utensils (*b. Shab.* 128a). As Jesus' emphasis on doing good on Sabbath shows, he highlights "doing" over negative restrictions but does not abrogate the Sabbath.

These incidents of healing are also cases of overcoming oppressive conditions related to maladies. Simply identifying maladies today as something "wrong," restricting the sick to confinement or quarantine, or putting people with diseases such as HIV-AIDS under judgment are scarcely any different.

Luke 6:12-49: Life in God's Commonwealth

The Text in Its Ancient Context

Prayer provides a setting for Jesus' selection of twelve disciples and his subsequent Sermon on the Plain. Praying suggests that Jesus is not independently self-sufficient. Rather, on the basis of his relationship with God, he chooses the Twelve and proclaims God's commonwealth (the program of 4:43). Here the Twelve play no role other than following, but the title "apostles" anticipates that they will be "sent" in the future.

The detail that Jesus looks at his *disciples* is a key to understanding his sermon. He describes their life in God's commonwealth, but the crowds also hear. Jesus highlights the poor from the outset of his speech (6:20), as did Mary (1:46-55), and as he did in his proclamation in Nazareth (4:18-19).

The programmatic 4:43 indicates that the Beatitudes describe life under God's commonwealth. Strikingly, blessings are announced in direct speech to Jesus' hearers ("you"). Luke's audience would likely have heard sympathetically as if Jesus were addressing them. Each blessing is expressed without a verb in the first half (common in Greek), but verb tenses vary in the explanatory half. God's care for the poor is clearly in the present (6:20). Thus it is a performative proclamation of God's blessing for the poor now (reiterating 4:18). Blessings for the hungry and those who weep are future (6:21), but Luke's audience certainly recalls Levi's banquet (5:29) as a present reality and anticipates feasting within Jesus' ministry, not merely beyond. Luke 6:22-23 breaks the terse form of the first three Beatitudes by adding a longer culmination of blessings for disciples as Jesus' marginalized followers when they face opposition, individually and collectively. As in the vindication of Israel's martyrs (6:23 calls to mind Israel's prophets and the Maccabean tradition), blessedness may indeed anticipate a future beyond this life, but the reward in heaven (a metaphor for vindication by God, Wolter, 251) is expressed without a verb and likely includes a relationship of confidence in and succor from God realized in Jesus' proclamation itself. Luke 6:23 also breaks the form by including an imperative: "Rejoice and skip for joy" (6:23, "rejoice and skip" together describe one act).

These blessings are balanced by an antiphony of woes. Again the address is directly to Jesus' hearers ("you"). The explanation of the woe to the rich is accounting language: "You have your receipt for what is due" (6:24). The explanations of the woe to those who eat well and laugh, like the second and third Beatitudes, are future (6:25), presumably near future. The longer, final woe balances the fourth Beatitude. Jesus exposes those who are highly regarded in the present as falsely deceived on the basis of "lessons of history" (6:26).

Jesus then shifts from performative declarations to imperatives. Thus God's commonwealth also includes directives for implementing blessings. Luke 6:27-38 is centered on relationships encapsulated in: "Do to others as you would have them do to you" (6:31). Because this is not "do to others as they do to you," it contravenes even mutuality and inverts retaliation into love, including accommodating to others. Second, it means mercy that surpasses what others deserve. Hearers of both Jesus and Luke would understand this in terms of concrete relationships in village or community life. Enacting this behavior does not depend on individual resolve but is inspired, motivated, and made possible by a relationship with a merciful God, like that between parent and child (6:35-36). Relationships with others involve relationships with God; relationships with God involve relationships with others. To be God's children means that behavior is begotten by God. The "great reward" in 6:35, as in 6:23, is a metaphor for vindication by God.

Luke 6:39-49 deals again with how behavior under God's commonwealth is inspired, motivated, and made possible by a relationship with the teacher (the God of mercy? or Jesus? 6:40), which also "opens one's eyes." The metaphors here turn hindered vision into following a teacher and orient hearers to tend to themselves rather than others. This relationship bears fruit like a tree (6:43-45). Luke's hearers then view Jesus as a mediator of God's commonwealth who proclaims how life is when God rules.

The Text in the Interpretive Tradition

Studied independently, the Beatitudes are generally understood as exhortations, although Luke's version contains only one imperative ("Rejoice and skip for joy," 6:23). The entire speech has also been interpreted as an "interim ethic" for a period before the imminent parousia (among others, Albert Schweitzer), or as an impossible ethic to demonstrate human inadequacy that evokes dependence upon God's mercy (among others, Luther), or as an intensification of Torah. When the Beatitudes are seen as an integral part of the speech in their Lukan context, they characterize life in God's commonwealth.

The Text in Contemporary Discussion

Some interpret the Beatitudes as addressed to the inner group of disciples to whom the blessings of God's commonwealth are proclaimed, whereas the imperatives regarding mutual relationships are spoken to the entire crowd. But the gathering of the crowd with the purpose of hearing Jesus (6:18) and the address of woes directly to the rich speak for an address to the entire group. Cases such as turning the other cheek are "focal instances" (Tannehill 1975) that provoke wide-ranging consideration far beyond one literal incident. They encourage not passive submission but active behaviors for God's children to take initiative from oppressors (Wink, 127).

Jesus' sermon has fueled discussions about the relationship of the indicative (performative declarations of God's blessing) and the imperative (commands). But the proclamation is nothing other than life under God's commonwealth in which relationships with God are integral to relationships with others—two dimensions that are hardly separate. Giving to those who ask (6:30, 34) exceeds mutuality; the initiative and control of goods lies not with the giver but with those in need. The imperative to be merciful in 6:36 is often understood as ethical imitation of God. On the other hand, the context has to do with a parent-child relationship. The relationship is not imitation as such but the behavior that a merciful parent begets in a child, as in the gender-specific proverb "like father, like son."

Inasmuch as peasants at the subsistence level constituted 90 percent of the population in Luke's world, the vast majority of the hearers of both Jesus and Luke were the poor. By contrast, for many of us in the so-called first world today who disproportionately consume the resources of the earth, it is disturbingly difficult to hear the Beatitudes with the ears of the poor (Bovon, 1:223), and we find ourselves bluntly challenged.

Luke 7:1-50: Deeds That Substantiate Jesus' Identity

The Text in Its Ancient Context

Luke 7 characterizes Jesus by what he does. Two remarkable deeds precede the Baptizer's question: "Are you the one who is coming or do we expect another?" (7:19-20). Jesus' response is then followed by a short discourse that elaborates his answer, and by the woman in Simon's house. Though the healing of a centurion's slave and the raising of a widow's son appear to drop precipitously into the narrative, they are integral to Jesus' response to the Baptizer. First, Jesus returns to Capernaum, where he previously had a remarkable ministry and achieved prominence (4:31-42). The centurion clearly plays a role in imperial systems—succinctly, he commands subordinates—but here he makes himself subservient to God's commonwealth. His slave exercises no agency but remains hidden behind the centurion and his friends, Jewish elders, and Jesus. The centurion controls everything from offstage, including Jesus' actions. Nevertheless, testimony about Jesus motivates him (7:3). So he sends elders, who present a positive picture of Israelite citizens (Green 1997, 286–87, views their appeal to reciprocity for the centurion's generosity negatively). They also portray the centurion positively. Through other friends, the centurion tells Jesus what to do and says more than Jesus (7:6-8). He acts with "power" in order to access Jesus' power. Jesus names this act "faith(fulness)," exceeding such acts among Israelites. Faith(fulness) is not confessed but dramatized. If hearers recall the men who took a paralytic to Jesus (5:19) and liken the elders to them (7:4-5), the comparison with Israel (7:9) does not indict Israel but produces amazement even for Jesus (there is no "disjunction between this Gentile and Israel" as Green [1997, 288] suggests). Previously, witnesses of Jesus' remarkable deeds were amazed; now Jesus is.

Jesus travels to Nain for another remarkable deed and this time takes the initiative (7:11-17). The incident is a traumatic funeral of a widow's only son. According to customs of patrilineal marriage, the woman's plight eclipses concern for the son. Without a husband or son, she is bereft of subsistence. In keeping with the good news of God's commonwealth, compassion motivates Jesus to touch the coffin. Surprisingly, he speaks to the dead youth with an imperative, commanding him to be raised (7:14-15). A crowd interprets Jesus' command as a prophecy, spoken for God whose favor comes to Israel (7:16), that is, God's commonwealth. This characterizes Jesus as a prophet *before* competing evaluations label him a "drunkard and glutton" (7:34) and Simon's skepticism about his prophetic identity (7:39). God's favor corresponds to Jesus' mission in 4:18, reinforces his prophetic character, and further associates his ministry with Elijah by parallels with 1 Kgs. 17:17-24. God's favor for *Israel* (7:16) speaks against taking the centurion's faith(fulness) in the previous episode as indicting Israel.

These deeds set the stage for the Baptizer's question, conveyed by messengers (*angeloi*, 7:24). The question whether Jesus is "the one who comes" picks up John's announcement in 3:16 of a more powerful one who comes but likely also alludes to general traditions of a figure who comes in God's name (see 19:38; Ps. 117:26 LXX). Jesus' response summarizes his deeds and reiterates his mission from Luke 4:18. Like John, Luke's hearers deduce Jesus' identity, as the one who comes, from what he does. Before Jesus answers, however, the narrator summarizes Jesus' deeds (7:21). In 4:18, Jesus anticipates giving sight to the blind, but the first reference to such an incident occurs in this summary. Thus, when Jesus recaps his deeds in 7:22, he can include restoration of sight as well as the raising of the dead from 7:11-16. The restoration of the centurion's slave, the raising of the dead youth in Nain, and the narrator's summary prepare for Jesus' answer to John.

Jesus' reference to *blessedness* for those who take no offense (7:23) likely picks up Ps. 117:26 LXX again. The negative statement regarding taking no offense expresses its positive counterpart: blessed are those whose actions dramatize their faith(fulness).

Jesus then elaborates his response to John. John's ministry was extraordinary, unlike some trivial reeds blowing in the wind, and was democratic, unlike elite royalty. Conspicuously, John included tax collectors (3:12; 7:29). Jesus reiterates John's task to prepare for one who comes (3:4, 16; 7:27). Demolishing social hierarchies (Wolter, 283), Jesus evaluates John as greater than all others. Second, he makes two comparisons. One is between the least and John in God's commonwealth (7:28). The other is between the way *some* Pharisees and lawyers and *some* tax collectors responded to God. The criterion for the comparison in both cases is God's justice (7:29-30), which John portrayed in socioeconomic terms (3:11-14). These tax collectors celebrated God's justice in forgiving them by accepting John's baptism.

Jesus gives a striking characterization to those who respond negatively to both John and Jesus. When he speaks about "this generation" in 7:31, he does not mean everyone of his epoch. "This generation" is literally "what is born from this." "Rejecting God's purpose" in 7:30 is personified as if it is their "daddy," in contrast to those who are the children of *Sophia*, who also is the personification of "Wisdom" (7:35). Although the reference to Pharisees and lawyers in 7:30 is general, they cannot be identified directly with those in 5:17, because here they are characterized by their response also to *John*. Jesus then consummates his characterization of specific Pharisees and lawyers who are present (addressing them directly in the second person, 7:34) with a proverb: "Sophia/Wisdom is vindicated on the basis of her children" (7:35). Sophia's children respond positively to John and Jesus as the antithesis of rejection by these Pharisees and lawyers. But the use of Sophia leaves room for weighty amplification (see the following section). Sophia's children include tax collectors who celebrated God's justice (7:29), but this also picks up the tradition of Wisdom as an attribute of God (Wis. 9:9-11).

The meal in Simon's house (Luke 7:36-50) also brackets John's question about Jesus' identity. Moreover, it is a case of Jesus' association with tax collectors and sinners. Although Jesus confronts Simon, Luke's audience would not overlook his initial hospitality. Jesus eats not only with tax collectors and sinners but also with Pharisees. But Simon's hospitality is interrupted by a woman with a reputation as a sinner. She performs an acted parable with her hair, tears, and ointment (7:38; e.g., like Jeremiah wearing a yoke [Jeremiah 27–28]). But the acted parable is subject to two interpretations. Simon interprets it as a violation of norms that calls into question Jesus' prophetic identity (Luke 7:39). Jesus interprets it as asserting the woman's restoration.

Simon's interchange with Jesus is marked by civility. He addresses Jesus as "teacher" ("rabbi"). Jesus tells a parable about a debtor who owes ten times as much as another. Proportionally, the greater debtor is more estranged from the creditor than the lesser. Simon participates in agreeing that forgiving both debts transforms the greater estrangement into greater affection. Jesus then contrasts the woman's actions with Simon's. In this comparison, Simon is not rebuked for not bathing Jesus' feet or kissing him or anointing him (7:44-46). Rather, this makes Simon analogous to the small debtor. Then Jesus overwhelmingly emphasizes the woman's forgiveness and indicates that her actions show great love for having been forgiven. In response to Simon's interior monologue (7:39), Jesus does know what kind of woman touched him. As the centurion dramatizes faith(fulness) at the beginning of the chapter, so does the woman at the end. She does not confess faith(fulness) but demonstrates it. The scene ends in restoration and peace for the woman. How does it end for Simon?

The Text in the Interpretive Tradition

Jesus' comparison of the centurion's faith(fulness) with Israel's is virtually always understood as a judgment on Israel in favor of gentiles. The centurion is a specific character already related to Israel and does not represent gentiles generally.

A strong interpretive tradition takes Jesus' remarkable deeds as manifesting his divinity. In the healing of the centurion's servant and the raising of the widow's son, Jesus does astonishingly little, however. The centurion especially contributes significant action. Both events point especially to Jesus as a prophet (see also 7:39) who speaks and acts for God. Luke's Christology is deduced from Jesus' functions (Cullmann). Similarly, faith(fulness) in this chapter is not confessional. It is deduced from actions.

The NRSV and many commentators take 7:29-30 to be the narrator's voice. It is equally possible that Jesus continues to speak. The word "this" is not in the Greek: Instead of: "All the people who heard *this*," read: "All the people who *heard including* the tax collectors affirmed God's justice . . . but the Pharisees and lawyers who refused John's baptism rejected God's purposes for themselves."

Does Jesus or the narrator affirm John's baptism? Whereas many interpreters take these words as representing Luke's view of Pharisees and lawyers in general, if Jesus is speaking, then it is clear that the Pharisees and lawyers here are individual characters who rejected God's purposes. This resists painting all Pharisees and lawyers in Luke with the same brush.

"This generation" in 7:31 is generally understood as a repetition of "those born of women" in 7:28 (note: the idiom emphasizes "birth"). Such a reading interprets this generation (7:31) apart from the context. Further, the basic meaning of *genea* (7:31) is not a "generation" (time period) but "lineage," "descent." Contextually, "this generation" has a referent—the Pharisees and lawyers who rejected God's purpose (7:30). At the end of the comparison, Jesus speaks of Sophia's children (7:35). The parallel at the beginning of the simile likewise has to do with parent and child: "To what will I compare people whose 'daddy' is 'rejecting God's purpose'?" (John the Baptist similarly characterizes those who reject God's purposes as "children of vipers," 3:7.)

The sudden appearance of Sophia in Jesus' pronouncement in 7:35 draws on a bank of traditions especially from Wisdom literature. In recent decades, the notion of drawing on the background of Wisdom traditions has achieved prominence especially through feminist interpretations. In Wis. 9:9-11 and elsewhere, Sophia has the status of a divine attribute. In Prov. 1:20-33 and 8:1-21, Sophia is a personified voice who calls for followers at the intersection of wisdom and evil.

Prominent interpreters hold that John is outside God's commonwealth (Conzelmann, 18–27; Wolter, 283). Some also consider "blessed is anyone who takes no offense at me" as a rebuke of John. Two matters make both unlikely. John's question and Jesus' response are in interplay with Ps. 117:26 LXX. "The one who comes" in the psalm is in interplay with John's question (Luke 7:19), and "*Blessed* is the one who comes" from the psalm is in interplay with 7:23. Second, the phrase "in God's commonwealth" (7:28) preferably modifies the verb rather than the "least": "In God's commonwealth the least is greater than John." The "least" who is "greater" demolishes hierarchies in God's commonwealth (see 22:26-27).

Simon the Pharisee is generally taken as negatively characterizing all Pharisees and as ironically participating with those who call Jesus a friend of tax collectors and sinners (7:34). Granted, his hospitality pales in comparison with the woman's, but he nevertheless hosts Jesus and Jesus responds actively. Simon's question to himself about Jesus' prophetic identity is answered in the passage. Was Simon convinced that Jesus was a prophet as Luke's hearers would be? Tradition notwithstanding, there is no basis in the text for identifying the woman who anoints Jesus, whom the narrator calls "a sinner," as a prostitute or as Mary Magdalene (see 8:2).

The Text in Contemporary Discussion

Many commentators note that the centurion and the widow pair a male and female, characteristic of Luke elsewhere. Nevertheless, the widow's meager characterization pales in comparison with the centurion's extended characterization.

John's question about "the one who comes" has been taken as equivalent to a messianic title (Mowinkel; Hahn, 380). Evidence for a stock title is lacking, but this does not detract from the allusion in 7:19, 23, to Ps. 117:26 LXX (quoted in Luke 19:39).

There is renewed interest today in pre-Lukan traditions. Multiple independent attestation of Jesus' table fellowship with tax collectors and sinners (e.g., Mark and Q) and agreement of friend and foe on such table fellowship (Jesus agrees with opponents, 7:34) make inclusive commensality strongly characteristic of the historical Jesus.

Traditional interpreters have construed Sophia as parallel to Jesus. But Elisabeth Schüssler Fiorenza has interpreted Sophia (Q 7:35) as reflecting an early Christian Wisdom theology in which both John and Jesus are among her children. Jesus in particular is "Divine *Sophia's* eminent prophet"—engendered and derivative from her (Schüssler Fiorenza, 139–44). For her, even Luke equates Jesus' messianic work with divine Sophia's (151). This heightens attention to feminine dimensions of God's character. Such dimensions pour beautifully and profoundly from Bobby McFerrin's "Twenty-Third Psalm" in the feminine. But lack of direct evidence in the text calls for reservation as to what is meant in Luke.

That slaveholders exploited slaves, including sexual exploitation, was a cultural commonplace. If interpreters note the centurion's slave's lack of voice and strain nevertheless to discern it, they might hear overtones of same-sex eroticism (Gowler, 116–18; similarly on Matthew's version; Jennings and Liew). This fits Jesus' inclusive relationships. If, however, such a voice is present, would the Israelite elders, who are positively characterized, also portray the centurion positively (Wolter, 269–70)?

Interpreters often call the woman in 7:37 a prostitute. Feminists and others object that this is gratuitous and prejudicial. Whatever her reputation, Jesus' affirmation of her forgiveness and his blessing of peace mean her restoration to proper communal relationships.

Jesus' interchange with Simon ends without resolution. Two views compete in studies of Pharisees in Luke. One sees them consistently characterized as pejorative even to the extent of reflecting anti-Judaism in Luke and views Simon as completely failing to offer Jesus hospitality—not even comparable to the lesser creditor. Another perspective sees Pharisees as characterized variously (not mere stereotypes), who, like Socrates' sophist interlocutors, are not straw men but competent interlocutors. Given Simon's role as host, the clarification of his doubt about Jesus' prophetic identity, and Jesus' parable, might he (and other guests, 7:49) also be persuaded? Indeed, Robert Tannehill asks, "Should We Love Simon the Pharisee?" (1994). Are interpreters today open to new possibilities for such Pharisees?

Luke 8:1-56: Seed and Soil, Discipleship and Kinship

The Text in Its Ancient Context

Luke 8:1 recalls 4:43 and makes this section a continuation of proclaiming the good news of God's commonwealth in other towns. New emphases fall on women associates, four of whom are named (see 23:55; 24:10) and who contravene customs by supporting men (8:1-3). Anticipating the parable of the seed and the soil, they correspond to seed growing in good soil.

Unproductive and abundantly productive soils in 8:4-8 echo relationships between plants/fruit and good/evil in 6:43-45. Nevertheless, the disciples request clarification. Jesus responds initially with the riddle of speaking in parables (8:10). God grants (divine passive) insiders knowledge of mysteries of God's commonwealth that are hidden from outsiders. Inconsistently, Jesus shifts from varieties of soil to relationships between seed and soil, corresponding to people shaped by divine or evil powers.

But this allegory is bracketed by metaphors that demand probing reflection. Mysteries of God's commonwealth (8:10) introduce the explanation (8:11-15), and it concludes with a lamp, correlated with hiddenness that will be disclosed and secrets that come to light (8:16-17). The result is a figuration between insider/outsider and mystery/light. Insiders who know mysteries of God's commonwealth are to disclose them to outsiders. Outsiders then become insiders. Insiders who do not disclose the mysteries become outsiders (8:18). Consequently, the mysteries are not esoteric!

Jesus' mother and siblings, who are outside (8:20), provide an instance of what constitutes insiders. Biological kinship warrants no priority over the crowd. Jesus' kinship derives not from human ancestry but from God: whoever derives life from God is God's child and therefore Jesus' kin ("elective kinship," Bovon, 1:315).

Though commonly understood as controlling nature, calming a storm at sea is also related to hearing and doing God's will (8:22-25). The key is two rebukes. Jesus rebukes the storm but also his disciples when he asks, "Where is your faith(fulness)?" The rebuke of the storm produces calm; the rebuke of the disciples produces fear and amazement. Faintness of faith(fulness) positions them perilously close to outsiders. Are they Jesus' kin?

Then a bizarre outsider becomes an insider (8:26-39). For the first and only time, Luke's Jesus leaves Israelite territory. He encounters a demoniac on the eastern side of the Sea of Galilee, likely a gentile, unclean—an extreme outsider who dwells not among the living but in tombs, as good as dead. As in other restorations, violations of norms (this time regarding gentiles and tomb impurity) are formidable. Also the demons name themselves "Legion," which the narrator associates with "many demons." But it is also Latin for many Roman soldiers. Moreover, how this demoniac plays out his insanity involves psychosocial manifestations of oppression (Theissen, 255–56). Indeed, Jewish people named the Romans who subjugated them "swine." They equated Roman legions with herding pigs, and a Qumran text belittles a legion for worshiping the emblem of swine on their standards and weapons (Annen, 184). The demons enter swine that bring about their own demise by jumping in the lake (symbolically?). The man then becomes an insider at Jesus' feet, who makes mysteries of God's commonwealth known to others. He hears God's word, does it, and is Jesus' kin.

Two intercalated healings juxtapose a prominent, named synagogue leader, who comes to Jesus face-to-face, with a nameless woman hidden in a crowd, who approaches from behind (8:41-56). He voices a desperate request for his "only" daughter (reminiscent of the widow's only son, 7:12); she expresses her desperate desire only as an internal monologue to herself. Twelve years of life-draining hemorrhages also juxtapose her to the voiceless twelve-year-old whose life is draining away. Indeed, Jesus calls the woman "daughter." Astonishingly, her healing occurs solely by her action. Jesus, as an enabler, senses it but does nothing. She violates norms about blood taboos and touching. Her internal voice also becomes public, and she tells her story. Jesus calls this "faith(fulness)"—not confessed, but dramatized. The moment her life is restored, the twelve-year-old loses hers. But Jesus implores Jairus not to give in to death. Mourners who do give in to death contrast with Jesus' insistence on life. Again, Jesus does little. Taking the daughter's hand and calling her "child," he entreats her to arise. He is an enabler; she acts and arises.

The Text in the Interpretive Tradition

At 8:2-3, social and economic dimensions certainly have to do with women among Jesus' disciples. Responsibility with respect to the "word" is often understood as a verbal message. But 8:15, 21, specifies doing. God's commonwealth is not confined to proclaiming good news. It is realizing good news, as in the Baptizer's call for fruits in socioeconomic terms (3:2-14). God's word for Jesus (5:1) also means restoration of marginalized people to community (4:18; ch. 5). The restoration of the demoniac, understood early and often as an allegory of salvation, includes his proclamation of what God did for him, including his reintegration into family and community.

The Text in Contemporary Discussion

Mary Ann Tolbert's interpretation of the parable of the seed and soil in Mark looks for characters in the rest of the Gospel who play out roles described in the parable (1989). The result is a particularly positive characterization of women. This holds also for Luke. The near context in 8:2-3 calls special attention to women disciples who bear fruit. Do their actions correspond to the grateful woman in Simon's house (7:35-50)?

But publicly women also have limited exposure and voice. The voiceless woman with the flow of blood transforms herself and achieves a public voice. When Jesus calls her "daughter," some take it as subordinating her. Alternatively, does this "daughter" anticipate 13:16, where another woman is called Abraham's daughter, which indicates reintegration into Israel's covenant community? Does it fit Jesus' understanding of "elective kinship" in 8:21?

Interpreters debate the relationship of the woman with the flow of blood to purity laws. One outcome is resistance to portraying Israelite culture negatively, so that the woman's healing becomes supersessionism, in which Jesus transcends oppressive Israelite society. But in both Israelite and Hellenistic cultures, a flow of blood was taboo, and as in other restorations in Luke, violation of norms is integral to the healing. But the woman's restoration to her *Israelite* community precludes supersessionism.

Luke 9: Disciples and Mission, Triumphs and Disappointments

The Text in Its Ancient Context

In 9:1-6, Jesus enables and sends the twelve to overcome oppressive powers and disease as manifestations of God's commonwealth. The context is clearly communal; they make no provisions for themselves, but live in mutuality with villagers. Jesus also anticipates opposition (recalling 2:34), and endorses a ritual that witnesses against opposition—shaking off the very vestiges of the town, a sign of how serious neglecting God's commonwealth is.

Luke 9:7-9 juxtaposes imperial systems with God's commonwealth by bracketing Herod's perplexity before and after by success in the apostles' mission. Rome's client ruler finds the success sensational enough to take notice (maintaining local order is his charge). Recalling the Baptizer's execution also makes the apostles take Herod seriously. Herod's imperial perspectives evaluate Jesus quite inadequately.

But the twelve are out of step. The feeding of the five thousand (9:12-17) is generally taken as an independent episode, but contextual connections are strong. In 9:3-4, the Twelve live in mutuality with villagers. Luke 9:12 inverts the situation. Villagers need sustenance from the Twelve. Indeed, the incident focuses on Jesus' command to them: "You give them something to eat" (9:13). Jesus enabled the Twelve to liberate and cure (9:1-2); now they claim inability. Jesus' enabling actions are unassuming—blessing and breaking meager provisions, the beginnings of any Israelite meal. This enables the Twelve to complete the task—they give "them" something to eat (9:17).

Characterizations of Jesus and the disciples are interdependent. Rumors provide Jesus a prophetic identity; Peter adds messianic identity (recalling 1:32-33). Jesus, however, immediately associates rejection and suffering with messianism and adds his first passion prediction. Clearly here, as elsewhere in Luke, Israelite leaders, necessarily collaborators with Rome, are involved in his suffering, but not *the people* as such. Identifying Jesus as God's Messiah adds to Peter's prominence, but discipleship is also qualified by following Jesus under the image of a cross. Crucifixion means Roman punishment designed to shame and terrorize resistors of imperial systems severely. Following Jesus does not avoid imperial systems. It means perseverance unto death. In Luke, who meets this qualification?

The transfiguration drives the interdependent characterization of Jesus and the disciples higher (9:28-36). The setting and scene—the mountain, the changed appearance, clothes as bright as "white lightning," Moses and Elijah glorified, Jesus' departure (*exodos*) to be accomplished in Jerusalem, the cloud, and the voice all evoke the numinous, which both reveals and conceals. The voice naming Jesus God's Son and commanding the disciples to heed him advances the identity of both. But the disciples are deficient, in a stupor and terrified. Peter speaks nonsense. At the end, all are dumbfounded.

Meanwhile, disciples at the foot of the mountain fare poorly. Jesus enabled them to cast out demons and cure (9:1-2). Now they are unable to heal another only son. Could Luke's audience discern who is included in Jesus' address to a "faithless and misbelieving generation" (9:41)? The specific charge in the *second person plural* to people who are *present* may include the father, certainly includes the disciples, but not Jesus' contemporaries generally. Again, Jesus is the enabler who heals, and restoration to family and community is explicit (9:42). Luke 9:43 again characterizes Jesus by his functions in relation to God.

Another ominous prediction again characterizes the disciples as fearful and lacking understanding (9:44). The following incident bears this out. They dispute their own prominence (9:46-48). Jesus corrects them by welcoming a child and by encouraging mutuality with people of low status. But then they do not accept another who is enabled in Jesus' *name* but whom John evaluates as an outsider. Again Jesus corrects: "Whoever is not against you is for you" (9:50).

Luke 9:51 shifts to a new period designated as the time for Jesus to be taken up, and Jerusalem emerges as Jesus' destination/destiny. Still, relationships with strangers, qualifications for following Jesus, and enabling disciples for mission follow long-established narrative trajectories (Bendemann 2001). Jerusalem fills in the itinerary that started in 4:43-44. In 9:52-55, James and John express another misunderstanding of relationships with Samaritans. Jesus rebukes them. In 9:57-62, Jesus challenges three potential followers. To the first, he portrays himself as homeless (the unpropertied class). Sharp sayings about the dead burying the dead and someone who looks back while plowing (self-contradictory) anticipate negative responses. Yet Luke leaves room to suppose that they might accept the challenges.

The Text in the Interpretive Tradition

The feeding of the five thousand is conventionally understood as a nature wonder. But emphasis falls on enabling the disciples to feed others. The crowd is unaware of and infers nothing about Jesus' power. Many interpreters have taken Peter's naming Jesus Messiah (8:20) as fulfilling Israelite expectations. But Israelite expectations varied greatly, and a suffering Messiah was unexpected. Persistent anti-Jewish interpretations of the transfiguration as showing that Jesus superseded Moses and Elijah are unwarranted. Because Jesus' glory is in the eyes of the beholders (Peter, James, and John), some interpreters shift the transformation to the disciples. But they remain woefully deficient. In spite of views that the transfiguration anticipates later two-nature Christology, it remains awesomely inexplicable.

A strong consensus takes 9:51 as introducing a central section/travel narrative. Alternatively, 9:51 specifies a destiny but continues Jesus' itinerary and mission from 4:43-44 (Bendemann).

The Text in Contemporary Discussion

The feeding of the five thousand as the disciples' feeding others shifts the focus from a nature wonder to a gift (Theissen, 45, 251). Luke underplays the multiplication of food, and focuses on mission in God's commonwealth: "You give them something to eat" (9:13). The twelve baskets of remnants signify that Jesus enables the Twelve to fulfill their mission (Fitzmyer 1981, 1:769). This fits thematically with Mary's joy over God's mercy in filling the hungry (1:53), Jesus' mission of good news to the poor (4:18), and blessedness for the poor who are fed (6:21) (see also feasting and eating, e.g., 5:27-39; 6:1-5). The plight of hunger today, exacerbated by using food as a tool for wealth and power over others, certainly indicts those who today claim to be disciples of the Jesus who enables mission: "You give them something to eat."

In Jesus' inversion of a dispute about greatness into welcoming a child with whom Jesus himself identifies, children achieve a paramount place in what it means to follow Jesus.

Jesus makes two separate remarks on discipleship (9:23-27, 57-62) that emphasize God's commonwealth first, last, and always. Between the transfiguration and the second remark, the problem of the need for Jesus to enable the disciples is again at issue in their inability to heal (9:37-43). Nevertheless, at the end of this healing, the greatness of God's commonwealth is apparent.

Luke 10: Manifesting God's Commonwealth in Contexts of Oppression

The Text in Its Ancient Context

Luke 10:1-12 extends Jesus' enabling. He commissions seventy-two others (seventy in the NRSV). Like the Twelve, the livelihood of the seventy-two depends on mutuality, and they heal and proclaim God's commonwealth. Three things are new: they go in pairs, they prepare for Jesus' visits, and God's commonwealth is at hand through them. The harvest anticipates success but comes with dangers—they are like lambs among wolves (10:2-3). But rejecting them incurs judgment because it is rejecting God (10:16).

As in the sermon in Luke 6, Jesus addresses woes against the unrepentant directly in the second person, mixing singular and plural (10:13-16). The plural may indicate the cities, and the singular may indict individuals among whom deeds of power are performed. Luke 10:16 legitimates the seventy-two: to listen to those whom Jesus' commissions is to listen to him. In 9:10, the narrator summarizes the apostles' success; in 10:17, they report in direct speech. This evokes Jesus' explanation of their power against hostility. His report of Satan's fall is parallel with the "enemy's" subjugation (10:18-19). Perhaps Luke's hearers construe this as mythological, but it is also contemporaneous with Jesus and the mission of the seventy-two. The enemy's power is tangible. From 1:71, 74, enemies are subjugators and involve imperial systems. In addition, Jesus' assurance that the names of the seventy-two *are written* in heaven (10:20) means that their part in God's commonwealth is not future but a present alternative to imperial systems.

Jesus uses kinship language (parent/child, five times) to confirm the present reality of God's commonwealth. The revelation of Jesus and God is also not future but present. The disciples' blessedness is similarly what they *have seen and heard* (10:21-24).

In contrast, a Torah teacher inquires about his *future*: "What do I do so that I will inherit eternal life?" (10:25). "Inherit" alerts Luke's hearers to God's promises of inheritance to Abraham's descendants (e.g., Gen 12:3; 17:3-8), which Israelite traditions pushed into a future "world to come." "Testing" implies a dialogue to discover answers (Wolter, 392). The lawyer, not Jesus, defines love of God and neighbor as the heart of Torah. In Jesus' response to the lawyer's challenge to delimit "neighbor," Luke's audience presumably hears the parable for the first time. In it, the sequence of a Levite following a priest anticipates a third Israelite who would pass by. But a Samaritan interloper throws open the question about who is neighbor to whom and subverts expectations. If hearers identify with the Samaritan, the parable is an astonishing example of transgressing barriers to help someone. If they identify with the wounded man, as the lawyer likely would, they are the ones needing help from someone deemed deficient. Again, the lawyer gives the answer. Luke's hearers obviously heard the story as persuasive. Did they ponder how the lawyer heard it? Further, this is a concrete story of life in God's commonwealth already.

Sheer sequence invites comparison of Martha and Mary (10:38-42) with the lawyer. Like the women in 8:2-3, Martha offers hospitality as envisioned in 9:4-6; 10:5-9. But she is anxious and troubled. Mary as a female learner is as astonishing as the Samaritan in the previous parable. Jesus affirms Mary's *choice* as "the good part." Linguistically, in comparing two choices, "the good part" may be heard as "the better part" (NRSV). The focus, however, is not on comparing the two women but on the "one thing" that is needful. This is what Mary chose.

The Text in the Interpretive Tradition

The announcement that God's commonwealth is at hand has generated discussions of whether it is already or not yet present. A present qualified by the future takes care of both (Wolter, 380–81).

Satan's fall is often understood as a mythological primordial event. Joel B. Green (1997, 419) pushes it toward the future. But Satan's fall is manifest in the success of the seventy-two, though struggles against evil continue. Interpreters conventionally categorize the parable of the compassionate Samaritan as an example. But if hearers identify with the wounded man, they play the role of needing help rather than providing it. Interpreters have long viewed Martha and Mary in terms of preference for submission to Jesus over hospitality. Emphasis has shifted to a contrast between distraction and listening to Jesus.

The Text in Contemporary Discussion

Because God's commonwealth is an alternative to Rome's, the dangers for the seventy-two are sociopolitical, like Jesus' crucifixion. Evil, however, exceeds its manifestations in imperialism. The lawyer's test question implies an honor-shame challenge that implies gain for one participant and loss for the other (Malina and Neyrey). But challenges also invite dialogue from which both may gain. The lawyer's attempt to "justify himself" may mean "ensuring what is right" (Robbins, 252). In any case, his interchange with Jesus explodes with astonishing new visions of reality, of inclusion and mutuality beyond ethnic, social, political, and religious differences. Parallels today both local and global are inescapable. Schüssler Fiorenza (62–73) takes Martha's *diakonia* ("serving [tables]" or "ministry") as preserving memories of her office of ministry among the earliest followers of Jesus, which later antifeminism (either Luke's or his precursors') repressed. But the contrast is between listening and distraction, not between listening and *diakonia* (Green 1997, 436).

Luke 11:1—13:9: Praying and Acting, Fairness and Injustice

The Text in Its Ancient Context

Teaching disciples to pray continues Jesus' enabling and aims at God's commonwealth in fullness—on earth as in heaven. Directly addressing God as "father" as a child to a parent is unusual (but see Sir. 23:1, 4), but fundamental to God's commonwealth. God's commonwealth entails table and community, food (a synecdoche for all of life) and forgiveness (the heart of community). In relation to God, sins are forgiven. In relation to others, debts are released (11:1-4) (Green 1997, 443). Then parables reinforce this parent-child bond—God is contrasted with a friend at midnight who gives, resistance notwithstanding, and with parents with human fallacies who give children good gifts. God's preeminent gift is the Holy Spirit (11:5-13).

Against this parent-child bond, Luke's audience encounters a competing identity for Jesus—an ally of the ruler of demons (11:15). Three arguments counter this: the proverbial civil-war "house divided against itself" (11:18-19), manifestations of God's commonwealth deriving from Jesus' bond with God (11:20), and binding the strong man (11:21-22). Another perspective identifies Jesus by his maternal relationship. Jesus gives preference to kinship with those who obey God (11:27-28; 8:21).

Judgment then invades a short sermon (11:29-36). The "generation" that Jesus characterizes as evil means not just his contemporaries but also their "lineage" from evil as if they are its children. His first point is about signs. As 11:15-16, 20, shows, signs are ambiguous. Interpretations vary. Beyond exorcisms that show his bond with God, Jesus appeals to Jonah and the queen of the South only to claim that God's commonwealth exceeds both. Nineveh's repentance occurred not from Jonah's positive proclamation but his warning of judgment.

Again Jesus eats not only with outcasts but also with Pharisees (11:37). This Pharisee is surprised that Jesus neglects washing, but makes no reprimand. Jesus contrasts body zones—clean outside does not mean clean inside (11:39-41). Suddenly he levels woes at Pharisees. He avoids criticizing their practices but emphasizes matters that they neglect: justice (mercy toward others, 11:41) and love of God (11:42). Assuming status above others incurs another woe (11:43). He characterizes them as covertly unclean, like unmarked graves—metaphorically similar to "clean outside does not mean clean inside" (11:44). He adds three woes against lawyers: loading people with burdens (how is unstipulated, 11:46); participants (vicariously and concretely) in violent treatment of messengers from God's Sophia/Wisdom (11:47-51); obfuscating knowledge in contrast to God's Sophia (11:52). After this, the summary of hostility against Jesus hardly surprises.

Jesus continues preparing disciples in Luke 12, warning them about the Pharisees' "yeast," which Luke glosses as hypocrisy (12:1). Hypocrisy is not merely outward behavior that conflicts with inner realities, but also accepting deceptive views of reality as genuine (see 11:42). Luke 12:2-3 reiterates the saying about hiddenness that will be disclosed from 8:17. There, it refers to positive revelation of mysteries of God's commonwealth; here, it is a negative judgment against hypocrisy. Astoundingly, this judgment is not against Pharisees but against disciples. A double message prepares them for persecution—first, *fearing* death and condemnation, and second, trusting God's care: "Do *not be afraid*; you are of more value than many sparrows" (12:4-7). Confessing Jesus assures his reciprocal affirmation before God; denials beget his denials (12:8-10). The context of interrelated imperial systems is again evident with reference to adjudication before synagogues, rulers, and authorities (12:11-12).

God's care is also the context for orientation toward material goods (12:13-20). First, Jesus refuses to settle a dispute about inheritance. Inheritances from father to son are developments from Abrahamic covenant promises that supposedly resulted in providing equitable access to resources of the land. The dispute means that either the plaintiff wants more or his brother refuses equitable access. Either way, Jesus presumes greed, which he reduces to absurdity with a "you cannot-take-it-with-you" parable.

Then, analogies from nature illustrate divine provisions for subsistence. Moreover, Jesus distinguishes God's commonwealth from the nations (12:30). Behind this lies Israel's covenant traditions of distribution of land and its resources that are qualitatively distinct from other nations. Here Luke's audience would understand imperial systems that exploited subsistence farmers—90 percent of the population—and funneled resources to the top 10 percent, and especially the top 2 percent (12:22-34). "Alms" as the complement to selling possessions means not mere "donations" but "merciful action" (12:33). This is but half of Jesus' message, which also has exhortations to diligence and warnings of judgment (12:35-59). Even these are punctuated with promises of blessing for fidelity. But figurations shift from nature to master-slave relationships, presuming that masters have prerogatives to bless and punish (12:37-38; 12:42-48). Slavery was a pervasive feature of Roman imperial systems that exploited the have-nots. In contrast to the conventional notion of oppression of slaves by the master, in 12:37 the master serves the slaves. In 12:45, like imperial collaborators, a slave enslaves other slaves. This too is a common feature of imperial oppression in which certain slaves become overseers of others. Both the slave and the master who punishes this slave play roles in oppressive imperial systems (see below on 17:7-10).

Jesus ends by portraying conflicts that God's commonwealth faces (12:49-59). Jesus comes with fire (12:49). The Baptizer associated fire with Jesus' baptism with the Spirit (3:16). But instead of baptizing, Jesus faces baptism (12:50). The range of associations with fire for Luke's audience would stretch from "enthusiasm" to "empowerment" to "purification" to "destruction." Here it is closely associated with division—surprisingly focused on households (12:52-53).

This portrait ends before a magistrate, a local imperial collaborator (12:57-59). Luke's audience would not assume that the accused is in the wrong. Magistrates favored elite Roman citizens over peasants (Garnsey, 128–41; Lintott, 97–123). So Jesus advises prudent accommodation to avoid debtor's prison. Such prudence also transfers to making judgments about God's commonwealth.

Luke 13:1-5 continues themes of judgment and repentance. Jesus' interlocutors report two rumors about unusual suffering and speculate about punishment for guilt. Pilate's massacre of Galileans instantiates imperial violence. The other is an accident at the tower of Siloam. At first glance, Jesus appears to dissociate sin from suffering. Actually, he intensifies it by leveling the playing field to include everyone and warning his hearers of punishment unless they repent.

But the following parable emphasizes "pastoral care" for opportunities to repent (13:6-9). A gardener cultivates and nourishes a tree so that it will bear fruit. The vineyard and fig tree are stock imagery for Israel and shalom. How will listeners transfer the meaning from the planter, the gardener, and the fruit to the situation of Jesus and God's commonwealth?

The Text in the Interpretive Tradition

Jesus claims no additional sign other than Jonah and the queen of the South because manifestations at hand are evident (11:29-32, see 12:54-56). Interpreters vary on whether that which is "here" is Jesus himself or God's commonwealth. Jesus' manifestations of God's commonwealth resolve these alternatives. "Alms" in modern terms inadequately translates *eleēmosynē* (12:33). It means "merciful action" far exceeding "donations." Eschatology is often understood as a map of the future. Eschatology in 12:35-48 functions for living appropriately in the present. The incident of Pilate's slaughtering Galileans at their temple sacrifices is not attested elsewhere, but it fits other acts of his violence that are.

The Text in Contemporary Discussion

Little in this section is explicit about imperial systems until the end of Luke 12. But responses of subjugated Israelites to Hellenistic and Roman domination heightened certain identity markers (circumcision, Sabbath, purity) above other aspects of Israel's heritage. Social control agents attempted to enforce these (11:46) (Bhabha, 3–5, 37, 41, 58, 162–64; Niebuhr, 21–23). Jesus' woes reflect debates among factions about such identity markers (11:37-54) and lament disregard shown to central aspects of Israel's heritage—justice and the love of God (11:42).

The so-called prosperity gospel takes 12:31 to mean that striving for God's commonwealth engenders wealth. Living in God's commonwealth ("It is your parent's good pleasure to give you the commonwealth," 12:32) in contrast to the world's nations (12:30-31) clearly contradicts this. It is elites in the world's nations that amassed wealth by exploiting the masses. Further, 12:22-31 has to do with subsistence living, not accumulating wealth.

Luke 12:35-59 is predominantly taken as anticipating the parousia. But emphasis still falls on mission in the present. The debtor before the magistrate (12:57-59) is generally understood as a parable of God's judgment. Alternatively, it means prudent accommodation to imperial systems.

Some interpreters view the reference to "one more year" in the parable of the fig tree (13:8) as a *last* opportunity for *Israel's* repentance that, from Luke's retrospective point of view, would no longer be available. This view was strongly supported until the last quarter of the twentieth century, when emphasis on the gardener's care achieved more prominence, but it is still advocated (Egelkraut, 206; Fitzmyer 1985, 2:1005–6).

Luke 13:10-35: Restoration and Inclusion in God's Commonwealth

The Text in Its Ancient Context

The context of the *healing* in 13:10-17 is *teaching*. Luke's audience perceives both. As liberation from Satan, the woman's healing manifests God's commonwealth (11:20-22). The synagogue plays a dual role. Under imperial systems, institutions have sociopsychic impact in maladies (Theissen, 255–56). But it also is a place for teaching and healing. The synagogue leader objects not to healing but to violating the Sabbath. Jesus challenges not the synagogue leader but the assembly: "hypocrites" (13:15). Hypocrisy is not playing an artificial role, but the failure to discern *God's work* on Sabbath (Green 1997, 524). Further, the woman emerges from marginality when Jesus names her uniquely "Abraham's daughter"—astonishingly, such a title for a woman is otherwise unknown. Jesus endorses the healing with village analogies about animal husbandry. Reference to Abraham also evokes God's promises to bless (1:54-55) that this healing fulfills. Luke 13:17 implies that Jesus persuades critics to join in rejoicing at *all* his remarkable deeds.

Jesus underscores this woman's liberation as manifesting God's commonwealth with two brief parables (13:18-20). First, a mustard seed produces a nesting place for birds. This may echo Ps. 84:4: "The sparrow finds a home, and the swallow a nest where she may lay her young." Moreover, this recalls God's care that exceeds concern for birds (Luke 12:24). Next, a woman leavens enough flour to feed 150 people (Nolland, 2:730). This also is not mere increase but the woman's accomplishment.

Luke 13:22 reiterates Jesus' programmatic mission to other cities (4:43-44) and his destination/destiny (9:51). Teaching is emphasized, but it depends on an interlocutor who presumes that Jesus will agree: "Only a few will be saved, won't they?" (13:23). Jesus concurs, but to the interlocutor's peril, Jesus includes him among those left out: "I say to *you* [plural]" (13:24). Then they see ancestors and prophets in God's commonwealth from the outside looking in (13:28). By contrast, numerous people from everywhere are eating inside. Those who imagine that others are excluded in favor of a few are themselves excluded.

Simultaneity links the next incident closely. After the prologue, the first word Luke's audience hears, in 1:5, is "Herod." The same name in 3:1 identifies his son, Antipas, who beheads the Baptizer (3:19-20). Some Pharisees (13:31), who are not antagonistic (Green 1997, 537–38), warn Jesus to avoid him. Herod is not merely curious (9:9) but presumes a ruler's right to dispose of Jesus. Jesus' epithet "fox" is adverse—no concession to shrewdness. His message for Herod (13:32-33) reiterates his itinerant mission and contests Herod's right of disposal over him.

Jesus travels to Jerusalem not to escape Herod's jurisdiction but to contest *Jerusalem's* jurisdiction. Jewish people are heirs of Abrahamic promises whom Jesus longs to *gather* like a hen her chicks. The deeds in 13:32 identify this gathering as God's commonwealth. The "forsaken house" refers to existing systems that are antithetical to God's commonwealth.

The Text in the Interpretive Tradition

The mustard seed and the yeast are often called growth parables, but this highlights only *growth*, whereas the figuration involves the *whole*. The lack of reference to the seed's size or the amount of leaven means that the comparison is not between small and large. Many interpreters take nesting birds in a mustard plant as sheer exaggeration. Still, the plant's specific species is beyond recovery. Some varieties grow as high as ten feet (BDAG). These parables highlight accomplishments of a man and a woman.

The Text in Contemporary Discussion

A change in setting notwithstanding, the woman's healing stands in continuity with the unfruitful fig tree (13:6-9) as a case of pastoral care for Abraham's descendants (Green 1989, 515). The mother of the seven sons in 4 Macc. 15:28 is identified as "the Abrahamite" (like "Israelite"), but not as Abraham's daughter as in Luke 13:16 (Brawley 1999, 120n36). Schüssler Fiorenza (1992, 209–10) objects that anti-Judaism is inscribed in Jesus' dialogue with the synagogue leader. In the setting, however, everyone is Jewish. Moreover, Jesus' concern is instantiating Israel's covenantal values. The narrow way and the closed door in 13:22-39 are often appealed to as limiting salvation to a devout remnant only. In the text, however, the door is closed for those who limit salvation, whereas the banquet in God's commonwealth is wide open. This raises a question for the popular *Left Behind* series: Who gets left behind?

Luke 14: Changing Social Relationships

The Text in Its Ancient Context

The primary setting for Luke 14 is a meal. Again a Pharisee hosts Jesus. Close scrutiny at meals regarding social status and ethics was the norm in antiquity. So watching Jesus (14:1) hardly means hostility. Indeed, Jesus likewise scrutinizes his companions (14:7). Meals were also occasions for thought-provoking discussions. It is appropriate, then, that Jesus raises the discussion topic of healing on Sabbath (14:3). He argues by curing a man with dropsy and defends this by giving his interlocutors the perspective of a parent or farmer who would rescue a child or ox from a well on Sabbath (similarly 13:15). The other guests mount no objection.

Luke's "parable" in 14:7 is actually an exhortation against seeking honor over others, based on a proverb that inverts honor and shame (14:11). Further, Jesus challenges his host not to invite elite guests with expectations of reciprocity, but the poor and afflicted, who cannot reciprocate. Astute hearers might note that the host partially complied by inviting Jesus and the man with dropsy, presumably without expecting reciprocity.

As expected, another guest introduces a discussion topic regarding dining in God's commonwealth (14:15). Jesus responds with a parable about someone whose invitation to a banquet is refused by people who are tied to possessions and family (14:18-20). The host replaces them with the poor and afflicted (as Jesus advises, 14:12-14) and demands that his house be filled with street people to the exclusion of the original invitees (14:16-24). Thus this host is "converted." He changes his social relationships by including people of low status (Braun, 98–131). His original invitation built a "fence" that excluded the lowly; now he builds a "bridge" to include them (Braun, 120, 126).

The topic of inclusion/exclusion of disciples then takes an arduous turn (14:25-35). Severe criteria for discipleship exclude virtually everyone. Luke's audience understands the reference to "hate" to mean the necessity to decide between God and family. Still, deciding *against* family members and life itself (14:26) exceeds Jesus' earlier definition of kinship among those who do God's will (8:19-21), but fits his warnings of family divisions (12:51-53). Abandoning all possessions (14:33) appears to conflict with the support Jesus and his disciples receive from women (8:2-3). Two parables also contradict these severe demands. The first is an analogy of *possessing sufficient economic resources* to complete a tower (14:28-30). The second calls for capitulation to a more numerous army with the supposition that *if resources were sufficient* there would be no capitulation (14:31-33). These analogies demonstrate that actions involve consequences, but poorly serve the specific conclusion of abandoning possessions. Salt that has lost saltiness is absurdly self-contradictory. If relations with family, possessions, and life itself empty salt of its saltiness, and if such salt is not worth a mound of feces, then it would seem that inclusion in discipleship is exceedingly unlikely. There are two hermeneutical clues to the scope of the exhortation: Hating family and life is glossed by reference to crucifixion (14:27), which literally was a consequence for resisting imperial systems. Further, the final comment hints that it is a figuration: "Let anyone with ears to hear listen" (14:35). The juxtaposition of crucifixion with the rejection of family is extreme but still conceivable. Because God's commonwealth requires an unrelenting decisiveness for Israel's heritage as an alternative to imperial systems, discipleship is arduous.

The Text in the Interpretive Tradition

Long traditions have supplied allegorical identities to the sequence of those invited to the banquet: for example, (1) Israel's leaders, (2) the Israelite populace, and (3) gentiles. The slaves who bring in the poor and afflicted are commonly understood as allegories of missions, first to Israel and then to gentiles. Alternatively, the parable is not allegorical, but deals with relationships with the poor and afflicted.

Read against a Septuagint background, hating family and life means making a decisive choice between God's commonwealth on one hand and family and life on the other (Wolter, 516–17). Many interpreters struggle in vain to explain how salt loses its saltiness. The saying is simply self-contradictory.

The Text in Contemporary Discussion

Dropsy (14:2) causes the body to retain fluid and paradoxically induces thirst. Some interpreters think the reference to dropsy is meant to parody Pharisees, some of whom are "lovers of money"

(16:14) (Braun, 26–42). This is excessive. Dropsy plays no role other than a malady to be cured. Furthermore, in other healings, maladies do not parody characters. Later rabbinic sources allow healing illnesses that are life-threatening on Sabbath (e.g., *m. Yoma* 8.6). Jesus' criterion of doing good on Sabbath is in continuity with such an attitude and extends it.

Willi Braun shows that the host in the parable is converted to change social relationships. "Hating one's life" (14:26) merits consideration that elsewhere in Luke the spirit of life drives *restoration* of health, justice, and peace.

Luke 15: Advocating Inclusion in God's Commonwealth against Resistance

The Text in Its Ancient Context

In Luke 15, some Pharisees and scribes murmur against Jesus' association with socially marginalized people. Jesus defends himself with three parables. The first puts his detractors in the shoes of a shepherd who rejoices over finding a lost sheep, makes divine rejoicing over one person who repents analogous, and thereby legitimates Jesus. The second makes a woman's search for a lost coin analogous to Jesus' mission and concludes, again, with divine joy over one person who repents. The first half of the third parable partially corresponds to the first two without an analogy to Jesus' mission. A father rejoices extravagantly over finding his son. All three parables subvert expectations. The shepherd irrationally forsakes ninety-nine sheep in dedication to one. In a patriarchal culture, the second makes female characters analogous to Jesus' mission and God's joy. The third evokes pathos when the desperate son expects to return, but only as his father's laborer. His father's extravagant joy and his restoration to sonship beyond anything he asked or thought are astonishing. This story turns not on the son's return, which fits a son who has learned his lesson, but on the father's welcome. Perhaps this echoes Ps. 103:13: God's love is like a father's.

But the third parable also has a second half. An older brother is contrariwise shocked over the celebration of his brother's return. His refusal to celebrate is reminiscent of those who rejected the banquet invitation (14:18-20; Wolter, 538). The father assures him of his love but gives priority to celebrating the other son's return. Not only has a lost person, like a sheep or coin, been found, but also a family member. This parable ends without closure. Did the older brother enter and celebrate? Can he remain his father's son without welcoming his brother? Were those who murmured in 15:1-2 persuaded?

The Text in the Interpretive Tradition

Since Adolf Jülicher (1888), most interpreters have considered the settings for the parables in the Gospels to be secondary. Thus they separate parables from their contexts in order to interpret them from Jesus' perspective. Joachim Jeremias (132) took the setting in 15:1-2 as essentially accurate and argued that these parables were not the gospel, but a defense of it. Other interpreters have reasoned that if these parables did not proclaim the gospel, where else could it be found?

In the third parable, the son's share of the inheritance is his patrimonial heritage, deriving from God's promise of land to Abraham's descendants. Israel distributed land among tribes and families.

Squandering this heritage in a foreign land abandons Israelite identity beyond feeding pigs. The break is not merely with the nuclear family but with the family of Abraham.

The Text in Contemporary Discussion

Interpreters often note that the older brother characterizes the younger negatively as squandering his possessions with prostitutes and designate his characterization as unreliable (Powell, 274). Typically, this transfers to also regarding as unreliable Luke's portrayal of Pharisees and scribes who unreliably accuse others. But narratives commonly fill in additional information progressively, and this characterization fills in the picture of "reckless living" in 15:13. This "completing analepsis" (later information that fills in an earlier gap) scarcely transfers to Pharisees and scribes.

The ratio of what is lost to the original unity is stepped up with each parable: one sheep of one hundred, one coin of ten, one son of two (Green 1997, 573, 576). Mark Allan Powell (265–87) designates the famine in 15:14 as a crucial detail that is generally disregarded in the prosperous Western world but would have been obvious in Luke's world, where famine was a menacing threat, and often a reality, and the squandering son fails to safeguard against such a world. Nevertheless, in that uncertain world, he is welcomed and safe in his father's house. In the imperial context, Rome's tribute system moved enormous amounts of grain from the East to the capital, often leaving local populations unable to accumulate surpluses against famines, which were thereby exacerbated. Such a world is contrasted with the father's house, a vivid analogy of the contrast between Rome's empire and God's commonwealth.

Luke 16: Children of Mammon and Children of God

The Text in Its Ancient Context

Luke 16 shifts Jesus' address from critics to disciples. A parable describes an economic delivery system featuring a rich man who acts unlike the father of the prodigal son. His broker squanders his property. So he dismisses him. The broker already manipulated accounts in his own favor and does the same for his patron's creditors so they will favor him. Even the rich patron praises his prudence. Jesus interrupts this story at 16:8 with the comparison typical of Luke's parables: Offspring of "this age"—that is, who derive their behavior from "this age"—are more prudent than offspring of light—who derive their behavior from "light." All the characters in the parable—the rich man, his broker, the debtors—are offspring of this age in contrast to offspring of light. For Luke, mammon in 16:9 is also an "offspring" of this age; that is, mammon is born from injustice. Jesus' exhortation to make friends by means of mammon that is born from injustice hinges on the oxymoron "eternal tents" (16:9). Tents as *temporary* shelters make this scathing irony (Porter; Brawley 1998, 820): Make friends by means of wealth that is born from injustice so that when it fails they will receive you in "eternal temporary shelters" (contra Nolland, 2:806). (Note: the rich man in 16:19-31 winds up *without* supporting friends.)

Jesus continues comparing faithfulness with injustice. In 16:11-12, he explicitly critiques faithlessness with respect to "unjust wealth" belonging to another. This excludes taking the broker's prudence in 16:8 as an example to emulate. Two worlds—mammon and God's commonwealth—are mutually exclusive (16:13).

Some Pharisees overhear and ridicule Jesus. Like the rich man in 16:1-8, their prudence regarding not only wealth but also honor (justifying themselves) makes them offspring of "this age." Jesus' response contrasts self-justification with God's perspective and insists that abominable conventions of honor-shame are incompatible with God's commonwealth (16:14-15).

Although Luke's audience could have taken Jesus' reference to the law and John as being discontinuous with the good news (contrasting "until then" with "now," 16:16), more likely, the law and John are starting points from which good news is now proclaimed. Therefore, Jesus affirms the abiding validity of law (16:17). Indeed, his interpretation of adultery in 16:18 intensifies law. Perhaps Luke's audience puzzled over entering God's commonwealth by force. "Force" could reflect the power of patron-client systems to compel reciprocity, to gain support by favoritism, to gain honor for oneself, and to accommodate to prudent rationales in contrast to the law, the prophets, and God's commonwealth.

This corresponds to the next parable, about a propertied member of the elite who scores splendidly in serving mammon, but poorly in terms of justice according to the law and prophets (16:19-31). He is the foil for a poor man who receives God's promises to Abraham's children. Lazarus is clearly Abraham's descendant; the rich man is not (see 3:8). The rich man pleads for his brothers in vain, because Abraham also affirms the abiding efficacy of the law and the prophets.

The Text in the Interpretive Tradition

Interpreters debate whether the "lord" in 16:8a is the rich man or Jesus. Clearly shifting from third person narration in the parable to first person exhortation, 16:9 begins with the word *kai*, which continues from 16:8b: "Because the children of this age are more shrewd than the children of light, I *also* say to you." Coherence also supports the patron as the lord of 16:8a. There is no verb in 16:16: "The law and the prophets until John" (NRSV supplies "in effect"). Many interpreters have argued that John belongs to a decisively separate time before Jesus. The trend today is toward continuity, supported by the abiding validity of the law (16:17-18). The good news of God's commonwealth is the law and the prophets (Nolland, 2:802).

The Text in Contemporary Discussion

More than dealing with possessions, the parable in 16:1-8 deals with economics in patronage and honor-shame systems. Especially it deals with deriving behavior from injustice. The broker is characterized not by the adjective "unjust" but by the genitive (*tēs adikias*, 16:8), which, as the "offspring of this age" and "offspring of light" (16:8) indicate, is a genitive of origin (Brawley 1998, 819). Another genitive of origin modifies mammon in 16:9. Prudent rationales fit patronage and honor-shame systems but are incompatible with God's commonwealth (similarly Green 1997, 597). Most interpreters value prudence positively here. The parable and Jesus' critique of honor-shame (justifying oneself) among Pharisees devalues prudence as a way of rationalizing injustice (16:15). The rich man and Lazarus is hardly about future judgment. Their deaths are past, and their relationships with Abraham are in the present.

Luke 17:1—18:8: Scandals and Faith(fulness) Less Than a Mustard Seed

The Text in Its Ancient Context

Jesus warns his disciples that it is impossible to avoid stumbling (*skandala*). Momentarily, Luke's audience might take this as their own stumbling, but 17:1 quickly shifts to causing another to stumble. A millstone around the neck is a radical punishment metaphor for causing one "little" one to stumble (17:2). This recalls the little children of 10:21, who know their parent and know they are God's children; that is, the "little flock" in 12:32, to whom God gives the commonwealth as fulfillment of promises to Abraham, and Lazarus from the preceding parable. Anyone familiar with Scripture might remember *skandala* that caused Israel to fall away from God. Suddenly Jesus turns to forgiveness. Failing to forgive is an instance of *skandala* (17:3-4).

Does 17:5 skip to another issue, or is faith(fulness) the condition for avoiding *skandala*? Repeatedly, Luke dramatizes faith(fulness) as action. The apostles' request implies a profusion of faith(fulness) beyond what they already have; Jesus reduces what they presume they have to *less than* a mustard seed (17:5-6).

Is the slave who does what is commanded a positive or negative example (17:7-10)? Hearers first occupy the role of a slave owner whose slave comes in from the field. They have a choice: invite the slave to the table or command him to serve the table. If the slave serves, would they, as slave owners, express gratitude? (parallel to 12:37). But precipitously, hearers are made to play roles not of slave owners but of unthanked slaves.

In sorting this out, hearers confront a story about ten lepers who encounter Jesus. Jesus does nothing except to say, "Go and show yourselves to the priests." On the way, they become clean (17:11-14). One returns to give thanks, and the narrator calls him a Samaritan (17:15-19). Jesus calls this faith(fulness); that is, the Samaritan dramatizes faith(fulness). The other nine treat Jesus as an unthanked slave, and now hearers perceive that Jesus' mustard-seed basic minimum is gratitude to God for God's works. Some Pharisees' question of *when* God's commonwealth comes (17:20-21) stands in continuity with this basic minimum. Jesus' answer is *where* as well as *when*. That is, he locates the commonwealth in the cleansed leper's gratitude as manifesting God's commonwealth in their midst.

Jesus then alerts his disciples to adversity in God's commonwealth. One stumbling block (*skandalon*) that leads astray is false messiahs (17:23-24). Jesus predicts a future final manifestation of God's commonwealth in himself, but only after suffering and rejection (17:24-37). This final manifestation is an unforeseen crisis demanding decisions in which some are saved (Noah, Lot) and others destroyed (Sodom, Lot's wife) (17:26-35). This prompts a question from Jesus' disciples: "Where?" Jesus answers in a riddle: where eagles gather around a corpse (17:37). Is it possible to unravel what *eagles* mean? (See below under "The Text in Contemporary Discussion.")

Luke 18:1-8 still addresses Jesus' disciples. Before narrating the parable, Luke interprets it: "It is necessary to pray always and not to despair." Maintaining hope (18:1) responds to the adversity predicted in 17:22-37. The judge, who does not fear God or respect people (18:3) and thus whose behavior is born from "injustice" (genitive of origin, 18:6), refuses to grant justice to a widow. He belongs to imperial systems that contrast with concerns for widows in Israel's Scriptures. Still, the woman's audacity would surprise hearers. The judge finally accedes to the widow's vexing persistence and grants her justice. Luke 18:8 reiterates the theme of faith(fulness) in 17:5-6, 19.

The Text in the Interpretive Tradition

Stumbling in 17:1 initially raises concern for personal failure. Such an element is present in 17:3-4, but in 17:1-2 the issue is causing others to stumble. Stumbling in the Septuagint means falling away from God.

The parable about a slave who does what is commanded, ending with "we are worthless slaves, we have done only what we ought to have done," is widely taken as Jesus' evaluation of his apostles who ask for increased faith, and the slave owner is likened to God, whose gratitude they should not expect. But if the parable is taken with the healing of ten lepers, and with 12:37 in the larger context, the unthanked slave corresponds also to Jesus, who is unthanked by nine out of ten lepers who are healed. Green (1997, 614) asserts that thanking a slave would put a master in debt to the slave. But the Samaritan leper who returns with thanksgiving does not obligate Jesus (17:16).

Interpreters have long debated whether *entos hymōn* in 17:21 means "in one's heart" or "among you." Questioning when God's commonwealth comes diverts some Pharisees from the cleansing of the lepers and searches in the wrong place for the wrong time. The NRSV implies a new setting by beginning 17:20 with "once." An alternate translation, "when he was asked," gives the Pharisees' question continuity with the context. There is no change in setting.

From the early church through the Middle Ages, the eagles in 17:37 were understood to be either angels or believers who are devoted to the body of Christ (O'Day).

Under the notion that parables have *one* central meaning, the parable of the widow and the unjust judge has been taken as *either* valuing the widow's persistence or contrasting God's readiness with the judge's reticence. Neither excludes the other.

The Text in Contemporary Discussion

Popular eschatology, such as the *Left Behind* series, often takes 17:22-37 to be descriptions of what some call the "rapture." First, the notion of rapture is not taken from any one biblical text but from a selective combination of texts picked here and there and removed from their contexts. Second, the language here is apocalyptic—vivid, imagistic figurations that create a sense of crisis *for the present*. The purpose is not to be a road map of the future (e.g., pilotless airplanes; see 17:34) but to encourage appropriate responsibility now.

Luke 17:37 repeats a Greek proverb (Ehrhardt) but substitutes "eagles" for the proverbial "vultures." Definitively, the text means "eagles" and not "vultures," as in recent English translations. Roman soldiers marched behind standards bearing eagles. Rome, like many nations today, depicted itself as an eagle. Jupiter's mascot was an eagle. Roman emperors likewise associated themselves with eagles, and the Septuagint repeatedly depicts empires that God uses to punish Israel as eagles. But God also brings to naught all such empires to reestablish shalom. Jerusalem's gathering, which Jesus desires in 13:34, is God's commonwealth (see on 13:32-34 above). The gathering of imperial eagles is Rome's kingdom. Christ's final manifestation reestablishes God's commonwealth against imperial systems, which are reduced to feeding on a corpse (Carter 2003).

Feminists and others (e.g., Cotter) champion the widow who asserts her rights against unjust, imperial, patriarchal systems, and they emphasize the way she dramatizes faith(fulness). Imperial studies note the verisimilar depiction of Roman courts, which favored elite Roman citizens over others (Garnsey, 128–41). "The parable is a burlesque of the whole justice system" (Cotter, 342). Praying with confidence that God grants justice is part and parcel of confronting injustice persistently, and vice versa.

Luke 18:9-34: Inclusion in and Exclusion from God's Commonwealth

The Text in Its Ancient Context

The parable in 18:9-14 revisits inclusion and exclusion. The addressees (some who trusted that they were right and despised others) are new. A Pharisee and a tax collector pray at the temple. Neither the Pharisee's gratitude for what differentiates him from others nor the tax collector's plea for God's mercy typify prayers of their group (Wolter, 593). Rather, group identity reflects social standing. Reminiscent of 13:23, in which it is presumed few will be saved and many will wind up outside, the first worshiper is not justified, the second is. Jesus, then, inverts honor and shame with a proverb (18:14).

The disciples, dangerously close to having a millstone hung around their necks (17:2), rebuke people who bring infants to Jesus. But following his own remarks in 17:3, Jesus rebukes them and declares that God's commonwealth belongs to little children (18:15-16, similarly 10:21). Three interpretations of receiving God's commonwealth "as a little child" are possible: receiving the commonwealth the way a child would; receiving it the way one accepts a child; receiving it by accepting a child (18:17). Interpreters profit from pondering each possibility without neglecting the others.

A rich ruler, obviously part of imperial systems, then asks the same question as the lawyer in 10:25: "What must I do to inherit eternal life?" (18:18). The question unavoidably interacts with receiving God's commonwealth as a child. Jesus' answer, similar to his response in 10:26, is: "What is written in the law?" (18:20). Jesus tells him to sell "whatever you have" and redistribute it among the poor, recalling 16:13: "You cannot serve God and mammon." The ruler's disillusionment evokes Jesus' parable: It is harder for the rich to enter God's commonwealth than for a camel to go through the eye of a needle (18:24-25). Some listeners deduce that no one can enter. Jesus then reiterates 1:37 with variations: "Human impossibilities are God's mighty deeds" (18:27).

Peter presents Jesus' followers as the rich ruler's counterpart. Jesus promises a double repayment for leaving home and family for God's commonwealth (18:29-30). In the world to come, it is eternal life. Repayment in the present is unspecified but already includes Jesus and present manifestations of God's commonwealth.

At 18:31, Jesus again reveals adversity to the Twelve. He forecasts being handed over to gentiles (Jewish people are not mentioned). A summary of his suffering and death follows. The Twelve do not understand.

The Text in the Interpretive Tradition

Many interpreters take the parable of two men praying in the temple as addressed to Pharisees. But the Pharisee who prays determines the addressees no more than the tax collector. In Luke 23, Jesus is mocked and Pilate threatens to flog him, echoing terms used in 18:32, though spitting is not mentioned. John Nolland's note (2:895) that handing Jesus over to gentiles breaks Jewish national solidarity fails to consider how indigenous ruling elites collaborate in imperial systems.

The Text in Contemporary Discussion

Social identity theory holds that members of groups exaggerate both in-group solidarity and distinctions from out-groups. Further, the social sciences identify honor as the pivotal value in antiquity. In this light, the Pharisee draws honor both from his in-group and by differentiation from tax collectors. The tax collector is inevitably a collaborator in imperial systems, but his prayer disavows norms of his group and implies changing group identity. As one whom God justifies (divine passive), he belongs to God's commonwealth.

Jesus' promise to the ruler of "treasure in heaven" (18:22) is parallel to God's commonwealth (18:24, 29), and it is a figurative circumlocution for God (Wolter, 600). Redistributing wealth as such does not accumulate treasure in heaven (18:22). Rather, the entire statement is a figuration for serving God rather than mammon.

Luke 18:35—19:27: The Commonwealth Jesus Brings and Ruling Systems

The Text in Its Ancient Context

Three episodes move toward Jesus' destination/destiny in Jerusalem: he heals a blind man as he approaches Jericho, encounters Zacchaeus in Jericho, and relates a parable as he nears Jerusalem. As Jesus approaches Jericho, a blind man calls him David's son and pleads for mercy, as did the tax collector in 18:13 (18:35-43). He is literally marginalized, off the road, begging. His insistent pleas break through efforts to silence him. Jesus issues only one word commanding him to do something: "See [again]!" The blind man's pleas in spite of protests dramatizes faith(fulness). He does see again and glorifies God, as did the Samaritan in 17:18. Unlike the ruler (18:22-23), he follows Jesus. Perhaps he also "sees" what the Twelve cannot understand (18:34) (Wolter, 607). The crowd, including those who protested the blind man's pleas, also sees anew and praises God (18:48).

In Jericho, Jesus encounters rich Zacchaeus, also marginalized as a chief tax collector/sinner (19:7). His office assures that he is a collaborator in imperial systems. He also wishes to "see" but faces two obstacles: a crowd and his short stature (19:3). He does one thing: he climbs a tree. As Zacchaeus's guest, Jesus enters another relationship with tax collectors/sinners that draws social protests (19:7). Zacchaeus reveals no motivation for changing relationships with mammon by redistributing half of his possessions among the poor and making fourfold reparation for defrauding (19:8-9). Jesus equates this change with salvation and the renewal of Zacchaeus's Abrahamic heritage (19:9-10). Like Abraham's daughter in 13:16, Zacchaeus is Abraham's son.

Jesus relates a story to a crowd traveling to Jerusalem that expects God's commonwealth to appear with Jesus' arrival there (19:11). In the story, a ruler in imperial systems gives ten slaves one mina (traditionally rendered "pound") each, with which they are to do business. Meanwhile, he goes to receive a kingdom (19:12-14), which some compatriots oppose. When he returns, he audits his slaves. Profits garner praise (19:16-23), but he disenfranchises a slave who safeguarded his mina

(19:26). Moreover, he slaughters the delegation that opposed him. The story is hardly about the minas and the slaves. It is a parable of a throne pretender who seeks and tries to maintain power. For Luke's audience, this likely was a gruesome analogy to Rome's empire—exploiting peasants, punishing unproductivity, and slaughtering opponents. Jesus distances himself from such a kingdom.

The Text in the Interpretive Tradition

From early Christian centuries, the blind man's naming Jesus David's son was understood as a christological confession fulfilling Scripture. It more directly recalls 1:32-33, 54-56, 69-73. Many interpreters emphasize Jesus' healing by the power of his word, but here the word is an imperative for the blind man to act: "look up/again." Some take Zacchaeus's expression of giving in the present tense as informing Jesus of what he already practices customarily (Fitzmyer 1985, 2:1225). But this runs aground on the future fourfold restitution of those he defrauded (19:8; also Wolter, 613–14). Interpreters have long noted parallels to Josephus's account of Herod Archelaus, who promised rewards to those who would support him in his attempts to consolidate power as a king (Josephus, *Ant.* 17.8.4–9.2). But then commentators virtually always take the parable as an allegory in which slaves correspond to people facing Jesus' parousia and judgment, including the eschatological destruction of his opponents, particularly Jerusalem and its rulers.

The Text in Contemporary Discussion

Restoring the blind man's sight in 18:35-43 involves defying attempts to keep the marginalized on the margin. Faith(fulness) here is not confessional but consists in persistent violations of impediments. Unlike others for whom Jesus performed remarkable deeds, the blind beggar is not merely reintegrated into community (Theissen, 52–53) but also follows Jesus. Recovery of Israel's covenant traditions is thematic for Luke, and in light of 1:32-33, 54-56, 69-73, "David's son" manifests God's fidelity to Abrahamic promises to bless. In Zacchaeus's case, Jesus overcomes social impediments in order to manifest that even an enlightened tax collector is Abraham's son. In light of how hard it is for a rich man to be saved (18:27), Zacchaeus is an instance of an impossibility in human hands that becomes God's mighty deed (Brawley 1998, 822). Zacchaeus's reversal follows Mary's inversion of rich and poor in 1:52-55, but it directly benefits the poor with something approaching mutuality. Overwhelmingly, interpreters of the parable on the minas and the slaves focus on praise of industrious discipleship. This produces a misfit of a harsh, greedy ruler disciplining unproductive disciples and opponents (cf. Herzog, 162–68). But parallels to Josephus's account of Archelaus make it rather a parable of a throne pretender that is analogous to imperial systems. Jesus presents these systems as the antithesis to God's commonwealth.

Luke 19:28—20:44: Ruling Systems in Jerusalem and the Things That Make for Peace

The Text in Its Ancient Context

Riding a donkey over his disciples' clothes, Jesus parodies royal parades and reprises Zech. 9:9 (Luke 19:28-40). In connection with the preceding parable of the throne pretender, this caricatures military acclamations. On the basis of deeds of good news for the poor and oppressed (19:37; cf. 4:18), Jesus' disciples ascribe a benediction to him as the king who comes in God's name (Ps. 117:26 LXX) and chant a doxology of God's peace (20:1). When some Pharisees protest, Jesus persistently follows the example of the blind beggar (18:38-39) and violates their objections (19:39-40).

Jesus is grim. He weeps. Jerusalem has not recognized what makes for peace—but faces disaster under destructive imperial systems (19:41-44).

The so-called cleansing of the temple is nothing of the sort. Rather, Jesus makes a *claim* on it as a house of prayer. The "den of robbers" (Jer. 7:11) insinuates the high-priestly party's place in imperial systems that reward elites and plunder the people (cf. Jer. 7:5-7). Jesus' claim for a place of prayer notwithstanding, he uses the temple for teaching and proclamation such that his teaching remains dramatically public (19:47; 20:1; see also 21:37-38; 22:53), again persistently violating opposition (19:45-48).

Luke 20 primarily reports consequences of Jesus' teaching. In a dispute about Jesus' source of power, Jesus makes his source comparable to John's. Beyond that, he refuses to answer (20:1-8). He narrates a parable, alluding to Isaiah's figuration of Israel as a vine (Isa. 5:1-7), about tenants of a vineyard who produce no fruit for the owner (20:9-19). This targets the high-priestly coterie (20:19). Avoiding a snare about paying tribute to Caesar, Jesus tantalizes hearers to ponder what belongs to God (20:20-25). An interchange with Sadducees on resurrection produces another riposte: "God is not the God of the dead but of the living" (20:27-38). Luke's audience would not consider all Jesus' interlocutors intractable because some agree with him (20:39). The Jesus whom Luke portrays in order to persuade the Gospel's audience also persuades his interlocutors. Jesus then takes his turn at posing a challenge: "How can people say that the Messiah is David's son?" Luke's audience might take this as denying the Messiah's Davidic lineage or as posing a riddle about *how* the Messiah can be both (20:41-44). Since Luke underlines both Jesus' Davidic lineage and his messiahship, a possible answer to how David's son can also be Messiah is by God's power (cf. Patte, 315–16).

The Text in the Interpretive Tradition

After 19:39, Pharisees disappear from Luke. Jesus' challengers become the high-priestly coterie. From earliest interpretations, debates have raged about *exousia* ("authority" or "power," 20:2, 8). The high-priestly party actually asks, "By what sort of *power* do you do these things? Who gave you this *power*?" (20:2). The *source of power* is the issue for both John and Jesus. Both lack *authority* (20:2-8).

Many interpreters understand the parable of the wicked tenants as rejecting Israel. But Luke correlates the tenants only with the high-priestly party (20:19), differentiated from the people in 19:48. The introduction for the trick question in 20:20 clearly spells out collaboration with the governor in imperial systems. Jesus' saying about tribute has been taken as indicating what in the United States is now called the separation of church and state. Jesus actually turns the question of tribute back on his interlocutors. The "Tiberius Denarius" of the time bears a "graven image" of the emperor with legends that label him "divine" and "high priest." The coin also belongs to mammon that derives from injustice (16:9, 11), and it recalls: "You cannot serve God and mammon" (16:13; similarly Green 1997, 716). The interlocutors are left to ponder their own question.

The Text in Contemporary Discussion

Jesus' disruption in the temple has strong support as a historical factor in his execution (E. P. Sanders, 253–68). The multitude's praise and benediction in 19:37-38 is christological but remains theocentric. That is, Jesus' deeds manifest God's power and produce praise of God. Arguments that the prediction of the siege of Jerusalem is an anachronistic reading of its devastation in 70 CE back into the life of Jesus are dubious. The prediction borrows from scriptural accounts of sieges (19:43-44) and is a logical deduction from imperial domination (Dodd 1947; Wolter, 634–35). Jesus' comparison of himself with John in 20:4 recalls John's economic and political emphases (3:10-14, 19-20). Prominent models for peace today presume that it is dependent on armed strength. In consideration of the larger context of Luke, the things that make for peace in 19:42 are good news for the poor and liberation from oppression.

Luke 20:45—21:38: The Demise of Injustice and God's Commonwealth

The Text in Its Ancient Context

Jesus turns to critiques of socioreligious conventions. Luke 20:45-47 does not condemn all scribes, but those who seek honor and abuse widows. The line of thought continues in 21:1-4 with rich people, like the scribes in 20:46, and a poor widow, who is like those abused in 20:47. In destitution, she casts her life (*bios*) into the temple treasury. She outshines the charity of elites but is hardly an example to emulate. Her offering is qualified by scribes who abuse widows and by Jesus' immediate prediction of the temple's destruction (21:4). She casts her *bios* into a collapsing institution.

Jesus' audience is unclear. He addresses disciples in 20:45, but others overhear. In 21:7, "they" ask when the collapse will occur. Nevertheless, the imperatives in 21:8 are directed to his followers. Jesus' response to inquiries about the time of the collapse is indeterminate, but he warns against deception from false claimants (21:8) or portentous events (21:9-11). Jesus warns of persecution in an unspecified period of time from control agents in imperial systems, kings, governors, synagogues, and prisons (21:12). This occasions exhortations for testimony that derives from a continuing relationship with Jesus (21:13-15).

Jesus paints the time of crisis in alarming tones: family and social conflict, military violence, hardships for pregnant women, mothers, and infants (21:20-24)—a time of punishment for, or justice against, evil (*ekdikēsis*). It is likely that Luke's audience had already witnessed some such, but would be puzzled by Jerusalem's rehabilitation after the time of the nations (21:24).

Suspense and uncertainly continue with Jesus' forecast of confusion over cosmic portents, natural disasters, and the shaking of heavenly powers (21:25-26). This becomes the setting for the ultimate manifestation of the son of man (21:27, alluding to Dan. 7:13). Violence and cosmic dissolution then turn into optimism, because as the ultimate manifestation approaches, evil powers fight violently but in vain. Increased violence signals how close they are to defeat (21:28-31). When Jesus says, "This generation will not pass away until all has taken place" (21:32), Luke's audience would have understood "this generation" to mean "the human race." Nolland (3:1009–10) takes "this generation" (21:32) as "Jesus' contemporaries," who obviously would have passed away before

Luke's audience heard these words. But the fundamental meaning of the Greek means "what is born" (= "all who live on earth" in 21:35). Wolter (682) is on track when he takes the Greek to mean the "human race."

The Text in the Interpretive Tradition

Scribes belong to an established group, but verse 46 is most properly understood as "those scribes who like to walk around in long robes." Rather than characterize all scribes, Jesus specifies those who seek honor but practice abuse (Nolland, 3:975–76; against Green 1997, 725). Abusing widows contravenes Torah stipulations to care for them. What "devouring houses" means is beyond recovery. *Bios* (21:4) means "life" or "sustenance for life." Luke is both looking back on events including the fall of Jerusalem and looking forward beyond his own time (Wolter, 672).

The Text in Contemporary Discussion

Although the poor widow's gift shames the rich, feminist and postcolonial interpreters (e.g., Sugirtharajah) correctly resist using her to encourage sacrificial giving. On scribes who abuse widows, Amy-Jill Levine objects appropriately to anti-Jewish attempts to negatively characterize all scribes and temple functionaries (oral presentation at Duke Divinity School, Durham, NC, February 20, 2013). On the other hand, critiques of elite collaborators in favor of preserving Israel's heritage are hardly anti-Jewish.

Luke 22:1—23:56: The Greatest Who Serves and the Power of Violence

The Text in Its Ancient Context

Luke's narrative changes abruptly at 22:1. Jesus' didactic encounters with people cease. Execution plots set the tone (22:2). Characters take sides—the high priests, Satan, and Judas over against Jesus, his disciples, and the people (22:2).

Sober realism modifies festivity (Passover recalls liberation *and* oppression). Jesus vows abstinence for the coming of God's commonwealth (22:18), presumably the final manifestation of the son of man from 21:27. Moreover, he interprets his final Passover as the giving of himself and a "new covenant." "New covenant" recollects both the Abrahamic covenant (synthesized with other covenant traditions) and Jer. 31:31, where it means not the replacement of but renewed consecration to Israel's covenant with God. Table solidarity fades, however, when Jesus announces Judas's betrayal (22:22).

Unexpectedly, the apostles reflect not God's commonwealth but imperial rulers—intrigue, betrayal, competition for priority (22:25). Jesus mandates God's commonwealth as a blunt alternative: "Not so for you" (22:26). Second, he inverts hierarchy into mutuality. He himself is "one who serves" (22:27).

Therefore, when Jesus confers his commonwealth on the apostles, Luke's audience understands his redefinition of rulers and thrones as mutuality (22:29-30). But when Jesus forecasts a satanic attack, the apostles' place in God's commonwealth again comes under threat (22:31-34). In 22:35-38, Jesus enigmatically advises his disciples to arm themselves, amending instructions in 9:3; 10:4. Earlier, they lived in mutuality; now they face animosity. Moreover, Jesus connects swords with fulfilling Scripture—they play the role of outlaws (22:37).

In 22:40, 46, Jesus and the apostles retreat to pray that they not enter into temptation, as in 11:4. Jesus himself appeals to God as Father. The cup metaphor for what lies ahead (22:41-42) also looks back to the new covenant (22:20). Both mean consecration to God. Grief already leads the apostles into temptation—instead of praying, they sleep (22:45).

With swords and failure at prayer, things turn topsy-turvy. Judas betrays Jesus with a kiss (22:47-48). All the apostles are willing to engage in swordplay. One actually does. They really do play the role of outlaws and mimic imperial violence. According to 22:37, this fulfills Scripture. By contrast, Jesus manifests God's commonwealth by stopping the swordplay and healing (22:49-51). Jesus' arrest confuses daylight and darkness (22:53).

While Jesus faces the high priest, Peter faces people of insignificant rank, and his promises of fidelity turn into denial (22:33, 54-62). The king who comes in the Lord's name (19:38) is mocked (22:63). The council demands that the one whose deeds manifested God's finger (11:20) confess whether he is the Messiah or not (22:67). When Jesus forecasts the manifestation of the son of man, the council ironically calls him "son of God." The interrogative "Are you the son of God?" can also be declarative: "You are the son of God." Jesus responds: "That [claim] is on your lips" (22:70). The testimony on their lips then becomes evidence against him.

In chapter 23, things remain topsy-turvy. Before Pilate, the high-priestly party accuses Jesus of being an insurgent king (23:2). Recalling the irony of "son of God" on the council's lips, Pilate's question, "Are you king of the Jewish people?" can also be declarative: "You are the king of the Jewish people." Jesus responds as he did to the council: "[That] is on your lips" (23:3). Herod's entrance (23:8) recalls repeated appearances in 3:1, 19-20; 9:7-9; 13:31-32. He and his soldiers mock Jesus as if he were a member of the ruling elite in elegant clothing (23:11).

In 23:22, Pilate declares Jesus innocent for the third time, but then delivers the verdict against him. Luke's audience could hardly have reacted positively to Pilate or Roman justice. Things are still topsy-turvy. Roman (in)justice condemns an innocent man (Lee, 100). Assertions of Jesus' innocence also follow the crucifixion: a victim crucified with him declares that Jesus has done nothing wrong (23:41); a Roman centurion declares him innocent (23:47); observers leave beating their breasts in remorse (23:48). Injustice is what Rome's systems look like. Leaders ridicule Jesus as saving others but unable to save himself, but unwittingly they deny the criterion of life in God's commonwealth: "Those who want to save their life will lose it" (9:24). Soldiers mock him as carnival king (23:36), daylight turns into darkness (23:44), the temple curtain separating sacred from profane is split (23:45). Like other temporary inversions at Jesus' crucifixion, there is no indication in Luke that the temple structure is abrogated. Note the resumption of activity in the temple in 24:53 as well as in Acts.

One thing contests utter absurdity. Quoting Ps. 30:6 LXX, Jesus commits his life to God (Luke 23:46). Luke's audience likely knew the psalm well enough to finish the verse: "Redeem me, Lord

God of truth." A few acquaintances watch, Joseph of Arimathea entombs Jesus' body, and some women prepare to pay last respects (23:49-56).

The Text in the Interpretive Tradition

Debates have raged over the meaning of "this is my body" (22:19). Roman Catholicism has held that without changing outward features, sacramental bread is transformed into Christ's body. Lutheranism speaks instead of Christ's presence in, with, and under the bread. Anything similar for the cup is impossible, because in Luke what is poured out is not blood but a new covenant (22:20). Luke attaches "do this in remembrance of me" only to the bread (22:19). Lack of a referent for "this" leaves uncertain what is to be done. Interpreters often take "remembrance" (*anamnēsis*) as making present what is remembered. This interpretation is a post–New Testament development (Brawley 1990a).

Accusations against Jesus before Pilate are political (23:2). Crucifixion was reserved for defiant slaves and unpacified foreigners. The mode of execution means that Jesus and the other two victims were executed as rebels. But Jesus' protest to his arrest as if he were a "brigand" (22:53) means that Jesus was executed "as if" he were a rebel.

The Text in Contemporary Discussion

The role of Jerusalem's populace in Jesus' execution is heavily debated. Identifying "the people" as the same group in every instance is problematic. Luke 22:2 separates the people from the high-priestly party. A crowd in 23:4 is the council of 22:66; 23:1. Their concern for "this place" associates them with the temple, and their perspective that Jesus stirs up "the [other] people" subtly differentiates them from "the people" (23:5). In 23:13, the context associates "the people" with the high priests. Pilate also says that he examined Jesus in the presence of this coalition (23:14), and thus they are the crowd of the council associated with the chief priests in 23:4. They are never identified as the Jewish people of Jerusalem (against Green 1997, 791; and Wolter, 745–46; Wolter softens this to "representatives"). The summary of opponents in 24:20 omits the people.

A closely related discussion interprets Luke not only as anti-Jewish but also pro-Roman. Postcolonial perspectives shed new light on this. Rome delegated control of local populations to native elite collaborators, whom Josephus identifies as "the high priests" (*Ant.* 20.251). Native collaborators may resist colonizers out of nationalistic concerns, but also support them in order to maintain privilege in colonial systems. In this light, Jesus' crucifixion is not a matter of theological ideology but of maintaining order (Lee, 95–96). From Mary's song (1:46-55) to Jesus' prescription for disciples in contrast to imperial systems (22:25-26), tensions with imperial systems in Luke is strong (Lee, 97). Although Jesus rejects rebellion, he proclaims God's commonwealth as an alternative to Rome's systems. Rome's systems claimed to bring justice to vanquished nations. By comparison, Pilate's verdict against Jesus in spite of declaring him innocent makes Rome's justice a travesty (Lee). Declarations of innocence also reflect negatively on Jewish people (Wolter, 688), but they are on the lips of Pilate, Herod (as Pilate alleges), a victim on a cross, and a Roman centurion. Pilate attempts to persuade the high priests, but they never treat Jesus as innocent of undermining imperial systems.

In the New Testament, "new covenant" occurs only in 1 Cor. 11:25, its parallel in Luke 22:20; 2 Cor. 3:6 (alluding to Jer. 31:31); and Heb. 8:8, 13, quoting Jer. 31:31-34. In spite of the prominence of "new" in Christian history and the scriptural canon, "covenant" in the New Testament virtually always (if not always) refers to Israel's covenant traditions. Jesus' new covenant as consecration of the heart, as in Jeremiah, is not discontinuous with Israel's heritage (also Green 1997, 763).

Postcolonialists have taken references to ruling (22:30) and swords (22:36, 49-50) as mimicry of Roman domination and violence. But before conferring thrones on the apostles, Jesus subverts imperial hierarchies (22:25-27). This subversion defies mimicry and redefines commonwealth and thrones as mutuality. The apostles' swordplay in 22:49-50 is imperial mimicry, which Jesus stops (22:51).

Luke portrays attempts of Jesus' opponents, from mockery to crucifixion, to reduce him to absurdity. Crucifixion is not only castigation but shaming to the uttermost. The other side of the story resists reduction to absurdity by irony and scriptural figurations (Brawley 1995, 42–60).

The other two victims crucified with Jesus (23:39-43) reflect the division among the people anticipated by Simeon (1:34-35). One mocks Jesus; the other declares him innocent. The second accepts crucifixion as deserved justice (v. 41) and thereby unjustly internalizes the values of the empire. Crucifixion was a vile form of capital punishment designed to terrorize resistors to the empire administered without "equality under the law" (compare executions of "terrorists" today). Traditionally, the second rebel has been called "penitent." But more than confess his deeds (v. 41), he confesses Jesus' commonwealth beyond the crucifixion before anyone else does (Wolter, 760): "Remember me when you come into your commonwealth" (v. 42). Jesus' reference to Paradise (v. 43) is too brief and inexact to build definitive pictures of the afterlife.

Luke 24: Resurrection

The Text in Its Ancient Context

After Jesus' violent crucifixion, Luke 24 opens with the softness of dawn. Women resume their solemn task, delayed by Sabbath, of anointing Jesus' body (23:56). Quickly, mysteriously, their unenviable but compassionate task is canceled, and incidents pile up for an eventful day. The stone—unmentioned earlier—is rolled away. "The" stone (24:2), with the definite article in its first reference, may presume familiarity with the tomb story or may be a cultural presumption that a stone would close the tomb. Jesus' body is absent. Two men (later called "messengers," *angeloi*, 24:23) in clothes shining like lightning startle them (24:1-4). The men ask a succinct question and jog memories: "Why are you seeking the one who lives among the dead? He is not here but has been raised. Remember what he told you." With the declaration "he is not here," the tomb loses significance (Green 1997, 836). For the women and Luke's audience, an empty tomb does not mean resurrection, and the messengers must interpret it by recalling Jesus' passion predictions (24:5-7). "He is risen" (24:5 NRSV) is a divine passive. "Has been raised" is preferable. Resurrection is God's act. The women's task is redefined. They had sought one who was dead among the dead. Astute listeners might have wondered if Jesus predicted his passion on occasions that are unnarrated because in 9:22; 18:31-34, he informed his disciples, not the women. But when the women remember, the predictions belong to their community just as to Luke's audience.

The women, who are named, report to a small but coherent community. The apostles consider their report nonsense. Because of the reminders of Jesus' passion predictions, made specifically to the apostles, their unbelief cannot be attributed to the low status of women in the culture (Green 1997, 840; against Nolland, 3:1193). Luke's audience knows that they are reliable (Tannehill 1986, 7–8, 21–22, 294). Somehow Peter (and others, 24:24) is a partial exception to the evaluation of the women as unreliable. He visits the tomb, sees some linen cloths, and goes home mystified (24:10-12).

Suddenly the story moves with two "of them" toward Emmaus. Their knowledge of "everything" is irony. They are unaware of Jesus' identity, and this "stranger" knows more than they. Reminiscent of Simeon and Anna (2:25, 38), they recount their hopes for Israel's redemption, now dashed: "We had hoped" (24:21). They reprise the five brothers in 16:31: they are unpersuaded, even though someone has been raised. Still, they ponder the women's report and mention others involved in Peter's experience at the tomb. In spite of the announcement that Jesus had been raised, they do not interpret the empty tomb as resurrection (24:13-24). Jesus, incognito, then provides a key for understanding. He interprets himself from Scripture but also interprets Scripture from himself. The essence of the interpretation is the Messiah's entering into glory after suffering (24:25-27). "Glory" in 24:26 means manifestations of God's power.

The travelers, probably husband and wife, extend the stranger hospitality (see 9:4-5). Reminiscent of Jesus' last supper (22:17-20) and feeding the five thousand (9:12-17), Jesus also plays the role of host in the home where he is the guest, blessing and breaking bread. In this act, they recognize the risen Jesus, but enigmatically, he vanishes (24:28-32). When they immediately return to Jerusalem, they find a coherent group, not scattered, but gathered like a family experiencing death. Luke's audience expects the two from Emmaus to tell their experience. Instead, the two listen as those in the group relate their experiences, including Jesus' appearance to Peter, which otherwise goes unnarrated (24:33-35).

Jesus astonishingly appears among them. He questions doubts, demonstrates his wounds and materiality (nails were unmentioned in Luke's crucifixion narrative), and eats (24:36-43). Then reviewing his ministry, he again interprets Scripture in terms of his suffering and resurrection (24:44-46). He also envisages this group's mission to proclaim repentance and forgiveness, which he universalizes and for which he promises empowerment (24:47-49). Listeners who also hear Acts 1:4-5 might retrospectively pick up allusions to Luke 11:13—God's eagerness to give the Holy Spirit to those who ask (Tannehill 1986, 239).

Luke succinctly recounts Jesus' ascension, accompanied by a benediction (24:50). This becomes the occasion for spontaneous worship reinforced by continual worship of God. Luke begins with Zechariah in the temple and ends with Jesus' followers likewise in the temple. In spite of Luke's quarrels with the high priesthood, his audience could not have taken the Gospel as antitemple.

The Text in the Interpretive Tradition

In contrast to the other Gospels, Luke locates all resurrection events in the environs of Jerusalem. Mark has no resurrection appearances, but anticipates them in Galilee. Matthew and John mix the locales. Luke's focus on Jerusalem likely has to do with the biblical perspective on Jerusalem as the center of the world, the point of contact between heaven and earth. When Gabriel appears in the temple, the first locale mentioned in Luke (1:8), he steps down from heaven at the central point of contact between heaven and earth. Although Gabriel also appears to Mary in Nazareth, the appearance in the temple emphasizes the direct contact of heaven and earth. At the end of Luke, Jesus ascends to heaven, also in the environs of Jerusalem. Further, Jesus' followers await the fulfillment of the promise of the Holy Spirit in Jerusalem, which in Acts, indeed, happens in Jerusalem (Brawley 1987, 118–32).

When Acts is taken into consideration, it is popular to argue for a shift of the center from Jerusalem to Rome. True, Paul winds up in Rome, but to make his destiny the destiny of the gospel is simply a category error. Beginning and ending the narrative in the temple, resurrection appearances in and around Jerusalem, and the ascension in the precinct of Jerusalem are part of Luke's emphasis on the validity of the good news as deriving from and centering on God.

The Text in Contemporary Discussion

Luke's empty tomb is not the basis for believing Jesus' resurrection. Various explanations for empty tombs are possible, and resurrection is usually not among them. The proclamation of the messengers provides the crucial interpretation. The empty tomb does not explain Jesus' resurrection; Jesus' resurrection explains it (Wolter, 770, 772). Even the proclamation remains incomplete without scriptural interpretations and resurrection appearances.

Schüssler Fiorenza (1992, 213) maintains that even though Luke reports the women at the tomb, he suppresses them by slighting their report (24:11) and ignoring resurrection appearances to them narrated elsewhere. Peter still holds first place in resurrection appearances in 24:34, although no narrative of it exists. The appearance to Peter even takes precedence over the Emmaus couple, likely husband and wife. Those who hear Luke's account of the place of women in Jesus' story should find it hard to understand how proclamation of the resurrection could ever have come about without women.

At the beginning, Luke presupposes and builds on a story of God's deeds that keep divine *promises* alive. The risen Jesus' last words in Luke instruct his followers to wait for what God has *promised* (24:49). Luke's audience waits with Jesus' followers to see how this will come to pass. Even without Acts as a sequel, they would expect the story of God's work to continue.

Works Cited

Alexander, Loveday. 1993. *The Preface to Luke's Gospel.* Cambridge: Cambridge University Press.

Annen, Franz. 1976. *Heil für die Heiden.* Frankfurt: Knecht.

Bendemann, Reinhard von. 2001. *Zwischen ΔΟΞΑ und ΣΤΑΥΡΟΣ.* Berlin: de Gruyter.

Bhabha, Homi. 1994. *The Location of Culture.* London: Routledge.

Bovon, François. 2002. *Luke: A Commentary on the Gospel of Luke.* Vol. 1. Trans. Christine M. Thomas. Minneapolis: Fortress Press.

Braun, Willi. 1995. *Feasting and Social Rhetoric.* Cambridge: Cambridge University Press.

Brawley, Robert. 1987. *Luke-Acts and the Jews.* Atlanta: Scholars Press.

———. 1990a. "*Anamnesis* and Absence in the Lord's Supper." *BTB* 20:139–46.

———. 1990b. *Centering on God*. Louisville: Westminster John Knox.

———. 1995. *Text to Text Pours Forth Speech*. Bloomington: Indiana University Press.

———. 1998. "Offspring and Parent." *SBLSP*, 2:807–30. Atlanta: Scholars Press.

———. 1999. "Abrahamic Covenant Traditions and the Characterization of God in Luke-Acts." In *The Unity of Luke-Acts*, edited by J. Verheyden, 109–32. Leuven: Peeters.

Brown, Raymond. 1979. *The Birth of the Messiah*. Garden City, NY: Doubleday.

Carter, Warren. 2000. *Matthew and the Margins*. Maryknoll, NY: Orbis.

———. 2003. "Are There Imperial Texts in the Class?" *JBL* 122:467–87.

———. 2006. *The Roman Empire in the New Testament*. Nashville: Abingdon.

Conzelmann, Hans. 1960. *The Theology of St. Luke*. New York: Harper & Bros.

Cotter, Wendy. 2005. "The Parable of the Feisty Widow and the Threatened Judge." *NTS* 51:328–43.

Cullmann, Oscar. 1963. *The Christology of the New Testament*. Philadelphia: Westminster.

Dodd, C. H. 1947. "The Fall of Jerusalem and the 'Abomination of Desolation.'" *JRS* 37:47–54.

———. 1961. *Parables of the Kingdom*. New York: Scribner.

Egelkraut, Helmuth. 1976. *Jesus' Mission to Jerusalem*. Frankfurt: Peter Lang.

Ehrhardt, Arnold. 1953. "Greek Proverbs in the Gospel." *HTR* 46:68–72.

Fitzmyer, Joseph. 1973. "The Virginal Conception of Jesus in the New Testament." *TS* 34:541–75.

———. 1981. *The Gospel According to Luke I–IX*. AB 28. Garden City, NY: Doubleday.

———. 1985. *The Gospel According to Luke X–XXIV*. AB 28A. Garden City, NY: Doubleday.

Garnsey, Peter. 1970. *Social Status and Legal Privilege in the Roman Empire*. Oxford: Clarendon.

Goulder, Michael. 1989. *Luke: A New Paradigm*. Sheffield: JSOT Press.

Gowler, David. 2003. "Text, Culture, and Ideology in Luke 17:1-10: A Dialogic Reading." In *Fabrics of Discourse: Essays in Honor of Vernon K. Robbins*, edited by David Gowler, L. Gregory Bloomquist, and Duane F. Watson, 89–125. Harrisburg, PA: Trinity Press International.

Green, Joel B. 1989. "Jesus and a Daughter of Abraham (Luke 13:10-17)." *CBQ* 51: 651–52.

———. 1997. *The Gospel of Luke*. NICNT. Grand Rapids: Eerdmans.

Hahn, Ferdinand. 1969. *The Titles of Jesus in Christology*. New York: World.

Herzog, William. 1994. *Parables of Subversive Speech*. Louisville: Westminster John Knox.

Jennings, Theodore, and Tat-Siong Benny Liew. 2004. "Mistaken Identities but Model Faith: Rereading the Centurion, the Chap, and the Christ in Matthew 8:5-13." *JBL* 123:467–94.

Jeremias, Joachim. 1972. *The Parables of Jesus*. New York: Scribner.

Jülicher, Adolf. 1888. *Die Gleichnisreden Jesu*. Freiburg: J. C. B. Mohr (Paul Siebeck).

Lee, Jae Won. 2011. "Pilate and the Crucifixion of Jesus in Luke-Acts." In *Luke-Acts and Empire*, edited by David Rhoads, David Esterline, and Jae Won Lee, 84–106. Eugene, OR: Pickwick.

Lintott, Andre. 1993. *Imperium Romanum: Politics and Administration*. London: Routledge.

Malina, Bruce, and Jerome Neyrey. 1991. "Honor and Shame in Luke-Acts." In *The Social World of Luke-Acts*, edited by Jerome Neyrey, 25–65. Peabody, MA: Hendrickson.

Mowinkel, Sigmund. 1956. *He That Cometh*. Oxford: Blackwell.

Niebuhr, Karl-Wilhelm. 1992. *Heidenapostel aus Israel*. Tübingen: Mohr Siebeck.

Nolland, John. 1993. *Luke 9:21—18:34* and *Luke 18:35—24:53*. WBC 35b-c; Dallas: Word Books.

O'Day, Gail R. 2004. "'There the ? Will Gather Together' (Luke 17:37)." In *Literary Encounters with the Reign of God*, edited by Sharon H. Ringe and H. C. Paul Kim, 288–303. New York: T&T Clark.

Patte, Daniel. 1987. *The Gospel according to Matthew*. Philadelphia: Fortress Press.

Porter, Stanley E. 1990. "The Parable of the Unjust Steward (Luke 16:1-13)." In *The Bible in Three Dimensions*, edited by David J. A. Clines, Stephen E. Fowl, and Stanley E. Porter, 127–53. Sheffield: Sheffield Academic Press.

Powell, Mark Allan. 2004. "The Forgotten Famine." In *Literary Encounters with the Reign of God*, edited by Sharon H. Ringe and H. C. Paul Kim, 265–87. New York: T&T Clark.

Reid, Barbara. 1996. *Choosing the Better Part*. Collegeville, MN: Liturgical Press.

Robbins, Vernon K. 2004. "The Sensory-Aesthetic Texture of the Compassionate Samaritan Parable." In *Literary Encounters with the Reign of God*, edited by Sharon H. Ringe and H. C. Paul Kim, 247–64. New York: T&T Clark.

Sanders, E. P. 1993. *The Historical Figure of Jesus*. New York: Penguin.

Sanders, E. P., and Margaret Davies. 1989. *Studying the Synoptic Gospels*. Philadelphia: Trinity Press International.

Sanders, Jack. 1987. *The Jews in Luke-Acts*. Philadelphia: Fortress.

Schaberg, Jane. 1987. *The Illegitimacy of Jesus*. San Francisco: Harper & Row.

Schlüssler Fiorenza, Elisabeth. 1992. *But She Said: Feminist Practices of Biblical Interpretation*. Boston: Beacon.

Scott, James. 2004. *Hidden Transcripts and the Art of Resistance*. Atlanta: Society of Biblical Literature.

De Ste. Croix, G. E. M. 1981. *The Class Struggle in the Ancient Greek World*. Ithaca, NY: Cornell University Press

Sugirtharajah, R. S. 1991–1992. "The Widow's Mite Revalued." *ExpTim* 103:42–43.

Tannehill, Robert. 1975. *The Sword of His Mouth*. Missoula, MT: Scholars Press.

———. 1986. *The Narrative Unity of Luke Acts*. Vol. 1. Philadelphia: Fortress Press.

———. 1994. "Should We Love Simon the Pharisee?" *CurTM* 21:424–33.

Theissen, Gerd. 1983. *The Miracle Stories of the Early Christian Tradition*. Philadelphia: Fortress Press.

Tolbert, Mary Ann. 1989. *Sowing the Gospel*. Minneapolis: Fortress Press.

Wink, Walter. 1992. *Engaging the Powers*. Minneapolis: Fortress Press.

Wire, Antoinnette. 1978. "The Structure of the Gospel Miracles Stories and Their Tellers." *Semeia* 11:83–113.

Wolter, Michael. 2008. *Das Lukasevangelium*. Tubingen: Mohr Siebeck.

John

Adele Reinhartz

Introduction

The Fourth Gospel is a study in contradictions: uplifting and infuriating; enigmatic and transparent; artful and inconsistent; profound and superficial; obscure and memorable. Commentators, from the ancient period to the present, often seek to smooth over the Gospel's inconsistencies and difficulties. It is these very contradictions, however, that have permitted readers throughout the centuries to find the Gospel both fascinating and meaningful to their own lives and situations.

The Gospel is most often associated with Ephesus in Asia Minor (today's Selçuk in Izmir province, Turkey), though an early version of the Gospel may have originated in Judea. Until the first publication of the Rylands Library Papyrus 52 in 1935, the Gospel was often dated to the mid-second century CE. P^{52} is an Egyptian codex fragment of John 18:31-33, 37-38, which has been reliably dated to 135–160 CE. Allowing for a period of several decades for circulation, a late first-century date for the Gospel's final version is likely.

The Book

The Gospel itself points to the unnamed Beloved Disciple, who makes his first appearance at the Last Supper (John 13), as the author of, or the authority behind, the Gospel (19:26-27, 35; 21:24). Traditionally, this disciple has been identified as John the son of Zebedee. This identification is unlikely, however. The Beloved Disciple is closely associated with Jerusalem and, according to the Gospel, had links to the high priest, an unlikely connection for Galilean fishermen such as the sons of Zebedee. The author of John's Gospel therefore remains unknown.

Another puzzle is John's relationship to the Synoptic Gospels. Clement of Alexandria (c. 150–211/216) asserted that John's Gospel was meant to supplement the Synoptics (Matthew, Mark, Luke; see Eusebius's fourth-century *Hist. eccl.* 6.14.7). Many modern scholars disagree. Although some Johannine stories are paralleled in the Synoptics (e.g., the feeding of the multitudes [6:1-14; cf. Matt. 14:13-21; Mark 16:32-44; Luke 9:10-17], Jesus' stroll on the water [6:16-21; cf. Matt. 14:22; Mark 6:45-51]), most of its episodes (e.g., the wedding at Cana [2:1-13], Jesus' encounter with the Samaritan woman [4:1-42], the raising of Lazarus [11:1-44]) are unique. Also unique is the Gospel's Christology, which emphasizes his existence prior to the world's creation and his identity as God's only-begotten Son. It is therefore unlikely that the Fourth Gospel drew directly on any of the Synoptics (Smith).

Despite the simplicity of its Greek, the Fourth Gospel is a literary masterpiece. It has a clear narrative structure built around Jesus' "signs" (miracle stories) and amplified by thematic discourses. It makes superb use of literary devices such as symbolism, irony, contrast, repetition, and misunderstanding. The book also, however, contains blatant discontinuities. For example, the story of the healing of a lame man, set in Jerusalem (ch. 5), is followed immediately by a note that places Jesus on the "other side of the Sea of Galilee" (6:1) without mentioning how and when he got there. In 14:31, Jesus tells his disciples to "Rise, let us be on our way," and then continues his lengthy discourse for two more chapters.

These awkward transitions suggest that the Gospel was heavily redacted before reaching its present form. The enumeration of two of the signs-stories (the "beginning of the signs," 2:11; "the second sign," 4:54) has been taken as evidence that the Gospel incorporated an earlier source consisting of a series of numbered miracle stories (Fortna; Von Wahlde). Theological inconsistencies may suggest that the Gospel was redacted several times in response to changing circumstances and ideas. There is currently, however, no manuscript evidence of redaction, with one exception: the story of the woman caught in adultery (7:53—8:13), which most scholars consider to be non-Johannine.

In its present form, the book divides easily into two parts: the Book of Signs (1:19—12:50), which is structured around a series of miracles or signs; and the Book of Glory (13:1—20:31), which begins with the Last Supper and ends with the resurrection appearances. The book is introduced by a prologue (1:1-18) and concludes with an epilogue (21:1-25).

The Hero

John's Jesus differs significantly from his Synoptic counterpart. He speaks in long discourses rather than pithy parables. While he heals the sick, feeds the multitudes, and walks on water, as in the Synoptics, he also speaks, only here, with Samaritans (John 4), raises the dead (John 11), and washes his disciples' feet (John 13).

These stark differences, and John's relatively late date, raise the question of this Gospel's value for historical Jesus research. Clement of Alexandria's (150–215 CE) famous description of the Gospel of John as the "spiritual Gospel" may imply that it is valuable for spiritual formation but not for historical understanding (Elowsky 2006, xix). The tendency to discount John as a source for the historical Jesus has been challenged in recent years, however (e.g., Fredriksen; Anderson, Just, and Thatcher).

The Story

The Gospel of John concerns a Galilean who gathers followers, performs miracles, teaches, rouses the ire of the Jewish leadership, and ends up before the Roman governor, who sentences him to death. In literary terms, this story is a tragedy because it ends in the wrongful execution of an innocent man. Because it is set in a specific time—the first third of the first century CE, when Pilate was the Roman governor of Judea and Caiaphas was high priest—and in specific geographical locations—the Galilee, Judea, and Samaria—the story can also be described as a historical tale (which is not to claim that it is historically accurate in its details).

This historical tale, however, is embedded in a larger cosmological story, about God's Son who existed with God before creation, came to dwell among humankind, and returned to God. In contrast to the historical tale, this cosmological tale is not bound in space and time but has the cosmos as its location and eternity as its time frame.

The two tales intersect at the incarnation (1:14) and the passion. The discourses draw the readers into the meanings of Jesus' signs within the cosmological tale. Indeed, the purpose of the Gospel is to help readers discern Jesus' cosmic significance within and through the signs "written in this book" (20:30-31).

The Message

The Gospel's main message is christological. John's Jesus is the preexistent Son of God, whom God sent into the world as God's agent, and the son of man, an apocalyptic figure who exercises judgment on God's behalf. Despite the prevalence of "son" language, the precise relationship between Jesus and God is uncertain. Is Jesus equivalent—in power, in majesty—to God? Does he have authority in himself, or is his authority derived from his relationship to the Father? Christology is closely linked to soteriology (the doctrine of salvation): those who believe in Jesus as the Christ and the Son of God will have "life in his name." John's Jesus insists that believers have eternal life in the present at the same time he promises eternal life in the future.

The most problematic element of John's message concerns the Jews and Judaism. The Gospel refers seventy times to *hoi Ioudaioi* ("the Jews"), far more than any other New Testament book. The Gospel makes ample use of the Hebrew Bible and has parallels to some postbiblical Jewish traditions. Yet its overall depiction of Jews and Judaism is negative. John's Jews are Jesus' archenemies. They interrogate him, challenge him, and pursue him unto death. In 8:44, Jesus tells a group of Jews that they have the devil as their father, an accusation that echoes through antisemitic literature to the present day. These negative statements may reflect a historical tension between the Johannine followers of Christ and the Jews who did not follow Christ, even if the details of their relationship cannot be determined.

The intended meaning and the best English translation of *hoi Ioudaioi* in the Gospel of John remain matters of considerable contention among scholars. Although most English translations use the term "the Jews," some scholars have argued vigorously for other options, such as "the Jewish authorities" (Von Wahlde) or, most prominently, "the Judeans" (Lowe; Mason; cf. Miller). These suggestions are motivated by what is seen as a discontinuity between the ancient *Ioudaioi*, with which the Gospel writer and audiences may have been familiar, and the modern "Jews" as known to contemporary readers and scholars of the Fourth Gospel. Some believe that using the term "Jews" for *hoi Ioudaioi* runs the risk of spreading antisemitism, given that many of the Gospel's references to *hoi Ioudaioi* are negative or even hostile. Translating *hoi Ioudaioi* as "the Jewish authorities," or "the leaders of the people," conveys the clear message that it is not the Jewish people as a whole who opposed Jesus or led to his death. Others argue that the *hoi Ioudaioi* of the first century were an ethnic group rather than a religious group. For that reason, it is preferable to translate the term as "the Judeans," an ethnic and geographic marker, rather than as "the Jews," which, in their view, refers to a group that practices the religion of "Judaism," which, some insist, did not yet exist at the time the Gospel was written (Mason). Both of these proposals are problematic. While in some contexts, such as 19:7, the term appears to refer to the authorities as distinct from the Jewish crowds, there are many passages in which the term clearly refers to the people as a whole (e.g., 2:13; 12:9). And while it may be true that the first-century *Ioudaioi* were distinguished by more than beliefs and practices that might be defined as "religious," the same is true of the modern term "Jew," which identifies not only those who actively engage in Jewish religious practices and customs but also secular Jews who explicitly reject those practices, as well as a broad spectrum of people in between. The best translation, therefore, remains "the Jews" (Reinhartz 2001a; Levine 2006, 162).

The Purpose and Audience

The Gospel's narrative, theology, message, and language suggest that it was written within and for a specifically "Johannine" group, perhaps the same group for which the Johannine epistles were composed (Painter). The community may have included Samaritans and gentiles alongside Jews, given that the Gospel draws on Jewish, Samaritan, and gentile traditions, ideas, and modes of expression.

Attempts at a detailed reconstruction of the community's historical circumstances have been based on the three verses (9:22; 12:42; 16:2) that refer to *aposynagōgoi* (people who are cast out of the synagogue). Some argue that these verses refer to an actual expulsion of Johannine followers from the synagogue on account of their faith in Christ (Martyn; Lincoln, 84). As the present commentary will explain, this hypothesis is problematic on historical and methodological grounds. Yet even if the expulsion theory is tenuous, the Gospel's hostility toward the Jews is real. It likely reflects a process of identity-formation on the part of the community, which also entailed efforts at differentiation from the Jewish community. This perspective does not excuse the Gospel's rhetoric, but it makes it possible to acknowledge the Gospel's place in the process by which Christianity became a separate religion, to appreciate the beauty of its language, and to recognize the spiritual power that it continues to have in the lives of many of its Christian readers.

The Commentary

The Fourth Gospel invites readers to insert ourselves into the text and even to a certain extent encourages us to become particular types of readers: compliant readers who will agree with the worldview it presents, and align themselves unequivocally with the light, life, and Spirit as defined in this Gospel and against the forces of darkness, death, and flesh, again as defined by John. But readers have a choice as to whether and how they insert themselves in this text, and it is often by resisting or challenging a compliant reading that we can truly engage with John's Gospel.

This commentary, like the others in this volume, will have three levels. The first level examines the text in its ancient context. In this level, we will take the position of a late first-century reader, while recognizing that bridging such a profound distance in time, space, culture, and language is ultimately impossible.

The second level, the text in the interpretive tradition, will comment on the text in the interpretive tradition. Because it is not possible in a brief commentary to do an exhaustive survey of the interpretive tradition, the comments here will focus primarily on how patristic readers understood certain key issues. The church fathers were keen and insightful readers of Scriptures. Although they often bent over backward to smooth over the contradictions with the Fourth Gospel and the differences between John and the Synoptics, their approaches to some of the text's difficulties can help illuminate our own understanding.

The third level, the text in contemporary discussion, considers some of the issues and questions raised by this text for our own place and time. The focus here will be on us as real readers. Because every real reader is different, the comments will necessarily reflect my own perspective as a Jewish scholar of the New Testament who is nevertheless respectful of those traditions and communities for which this Gospel is canonical. My starting point is the conviction that while the Gospel attempts to steer us in the direction of compliance, it is by resisting that pull and critical questioning that will lead us to a deeper understanding and engagement with the text, whatever our personal religious beliefs and commitments.

References to "John" are not meant to be taken as statements of authorship but simply as a shorthand for the name of the book. Biblical quotations are from the New Revised Standard Version, unless otherwise stated. References to patristic sources in the second level of commentary are from *The Ancient Commentary to the Scriptures* (Elowsky 2006; 2007), unless otherwise noted.

John 1:1-18: The Prologue

The Text in Its Ancient Context

The opening of John's Gospel may surprise first-time readers familiar with the opening chapters of Matthew and Luke. Absent are the virgin Mary, the manger, the magi, and all other elements of the "Christmas story." Instead, the prologue situates Jesus within the relationship between God and humankind that begins with Genesis, and proclaims the universal scope and significance of the Gospel's salvation story. The prologue's opening words, "In the beginning," quote the opening of the biblical book of Genesis (Gen. 1:1). The quotation signals that what follows is not just another biography but a story of life-giving significance for all creation.

Poetic Style

The prologue makes use of "staircase parallelism," in which an important word at the end of one line is taken up at the beginning of the next: "In the beginning was the *Word*, and the *Word* was with God" (1:1); "in him was *life*, and the *life* was the *light* of all people. The *light* shines in the darkness" (1:4-5). Some view this poetic style as evidence that the prologue was a pre-Johannine, independent hymn that was incorporated into the Gospel and adapted to serve as its introduction.

Wisdom Imagery

The prologue's "Word," though masculine in both grammatical and human form, is remarkably similar to "Lady Wisdom" of biblical and postbiblical Wisdom literature. In Prov. 8:22-31, Wisdom describes her role in the creation of the world, and the intimate delight of her relationship with God (8:30-31). Wisdom and Logos are closely linked in the writings of the Alexandrian Jewish philosopher Philo (20 BCE–50 CE) and the Aramaic targumim, in which God's assistant is the *memra*, a masculine term meaning "word." This prior linking suggests that the fluidity between feminine Wisdom and masculine Logos is not the Gospel's innovation.

The phrase "lived among us" (NRSV) is more literally, and vividly, translated as "tabernacled among us," thereby preserving the allusion to the Shekinah, the divine presence (cf. *Tg. Onq.* at Deut. 12:5), and the tabernacle that the Israelites constructed in the wilderness (e.g., Exod. 25:9), in which God's presence was uniquely palpable.

The prologue also introduces key metaphors, figures, and themes that will be developed in the Gospel's stories and discourses. The metaphors include "light" and "life" to describe Jesus and the opportunity he will provide to humankind, and "world," a multilayered term—*cosmos*, in Greek—that can refer to the physical world, to humankind, but also more narrowly to those who refuse to believe. John 1:6-8 refers to John the Baptist as the one who testifies to the "light" but is not himself the light. John 1:17 contrasts the law that was given through Moses with the grace and truth now given through Jesus Christ.

Finally, the prologue draws its imagined or ideal audience into the Gospel's narrative and theological world. The first person plural in 1:14—"we have seen his glory, the glory as of a father's only son, full of grace and truth"—situates the reader alongside the narrator as a member of the group that, in contrast to Jesus' own people, "received him, . . . believed in his name," and therefore became "children of God" (1:12-13).

The Text in the Interpretive Tradition

The church fathers viewed the Johannine account of the Word as complementary to the infancy narratives of Matthew and Luke. Augustine (354–430 CE) commented that Christ's dual nature required two births, one divine—described in John—and one human—described in Matthew and Luke (*Serm.* 196.1; Elowsky 2006, 3). His contemporary Jerome (347–420) stressed his inability to comprehend how the Word was made flesh, admitting, "The doctrine from God, I have; the science of it, I do not have" (*Homily* 87, On John 1:1-14; Elowsky 2006, 41).

The opening lines of the prologue have fired the imagination since ancient times. Their "celestial flights" led to the use of the eagle to represent the Fourth Gospel (R. E. Brown 1966, 18). The words were thought to have healing power, and for that reason were used in long-standing custom of the Western church as a benediction over the sick and over newly baptized children and as amulets to protect against illness (R. E. Brown 1966, 18).

The Text in Contemporary Discussion

The poetic beauty of the prologue can make the human spirit soar and provide a glimpse of the cosmic context of our mundane existence. But its binary contrasts—between light and darkness,

Moses and Jesus, law and truth, acceptance and rejection—also construct a polarized worldview that is both supersessionist and hierarchical. The claim that Jesus—the Word—provides the only path to knowledge of God explicitly invalidates any belief system, including Judaism, that does not include faith in Jesus as the Christ and Savior. By occupying the compliant reading position that the prologue, through its use of the first person plural and other techniques, prescribes, we become complicit in this invalidation.

But we are not required to be compliant readers in order to understand the prologue, or the Gospel as a whole, and appreciate its beauty. Although the Gospel narrator steers us relentlessly toward compliance, we as readers are autonomous and therefore free to choose our own subject positions, to resist the prescribed response, accept it, or modify it, to investigate what may lie behind the polarizing rhetoric, and to raise our own questions, at the same time that we appreciate the Gospel's language and ideas.

The Book of Signs (1:19—12:50)

1:19-34: The Testimony of John the Baptist

The Text in Its Ancient Context

The Book of Signs (1:19—12:50) opens with priests and Levites from Jerusalem interrogating John the Baptist. To their open-ended question, "Who are you?" John responds more specifically that he is neither the Messiah, nor Elijah, nor the prophet. He is merely the forerunner of a far worthier man, "the voice in the wilderness" who cries, "Make straight the way of the Lord." The quotation of Isa. 40:3 is taken from the Greek version (Septuagint) in which *the voice* is "in the wilderness," rather than the Hebrew (Masoretic text) version, in which not the voice but *the way of the Lord* is in the wilderness.

Jesus makes his announced appearance the next day. John continues his testimony by describing a past occurrence: the descent of the Spirit on Jesus, and Jesus' identification as the one who "baptizes with the Holy Spirit" (1:33). The Fourth Gospel does not recount Jesus' own baptism, which in the Synoptics is the occasion on which the dove, or the Holy Spirit, descends on Jesus.

The Text in the Interpretive Tradition

The Gospel's omission of the baptism account may reflect some discomfort with the notion that the one who removes the world's sin (1:29) would have been baptized by John. The church fathers read the baptism back into the Johannine narrative. John Chrysostom (347–407) explained that baptism allowed John to testify publicly, and provided Jesus with his first disciples (*Homilies on the Gospel of John* 17.1–2; Elowsky 2006, 68).

The Text in Contemporary Discussion

Implicit in John's account is the story of a master—the Baptist—who gradually lost his following to a former disciple. The Baptist is remarkably gracious about Jesus' ascendancy, and anxious that both the authorities and his own followers know the truth. The historicity of this subtext is anyone's guess, but the scenario itself is not uncommon in religious and many other contexts. The passage provides an opening for thinking about how power, authority, and leadership can shift within and between communities, and how such changes are best handled.

1:35-51: Call of the Disciples

The Text in Its Ancient Context

John the Baptist testifies to two disciples who then follow Jesus, converse with him, and believe. One of those two disciples, Andrew, testifies to his brother Simon. Simon comes to Jesus, who renames him Cephas (Peter; 1:42). Jesus then travels to the Galilee and finds Philip (1:43), who then testifies to Nathanael. Nathanael is initially skeptical but then comes to Jesus and, astounded by Jesus' prophetic abilities, exclaims: "Rabbi, you are the Son of God! You are the King of Israel!" (1:49). With the exception of Philip, Jesus does not actively recruit the disciples. Rather, one disciple testifies to another, who then comes to Jesus for a personal encounter.

The sequence concludes with a prophecy by Jesus to Nathanael that he "will see heaven opened and the angels of God ascending and descending upon the Son of Man" (1:51), an allusion to Jacob's ladder (Genesis 28). The son of man title is a direct translation from the Aramaic *bar nasha*, which literally means a human being. But in this Gospel, the title refers to Jesus' role in the cosmos and his relationship to God.

The Text in the Interpretive Tradition

For Chrysostom, Simon's name change (1:42) demonstrates Jesus' divine identity: "He does this to show that it was he who gave the old covenant, that it was he who altered names, who called Abram 'Abraham,' and Sarai 'Sarah' and Jacob 'Israel.'" The difference is that in these cases, each person received a different name, whereas "now we all have one name, that which is greater than any. We are called 'Christians,' and 'sons of God' and 'friends' and [his] 'body'" (*Homilies on the Gospel of John* 19.2–3; Elowsky 2006, 82). Chrysostom's comment alludes to (among other passages) John 5, 10, and 11, in which Jesus calls the dead, his sheep, and Lazarus by name, and in doing so, renews their lives. The same may also be true for Simon, whose life is renewed when he meets Jesus.

The Text in Contemporary Discussion

The paradigm of the call, whereby discipleship is initiated through personal testimony, ascribes equal importance to the human witness and to the divine, and it has served as the model for Christian evangelizing activity for almost two millennia. But those on the receiving end today, whether from door-to-door missionaries or from well-meaning acquaintances, can experience evangelizing activities—and the assumption of some that the only route to a good life is faith in Christ—as at best an intrusion and at worst as offensive. Indeed, toward the end of the twentieth century, a number of Christian communions officially renounced the cause of "evangelizing" Jews, thus opening the door to more mutual conversation.

2:1-12: Jesus' First Sign: Wedding at Cana

The Text in Its Ancient Context

Jesus' public ministry begins when he turns water into wine at a wedding in the Galilean town of Cana, approximately nine miles (fifteen kilometers) north of Nazareth. In referring to this act as the "first of his signs," the narrator creates an expectation that there will be more signs, perhaps indeed an entire series of them, and also signals that these acts are not mere miracles, designed to demonstrate Jesus' ability to overturn the natural order of things, but signs that point the way to something important: the cosmological tale.

Jesus' mother spurs Jesus into action by mentioning that the wine has run out. She remains unnamed here (as throughout this Gospel), but has confidence in his ability to rectify the problem. Jesus responds: "Woman, what concern is that to you and to me? My hour has not yet come" (2:4). But she is not put off by Jesus' apparent refusal (2:4) and instructs the servants to do whatever Jesus says. Modern readers may bristle at the idea of a young man calling his mother "woman," but as the young man is Jesus, commentators have alternative explanations.

In this case, however, we may safely acquit Jesus of the charge of disrespect. Jesus consistently prefaces his revelations to women—the Samaritan woman (4:21), Jesus' mother again (19:26), and Mary Magdalene (20:13, 15)—in this way. Rather than a marker of social distance, the term "woman" functions like "behold" or "truly, truly I say to you" and parallels the form Jesus uses to address God as Father. Indeed, Jesus makes revelatory statements to individual women perhaps even more frequently, and with less ambivalence, than he does to men. In addition to the three women just mentioned, he reveals his truths to Mary and Martha of Bethany (11:25; 12:7). This motif renders the Gospel of John amenable to feministic historical, literary, and theological interpretation (see the collected essays in Levine 2003).

The passage also introduces the term "hour," which appears in several different formulations throughout the Gospel. The reference is to the time of Jesus' death and glorification. The messianic and salvific echoes in this passage may also be conveyed by the comment that it happened on the third day. While this may simply be a chronological marker indicating that it was the third day after the preceding event—Jesus' comments to Nathanael—it may equally foreshadow the resurrection, just as the wedding may allude to the messianic banquet, the feast that will celebrate the inauguration of God's rule (Kobel, 85–86). The passage shows that first-century Jews practiced ritual hand-washing prior to eating a meal; the practice is otherwise known from later rabbinic sources (*b. Ber.* 53b, *b. Shab.* 62b). The "bridegroom" is a double entendre that refers literally to the Cana bridegroom but, in the cosmological setting of the Gospel, also alludes to Jesus as the eschatological bridegroom (cf. 4:29).

The Text in the Interpretive Tradition

Like modern commentators, the church fathers attempted to explain Jesus' apparent rudeness. Bede (672/673–735) stated categorically that "he would not dishonor his mother, since he orders us to honor our father and mother" (*Homilies on the Gospels* 1.14; Elowsky 2006, 95). Chrysostom too insists that Jesus honors his mother, on the basis of Luke 2:51, and provides a helpful general principle governing filial obligation: we must be subject to our parents but only as long as they "throw no obstacle in the way of God's commands." But "when they demand anything at an unseasonable time or cut us off from spiritual things," we are not to comply (*Homilies on the Gospel of John* 21.2; Elowsky 2006, 91).

The Text in Contemporary Discussion

The fact that this Gospel can proclaim an exalted view of Christ without an annunciation scene raises the question of whether the belief in Mary's virginity is indeed essential to Christian faith.

Also striking in this passage is the notion of abundance. While many are accustomed to bounty in the material aspects of daily life, this passage can serve as a reminder that for some, abundance is an experience as rare as a wedding celebration.

2:13-25: Jesus' Sign of Authority over the Temple

The Text in Its Ancient Context

In the Synoptics, the cleansing of the temple occurs at the end of Jesus' ministry and spurs the Jewish authorities' decision to press for Jesus' death (Matt. 21:17; Mark 11:15-19; Luke 9:45-48). In John, however, this episode is Jesus' first public appearance. The presence of merchants and money-changers in the temple precinct may seem an affront to the dignity and holy nature of the temple. Prior to the temple's destruction (70 CE), however, Jewish worship was carried out primarily through regular sacrifices. During the three pilgrimage festivals (Tabernacles, Passover, Weeks), pilgrims needed sacrificial animals and birds, and had to change their local currency into the Tyrian half-shekel for the temple tax (Exod. 30:11-16). Merchants and money-changers were needed. Why, then, did Jesus create a scene?

For this Gospel, one answer lies in Ps. 69:9: "Zeal for your house will consume me." The episode asserts Jesus' entitlement to his father's house, by virtue of his role as the Son of God. At the same time, when Jesus challenges the Jews to "destroy this temple, and in three days I will raise it up" (2:19), the narrator explains, he did not intend the physical temple but rather the temple of his body.

The Text in the Interpretive Tradition

To smooth over the contradiction between John and the Synoptics, the church fathers posit two "cleansing" events (Elowsky 2006, 101). Augustine uses the occasion to chastise "those who seek their own interests in the church rather than those of Jesus Christ" and warns: "Let them beware of the scourge of ropes. The dove is not for sale; it is given gratis, for it is called grace" (*Tract. Ev. Jo.* 10.6.1–3; Elowsky 2006, 101).

The Text in Contemporary Discussion

The temple scene is shocking due to the uncharacteristic violence and hot emotion that it attributes to this otherwise cool, calm, and collected Savior. One cannot but wonder if a less violent act might have served to state Jesus' claim to his Father's house. It may be that the Gospel reflects the post-70 era, when the temple no longer stood, the sacrifices no longer took place, and the evangelist or community had only vague knowledge of the pilgrimage festivals. But the passage raises the more fundamental question of when, if ever, and under what circumstances, if at all, it is appropriate to use a violent act to demonstrate sovereignty, ownership, or entitlement.

3:1-21: Nicodemus

The Text in Its Ancient Context

Jesus' first extended discourse is a dialogue with a Pharisaic leader named Nicodemus, who comes under the cover of darkness. To him, Jesus utters the now famous words: "No one can see the kingdom of God without being born from above" (3:3), or born again (the source for the term "born-again Christianity"). Interpreting this saying literally, Nicodemus wonders how one can reenter the womb and be reborn. But Jesus was referring to spiritual, not physical, rebirth.

It is difficult to discern where Jesus' discourse ends and the narrator's commentary begins. Greek manuscripts do not include punctuation, but many commentators argue that verses 16-21 belong to the narrator because they refer to "the Son" in the third person. But perhaps this problem does not demand resolution. In this Gospel, Jesus' discourses and the narrator's commentaries are similar in theology and in phraseology, thereby suggesting a complete congruency between Jesus' words and the narrator's comments.

The Text in the Interpretive Tradition

For most church fathers, rebirth was associated with baptism, which, accompanied by repentance, resulted in the remission of former sins (Justin Martyr, *1 Apol.* 61; Gregory of Nazianzus, *On Holy Baptism*, Oration 40.8; Elowsky 2006, 109, 111). Hilary of Poitiers (300–368) attempts to explain how God's sacrifice of his only Son can express divine love for the world: "Gifts of price are the evidence of affection: the greatness of the surrender is evidence of the greatness of the love. God, who loved the world, gave no adopted son but his own, his only begotten [Son]" (*On the Trinity* 6.40; Elowsky 2006, 126).

The Text in Contemporary Discussion

The idea of human sacrifice—especially of one's own child—as an expression of love seems counterintuitive. Its roots are buried in the sacrificial systems that were the dominant form of worship in many ancient cultures. Yet even in the Hebrew Bible, the idea of sacrificing a beloved child is shocking, as in Judges 11, in which the warrior Jephthah vows to sacrifice the first thing—person—that comes out of his house to greet him if he wins a battle (Judg. 11:31). A closer parallel is the "binding" of Isaac. In Genesis 22, God orders Abraham to sacrifice his only son, the one whom he loves, Isaac, but Abraham receives a last-minute reprieve. By contrast, the Fourth Gospel insists, God went all the way. If Abraham was motivated by love of God to obey such a difficult order, how much more meaningful is God's sacrifice, which was motivated by love of the world? Nevertheless, God's loss is not absolute, because his Son is resurrected, and returns to live with him.

3:22-36: Jesus the Baptizer

The Text in Its Ancient Context

In John's Gospel, the ministries of Jesus and John the Baptist overlap and, indeed, are competitors. The Fourth Gospel has the Baptist reassure his disciples that it is not only inevitable but actually essential that Jesus' followers outnumber the Baptist's disciples (3:30). From this point onward, the Baptist is absent from the Gospel narrative.

The Text in the Interpretive Tradition

Bede used this text as an opportunity to speak about the church "gathered from among all nations," which he calls "a virgin pure of heart, perfect in love, bound to him in the bond of peace, in chastity of body and soul and in the unity of the Catholic faith. . . . Our Lord therefore committed his bride to his friends who are the preachers of the true gospel" (*Exposition on the Gospel of John* 3; Elowsky 2006, 135).

The Text in Contemporary Discussion

We may speculate that it may not have been easy to differentiate the followers of Jesus from the followers of other figures such as the Baptist. Non-Christians often have the same difficulty when surveying the Christian landscape today. The Baptist's deferential behavior raises the question of how competing groups are to relate to one another.

4:1-42: The Samaritan Woman

The Text in Its Ancient Context

Chapter 4 opens on a troubling note: Jesus must leave the vicinity because the Pharisees have heard about his baptizing activity. The narrator clarifies that it was the disciples, and not Jesus himself, who baptized, but the significance of this distinction is unclear given that they were acting on Jesus' behalf. The focus of this chapter, however, is on the rest stop that Jesus takes in the Samaritan town of Sychar en route to the Galilee. Sitting by a well, he asks a Samaritan woman for water, and at the end of their conversation, the woman returns to her city without her water jar, as an apostle of the Messiah (4:29).

Jesus and the woman are alone, as Jesus' disciples had gone into the city to buy food (4:8). The Samaritan woman is surprised by Jesus' request for water, for, as the narrator comments, Jews do not share with Samaritans. Jesus offers her living water—far superior to the well water that she can give him—and then inquires about her husband. He reveals his detailed knowledge of her unusual situation: she has already had five husbands "and the one you have now is not your husband" (4:18). Rather than take offense, the woman proclaims him to be a prophet. She asks about a difference between Jews and Samaritans, concerning the location for worship: Gerizim or Jerusalem? Jesus initially affirms the contrast between Jews and Samaritans: "You worship what you do not know; we worship what we know, for salvation is from the Jews." He then prophesies a time when worship will concentrate in neither location but in Jesus himself. The woman discerns that he may be the Messiah. The disciples return, and, while surprised that he is speaking with a woman, they do not confront him. Their surprise is in itself surprising, for the Gospel gives no indication that Jesus refrained from speaking to women.

The episode is reminiscent of the biblical stories in which boy meets girl at well (4:12; see Gen. 24:15-31; 29:9-13; Exod. 2:16-21). The present encounter does not end in betrothal but in something much greater: the promise, or assurance, of eternal life (Eslinger). In speaking with the Samaritan woman, Jesus transgresses boundaries of both gender and ethnicity. The scene also implies that there may have been Samaritans among the Gospel's intended readership.

The disciples bring food. Just as he redefined water from the mundane to the eternal, so does Jesus elevate the notion of food from physical to spiritual nourishment: doing his Father's will. He continues enigmatically: "Four months more, then comes the harvest," which the disciples will reap though they did not plant the field. The episode draws to a close when the Samaritans to whom the woman has testified invite Jesus to stay with them. Afterward, they declare that their faith is no longer because of her words but because of their encounter. This episode echoes the pattern of the call of the disciples: the Samaritan woman meets Jesus, testifies to others, who encounter Jesus in person and declare their faith. The passage presumes the readers' knowledge that the Samaritans, like the Jews, believed in the eventual coming of a savior figure, whom the Samaritans called *Taheb* (Crown, Pummer, and Tal, 224–26).

The Text in the Interpretive Tradition

In leaving Judea, Chrysostom explains, Christ aimed "to take away their malice and soften their envy." Although in a confrontation Jesus could have prevented the Jews from hurting him, he preferred to do things "in a human way" so that people would "believe his incarnation" (*Homilies on the Gospel of John* 31.3; Elowsky 2006, 141). Augustine adds that Jesus "wanted to provide himself as an example for believers in time to come, that it was no sin for a servant of God to seek refuge from the fury of persecutors" (*Tract. Ev. Jo.* 15.2; Elowsky 2006, 142).

Scholars who attempt to soften the Gospel's harsh verdict on the Jews point to Jesus' statement in 4:22 that "salvation is from the Jews." The church fathers were not similarly motivated but nevertheless came up with the most logical interpretation of this verse: that it refers to Jesus' own Jewish origins. As Augustine notes, "Of what lineage was Christ born? Of the Jews. . . . He did not say, after all, 'salvation is for the Jews' but 'salvation is from the Jews'" (*Serm.* 375.1; Elowsky 2006, 159).

For Origen, the woman is an apostle and a role model, "for by recording the woman's commendation for those capable of reading with understanding, the Evangelist challenges us to this goal" (*Comm. Jo.* 13.169; Elowsky 2006, 166). Chrysostom admires her for exhibiting "the actions of an apostle, preaching the gospel to everyone she could and calling them to Jesus. She even drew out a whole city to hear him" (*Homilies on the Gospel of John* 32.1; Elowsky 2006, 154).

The Text in Contemporary Discussion

The Gospel implies that the message of Jesus as Son of God and Savior is open to all regardless of gender and ethnicity, and overcomes both sets of socially constructed boundaries. Jesus' discourse also decouples true worship from any specific location. In doing so, he establishes a framework for a universal mode of covenantal relationship with God where women and men, Jews, Samaritans and gentiles, can worship where they are, united in a community whose salvific agent came "from the Jews." Christian "universalism" has often been contrasted favorably with Jewish "particularism," suggesting that Christianity is broad and accepting while Judaism is narrow and exclusivistic. Open and welcoming as this message sounds, the insistence on one single path or "way" (cf. 14:6) to covenantal relationship with God in itself is an exclusive message that invalidates other choices.

4:43-54: Second Sign: Healing of the Official's Son

The Text in Its Ancient Context

After his stay with the Samaritans, Jesus continues his journey to the Galilee, as the narrator maintains a quiet sense of danger with the proverb—"a prophet has no honor in the prophet's own country" (see Matt. 13:53-58; Mark 6:1-6; Luke 4:22-24; *Gos. Thom.* 31).

An official asks Jesus to come down to Capernaum to heal his son. Jesus refuses but assures the man that his son will live. As the man departs, his slaves (or servants) meet him with the good news of his son's recovery, and they all become believers. Jesus has healed the son by words and from a distance. The narrative describes this act as Jesus' second Cana sign—an enumeration important for the hypothesis that the Gospel made use of a preexisting "signs source"—but Jesus criticizes the nobleman for requiring a sign in order to believe: "Unless you see signs and wonders you will not believe" (4:48). Although addressed to an individual, the verb "you see" is not singular but plural. This warning is intended for all readers, not only this distraught father.

The Text in the Interpretive Tradition

Chrysostom comments on the weakness of the official's faith, who needed confirmation before believing fully. Chrysostom dismisses the official's approach to Jesus as "nothing special, for parents often are so carried away by their affection that they consult not only those physicians they depend on, but even people they do not depend on at all." The lesson? Do not wait for miracles or lose faith when prayers are not answered, for those whom God loves he also chastens (*Homilies on the Gospel of John* 35.2–3; Elowsky 2006, 174).

The Text in Contemporary Discussion

Chrysostom accurately describes the frame of mind of someone whose loved one is ill. But Jesus' rebuke also fits into a major Johannine theme: the tension between hearing and seeing. A second tension, between presence and absence, is also not fully resolved. Despite Jesus' words in 4:48, the Gospel continues to present signs and wonders that, if properly—cosmologically—understood, can be a basis for faith. The tension is by no means limited to this Gospel, or to issues of faith, but permeates our own lives due to the rapid growth of digital communication. Do email and Skype overcome absence or contribute to alienation? Are Facebook friendships real or illusory? Do virtual experiences interfere with or enhance our "real" relationships? Although our digital dilemmas were not even remotely anticipated in the first century, the followers of Jesus who lived after his death had to grapple with presence and absence as well. How is a would-be believer to have a personal encounter with Christ in the years after the crucifixion? And how are leaders such as Paul supposed to interact with the communities they founded throughout the region? For Paul, and many others, it was the written word that would serve as their mode of virtual presence, substituting for the real presence of Jesus, and themselves, in a post-Easter world.

5:1-47: Healing on the Sabbath

The Text in Its Ancient Context

Although the term *sēmeion* is not used, the healing of the lame man, like the two Cana miracles, is a sign that reveals Jesus' identity and relationship to the Father to those who can understand the cosmological story beneath the narrative's surface. The sign takes place on an unnamed Jewish pilgrimage festival and displays a detailed knowledge of the temple area, corroborated by the modern discovery of a second-century healing sanctuary and pool with five porticoes in this approximate location (Freund, Arav, and Bethsaida Excavations Project). The explanation of how healing took place at the pool—an angel of the Lord used to come down in the pool, the water was stirred up, and the first to enter would be healed (5:3)—was known to Tertullian (160–225) and to Chrysostom, but because it is absent from the earliest manuscripts, it is not considered original to the Gospel.

This sign marks an escalation in the conflict with the Jewish authorities. Jewish law permitted violation of the Sabbath to save a life, but in healing a chronically disabled man, the Johannine Jesus was deliberately provoking the authorities. Indeed, the narrator insists that it was because of such Sabbath activities that the Jews began to persecute Jesus (5:16).

The primary conflict, however, is christological. Jesus' response to the Jews' concerns about Sabbath violation is provocative: "My Father is still working, and I also am working." Because birth, growth, death, and other natural processes did not cease on the Sabbath, Philo of Alexandria commented that though God rested on the seventh day of creation, God works on the weekly Sabbath while Jews do not (Philo, *Cher.* 86–90; *Leg.* 1.5–6). In the context of this ancient debate, Jesus' act of healing shows not that the Sabbath is invalid but that, like his Father, he does not stop his divine work.

For the Jews as presented in John's Gospel, this claim is blasphemy and they sought "all the more to kill him, because he was not only breaking the sabbath, but was also calling God his own Father, thereby making himself equal to God" (5:18). The sign is followed by a discourse devoted to two main topics: the Son's divine work of judgment and raising the dead; and the various witnesses to Jesus' identity as God's Son, such as John the Baptist, God, and the Scriptures. The entire discourse has a forensic, judicial tone to it, and concludes with Jesus' judgment on the Jews who have confronted him: by persecuting Jesus, they show their alienation from God.

The Text in the Interpretive Tradition

Although the Johannine Jesus was not inciting Jews to violate the Sabbath, Cyril of Alexandria (376–444) suggests that with faith and new life in Christ, "it was necessary that the old letter of the law should become of no effect and that the typical worship in shadows and empty Jewish customs should be rejected" (*Commentary on the Gospel of John* 2.5; Elowsky 2006, 183).

The Text in Contemporary Discussion

As Cyril's comments show, John 5 is often (incorrectly) taken as evidence that Jesus abrogated Sabbath observance. Christians and others often view the Jewish Sabbath regulations as restrictive, overly ritualistic, and outmoded. Far from disrupting modern life, however, the Sabbath provides the rest, respite, and temporary retreat from the noise, rush, and anxiety of daily life. Jews who observe the Sabbath experience it as the sanctification of time, as a foretaste of the world to come, a day of spiritual and physical renewal (Heschel). The restrictions on work, travel, and other activities are what make that experience possible.

6:1-21: A Fifth Sign: Feeding of the Multitudes and Walking on Water

The Text in Its Ancient Context

John 6 begins with a sign (although, again, the term *sēmeion* is not used) familiar from the Synoptic Gospels: the feeding of the multitudes, also known as the feeding of the five thousand (see Matt. 14:13-21; Mark 16.32-44; Luke 9:10-17) or the multiplication of the loaves and fishes. The note that "after this Jesus went to the other side of the Sea of Galilee," also called the "Sea of Tiberias," is puzzling, as in the immediately preceding passage Jesus is in Jerusalem, far from the Galilee. The transition to this passage has often been seen as evidence of a redactional process of composition. By remaining in Galilee for the Passover, Jesus fulfills the prophecy to the Samaritan woman, that soon people would worship God neither on Gerizim nor in Jerusalem, but through Jesus (Reinhartz 1989). As in the Synoptics, the feeding miracle is followed by Jesus' walking on water, suggesting that these two events were linked from a very early point in the tradition.

The Text in the Interpretive Tradition

As Chrysostom notes, this sign differs from the others thus far recounted in that Jesus gives thanks before performing the miracle. Chrysostom derives from this the principle that it is proper to give thanks to God before eating, perhaps without realizing that Jesus was following the Jewish practice of blessing the bread before a meal. Chrysostom also criticizes the eagerness of the crowd to eat, when earlier they were ready to kill Jesus for his behavior during the feast (*Homilies on the Gospel of John* 42.3; Elowsky 2006, 214).

The Text in Contemporary Discussion

As at the wedding at Cana, the theme in the feeding story is abundance, stunning in its quality, quantity, and its very existence. Jesus' concern for feeding the crowd comes as a surprise, for there is no sign that they expect him to provide lunch. The story would seem to demonstrate responsibility toward the hungry. The crowd does not ask to be fed; rather, it is Jesus who takes this daunting task upon himself. The story emphasizes the wonder inherent in Jesus' ability to feed such a big crowd with a mere five loaves and two fish, but perhaps the larger miracle is the concern to provide for others in the first place. Many ordinary individuals are capable of doing the same. And yet, the discourse that follows does not address this theme but, on the contrary, directs attention away from human needs and responsibilities and focuses instead on forms of "spiritual nourishment" that many in that same crowd refuse or are unable to digest.

6:22-71: The Bread of Life Discourse

The Text in Its Ancient Context

Those who had eaten their fill finally catch up with Jesus in Capernaum. Playing on the contrast between material food and spiritual food, Jesus criticizes them for eating their fill without understanding the deeper meaning of the experience. The people cannot accept that the true and divine bread is Jesus himself. Even more shocking, however, is the next revelation: Just as people eat bread to sustain their bodies, so must they eat the bread of life in order to sustain their spirits and gain eternal life. Jesus shocks them by warning: "Unless you eat the flesh of the Son of Man and drink his blood, you have no life in you" (6:51-54).

On the surface, and no doubt also to the incredulous crowds, this assertion sounds uncomfortably cannibalistic. But in Christian theology, the passage has often been interpreted in eucharistic terms. It is difficult, however, to pin this discourse down to a single meaning, for its language is reminiscent also of the Passover as the season of salvation, and of pagan rituals of theophagy—eating of God—associated with the Greco-Roman mystery cults of Demeter and Dionysus (Kobel, 234–36, 247), and because the Eucharist plays no part in the Johannine account of the Last Supper (John 13).

Many followers leave, but the Twelve remain, for they "have come to believe and know that you are the Holy One of God" (6:69). Jesus seems reassured, and in turn reassures them that he has chosen them, but introduces a sinister note: "Yet one of you is a devil" (6:70). The narrator reveals information not yet known to the disciples: the betrayer is one of them, Judas Iscariot (6:71).

The Text in the Interpretive Tradition

The eucharistic interpretation of the discourse was widespread among the church fathers. Cyril of Jerusalem compares the bread of life to the showbread that was part of temple worship. The showbread, however, belonged to the "old covenant" that has now been replaced by the "new covenant" in which "the bread of heaven and the cup of salvation . . . sanctify body and soul" (*Mystagogical Lectures* 4.4–6; Elowsky 2006, 239). He notes that "the person who receives the flesh of our Savior Christ and drinks his precious blood . . . shall be one with him" (*Commentary on the Gospel of John* 4.2; Elowsky 2006, 241).

The Text in Contemporary Discussion

Eating the body and drinking the blood can also refer to consuming Jesus' words and teachings, which provide the nourishment needed to grow and thrive spiritually (Phillips). Just as the food and drink we ingest have a profound effect on health, state of mind, mood, and ability to function in the world, so can the books we read, the conversations we have, and all our worldly encounters change us, nourish us, and help us make our way in the world. But not all words will be beneficial, or equally beneficial, to all.

7:1-52: Festival of Tabernacles

The Text in Its Ancient Context

John 7 takes place during yet another pilgrimage festival, Tabernacles. During this harvest festival, families and communities are required to live in booths reminiscent of the temporary dwellings in which the Israelites lived during their forty-year wandering in the desert.

When Jesus' brothers urge him to go, he refuses, "for my time has not yet fully come" (7:8). Yet once his brothers leave, Jesus secretly goes as well. In any other story, this about-face would be seen as deception. Commentators are reluctant, however, to view Jesus in this light, and suggest that his earlier refusal was misunderstood by his brothers: Jesus was not refusing to go to Jerusalem, but asserting that it was not his time to "go up" to his Father (R. E. Brown 1966, 308). This is far from convincing, as it does not account for why he went up to Jerusalem "in secret."

The scene then shifts to Jerusalem, and introduces a refrain that extends throughout this and the following chapters: a division among the Jewish crowds as to Jesus' identity. Some defend him as a good man, others condemn him as a deceiver. When Jesus finally arrives, in the middle of the festival, his teachings astonish the people, but the narrator does not reveal those teachings to the reader. The crowds propose a criterion for discerning whether Jesus is the Messiah: "We know where this man is from; but when the Messiah comes, no one will know where he is from" (7:27). This may be an allusion to the tradition of the "hidden messiah," one of several different strands of messianic expectation in the first century (see *1 Enoch* 46:1-3). Yet, from the point of view of the Gospel and the Johannine Jesus, their knowledge is inadequate and misguided. For Jesus does not fundamentally come from Nazareth but from God. For this reason, he fulfills "hidden messiah" criteria, as the readers, but not the crowds, are aware.

The split in the crowd alarms the Pharisees, and they and the chief priests send the temple police to arrest him (7:32). At the same time, Jesus predicts his imminent departure, and prophesies that "you will search for me, but you will not find me; and where I am, you cannot come" (7:34). In a typically Johannine move, the crowds understand, or rather, misunderstand him to be speaking literally, and wonder whether he intends to "go to the Dispersion among the Greeks and teach the Greeks?" (7:35). The reader knows that Jesus is referring to his return to the Father, but the statement may also be an ironic hint that the Word has spread from Judea and Galilee to the gentile communities of the Diaspora.

Each day of the Tabernacles festival is marked by a procession including prayers for deliverance, called Hosannas. The last day was (and still is) called the "great" Hosanna. On this day, Jesus offers "living water" to all. This may be an allusion to the custom during Tabernacles of carrying a golden pitcher of water from the pool of Siloam to the temple as a reminder of the water drawn from the rock in the desert (Num. 20:2-13) and as a symbol of hope for messianic deliverance (Isa. 12:3).

The temple police, sent by the Jewish authorities to arrest Jesus, return empty-handed but astonished: "Never has anyone spoken like this!" (7:46). Nicodemus urges that Jesus be heard out before judgment is passed. The others mock Nicodemus: "Surely you are not also from Galilee, are you? Search and you will see that no prophet is to arise from Galilee" (7:52). The authorities will not be deterred from seeking his death.

The Text in the Interpretive Tradition

The church fathers were unsure what to make of Nicodemus's behavior. Theodore of Mopsuestia (350–428) believes that Nicodemus did not defend Jesus vociferously enough (*Commentary on John* 3.7.52; Elowsky 2006, 271), but Cyril of Alexandria counts Nicodemus among Jesus' secret believers (*Commentary on the Gospel of John* 5.2; Elowsky 2006, 271).

The Text in Contemporary Discussion

Jesus' duplicity in relation to his brothers adds unexpected depth to this two-dimensional figure. His duplicity was less of a problem for the Gospel writer than for modern commentators. While the desire for an unsullied Jesus is understandable, it is at odds with a Christology that views him as both human and divine. It is unfortunate that so few commentators allow him any of the foibles that help make human beings interesting, if also at times irritating or exasperating. How refreshing it would be to imagine Jesus deliberately deceiving his brothers because he does not want to go to Jerusalem with them! Would this behavior make Jesus any less Christlike? The point is raised most sharply in comparison with the great figures of the Hebrew Bible—Abraham, Moses, David—all mentioned in the Fourth Gospel, and all of whom are portrayed in the Bible as using guile to achieve their purposes.

7:53—8:11: The Adulterous Woman

The Text in Its Ancient Context

The story of the adulterous woman is a non-Johannine interpolation, appearing in some ancient manuscripts after Luke 21:38, where it fits the narrative context quite well, and in others at its present spot, where it interrupts the Johannine narrative. In this story, Jesus exposes the hypocrisy of the scribes and Pharisees who intend to stone the woman for adultery yet are themselves sinful. Before confronting the leaders, Jesus bends down and writes something with his finger (8:6). What he actually wrote is unknown, but the mention of writing may allude to Jer. 17:13, which declares that those who depart from God shall be written in the earth. Jesus sends the woman on her way without condemnation but adjures her to refrain from sin.

The Text in the Interpretive Tradition

Augustine, like Jerome, knows that the story is absent from some manuscripts of John but believes that it was excised by weak men who fear that their wives would interpret Jesus' injunction to the woman as "liberty to sin with impunity." He also strongly criticizes men who refuse to accept that the prohibition of adultery extends to them as well (*On Adulterous Marriages* 2.7.6, 2.8.7; Elowsky 2006, 276).

The Text in Contemporary Discussion

This non-Johannine story provides occasion for further reflection on the imperfections of human nature. There is an irony in the passage that often escapes notice. Jesus challenges the scribes: "Let anyone among you who is without sin be the first to throw a stone at her" (8:7). By challenging anyone "among you," Jesus excludes himself as a potential stone-thrower. Implicit but not stated is that, for the New Testament authors, Jesus himself would have been the only person present who was without sin, and yet he does not lift a finger against her. Rather than judging and sentencing the woman, he judges those who would punish her. Missing from the passage, however, is any attribution of responsibility to the man with whom she committed this transgression. This is striking in light of Deuteronomy's explicit statement that both the man and the woman shall be punished (Deut. 22:22).

8:12-59: Confrontation with the Jews

The Text in Its Ancient Context

This lengthy polemical discourse revolves around two major issues: Jesus' identity and Jewish identity markers. At stake is the fundamental notion of covenant: on what basis does one enter into and maintain a covenantal relationship with God?

In John, Jesus' Jewish identity is not signaled explicitly—he is called a *Ioudaios* only once (4:9)—but it is implied by his participation in the Jewish festivals, his use of biblical quotations, and the locations of his activity. In 8:17, however, the Johannine Jesus distances himself from Judaism, when he declares to the Pharisees, "In *your* law it is written that the testimony of two witnesses is valid" (emphasis added). Perhaps Jesus is simply declaring that as the preexistent son of God, the Torah does not apply to him.

At the outset, Jesus' interlocutors are described as Pharisees, but soon his partners in dialogue are referred to simply as "the Jews" (8:22). Much of the discourse alludes to the Abraham story and to God's covenantal promises to the patriarch (Genesis 12; 15). In 8:33, the Jews claim that they are children of Abraham (see Gen. 12:2; Deut. 14:1), and that they have never been enslaved. Although commentators contend that the Jews were lying by deliberately ignoring their enslavement in Egypt prior to the exodus, it is likely that their claim refers not to slavery but to idolatry, which involves "serving" gods other than the one God of Israel (see Jer. 2:10-14; Reinhartz 2001b).

The second element concerns Ishmael, the slave Hagar's son, and Isaac, the son who inherits the covenant promises. In Genesis, it is the Israelites who descend from Isaac; postbiblical Jews claimed this lineage as well. Paul, however, argued that it was believers in Christ who descend from Sarah, and nonbelievers who are the slaves (Galatians 4). John does not develop the "allegory," but in 8:35 he describes sonship as a consequence of faith in Christ, not as a birthright. Jesus himself is the true "son" who belongs in the temple, in contrast to the Jews, who serve in the temple but do not inherit it.

Evidence that the Jews have lost their Abrahamic lineage lies in their rejection of Christ, in contrast to Abraham, who welcomed the three divinely sent guests to his tent in Genesis 18. Finally, Jesus claims that because they murder and lie, the Jews are not children of God, but "from your father the devil" (8:44). The argument regarding Abrahamic and divine/demonic sonship rests on the idea that children will behave like their parents, an assumption that is not borne out by experience.

The Jews respond with their own accusations: Jesus is a Samaritan and has a demon (8:48). Jesus does not respond to the Samaritan charge and simply denies that he has a demon. But he makes a shocking statement that persuades them that he is indeed possessed: "whoever keeps my word will never see death" (8:51). This claim turns the conversation back to Abraham, as the Jews ask: "Are you greater than our father Abraham, who died?" (8:52). Jesus declares that Abraham rejoiced at "his day," and that he existed before Abraham. These statements may allude to Jesus' preexistence, as well as to the traditions described in the pseudepigraphical *Testament of Abraham*, in which God gives Abraham a tour of the heavens and provides him with knowledge of the final judgment. Predictably, the chapter ends with the Jews' attempt to stone Jesus.

The Text in the Interpretive Tradition

The church fathers hope for the conversion of some Jews. Cyril states that "we must not think that all the Jews were utterly immersed in ill-tempered foolishness"; some came to faith while others were dissuaded by the "unholy scribes and Pharisees whose boundless unbelief stirred the others to wrath and intemperately kindled them to bloodthirstiness" (*Commentary on the Gospel of John* 6.1; Elowsky 2006, 309).

In claiming never to have been enslaved, Augustine insists, the Jews were lying ingrates. "Wasn't Joseph sold? Weren't the holy prophets led into captivity? And again, didn't that very nation, when making bricks in Egypt, also serve hard rulers, not only in gold and silver but also in clay? If you were never in bondage to anyone, ungrateful people, why is it that God is continually reminding you that he delivered you from the house of bondage? . . . [and how] were you now paying tribute to the Romans, out of which also you formed a trap for the truth himself, as if to ensnare him?" (*Tract. Ev. Jo.* 41.2; Elowsky 2006, 296).

The Text in Contemporary Discussion

The unfortunate link between the Jews and the devil in 8:44 has spawned a potent antisemitic symbol. As a Jew, I would urge Christians to acknowledge and wrestle with this aspect of the text. What does it mean that texts like this are present in canonized literature? Does it make it better to understand these discourses, not as belonging to the historical Jesus, but as reflecting a flawed and ideologically motivated author and community? As some Christian churches have begun to ask, should such texts continue to be read in Christian worship?

9:1-41: A Sixth Sign: Healing of the Blind Man

The Text in Its Ancient Context

On seeing a man born blind, the disciples ask Jesus about whose sin caused his blindness: the man or his parents? Neither, says Jesus. The man was born blind so that Jesus might heal him and thereby perform a sign (though, again, the term *sēmeion* is not used) that testifies to the divine glory and his identity as God's Son. The man's journey from blindness to sight symbolizes the journey from unbelief to belief. Like the healing of the lame man, the sign, also done on the Sabbath, causes a division among the people. The formerly blind man is taken to the Pharisees for investigation. As in John 8, the term "Pharisees" for Jesus' interrogators drops out in favor of "the Jews," a change that blurs the distinctions between the general term and the subset of Jewish leaders. The Jews now call the man's parents as witnesses, but they prove reluctant to respond directly to questions, because "they were afraid of the Jews; for the Jews had already agreed that anyone who confessed Jesus to be the Messiah would be put out of the synagogue" (9:22).

Using a two-level reading method, many scholars argue that John 9, and the Gospel as a whole, tell not only a story of Jesus but also the story of the Johannine community, specifically the expulsion of Johannine believers from the synagogue for confessing Jesus to be the Messiah. This expulsion is seen as the rationale for the Gospel's often harsh words about the Jews, as well as an important milestone in the "parting of the ways" between Judaism and Christianity. External corroboration has often been sought in the liturgical "blessing" (curse) on the heretics, *Birkat ha-Minim*, that was added to the daily liturgy. The theory is that in the late first century, Jewish authorities added this curse as a way of flushing undesirables such as Jewish Christ-confessors out of the worship service and thereby from the community as a whole (Martyn).

Recent research, however, has revealed no first-century manuscript evidence for *Birkat ha-Minim*. Nor is there evidence that belief in an individual's messianic identity would have been a basis for exclusion. Indeed, in 132–135 CE, Rabbi Akiva is said to have made similar claims for Simeon Bar Kosiba, yet Akiva's high status did not suffer as a result. Rather than a coded reference to the expulsion of the Johannine community from the synagogue, 9:22 may well be a strategy for forging a community identity outside of and separate from Judaism.

Jesus provides the symbolic, cosmological meaning of this sign: "I came into this world for judgment so that those who do not see may see, and those who do see may become blind" (9:39). The Pharisees—here again, the more specific term is used—object to being called blind, but Jesus insists: "If you were blind, you would not have sin. But now that you say, 'We see,' your sin remains" (9:41).

The Text in the Interpretive Tradition

Augustine makes much less of the expulsion in 9:22 than do modern scholars. Reading the complete separation of Judaism and Christianity back into the Gospel, he explains that "it was no disadvantage to be put out of the synagogue since the one they cast out, Christ received" (*Tract. Ev. Jo.* 44.10; Elowsky 2006, 331).

Augustine and Cyril of Alexandria use this Sabbath healing as an opportunity to distinguish between the "carnal" Sabbath observed by Jews and the spiritual Sabbath observed by Christ. Augustine explains that the Pharisees were wrong to accuse Jesus of profaning the Sabbath. "On the contrary, he kept it because he was without sin; to observe the sabbath spiritually is to have no sin . . . But these men, who neither could see nor were anointed, observed the sabbath carnally but profaned it spiritually" (*Tract. Ev. Jo.* 44.9; Elowsky 2006, 330).

The Text in Contemporary Discussion

The reference to expulsion, however it is interpreted, provides an opportunity to think about the frequent experience of schism within faith-based or other communities. The separation of a subgroup from the main community may be perceived as a departure by those who remain within and as an expulsion from those who leave. Drawing on our own experiences allows us to consider a range of possibilities that acknowledge the efforts of early groups of Christ-followers to create new communities within which they could give full expression to their convictions.

10:1-42: The Good Shepherd

The Text in Its Ancient Context

The Johannine Jesus, unlike his Synoptic counterpart, does not speak in parables. In John 10, however, he employs the "figure" (Gk. *paroimia*) of the shepherd who calls his sheep by name and leads them out of the sheepfold. This is a pastoral, everyday scenario that lends itself readily to a cosmological interpretation.

The shepherd is a well-known biblical metaphor for leaders, divine and human, such as Moses (Exod. 3:1), David (2 Sam. 5:2), and God (Psalm 23). The language (hearing the voice, calling the sheep by name, leading them out) recalls John 5:28, in which Jesus promises that "all who are in their graves will hear his voice and will come out" and anticipates 11:43, in which Jesus calls Lazarus by name out of his grave. These references to death raise the intriguing possibility that the passage alludes to the "harrowing of hell," the belief that Jesus spent the days between his crucifixion and resurrection in Hades bringing the dead to faith (Reinhartz 1992).

Jesus also refers to "other sheep that do not belong to this fold" (10:16), perhaps an allusion to members of the Johannine community—believers—who are not of Jewish origin. This discourse, too, took place during the early winter festival, Hanukkah (Dedication). This festival commemorates the rededication of the temple (164 BCE), after it had been desecrated by the Seleucid king Antiochus IV (1 Macc. 4:52-59). Again the Jews attempt to stone him, this time for blasphemy, "because you, though only a human being, are making yourself God" (10:33). Jesus responds as a true rabbi, with a biblical verse: "Is it not written in your law, 'I said, you are gods'?" (10:35). Here, too, Jesus distances himself from the Torah, even as he brings it as a witness to the truth of his own words and identity.

The Text in the Interpretive Tradition

The church fathers interpreted the prophecy that in the future "there will be one flock and one shepherd" (10:16) as a reference to gentile Christians. As Theodore of Mopsuestia points out, "many among the Gentiles as well as many among the Jews are destined to gather together into a single church and to acknowledge one shepherd and one lord, who is Christ" (*Commentary on John* 4.10.216; Elowsky 2007, 35).

The Text in Contemporary Discussion

The inclusion of other sheep projects the ideal of a single, universal community united by faith in Christ. Yet a similarly universal and totalizing image in the Hebrew Bible, the Tower of Babel, is broken up by God, who is critical of the endeavor. In the twentieth and twenty-first centuries, many Western countries have become ever more diverse, ethnically, religiously, culturally, and linguistically. Some see this development as disturbing. Others, however, view the diversity as enriching and exciting. The principles of acceptance and mutual respect are often lacking in universalizing ideologies or homogeneous communities, but are necessary for living in communities characterized by diversity.

11:1-54: A Seventh Sign: Raising of Lazarus

The Text in Its Ancient Context

When Jesus learns of Lazarus's serious illness, he makes the surprising decision to remain where he is instead of rushing to his friend's bedside. As the story proceeds, the reason for the delay becomes clear: Jesus is waiting for Lazarus to die so that he can raise him up and thereby glorify God.

By the time Jesus arrives, Lazarus has been dead and buried for four days. Mary and Martha are mourning in the company of "many of the Jews" (11:19). Each sister reproaches Jesus for not coming sooner. Jesus promises Martha that Lazarus will rise again, and declares famously, "I am the resurrection and the life. Those who believe in me, even though they die, will live, and everyone who lives and believes in me will never die" (11:25-26). Martha responds with a full confession of faith: "Yes, Lord, I believe that you are the Messiah, the Son of God, the one coming into the world" (11:27).

Upon seeing Mary, Jesus "was greatly disturbed in spirit, and deeply moved" (11:33). When he sees the tomb, he weeps (11:35). In the first century, Jews were buried in linen shrouds and their bodies laid in a sealed tomb so that the flesh would decompose. After a period of eleven months, the tomb would be unsealed, and the bones would be placed in an ossuary (bone box) and stored on a shelf in the tomb (Hachlili). In the days after burial, however, removing the stone would release the stench of decomposition. Jesus gives thanks to God and clarifies that his prayer is "for the sake of the crowd standing here, so that they may believe that you sent me" (11:41). In doing so, he attributes the miracle not to his own innate power but to God. He then calls out—like the shepherd would to the sheep in John 10—"Lazarus, come out!" thereby fulfilling the prophecy in 5:28-29, that the dead will hear the voice of the Son of God and come out of their tombs (11:43). Lazarus's revival foreshadows Jesus' own.

Some Jews believe, but others go to the Pharisees, who call a meeting of the council (11:47) out of concern that "Romans will come and destroy both our holy place [the temple] and our nation" (11:48). The Gospel may be suggesting that the Jewish authorities viewed faith in Jesus as a loss of attachment to God, which God would punish by allowing Rome to destroy the temple, just as the Hebrew Bible believed that God had sent the Assyrians and Babylonians to punish the Jews for turning away from the covenant (2 Kgs. 21:14-15). In the Maccabean era, a similar explanation was used to explain how Antiochus IV succeeded in desecrating God's temple (2 Macc. 5:15-20). A second possibility is that widespread belief of Jews in Jesus might make Rome fear rebellion or civil war, and therefore prompt Rome to move quickly by moving against the temple.

In response, Caiaphas (high priest 18–36 CE; Josephus, *Ant.* 18.90–95) reminds the council that "it is better for you to have one man die for the people than to have the whole nation destroyed" (11:50). The narrator interprets this comment as an unwitting prophecy that Jesus would die for the nation (11:51) and "to gather into one the dispersed children of God" (11:52). While Caiaphas is often depicted as the mastermind behind Jesus' death, his comment is a general principle and does not convey animosity toward Jesus. Jesus again withdraws, this time to the town of Ephraim, where he remains with the disciples (11:54).

The Text in the Interpretive Tradition

Chrysostom saw a contradiction between the expulsion mentioned in 9:22 and the presence of Jews in the home of Mary and Martha. He asks: "How could the Jews console the loved ones of Christ, when they had resolved that whoever confessed Christ should be put out of the synagogue?" He suggests that "perhaps the extreme affliction of the sisters excited their sympathy, or they wished to show respect for their rank. Or perhaps those who came were of the better sort, as we find that many of them believed" (*Hom. Jo.* 62.2; Elowsky 2007, 12).

Origen asks a more theological question: If Caiaphas was wicked, and therefore, by definition, did not possess the Holy Spirit, how could he utter a true prophecy? Perhaps Caiaphas was simply speaking unintentionally, as everyone does at times. In the end, however, he cannot deny that the prophecy was from the Holy Spirit, even as he refuses to commit himself fully to this idea: "I do not in the least maintain that this was the case, but leave it to readers to decide what one must recognize as correct concerning Caiaphas, and the fact that he has been moved by the Spirit" (*Comm. Jo.* 28.191; Origen, 332).

The Text in Contemporary Discussion

As with the Gospel as a whole, it is important to remember that the passage is little concerned with accurate reportage but obsessed with Christology. The speech placed in Caiaphas's mouth describes Jesus as the scapegoat. On the annual Day of Atonement, the high priest symbolically cleansed the nation of sin by loading the people's sins onto the goat and sending it into the desert. Caiaphas's words also recall the Christian interpretation of the temple's destruction as a consequence of the Jews' role in the passion and prophesy the messianic ingathering of all peoples joined by faith in Christ.

The congruence of the high priest's words with the Gospel's own theological interests does not of course say anything one way or another about the historicity of the events or words. But they should caution us on the need to read critically, and to remember that even the texts we consider sacred or that mean much to us cannot be disentangled from their historical contexts or the interests of their authors.

11:55—12:11: The Anointing of Jesus at Bethany

The Text in Its Ancient Context

Prior to the third and final Passover of Jesus' public ministry, Jesus eats dinner with the Bethany siblings. At this dinner, Mary anoints Jesus' feet with expensive perfume and wipes his feet with her hair. (This story parallels but does not duplicate the Synoptic story of an unnamed woman who anoints Jesus at the home of Simon the Pharisee; see Matt. 26:6; Mark 14:3; Luke 7:36.) Judas protests that it would have been better to sell the perfume and give the proceeds to the poor.

Jesus responds that the anointing foreshadows his impending death; the poor remain, but Jesus will soon depart.

The Text in the Interpretive Tradition

The church fathers struggled with the question of Judas's moral status. If he was always evil, how could he have been chosen as a disciple? If he became evil only at the end, why would not his association with Jesus have saved him from himself? Augustine's view is that "Judas did not become perverted only at the time when he yielded to the bribery of the Jews and betrayed his Lord. . . . But he was already a thief, already lost, and he followed our Lord in body but not with his heart" (*Tract. Ev. Jo.* 50.10-11; Elowsky 2007, 46).

The Text in Contemporary Discussion

Although Jesus rebukes Judas for commenting on the expense of the ointment, the narrator indirectly acknowledges the validity of the concern, but dismisses it due to the source, for Judas "said this not because he cared about the poor but because he was a thief" (12:6). Yet Jesus' rebuke, "you always have the poor with you, but you do not always have me" (12:8), is problematic, as it places a higher priority on the symbolic preparations for his death (12:7) than on the needs of others. In contemporary society, it can also be difficult to balance the desire to honor individuals or occasions with the responsibility to help the less fortunate.

12:12-50: The Triumphal Entry and End of Jesus' Public Ministry

The Text in Its Ancient Context

Jesus' entry (cf. Matt. 21:1; Mark 11:1; Luke 19:28) is the high point of his ministry, as he is greeted by jubilant crowds waving palm branches and proclaiming him the king of Israel (12:13). This demonstration would have given the Romans ample reason to be concerned about the royal claims made for, if not quite by, Jesus, and to justify a verdict of treason punishable by crucifixion. The Gospel puts this act in a cosmological context, which the disciples do not understand until after his death and glorification (12:16), while the alarm of the Pharisees increases (12:19).

Jesus' triumphal entry is witnessed not only by Jewish crowds and authorities but also by "Greeks" who have gone up to Jerusalem to worship at the festival (12:20). Although it is possible that these were Greek-speaking Jews, Jesus' reaction suggests that they were non-Jews. It was not uncommon for gentiles to attend the temple; indeed, Herod's temple included a Court of the Gentiles (Schmidt 2001, 79). These Greeks approach Philip, who in turn tells Andrew, and they both tell Jesus (12:21). In contrast to the call of the disciples and the Samaritan woman, Jesus refuses to encounter them directly but instead announces that "the hour has come for the Son of Man to be glorified" (12:24). The question of whether gentiles can be part of this new movement is therefore postponed until after Jesus' death. In contrast to the Synoptics, in which Jesus prays that the Father remove this cup from him during the dark night at Gethsemane (Matt. 26:39; Mark 14:36; Luke 22:42), John's Jesus braces for his death: "it is for this reason that I have come to this hour" (12:27). He accepts that he must die in order to fulfill his divine mission and return to the Father.

Nevertheless, he does request something from God: "Father, glorify your name" (12:28). God responds immediately: "I have glorified it, and I will glorify it again" (12:28). Jesus gives the people one last chance to understand his cosmological significance (12:32-36), but they refuse. He hides and departs from them. Even so, the narrator states, many authorities did believe in him but were afraid to confess openly for fear of expulsion from the synagogue (12:42).

The Text in the Interpretive Tradition

Augustine contrasts the Jewish and gentile response to Jesus: "Look how the Jews want to kill him, the Gentiles to see him. But they also were there with the Jews who cried, 'Blessed is he who comes in the name of the Lord, the king of Israel.' Here then are both those of the circumcision and those of the uncircumcision, once so wide apart, coming together like two walls and meeting in the one faith of Christ by the kiss of peace" (*Tract. Ev. Jo.* 51.8; Elowsky 2007, 58). Augustine's interpretation reflects a perspective grounded in the letters of Paul, who provided a theological rationale for the inclusion of the gentiles among God's covenant people (Gal. 4:5; Romans 9–11).

The Text in Contemporary Discussion

Some scholars suggest that the gentiles who want to see Jesus represent the gentile members of the Johannine community (R. E. Brown 1979, 55), and can encourage reflection about the challenges involved in heterogeneous communities when it comes to self-definition. The gentiles who became part of the Jesus community encountered a worldview different from their culture of origin, but they also brought new ideas and customs. The challenge is to allow the group identity to expand and change in response. It is likely that the Gospel exposes some of the negotiations that had to take place in order to forge an identity for its ethnically mixed audience, and the same is true of communities today.

The Book of Glory (13:1—20:31)

13:1-38: Final Dinner

The Text in Its Ancient Context

Whereas in the Synoptics (Matt. 26:26-29; Mark 14:22-25; Luke 22:13-20) Jesus' final meal with the disciples is a Passover seder—the ritual Passover meal that, in the period when the temple was standing, was convened for the eating of the Passover sacrifice—and is marked by the institution of the Eucharist, the Last Supper in John is not a Passover seder but takes place the day before the Passover begins, and it features not the Eucharist but a ritual foot washing.

The pre-Passover timing of this meal, and of the passion narrative as a whole, transforms Jesus' own death into the Passover sacrifice, as it takes place several hours before the festival begins, at the time when the Passover lamb would be slaughtered (R. E. Brown 1970, 556; *m. Pesach* 5.1). The chronology may therefore be theologically motivated, but at the same time, it is also more plausible historically than the Synoptic timing. The Synoptic narrative indicates that the Jewish council put

Jesus on trial during the night of the Passover festival itself, a highly unlikely circumstance given that this would have constituted a violation of Jewish law (Sanders, 298).

The passage raises the interesting but ultimately unanswerable question of whether there were ancient communities of Christ-confessors who rejected or perhaps were not aware of the eucharistic practices of other churches. The eucharistic allusions in the Bread of Life discourse (John 6) would suggest knowledge of this practice, but its absence from the Last Supper story casts doubt on this group's practices.

The narrator provides three crucial pieces of information in the first two verses: Jesus' hour "to depart from this world and go to the Father" has finally come; Jesus would love "his own" to the end (13:1); and "the devil had already put it into the heart of Judas son of Simon Iscariot to betray him" (13:2).

At the table, Jesus explains that just as he had washed the disciples' feet, so also should they wash each other's feet (13:12-13). This was to be an egalitarian act, for "servants are not greater than their master, nor are messengers greater than the one who sent them" (13:16). Jesus surprises his disciples when he prepares them for the betrayal. Though readers have known the betrayer's identity since John 6 (and, likely, before they read or heard this Gospel at all), not so the disciples.

The narrator now introduces a new character: the disciple whom Jesus loved (13:23). If he is new to the readers, he is not new to Jesus. Indeed, he is an intimate friend, not only because he is loved by Jesus—as all the disciples are—but because he reclines next to Jesus, in his bosom, just as Jesus does with God the Father (1:18). This intimacy is acknowledged by Peter, who asks the disciple to address Jesus on his behalf. Jesus hands bread to Judas, who departs, thereby sealing Jesus' fate.

The Gospel returns to the outline of the story shared by all four Gospels, in which Jesus prophesies that Peter will deny him three times (13:38). Before that point, however, he introduces the commandment to "love one another" (13:34). The love commandment sounds expansive, uplifting, and generous, and in this regard it echoes a saying that the rabbinic tractate *The Sayings of the Fathers* attributes to the Pharisaic teacher Hillel: "Be of the followers of Aaron, loving peace, pursuing peace, loving your fellow human beings and bringing them to Torah" (*Abot* 1.12). Nevertheless, the fact that the commandment is given only to the disciples implies that the love is meant only for those who are within the community (Meier, 559).

The Text in the Interpretive Tradition

The church fathers accepted the identification of the Beloved Disciple as John son of Zebedee and proposed various solutions to the problem of his anonymity in the Gospel. Augustine explains that "it was a custom of the sacred writer, when he came to anything relating to himself, to speak of himself as if he were speaking of another. He would give himself a place in the flow of the narrative so that he became one who was the recorder of public events rather than making himself the subject of his preaching" (*Tract. Ev. Jo.* 61.4; Elowsky 2007, 103).

The more important issue concerns Judas's moral culpability. If the devil had put the idea of betrayal into Judas's heart, to what extent is Judas to blame? Does Jesus bear some responsibility as the one who chose his disciples, including the betrayer? Cyril of Alexandria appeals to the principle of freedom of choice in addressing these questions: "Christ chose Judas and associated him with the holy disciples, since at first he certainly possessed the capacity for discipleship. But when, after the temptations of Satan succeeded in making him captive to base greediness for gain, when he was conquered by passion and had become by this means a traitor, then he was rejected by God. This, therefore, was in no way the fault of him who called this man to be an apostle. For it lay in the power of Judas to have saved himself from falling" (*Commentary on the Gospel of John* 9; Elowsky 2007, 99).

Perhaps the most famous interpretation of John's Last Supper is Leonardo da Vinci's mural painting in the refectory in the convent of Santa Maria Della Grazie, Milan (1495–1498). Leonardo catches the dinner party just at the moment that Jesus declares: "One of you will betray me" (13:21). He captures the astonishment and fear on the disciples' faces and their attempts to excuse themselves. Judas is posed to accept the bread, and the Beloved Disciple, portrayed as a young, beardless man, reclines on Jesus, in a pose that prompted the novelist Dan Brown to speculate that this was really Mary Magdalene (D. Brown; Ehrman).

The Text in Contemporary Discussion

Jesus' explanation of the foot washing implies a radical egalitarianism that erases the hierarchies of master-servant and teacher-disciple. This egalitarianism was not incorporated into the institutional structures of the church, but the Johannine passage may open up such possibilities for contemporary communities. Appealing as it might be, however, this model is not without its issues. How does the humility inherent in the act of foot washing mesh with the insistence on Jesus' divine identity? Another issue concerns the question of gender. The text does not specify whether the dinner party also included women, and it therefore lends itself to either interpretation. If the Gospels are to be taken as a source for Christian community—an assumption that is often made but that could be queried nonetheless—John 13 provides some opening for a less hierarchical institution.

14:1—16:33: Farewell Discourses

The Text in Its Ancient Context

After dinner, Jesus speaks for three full chapters. These Farewell Discourses prepare his disciples for his death and for moving forward without him.

Images. The discourses contain several images that make his message more vivid. The first describes "his father's house" as a mansion with many rooms. Jesus promises that he will return and take them to this house (14:2). There may be an allusion here to the Jewish *hekhalot* ("palaces") tradition, involving stories in which a seer visits the heavenly realm and explores its different rooms (see the chariot vision in Ezekiel 1 and *1 Enoch* 17–18). More immediately, the verse also alludes to the temple, which Jesus called his Father's house in 2:16, and to the son/slave contrast in 8:35. Jesus insists that this house can be reached in only one way: "I am the way, and the truth, and the life. No one comes to the Father except through me" (14:6).

A second vivid image is found in 15:1-6, in which Jesus declares himself to be the true vine, and God the vine grower. This vividly illustrates the central tenets of Johannine Christology: that God has planted his creation, the vine, in the world and continues to tend it so that it will bear fruit. The branches—the disciples—must not only gather followers but also ensure the quality of the wine, that is, of the faith in Jesus. Those that cannot bear fruit are pruned. This may be a veiled reference to Judas, the disciple who has been removed from the Twelve. Essential to the production is mutual indwelling; the branch cannot bear fruit except as part of the vine. Jesus exhorts: "Abide in me as I abide in you" (15:4).

Finally, Jesus reassures the disciples using a common apocalyptic motif: the woman in labor, e.g., Rev. 12:2; cf. Isa. 13:8). In the short term, they will "weep and mourn" while the hate-filled world rejoices. But in the larger, cosmic context, it is the disciples who will rejoice, like a woman is in pain during labor but rejoices when the child is born (16:21).

The Love commandment. In chapter 13, Jesus adjures the disciples to love one another. This commandment is repeated and amplified in John 15. The greatest love is "to lay down one's life for one's friends" (15:13). Now that he has revealed all to them, his disciples are his friends. Yet he remains their leader, whose commandments—to go and bear fruit that will last (15:15)—must be obeyed. The idea of dying for one's friends is also expressed in Aristotle's extensive comments on friendship in the *Nicomachean Ethics* 9.1169a. The question, however, is, What constitutes love, and who are the friends (cf. Luke 10:29)?

The Paraclete. Those who are addressed by the love commandment, in turn, will receive another "Advocate" (or Paraclete: Gk. *paraklētos*), who will remain with the disciples forever. The Advocate is the Holy Spirit; he will be sent by the Father, and he will teach the disciples, and remind them of what Jesus said to them in his life. He will testify on Jesus' behalf, and prove the world wrong about sin and righteousness and judgment (16:8). For this reason, Jesus' departure is not only necessary but also beneficial; otherwise, the Advocate will not come (16:7). It is unclear whether the Paraclete will work through the community's leadership, through prophecy, or through other "spiritual gifts" as discussed by Paul in 1 Corinthians 12–14. Nevertheless, the promise of the Paraclete implies the existence of a community that already believes it possesses additional knowledge and authority that has come to them through and after Jesus' death and ascension to God.

Persecution. Alongside these benefits, however, the disciples are warned to expect persecution (15:21) and even death (16:2). The context implies Jewish responsibility for this suffering, but this is not supported by the historical record. This section contributes to the arguments some have made that the Gospel is a martyr's text, intended to give comfort and strength to those who face persecution (Moss).

The Text in the Interpretive Tradition

With regard to 14:2, Augustine suggests that Jesus is "preparing the dwellings by preparing for them the dwellers. As, for instance, when he said, 'In my Father's house are many dwellings.' What else can we suppose the house of God to mean but the temple of God? And what that is, ask the apostle, and he will reply, 'For the temple of God is holy, which temple you are.' This is also the kingdom of God that the Son is yet to deliver up to the Father" (*Tract. Ev. Jo.* 68.2; Elowsky 2007, 121).

The Text in Contemporary Discussion

The love commandment is often quoted to assure non-Christians that love is the essence of the Christian message. Yet within its context, in which Jesus, for the first time, is speaking to the disciples alone and not to a crowd, and warning them of persecution, it seems that this love is turning inward, and characterizing friendship within the community rather than humankind more generally.

17:1-26: Jesus' Prayer

The Text in Its Ancient Context

After these final words to the disciples, Jesus prays to God, not for his own benefit, or for God's, but for those who are listening in, whether directly, as the disciples, or through the written word, as the book's readers or listeners. In contrast to the Synoptic Savior, the Johannine Jesus anticipates his fate with satisfaction and joy, as it marks his return to the glory that he enjoyed with God before the world existed (17:5). In alluding to the prologue, this prayer provides a brief reprieve from the gritty account of the passion, which they are about to read, and recalls the cosmic significance of the narrative as a whole.

The prayer advocates for the disciples, seeks God's protection for them, and thereby reassures them of the joyous end that will await them after their pain and persecution will end. He gives their credentials—they were given to them by God, they kept God's word (quite literally, perhaps: they have kept Jesus, the Logos, safe, 17:6), and they know that Jesus came from God (17:8). Jesus differentiates sharply between those who are "his own" and those who are not. Though his disciples live in the world, they do not belong to the world.

Jesus concludes with a statement of the unity among Father, Son, and believers, and the prayer that the disciples shall indeed enter into the glory "which you have given me because you loved me before the foundation of the world" (17:24). This concludes the revelatory part of the Gospel, and it ends as it begins, with a statement about Jesus' preexistence and the cosmic context for his earthly mission.

The Text in the Interpretive Tradition

How does one live in the world but not be of the world? The *Letter to Diognetus* (late second century) explains by analogy: "What the soul is to the body, Christians are to the world. The soul is dispersed through all the members of the body, and Christians throughout the cities of the world. The soul dwells in the body but is not of the body. Likewise, Christians dwell in the world but are not of the world. The soul, which is invisible, is confined in the body, which is visible. In the same way, Christians are recognized as being in the world, and yet their religion remains invisible" (*Letter to Diognetus* 6; Elowsky 2007, 244).

Cyril of Alexandria has a more pragmatic explanation: "Christ does not wish for the apostles to be set free of human affairs or to be rid of life in the body when they have not yet finished the course of their apostleship or distinguished themselves by the virtues of a godly life. Rather, his desire is to see them live their lives in the company of people in the world and guide the footsteps of those who are his to a state of life well pleasing to God. After they have done this, then at last, with the glory they have achieved, they will be carried into the heavenly city and dwell with the company of the holy angels" (*Commentary on the Gospel of John* 11.9; Elowsky 2007, 250).

The Text in Contemporary Discussion

Jesus prays that the disciples will transmit Jesus' message to the world after he is gone, perhaps aided by the Paraclete. Yet it is rare, or perhaps impossible, for the message to remain the same over time. The churches that developed after Jesus' death, including the Johannine community itself, may have perceived themselves in continuity with Jesus (even when in conflict with each other), but they departed from his teachings in significant ways, including the egalitarianism implied in chapter 13.

18:1—19:16a: Betrayal, Trials, and Denial

The Text in Its Ancient Context

John's account of the events that led directly to Jesus' death are similar in outline, though not always in detail, with the Synoptic versions, suggesting to many scholars that the passion narrative was the first lengthy narrative unit in the Gospel tradition.

Immediately after the prayer, Jesus steps into the garden across the Kidron Valley (18:1), where he is immediately met by Judas, along with a detachment of soldiers and police of the Jewish authorities (18:2-3). There is no "Judas' kiss" (cf. Matt. 26:48; Mark 14:44; Luke 22:47-48). Rather than wait for Judas to identify him, Jesus steps forward and asks, "Whom are you looking for?" (18:4). This echoes the question he first asked of the Baptist's disciples (1:38). Jesus identifies himself simply with "I am he," recalling yet again God's self-identification in Exod. 3:14. Once in custody, he endures an interrogation before a high-priestly authority. In contrast to Mark and Matthew, however, this authority is not the high priest himself—whom Matthew names but Mark leaves anonymous—but Caiaphas's father-in-law, Annas. The episode has led to considerable speculation concerning Annas's ongoing role in and influence over high-priestly matters.

The "high priest" is most interested in Jesus' disciples and teachings. As usual, Jesus responds indirectly: "I have spoken openly to the world; I have always taught in synagogues and in the temple, where all the Jews come together. I have said nothing in secret" (18:20). Jesus' assertion is borne out by his earlier activity. In fact, until the Farewell Discourses, Jesus has taught only crowds, and often in the synagogue or the temple.

Intercut with this interrogation is the story of Peter's denial. By its end, Jesus is presumably in Caiaphas's custody, but what, if anything, occurred between them is not divulged.

The decisive event in the passion sequence, however, is the trial before Pilate. John's Pilate is extremely reluctant to condemn Jesus. He asks Jesus' Jewish captors: "What accusation do you bring against this man?" (18:29). Like Jesus, they do not answer directly, but simply say that had he not been a criminal they would not have handed him over. Pilate suggests that he give Jesus over to them for judgment, but they remind him that it is only Rome that can hand down the death penalty. The narrator points out the necessity of crucifixion to fulfill Jesus' prophecy about his mode of death (18:32).

Because the Jews must remain outside to avoid pre-Passover ritual defilement (18:28), Pilate goes back and forth between them and Jesus. He confronts Jesus with the claim that he is king of the Jews. Jesus poses a question of his own: "Do you ask this on your own, or did others tell you about me?" (18:34). Pilate reminds him that it is his own people who have handed him over, and now asks more generally, "What have you done?" (18:35). Jesus then responds, enigmatically, to the previous question: "My kingdom is not from this world," for his disciples are not fighting on his behalf (18:36). Pilate struggles to comprehend: "So you are a king?" (18:37). But Jesus, as always, avoids a direct answer: "You say that I am a king." As for what he says, "For this I was born, and for this I came into the world, to testify to the truth" (18:37), setting the stage for Pilate's famous but cryptic question: "What is truth?" (18:38). Without awaiting a response, Pilate goes back out to the Jews and declares that he finds no reason to prosecute Jesus.

Instead of releasing Jesus, however, he offers the crowds a choice between Jesus and Barabbas. Although the Gospel describes this as a Passover custom (18:39), there is no evidence for it outside the Gospels' passion accounts (cf. Matt. 27:15; Mark 15.6; Luke 23:17). The Jews insist on Barabbas. Barabbas is described as a *lēstēs* (18:40), which can mean "robber" or "bandit." In the writings of Josephus, the term is used to describe guerrilla fighters who both stole and incited violence against Rome (*War* 2.253–54). The fact that Barabbas was sentenced to crucifixion, a punishment normally reserved for those convicted of treason, may imply that he was such a fighter, rather than a mere thief.

And still the death sentence is not passed. Pilate has Jesus flogged and then finally brings him out to face his accusers: "Behold the man" (19:5 KJV). The chief priests and police cry out for his crucifixion, as Pilate insists a third time: "I find no case against him" (19:6). The Jews again insist that he has broken their law by claiming to be Son of God, a claim that leads Pilate to approach Jesus again: "Where are you from?" (19:9). In this way, the Gospel reminds the reader of the messianic criterion of unknown origins that has been woven through the narrative.

Jesus does not respond until Pilate threatens him: "Do you not know that I have power to release you, and power to crucify you?" (19:10). But Jesus denies that Pilate has any independent power; rather, "the one who handed me over to you is guilty of a greater sin." (19:11). If Jesus' death by crucifixion is essential to the fulfillment of his mission and his return to God, why is Pilate blameless but the Jewish authorities guilty? Finally, Pilate relents and hands Jesus over to be crucified (18:16a).

As in the Synoptics, Pilate is extremely reluctant to condemn Jesus, and uses several tactics—deflection, negation—to extricate himself from the situation. In contrast to the Synoptics, however, John's Gospel suggests that Pilate was more interested in and engaged with Jesus beyond his potential to stir up a crowd. This interest is conveyed, first, by his question: "What is truth?" to which Jesus, continuing his near silence, does not respond (18:38). A second hint is found in the formality with which he presents Jesus, now wearing the crown of thorns and "royal" robe, to the crowd. The King James Version captures the nuance of the Greek, with its translation: "Behold the man" (19:5); even more striking is the famous Latin phrase of the Vulgate: "Ecce homo." The third, occurring in the next section, is the *titulus* that proclaims Jesus the king of the Jews, and his insistence on this wording in the face of the chief priests' protests (19:21-22).

Pilate's interest can be read in two different ways: as a tacit but sincere acknowledgment of Jesus' royal status (with acceptance of Jesus' declaration that he is the head of a kingdom that is not from this world, 18:36), and as irony intended to humiliate Jesus (as the soldiers did when robing and crowning him; 19:2-3) and to mock the royal claims made on his behalf.

The Text in the Interpretive Tradition

Augustine opted for the former view. He not only exonerated the Roman governor but also drew him in as a witness to the "truth," suggesting that the "truth" that Jesus was the king of the Jews was inscribed in Pilate's heart, as it was on the *titulus* (*Tract. Ev. Jo.* 115.5; Elowsky 2007, 294).

Cyril of Alexandria has a less elevated view of the governor: "When he called Jesus king of the Jews, he spoke in jest and tried to abate by ridicule the anger of the furious mob. He also clearly showed that this particular accusation was brought in vain. A Roman officer would never have thought a man condemned of plotting for a kingdom and revolution against Rome worthy to be released. He bore witness, then, to Jesus' utter innocence by the very reasons he gave for Jesus' release" (*Commentary on the Gospel of John* 12; Elowsky 2007, 294).

The Text in Contemporary Discussion

The trial narrative is a case study on the use of intimidation in legal and political processes. This theme operates not only on the story level—the Jews intimidating Pilate into sentencing Jesus to death—but also in the potential impact of the Gospel on its ideal readers: to leave them with no alternative but to blame the Jews for Jesus' death.

19:16b-42 Crucifixion and Burial

The Text in Its Ancient Context

The events wind to their inevitable conclusion. The crucifixion field is here called Golgotha, an Aramaic term meaning "The Place of the Skull" (19:17). A trilingual *titulus*—in Hebrew, Latin, and Greek—is placed on the cross, reading "Jesus of Nazareth, the King of the Jews." The chief priests object to the wording, arguing that it should read, "This man said, I am King of the Jews" (19:21), but Pilate refuses to change it, thereby indirectly acknowledging Jesus' sovereignty (19:22). The trilingual nature of the *titulus* testifies to the diversity that the Gospel writer presumed was the case in Jerusalem.

Even on the cross, Jesus maintains his presence of mind. The narrator notes that three women are standing near the cross: his mother, his aunt, and Mary Magdalene (19:25). From the cross, Jesus tells his mother, "Woman, here is your son," and says to the disciple, "Here is your mother" (19:26-27). On the face of it, Jesus is here showing his filial solicitude by ensuring that his mother will be cared for after his death. But interpreters have more often sought symbolic interpretations. It seems clear that the Beloved Disciple represents the ideal believer, but who or what would the mother represent? R. H. Strachan (319) suggests that she symbolizes the Jewish heritage that is now being entrusted to Christians; for Bultmann (673), she represents Jewish Christianity, now entrusted to gentile Christianity. Raymond Brown (1970, 925–26), drawing on the imagery of John 16:21, suggests that she evokes "Lady Zion," who brings forth a new people in the messianic age that Jesus' death ushers in. This interpretation ties in well with the promise that believers will be reborn (3:3) as children of God (1:12-13); nevertheless, the absence of any references to a maternal figure in these other contexts makes it difficult to conclude that this is meaning the evangelist or his first readers would have read into or out of this scene.

At the point of his death, the narrator says, Jesus declares his thirst, to fulfill Scripture (Ps. 69:21). He sips wine from a sponge on a hyssop branch, declares, "It is finished," bows his head, and gives up his spirit (19:30). In this moment, as throughout the Gospel, Jesus fully and calmly accepts the necessity of his death to the fulfillment of God's will and his own return to the Father. Interestingly, despite the numerous scenes involving food and drink, it is only at the moment before his death that Jesus himself explicitly consumes food or drink (Kobel, 301–6). The reference to hyssop recalls the Passover sacrifice, as it was used to mark the doorposts before the exodus (Exod. 12:22). Its mention here recalls the theme, distinct to this Gospel, of Jesus as the Passover sacrifice. This identification of Jesus as the Passover lamb is further strengthened by the fact that, unlike the other men crucified alongside him, Jesus did not have his legs broken (19:31-32). The narrator explains that this was because he was already dead (19:33). But in keeping his legs intact, the Roman soldiers also (inadvertently) ensure his acceptability as a Passover sacrifice, which had to be "without blemish" (Exod. 12:5).

After his death, Jesus' side is pierced, and "at once blood and water came out" (19:34). What this means from a physiological point of view has been much discussed but remains unclear (Wilkinson). Like many other elements of this Gospel, however, the scene has a symbolic meaning, perhaps alluding to the spiritually cleansing role of water in baptism and foot washing. The passage may also link back to 7:38, in which Jesus quotes a Scripture (the source is unclear, but Prov. 18:4; Isa. 58:11; and Sir. 24:30-33 have been suggested)—"Out of the believer's heart shall flow rivers of living water"—that the narrator interprets as a reference to the Spirit. If so, the scene may be christological, proclaiming Jesus as both human (blood) and divine (water). The blood may also suggest a eucharistic interpretation, whereby believers are able to imbibe Christ by virtue of his death on the cross. To emphasize the importance of this event, the narrator stresses the reliability of the witness, referring to the Beloved Disciple (19:35). A secret disciple, Joseph of Arimathea, along with Nicodemus, anoints and wraps Jesus' body and buries it in the garden near Golgotha. This passage lends credence to the view that Nicodemus, too, was a secret disciple. The preparation for Passover, the season of salvation, has been completed; the lamb has been sacrificed, his mission in the world accomplished, and his return to the Father assured.

The Text in the Interpretive Tradition

Augustine indicates that a trilingual *titulus* was needed: "the Hebrew because of the Jews who gloried in the law of God; the Greek, because of the wise people among the gentiles; and the Latin, because of the Romans who at that very time were exercising sovereign power over many, in fact, over almost all countries" (*Tract. Ev. Jo.* 117.4; Elowsky 2007, 311). He also expands on the motif of Pilate as a convert. The governor was "the wild olive [see Rom. 11:17] to be grafted on, while the leaders of the Jews represented the broken-off branches" (*Serm.* 218.7; Elowsky 2007, 312). In this passage, Augustine is expanding on the Gospel's clues that Pilate was attracted to Jesus' message.

The Text in Contemporary Discussion

The crucifixion scene is perhaps the most poignant in the entire Gospel tradition. For John, it is in Jesus' death that he is most completely and profoundly both human and divine. His calm acceptance has served as a model for martyrs—those who must, or choose to die for their beliefs—from the early Christian period to the present day (Chilton), even as the Gospel's eschatology, which assures believers that they will follow Jesus to the rooms he has prepared for them in his Father's house, made it possible for Christians to face death calmly in times of persecution.

20:1-18: Mary Magdalene and the Gardener

The Text in Its Ancient Context

The Gospels are silent on the period of time between Jesus' burial and the discovery of the empty tomb, but all depict women as the ones who discover the empty tomb on Sunday morning. In John, Mary Magdalene comes alone, sees that the stone is rolled away, and runs to tell Peter and the "other" disciple that "they" have removed the body (20:2). The two men run to the tomb. The other disciple reaches the tomb first, but it is Peter who enters first. When the other disciple goes in, he believes. *What* he believes, however, is not specified. The narrator does not help clarify matters when he states that "as yet they did not understand the scripture, that he must rise from the dead" (20:9), for there is no specific biblical quotation to this effect. The two men return to their homes, but Mary remains weeping at the tomb. She then looks in and sees two angels (20:11-12), who ask, "Woman, why are you weeping?" She turns and sees Jesus but does not recognize him. He asks, "Whom are you looking for?" the same question he asked the Baptist's followers (1:38) and the forces who had come to arrest him (19:7). Mary mistakes him for the gardener and politely asks him to tell her where he put the body, so that she can take it away. He then calls her by name, as he had called Lazarus, and reveals his identity to her. She responds "Rabbouni!" which the narrator explains as meaning Teacher in Hebrew, though in fact it is Aramaic (20:16). He then tells her not to hold on to him; whether Mary had already touched him, or was merely reaching out to do so, is not stated, but the reason is "because I have not yet ascended to the Father" (20:17). Jesus' reason suggests that he is undergoing a process of change with regard to his corporeality that physical contact might interrupt. At the same time, one cannot ignore the hint of sexual tension in the scene. Mary's search for Jesus' body echoes the language of the Song of Solomon (Song of Songs), in which the female lover searches for her groom (see esp. Song of Sol. 3:1-4). Other parallels include the reference to "peering in" (John 20:5; Song of Sol. 2:9) and the use of spices (John 19:39; Song of Sol. 1:12; 3:6) (Reinhartz 1999). This is not to say that John portrayed Mary and Jesus as physical lovers. Even in the first century, the Song of Songs had acquired a spiritual interpretation as an allegory of the love between God and the covenant people, and it is likely that this allegory lies in the foreground of the Gospel's allusions to the Song of Songs. At the same time, this section has been one source of the speculation found in second-century and later sources of a special relationship between Jesus and Mary Magdalene that is expressed explicitly in the *Gospel of Thomas*, the *Gospel of Philip*, and the *Gospel of Mary* (Schaberg; King).

More important, he gives her a special mission: to go to "my brothers"—the male disciples—and tell them that he is ascending to the Father (20:17). She does so, saying, "I have seen the Lord" (20:18). Their response, if any, is not recorded.

The Text in the Interpretive Tradition

Rufinus of Aquileia (340–410) noted the story's echoes of the Song of Songs, which he interprets, alongside passages from the Psalms, the Prophets, and, indeed, all of Scripture, as a prophecy of the resurrection: "This was foretold in the Song of Songs: 'on my bed I sought the one my soul loves. I sought him in the night and did not find him' [Song of Sol. 3:1]. Of those also who found him and held him by the feet, it is foretold, in the same book, 'I will hold the one my soul loves and will not let him go' [Song of Sol. 3:4]" (*Commentary on the Apostles' Creed* 30; Elowsky 2007, 344).

The Text in Contemporary Discussion

The Song of Songs allusions subtly place Mary and Jesus in the role of lovers, a hint that is reinforced when he does not permit her to touch him. Whatever their historical relationship was, it has been transformed by his death. More important for contemporary purposes is to note that Mary is an "apostle to the apostles." This description is thought to have originated in the *Commentary on the Song of Songs* 25.6 (Cerrato, 191) written by (or perhaps attributed to) Hippolytus of Rome (170–235) (Haskins, 65; Ernst, 95–117). This point reinforces the theme of egalitarianism found in Jesus' encounter with the Samaritan woman (also an apostle), and in the foot washing at the Last Supper. But in contrast to the Samaritan woman, there is no evidence that Mary's testimony had any effect on the disciples. This silence replicates the difficulty that some women have experienced in being respected and trusted for their knowledge. Even if the (male) disciples' response is not evident, the Gospel itself is a vehicle through which her testimony can be appreciated.

20:19-29: Appearances to the Disciples

The Text in Its Ancient Context

That evening, Jesus materializes in the room in which the disciples are hiding from the Jews and announces his presence with a traditional greeting: "Peace be with you" (20:19; cf. Tob. 12:47). He identifies himself by showing his hands and side, commissions them to carry on his work (20:21), and, emulating God's act of creating Adam (Gen. 2:7), he breathes the Holy Spirit onto them. One disciple, who has come to be known as "Doubting" Thomas because of this scene, was absent and refuses to believe, "Unless I see the mark of the nails in his hands, and put my finger in the mark of the nails and my hand in his side" (2:25). The following week, Jesus reappears. Whereas Mary was forbidden from touching Jesus, Thomas is now invited to do so, raising the question of Jesus' post-crucifixion corporeality. Throughout the Gospel, Jesus' crucifixion has been described as an exaltation (e.g., 3:14), suggesting that his death is simultaneously his return to the Father. If the ascension is a return to the same preexistent state that the Word had before it (or he) was made flesh (1:14), then it is reasonable to think that it also marks a return to a noncorporeal existence. His ability to enter the room despite the locked doors also implies incorporeality. And yet, he invites Thomas to touch him. The inconsistency with regard to the status of Jesus' body has suggested to some scholars that the Thomas story is a secondary addition (R. E. Brown 1970, 1032). This is certainly plausible, particularly in light of 20:29, which is obviously addressed to the Gospel's audiences. The narrative is silent as to whether Thomas does touch Jesus, but he immediately confesses his faith: "My Lord and my God!" (2:28). Jesus gently chides him: "Have you believed because you have seen me? Blessed are those who have not seen and yet have come to believe" (20:29). This passage brings to fruition the pattern that began with the call of the first disciples: the emphasis on believing through the testimony of others. In chiding Thomas, Jesus is addressing later readers who cannot see Jesus directly but who have access to the reliable testimony of the Gospel (see 19:35) as a basis for faith. The story therefore reinforces the authority of the Gospel as a source for its readers' christological understanding and therefore also their salvation.

The Text in the Interpretive Tradition

Gregory the Great (540–604) suggested that "the unbelief of Thomas is more profitable to our faith than the belief of the other disciples. For the touch by which he is brought to believe confirms our minds in belief, beyond all question" (*Forty Gospel Homilies* 26; Elowsky 2007, 367). Leo the Great (400–461) acknowledges the difficulty of believing without seeing, but argues that "it is the strength of great minds and the light of firmly faithful souls unhesitatingly to believe what is not seen with the bodily sight and to focus your affections where you cannot direct your gaze" (*Sermon* 74.1; Elowsky 2007, 374).

The Text in Contemporary Discussion

Jesus' remark to Thomas provides space for considering the relationship between the written word and historical, philosophical, and spiritual truths. The norms of historiographical writing have changed since the late first century; we now expect historians and biographers to report the facts and not only their interpretations thereof. Nevertheless, every attempt to convey facts also entails shaping those facts into a story, which in turn complicates its relationship to fact. No wonder that Thomas would not believe something so unusual as resurrection without seeing the evidence for himself. And yet, as the story itself emphasizes, there are many occasions when we must rely on the testimony of others, even in matters of crucial importance to our own well-being.

20:30-31 Conclusion and Statement of Purpose

The Text in Its Ancient Context

Although it is followed by a final chapter, John 20:30-31 is the conclusion and statement of purpose of the Gospel as a whole. The passage acknowledges that the Gospel presents only a selection of Jesus' many acts and directs our attention to the disciples as the primary witnesses. Like 4:48, the passage is aimed directly at the readers or listeners. What is remarkable about this passage is the important role that it envisages for "this book" in the lives of its audiences.

On the surface, the intent of these verses is clear: to persuade "you" that Jesus is the Messiah, the Son of God, and thereby to lead "you" to eternal life. But the meaning is murkier than one might suppose, due to a textual variant in 20:31: "so that you may [come to] believe" (NRSV). The conjunction "so that" requires a verb in the subjunctive mood (English: "may" or "might"). The oldest manuscripts have the verb "believe" in the present subjunctive form, meaning "that you may continue to believe." This variant implies that the Gospel was written in order to deepen the faith of an audience that already professes belief in Christ. Other manuscripts, however, have the verb in the aorist subjunctive, meaning "that you may come to believe." This variant suggests that the Gospel was written in order to persuade nonbelievers to become believers; in other words, for missionary purposes. Although the New Revised Standard Version has chosen the latter reading in its translation, the scholarly consensus is that the Gospel is not a missionary document, because its language and concepts are better understood as addressing insiders rather than outsiders.

The Text in the Interpretive Tradition

For Origen, reading Jesus' words in the Gospels was tantamount to hearing him directly. He comments that "the Samaritans renounce their faith that was based on the speech of the woman when they discover that hearing the Savior himself is better than that faith . . . Heracleon says, 'People believe in the Savior first by being led by people. But whenever they read his words, they no longer believe because of human testimony alone, but because of the truth itself'" (*Comm. Jo.* 13.353; Elowsky 2006, 170).

The Text in Contemporary Discussion

The Gospel's statement of purpose, like the prologue, calls on readers to situate themselves within the Gospel, that is, to be the "you" that the Gospel is addressing. This "you" is an idealized, fully compliant reader who will situate him- or herself alongside the narrator, the disciples, the Samaritan woman, and other positive characters. Such a reader will not only accept that Jesus is the Christ and Son of God as described in the Gospel but also take on the negative representation of the unbelieving world—represented by "the Jews"—that runs throughout the narrative. Real readers, however, have a choice as to whether or how much of the Gospel to take on in their own personal faith and spiritual journey. Christian readers may choose to accept some sections and resist others. Non-Christian readers may resist the fundamental message but nevertheless engage with other elements of the Gospel, such as its rich symbolism or its positive representation of women.

21:1-25: Epilogue

The Text in Its Ancient Context

On the basis of its content and literary style, this chapter has sometimes been viewed as a later, non-Johannine addition. Unlike 7:53—8:11, however, the manuscript evidence does not show that it circulated separately from the rest of the Gospel or that the Gospel originally ended with chapter 20. Nevertheless, it presents a somewhat different image of the disciples than the rest of the Gospel.

The chapter recounts Jesus' third and final postresurrection appearance, during the disciples' fishing expedition by the Sea of Galilee. Until Jesus appears, the fish are not biting, but when he instructs them about where to cast the net, their haul is huge: 153 large fish. They cook and eat some with bread, in a scene that recalls the multiplication of the loaves and fishes (John 6).

After breakfast, Jesus asks Peter three times whether Peter loves him, and instructs him to tend the flock (20:15-17). In doing so, Jesus erases the shame of the threefold denial, and installs Peter as the shepherd who will lead them in Jesus' absence. The reemergence of the shepherd and sheep metaphor clashes with the fishing symbolism, though both sets of images are used in the Gospel to refer to the gathering of believers and followers. Also jarring is the elevation of Peter over the Beloved Disciple, who has been Jesus' closest follower to this point. Jesus concludes his charge to Peter with an enigmatic prophecy: "when you were younger, you used to fasten your own belt and to go wherever you wished. But when you grow old, you will stretch out your hands, and someone else will fasten a belt around you and take you where you do not wish to go" (21:18). The narrator attempts to clarify that Jesus "said this to indicate the kind of death by which he would glorify God" (21:19).

Peter then asks: what about the Beloved Disciple (21:20)? This question elicits an even more opaque response: "If it is my will that he remain until I come, what is that to you? Follow me!" (21:22). The narrator carefully explains that Jesus has used a conditional formulation ("If it is my will . . .") that does not necessarily promise that the disciple will live, but neither does it declare his death. Many have speculated that the Beloved Disciple, while portrayed in an idealized fashion, was the founder and leader of the Johannine community (R. E. Brown 1979). If so, the story suggests that by the time of writing (or perhaps the time of the final redaction), the disciple had already died. Nevertheless, the narrator asserts that "this is the disciple who is testifying to these things and has written them, and we know that his testimony is true" (21:24).

While some have suggested that John 21 was a later addition to the Gospel, the majority opinion views it as original to the final version of the Gospel (for discussion see Köstenberger, 582–86). Even if it was written or redacted by the same person or group that is responsible for the rest of the Gospel, the ending may serve to bring this Gospel closer to the Synoptics, in which Peter is the disciple closest to Jesus.

The Text in the Interpretive Tradition

The precise number of fish has encouraged considerable speculation. Ammonius (fifth century) suggests that "the hundred can be understood to mean the fullness of the Gentiles. The fifty refers to the elect of Israel who have been saved. And the three set one's mind on the revelation of the holy Trinity, to whose glory the life of the believers who were caught in the dragnet is naturally connected" (*Fragments on John* 637; Elowsky 2007, 381).

Augustine offers a more complex calculation: "When to the number of 10, representing the Law, we add the Holy Spirit as represented by 7, we have 17. And when this number is used for the adding together of every serial number it contains, from 1 up to itself, the sum amounts to 153. . . . All therefore who are sharers in such grace are symbolized by this number. . . . This number has, besides, three times over, the number of 50, and 3 in addition, with reference to the mystery of the Trinity; while, again, the number of 50 is made up by multiplying 7 by 7, with the addition of 1. . . . And we know that it was the fiftieth day after our Lord's ascension that the Holy Spirit was sent, for whom the disciples were commanded to wait according to the promise. It was not, then, without a purpose that these fishes were descried as so many in number and so large in size" (*Tract. Ev. Jo.*122.8–9; Elowsky 2007, 382).

The Text in Contemporary Discussion

The epilogue rehabilitates Peter, who had played second fiddle to the Beloved Disciple since chapter 13. This may well be the result of changing circumstances in the Johannine community—the death of its founder—but it also speaks to the ways in which narratives confer authority and how succession is managed.

From beginning to end, this Gospel keeps a steady eye on its readers or hearers. Whether the evangelist envisaged an audience beyond the late first-century community to which it was most immediately addressed is not known. From a vantage point some two millennia later, however, it is clear that the Gospel of John has engaged, inspired, and challenged many readers in many eras, locations, and situations, and continues today to provide ample material for grappling with the fundamental historical, spiritual, and theological questions of human existence.

Works Cited

Anderson, Paul N., Felix Just, and Tom Thatcher. 2007. *John, Jesus, and History*. Atlanta: Society of Biblical Literature.

Brown, Dan. 2003. *The Da Vinci Code: A Novel*. New York: Doubleday.

Brown, Raymond Edward. 1966. *The Gospel according to John I–XII*. AB 29. Garden City, NY: Doubleday.

———. 1970. *The Gospel according to John XIII–XXI*. AB 29a. Garden City, NY: Doubleday.

———. 1979. *The Community of the Beloved Disciple*. New York: Paulist.

Bultmann, Rudolf. 1971. *The Gospel of John: A Commentary*. Philadelphia: Westminster.

Cerrato, J. A. 2002. *Hippolytus between East and West: The Commentaries and the Provenance of the Corpus*. Oxford: Oxford University Press.

Chilton, Bruce. 2008. *Abraham's Curse: The Roots of Violence in Judaism, Christianity, and Islam*. New York: Doubleday.

Crown, Alan David, Reinhard Pummer, and Abraham Tal. 1993. *A Companion to Samaritan Studies*. Tübingen: Mohr Siebeck.

Ehrman, Bart D. 2004. *Truth and Fiction in The Da Vinci Code: A Historian Reveals What We Really Know about Jesus, Mary Magdalene, and Constantine*. Oxford: Oxford University Press.

Elowsky, Joel C. 2006. *John 1–10*. Ancient Christian Commentary on Scripture, New Testament 4a. Downers Grove, IL: InterVarsity Press.

———. 2007. *John 11–21*. Ancient Christian Commentary on Scripture, New Testament 4b. Downers Grove, IL: InterVarsity Press.

Ernst, Allie M. 2009. *Martha from the Margins: The Authority of Martha in Early Christian Tradition*. Leiden: Brill.

Eslinger, Lyle. 1987. "The Wooing of the Woman at the Well: Jesus, the Reader and Reader-Response Criticism." *Literature and Theology* 1, no. 2:167–83.

Fortna, Robert Tomson. 1970. *The Gospel of Signs: A Reconstruction of the Narrative Source Underlying the Fourth Gospel.* London: Cambridge University Press.

Fredriksen, Paula. 1999. *Jesus of Nazareth, King of the Jews: A Jewish Life and the Emergence of Christianity*. New York: Knopf.

Freund, Richard A., Rami Arav, and Bethsaida Excavations Project. 1995. *Bethsaida: A City by the North Shore of the Sea of Galilee*. Kirksville, MO: Truman State University Press.

Hachlili, Rachel. 2005. *Jewish Funerary Customs, Practices and Rites in the Second Temple Period*. Leiden: Brill.

Haskins, Susan. 1994. *Mary Magdalen: Myth and Metaphor*. New York: Harcourt, Brace.

Heschel, Abraham Joshua. 1951. *The Sabbath, Its Meaning for Modern Man*. New York: Farrar, Straus and Young.

King, Karen L. 2003. *The Gospel of Mary of Magdala: Jesus and the First Woman Apostle*. Santa Rosa, CA: Polebridge.

Kobel, Esther. 2011. *Dining with John: Communal Meals and Identity Formation in the Fourth Gospel and Its Historical and Cultural Context*. Leiden: Brill.

Köstenberger, Andreas J. 2004. *John*. Baker Exegetical Commentary on the New Testament. Grand Rapids: Baker Academic.

Levine, Amy-Jill. 2003. *A Feminist Companion to John*. 2 vols. London: Sheffield Academic Press.

———. 2006. *The Misunderstood Jew: The Church and the Scandal of the Jewish Jesus*. San Francisco: HarperSanFrancisco.

Lincoln, Andrew T. 2005. *The Gospel according to Saint John*. Peabody, MA: Hendrickson.

Lowe, Malcolm F. 1976. "Who Were the 'Ioudaioi'?" *NovT* 18, no. 2:101–30.

Martyn, J. Louis. 2003. *History and Theology in the Fourth Gospel.* 3rd ed. NTL. Louisville: Westminster John Knox.

Mason, Steve. 2007. "Jews, Judaeans, Judaizing, Judaism: Problems of Categorization in Ancient History." *JSJ* 38:457–512.

Meier, John P. 2009. *A Marginal Jew: Rethinking the Historical Jesus.* Vol. 4, *Law and Love*. New Haven: Yale University Press.

Miller, David. 2010. "The Meaning of Ioudaios and Its Relationship to Other Group Labels in Ancient 'Judaism.'" *Currents in Biblical Research* 9, no. 1:98–126.

Moss, Candida R. 2010. *The Other Christs: Imitating Jesus in Ancient Christian Ideologies of Martyrdom*. New York: Oxford University Press.

Origen. 1993. *Commentary on the Gospel according to John. Books 13–32.* Translated by Ronald E. Heine. Washington, DC: Catholic University of America Press.

Painter, John. 2010. "Johannine Literature: The Gospel and Letters of John." In *The Blackwell Companion to the New Testament*, edited by David Edward Aune, 344–72. Malden, MA: Wiley-Blackwell.

Phillips, Gary A. 1979. "'This Is a Hard Saying; Who Can Be a Listener to It?' The Creation of the Reader in John 6." In *SBLSP*, edited by Paul Achtemeier, 185–96. Missoula, MT: Scholars Press.

Reinhartz, Adele. 1989. "Great Expectations: A Reader-Oriented Approach to Johannine Christology and Eschatology." *Literature and Theology* 3, no. 1:61–76.

———. 1992. *The Word in the World: The Cosmological Tale in the Fourth Gospel.* Atlanta: Scholars Press.

———. 1999. "To Love the Lord: An Intertextual Reading of John 20." In *The Labour of Reading: Essays in Honour of Robert C. Culley*, edited by Fiona Bladk, Roland Boer, Christian Kelm, and Erin Runions, 56–69. SemeiaSt. Atlanta: Scholars Press.

———. 2001a. "'Jews' and Jews in the Fourth Gospel." In *Anti-Judaism and the Fourth Gospel: Papers of the Leuven Colloquium, 2000*, edited by R. Bieringer, Didier Pollefeyt, and F. Vandecasteele-Vanneuville, 341–56. Assen, the Netherlands: Royal Van Gorcum.

———. 2001b. "John 8:31-59 from a Jewish Perspective." In *Remembering for the Future 2000: The Holocaust in an Age of Genocides*, edited by John K. Roth and Elisabeth Maxwell-Meynard, 2:787–97. London: Palgrave.

Sanders, E. P. 1985. *Jesus and Judaism*. Philadelphia: Fortress Press.

Schaberg, Jane. 2002. *The Resurrection of Mary Magdalene: Legends, Apocrypha, and the Christian Testament.* New York: Continuum.

Schmidt, Francis. 2001. *How the Temple Thinks: Identity and Social Cohesion in Ancient Judaism*. Sheffield: Sheffield Academic Press.

Smith, D. Moody. 2001. *John among the Gospels*. Columbia: University of South Carolina Press.

Strachan, R. H. 1941. *The Fourth Gospel, Its Significance and Environment*. London: Student Christian Movement Press.

Von Wahlde, Urban C. 1989. *The Earliest Version of John's Gospel: Recovering the Gospel of Signs*. Wilmington, DE: Michael Glazier.

———. 2000. "'The Jews' in the Gospel of John: Fifteen Years of Research (1983–1998)." *ETL* 76:30–55.

Wilkinson, John. 1975. "Incident of the Blood and Water in John 19:34." *Scottish Journal of Theology* 28, no. 2:149–72.

ACTS AS A HISTORY OF THE EARLY CHURCH

Demetrius K. Williams

If the Gospel of Luke and the Acts of the Apostles were written by the same person—the view taken here, though it is a controversial matter to which we will return below—the author has the distinction of being the only writer of a Gospel to provide a sequel. Acts offered to the early church an account of Christian origins and an edifying narration of the spread of the gospel, chronicling the notable deeds and challenges of the first generation of Jesus-followers and addressing several issues confronting the early church in its infancy, the most pressing of which were the social and theological challenges resulting from expansion (i.e., the inclusion of gentiles); the early church's relationship with Judaism; and its spread into and navigation of the cultural and political environment of Rome (C. Matthews, 183). The commentary that follows will trace these themes through the work; this essay will discuss Acts as the single historical writing in the New Testament.

The designation "Luke-Acts" considers the Gospel and Acts together as a single two-volume literary project, though these were separated early on in the ecclesial tradition: there are no extant manuscripts or canon lists in which they appear joined together. The patristic writers treated Luke and Acts separately, although they acknowledged their common authorship. Their separation was likely a result of the different literary types and functions of the two documents within the canon (which is organized by genre, Gospels, History, Letters, Apocalypse). The Gospel of Luke is similar to the other Gospels, but Acts more closely resembles other well-known literary genres in the ancient world, historical writings in general, but also the ancient romance genre that included travel, shipwreck, and danger. On the one hand, Luke provides both a kind of ancient "biography" of the founder (Jesus) and as an introduction to the deeds of the first generation of Jesus' followers as depicted in Acts. The latter writing, on the other hand, serves as an introduction to the letters of Paul, even though it was likely written decades later than they. (Note, too, that the letters ordinarily begin with Paul's Letter to the Romans and that Acts ends with Paul in Rome, openly preaching the gospel without hindrance.) Their separation within the canon allows the two writings to perform these different literary and ecclesial functions (Johnson, 187–88).

While Luke-Acts is generally believed to be the work of a single author, the traditional attribution of these writings to Luke—"the beloved physician" and companion of Paul (see Col. 4:14; Philem. 24; 2 Tim. 4:11)—has been challenged. Neither the Gospel nor the Acts includes a name in the superscription of the earliest manuscripts. (Superscriptions were added to the Gospels in the early second century, during heated ecclesial debates concerning to whom "the Scriptures" belonged—the emerging proto-orthodox movement, or the "heretics," or even to Judaism, for that matter, as we see being argued in the *Epistle of Barnabas*.) As in the commentary, I refer here to the author as "Luke" as a matter of convenience (Williams 2007, 213).

Dating the Acts of the Apostles

Different proposed dates for Acts correspond to very different understandings of the character and purpose of the writing. Three distinct periods have emerged as prominent candidates: early (62–70 CE), intermediate (80–90 CE), and late (110–150 CE; Tyson, 1–23; Drane, 245–47).

Those scholars who prefer an early date believe Paul's arrival and sojourn in Rome (Acts 28) most likely occurred between 58 and 60 CE. On this view, the author of Acts, who included ample and detailed descriptions of Paul's earlier trials, did not provide a description of the final trial in Rome or its outcome because Acts was written before that trial took place. This would also explain why Acts does not mention any of Paul's letters, since they had not been collected and circulated at so early a date. Further, the so-called we-sections (Acts 16:10-17; 20:5-15; 21:1-18; 27:1-28), which appear to imply that the narrator was present with Paul as an "eyewitness" on a number of important occasions, are taken as evidence that at least chapters 13–28 depend on a firsthand report, and the character of these chapters is taken to suggest the historical reliability of the book as a whole. The author's intention presumably was to document and describe the spread of the gospel from Jerusalem to Rome, and once Paul arrived at this destination, that task was completed.

Scholars who favor an intermediate date for Acts point out that while the Roman destruction of Jerusalem and its temple in 70 CE is not mentioned in Acts, it is alluded to in the Gospel of Luke (21:20-24). Furthermore, if Luke used the Gospel of Mark, which was arguably written between 66 and 70 CE, Luke-Acts could not have been written before this time. These scholars propose a date before 90 CE, however, because the author does not seem to know of Paul's letters, which were presumably collected and being circulated by that date. This dating, perhaps in the mid-70s to mid-80s, casts doubt on arguments for an "eyewitness" account of the life of Paul. The author is arguably a generation removed from the persons and events about which he writes, and while he devotes considerable attention to Paul, he fails to mention important aspects of the apostle's teaching; for example, his preaching of justification by faith for gentiles (Galatians 3 and Romans 4), or the validity of his identity as an apostle (see 1 Corinthians 9; 2 Corinthians 3; Rom. 1:1). (The criteria for being an apostle in Acts 1:21-22 implicitly exclude Paul, notwithstanding Acts 14:4, 14, where

Paul and Barnabas are called apostles—perhaps reflecting a source used by the author and not his own view.) On this view, it would have been highly unlikely for an author who had been Paul's close associate and companion to have overlooked or excluded these and other essential Pauline concerns. Furthermore, Acts expresses attitudes and beliefs that became common in the postapostolic age and tends to smooth over tensions in the early church, portraying the apostles as unified and in mutual agreement in matters over which Paul's letters indicate tension and debate.

Scholars who prefer a late date for the composition of Acts (110–150 CE) observe that Acts seems to be unknown before the last half of the second century; the first unquestionable witness to Acts is the church leader Irenaeus (fl. c. 180 CE). Further, the author of Acts was apparently acquainted with Josephus's *Antiquities of the Jews* (ca. 93–94 CE): we may compare the mention of Theudas in Acts 5:36-37 and of the Egyptian troublemaker in Acts 21:38 with Josephus's description of related events in *Antiquities* 20.5.1. Positioning Acts between the times of Josephus and Irenaeus yields a period between 110 CE and 150 CE. In contrast to advocates of earlier dating, some recent studies have argued that the author of Acts was quite aware of the Pauline Letters (Pervo 2006), especially Galatians (Leppä). Indeed, it has been argued that Acts was written to subvert at least one possible second-century interpretation of Galatians. Although there are verbal and conceptual similarities between Acts 15 and Galatians 2 (Walker 1985; 1998), there are also marked differences, as Acts conveys more unified and harmonious relationships between Paul and the Jerusalem apostles. One explanation is that the author of Acts sought to counteract the notion of a radical break between law (Torah) and gospel that could be inferred from an "improper" reading of Galatians, as for example by Marcion or his followers. In contrast to Marcion's separation of Jesus from Israel's Scriptures, Acts depicts Peter, Paul, and other believers proclaiming that Jesus as their fulfillment. While Marcion claimed that Paul was the only true apostle, Peter and the others being "false apostles," Acts portrays Paul as in total agreement with the other apostles and even subservient to them; portrays Peter (not Paul) as the first to initiate preaching to the gentiles (Acts 10:1—11:18); and even defines apostleship in a way that excludes Paul (Acts 1:22-24). While Marcion attributed to Paul a radical distinction between law and grace, the dispensation of the law (Torah) having come to an end with the coming of Christ (see Gal. 3:23; Rom. 10:4), Acts characterized Paul as a Torah-observant Jew and a devout Pharisee, even portraying him as circumcising Timothy "because of the Jews" (Acts 16:1-4). Recent studies take these aspects of the narrative as evidence that Acts was written in direct opposition to Marcionite teaching and belongs alongside other anti-Marcionite figures like Justin Martyr (c. 140s CE). Indeed, Acts appears to share aspects of the thought-world of early second-century writings including those of Justin, 4 Maccabees (c. 100 CE), the letters of Ignatius of Antioch (c. 110 CE), and the *Martyrdom of Polycarp* (c. 150 CE), and appears a close relative of the apocryphal *Acts of Paul*, both in terms of genre and dating (S. Matthews, 5–6; see also Gregory; Mount; Tyson; and Skarsaune).

A late date for Acts has obvious implications for its relationship to the Gospel of Luke. The facts (mentioned above) that no extant manuscripts or canon lists ever joined the two writings together and that patristic writers discussed them separately suggest to some scholars that we should exercise caution in claims regarding the assumed unity of authorship (Parsons and Pervo; Walters). Patricia Walters argues that literary seams and redactional summaries in Luke-Acts, which have usually been attributed to a single author's use of different sources, should instead be attributed to the work of different authors. Lexical and theological thematic differences between the writings are too great, she argues, to be accounted for as the result of different genres (gospel, acts) or a shift in narrative style. She proposes dating the Gospel to the first century, but Acts to the second.

The diversity of these arguments means that a precise date for Acts still cannot be determined with certainty. What is certain is that decisions about the date of Acts shape the various ways we read it: as a history of the first Christian generation from the 60s or 70s, incorporating "eyewitness" accounts; as a second-generation (70s–80s) account of Christianity's movement away from its Jewish roots to become a largely gentile movement; or as a second-century (110–150) effort to combat Marcionite teachings.

The Genre of Acts

Traditionally, there was little dispute among New Testament interpreters that the author of Acts was a historian by intention, making Acts the only intentionally historical writing in the New Testament (Conzelmann, xl). As historical-critical perspectives have developed, however, the discussion has become more nuanced. After acknowledging that Luke intended to write a historical narrative, scholars have asked whether he was a good or bad historian (Johnson, 190). Acts has been severely criticized regarding its historical value and accuracy, a dispute that not long ago made it "the storm centre of modern New Testament study" (Marshall, 13, after Unnik). The first criticisms of the historicity of Acts arose from the mid-nineteenth-century Tübingen school, led by Ferdinand Christian Baur, whose stated singular purpose in investigating the New Testament was to "comprehend the historically given in its pure objectivity as far as it is generally possible" (Baur, vi–viii). This new emphasis on "historicity" and historical "objectivity" (though in some tension with Hegel's dialectical philosophy of history) led members of the Tübingen School to assert that Acts was merely a piece of Christian propaganda literature, written in the early second century and entirely unreliable as a historical document (see Munck, lv). This assessment has been reasserted among some contemporary scholars: for example, Gerd Lüdemann wrote that the "straight-line" arrangement of the narrative "clearly oversimplifies the actual order of events," and so "cannot furnish the basis for a valid history of early first-century Christianity" (Lüdemann 2008, 71; 2005). It is perhaps more appropriate, Lüdemann asserts, to view Acts as a combination of both historical fact and historical fiction (Lüdemann 2008, 65). Acts may not be completely unreliable—it appears to have embedded within it traditions that may contain a kernel of historical fact—but each episode must be critically evaluated to ascertain the historical value of the traditions behind it.

Other interpreters have emphasized the entertaining aspect of Acts and classified it among the historical novels of antiquity (Pervo 1987, 11, 137–38); Howard Clark Kee describes it as a "novelistic drama" (Kee, 1). This designation further blurs the characterization of Acts as history because the measure of a genre's entertainment value does not allow us to distinguish works of ancient history from ancient novels. As Emilio Gabba notes in this regard, "in the same climate of paradoxographical literature the 'novel' is born and develops; the novel in antiquity is in fact a form of history"

(Gabba, 15). While accuracy, objectivity, and critical assessment are expected today of the modern historian—"accuracy about the facts together with some accurate, and as far as possible objective, assessment about what the facts signify; in other words, some interpretation of what happened, in the economic and social as well as the political and military spheres" (Grant, 2)—ancient principles of historiography were different. To be sure, in antiquity, the craft of writing history also dealt with events regarded as important and noteworthy. But "ancient history was written according to principles, interests, aims, and tastes of great diversity. Works of history in antiquity were composed according to its intended audience, and different types of history aimed at different readers, had different aims, were composed according to different principles" (Gabba, 3). Ancient historiography, therefore, should not be understood according our contemporary sense of factual reporting, but as "literary artistry," because the first duty of any historian was to be an artist. In Lucian's opinion (120–180 CE), a good historian had to have "powers of expression" (*On Writing History* 34). In short, then, an ancient historian had to weave stories that would, first and foremost, entertain, and for this purpose, historical precision and detailed accuracy were secondary, if not totally disregarded. Even if we measure Acts against the standard of ancient historiography as found, for example, in the works of Thucydides (460–400 BCE)—whose survey of causes and effects, goal of impartiality in securing and evaluating evidence from both sides of an issue, and rigorous accuracy of detail in separating truth from falsehood established ancient scientific standards (though these were not maintained by his successors: "in the end, the demands of artistry gained precedence over those of science" [Grant, 8, 95]) and constitute perhaps the closest approximation to the contemporary ideal of history-writing—Acts suffers in the comparison, for it lacks some of the basic characteristics of a historical work as found in Thucydides. Some scholars have therefore asserted that Acts is not historical, and that its author is not the first Christian historian (Kümmel, 161–62).

Some scholars have asked whether the question of genre would be resolved if the entire literary project of Luke-Acts were considered and assessed together (Rothschild; Ehrman, 155). Attempts to classify the literary genre of Luke-Acts have included "theological history" (Maddox, 16), "apologetic historiography" (Sterling, 374; Doughty), and Greco-Roman biography, composed of an admixture of two subtypes (Talbert, 134). But since the two writings are structured and organized quite differently, as was recognized early on in the ecclesial tradition that treated and placed them separately, efforts to categorize the conjoined work have not proved generally convincing.

It is nevertheless commonly recognized that the book of Acts is concerned, in organization and intention, with a sequential development of the early Christian movement and with recounting the deeds of important figures in that development. The narrative is set within a chronological framework that begins with the origin of the movement, noting its spread and development using "synchronisms" (DeSilva, 349)—that is, attempts to correlate an event with different methods of dating; for example, the reigns of kings, the tenure of governors, or the Jewish high priesthood. In these respects, Acts resembles other kinds of histories produced in antiquity that used similar literary features to recount the lives of key leaders, significant incidents in the life of a particular city or region, or momentous events (major wars, for example) in a nation's history. Such histories could be arranged according to a particular topic, or presented in a chronological sequence (Polybius). This could be restricted to a single, albeit complicated event, such as in Thucydides' account of the

Peloponnesian War, or as a series of interrelated events, as in Polybius's account of Rome's ascendance over the Mediterranean world. Some historical narratives covered the salient events in the memory of a nation, designed particularly to show how the character and identity of a people or nation was established and how they came to be. (For example, Josephus's twenty-volume *Antiquities of the Jews* sketches the significant events, beginning with Adam and Eve and continuing to Josephus's own day, in the history of Judaism.) Contemporary historians sometimes call this genre a "general history" or a "historical monograph." These ancient histories commonly had a number of principal characters and tended to employ a wide range of subgenres, such as travel narratives, anecdotes, private letters, dialogues, and public speeches. For the most part, ancient Greco-Roman histories were creative literary productions and were not concerned necessarily with exacting certitude with regard to dates or facts. Historians exercised creative freedom in how they compiled and communicated their information (Ehrman, 155). Thus the ancient view of history was not unified, and historians in the Greco-Roman world produced a variety of differing literature that was designated as history. Moreover, for many ancient historians, the relevant criteria for historical narratives were similarity, plausibility, and persuasiveness. Acts seems most closely to correspond to these designations in that it provides a single, orderly account that sketches the salient events of the history of the Jesus movement, from its origins to a point in the not-too-distant past, to show how the Christian identity as a new genus or people was established (Palmer).

The act of persuasion requires the use of language intentionally and purposefully crafted to convey meaning and appeal. Contemporary historians increasingly recognize that *language* shapes and creates the past; the basic events of human experience do not in and of themselves possess the qualities of coherence, unity, integrity, connectivity, comprehensiveness, and closure (S. Matthews, 20–24). Human ingenuity and creativity impose these formal narrative qualities on events and experience. Consequently, all written histories, whether ancient or modem, cannot be viewed as objective and unbiased accounts of what "really happened in the past." Ancient and modern historians out of necessity pick and choose what to recount and what to present as significant or noteworthy. In this selection process, it is certain that a historian narrates events, intentionally or not, in such a way that exposes his or her priorities, values, beliefs, and interpretation of those events (Ehrman, 155). In contemporary postmodern thought, it is recognized that *this is the ideological work that ancient (and modern) narratives do* (S. Matthews, 21). This important shift in perspective for understanding ancient historical writings has potential to aid the contemporary reader in reading the Acts of the Apostles.

Contemporary Options for Reading Acts: Ideological, Postcolonial, and Postmodern Perspectives

While standard historical and literary approaches have provided important insights into the text of Acts, the theology of Luke-Acts, and important themes and motifs in the narrative, a number of newer "reading perspectives" and interpretive frameworks offer insights into the ways in which narrators both ancient and modern encode their own (and their group's) priorities, agendas, values, beliefs, and biases into the stories they tell.

Ideological critics help us to understand that the "raw events" of the past are to be distinguished from historical narration about those events, giving them meaning. The writing of history involves perspective, opinion, interpretation, and organization as the historian connects events with a particular purpose in mind. History is not possible without discourse (Dijk, 120–21); "history as a discourse attempts to wrest and provide meaning out of events that inform the development or making of culture, nation building, and processes by which ethnoracial identity is constructed" (S. Matthews, 4). Ancient (and contemporary) historical narratives are perspectival and bound up with views of authority and social order, not always as it is, but as it ought to be. In these ways, historical writings and narratives are ideological—they express vested interests whether consciously or only implicitly. Because "no one can write entirely objective history, we must be ever alert to identify ideology when it plays a recognizable role" in Luke-Acts as well (Lüdemann 2008, 66).

"[As] the basis of a social group's self-image, ideologies organize its identity, actions, and resources as well as its relations to other social groups" (Dijk, 115). So, ideology is not necessarily negative; all human groups are implicated in it. However, the social, political, and religious impact of ideology becomes more acute with regard to empires and imperial or colonial regimes that seek to promote and impose their values on other nations or peoples. Although military power usually was (and is) used to maintain control, the political and social mechanisms of empire are also extended through social, cultural, religious, and political constructs that promote acceptance and a sense that the hegemony is "natural" (Punt, 192). The Roman Empire provides an appropriate example of the material reality through which ideology is imposed, through the use of images (the ancient mass media)—statues, monuments, coins, and temples (Lopez)—and through inscriptions and literature, especially the imperial patronage of historical narratives that promoted and legitimized the empire and imperial prerogatives. Such propagandistic images and historical literature, whether conscious or unconscious or by means subtle or overt, portray the reality, values, and benefits of empire (as natural or divinely instituted), expressed through *a unifying cultural ideal*, or in contemporary postmodern nomenclature, through a "grand-narrative" (Flax). In postmodern thought, a grand-narrative (or meta- or master narrative) is "a global or totalizing cultural narrative schema which orders and explains knowledge and experience" (Stephens and McCallum, 1). All aspects of societies depend on these grand-narratives. Therefore, a grand-narrative is a story that encompasses and explains other "little stories" within totalizing schemes (Lyotard, xxiii–xxiv).

At this point, postmodern thought converges with postcolonial and ideological investigation. Not only social groups but also national and imperial regimes produce grand-narratives that universalize, characterize, and promote their politics, worldviews, identities, and values. These grand-narratives inevitably mask contradictions and inconsistencies inherent in a regime's practice or organization. For example, a grand-narrative is implicit in the statement in the American Declaration of Independence that "We hold these truths to be self-evident, that all men are created equal, that they are endowed by their Creator with certain unalienable Rights, that among these are Life, Liberty and the pursuit of Happiness." The ideal stated here is the foundation of American democratic politics, institutions, and society, but we know that it has also masked inconsistencies of racism, slavery, sexism, and classism (among other things). Postmodern examinations attempt to expose and critique such inconsistencies (Flax, 41). Postcolonial analysis engages in "ideological reflection on the discourse and practice of imperialism and colonialism," recognizing that the shadow of empire stands behind and within the construction of ancient texts (Segovia, 126). An ideological-critical lens is essential to both perspectives because ideological analysis explores the relationship between rhetoric and power (Bible and Culture Collective, 274). Postmodern, postcolonial, and ideological-critical perspectives resonate in biblical studies because the biblical texts were written in the shadow of empire and are at once rhetorical and ideological: that is, they too seek to persuade, they espouse certain values and beliefs, they interpret the meaning of certain events, and they limit and constrain their readers in multiple ways (DeSilva, 678–79). These perspectives allow new angles of vision on Luke-Acts as a historical project.

Luke as a Historian of the Early Church

We may consider Acts a work of ancient ecclesial history. In the prologue to Luke (1:1-4), the author expresses what we may take as his purpose for Acts as well (see Acts 1:1; Stott, 22). He informs his reader that he has examined and explored both written and oral sources (Luke 1:1-3), presumably attempting to use them "critically"; that is, collecting information and relating it to his story (an "orderly account" or "narrative," 1:3). We may also understand Acts as interacting with other grand-narratives. Luke-Acts draws connections among events in the origins of the Christian movement (beginning with characters rooted in Judaism), the teaching and deeds of Jesus, the proclamation and actions of the apostles, and the later experiences of the churches. He relates these, further, to Israel's Scriptures, casting the emergence of Jesus and the early Christian movement as a fulfillment of biblical prophecy and thus continuing the heritage of Israel. He also indicates that his story coincides with the period of the emergent glory of the Roman Empire and its civilizing mission (see Brunt, 25–35), stipulating that Jesus was born under the reign of the first Roman emperor, Caesar Augustus (Luke 2:1); while Quirinius was governor of Syria (2:2) and King Herod the Great ruled Judea (1:5); his ministry began during the reign of Tiberias Caesar (Luke 3:1); and he was crucified under the procurator Pontius Pilate (Luke 23:24-25), while Tiberias was still in power. Acts tells the story of the early church within the framework of the larger Roman context as well, in Judea and Syria (Herod Agrippa, Acts 12:20-22; procurators Antonius Felix, Acts 23:24, and Porcius Festus, Acts 25:1; King Herod Agrippa II, Acts 25:13), Asia Minor (*Asiarchs* or officials in the province of Asia, Acts 19:31), and Europe (the proconsul Gallio, Acts 18:12-17). Luke must have known that Rome, too, had its "gospel" (an inscription from 9 BCE in Priene, Asia Minor references the "good news [*euangelia*] of Augustus"; see Deissmann, 366) that promoted the *Pax Romana* ("peace of Rome"), its "savior" (the reigning Caesar), and a driving mission to dominate and to civilize the world as part of its ideology (as expressed in Virgil's *Aeneid*, 29–19 BCE; Horsley 2003, 12). Indeed, Theophilus, to whom Luke-Acts is dedicated, may have been a Roman patron: the address "most excellent Theophilus" echoes the use "most excellent" used to address a governor of a province (Acts 23:26; 24:3; 26:25). (Theophilus, literally translated "lover of God" or "beloved of God," might also simply be a code name for all Christians: Ehrman, 115–17.) One narrative strategy in the work is to show that, although Judaism (and emerging Christianity) are insignificant in the eyes of Rome, providence is being mediated through the traditions of Israel, *not* those of Rome; it is by means of the gospel of Christ that God is bringing about a new world order, and the apostles are God's agents (Horsley 1997, 206–14, 242–52; 2003, 132–33).

Luke's sources for Acts were limited, so far as contemporary scholars can detect them at all; the whole work is so consistent in style that detecting sources behind the narrative is a matter of deduction (or educated guesswork). Nevertheless, scholars have suspected at least three possible sources: (1) traditions about Peter (and Stephen and Philip) and the Jerusalem church; (2) an "eyewitness" travelogue recounting a portion of Paul's missionary journeys, beginning in chapter 16; and (3) traditions about Paul's conversion and early experiences (Dupont; Hemer, 308–64; Barrett, 1:49–56, 2:xxiv–xxxii). Given the apparent limitations of these sources, Luke can describe some events in detail, but must skip over others, on occasion leaving gaps of several years at a time. This aspect of his narrative resembles the Greek historians Xenophon and Plutarch, who presented a selection of a hero's acts, emphasizing historical vignettes that set forth the hero's character. Most of his narrative is dominated by the towering personalities of Peter and Paul, indicating that Acts is not a simple chronicle, but a portrayal of the character of figures in the early church (Baker, 884).

In piecing together his narrative, Luke exhibits a historian's instinct for chronology and causality: "he makes connections between events, so that a thread of purpose runs through his narrative" (Johnson, 190). That purpose is stated in Acts 1:8, where Jesus tells the disciples, "But you will receive power when the Holy Spirit has come upon you; and you will be my witnesses in Jerusalem, in all Judea and Samaria, and to the ends of the earth." This singular purpose, to explicate the spread of the gospel from Jerusalem to Rome, connects the seemingly disparate pieces into a cohesive whole (Witherington, 1).

Movement from Jerusalem to Rome and the Portrayal of the Apostles

Some scholars have attempted to outline Acts according to the geographical schema in Acts 1:8. But although Luke begins his narrative in Jerusalem, he does not follow the precise sequence in Acts 1:8: Philip's missionary efforts in Samaria (Acts 8:5-25) are narrated before Peter's work in Judea (Acts 9:31—10:48). A little later, the story moves back and forth from Antioch to Jerusalem (11:19-30; 12:1-25). Then, once Paul's missionary work begins, the narrative moves from Europe to Asia, and then back to Jerusalem again. Finally, the book ends with Paul in Rome, which might have been regarded by Luke's readers as the center of the Roman Empire, but certainly not "the ends of the earth." These minor incongruencies are secondary to the overarching theological (or ideological) purpose reflected in the narrative of the gospel's spread from Jerusalem to Rome. This spread represents Luke's conception of salvation history; that is, the sweep of missionary activity throughout the Roman Empire, beginning in Jerusalem and then to the broader Judean regions (chs. 1–8), expands and gains new converts through the Hellenists' mission to the gentiles (which includes Paul and Barnabas, chs. 11–15), and ends with the mission of Paul in Rome (chs. 16–28), thus fulfilling the history of salvation.

This salvation-historical schema has a significant intertextual reference in Isaiah 40–66. Like the postexilic Second Isaiah, Luke is attempting to redefine and rebuild the people of God after the distress and destruction of the first Jewish-Roman War in 66–70 CE (by rewriting the "Isaianic new exodus": Pao). Scholars have noted that Acts often quotes from the Septuagint, and especially Isaiah (Acts 7:49-50; 8:32-33; 13:34, 47; 28:26-27); however, there are other implicit allusions as well. Some of the most important allusions refer to the power of God's word (Isa. 40:6-8; cf. Acts 6:7; 12:24; 19:20), the centrality of Jerusalem (Isa. 40:9-11; cf. Acts 1:4-5), the work and power of the Holy Spirit (Isa. 42:1; 44:1-4; 61:1-2; cf. Acts 2:1-4; 10:38; 13:1-4), and the (re-)creation of God's people that will include both Jews and gentiles (Isa. 43:15-21; 49:6; cf. Acts 10:44-48; 14:1; 15:12-31) and will also include previous outcasts like eunuchs (Isa. 56:4-5, 8; cf. Acts 8:26-40). Interestingly, Acts 1:8 captures a number of the main elements of Isaiah 40–55: "the geographical sequence of the verse signifies the centrality of Jerusalem ('in Jerusalem [first]'), the reunification of Israel ('in all Judea and Samaria'), and the inclusion of Gentiles ('and to the ends of the earth'). This verse is further sandwiched by two references to the focus of the Isaianic new exodus: Israel's restoration or reconstitution" (Liew, 420–21). The disciples' question in Acts 1:6 prompts Jesus' "programmatic promise," and for Luke, the apostles have a signal role in fulfilling that promise.

Given the limited narrative portrayal of all the apostles, the title "Acts of the Apostles" is a bit misleading. The writing could be more accurately titled the "Acts of Peter and Paul" because they play particularly prominent roles, Peter especially in Acts 1–12, 15, and Paul in Acts 9 and 13–28. The apostles James and John play only minor roles, and the other apostles, no significant role at all. If we think of them as implicitly subsumed under Peter, the result is a roughly symmetric presentation in which Peter (and the other apostles) are guarantors of Jesus' ministry and, as authorized witnesses, provide continuity for the church's continuing mission through Paul. Peter is clearly the leader and chief spokesman of the group; his preaching founds the church (Acts 2), authorizes and ordains new leaders (Acts 6), and guards and regulates the transmission of the Holy Spirit (Acts 8). His missionary work, not Paul's, opens the door to gentile integration into the community (Acts 10). The Jerusalem Conference (Acts 15), narrated at the midpoint of the book, represents a pivotal point in the spread of the gospel, separating the Jerusalem period of the church (under the leadership and authority of Peter) from the expanding outreach to the gentiles; it provides the presupposition and legitimacy for Paul's independent mission after his separation from Barnabas (also in Acts 15). Whether or not this narration reflects history "as it actually happened," it gives rhetorical foundation and validation to Paul's mission, showing that it is congruent with and legitimized by the earlier apostles, especially Peter and James (who defend gentile freedom from the law; compare the impression left in Galatians 2). The central place of the Jerusalem Conference has salvation-historical significance (Lüdemann 2003, 68–69).

The Construction of Christian Identity

In Acts, the good news is proclaimed to rich and poor, slave and free, high and low, Greek and Roman, Jew and gentile. Evidently Luke sought to portray the gospel as available to all peoples (cf. Gal. 3:27-28), an agenda expressed most vividly in Acts 2:16-21—a passage that advances the imperative of Acts 1:8. Luke describes the day of Pentecost as the fulfillment of the prophet Joel's prophecy regarding the descent of the Holy Spirit; indeed, that prophecy expresses the "grand narrative" in Luke by promising universal inclusion of all peoples into the covenant people Israel. Through the proclamation and promise of the gospel, the former barriers of age, race and ethnicity, class, status, and gender were eradicated by the coming of the Holy Spirit, thus grounding the new movement's identity and purpose (Williams 2009, 289–93). Although the Pentecost event, like Joel's prophecy, describes the experience of "ethnically diverse" Jews, in Acts the event foreshadows the eventual integration of gentiles in the promise of the Holy Spirit—a theme that receives significant development later in Acts (see 8:26—15:35), perhaps signifying a protracted struggle in the church. The integration of gentiles depends on the giving and receiving of the Holy Spirit (10:34), who also functions as the "eraser" of ethnic difference (15:8-9).

Because Luke also believes that God is faithful to God's promises, however, and that certain patterns in history indicate the regularity of divine providence, the early part of the narrative depicts the work of mission and evangelism as restricted to Palestinian or Hellenistic Jews. Missionary activity is carried out by Jewish figures like Peter, Philip, Barnabas, and Paul (and a few "minor" missionaries like the Hellenist Jews in Acts 11, Priscilla and Aquila, and the Alexandrian Jew Apollos, whom they "instructed more accurately in the faith," 18:1-2, 24-26). Luke never recounts the missionary activity or preaching of any non-Jewish convert. "This ethnic monopoly (a kind of 'glass ceiling' for Gentile followers?) may explain why Paul circumcises Timothy, who has a Greek father and a Jewish mother (16:13). . . . What distinguishes him is that Paul desires to make him a missionary partner (16:3)" (Liew, 422).

In addition, one observes that Luke does not depict the Holy Spirit as bestowed on all converts without distinction. In Acts, faith in Christ without reception of the Holy Spirit represents only incomplete or partial integration into the community (8:14-17; 18:24—19:7). "The presence of the Spirit is seen as the distinguishing mark of Christianity—it is what makes a person a Christian. . . . The Spirit, then, is the *sine qua non* for being a Christian, not merely a means by which one gets a spiritual booster shot subsequent to conversion" (Witherington, 140). The Samaritans experience a delay between their baptism and their receiving of the Holy Spirit (8:16); the Ephesians receive the Holy Spirit closely following their baptism (19:5-6); and the Holy Spirit comes upon the centurion at Caesarea, Cornelius, and his household even before they are baptized (10:44-48; Liew, 420–21), causing some scholars to term this event "the Gentile Pentecost" (Witherington, 134). There is no mention of the Ethiopian convert in chapter 8 receiving the Holy Spirit, however; the Spirit instead moves on Philip as he and the Ethiopian are rising from the baptismal waters, transporting Philip to a new locale (8:38-40). Accordingly, the black Ethiopian's incorporation into Christ appears incomplete, while the nonblack European's incorporation is complete. This may be (as some contemporary scholars have suggested) because Luke seeks to complete the "Acts of Philip" before moving to his next subjects, Paul's "conversion" (ch. 9) and Peter's initiation of the gentile mission (ch. 10; Haenchen, 309–17). Or perhaps Luke used the Ethiopian eunuch positively to express the fulfillment of Isaiah (56:4-5, 8), which promises God's salvation and honor to the eunuch (González, 117–18). Or perhaps we see here an aspect of Luke's ideology regarding authority: although Philip initiated the Samaritan mission, the Holy Spirit was not given until Peter arrived (ch. 8); likewise, although Philip baptized the Ethiopian eunuch, he was not authorized (according to Luke) to transmit or confer the Holy Spirit. These explanations may not mitigate the impression that Luke values the conversion of a European—a Roman centurion—over a black African who presumably "outranks" him—an official of the Candace.

The issue of gender offers another example of Luke's inconsistency. The quotation from Joel names "prophesying daughters," but neither the prophesying of non-Jews nor of women is narrated in Acts; only that of sons of Israel. Luke and Acts are generally held to be the New Testament writings most affirming of women, but as Beverly Roberts Gaventa asks, "What ever happened to the prophesying daughters?" Several women are mentioned by name, like Tabitha, Mary (mother of John Mark), Lydia, and Damaris, among the believers; but they are not given voice. The first woman to speak in the narrative, Sapphira, is also the last (Acts 5:8; Gaventa, 49). When we at last encounter Philip's four unmarried daughters (21:9), we are told that they prophesy, but hear not a word from them; instead, we hear from Agabus, who has come down from Judea, some distance away, to warn Paul of the danger awaiting him in Judea (Acts 21:11). The silence even of prophesying daughters subtly reveals Luke's views of masculinity (Gaventa, 56–58). Women are not independent missionaries and preachers; rather, they support the male apostle's missionary activity as coworkers and patrons (even Prisca/Priscilla must accompany her husband: Schüssler Fiorenza, 161).

Nor does Luke narrate prophesying slaves (the last element in Joel's prophecy). Twice, female slaves are given voice, although briefly. Rhoda, a house slave, encounters Peter, but her testimony about him is initially rejected by those in her owner's household (Acts 12:6-17). Paul exorcizes a spirit of divination from an unnamed slave girl (who stands outside the circle of believers), who declares the truth about his mission and message (though this is not described as prophecy); but she too is silenced and is not offered the message of salvation after the exorcism (Acts 16:16-18). Thus, while Luke includes several accounts of women and of slaves in Acts, his narrative effectively suppresses roles that conflict with his own treatment of the church and his understanding of authority. For him, "male characters circumscribe female identity in the text, developing the 'domestic' characterization of women whereby premium Roman imperial values are demonstrated for leadership" (Penner and Vander Stichele, 198).

A postmodern reading of all these issues recognizes that Luke utilized Joel's prophecy to express his grand-narrative that the bestowal of the Holy Spirit on "all flesh" embraces all racial and ethnic diversity, without regard to geographical location, language, or nationality (Witherington, 71–72). This promise of universal fulfillment nevertheless masked certain inconsistencies: Luke did not understand it to eliminate or radically to realign sex and class barriers, but only to validate the incorporation of gentiles into the covenant promises of the people Israel. In the end, a postmodern reader might critique such inconsistencies by observing that Luke's idea of embracing all ethnic diversity accorded with the values of the Roman Empire: it embraced ethnic diversity without demolishing Roman social convention or the hierarchical ordering of society (Williams 2009).

Luke's project, then, might be described as attempting to redefine and rebuild the people of God after the distress of the first Jewish-Roman War; he attempted to establish the church as the newly constituted Israel, composed of believing Jews and gentiles as the true heirs of Israel (Pao). He pursued this goal by using Joel's prophecy as his grand-narrative. In this endeavor, he also had some other scriptural precedents, for example, Isaiah 40–55. Thus one could also describe Luke's efforts as attempting to present his version of the fulfillment of the promises of Isaiah, which resulted in two distinct social/religious entities called Judaism and Christianity. Although according to Acts 11:26, believers are called "Christian" for the first time in Antioch during the apostolic age, the absence of the term *Christianoi* in any literature, from within or without the Jesus movement, until the early second century leads most scholars to conclude the term was *not* a common name for members of the movement before that point. Luke's effort is an early endeavor to form a distinct identity that will not be firmly established for some centuries (S. Matthews, 7).

Acts and the "Break" with Judaism: "Jews" as Agents of Persecution

Luke's ethnic interests are also exhibited in the way he explains Christianity's move from its Jewish foundations to spread to the gentile world. The process can be described in terms of hierarchical authority: the chain of succession established in Acts moves from God to Jesus, from Jesus to Peter and the other disciples, then from the Jerusalem church to the Hellenistic church, which influences Stephen, and then Paul and Barnabas, who continue the mission to the gentiles. The progression of "the Way" also happens geographically, moving from Jerusalem to Judea and Samaria and unto the ends of the earth. These themes are combined in a narrative in which Christianity emerges and diverges from Judaism quickly and decisively. The Hellenistic wing of the "Way" initiates the development of a new identity for Jewish and gentile followers of Jesus that is different from that of Judaism (Acts 11:26). Paul's final speech to the Jews in Rome represents a decisive break between Jews and gentile followers of the Way, already in the lifetime of Paul himself (28:25-28). Luke marks the beginning of this transition by Stephen's death at the hands of a disorderly and unruly mob of Jews, a device so influential that the fourth-century church leader Eusebius of Caesarea would emulate it, reinscribing the narrative of Acts "by which originary martyrdom is linked to the creation of two distinct social groups," Stephen's death igniting "the 'first and great' persecution of one distinct social group, the Jerusalem *ekklesia* by another, 'the Jews'" (S. Matthews, 9, citing *Hist. eccl.* 2.1.8). Thus Acts constructs the identity of nonbelieving Jews (Acts 14:2) as agents of violence, and Christian identity as those who suffer at the hands of Jews.

Luke's earlier portrayal of his narrative hero, Saul of Tarsus, as a radical defender of (Pharisaic) Judaism and a zealous persecutor of the Christians, places him "present and accounted for" at the murder of Stephen. After his "conversion," in solidarity with his new identity and community with the Hellenists Jews whom he formerly opposed, Paul would suffer at the hands of the (unbelieving) Jews (9:23; 13:50; 14:2, 14, 19; 17:5; 20:3, 19; 21:11, 27; 23:12, 20, 27; 26:21). Luke's construction of two categories, persecutor and persecuted, requires that although Paul is still a Jew (21:39; 22:3), he is a persecuted one (because he believes in Jesus as the Messiah). At the beginning of his missionary travels and preaching, he preached to gentiles only under compulsion, that is, only after the Jews rejected his gospel (13:46-7; 18:5-6). Luke defends Paul against accusations that he preached against Judaism; he did not (Luke insists) teach Jews to abandon their traditions. As a matter of fact, Luke shows that Paul participated in Jewish rituals both in Ephesus and in Jerusalem (Acts 21:17-26; 16:1-3, which may be compared with Gal. 2:1-5, where Paul was *not* inclined to perform such a gesture). Not all Jews are depicted as persecutors of Christians, however; those who at least are willing "to search the scriptures" and withhold judgment are presented as civil and rational (Acts 17:11, 17; 14:4; 19:10). In the end, nonetheless, Luke's portrayal of a break with Judaism, initiated by Stephen's death, is swift and contingent on violence. Luke's distinction between the "persecuting Jew" and the "victimized Christian" has been reinscribed to some degree in modern scholarship, which still buys unsuspectingly into Luke's binary master-narrative of Christian origins (S. Matthews, 8).

Portrayal of Roman Characters

Unlike the depiction in Acts of some Jews as violent persecutors of Christians, some Roman characters are virtually absolved from violence. Roman magistrates and other officials are depicted as reasonable in their comportment and equitable in their judgments (but not all: Gallio does nothing to quell a riot [Acts 18:17]; Felix obstructs justice waiting for a bribe [Acts 24:26]). Even military personnel, for the most part, are depicted quite positively, even when carrying out orders (Acts 22:24-26). This was evident already in Luke, particularly in the trial of Jesus (which prefigures the Roman treatment of Paul in Acts) and his crucifixion. In Luke's account of Jesus' execution (Luke 23), it was "the Jews" who carried out the act—not the Romans. Luke omits the scene in which Jesus was scourged by Romans (cf. Mark 15:14; par. Matt. 27:26); Pilate reluctantly hands Jesus over to the will of the Jews (Luke 23:25), and it is they who lead him away (23:26) and crucify him (23:33). In Luke's narrative, those who call out for Jesus' death also judge and condemn him. As Lüdemann observes, "In literary terms, the way [Luke] uses others to relieve the Roman authorities of responsibility for the condemnation of Jesus and the actual crucifixion is a *tour de force*; in historical and theological terms, it is a *monstrosity*. Indeed, historical truth comes in a distant second to the evangelist's zeal in promoting his ecclesiastical program" (Lüdemann 2008, 71). Note, too, the elimination of the sort of cruelty in the report of Jesus' execution that appears in other reports and descriptions of the Roman practice of crucifixion (Hengel).

While Luke evidently attempted to play down the actual role and brutality of the Romans in such events, he could not simply ignore the death of Jesus. His narrative strategy did allow him to ignore and exclude a portrayal of Paul's death, however, and since Paul suffered like Jesus "at the hand of the Jews," Luke could continue his positive presentation of Roman characters. Having exonerated the Roman participation in the crucifixion of Jesus, Luke depicts the Roman soldiers involved in Paul's arrest in Jerusalem, and the subsequent negotiations, as protective of Paul and reasonable in a threatening situation (except in the two cases noted above). The Jews, on the other hand, are generally portrayed for the most part as hostile and riotous in their behavior, from which the Romans must protect Paul. This idyllic narrative depiction of the Romans masks the actual role and historical realities of Roman imperial power, as well as the violence it unleashed generally against colonized peoples in the Mediterranean world under its dominion (including Jews and "Christians" alike). Although Luke knows that the Roman state eventually executed Paul, he chose not to report the fact, instead closing the narrative of Acts with Paul being privileged by the Romans to preach the gospel without any hindrance. The historical reality was that Paul was never set free but rather was executed under Roman decree. Luke does not recount the story of Paul's violent death, perhaps because he did not consider it edifying, or because ending on the note of Paul's unhindered freedom to preach opened up possibilities for the church even under severe threats to its life. It seems, then, that Luke created a theologically (or ideologically) grounded picture of the Roman state in order to secure present and future privileges of unhindered preaching for the church.

It appears, then, that despite apparent tensions with the Roman imperial grand-narrative, as described above, the author of Luke-Acts also avoids the presentation of episodes that might raise those tensions to the level of an explicit conflict of values. In other ways, the author appears to participate in some of the values of Roman imperial culture. In this regard, Mariann Bonz has observed aspects of a remarkable but seldom-recognized intertextuality with Virgil's *Aeneid.* Virgil presents the legendary Trojan hero Aeneas escaping from the flaming ruins of Troy to bring to Italy the best values of Trojan piety and honor; the explicit consequence is that the Romans of the Augustan age, descendants of Aeneas, are ordained by the gods to act out those values by exercising their divine right to dominate the world. In some ways, Bonz argues, Luke appears to imitate Virgil, presenting the Christians as a new people destined to spread (from east to west, even to Rome) and "conquer" the world. The Christians emerge in Acts as heirs of the very best of the Jewish tradition, who, after the suffering of the first Jewish Revolt and the destruction of Jerusalem, are given the right and privilege to rebuild the nation of Israel (Bonz, 182).

It is in Luke's apparent imitation of Roman values that we gain a picture of his own participation in the Roman construction of masculinity as well. The "imperial atmosphere of masculine comportment and display, quintessential in the formation of [Acts'] narrative flow, also reflects on Luke's own manly performance." Moreover, "the speaking voice in Acts is clearly a powerful male-gendered voice, which finally says something about Luke and the masculine image he projects through inscribing it on the narrative community and especially its leaders, with whom Luke seems to identify the most, given the role they play in proclaiming *his* gospel" (Penner and Vander Stichele, 202 [emphasis original]). On this view, Luke has portrayed the Romans so positively because, although he proposes a narrative in which divine providence is carried forward by another people—the new people created by a restored Israel joined with believing gentiles obedient to Israel's Messiah—he nevertheless ultimately upholds the Roman values of *virtus* and *imperium,* which encompass the virtues of social order and masculinity. Luke depicts acts of speech and behavior that comply with the social values of a (male) Roman elite, which may show us just how closely the author himself comports with those values.

Reading Luke-Acts Today

Luke clearly sought to accomplish several goals in his account of the origins of the early church. The preceding discussion shows that different contemporary interpreters perceive different possible agendas in his writing, both explicit and also the implicit values of conflicting grand-narratives in Luke's environment.

Like the author of Luke-Acts, the modern reader also brings to the reading of this work his or her own view(s) of the world, biases, agendas, and participation in the often implicit grand-narratives of our own time. By attending to these possibilities, we may discover in reading Acts our own values and also our own inconsistencies, for as Louis Althusser has warned: "there is no such thing as an innocent reading, we must say what readings we are guilty of" (Althusser, 14).

Works Cited

Althusser, Louis B. 1975. *Reading Capital.* Translated by Bruce Brewster. London: New Left Books.

Baker, William H. 1989. "Acts." In *Evangelical Commentary on the Bible*, edited by Walter Elwell, 884. Grand Rapids: Baker.

Barrett, C. K. 1994. *Acts of the Apostles.* 2 vols. ICC. Edinburgh: T&T Clark.

Baur, Ferdinand Christian. 1853. *Das Christentum.* Tübingen.

Bible and Culture Collective. 1995. *The Postmodern Bible.* New Haven: Yale University Press.

Bonz, Mariann Palmer. 2000. *The Past as Legacy: Luke-Acts and Ancient Epic.* Minneapolis: Fortress Press.

Brunt, P. A. 1997. "*Laus Imperii.*" In *Paul and Empire: Religion and Power in Roman Imperial Society*, edited by Richard A. Horsley, 433–80. Harrisburg, PA: Trinity Press.

Conzelmann, Hans. 1987. *Acts of the Apostles.* Edited by Eldon Jay Epps and Christopher R. Matthews. Philadelphia: Fortress Press.

Deissmann, Adolf. 1927. *Light from the Ancient East.* New York: Harper & Row.

DeSilva, David A. 2004. *Introduction to the New Testament: Contexts, Methods and Ministry Formation.* Downers Grove, IL: Intervarsity Press.

Dijk, Teun A. van. 2006. "Ideology and Discourse Analysis." *Journal of Political Ideologies* 11, no. 2 (June): 115–40.

Doughty, Darrell J. 1997. "Luke's Story of Paul in Corinth: Fictional History in Acts 18—Historical Criticism or Apologetic Historicizing?" *Journal of Higher Criticism* 4, no. 1 (Spring): 3–54.

Drane, John. 2011. *Introducing the New Testament.* 3rd ed. Minneapolis: Fortress Press.

Dupont, J. 1961. *The Sources of Acts.* Translated by K. Pond. New York: Herder and Herder.

Ehrman, Bart D. 2012. *The New Testament: A Historical Introduction to the Early Christian Writings.* 5th ed. Oxford: Oxford University Press.

Flax, Jane. 1990. "Postmodernism and Gender Relations in Feminist Theory." In *Feminist/Postmodernism*, edited by Linda J. Nicholson, 621–43. London: Routledge.

Gabba, Emilio. 1983. "Literature." In *Sources for Ancient History*, edited by Michael Crawford, 1–79. Cambridge: Cambridge University Press.

Gaventa, Beverly Roberts. 2004. "What Ever Happened to the Prophesying Daughters?" In *A Feminist Companion to the Acts of the Apostles*, edited by Amy-Jill Levine, 49–60. Cleveland: Pilgrim.

Grant, Michael. 1995. *Greek and Roman Historians: Information and Misinformation.* New York: Routledge.

Gregory, Andrew. 2003. *The Reception of Luke and Acts in the Period before Irenaeus: Looking for Luke in the Second Century.* Tübingen: Mohr.

González, Justo L. 2001. *Acts: The Gospel of the Spirit.* Maryknoll, NY: Orbis.

Haenchen, Ernst. 1971. *Acts of the Apostles: A Commentary.* Philadelphia: Westminster.

Hemer, Colin J. 1989. *The Book of Acts in the Setting of Hellenistic History.* Edited by C. Gempf. Tübingen: Mohr Siebeck.

Hengel, Martin. 1977. *Crucifixion in the Ancient World and the Folly of the Cross*. Philadelphia: Fortress Press.

Hodgson, P. C. 1966. *The Formation of Historical Theology: A Study of F. C. Baur.* New York: Harper.

Horsley, Richard A., ed. 1997. *Paul and Empire: Religion and Power in Roman Imperial Society.* Harrisburg, PA: Trinity Press International.

———. 2003. *Jesus and Empire: The Kingdom of God and the New World Disorder*. Harrisburg, PA: Trinity Press International.

Johnson, Luke Timothy. 2010. *The Writings of the New Testament.* 3rd ed. Minneapolis: Fortress Press.

Kee, Howard Clark, 1990. *Good News to the Ends of the Earth: The Theology of Acts.* Philadelphia: Trinity Press International.

Kummel, Werner. G. 1987. *Introduction to the New Testament.* Rev. ed. London: SCM.

Leppä, Heikki. 2002. "Luke's Critical Use of Galatians." PhD diss., University of Helsinki.

Liew, Tat-siong Benny. 2004. "Acts." In *Global Bible Commentary*, edited by Daniel Patte, 419–28. Nashville: Abingdon.

Lopez, Davina C. 2012. "Visual Perspectives: Imag(in)ing the Big Picture." In *Studying Paul's Letters: Contemporary Perspectives and Methods*, edited by Joseph Marchal, 93–116. Minneapolis: Fortress Press.

Lüdemann, Gerd. 1989. *Early Christianity according to the Traditions in Acts.* London: SCM.

———. 2005. *The Acts of the Apostles: What Really Happened in the Earliest Days of the Church.* Amherst, NY: Prometheus.

———. 2008. "Acts of Impropriety: The Imbalance of History and Theology in Luke-Acts." *TJT* 24, no. 1:65–79.

Lyotard, Jean-François. 1979. *The Postmodern Condition: A Report on Knowledge.* Manchester: Manchester University Press.

Maddox, R. 1982. *The Purpose of Luke-Acts.* Edinburgh: T&T Clark.

Marshall, I. Howard. 1984. *Luke—Historian and Theologian*. Exeter: Paternoster.

Matthews, Christopher R. 2001. "Acts of the Apostles." In *The New Oxford Annotated Bible: NRSV with the Apocrypha*, edited by Michael D. Coogan, 1919–71. 3rd ed. Oxford: Oxford University Press.

Matthews, Shelly. 2010. *Perfect Martyr: The Stoning of Stephen and the Construction of Christian Identity.* Oxford: Oxford University Press.

Mount, Christopher. 2002. *Pauline Christianity: Luke-Acts and the Legacy of Paul.* NovTSup 104. Leiden: Brill.

Munck, J. 1986. *The Acts of the Apostles.* AB 31. New York: Doubleday.

Palmer, Darryl W. 1992. "Acts as the Historical Monograph." *TynBul* 43, no. 2:373–88.

Pao, David C. 2002. *Acts and the Isaianic New Exodus*. WUANT 2. Tubingen: Mohr Siebeck.

Parsons, Mikeal C., and Richard I. Pervo. 1993. *Rethinking the Unity of Luke and Acts*. Minneapolis: Fortress.

Penner, Todd, and Caroline Vander Stichele. 2004. "Gendering Violence: Patterns of Power and Constructs of Masculinity in the Acts of the Apostles." In *A Feminist Companion to the Acts of the Apostles*, edited by Amy-Jill Levine, 98–104. Cleveland: Pilgrim.

Pervo, Richard. 1987. *Profit with Delight: The Literary Genre of the Acts of the Apostle.* Philadelphia: Fortress Press.

———. 2006. *Dating Acts: Between the Evangelists and the Apologists*. Santa Rosa, CA: Polebridge.

Punt, Jeremy. 2012. "Postcolonial Approaches: Negotiating Empire Then and Now." In *Studying Paul's Letters: Contemporary Perspectives and Methods*, edited by Joseph Marchal, 191–208. Minneapolis: Fortress Press.

Rothschild, Clare K. 2004. *Luke-Acts and the Rhetoric of History: An Investigation of Early Christian Historiography.* Tübingen: Mohr Siebeck.

Sacks, Kenneth. 1981. *Polybius on the Writing of History.* Berkeley: University of California Press.

Schüssler Fiorenza, Elisabeth. 1989. *In Memory of Her: A Feminist Theological Reconstruction of Christian Origins.* New York: Crossroad.

Segovia, Fernando F. 2000. *Decolonizing Biblical Studies: A View from the Margins.* Maryknoll, NY: Orbis.

Skarsaune, Oskar. 1987. *The Proof from Prophecy: A Study in Justin Martyr's Proof-Text Tradition: Text-Type, Provenance, Theological Profile.* NovTSup 56. Leiden: Brill.

Stephens, John, and Robyn McCallum. 1998. *Retelling Stories, Framing Culture: Traditional Story and Metanarratives in Children's Literature.* New York: Routledge.

Sterling, G. E. 1992. *Historiography and Self-Definition: Josephus, Luke-Acts and Apologetic Historiography.* Leiden: Brill.

Stott, John R. W. 1990. *The Message of Acts.* Leicester: Inter-Varsity Press.

Talbert, C. H. 1977. *What Is a Gospel? The Genre of the Canonical Gospels.* Philadelphia: Fortress Press.

Tyson, Joseph. 2006. *Marcion and Luke-Acts: A Defining Struggle.* Columbia: South Carolina University Press.

Unnik, W. C. van. 1980. "Luke-Acts a Storm Center in Contemporary Scholarship." In *Studies in Luke-Acts*, edited by Leander. E. Keck and J. Louis Martyn, 15–32. Philadelphia: Fortress Press.

Walker, William O., Jr. 1985. "Acts and the Pauline Corpus Reconsidered." *JSNT* 24:3–23.

———. 1998. "Acts and the Pauline Corpus Revisited: Peter's Speech at the Jerusalem Conference." In *Literary Studies in Luke-Acts: Essays in Honor of Joseph B. Tyson*, edited by Richard P. Thompson and Thomas E. Phillips, 77–86. Macon, GA: Mercer University Press.

Walters, Patricia. 2009. *The Assumed Authorial Unity of Luke and Acts: A Reassessment of the Evidence.* Cambridge: Cambridge University Press.

Williams, Demetrius K. 2007. "Acts of the Apostles." In *True to Our Native Land: An African American New Testament Commentary*, edited by Brian Blount, 213–48. Minneapolis: Fortress Press.

———. 2009. "'Upon All Flesh': Acts 2, African Americans and Intersectional Realities." In *They Were All Together in One Place: Toward Minority Biblical Criticism*, edited by Randall C. Bailey, Tat-siong Benny Liew, and Fernando F. Segovia, 289–310. Atlanta: Society of Biblical Literature.

Witherington, Ben, III. 1998. *Acts: A Socio-Historical Commentary.* Grand Rapids: Eerdmans.

THE ACTS OF THE APOSTLES

Michal Beth Dinkler

Introduction

The Acts of the Apostles is unique in the New Testament as the only sequel to a prior narrative (Luke's Gospel). Although the precise relationship between the Gospel and Acts remains under debate, most scholars agree that the same author wrote both volumes. Despite traditional accounts attributing this work to Paul's companion "Luke, the beloved physician" (Col. 4:14), in truth, the historical identity of this anonymous author remains unknown. He will be called "Luke" here simply for convenience.

Though the author was not a historian in any modern sense of the word, he clearly was concerned to give his addressee Theophilus a verifiable, orderly, historiographical account of Jesus' life and the subsequent spread of the early Jesus movement (Luke 1:1-4; Acts 1:1-2; Sterling). He was conversant with Roman administrative practices, and also clearly educated, writing in sophisticated Greek prose and alluding to Greco-Roman literature, as well as Jewish Scripture and traditions.

Recently, scholars have reopened the question of when Acts was written, suggesting that a composition date during the mid-second century CE (c. 110–130) is more likely than the traditional consensus dating Acts between 80–100 CE (Tyson; Pervo). The authorship and date of composition obviously influence our consideration of the historicity of Acts. The traditional view that Luke was Paul's companion lent credence to the sections of Acts that refer to Paul, a view further bolstered by the so-called we-passages, in which the narrator speaks in the first-person plural (16:10-17; 20:5—21:18; 27:1—28:16). In the second century CE, Irenaeus took the we-passages as proof that the author was an eyewitness of the events narrated (*Adv. haer.* 3.1–14). This view reigned until the eighteenth century, when historical-critical scholars (e.g., redaction, source, and form critics) mined the we-passages for evidence of Luke's multiple sources. In the nineteenth century, Bruno Bauer suggested that "we" narration established reliability within a fictional narrative world.

Contemporary scholars tend not to see the we-passages as evidence of historicity, but rather as the conventional ancient style for narrating sea voyages (Robbins), or as a means of legitimating Paul (Campbell). The ambiguities surrounding the historical identity of the author have led most scholars today to reject the previously common practice of using Acts to establish the historicity or chronology of the Pauline Letters.

Like reconstructions of the Lukan author, conjectures about the location of composition and intended audience must be tentative. Commentators have offered intriguing proposals regarding the identity of the "most excellent" Theophilus (Luke 1:3). As Luke uses "most excellent" elsewhere to refer to Roman leaders (Acts 23:26; 24:3; 26:25), perhaps Theophilus is a Roman patron who commissioned these narratives; alternatively, "Theophilus," which literally means "God-lover," could refer symbolically to anyone who loves God. In any case, it seems clear that Luke wrote Acts to be read more broadly than by one person.

Specific scholarly suggestions tend to link Luke's intended audience with a particular rhetorical purpose: Luke wrote to Jewish Christians in order to legitimate Paul, to Christians in Rome to commend the Roman Empire, or to Roman officials to defend Christianity. All we can say with certainty is that Acts can be situated within the first- or second-century-CE Mediterranean world, which means the implied audience would be familiar with basic sociocultural, political, geographical, and religious norms associated with life in the Roman Empire.

Scholars have consistently emphasized one dominant theme in Luke's two-volume work: salvation to the ends of the earth. Typically, Acts 1:8 is viewed as the quintessential Lukan formulation of universal salvation, and as an outline for the book of Acts as a whole. Other themes commonly identified in Luke-Acts include Christians' relationships with marginalized "others" (e.g., the poor, women, and Jews), proper uses of wealth, fulfillment of prophecy, the divine will and human response, the church (its growth, leadership, eschatological role, and ecclesiological practices), and the gift of the Holy Spirit. For more detail on these and other critical debates in Acts scholarship, see the preceding essay in this volume.

Given the extent of the narrative, it is helpful to keep a broad outline of the story in mind:

Acts 1:1—6:7: The Birth of the Church and Witness to Jerusalem
Acts 6:8—9:31: Spreading Beyond Jerusalem: Samaria and Judea
Acts 9:32—12:25: Bridge to the Gentiles: Expansion into Antioch
Acts 13:1—15:35: Expanding to the "Ends of the Earth": Asia Minor
Acts 15:36—21:16: Expanding to the "Ends of the Earth": Europe
Acts 21:17—28:31: At Long Last: The Movement Reaches Rome

1:1-26: Prologue and Introduction

The Text in Its Ancient Context

The stereotypically formal Greco-Roman dedication to Theophilus mirrors that of the Gospel (Luke 1:1-4). Thus the foreword (1:1-5) and ascension story (1:6-11; cf. Luke 24:44-53) function as a bridge, establishing continuity with Luke's Gospel and looking ahead to the story's next phase.

Many see Acts 1:8 as programmatic for the entire book: Acts recounts the worldwide spread of the gospel.

Jesus' ascension in Acts (1:6-11) differs slightly from the Gospel account (Luke 24:50-53). This version shifts the focus from Jesus to the apostles and postpones the Parousia (which supports Conzelmann's controversial contention that Luke wrote to explain the Parousia's delay). Acts 1:3 is the only mention in the New Testament of forty days between Jesus' resurrection and ascension (though this may be idiomatic for "a long time").

Continuities exist as well; the account reinforces several key Lukan themes. First, the passive form of the Greek verb *epērthē* ("he was lifted up") establishes that God governs the narrative's events. God's sovereignty is so strong in Luke-Acts that the acts of Luke's characters have been called "the twitching of human puppets" (Haenchen, 361). Second, Jesus promises the Holy Spirit (1:8), whom many consider the main character in Acts. Third, Acts 1:9 recalls Jesus' prediction of the son of man's return (Luke 21:27), and is consistent with other New Testament texts (Matt. 26:64; Mark 14:62; Rev. 1:7; 14:14).

The account resonates with other ancient ascension narratives. For example, Gen. 5:24 implies that Enoch ascends into heaven, and in the Jewish mystical texts *1* and *3 Enoch*, he transforms into an angel. In 2 Kgs. 2:11, the prophet Elijah ascends into heaven on a chariot of fire, and in *Joseph and Aseneth* 17.7–8, an angel rides a chariot to heaven. Acts 1:9-11 especially resembles Josephus's depiction of Moses' ascension in *Antiquities* 4.326.

Following Jesus' ascension, Peter makes the first of twenty-four public speeches in Acts (1:16-22). Speeches in Acts establish Luke's literary artistry, interpret theological themes for readers, and propel the plot. In this, Luke resembles ancient historians, who used speeches to emphasize themes and move the narrative forward.

Peter cites Pss. 69:25 and 109:8, effectively casting Judas as God's enemy and making his replacement a divine necessity. Luke's readers already know that Judas betrayed Jesus (Luke 22:47-53), but here, they learn of Judas's bloody death (cf. Matt. 27:3-10). After praying and casting lots, the disciples choose Matthias (1:21-26), who is otherwise unimportant, as he is unmentioned elsewhere in the New Testament. What matters is the unbroken apostolic witness of Jesus' ministry; the number twelve maintains symbolic continuity with Israel's twelve patriarchs, whom the twelve apostles will eventually judge (Luke 22:30).

The Text in the Interpretive Tradition

In the second and third centuries, Christian apologists such as Justin Martyr, Tertullian, and Origen further developed the doctrinal and theological importance of Christ's ascension when defending against those who denied that it had happened at all. Athanasius insisted that Jesus' ascent is the natural corollary to the incarnation, as it ends Christ's bodily humiliation and begins his heavenly exaltation. Jesus' ascension also appears repeatedly in early creedal formulas (e.g., the Apostles', Nicene, and Athanasian Creeds). In the Qur'an, Jesus does not die at all; he ascends into heaven alive.

Pictorial renditions through the centuries reflect the inherent difficulties in representing Jesus' ascension. Early Christian artists struggled with how to depict Jesus' earthly absence (which paradoxically points to his heavenly presence), often resorting to static scenes of Jesus on clouds above his disciples. Eventually, a new kind of visual rhetoric arose as artists depicted the scene from below, with only Jesus' feet visible (e.g., Albrecht Dürer's famous sixteenth-century woodcut).

In the thirteenth century, Thomas Aquinas emphasized that Christ's ascension prepares the way for the ascension of all believers. Later, sixteenth-century Reformers picked up on a similar theme; Calvin interpreted Jesus' ascension as evidence that Christians are *already* victorious through Christ (*Institutes* 2.16).

Luther and Zwingli drew different conclusions about the Eucharist based on Jesus' ascension: for Zwingli, Christ's body is located with the Father and therefore cannot literally be present at the Eucharist. For Luther, however, the Father's right hand symbolizes a place of power, not a physical location; thus, Luther argued, Christ is literally present whenever Christians celebrate the Lord's Supper.

The Text in Contemporary Discussion

The symbolic geographic movement of the Gospel from Jerusalem to Rome presents a hermeneutical challenge for modern interreligious dialogue, since it easily lends itself to a supersessionist theology: Jerusalem (representing Judaism) is superseded by the power of Rome (representing Christianity). Furthermore, twentieth-century evangelist Billy Graham referred to Acts 1:8 when calling Christians to "win the whole world for Christ." Does "winning the whole world for Christ" facilitate Western triumphalism?

Some consider the call to spread the gospel "to the ends of the earth" as an indication that the Christian message is superior to and ought to supplant all other religious traditions. Such religious triumphalism, which was inextricably wedded to Western colonial expansion, often assumes that to do missionary work Christians must be foreigners in a strange land; however, the early Christian movement "begins in Jerusalem," suggesting that empowered by the Spirit, Christians can and should also witness at home (Kanyoro).

Jesus' promise that God's reign transcends expectations can also challenge marginalized people groups today. For example, Justo González warns that if US Hispanics overemphasize God's coming reign, they will neglect their global witness. Does Acts teach that the church should prepare for an imminent Judgment Day, or maintain tradition in the face of an indefinitely delayed eschatology?

Some take Acts 1:12-26 as a fixed prescription for church leadership. According to the Catholic Church, apostolic succession originates here, guaranteeing doctrinal teachings through the bishops' unbroken lineage. In contrast, Ernst Kasëmann famously disparaged Acts' "early catholicism" (Frühkatholizismus), by which he meant a departure from the "true" gospel's egalitarianism. Most scholars today emphasize that Acts describes leaders adapting to changing circumstances.

Recently, Luke's contradictory gender constructions have provoked a spate of scholarly studies. On the one hand, Acts 9:36 is the only time a woman is explicitly labeled a "disciple" in the New Testament (Tabitha; cf. Rom. 16:7), and other women play important roles in the Christian community (1:14; 2:17-18; 12:2; 16:13-15; 18:18, 26; see Josephus, *Ant.* 4:219 on rejecting a woman's legal witness). Thus many believe Acts supports women's church leadership (Pierce, Groothuis, and

Fee). However, Acts also silences women: they are rarely quoted, men remain in command, and Peter stipulates that Judas's replacement be male (1:21). Therefore, others find it futile to try and reclaim Acts for feminist causes (Schaberg).

A more basic question underlies these discussions: Should an ancient narrative be a contemporary imperative? If so, how should interpreters discern which narrative elements are relevant and/or normative for their situation(s)?

2:1-47: The Day of Pentecost

The Text in Its Ancient Context

The miraculous outpouring of the Holy Spirit on Pentecost (2:1-13) fulfills Jesus' prophecies (Luke 24:49; Acts 1:4-5) and formally inaugurates the messianic community. Luke is beholden to Jewish tradition: Hellenistic Jews gave the name "Pentecost" ("fiftieth") to the Jewish "Festival of Weeks" (Shevuot), which occurred fifty days after Passover. Originally a harvest festival, Pentecost eventually celebrated the giving of the Mosaic law. The onlookers' comprehension of the multiple languages likely echoes the rabbinic legend that God gave the Sinaitic law in seventy languages for the world's seventy nations (compare *glōssolalia*, which requires interpretation; 1 Cor. 14:1-25; see Philo, *De decalogo* 9–11). The sound of rushing wind and the tongues "as of fire" evoke Hebrew Bible theophanies (Gen. 2:7; Exod. 3:2; 13:21; 19:18; Ps. 33:6; cf. Isa. 5:24).

The onlookers are devout Diaspora Jews living in Jerusalem (2:5). This is the first instance in Acts of *Ioudaios*, a difficult word to translate since it has multiple overlapping referents: geographic, religious, and ethnic. The subsequent list of nations (2:9-11) resembles lists found in ancient astrological and historical writings. Scholars have proposed several direct sources (e.g., Genesis 10 and Philo's *Embassy to Gaius* 281–82). Aside from questions of translation and derivation, juxtaposing *Ioudaios* and the list of nations at the start of Acts substantiates the Lukan message that the gospel came first to the Jews, then spread throughout the world.

As is common in Luke-Acts, bystanders misinterpret the events (2:13). In the Gospel, those who misunderstand are typically closest to Jesus (2:43, 50; 9:10-17, 28-36, 37-42, 44-45, 49-50, 54-55, 57-62). In Acts, outsiders misunderstand, often about a character's identity (3:17; 7:25; 8:18-24; 13:27; 14:11-13; 19:14-16; 22:9; cf. 21:17-26). Characters' ignorance frequently introduces dramatic irony (when characters know less than the readers), thus privileging readers and solidifying insider-outsider boundaries. Lukan characters often unwittingly voice the narrator's—and ultimately God's—perspective (cf. 5:39).

Peter instructs the witnesses to "listen carefully" (2:14). Using a complex of seeing- and hearing-related words, Luke consistently commends listening well. Peter interprets Pentecost as a fulfillment of prophecy (2:16; a slightly modified citation from Joel 2:28-32 LXX), thereby connecting the indwelling of the Spirit with the prophetic task established in the Hebrew Bible. As a result of these events, three thousand join the nascent Jesus movement (first labeled "Christian" in Antioch; see 11:26).

The Text in the Interpretive Tradition

Patristic preachers like Cyprian and John Chrysostom used an idealized Acts 2 community to castigate their congregations' divisiveness. Fourth-century monastics like Basil the Great appropriated Acts 2:44-45 for the apostolic life (*vita apostolica*), including a vow of poverty. This passage also inspired Thomas More's *Utopia* (sixteenth century) and Marx and Engels's *Communist Manifesto* (nineteenth century). As a result, it was common in the twentieth-century view to assert that early Christians were "communists." Despite the fact that communist thinkers appealed to early Christian practice to develop and support their ideological system, labeling early Christians "communist" is anachronistic.

By the fifth century CE, the Feast of Pentecost had become a liturgical tradition distinct from Easter; Eastern churches held that the church was born at Jesus' resurrection, while Western churches considered Pentecost the church's birth.

Pentecost has sparked many debates over pneumatology: Post-Reformation theologians (sixteenth century) and Princeton theologians like B. B. Warfield (nineteenth century) advanced a cessationist view (charismata have ceased), whereas others insist that demonic deliverance, divine healing, and ecstatic prophecy continue. According to Charles Parham (1873–1929), missionaries who speak in tongues need not study foreign languages. Pentecostals and members of the Holiness movement (early twentieth century) took glossolalia as evidence of true faith and, often, the dissolution of racial barriers. The Pentecostal movement initially was interracial (e.g., the Azusa Street Revival of 1906–1909).

The Text in Contemporary Discussion

A nostalgic, romanticized image of early Christian unity continues. Commentators often write that Pentecost overturns the Tower of Babel story (Gen. 11:1-9) and that the Holy Spirit brings concord (Acts 2:44-45). Many Christians today assume that while contemporary Christians are divided, the early church enjoyed uncomplicated *koinōnia* ("fellowship": a praised virtue in Hellenistic literature). For instance, the Barna Research Group reports that the "house church movement" is growing worldwide. The movement rejects ecclesiastical structures and ordained clergy in favor of meeting in private homes; this is supposedly modeled on the early Christians (Acts 2:42; 5:42; 12:12; 16:40; 20:20), though advocates of the movement often overlook how Roman households were bustling hubs of activity, with business conducted in the *tablinum* ("office"), and daily offerings left in the *lararium* ("shrine"). The earliest house churches did not meet in solely private spaces. The Holy Spirit's coming also led to believers sharing their resources (Acts 2:44-45); since the 1960s, liberation theologians have referenced Acts 2 to advocate for sharing material wealth with poor people.

For others, Pentecost is not an overturning, but simply a new iteration of Babel, since the disciples speak local dialects (not one common language), and they again scatter throughout the earth. How one interprets Pentecost influences missions and diversity in the church today. For instance, some Christian missionaries seek to assimilate, or "speak the language" of other cultures, while others believe a truly "globalized" Christianity will transcend cultural differences. Does the Holy

Spirit erase ethnic/racial differences and subvert human-made hierarchies? Does Pentecost add a welcoming, multiethnic element to Christianity that churches today should celebrate and emulate?

Relatedly, if Pentecost overcomes humanity's fragmentation, as Rome also purported to do, does this imply that early Christians appropriated Roman imperialistic propaganda (Gilbert)? Does Luke reinscribe hierarchical values? If so, do Christians today perpetuate similarly problematic ideologies?

Luke utilizes the prevailing discourses of his time in his own form of what Denise Buell calls "ethnic reasoning." Recognizing that race and ethnicity are socially shaped, discursive constructions, rather than fixed, stable categories complexifies Luke's universalism. How have Christians used the fluid categories of race/ethnicity apologetically, as evidence of Christianity's multicultural appeal?

In the United States, racial-ethnic minorities are becoming the majority. How does, or should, this influence American churches, which remain predominantly segregated? Are ethnically homogenous congregations blind to their own racialized assumptions and systemic sin, or are they rightly respecting differences between people groups?

3:1—6:7: The Church in Jerusalem

The Text in Its Ancient Context

Peter's healing of the lame man (3:1-11) provides the first instance of the "wonders and signs" mentioned earlier (2:43). The miracle recalls Jesus' healings (Luke 7:22) and the prophetic tradition that at Israel's redemption the lame will "leap like a deer" (Isa. 35:6). In ancient society, those with disabilities often were ridiculed and associated with sin; Peter communicates that *all* people, regardless of appearance or ability, are welcome in God's kingdom.

Four times, Luke says the witnesses are astonished (3:10-12). This further develops an established Lukan theme: in Luke's Gospel, God amazes people (1:63; 2:18, 33), then Jesus does (4:22, 32, 36; 5:24-26); and now in Acts, the disciples engender amazement, implicitly linking them to God and Jesus, and heightening their authority in the narrative.

Peter's prophetic speech (3:12-26) echoes the one he gave at Pentecost: again, he addresses a misunderstanding, clarifies the miracle's divine origin, and demonstrates that Jesus fulfills messianic prophecies. Contrary to a common Jewish conviction, welcoming gentiles fulfills the Abrahamic covenant (3:25).

While the "people" respond gladly, the Jewish authorities become angry. In Luke's Gospel, the Pharisees *and* Sadducees oppose Jesus, but in Acts, the main opponents are the Sadducees. The descriptions of the Sadducees in Acts (4:1; 5:17; 23:6-8) cohere with Josephus's account that they are the aristocratic temple priesthood, the majority party of the Sanhedrin (*Ant.* 13:297–98). Testifying before the Jerusalem Council (4:1-22), Peter fulfills Jesus' promise (Luke 12:11-12).

Luke then adds to the picture of Christian communal life (cf. 2:43-47). The disciples' prayers are immediately answered (4:23-31), in a clear echo of Pentecost (cf. 2:1-4); unified in "heart and soul" (4:32), they voluntarily share possessions (4:33-37), thereby implementing Jesus' commands (Luke 12:33; 18:22), in contrast to typical Mediterranean patron-client relations (Moxnes). Correct use of possessions is a common Lukan theme (Seccombe). The phrase "heart and soul" may draw on Deuteronomy (4:29; 6:5; 10:12; 11:13; 26:16), and/or echo traditional Greek proverbs (*Nic. Eth.* 9.8.2).

And yet, this idyllic communal portrait does not last. Unlike Barnabas (4:36-37), Ananias and Sapphira refuse to surrender their possessions and lie about their hoarding (5:1-11). Similar to Achan, whose deceit results in his divinely sanctioned death (Josh. 7:16-26), God strikes Ananias and Sapphira dead. Ironically, after refusing to place all their money "at the apostles' feet" (5:2; cf. 4:35-37), this is precisely where Sapphira dies (5:10). The divine retribution legitimates the apostles' authority (5:11).

Acts 5:17-26 is the first of three miraculous prison escapes in Acts (cf. 12:6-11; 16:25-27). Again, the Jerusalem Council attempts to thwart the spread of the gospel. Again, the apostles refuse to be silenced, citing a well-known Greek proverb and common Jewish admonition that they obey God, not humans (5:29; cf. Plato, *Apology* 29D; Deut. 4:30; 8:20; 9:23; 30:2). The Pharisee Gamaliel's intervention pacifies the Jewish authorities (5:39) and immediately proves prophetic, as the apostles continue preaching (5:42).

In line with Jewish practice (Deut. 14:28-29; 24:17-21; 26:12-13; Isa. 1:17-23), the early church cared for widows (6:1-7), who were particularly vulnerable in such a patriarchal culture (Moxnes). Luke's Gospel repeatedly refers to widows (7:11-17; 9:39; 18:1-8; 20:47). Historically, the presence of Greek-speaking Hellenistic Christians and Aramaic-speaking Hebrew Christians is likely, given Jerusalem's diversity and hellenization's long-standing influence throughout the empire (cf. 1 Macc. 1:11-15). When choosing overseers for daily food distribution, the apostles pray (cf. 1:12-26) and lay hands on the seven (6:6), evoking Joshua's commissioning (Num. 27:18-23). They repeat the practice later (8:15-19; 9:12-17; 13:2-3).

Six summary statements like 6:7 punctuate the Acts narrative (cf. 9:31; 12:24; 16:5; 19:20; 28:31), reiterating and deepening the inseparable link between God's unstoppable word and the growth of the church. Each of the six resulting panels shows the movement of the gospel into a different geographical region.

The Text in the Interpretive Tradition

Proponents of the traditional view that Luke was a physician long believed Acts 3:1-11 demonstrated unique medical knowledge (e.g., W. K. Hobart [*The Medical Language of St. Luke*, 1882]). However, in 1920, Henry Cadbury convincingly demonstrated that such vocabulary was common in ancient literature.

As with Acts 2:42-47, patristic sermons (e.g., Cyprian, Chrysostom) take the common life described in 4:32-37 as a normative historical reality and a paradigmatic example of Christian generosity and unanimity. In contrast to this ideal, church fathers condemned Ananias and Sapphira as greed personified (e.g., Maximus of Turin).

Patristic interpreters produced panegyrics of Peter based on this section of Acts: Peter is the divinely appointed miracle-worker and defender of the faith nonpareil. Cyprian cites Peter's lack of money (3:6) to denounce greed. The Venerable Bede taught that the church, who "walks upright" (Peter), must raise Israel, who "limps" without the gospel (the lame man). The Catholic Church sees Peter as Rome's first bishop, from whom infallible papal authority descends. Ironically, throughout the sixteenth through the eighteenth centuries, English Dissenters used Acts 4:19 to justify leaving the Church of England (which was originally established to oppose papal authority).

Supporters of the church's rigid hierarchical structure in the Middle Ages used Acts 6:1-7 (and 20:17, 28) to defend formal ecclesiastical offices. For medieval theologians, institutionalization was necessary to stave off false teachings and to manage the church's increasingly differentiated ministries.

The Text in Contemporary Discussion

Recent advances in disability studies focus on the lame man. Although scholars debate whether first-century-CE laws banned those with disabilities from the temple, in Acts, the man enters the temple only after he is healed. The key question is whether the story demeans or emancipates those with disabilities: Does God overturn human discrimination? Or does Luke reinscribe the polemics of ancient physiognomy (systematically connecting physical features with one's inner disposition) by implying that one must be physically able to be spiritually acceptable?

Although Ananias and Sapphira's deaths offend modern sensibilities, most commentators conclude that they deserved their punishment. Recently, scholars have warned against uncritically accepting the text's ideology that Christian violence is divinely sanctioned "justice," whereas outsider violence against Christians is unjust. The theme of unrighteous outsiders persecuting righteous insiders appears throughout ancient literature, including the Dead Sea Scrolls and the Hebrew Bible. Furthermore, in Acts, violence is gendered: perpetrators (on both sides) are male, but the text effeminizes "outsiders" (e.g., Acts 19:21-41) and glorifies "insider" (i.e., Christian male) violence.

Violence in Acts also raises the complicated question of Jewish-Christian relations. Scholars often single out depiction in Acts of the Pharisees as relatively positive. The *Catechism of the Catholic Church* refers to Acts 6:7 to affirm that Jews are not responsible for Jesus' death. Others challenge what they see as anti-Jewish rhetoric in Acts (e.g., 13:44-52), objecting that those stereotypes are dehumanizing, overly simple, and historically inaccurate.

Acts 6:1-7 both affirms and undermines women: on the one hand, Luke insists that the church must care for socioeconomically disadvantaged women; on the other hand, this perpetuates female dependence on a male-run ecclesiastical institution, perhaps squelching widows' autonomy (Price). Clearly, early Christians were ambivalent over widows' relative power and sexuality (cf. 1 Tim. 5:9-16). Acts 6:1-7 also records divisions of ministerial labors that eventually became gender-based (e.g., ministries of the word are for males, service ministries are for females).

6:8—8:3: The Persecution and Martyrdom of Stephen

The Text in Its Ancient Context

In the previous section (6:1-7), the disciples in Jerusalem chose seven leaders to resolve an internal conflict. Here, the conflict begins to move outward, as diasporic Jews from Asia Minor (Cilicia and Asia) and Africa (freed slaves from Cyrene and Alexandria) arrest one of the chosen seven (Stephen). The Lukan narrator underscores the injustice of their accusations by emphasizing Stephen's grace and power (6:8), wisdom through the Spirit (6:10), and angelic innocence (6:15)—attributes associated with God's chosen leaders enacting the divine plan (7:22, 25).

Several significant parallels exist between these scenes and Jesus' passion in the Gospel: like Jesus, Stephen is falsely accused of speaking against Moses, opposing Jewish customs, and blaspheming. Both Jesus and Stephen refer to the son of man at God's right hand (7:55; cf. Luke 22:69), both ask God to forgive their tormentors (7:60; cf. Luke 23:34), and Stephen commends his spirit to Jesus (7:59), just as Jesus commended his spirit to God (Luke 23:46). Rhetorically, these recurrences link the sufferings of Christians back to the sufferings of Jesus' passion.

There is a crucial distinction, however. Whereas Jesus himself remains silent before Herod (Luke 23:9), Stephen eloquently refutes the charges against him (Acts 6:9-12); presumably, as Stephen speaks, Jesus is fulfilling his promise to provide the words (Luke 21:14-15). Stephen recounts the establishment of God's covenant, summarizes Israel's history, and draws extensively on the patriarchal stories (with some divergences from Genesis). The attentive reader knows that with Stephen as his mouthpiece, Luke is adding a new layer of meaning to these familiar accounts. For example, Stephen's citation of Deut. 18:15 contains a pun: God fulfilled the promise to "raise up" a prophet like Moses—literally and figuratively—in Jesus (cf. 3:22). Stephen's speech also advances a crucial Lukan theme: the state of one's heart determines whether one will receive the divine word (cf. Luke 8:4-21; 10:24). The Lukan narrator's ideological conviction is placed in Stephen's mouth: the Jews reject Moses, the law, and the prophets due to their "uncircumcised" hearts and ears (7:51). Without Gamaliel to appease the authorities (see 5:34-40), the confrontation escalates and Stephen becomes the first Christian martyr. Ironically, by executing him, the people prove Stephen's point that the Jews reject God's prophets; the narrative rhetoric thereby authorizes Stephen and his message.

Acts 7:58 records the most famous witness of Stephen's killing: Saul of Tarsus in Cilicia, later called Paul (a Roman name). Saul, a member of the Jewish Diaspora and committed Pharisee, most likely was named for Israel's great king. As Acts repeatedly attests, Saul zealously sought to exterminate the early Jesus movement (7:58; 8:1; 9:1-2, 5, 13-14, 21; 22:4-5, 7, 19; 26:9-11, 14). According to the Lukan narrative, Stephen's death inaugurated a "severe persecution," scattering the Jerusalem church throughout Judea and Samaria (8:1).

The Text in the Interpretive Tradition

Non-Christian martyrdoms symbolically associated crowns with the "victory" of martyrdom and immortality prior to Stephen's execution. Nevertheless, traditional Christian history dubs Stephen (whose name means "crown") the "Protomartyr"—the first in a long line of Christians "crowned" with martyrdom in imitation of Christ. For instance, the early account of the martyrdoms in Lyons and Vienna refers to Stephen (Eusebius, *Hist. eccl.* 5:2:5).

By the fourth and fifth centuries, once Acts was canonized, church fathers like Gregory of Nyssa, Hesychius of Jerusalem, and Augustine of Hippo often referred to Stephen's martyrdom in their homilies, lauding his effective preaching, his service as a deacon, and his patience when persecuted. Though the Catholic Church never officially canonized Stephen, he is recognized as a saint; Christian iconography depicts him with stones and a crown.

The famous *Foxe's Book of Martyrs*, originally published in 1563, chronicles Christian martyrdoms from Jesus through the Inquisitions (twelfth–thirteenth centuries) and the Protestant Reformation (fourteenth–sixteenth centuries); subsequent editions added the Church of England's split from the Catholic Church (1559) and nineteenth-century American missionaries like Adoniram Judson. *Foxe's Book of Martyrs* shaped the West's collective Christian consciousness, including the complex legacy of Christian self-identification as the legitimate heirs and correct interpreters of Jewish traditions and Scriptures. For centuries, claims that the Jews rejected the true Messiah, killing Jesus and then his followers, have fueled antisemitism, including Luther's highly influential *Von den Juden und Ihren Lügen* (*On the Jews and Their Lies*, pub. 1543), and the Nazis' "ethnic cleansings" (1939–1945).

The Text in Contemporary Discussion

Acts is particularly virulent in its anti-Jewish polemic. Stephen blames Jesus' crucifixion and early Christian persecution entirely on the Jews (7:51-60). Since passages like this have fueled antisemitic atrocities like the Holocaust, many question whether this is the "word of God," and whether such passages should be read in church. Are the *Lutheran Lectionary for Mass* and *The Revised Common Lectionary* right to include them in the liturgy, or should clergy avoid them?

Recently, scholars have debated the historical origins of the Christian martyrdom tradition. Some, following William Frend, argue that Christian martyrdom accounts have literary precedents in the Jewish Maccabean genre (1965); Glen Bowersock, however, contends that Christian martyrdom was an entirely new phenomenon that arose from early Christian interactions with Romans, who venerated suicide (1995). Still others, such as Daniel Boyarin, argue that the Christian martyrological narratives reveal the contested nature of Jews' and Christians' close interconnectedness at the time, and their efforts to construct separate categories of identity (1999). Relatedly, scholars like Judith Perkins and Candida Moss fundamentally challenge the traditional notion that early Christians faced pervasive, consistent persecution, since most extant accounts come from the church historian Eusebius, who wrote during Constantine's pro-Christian reign and consistently disparaged earlier emperors as anti-Christian (fourth century CE). Other historical records indicate that individual governors held localized freedom regarding Christian persecution, and mass apostasy was far more common than actual martyrdoms. Scholars like Elizabeth Castelli bracket historiographical considerations, focusing on the dynamic role of power negotiations and hagiographical memories in early Christian identity formation (2004).

Nevertheless, the narrative of unjust Christian martyrdom at the hands of outside persecutors remains powerful; Christian self-sacrifice today is often cast in the same mold as the ancient accounts. The Voice of the Martyrs, an American nonprofit organization, seeks to encourage those who are "persecuted for their faith in Christ" and distributes Bibles in "hostile nations"; innocent deaths, as in the Columbine massacre (April 20, 1999) and the World Trade Center attacks (September 11, 2001), are deemed martyrdoms and used as rallying cries against America's "enemies." There is a danger when such views legitimate unethical violence and racial profiling, or perpetuate stereotypes of entire populations as "anti-Christian."

8:4-40: The Ministry of Philip

The Text in Its Ancient Context

The "severe persecution" begun at Stephen's martyrdom ultimately enables the fulfillment of Jesus' promise in Acts 1:8, since it leads Philip (one of the seven chosen in 6:1-7) to preach in Samaria (8:4). As part of a pervasive motif advocating for the outcasts of society, Luke's Gospel gives special attention to Samaritans, whom Jews despised for insisting that they were the true preservers of the Mosaic law (Luke 10:30-37; 17:11-19). Entrance into Samaria thus establishes connective tissue with the Gospel and represents a significant moment in the expansion of the church.

Simon, Philip's literary foil, has duped the Samaritans with magic, which for Luke represents the cosmic drama between God's forces and the forces of evil (8:4-25). Despite his baptism (8:13), Simon is not transformed; failing to distinguish between miracles and magic, he tries to buy the Spirit's power (8:18-24). The narrative rhetoric here emphasizes two common Lukan themes: the danger of magic and the danger of wealth.

Though the gentile mission does not formally begin until chapter 10, Acts 8:26-40 depicts the first gentile conversion. Philip overhears an Ethiopian eunuch reading aloud (following the ancient custom) from the Isaianic scroll (most likely the Septuagint version). The Ethiopian eunuch is an outsider on multiple counts: In the Greco-Roman geographical imagination, Ethiopia was the end of the world (whereas Rome was its navel, or *omphalos*). The eunuch's conversion fulfills Acts 1:8 and demonstrates that the Spirit reaches all who are "far away" (*makran*, 2:39; in Greek literature, *makran* often refers to Ethiopians). Ancient writers like Herodotus, Strabo, and Homer describe Ethiopians as the original race, handsome and dark. Several ancient physiognomic handbooks, which outline how physical features reflect moral character, depict Ethiopians as cowardly (Parsons, 119).

The term *eunuch* could simply indicate his official title (cf. Gen. 39:1 LXX) as finance minister for the Candace (the title for queens of Ethiopian Meroë). If *eunuch* indicates that he was castrated, then he was "other" physically, as well. First-century society demonized eunuchs, associating honor with masculinity and shame with femininity. Further, if he was castrated, he could not be a Jew, despite his interest in Israel's religion (8:27-28; Lev. 21:20; Deut. 23:1; Josephus, *Ant.* 4.290–91). Overall, the eunuch's conversion epitomizes the Lukan themes of universalism and social justice: the gospel reaches the marginalized.

As elsewhere in Luke-Acts, the Holy Spirit directs events on the Gaza road (8:26, 29, 39). This detail characterizes Philip as a prophet like Elijah, whom the Spirit leads similarly (1 Kgs. 18:46). The passage cited (Isa. 53:7-8) refers to the sacrificial lamb, who (like Jesus before Herod; Luke 23:9) "does not open his mouth" (8:32); in contrast, Philip "opens his mouth" (8:35) and explains the Scriptures, just as the risen Jesus did on the Emmaus road (Luke 24:27). Philip baptizes the eunuch, ritually reversing his debased status. The *katabasis-anabasis* language here (8:38-39) is common in Greco-Roman mythology (e.g., Theseus, Heracles, and Orpheus travel "down" to Hades and "come up" again), and may have contributed to the Christian concept of baptism as a death and rebirth. The eunuch rejoices (8:39), a common response to the gospel in Acts. The Spirit "snatches up" Philip, depositing him in Azotus, a city over twenty miles north (8:38-39). Few instances of miraculous disappearances occur in Luke-Acts (cf. Luke 9:28-36; 24:31; Acts 1:9), though they are common elsewhere in ancient literature (e.g., Mars takes Romulus up into heaven in Dionysius of Halicarnassus, *Ant. Rom.* 2.56.2; Aphrodite "snatches" Paris in Homer, *Il.* 3.380–83). The Hebrew Bible similarly depicts God's Spirit transferring prophets to new locations (1 Kgs. 18:12; 2 Kgs. 2:11-12, 16; Ezek. 3:14; 8:3; 11:1, 24; 43:5). Philip settles in Caesarea, which is where we find him thirteen chapters later (Acts 21:8).

The Text in the Interpretive Tradition

The church fathers were troubled by Simon's "wickedness" following baptism (8:22). The Venerable Bede posited that Simon feigned receiving the Spirit (CS 117:79), while Augustine concluded that baptizing someone evil results in evil, even if the baptizer is holy (FC 79:19). Simon appears elsewhere in Christian literature as Simon Magus (a Greek title meaning magician), who, traveling with a woman named Helena, was the ultimate heretic (e.g., Irenaeus, *Adv. haer.* 1.23.1-4).

Ferdinand Christian Baur, leader of the so-called Tübingen School of theology (nineteenth century), drew attention to references to Simon Magus in the Clementine literature and Apocryphal Acts, suggesting that Simon Magus was an alternative name for Paul. Building on the Hegelian dialectic, Baur held that the hierarchical "Catholic Christianity" of the second century CE represented the synthesis of Jewish Petrine Christianity (thesis) and gentile Pauline Christianity (antithesis).

Many patristic commentators held that the eunuch exemplifies the ideal response to the Christian message: he studies Scripture and, despite his high political station, humbly asks for help. Later Christian tradition taught that he was the first missionary to Africa. The eunuch's conversion also posed hermeneutical problems, however. Early Christian apologists like Justin recognized that ideal non-Christian readers *should* ask questions like the eunuch's (8:34), but they also believed that only Christian readers *can* ask them.

Acts 8:37 also presents a text-critical issue: though clearly not original, several manuscripts add a liturgical gloss with a baptismal formula: "He said to him, 'If you believe with your whole heart, you may.' He replied, 'I believe that Jesus Christ is the Son of God.'" Modern translations omit the verse number or put it in parentheses.

The Text in Contemporary Discussion

Conservative Christians in the West have revived the ancient Christian polemic against magic, believing that popular narratives about magic (e.g., J.K. Rowling's *Harry Potter* series) expose children to evil. African Christians offer a unique perspective on Simon's magical worldview because many Africans generate revenue by practicing magic today; although Simon's attempt to buy the Holy Spirit's power makes good financial sense in such a context, African Christian leaders condemn magic and superstition.

Many African churches uphold the tradition that the Ethiopian eunuch was the first African missionary; we do know the gospel reached the African continent early, and some of the earliest complete Bible translations were produced there.

Often, Christians take the Ethiopian eunuch's conversion as evidence of Christianity's countercultural inclusivity. Though the eunuch customarily stands outside acceptable society, the reference to Isa. 53:7-8 (LXX) affirms that foreigners will be restored to the people of God (cf. Isa. 56:3-5). From this perspective, Acts 8:33 commends the pursuit of justice in all contexts of humiliation, including ours today. Some consider this text redemptive for LGBTQ Christians, calling Christian communities to accept those who cannot/do not have children or engage in heterosexual intercourse (Wilson).

Liberation and womanist theologians commend a hermeneutic of suspicion instead. For them, ethnic difference is used as a polemical device marking outsiders, which is especially evident when comparing the Ethiopian eunuch's conversion to that of the Roman Cornelius (Acts 10:1-48). Ethno-political language and heterosexist ideologies suggest that early Christians simply adopted Rome's discursive strategies, marginalizing those outside of Rome.

The same dialectic remains operative today: On the one hand, the eunuch is an example of a marginalized minority who converts to Christianity; the example itself implicitly invites minorities today to imagine themselves as followers of Jesus as well. On the other hand, despite his conversion, the eunuch's marginal status does not change, in the story or in subsequent Christian history.

The overwhelming majority of Christian artwork depicts Jesus and his closest followers as white Europeans, which (despite many beloved iconic images) is historically inaccurate and perpetuates Eurocentric notions of racial superiority. We can see the continued power of this racialized image of Jesus and his followers in the fact that when Barack Obama was elected president of the United States in 2009, Afrocentric depictions of a black Christ that circulated on the Internet provoked the ire of many Americans.

Larger questions thus remain: can Acts 8:26-40 empower contemporary faith communities to challenge all forms of oppression? Or is the text inherently racist and/or sexist? Is Christianity a "white man's religion," as members of the Nation of Islam and others contend? How do biblical tropes that marginalize the "other" function today?

9:1-31: The Call of Saul/Paul

The Text in Its Ancient Context

In this highly dramatic episode, Saul, vigorous persecutor of Jesus' disciples, experiences a divine epiphany on the road to Damascus, in Syria. We are not told how the gospel has reached Damascus, only that Saul is on his way there to persecute followers of Jesus, and that his reputation precedes him. Ananias's parallel vision directs him to lay hands on Saul to restore his sight (cf. 4:30; 5:12; 8:17). Ananias's obedience and familial greeting (9:17-19), along with Barnabas's testimony (9:27), corroborate God's acceptance of Saul and validate Saul's claim to apostleship.

Luke's third-person account of Saul's transformation here differs slightly from the first-person versions recounted later in Acts (22:1-16; 26:9-18), and in Paul's letters (1 Cor. 15:3-8; Gal. 1:11-16). The Christophany contains typical features of Jewish theophany-type scenes, including a fall (cf. Ezek. 1:28; Dan. 8:17, 10:9), a bright light (cf. 4 Macc. 4:10, *Joseph and Aseneth* 14.1–2), and a vision only the recipient sees (cf. Dan. 10:7; Ezek. 1:28). There are also verbal echoes of the legend in 2 Maccabees 3, where a persecutor, Heliodorus, falls to the ground in darkness, "converts," and testifies to God's power.

Ironically in light of his previous witness of Stephen's martyrdom (7:58), Saul steps into the gap left by Stephen's death, taking a central leadership role in the Christian community. As such, this represents a major turning point in the narrative. For Luke, Saul's shifting role is inevitable: he is God's "chosen vessel" (9:15), instantiating the Lukan theme of divine necessity (what Cosgrove calls "the divine *dei*").

The Text in the Interpretive Tradition

For some early Christians, Acts 9:1-31 was literally prescriptive: Saul's fast prepared him for baptism, which is necessary for salvation (e.g., Justin, *1 Apol.* 61; Tertullian, *Bapt.* 20). Later commentators often read Saul's conversion story more symbolically. For instance, to the Venerable Bede (seventh century CE), Saul's blindness represents the darkness of sin, which is then overcome by the light of faith. The three days of blindness teach Saul that he was wrong to doubt Jesus' resurrection on the third day.

Many influential Christian theologians have read Saul's Damascus vision as an archetype for Christian conversion. For example, Augustine's own famous garden conversion in 386 CE led him to read Saul's conversion as God's "violent capture of a rebel will." Medieval illustrations portray a wolf changing into a lamb, or a toppled horseman, both of which represent the rebellious human will being forcefully transformed. In the sixteenth century, Luther preached that Saul's conversion is a paradigm of Christian faith: failure to keep God's law leads to deep shame. Conversion, which frees one from the devil's grasp, is the result of God's prevenient grace alone. Luther contrasted Saul's transformation with the so-called papists who, like Saul before his conversion, persecuted the Reformers (the "true" Christians).

The Text in Contemporary Discussion

This passage is at the center of ongoing debates about Saul's identity and how his conversion experience should influence Christianity today (e.g., Longenecker). Luther's depictions of Saul's conflicted conscience contributed directly to current Christian conceptions of sin, grace, and salvation. Still, scholars attuned to anthropological and social-scientific concerns caution Western readers not to overly psychologize Saul's Damascus-road experience; the social implications of Saul's "conversion" were just as important as his interior state. Ananias's astounding willingness to forgive Saul, and Barnabas's commendation, serve as a welcoming entrée into the community of Jesus-followers, some of whom likely suffered at Saul's hands. Accordingly, contemporary readers should be wary of reading an individualized psychological pattern into Saul's transformation as normative, as Luther did.

In colloquial English, we often use the proverbial "Damascus experience" to describe any abrupt change of mind, as when a politician suddenly reverses her position on an issue. Despite idiomatic usage, some scholars object to the word *conversion*, since Saul never denounced his Jewish identity. The new perspective on Paul insists that Saul did not "convert" to a new religion; rather, this prophetic "call" or "commissioning" (akin to Isa. 6:1-13) allowed Saul to maintain his Judaism. By recognizing Jesus as the Jewish Messiah, Saul simply transferred to another Jewish sect (Segal).

For Luke, did Saul's "conversion" liberate his soul from the torturous Mosaic law? Those who interrogate anti-Jewish strains in Christian rhetoric point out that this view easily engenders supersessionism and xenophobia. What is at stake when Christians take Saul's pre-"conversion" violence against Christians as characteristic of all Jews? Relatedly, does Saul's gentile mission *replace* a failed mission to Israel (Sanders)? If so, is Acts inherently antisemitic? Or does the gentile mission *complete* the mission to Israel, as implied in prophetic passages like Isa. 49:6 (Jervell)?

9:32—11:18: The Ministry of Peter

The Text in Its Ancient Context

In 9:32, Luke reintroduces Peter, who takes the gospel westward to Lydda (on the Plain of Sharon) and Joppa (9:32, 36). Peter's healing of Tabitha (Dorcas in Greek) fits the form of ancient miracle-type scenes (Bultmann's *Wundergeschichten*): a description of the circumstances (9:37), the miracle (9:40), a corroborating sign (9:40), and/or the witnesses' response (9:42). Raising the dead establishes continuity between prophets in the Hebrew Bible (1 Kgs. 17:17-24; 2 Kgs. 4:32-37), Jesus in the Gospel (Luke 7:11-17; 8:41-42, 49-56), and the apostles in Acts. The story has intertextual resonances with Luke 8:49-56, where Jesus raises Jairus's daughter; Jesus' instruction in the Markan parallel (5:35-43), *Talitha, koum* ("Little girl, I say to you, get up") also sounds similar to Peter's instruction, *Tabitha, anastēthi* ("Tabitha, get up," Acts 9:40).

Acts 9:36 is the only instance of the feminine noun for "disciple" (*mathētria*) in the New Testament (a *hapax legomenon*). Scholars often assume, based on 9:39, 41, that Tabitha was a widow, though the text never explicitly states this. Tabitha cares for the poor (9:36), a description Luke also uses to describe Cornelius in the next section (10:2, 4).

Like Tabitha, Cornelius is a sympathetic character with financial means. As a centurion, he commands one hundred men in the Roman army's Italian cohort (likely an anachronistic reference, since it is not attested elsewhere until 69 CE). Cornelius lives in Caesarea Maritima, the Roman capital of Judea, where Herod the Great had several pet building projects (see Josephus, *Ant.* 15.9.6 [15.331–41]). As an influential paterfamilias, Cornelius commands a large household (10:7).

Described as a devout gentile who "fears God" and prays continuously (10:2), Cornelius may be a "God-fearer," a category of gentiles who worshiped God and followed Jewish customs, without being proselytes. Some question the existence of God-fearers as a distinct historical category, though inscriptional evidence seems to indicate that "God-fearers" were active in synagogues, often as benefactors. In Acts, such gentiles resemble devout Jews (13:16, 26; 16:14; 18:7). Like Mary (Luke 1:26-38) and Ananias (Acts 9:10-17), Cornelius receives an angelic visitation at the ninth hour (three o'clock), the hour of prayer (10:3; cf. 3:1).

When the spotlight shifts to Peter, Luke highlights a main obstacle to gentile inclusion in the messianic assembly: their ritual uncleanness. Although no purity laws forbade Jewish table fellowship with gentiles, social taboos clearly discouraged such associations. Within the narrative, interactions between Jews and gentiles are vigorously contested. Peter's vision leads to the first of four household conversions in Acts (see also 16:11-15, 25-34; 18:1-11), and to Peter's own "conversion" to a new point of view regarding Jew-gentile relations (Parsons, 141); after some reticence, Peter finally grasps God's impartiality (10:34).

The significant amount of repetition throughout chapters 10–11 accentuates the importance of this narrative moment, when gentiles are officially welcomed into the people of God. In a recapitulation of the Pentecost event, the Holy Spirit descends on the gentiles (10:44-48). Upon Peter's return to Jerusalem, he recounts his vision (11:1-18; cf. 10:9-16). Similar to Luke's own storytelling (Luke 1:3), Peter describes events "step by step" (11:4), adding his own interpretive emphasis on God's role in establishing the gentile mission. Just as Jesus' opponents are silenced in Luke's Gospel (Luke 14:1-6), Peter's criticizers are silenced; unlike Jesus' antagonists, however, Peter's interlocutors eventually praise God (11:18).

The Text in the Interpretive Tradition

Chrysostom and Basil the Great enjoined their congregants to emulate Tabitha's virtuous behavior. During the Protestant Reformation, Calvin taught that faith preceded Tabitha's good works.

Cornelius's baptism (10:44-48) appeared in third-century doctrinal debates over the (re)baptism of "heretics," apostates who left the church in the face of Roman persecution. Cyprian ("pope" of Carthage) wrote a letter to Stephen ("pope" of Rome) in which he argued that Cornelius's baptism *after* receiving the Spirit commends (re)baptism (*Epist.* 72). Christian thinkers also referred to the household conversions in Acts to support infant baptism (which was widespread by the third century CE), assuming that children were present whenever entire households are mentioned.

Origen's and Augustine's different readings of Cornelius's angelic visitation were important in theological disputes over free will and divine grace (e.g., the semi-Pelagian controversy). For Origen, Cornelius merits an angelic visitation because he is charitable (10:2), but for Augustine, God's prevenient grace led to Cornelius's good works.

Fierce debates arose in late antiquity between the Antiochene "school" of intellectuals like Chrysostom, Diodore of Tarsus, and Theodore of Mopsuestia, who read Scripture literally, and those of the Alexandrian "school" like Origen and Clement of Alexandria, who read allegorically. Surprisingly, Antiochene interpreters read Peter's vision (10:9-16) allegorically (the animals represent incorporating gentiles into God's people), while Origen took it literally (the animals represent overturned Jewish dietary restrictions).

In the fourth- and fifth-century trinitarian and christological controversies, Western adoptionists took Peter's reference to God's "anointing" Jesus (10:38) as evidence that Jesus is subordinate to the Father; the now-orthodox interpretation is that Jesus' unction concerns only his humanity.

Nineteenth-century African American preachers appropriated Peter's assertions (10:34-36) to denounce prejudice. This text thus undergirded Christian objections to white supremacists, who preferred New Testament texts like Philemon.

The Text in Contemporary Discussion

Feminist reception history oscillates between celebrating female difference and insisting females are no different from males. Some feminist scholars celebrate Tabitha's status as a "disciple" (*mathētria*), lamenting "malestream" scholarship's dismissal of this title. Further, Lukan scholars often consider the successive healings of Aeneas and Tabitha (9:32-43) as an instance of the "gender pairs" that are a signature feature of Luke's work (e.g., Luke 1:11-20/26-38, 46-55/67-79; 2:25-35/36-38; 8:40-56; 11:31-32; 13:16/19:9; 13:18-21; 15:3-7/8-10). They reference this so-called dual-witness motif as evidence of Luke's emphasis on gender equality. Acts contains fewer gender pairs, but frequently notes that "both men and women" belong to the Christian community (5:14; 8:3, 12; 9:2, 36; 22:4; cf. 9:2; 17:12). On the other hand, praising Tabitha "has a dark side" when her service-oriented good deeds are contrasted with the depictions in Acts of preaching and teaching as male activities (Anderson, 33).

The baptisms in Cornelius's household continue to factor into disputes over infant baptism versus believers' baptism. Although most churches today (Catholic, Protestant, and Orthodox) baptize infants, certain denominations (e.g., Baptists, Pentecostals) only baptize adults. The Church of Jesus Christ of Latter-day Saints holds that infants are sinless; they do not baptize until the age of eight (*Doctrine and Covenants* 68:27).

House-church advocates consider the conversions of Cornelius's household a missiological model for decentralized, autonomous church planting today. One operative question is whether patriarchy should characterize the church. Some hold that the apostolic home-fellowship model marks the climax of progressive revelation, overturning the patriarchy of the old covenant and erasing all sociocultural and ethnic differences; women lead house churches around the world (e.g., in China, women lead an estimated two-thirds of Christian churches). Others, however, point out that Cornelius remains the paterfamilias, the Roman patriarch in charge of the household; some Christians take this *normal* historical reality as *normative*, believing that Christians ought to embrace God-ordained, male-led hierarchy.

11:19—12:25: God Protects the Jerusalem Church

The Text in Its Ancient Context

The summary in 11:19-21 serves several narrative purposes: first, the mention of Stephen's martyrdom subtly reminds readers of Saul (9:1-31). Second, Luke introduces Antioch, Saul's home base during his missionary journeys. As the Roman government's seat in Syria and a cosmopolitan intellectual center, Antioch is an appropriate place for the gospel to reach the "Hellenists"/"Greeks" (manuscripts vary at 11:20). The appellation "Christian" was a label given by outsiders (11:26; cf. 26:28); Luke prefers "the Way" (see 9:2; 19:9, 23; 22:4; 24:14, 22).

Luke seeks to integrate the Christian narrative into Greco-Roman historiographical accounts: in 11:28, he mentions Claudius's reign (41–54 CE) and a famine in Judea (Josephus records one c. 45–48 CE in *Ant.* 20.51–53) that threatens the "whole inhabited world" (11:28); this may be hyperbolic, or it may refer to the Roman Empire, purportedly the "whole world" to its inhabitants (cf. 17:6; 24:5).

The famine-relief mission frames the following unit (11:30—12:25), where God protects Peter from King Herod Agrippa I, son of Herod Antipas and grandson of Herod the Great (both mentioned in the Gospel; Luke 1:5; 3:1, 19-20; 9:7-9; 13:31; 23:8-15). As Rome's vassal king, Agrippa's relationship with the Jews was contentious; he hopes arresting Peter will placate them. The note that this occurred during the Feast of Unleavened Bread alludes to Jesus' arrest (cf. Luke 22:1-7) and explains why Peter's execution is delayed.

The second of three miraculous prison escapes in Acts (12:5-11; cf. 5:17-21; 16:23-40) utilizes exodus language and stock images from prison escapes elsewhere (e.g., chains falling off, angelic intervention, gates opening automatically, walking past sleeping guards). Form critics posit dependence on Euripides' *Bacchae*, Dan. 3:1-30, Artapanus's depiction of Moses, and/or Homer's *Iliad* (MacDonald, 121–45). The scene also recalls Jesus' resurrection (Luke 24). Acts emphasizes God's sovereignty over attempts to arrest (!) the spread of the gospel.

In a uniquely humorous moment, a slave named Rhoda recognizes Peter's voice at Mary's door, but rather than opening the door, she runs to tell the disciples. As happens repeatedly in Luke-Acts, the recipients of good news misconstrue it as nonsense (12:15; cf. Luke 24:11; Acts 2:13-15; 26:24); their response reflects an ancient belief that a guardian angel appears when one dies (12:15). Of course, Peter's miraculous escape story vindicates Rhoda.

The guards' panic at Peter's absence is warranted (12:18; cf. 5:21-24), given Agrippa's tyrannical reaction: he cross-examines and executes them (12:19); following Roman law, guards typically received the punishment intended for escaped prisoners (*Code of Justinian* 9.4.4).

The final scene starring Agrippa (12:20-25) highlights his unexplained anger with the people of Tyre and Sidon on the Phoenician coast, who seek reconciliation (likely bribing the king's assistant) for economic reasons (12:20). In Josephus's account of this event, Agrippa's speech (12:21) occurs at a festival honoring Caesar in Caesarea. As was common in the ruler cult, the crowd declares Agrippa's voice divine (12:22); according to Josephus, they do so because of his silver robes (*Ant.* 19.346). Whereas the apostles redirect praise toward God (see 3:12-13; 10:25-26; 14:13-15), Agrippa accepts the flattery and (ironically, since the crowd considers him immortal) dies by worms (cf. Jth. 16:17; 2 Macc. 9:9). Agrippa's demise reflects the ancient trope of a tyrant's downfall, and fulfills Mary's prophecy (Luke 1:52).

God's word (here, a metonymy for believers) remains unstoppable (12:24). When Barnabas and Saul return (12:25), the episode comes full circle and the main protagonist shifts from Peter (often called "apostle to the Jews") to Saul (usually dubbed "apostle to the Gentiles"). Peter is only mentioned again in 15:7.

The Text in the Interpretive Tradition

Antioch has been called Christianity's birthplace, since believers were first called "Christians" there (11:26) and the Antiochene church sponsored Saul's initial missionary journey (13:1-3). This gave Chrysostom great pride, since Antioch was his hometown. Antiochene Christians also sent many bishops to the Councils of Nicaea and Chalcedon, and generated "canon" lists similar to our contemporary New Testament.

Church fathers emphasized moral formation in this section of Acts. For instance, Chrysostom pointed to the Antiochene church when chastising his congregants for neglecting the poor. This moralizing also led ante-Nicene Christians to wrestle with Agrippa's execution of the innocent prison guards (12:18-19), often concluding that God would overturn such injustices upon Jesus' return. Agrippa's portrayal in Acts contrasts with Jewish tradition, where he is fair and generous (*Ant.* 19.330).

This subunit of Acts gave rise to several important Christian traditions. Postapostolic Christians identified John Mark (12:12) as the author of Mark's Gospel and founder of the Alexandrian church. James (12:17), later called "James the Just," brother of Christ and leader of the Jerusalem church, became legendary for his piety. In the second century, Hegesippus famously reported that James's knees were like a camel's from constant praying. According to Catholic tradition, James is patron saint of Spain, where he was sent to evangelize. Catholics also believe the vague reference to "another place" in Acts 12:17 refers to Rome, where Peter was the first pope. (Later texts explicitly connect Peter with Rome; see 1 Pet. 5:13; *1 Clement* 5.4; *Acts of Peter* 7.)

Despite Baur's distinction between Peter and Paul, Christian tradition venerates them together: iconography depicts them as pillars of the church, often with Jesus giving Peter the keys to the kingdom (the *donatio clavium*) and Paul the law in a scroll (the *traditio legis*).

The Text in Contemporary Discussion

The summary in 11:19-21 signals a new challenge for the church: community integration. Despite the reference to peaceful growth in 9:31, the bulk of Acts points to barriers to full integration among early Christian converts. Recently, minority biblical criticism has identified similar concerns among minorities today, as their membership in American society hinges on loyalty to ideologies like capitalism or individualism (Liew). What do contemporary Christian groups establish as qualifications for inclusion? How should the Lukan narrative's treatments of cultural integration influence church membership (broadly conceived) today? How can scriptural discourses around insider/outsider boundaries inform ecclesial traditions and practices in today's communities?

An important corollary is whether Luke wrote to bolster insiders' faith, or to defend Christianity's political innocuousness to Roman outsiders (the *apologia pro ecclesia* hypothesis). Here, distinguishing among multiple potential audiences is helpful. Even as stories are embedded within particular communities, they are never fixed in only *one* sociohistorical situation. Readers' presuppositions and experiences predispose them to understand texts in unique ways. While Luke's earliest readers probably all understood Roman imperial practices, "outsiders" likely interpreted the narrative differently from "insiders."

13:1—14:28: Paul's First Missionary Journey

The Text in Its Ancient Context

Acts 13:1-3 is a pivotal dividing point: chapters 1–12 focus on Peter and Jerusalem, while chapters 13–28 describe Paul's mission to the "ends of the earth," beginning with Asia Minor. Following the biblical topos of name changes consonant with role changes, Saul is called Paul from 13:9; once the

Spirit appoints Paul and Barnabas, they are commissioned in what appears to be a formal ceremony (13:3). Inaugurating the first of three Pauline missionary journeys, Paul and Barnabas travel with John Mark to the island of Cyprus, where they establish a pattern repeated throughout the journeys: they begin in the synagogues, gentiles convert, and Jews drive them out with (threats of) violence.

They arrive in Paphos on the southwestern Cyprian coast—seat of the Roman proconsul Sergius Paulus—indicating they have traversed the entire island. Paul's encounter with the magician Bar-Jesus (whose name, ironically, means "son of Jesus") resembles Stephen's confrontation with Simon (8:4-25). Paul's condemnation echoes the denunciations of magic in the Hebrew Bible. Bar-Jesus' blindness subtly recalls Paul's own temporary blindness (9:1-30) and reinforces the Lukan theme of divine fulfillment. Consider the ironies: Paul, called to open the eyes of the gentiles, casts one into further darkness. Whereas Paul was sent to "Straight Street" (9:6-11), Bar-Jesus makes the Lord's straight paths crooked (13:10). Bar-Jesus' attempts to lead the proconsul astray spiritually result in his own need to be led physically (13:11).

Paul (*sans* John Mark; 13:13) reaches Antioch of Pisidia (distinct from Antioch of Syria), in the Roman province of Galatia. He begins the first of his three major sermons by surveying Israelite history, and ends with the gospel (13:14-52). The parallels between this and other apostles' sermons unify the narrative, establishing and interpreting theological themes for readers (Soards). This episode also recalls Jesus' Nazareth sermon (Luke 4:16-30) in both content and result (13:50-52; cf. Luke 4:28-29). The apostles leave (13:51-52), shaking dust off their feet in protest (cf. Luke 9:5; 12:10-11).

Events in Iconium (14:1-7) repeat what is by now a familiar progression: the "apostles" (the designation extends here beyond the Twelve; 14:4, 14; cf. 1:2; 2:37; 4:33; 5:29; 9:27; 15:2; 16:4) begin in the synagogue, gentiles convert, and some Jews become violent. Paul avoids being stoned in Iconium, but he is not so fortunate in the next vignette, set in the Roman colony of Lystra (14:8-20). Following Jesus' and Peter's examples, Paul heals a lame man (cf. Luke 5:17-26; Acts 3:1-10). These intratextual echoes bolster Paul's legitimacy as God's agent. The witnesses' conclusion that Paul and Barnabas are Hermes and Zeus incarnate (the messenger god and sky god, respectively) is unsurprising in light of the widespread ancient notion—reflected in the Homeric epics and Ovid's *Metamorphosis* 8.611–724—that the gods disguised themselves as strangers.

Paul and Barnabas, rending their clothes in grief, redirect the exaltations to the "living God" (cf. 2 Kgs. 19:4, 16; Dan. 6:20, 26). The Lycaonians and Jews from Antioch and Iconium stone Paul and leave him for dead; ironically, given that Paul rejects attributions of immortality, he inexplicably "gets up" and leaves (14:19-20). This is particularly striking when compared with Agrippa's death (12:20-23).

Paul's first journey ends with many converts and no persecution in Derbe, on the outskirts of imperial territory (14:21-28). Returning to their Antiochene sponsors, Paul and Barnabas bravely revisit Lystra and Iconium, where they had been violently opposed. In a brief (anachronistic?) note, Luke reports that they elect presbyters in every church.

The Text in the Interpretive Tradition

Paul's evangelistic efforts as a traveling missionary have been reimagined and imitated over time. In the second and third centuries, for example, the apocryphal Acts expanded on the canonical profiles of the apostles. Although the apocryphal Acts tend to reflect the framework of the canonical Gospels rather than the canonical Acts, some were built around a similarly episodic travel-narrative structure, with different itineraries and casts of characters (Bovon). The *Acts of Paul* describes Paul traversing the major Mediterranean cities, where he preaches, performs miracles, and encounters opposition. One excerpt, the *Acts of Paul and Thecla*, contains the earliest extant physical description of Paul (short, bald, with a long nose and large eyes). This description typifies subsequent depictions of Paul in Christian paintings and iconography.

For Chrysostom, Paul epitomized pedagogical prowess, using different rhetorical strategies for different audiences. For instance, Chrysostom explained why Paul blinded Bar-Jesus (13:11) by pointing to the plague of boils in Egypt (Exod. 9:8-12): Paul used blindness just as God used the boils—to teach, not to punish.

Commitment to the Protestant doctrine of *sola scriptura*, along with a desire to model evangelistic efforts on a fixed Pauline paradigm, led nineteenth-century interpreters to divide Paul's travels into three separate "missionary journeys," a threefold division still popular today (but likely foreign to Paul himself).

The Text in Contemporary Discussion

Postcolonial scholars recognize that modern missionaries' Eurocentric interpretations of Paul's journeys served their own colonizing interests; they used Acts to construct totalizing binaries—"center versus margins," "civilized versus uncivilized," and "enlightened versus superstitious"—that are too reductionistic to represent the ambivalences inherent in every time and culture. Dehumanizing stereotypes are not limited to earlier generations; some biblical scholars today adopt racialized rhetoric and supersessionist ideologies. For example, stereotypes of the Lycaonians as Mediterranean "hicks" betray scholars' "Orientalizing" tendencies (Wordelman, 205).

Some call Christians to repent and reject racist, anti-Jewish rhetoric in Acts (e.g., 13:44-52), while others point to Paul's blinding of Bar-Jesus (13:11) as another Lukan instance of justified Christian violence against outsiders. These views provoke hermeneutical questions: if we aim to read Acts within its cultural, sociohistorical contexts, but Acts uses fixed categories and essentializing language, should we accept these as evidence of how the implied author or audiences conceptualized their world? Or should we assume that this rhetoric masks Luke's internalization of the imperialist agenda? Should we counter authoritarian claims to hegemony by uncovering the text's unspoken ambiguities? Do these approaches simply represent different readers' goals (i.e., discovering Luke's intentions versus exposing inconsistencies in Acts)? Are these goals at odds with one another, does one presuppose the other, or do or can they complement each other?

15:1-35: The Jerusalem Controversy

The Text in Its Ancient Context

The Jerusalem Council (15:1-35) publicly legitimates the gentile mission, which started privately with the Ethiopian eunuch's conversion in Acts 8, and began to spread with Cornelius's conversion and Peter's defense in Acts 10–11. This is the first formal council convened to address the complexities that arose as gentiles increasingly joined the inchoate Christian community; early Christian identity-construction involved significant disputes about covenant-related issues such as food sacrificed to idols, the Mosaic law, and circumcision. The precipitating event is that Pharisaic Judaizers in Antioch want to circumcise gentiles. Paul and Barnabas, unable to resolve this dispute alone, seek the advice of the Jerusalem "apostles and elders" (mentioned five times in the chapter; 15:2, 4, 6, 22, 23).

The account paints a picture of both dissension and decorum. On the one hand, "much debate" occurs (15:7); on the other hand, the apostles listen attentively (15:12), and James waits patiently to speak (15:13). Contrast this insider assembly's dignified tone with outsiders' unruly mayhem and intentional interruptions elsewhere (18:12-17; 19:23-41). Although Luke attests to tensions among early Christians, their mode of resolving disputes adheres to Greco-Roman standards of masculine comportment, including self-restraint and propriety; in this way, Luke's storytelling reflects and reinforces the gendered sociocultural ideologies of the Greco-Roman environment, as he constructs early Christian insider-outsider boundary markers.

Acts 15:6-21 follows a trifold legitimating sequence. First, Peter (absent from the story since Acts 12) reappears with a judicial speech that further develops themes established in Cornelius's conversion story, especially that of divine choice. Salvation comes through grace, as a gift for *both* Jewish and gentile believers, not through the "yoke" of the law (15:11). Peter's speech, recounted in direct discourse for emphasis, appeals to recent events of which the church leaders are well aware. Second, Paul and Barnabas attest to the visible "signs and wonders" (cf. 14:3) that God has performed among the gentiles. In the Gospel and Acts, miraculous "signs" follow and verify God's communication (Luke 2:12, 34; 11:16, 29, 30; 21:7, 11, 25; 23:8; Acts 2:19, 22, 43; 4:30; 5:12; 6:8; 7:36; 8:6, 13; 14:3). Finally, James's speech provides scriptural warrant for the gentile mission, referencing Amos 9:11-12 (LXX), and Lev. 17:8—18:26 concerning "aliens" among the Jews. Rhetorically, each phase in this progression provides a different basis for the gentile mission experience, miracles, and Scripture. All three point to the gentile mission as God's original plan, and to God's initiative in bringing it about.

The group drafts a letter (15:22-29) stipulating two major decisions: gentile Christians need not be circumcised, but they ought to abstain from fornication, blood, and things strangled or polluted by idols (Exod. 34:15-16; Lev. 3:17; 17:3-14; 18:6-30; Deut. 12:16-27). Though the issue arose in Antioch, the letter is addressed to Antioch, Syria, and Cilicia (15:23), subtly underscoring the Jerusalem church's widespread influence. Paul and Barnabas return to the Antiochene Christians (15:35), who rejoice at the verdict, providing closure for this watershed event in the early church.

The Text in the Interpretive Tradition

The legacy of James and the Jerusalem Council extended in narrative form into noncanonical accounts like the *Ascents of James* (probably preserved in *Ps.-Clem. Rec.* 1.43–44). The council (15:1-35) also figured prominently in later theological discussions: while some emphasized the council's format as a normative process for handling church conflict, others developed the implications of its resolutions.

Early Christian apologists marshaled Acts 15:1-35 as evidence against so-called heretics. Responding to Celsus's charge that Christianity was disunified, Origen pointed to Acts 15 as proof that the Holy Spirit resolves Christian disputes (*C. Cels.* 3.10–11). Chrysostom considered the account an ecclesiological model for theological decision making: ecumenical councils should be orderly, with all participants submitting to the bishop (*Hom. Act.* 33).

Interpreters' views of the Jews determined their assessment of the Jerusalem Council's decisions. For the Venerable Bede, the council attested to early Christian respect for Judaism. Others took it as a rejection of Judaism. During the Reformation, Luther cited Acts 15 to denounce the Jews' "works-based theology." Relatedly, opponents of infant baptism argued that, since salvation is through grace, unbaptized infants go to heaven (15:11). Catholics point to Acts 15 as evidence of the development of doctrine: contrary to the Protestant principle of *sola scriptura*, in this view, the Holy Spirit reveals truth progressively, which church leaders safeguard through tradition.

During the modern period, the difficulties with reconciling Acts 15 and Gal. 2:1-10 based on modern historiographical standards raised larger issues of the historicity and relationship between Acts and Paul's letters. Some harmonized the two accounts and ignored discrepancies, while others considered them two separate events; still others took the differences as evidence of the story's historical unreliability.

The Text in Contemporary Discussion

Missiologists frequently cite Acts 15 when considering how to communicate the gospel across cultural boundaries. Is the Christian message universal, or does every unique culture require its own contextualized form of the gospel message?

Some look to Acts 15 as a hermeneutical model, asking: What is the Holy Spirit's relationship to the Word of God? How do/should Christians appropriate Scripture for new situations like those raised by modern birth control, Internet use, stem cell research, or weapons of mass destruction? Some apply the text directly to contemporary situations, like Jehovah's Witnesses, who refuse blood transfusions based on Acts 15:29: Others believe each new age requires fresh Spirit-led discernment. Interpreters also disagree about whether Acts 15 condones or vilifies interpretive plurality. On the one hand, characters express multiple viewpoints in a respectful dialogue with a peaceful resolution. On the other hand, the leadership's final decision effectively suppresses the other faction's views. Certain scholars believe Acts 15 is a distinctly formative event in the life of the early church, and thus not paradigmatic for today.

Acts 15 has important implications for contemporary Jewish-Christian relations. Many scholars have labeled Acts antisemitic, since repeatedly, Jews oppose the gospel, while gentiles accept it (cf. 13:44-46; 18:6; 28:25-28). The Jerusalem Council also rejects a fundamental distinguishing feature of the nation of Israel (circumcision), and affirms salvation for Jews and gentiles alike (15:11). On the other hand, the council maintains certain purity laws and, although gentiles convert, Luke never shows them as leaders. A few scholars describe Luke as Jewish and pro-Israel.

While twentieth-century scholars found inconsistencies between Acts 15 and Galatians 2 to be problematic, interpreters today recognize that rhetorical exigencies engender different kinds of narratives; thus it can be more productive to ask how each writing functions rhetorically. This, of course, raises larger questions about doing "history" using the New Testament texts. What does it mean to reconstruct historical circumstances with limited sources, especially when ancient concepts of "history" differ from ours?

15:36—18:21: Paul's Second Missionary Journey

The Text in Its Ancient Context

Paul's second journey moves through Philippi (16:11-40), Thessalonica and Beroea (17:1-15), Athens (17:16-34), and Corinth (18:1-18). Thus the expansion in the narrative to "the ends of the earth" now extends into Europe. The trip begins inauspiciously: in the so-called Antioch incident, Paul and Barnabas part ways (15:36-40), and Acts does not record them together again. Instead, Paul invites Timothy, who—with a Jewish-Christian mother and a Greek father—embodies Lukan universalism. Paul's unnecessary circumcision of Timothy (16:3; cf. 15:1-35) illustrates how he adapts evangelistic strategies for different audiences (16:1-5). Multiple references to divine guidance (16:6-10) establish that God chooses Paul's destinations.

At 16:10, the narration inexplicably shifts from an anonymous third-person external point of view to a first-person plural internal perspective. Though the Gospel and Acts both begin with first-person direct address (Luke 1:1-4; Acts 1:1), the "we-passages" (see 20:5-21:18; 27:1-28:16) are famously enigmatic. In Acts, they coincide with sea voyages (Robbins).

Luke calls Paul's first destination—Philippi—the "foremost city" of Macedonia (16:11-12), which is odd, since Thessalonica was Macedonia's capital. The Philippian mission is framed by references to Lydia of Thyatira (which had a famous purple dyeing industry; 16:14-15, 40): Lydia deals in purple cloth, a luxury item. She and her household become the first converts in Europe; the reference to her household likely indicates that she is unmarried and wealthy. Her conversion thus illustrates the spread of the gospel to prominent elites. Repeated narrative articulations of the gospel's spread to a variety of people create coherence across Luke's episodic narrative.

Sandwiched between mentions of Lydia is a pericope about someone on the opposite end of the social scale: a slave girl with a "pythonic spirit" whose prophetic abilities generate revenue for her masters (16:16). The pythonic spirit alludes to the oracle of Apollo at Delphi, a staple of popular Roman religion that was inextricably linked to the city's economy. Following Paul and Silas's exorcism of the slave girl against her masters' wishes, the magistrates (the Roman colony's chief officials) imprison the two apostles, who miraculously escape. Unlike the other prison escapes in Acts (see 5:19-21; 12:6-11), this one results in the conversions of the jailor and his household (16:25-34).

In both Thessalonica and Beroea, Christianity draws converts (17:4, 12). However, in Thessalonica, Christians are accused of "turning the world upside down"—an ironic charge, given that *the mob* disturbs the peace (17:5-6). In contrast, Jews in Beroea respond positively, verifying Paul's claims with the Scriptures (17:11).

Athens was a major urban center marked by religious fervor and intellectual curiosity. Luke describes Athens as "full of idols" (17:16) because Athenian public spaces were crowded with statuary, temples, iconography, and altars to the emperor and pagan gods. Unlike other public speeches in

Acts, which are addressed to Jews, Paul addresses the Areopagus, Athens's elite administrative body (17:16-31). Tailoring his apologetic strategies accordingly, Paul speaks in classical Greek oratorical style and addresses Epicurean and Stoic philosophies. His language resembles the Athenians' charge against Socrates in Plato's *Apology* (17:18), and he cites the third-century-BCE Greek poet Aratus (17:24-29). The conversions of members of the Areopagus demonstrate Paul's rhetorical effectiveness (17:34).

Corinth, the Roman capital of Achaia, was a thriving commercial center; strategically located on the Isthmus of Corinth, the city controlled major trade routes between Asia and Rome. Paul's meeting before Gallio (the Roman proconsul governing Achaia c. 51–53 CE) suggests Corinth's administrative importance as well. In a rare temporal marker, Luke reports that Paul stays in Corinth for a year and six months (18:11), where he meets Prisca (Priscilla is the diminutive) and Aquila (18:2-26). Ancient literature rarely lists the woman's name first (18:18, 26); doing so may indicate that Priscilla was of higher social status than Aquila. Paul cuts his hair in Cenchraea (eastern Corinth; 18:18) due to an unknown vow (cf. 21:23-24); it may be the Nazirite vow (Num. 6:1-21).

The Text in the Interpretive Tradition

Paul's split with Barnabas (15:39) posed a challenge for those who emphasized early Christian harmony; for Calvin, Paul's refusal to compromise marked his zeal for the gospel.

Proponents of infant baptism supported their case by appealing to the household conversions in 16:11-15 and 16:25-34.

In line with his stereotypically anti-Jewish polemic, Chrysostom insisted that Paul only circumcised Timothy to gain a hearing with the Jews, not because he respected Jewish laws.

Later texts mimicked Paul's Areopagus address, as in the apocryphal *Acts of Philip* 2, where Philip similarly appears before the Athenian philosophers. Others have hailed it as a missiological manifesto, emphasizing that the speech is addressed to non-Jews. Nineteenth-century abolitionists used it (esp. 17:26) as a prophetic call for racial justice. However, early twentieth-century scholars like Martin Dibelius denigrated the Areopagus speech as an un-Pauline capitulation to educated pagan elites.

The Text in Contemporary Discussion

Jewish orthodoxy is not the primary issue at stake in Timothy's circumcision (16:1-3; cf. 15:1-35; 16:4-5); texts like Philo's writings and *Joseph and Aseneth* attest that circumcision was already debated in Paul's day. Rather, this passage reminds us that religious identities are always negotiated and configured on the body. How are physical bodies variously employed in Christian discourses today? How do assumptions about the body inform contemporary Christian theology, and how does embodiment influence contemporary Christian practice?

Lydia and the slave girl have been read as "border women" in "land possession type scenes" (a traveling hero and a "native" woman) that simultaneously highlight Paul's foreignness and legitimate his ideological conquest (Staley). Laura Nasrallah suggests another intriguing parallel: Paul's travels create a Christian form of the Panhellenion—a mid-second-century league of Greek cities Hadrian established to promote unity. Expansionist discourses like this helped to shape American concepts like "Manifest Destiny" and divinely mandated territorial expansion, which continue to inform US imperialism and post-9/11 political rhetoric.

For some scholars, Luke subordinates both Lydia (16:13-15) and the slave girl (16:16-18) to Paul, demonstrating that Christian communities do not threaten the patriarchal values of the Roman social order. Merely a pawn in the power contest between her masters and Paul, the slave girl herself is inconsequential. Many African American scholars have pointed out that this reinscribes oppressive slave ideologies.

Some hail Paul's Areopagus speech (17:16-31) as a model for interreligious dialogue. The Native American Lifeway Adult Bible Study argues that unlike early European settlers in America, Paul never forced his beliefs on others; observing them, he developed his approach accordingly (17:22-23). Larger questions arise: How does Paul portray the essence of Christian identity when speaking with the Athenians (17:28-29), and (how) does this differ from the way Christian identity is portrayed elsewhere in Acts? How does/should Christianity influence minority acculturation today? How should Christians from different ethnic and cultural backgrounds relate to one another? Is Christianity a homogenizing force in our world? Should it be?

Paul's upbringing in Tarsus (a university city) and his Roman citizenship presumably increased his stature before the Athenian intellectuals. By adopting their discourse, is Paul practicing effective evangelism, or compromising the gospel? Should Christians regard Paul here as a model to be emulated, or a cause for caution? More broadly, when leaders in education, politics, news and entertainment media, and other forums adapt their message to the medium, are they communicating responsibly, or perpetuating patterns of power and privilege?

18:22—21:16: Paul's Third Missionary Journey

The Text in Its Ancient Context

Paul's third missionary journey begins in Ephesus, the capital of Asia and probably the third-largest city in the empire behind Rome and Alexandria. Situated on multiple land routes and a major seaport, Ephesus was a center of international trade. Filled with notable buildings and multiple agoras, inscriptions describe Ephesus's great wealth and importance. Paul spends the most time in Ephesus (two years and three months; 19:8, 10), and even if 19:10 is hyperbolic from the perspective of historical reconstruction, the narrative portrays this as the culmination of his evangelistic efforts.

Creating narrative continuity with the foregoing section, where Priscilla and Aquila are mentioned (18:18-21), Luke sets the stage in Ephesus with a story about the couple's ministry to Apollos (18:24-28). Right away, the narrative associates Apollos with the apostles, as he speaks boldly in the synagogue (18:26). Bold speech—*parrēsia*—characterizes true discipleship in Acts (9:27-28; 13:46; 14:3; 19:8; 26:26). Rightly receiving Priscilla and Aquila's instruction, Apollos preaches in Achaia (19:27-28). This progression of the right disposition, correct reception of God's word, and faithful proclamation is a central Lukan paradigm for discipleship.

Acts 19:10-20, framed by references to the "word of the Lord" (19:10, 20), contrasts God's power (e.g., Paul's miracles in 19:11-12) with magic, which was particularly pervasive in Ephesus.

Jewish exorcists, attempting to use Jesus' name as an incantation, are overtaken; the event, like Bar-Jesus' defeat (13:6-11), causes amazement and widespread conversion. Those who practiced magic burn their books (instruction manuals in the art of magic), publicly renouncing that way of life in favor of the Christian Way (19:19-20). As is familiar by this point in Acts, success begets opposition. Employing a common figure of speech called litotes (an understatement using a double negative to make an affirmative statement), Luke describes "no little" public disturbance (19:23; cf. 12:18-19; 15:2; 19:23-24; 20:12; 27:20).

Having established that the Christian God is more powerful than generic magic, Luke turns to the locale-specific goddess Artemis, whose Ephesian cult was well known in antiquity. It would be difficult to overstate the importance of the cult of Artemis to the Ephesian worldview. Numerous inscriptions, coinage, literary artifacts, and the enormous temple of Artemis itself (one of the Seven Wonders of the Ancient World) attest to the Ephesians' conviction that they enjoyed a unique covenant relationship with their patron goddess. Worship of Artemis was considered necessary for the city's economic stability, as she sent the harvest and guarded the city's welfare. The temple was not only a spiritual sanctuary but also a bank, lending money, charging interest, and housing Artemis's own large financial estate (on the temple as a bank, see Strabo, *Geog.* 14.1.21–29).

For economic and spiritual reasons, Demetrius incites a riot (19:24-28). In what becomes a major public spectacle, the believers face a confused (19:29, 32), angry mob in the Ephesian theater (which held nearly twenty-five thousand people and still stands today). The mob exemplifies the opposite of classical Greco-Roman decorum and orderliness (cf. the Christian assembly in 15:1-35). Paul's third great missionary journey ends when the town clerk indirectly vindicates Paul and dispels the crowd.

Paul's journey to Rome parallels the Lukan passion narrative: the reference to the days of unleavened bread (20:6) mirrors references to Passover in Luke 22:1, 7; the mention of breaking bread in an upper room (20:7, 8) recalls Jesus' Last Supper (Luke 22:7-14); Eutychus's sleepiness (20:9) may allude to the disciples' sleeping in Gethsemane (Luke 22:45-46). The believers' failures to dissuade Paul from his inexorable march toward Rome (21:4, 12) parallel Jesus' Spirit-led journey to Jerusalem. Paul is further likened to Jesus (and Peter) when he raises Eutychus from the dead (20:10; cf. Luke 7:15; 8:52-55; Acts 9:36-42).

The Text in the Interpretive Tradition

Following the Reformation, early Baptists pointed to John's baptism of repentance (19:3-4) and the baptism of Ephesian believers (19:5) to argue for believers' baptism. They stressed the importance of personal repentance and individual accountability.

Priscilla's apparently prominent role in teaching Apollos (18:24-28) gave rise to several legendary accounts, including the belief that a fourth-century church (Saint Priscae) was built on the site of her house church in Rome (cf. 1 Cor. 16:19). In 1900, Adolf von Harnack even posited that Priscilla wrote the book of Hebrews.

Although Christians officially excluded women from leadership roles for centuries, examples like Lydia and Priscilla demonstrate that there were women leaders even in the early church.

Widespread evidence such as tombstone inscriptions attest to women priests from the third through the ninth centuries, and women prophets were active in early church life. Tertullian (e.g., *De anima* 9.4), Cyprian (e.g., *Epistle* 74.10), and the Nag Hammadi poem *Thunder, Perfect Mind* all mention unnamed women prophets. In the second century, Montanus's female colleagues Prisca and Quintilla influenced the rise of the New Prophecy, or Montanism.

According to the church historian Eusebius in the fourth century (*Hist. eccl.* 3.31.3–4), a tradition dating to the second century held that Philip's daughters of Acts 21:8-9 moved to Hierapolis in Phrygia. Several later traditions claim that the women eventually married.

Twentieth-century advocates of women's ordination proclaimed a theology of liberation based partly on the view that Philip's prophesying daughters fulfilled the prophecy in Joel 2:28 (cf. Acts 2:17) and served as "leaders for the church in Caesarea" (Torjesen, 27–28). Readers in Papua New Guinea were distracted by the description of Philip's daughters as unmarried (21:9), since in that culture, everyone marries (Clark, 208); this illustrates Hans-Georg Gadamer's well-known claim that all interpretations reflect the interpreter's sociocultural situatedness.

The Text in Contemporary Discussion

Women's roles in the Christian community continue to garner scholarly and popular attention. Some believe Lydia and Priscilla point to a Lukan emphasis on women's leadership. Others counter that when women are rhetorical tools with which men think, even positive portrayals of women legitimate patriarchal control. Though Luke mentions Philip's prophesying daughters, he quotes only Agabus's prophecy (21:9-11). Note, too, that Philip's daughters remain anonymous, while the male prophet is named (21:10; cf. 11:28). This is unsurprising: although low-status characters played integral roles in society, they generally remain unnamed in ancient literature. The point is to acknowledge that gender-based ideological implications underlie Luke's narrative; Acts both recognizes and represses women's ministries (Seim).

Philip's daughters also raise the issue of virginity, which was much lauded in early Christian contexts (the Greek word *parthenos* can be translated "unmarried" or "virgin," 21:9). Some contemporary scholars argue that praise for female virginity points to negative presuppositions regarding femininity, while affirmations of celibate female leaders in the church subtly reinscribe patriarchal biases.

Many conservatives and liberals accept a unilinear paradigm of "decline," in which early Christians were egalitarians, while later Christians marginalized women as institutionalism increased. Recently, scholars have critiqued three common dichotomies imposed on historical reconstructions of early Christianity: patriarchy versus the discipleship of equals; public versus private; ascetic versus domestic lifestyles. Each category is more complex historically than typically assumed.

These discussions provoke crucial questions: How might understanding early Christian history as ambiguous and polyphonic affect women's roles in churches today? How do biblical translations communicate specific ideologies? For instance, the NRSV, NIV, ESV, NASB, and ASV translate *gynai* (21:5) as "wives" instead of "women." Both are linguistically possible, but "wives" subordinates women to their husbands and limits women's involvement in the early church.

21:17—23:35: Events in Jerusalem

The Text in Its Ancient Context

Estimates of the number of Jews in Jerusalem at Paul's time range from twenty thousand to fifty thousand. According to Luke, many thousands of these Jews have become believers, but they remain "zealous for the law" (this description recalls the passionate commitment to Yahweh and Israel that typifies many heroic Jewish figures: Num. 25:6-13; Judg. 9:2-4; 1 Kgs. 18:40; 1 Macc. 2:23-27, 49-68; cf. Paul's self-description in 22:3). For them, Paul's teachings threaten Israel's distinctive boundaries, but this does not fit the narrator's characterization of Paul; by Acts 21, he has circumcised Timothy (16:3), shaved his hair (18:18), and observed Jewish holidays (20:16). Still, he agrees to demonstrate his respect for the Mosaic law publicly, so that the Jewish believers might observe him for themselves (21:23-26).

Though Paul appears to appease the Jewish Christians, events repeat themselves when a mob of outsiders (Jews from Asia) challenges him. The description is remarkably similar to the riot in Ephesus: the crowds are in an "uproar," shouting confusedly as they seize Paul and drag him outside the temple (21:30-32; cf. 19:29-32). The two scenes also differ: unlike the proconsul Gallio, who dismissed a similar dispute as an inter-Jewish quarrel and allowed a man to be beaten (18:12:17), officers in Jerusalem control the situation, protect Paul (21:31-35; 23:10), and allow him to defend himself (21:40). Paul chooses his content and his language wisely (first, Greek to the tribune, 21:37, then Aramaic to the crowd, 21:40; 22:2), identifying himself in terms appropriate for each audience. Paul's exchange with the tribune picks up the Lukan motif of misunderstood identity.

Paul's defense in Jerusalem (22:1-21) retrospectively recounts his Damascus experience for the second time (cf. 9:1-31), now from his first-person perspective, and with several changes that appeal to a Jewish audience. Effectively concluding his earlier defense, Paul takes advantage of the well-known dispute between Pharisees and Sadducees over resurrection to provoke violent controversy between them (23:6-10). Even as the Jews accuse Paul of rejecting their teachings (21:28), his intimate knowledge of Jewish teachings protects him. A divine pronouncement that Paul will testify in Rome (23:11) sets the stage for the journey to Rome, which occupies the rest of the narrative.

The Jews then hatch the most elaborate plot yet to kill Paul; whereas Luke briefly describes earlier attempts on Paul's life (9:23-25, 29-30; 14:19; 20:3, 19; 21:31), this premeditated conspiracy—and Paul's escape—are related in much greater detail. The dramatic tension mounts as a large group vows to achieve their goal (23:12-15). Paul's nephew (otherwise unknown in early Christian literature) warns Paul and informs the tribune about the plot (23:16-22). The tribune (whose name, Claudius Lysias, the reader finally learns in 23:26) goes to great lengths to protect Paul: nearly five hundred men—probably Lukan hyperbole to increase suspense—escort Paul through the night to Caesarea, where he appears before Felix (23:23-35).

The Text in the Interpretive Tradition

Second- and third-century martyrdom accounts demonstrate that the right response to suffering was a point of contention for Jesus-followers. Though Christian apologists like Tertullian argued that martyrdom is a Christian duty, Paul's detailed escape plan (23:12-35) supported Christian exhortations *not* to volunteer for martyrdom (e.g., *Mart. Pol.* 4.1).

For Augustine, Paul's claim to Roman citizenship (22:22-29) exemplifies Jesus' injunction to turn the other cheek (Luke 6:29). Augustine viewed the scene as juxtaposing heavenly and worldly values: the tribune disregards the heavenly honor that Paul values most (salvation), but respects the earthly honor that Paul values least (citizenship).

In the nineteenth century, debates raged over whether to translate the Greek word *baptizein* in verses like 22:16 as "wash" or "immerse," with obvious doctrinal implications accompanying each choice. Bible Societies that sought to translate biblical texts "directly" without promoting specific doctrines found this problematic.

The Text in Contemporary Discussion

Postcolonial thinkers who interrogate race and ethnicity in biblical texts assert that Acts 21:37—22:29 epitomizes Paul's *hybridity* (the mixtures and interdependences created in liminal spaces of boundary crossings). Paul is a Jew and a Roman citizen, Hebraic and Hellenic—as Daniel Boyarin puts it, he is a "Jewgreek" (1994, 79). Paul speaks Hebrew, claims his education under Gamaliel, and insists on his prior obedience to the Jewish authorities. And yet, he also invokes his Roman citizenship. With great rhetorical skill, Paul strategically highlights certain aspects of his identity based on each discursive situation.

Paul's conversation with the tribune illuminates ancient conceptions of social class. The tribune paid for his citizenship, whereas Paul was born a citizen (22:28). Although we lack statistics on the Roman economy (especially from rural areas, where most poverty exists), historians agree that Roman social status was relatively fluid. Routes for upward mobility such as manumission meant the same person could be assessed using different criteria, such as wealth, juridical status, education, and so on. A slave could be better educated than his master; citizenship did not imply wealth. A more nuanced picture of early Christian socioeconomic realities should inform our readings of Paul's identity claims.

24:1—26:32: Events in Caesarea

The Text in Its Ancient Context

Although ancient accounts describe Felix as corrupt, Acts at first characterizes him positively: "well-informed about the Way" (24:22), he gives Paul a fair hearing and liberty while in custody (24:10-24). Still, for two years (24:27), he stalls (24:22), hoping for a bribe (24:26). Luke mentions Felix's wife Drusilla (24:24), whom many readers would have known he pursued while she was married to Azizus of Emesa. And Felix keeps Paul in captivity when Festus succeeds him, hoping to ingratiate himself with the Jews (24:27). Perhaps this explains why Felix becomes "frightened" when Paul describes divine judgment (24:25).

Festus also wants to appease the Jews (25:9), a detail that attests to their power in the region. Nevertheless, in keeping with Luke's positive portrayals of Roman authorities (Luke 23:4, 14, 15,

20, 22, 41, 47; Acts 18:14-16; 19:37-41; 23:29), Festus listens to Paul's defense and agrees to his request to go to Rome (25:8-12). This long-anticipated journey is delayed by the arrival of King Herod Agrippa II (son of Herod Agrippa, cf. 12:1-4) and his sister Bernice (with whom Agrippa reportedly had an incestuous relationship).

Their arrival prompts the fourth cycle of Jewish accusations and Paul's sophisticated rhetorical maneuvering in his own defense (22:1-21; 24:10-21; 25:8-11; 26:2-29). In each case, Paul's forensic rhetoric serves two chief purposes: he depicts Jesus as the Jewish Messiah and legitimates his own apostolic ministry. The accusations levied against Paul instantiate the Lukan theme of Jesus'—and his disciples'—innocence.

Paul's trials before the authorities recall Jesus' trials, albeit with an important distinction: whereas Jesus remains silent before Herod (Luke 23:6-12), Paul, like Stephen in Acts 6:8—8:3, vehemently defends himself; perhaps he receives the words from Jesus himself (Luke 21:12-15).

The recapitulated episodes in Acts 25–26 are not simply the scene repetitions that are common in episodic narratives; rather, a sense of suspense and intrigue accrues as the stature and power of those who hear Paul's defense increases. More is at stake with each successive trial. The elaborate public ceremony (25:23) before King Agrippa and Bernice is the climactic moment on Paul's inexorable journey to Rome, ending with Agrippa's consternation over why Paul appealed to Caesar (26:32).

The Text in the Interpretive Tradition

Early Christian martyrdom accounts conventionally portray the martyr pronouncing judgment on the accusers and/or confessing her or his identity as a Christian. Early Christians did not appear to understand Jesus' silence on trial as a paradigmatic model; they followed Paul's example instead.

Many centuries later, the modern missionary movement drew on Paul's example to legitimize missionary expansion and, concomitantly, European colonization. Parachurch Bible societies, translation efforts, and formal missionary societies were founded and flourished following William Carey's famous sermon in 1793; Carey, along with missionaries like Adoniram Judson, defended the historicity of Acts and appealed to Paul's missionary journeys as an ideal missionizing blueprint: choose destinations strategically, establish churches, train local leaders, and vehemently defend the faith.

The Text in Contemporary Discussion

Acts 26:12-18 contains the third recounting of Paul's Damascus experience (cf. 9:1-31; 22:1-21). Following Ernst Haenchen, most contemporary scholars abandoned the attempt to identify disparate sources behind the accounts of Paul's Damascus road experience; instead, they consider the differences between the accounts as evidence of the author's specific theological and stylistic emphases at various points in the story. For instance, the third rendition of the story in Acts contains fewer details about the event itself (e.g., Ananias is removed entirely), and a greater emphasis on its symbolic dimensions: Paul draws stark lines between good and evil (and Christian and Jew), extending the description of his prior persecution of Christians (26:9-11), and using the language of light and dark to connect himself with Christ (26:13, 18, 23).

Acts 24:1—26:32 spotlights the Roman governmental authorities (Felix, Festus, Agrippa, and Bernice). Luke-Acts is clearly preoccupied with power; however, whether Luke presents a consistently pro- or anti-imperialist agenda continues to be a site of rigorous scholarly contestation. The crux of the debate is whether Luke is sympathetic toward or fundamentally opposed to Roman rule. Some argue that Acts openly rejects all forms of hegemony; others suggest that like many colonized peoples, Luke internalized and replicated Rome's imperialist ideology, only dissenting via what James Scott famously called "hidden transcripts," or private, everyday speech countering hegemonic discourse.

Postcolonial theorists have challenged the common tendency to portray the Roman Empire and early Christianity as monolithic, reified categories: the antagonistic colonizing Roman authorities as clearly opposed to the (resistant or complicit) colonized Christians. Postcolonial thinkers destabilize the simplistic colonizer/colonized binary by recognizing what Homi Bhabha dubs "colonial ambivalence"—the oscillation between desire and denigration that occurs within colonizer and colonized, invariably implicating both in contested discourses about identity. Colonialism is never unilateral. Like many colonized people today, early Christians lived within multiple contexts; Acts testifies to early Christian attempts to revise inherited stories and negotiate a coherent identity in conversation with other texts and other communities. Furthermore, the relationships between the Roman authorities and "native populations" were inconsistent across the empire. Can we move beyond essentialist caricatures of the oppressive Roman Empire and oppressed Christians? What implications might attention to ambivalence, misrepresentation, and inconsistencies have for marginalized communities across the globe?

27:1—28:31: Paul's Trip to Rome and Conclusion

The Text in Its Ancient Context

The last two chapters of Acts are recounted almost entirely in the first person plural (27:1—28:16). Paul's journey to Rome has all the makings of an epic adventure tale—a sea voyage, storms, shipwreck, an exotic location with island "natives," miraculous healings, and heroism in the face of danger. As the voyage begins, the narrator notes that "the Fast" (the Day of Atonement) has passed, indicating the season is autumn. This detail and Paul's prophetic warning (27:10) create a foreboding sense of impending calamity. Indeed, the situation goes from bad to worse when the ship runs aground on Malta, an island south of Sicily (28:1). Luke's harrowing account of the struggle to reach shore is vivid and detailed (27:39-44). The shipwreck and the soldiers' plan to kill all the prisoners (27:42) make it even more astounding that everyone survives (27:44). In the narrative fulfillment of Paul's vision (27:22-26), Luke again demonstrates that God's plan inevitably comes to fruition.

The voyage is rich with intertextual traces of Homeric epic, Greco-Roman literature, the Hebrew Bible (including Isaiah), and Virgil's *Aeneid* (Bonz). In Chariton's ancient Greek novel *Chareas and Callirhoe*, which is roughly contemporaneous to Acts, a travel narrative provides the impetus for plot development. Legal trials fulfill similar functions in the Greek novels and Acts; courtroom scenes are particularly conducive for communicating ideologies because they establish a rhetorical winner and loser. Whereas ancient Greek novels record crimes of passion, Acts records "crimes" against Christianity; Luke uses this juridical trope to emphasize that when the apostles stand trial, the view they espouse is true. Other parallels exist, as well; Petronius's early Latin novel *Satyricon* explicitly references the early Christian rite of the Lord's Supper, while Paul's breaking of bread in Acts 27:35 clearly has eucharistic undertones (cf. Luke 22:19).

On Malta, the "natives" warmly welcome the newcomers (28:2, 7, 10); foreign hospitality extended to shipwrecked protagonists is a trope from the ancient novels that Luke appropriates to illustrate Christian benevolence. Despite the Maltans' misunderstandings (28:4-6), Paul heals their sick (28:8-9). The group departs on an Alexandrian ship probably carrying grain, as Rome imported grain from Egypt (cf. 27:38). Zeus's sons Castor and Pollux ("the Twin Brothers" on the ship's figurehead, 28:11) were thought to provide protection at sea; the irony that an ideal Lukan reader will discern is that only the Christian God provides true protection.

Typical narrative plots follow the climax with a denouement—a falling action that provides closure. Acts ends with Paul under what we today call "house arrest": with only one guard, he enjoys remarkable freedom (28:16). Though tradition tells of Paul's beheading in Rome around 64–65 CE (and Luke alludes to it in 19:21; 20:22-25; 23:11; 26:32; 27:24), this is not how Luke ends his story. Rather, Acts concludes on a triumphant note. The disciples have fulfilled Christ's programmatic commissioning (1:8): the message has finally reached Rome, the capital of the empire and (according to Roman ideology) the center of the *oikoumenē* (the inhabited world).

The Text in the Interpretive Tradition

As the first generation of Christians passed away, tradition became the crucial ideological battleground. In response to Marcion and others, proto-orthodox Christians of the second through fourth centuries generated many pseudepigraphical works to build on existing details and fill the lacunae in Acts. For instance, most accounts utilize the depiction in Acts of Paul as a Roman citizen (21:39; 22:25-29; 23:27); however, whereas the canonical Acts implies (but does not state) that Paul is martyred in Rome, in the apocryphal *Acts of Paul*, the beheaded Paul appears to Nero, promising divine vengeance.

Martin Luther's Heidelberg Disputation (1518) coined the terms "theology of glory" and "theology of the cross" to contrast salvation based on human effort (*theologia gloriae*) with salvation based on Christ's sacrifice on the cross (*theologia crucis*). Luke has long been read as a theology of glory, partly because it ends with Paul preaching "without hindrance" in Rome (28:31). Still, persecutions punctuate Paul's journeys; he arrives in Rome because he refuses to avoid suffering, which the Holy Spirit has predicted repeatedly (cf. 20:22-24; 21:11-13).

The Text in Contemporary Discussion

Acts 28:27-28 reiterates that God's salvation is for the gentiles. Is the mission to the Jews permanently over, thereby replacing one form of particularism (Jewish salvation) with another (gentile salvation)? Or does this simply reinforce that God has ordained the gentile mission and the gospel must spread to all people?

Our final picture of Paul epitomizes several Lukan motifs—the gentile mission, the unstoppable divine will, rightly receiving God's Word, and boldly proclaiming the gospel as a constitutive component of discipleship. In a sense, then, the final installment provides closure, reinforcing ideological commitments that are discernible throughout the entire narrative.

And yet, Acts also remains famously open-ended. Though ancient historians extolled the virtues of completing one's narrative (e.g., Dionysius, *Thuc.* 16.847), Luke's ending generates openness in several ways. Paul's visitors in Rome have mixed reactions to the gospel (28:24-25), Jesus does not reappear as promised (1:11), and the reader never hears of Paul's fate after his two years in captivity (28:30). Neither does Luke relate the ending of other main characters' stories, like Barnabas or Peter. And although the book begins with a personal address (1:1), there is no concluding second-person farewell, as in the epistles (cf. Rom. 16:21-7; 1 Cor. 16:19-24; Eph. 6:23-24; Phil. 4:20-23; Col. 4:7-18). Does the final word of Acts—a Greek adverb meaning "without hindrance"—hint that the church's work is over, or just beginning?

Discussing this inconclusive ending, some scholars have suggested that Luke intended to write a third volume, that he ran out of space on his scroll, or that he was ignorant of Paul's fate. More generally, if the ending of Acts implies that the gospel will continue to spread, what are the implications for Christian disciples today? What forms of interference limit the spread of the gospel, and how are Christians called to overcome them?

Ancient rhetors like Cicero (*De or.* 2:41:177) and Plutarch (*Mor.* 1.45E) believed open-endedness engaged readers by allowing them to linger longer over the story. In modern psychological terms, this is an instance of the Zeigarnik Effect: what remains unfinished is better remembered. The open-endedness of Acts implicitly situates the reader in Theophilus's position: the reader must decide how to respond to this dynamic, challenging, and beautifully complex early Christian narrative.

Works Cited

Anderson, Janice Capel. 2004. "Reading Tabitha: A Feminist Reception History." In *A Feminist Companion to the Acts of the Apostles*, edited by Amy-Jill Levine, 22–48: New York: T&T Clark.

Bhabha, Homi. 1994. "Of Mimicry and Man: The Ambivalence of Colonial Discourse." In *The Location of Culture*. London: Routledge.

Bonz, Marianne P. 2000. *The Past as Legacy: Luke-Acts and Ancient Epic*. Minneapolis: Fortress Press.

Bovon, François. 2003. "Canonical and Apocryphal Acts of Apostles." *JECS* 11: 165-94.

Bowersock, Glen. 1995. *Martyrdom and Rome*. Cambridge: Cambridge University Press.

Boyarin, Daniel. 1999. *Dying for God: Martyrdom and the Making of Christianity and Judaism*. Stanford: Stanford University Press.

———. 1994. *A Radical Jew: Paul and the Politics of Identity*. Berkeley: University of California Press.

Buell, Denise Kimber. 2005. *Why This New Race? Ethnic Reasoning in Early Christianity*. New York: Columbia University Press.

Campbell, William Sanger. 2007. *The "We" Passages in the Acts of the Apostles: The Narrator as Narrative Character*. Atlanta: Society of Biblical Literature.

Castelli, Elizabeth A. 2004. *Martyrdom and Memory: Early Christian Culture Making*. New York: Columbia University Press, 2004.

Clark, David. 2011. "Linguistic and Cultural Influences on Interpretation in Translations of the Bible." In *The Oxford Handbook of the Reception History of the Bible*, edited by Michael Lieb and Emma Mason, 200–213. Oxford: Oxford University Press.

Cosgrove, Charles. 1984. "The Divine DEI in Luke-Acts." *Novum Testamentum* 26: 168-90.

Frend, W. H. C. 1965. *Martyrdom and Persecution in the Early Church: A Study of a Conflict from the Maccabees to Donatus*. Oxford: Basil Blackwell.

Gadamer, Hans-Georg. 1960. *Wahrheit und Methode*. Tübingen: J. C. B. Mohr.

Gilbert, Gary. 2002. "The List of Nations in Acts 2: Roman Propaganda and the Lukan Response." *JBL* 121:497–529.

González, Justo L. 2001. *Acts: The Gospel of the Spirit*. Maryknoll, NY: Orbis.

Haenchen, Ernst. 1971. *The Acts of the Apostles*. Translated by Bernard Noble et al. Philadelphia: Westminster.

Jervell, Jacob. 1972. *Luke and the People of God*. Minneapolis: Fortress Press.

Kanyoro, Musimbi. 2004: "Thinking Mission in Africa." In *A Feminist Companion to the Acts of the Apostles*, edited by Amy-Jill Levine, 61–70. New York: T&T Clark.

Liew, Tat-siong Benny. 2004. "Acts." In *Global Bible Commentary*, edited by Daniel Patte, 419–28. Nashville: Abingdon.

Longenecker, Bruce, ed. 1997. *The Road from Damascus*. Grand Rapids: Eerdmans.

MacDonald, Dennis. 2003. *Does the New Testament Imitate Homer? Four Cases from the Acts of the Apostles*. New Haven: Yale University Press.

Moxnes, Halvor. 1991. "Patron-Client Relations and the New Community in Luke-Acts." In *The Social World of Luke-Acts: Models for Interpretation*, edited by Jerome H. Neyrey, 241–68. Peabody, MA: Hendrickson.

Nasrallah, Laura S. 2008: "The Acts of the Apostles, Greek Cities, and Hadrian's Panhellenion." *JBL* 127:533–65.

Parsons, Mikael C. 2008. *Acts*. Paideia. Grand Rapids: Baker Academic.

Pierce, Ronald W., Rebecca Merrill Groothuis, and Gordon D. Fee, eds. 2004. *Discovering Biblical Equality: Complementarity without Hierarchy*. Downers Grove, IL: InterVarsity Press.

Pervo, Richard. 2006: *Dating Acts: Between the Evangelists and the Apologists*. Santa Rosa, CA: Polebridge.

Price, Robert. 1997. *The Widow Traditions in Luke-Acts: A Feminist-Critical Scrutiny*. SBLDS 155. Atlanta: Scholars Press.

Robbins, Vernon. 1975. "The We-Passages in Acts and Ancient Sea Voyages." *BR* 20:5–18.

Sanders, Jack T. 1987. *The Jews in Luke-Acts*. London: SCM.

Schaberg, Jane. 1998. "Luke." In *Women's Bible Commentary*, edited by Carol A. Newsom, Sharon H. Ringe, and Jacqueline E. Lapsley, 363–80. Louisville: Westminster John Knox.

Scott, James. 1990. *Domination and the Arts of Resistance: Hidden Transcripts*. New Haven: Yale University Press.

Seccombe, David. 1982. *Possessions and the Poor in Luke-Acts*. Linz: A. Fuchs.

Segal, Alan. 1990. *Paul the Convert: The Apostolate and Apostasy of Saul the Pharisee*. New Haven: Yale University Press.

Seim, Turid Karlsen. 1994. *The Double Message: Patterns of Gender in Luke-Acts*. Edinburgh: T&T Clark.

Soards, Marion L. 1994. *The Speeches in Acts: Their Content, Context, and Concerns*. Louisville: Westminster John Knox.

Staley, Jeffrey L. 1999. "Changing Woman: Postcolonial Reflections on Acts 16:6-40." *JSNT* 73:113–35.

Sterling, Gregory. 1992. *Historiography and Self-Definition: Josephus, Luke-Acts and Apologetic Historiography*. NovTSup 64. Leiden: Brill.

Torjesen, Karen Jo. 1993. *When Women Were Priests: Women's Leadership in the Early Church and the Scandal of Their Subordination in the Rise of Christianity.* San Francisco: HarperSanFrancisco.

Tyson, Joseph. 2006. *Marcion and Luke-Acts: A Defining Struggle.* Columbia: University of South Carolina Press.

Wilson, Nancy. 1995. *Our Tribe: Queer Folks, God, Jesus, and the Bible.* San Francisco: HarperSanFrancisco.

Wordelman, Amy L. 2003. "Cultural Divides and Dual Realities: A Greco-Roman Context for Acts 14." In *Contextualizing Acts: Lukan Narrative and Greco-Roman Discourse*, edited by Todd Penner and Caroline Vander Stichele, 205–32. Atlanta: Scholars Press.